PENGUIN BOOKS

DEATH IN HAMBURG

Richard J. Evans was born in Woodford, Essex, in 1947. He studied at Jesus College, Oxford, where he took a first-class degree in modern history in 1969, and went on to take a D.Phil. at St Antony's College, Oxford, in 1972. After teaching in the History Department at the University of Stirling, he moved in 1976 to the University of East Anglia, Norwich, where he was Professor of European History from 1983 to 1989. He is currently Professor of History at Birkbeck College, University of London. He has spent many years living and researching in Germany, including a period at the Free University of Berlin as Research Fellow of the Alexander von Humboldt Foundation, and he also taught in New York, as Visiting Associate Professor of European History at Columbia University, in 1980. His books include *The Feminists* (1977), *Rethinking German History* (1987) and *In Hitler's Shadow* (1989), and his work has been translated into many languages, including French, German, Italian, Japanese, Spanish and Swedish. He is married with one daughter and lives in Norfolk.

DEATH IN HAMBURG

*Society and Politics in
the Cholera Years
1830–1910*

RICHARD J. EVANS

PENGUIN BOOKS

PENGUIN BOOKS

Published by the Penguin Group
27 Wrights Lane, London w8 5TZ, England
Viking Penguin Inc., 375 Hudson Street, New York, New York 10014, USA
Penguin Books Australia Ltd, Ringwood, Victoria, Australia
Penguin Books Canada Ltd, 2801 John Street, Markham, Ontario, Canada L3R 1B4
Penguin Books (NZ) Ltd, 182–190 Wairau Road, Auckland 10, New Zealand

Penguin Books Ltd, Registered Offices: Harmondsworth, Middlesex, England

First published in Great Britain by Oxford University Press 1987
First published in the USA by Oxford University Press 1987
Published in Penguin Books 1990
1 3 5 7 9 10 8 6 4 2

Printed in England by Clays Ltd, St Ives plc

FOR THE FRIENDS, PAST AND PRESENT,
WITH WHOM I HAVE ENJOYED LIFE IN
HAMBURG.

PREFACE

THIS is a book about the inner life of a great European city at the height of the industrial age. It tells the story of how, as the city grew from a modest though substantial seaport into a massive modern conurbation in the course of the nineteenth century, the problems of keeping its inhabitants alive and well, of supplying them with clean water, fresh air, pure food, and all the other basic requirements of human existence became steadily more acute, and led in the end to catastrophe. It shows how the solution of these problems was closely bound up with structures of social inequality and social conflict in the city, and how these also changed as the city became larger and more complex. Social conflicts found an outlet in political struggles, and these too play an important part in the events which the book narrates. The climax and centre-piece of the story is formed by the great cholera epidemic which affected Hamburg alone of all the cities and towns of Western Europe in 1892. Nearly ten thousand people died in this disaster in the space of little more than six weeks; and the ways in which the city coped, or failed to cope, with the catastrophe, and the effects it had on the life of the city afterwards, have parallels and lessons for the medical problems and urban disasters of a century later, in the age of AIDS and the nuclear peril.

The book, therefore, stands in the long line of 'plague literature' that runs from Boccaccio through Defoe and on to Camus and André Brink.[1] In writing it I have become increasingly conscious of the forms and conventions which this genre imposes on the author, and which have found their way into a large part of the more strictly historical literature on the subject, from Jean-Noël Biraben's *Les hommes et la peste* and Paul Slack's *The Impact of Plague in Tudor and Stuart England* to studies of more modern epidemics such as Michael Durey's work on cholera in Britain or Alfred Crosby's account of influenza in 1918–19.[2] The uncovering of the negligence and duplicity of the authorities, the leisurely recounting of causes, influences, and premonitions followed by a swift narrative of the disaster itself, the shifting of focus from the collective to the individual and back again, the cathartic stock-taking after the event:

---

[1] G. Boccaccio, *The Decameron* (London, n.d.); D. Defoe, *A Journal of the Plague Year* (London, 1722, repr. 1966); A. Camus, *La Peste* (Paris, 1947); A. Brink, *The Wall of the Plague* (London, 1984); see also D. Steel, 'Plague Writing. From Boccaccio to Camus,' *Journal of European Studies*, 11 (1981), 88–110.

[2] J.–N. Biraben, *Les Hommes et la Peste en France et dans les Pays Européens et Méditerranéans* (Paris, 2 vols., 1975–6); P. Slack, *The Impact of Plague in Tudor and Stuart England* (London, 1985); M. Durey, *The Return of the Plague: British Society and the Cholera 1831–32* (Dublin, 1979); A. Crosby, *Epidemic and Peace 1918* (Westport, Conn., 1976).

all these characteristic features of plague literature have done much to dictate the structure of this book.

But a reading of plague literature also made me aware of the metaphorical uses of epidemics, expressed directly and with unforgettable power in the classic work of Albert Camus, more abstractly and obliquely in the novella of Thomas Mann which suggested the title to this book.[3] The American critic Susan Sontag has recently warned of the dangers of using illness as a metaphor, but her warnings are based on an understanding of medical science which, as I hope to show, is at best simplistic, at worst, naive.[4] This book too, therefore, can also be understood in a metaphorical sense. More died in Hamburg in 1892 than just people. The epidemic, as one local inhabitant who lived through it observed, was the dividing-point between the old and the new; in particular, it struck the death-knell for the old system of amateur government by local notables under which Hamburg had previously been ruled. It marked, even if it was not alone in bringing about, the victory of Prussianism over liberalism, the triumph of state intervention over *laissez-faire*. It formed a significant, symbolic moment in the history of the German middle classes, and set the scene for their entry into the twentieth century. These metaphorical resonances of the book's theme indicate, I hope, that its central concerns go far beyond the mere depiction of urban disaster.

When I began the research for this book in the late 1970s, I little realized that it would take nearly a decade to complete. I was drawn to the history of Hamburg partly by a feeling that it was time to do something to counteract the narrow Prussocentrism of much writing on German history at the time, and partly by an existing interest in the social history of German liberalism. My starting-point was the reputation of Hamburg, Germany's second-largest city after Berlin, as a 'foreign body' in the German Empire, an 'English' town in a continental setting. Hamburg, I thought, could be used as a kind of historical laboratory in which to test common notions of the contrast between England and Germany. It was not only a municipality, but also a 'free city' for much of the nineteenth century, an autonomous state within the German Confederation and after 1870 within the German Empire. Most important of all, it was ruled by liberal, middle-class merchants. It could be used therefore to try and answer by a case-study one of the great 'if' questions of modern German historiography: if the bourgeoisie had conquered political power in 1848 or thereafter, would there have been a more just, a more equal, a more liberal, a more democratic, a more rational society? Or would things have been more or less the same as they turned out to be anyway?

Initially I hoped to answer these questions through a brief cross-sectional study of the 1890s and the early 1900s, but as I worked through the very extensive source material in the Hamburg state archives I was drawn

[3] Camus, *La Peste;* Thomas Mann, *Death in Venice* (Harmondsworth, 1955).
[4] Susan Sontag, *Illness as Metaphor* (Harmondsworth, 1983).

irresistibly further back in time, and this is the principal reason why the book has taken so long to complete. In its final form, presented here, it is constructed at three levels of analysis, of increasing specificity, each informing the other. At the most general level, it attempts an outline of the city's social and political history in the nineteenth century, approached through class conflict and the relations of state and society. My understanding of these by no means unproblematical concepts will, I hope, become clear in the course of the first chapter. A second level of the book pursues these general issues into a case-study of the history of the urban environment and its relation to death and disease. It asks not only how Hamburg's rapid growth affected the life and health of its inhabitants, but also how its effects were perceived by different sectors of the population. These questions were raised in a particularly acute form by the great cholera epidemics which afflicted the city in no fewer than sixteen different years between 1831 and 1892, and which had an impact on society and politics in Hamburg over the whole period from 1830 to 1910, an impact which justifies their description as 'the cholera years' in the subtitle to this book. Broadly speaking, coverage becomes thicker and more detailed towards the end of the period. This leads to the third, most detailed level of the book, the narrative of the cholera epidemic of 1892.

The 1892 cholera epidemic generated a vast amount of source material, from memoirs, diaries, letters, newspaper articles, and photographs to official commissions of enquiry, statistical investigations, reports of charitable and voluntary associations, and of course massive additions to the files of the government departments which had to deal with it. In the epidemic, the workings of state and society, the structures of social inequality, the variety of values and beliefs, the physical contours of everyday life, the formal ideologies and informal ambitions of political organizations, were all thrown into sharp and detailed relief. Another way of understanding the structure of this book, therefore, is to see it as consisting of a horizontal cross-section through the structures of life in the city taken during six weeks in the late summer of 1892, interlocking with a longitudinal analysis which traces back every causal element in the epidemic to its origins early in the nineteenth century and takes its aftermath and consequences on into the twentieth. Each of the first twelve sections in the book thus takes one strand in the causal knot and follows it through to the eve of the 1892 epidemic, while the remaining twelve sections, beginning with the first part of Chapter 4, present an intensive analysis of the epidemic itself and discuss its significance in the light of the general questions posed at the outset.

These procedures, and the immense richness of the source material on which they rest, make it possible to re-create in unprecedented detail the inner life of a great German city in the nineteenth century. In recent years there has been a vast outpouring of research on the history of everyday life in Germany. Much of it has been focused at a very detailed, local level. This development has not been without its critics, and I hope in this book not only to present to an English-speaking audience a wide range of evidence in this field, but also perhaps to show why it is important that it be studied. In the broadest sense, it allows us to reflect on many aspects of the human condition that are important to a modern readership despite their customary neglect by professional historians: just as important, however, is the recognition that political behaviour and aspirations are rooted in the structures and experiences of daily life; they do not simply exist in some isolated, autonomous sphere of their own. In the same way, although this book also approaches the past 'from below,' I mean this in the sense that its basic sympathies lie with the mass of the people, rather than with the few who governed them; I do not mean either that it neglects the upper reaches of society and the state, or that it makes no attempt to recover the inner world of Hamburg's dominant classes with as much sympathy as I can muster.

Inevitably, a book conceived along these lines cuts across many conventional boundaries, from social geography and the history of living standards to labour history and the history of the physical environment. It is emphatically not a specialist work of medical history. It approaches the history of medicine and disease from the point of view of the social historian, and locates these subjects in their contemporary social and political context rather than in the long-term development of medical science as it appears from the vantage-point of the present. In writing this book, I have been influenced by social histories of cholera in America, Britain, France, and Russia which have appeared over the last twenty-five years; no such study exists as yet for Germany, and by examining comparative material, especially for Prussia, I hope to go some way towards providing one in the course of this book. Not only specialists in the history of medicine, but also in a whole range of the other subdisciplines into which historical research unfortunately seems to be disintegrating today, from the history of housing to the history of population, will have to forgive my intrusion into their particular areas of expertise; but perhaps they may also learn something by seeing their own concerns placed in a more general context and viewed, as it were, with an outsider's eye.

If this is not a work of specialized medical history, neither, despite appearances, is it primarily conceived as a study in quantitative history. In order to establish the contours of social inequality in the city, I have found it necessary to include some statistical analysis, but in view of the many problems presented by this material, I have tried to place this analysis firmly in a qualitative context. Elaborate statistical procedures did not seem in the end to promise rewards commensurate with the work involved in applying them, so I have contented myself with only a very simple level of statistical testing. In order to ease the task of the reader unfamiliar with quantitative material or with the areas dealt with in this book, I have tried to avoid technicalities and to present as many of the statistics as possible in the form of easily digestible maps, histograms, and other graphic devices. Detailed discussion of the problems encountered in compiling the statistics, and the techniques used in analysing them, has been banished to an Appendix. Nevertheless, in a book of this length, based to a considerable extent on unpublished manuscript sources, the scholarly apparatus is inevitably rather unwieldy. I have attempted to keep it in check by restricting it to a minimum. The footnotes are deliberately conceived as references which will enable the reader to gain an impression of the kind of sources on which statements in the text are based, and to locate them and check them if so desired. With a very few exceptions, they are not intended to provide space for discussion of matters of secondary interest; still less are they designed to provide complete bibliographies of the secondary literature on all the subjects dealt with. Similarly, the bibliography is rigorously restricted to sources found useful for the analysis and cited in the book. Additional references can easily be pursued through the monographs and research surveys mentioned in the footnotes. At the end of the book, the index gives the modern place-names alongside the contemporary ones used in the text (especially important where national boundaries have changed).

In a project as wide-ranging as the present one, the author is more than usually dependent on the help of others. My first acknowledgment must be to my own institution, the University of East Anglia, which has not only given me the time and the facilities with which to carry out the research, but has also borne the brunt of the financial costs through a series of generous grants from the Special Travel and Research Fund of the School of Modern Languages and European History. At a time of general cut-backs and economies in the British university system, I have indeed been fortunate to belong to an institution that still has the courage to support research in the humanities and social sciences from its own resources, at some cost to itself in other respects. I am also indebted to the University of Hamburg for providing me with accommodation in its Gästehaus on my numerous research visits between 1978 and 1985, to the Institut für europäische Geschichte, Mainz, and its Director, Professor Dr Karl Otmar, Freiherr von Aretin, for providing me with a peaceful and collegial atmosphere in which the final stages of writing could be completed, to the Alexander von Humboldt Foundation for generous financial support which enabled me to devote some time to this book while working on another, related project, and to the British Academy for supporting my research at a crucial stage earlier on.

In the course of my work, I was fortunate to be able to attend the first conference held in Germany on the social history of medicine, at the Zentrum für interdisziplinäre Forschung at the University of Bielefeld, and I am grateful to the organizers, Prof. Alfons Labisch and Prof. Reinhard Spree, for allowing me to attend. I also learned much from the first conference of the Hamburg

Arbeitskreis für Regionalgeschichte, held in 1982, and from the meetings of the UEA Research Seminar in Modern German Social History, which have helped form my views in more ways than may be readily apparent from the contents of this book. A number of seminar audiences have listened patiently to chapters as they were in the course of being written, and many of their comments and suggestions have found their way into the text in one form or another. I am especially indebted to the tolerance with which my first faltering steps in the direction of medical and demographic history were received by the seminars of the Wellcome Unit for the History of Medicine at Oxford and the Demographic Database at Umeå University in Sweden; I also benefited from the discussion of some of the arguments and evidence presented in this book at the joint UEA–Hamburg Historians' Colloquium in Hamburg, the Institute for European Population Studies at the University of Liverpool, the Demographic and Family History Seminar organized by Richard Smith at All Souls' College, Oxford, the German History Seminar run by Anthony Nicholls and Hartmut Pogge-von Strandmann at St Antony's College, Oxford, the eighth UEA Research Seminar in Modern German Social History, held in Norwich in 1985, and seminars or lectures at the State University of California (Long Beach), the University of California at Riverside, the Institut für europäische Geschichte in Mainz, the Universities of Bielefeld, Düsseldorf, and Essen and the Ruhr University Bochum. My thanks go to all those who organized and participated in these discussions: many of their suggestions have had a material part in the shaping of this book and the arguments advanced in it.

Many individuals and institutions helped in various ways during the research for this book. Peter Loewenberg not only organized a most stimulating evening's discussion at his home in Westwood, Los Angeles, but also drew my attention to the fictionalized account of the 1892 epidemic by his grandfather, Jakob Loewenberg, a member of a 'sanitary column' in the city: Helga Kutz-Bauer also lent me a novel on the epidemic, by Paul Schurek. I am deeply indebted to them both, as I am to Mrs Ruth Evans (Oxford), who most kindly allowed me to see the Mönckeberg family papers in her possession. More formal acknowledgements for permission to cite documentary material are due to Carmen, Countess Finck von Finckenstein-Jelmini, and Dr Edgar Petersen, while the directors and staff of the University of East Anglia Library, the Library of the Wellcome Institute for the History of Medicine (London), the Kirchenarchiv Hamburg, the Staatsarchiv Bremen, the Bundesarchiv Koblenz, the Stadtarchiv Berlin (Hauptstadt der DDR), the Geheimes Staatsarchiv Preussischer Kulturbesitz, Berlin-Dahlem, and the Staatsarchiv der Freien und Hansestadt Hamburg, have all gone out of their way to help my enquiries and provide material: I am very pleased to have the opportunity here of conveying my gratitude to them all. I am also grateful for permission to reproduce the illustrations provided by the sources noted in the List of Plates below.

There are a few special debts of gratitude which I owe to a number of people, though I can scarcely hope to repay them all. First of all I would like to thank Claus Stukenbrock, of the Staatsarchiv Hamburg, for the patience and generosity with which he has made available to me his unrivalled knowledge of the archival material relating to the social history of the city in the period with which I am concerned. Over the past two decades he has earned the gratitude of more than one generation of researchers, and without his help and guidance, this book, perhaps more than most, could never have been completed. Secondly, I am very grateful to Arthur Imhof (Free University of Berlin) for his encouragement in the early stages of this project, and more particularly for showing me by the example of his own work that statistical material can be made easy to digest by presenting it in graphic form. Special thanks are due in this respect to Ian Brooke, of the Graphics Unit at the University of East Anglia, for his tireless and patient work in drawing the artwork that forms such an important element in this book, and for putting up over a period of years with a task that must have seemed endless at times. Whatever clarity the book has in its presentation of the statistics is largely due to him. And if the statistical analysis itself is in any way persuasive, much of the credit must go to Joanna Bourke (Canberra) who provided much-needed help at the last minute. Paul Weindling (Oxford) has freely given of his time and resources in supplying me with references, offprints, photocopies, and encouragement in the field in which he is himself a leading authority, as well as providing critical comments on a large part of the final typescript. If his efforts to educate me in matters of German medical history have been less than completely successful, then I only have myself to blame. John Breuilly (Manchester) has also put me greatly in his debt by his characteristic generosity in sharing the materials and expertise which he has accumulated in his long years of studying Hamburg in the early and middle part of the nineteenth century. Logie Barrow provided generous hospitality during my research in Bremen and I owe a great deal to him for his constant encouragement of the project. Lynn Abrams, Cathleen Catt, Barry Doyle and Graham Ford sustained me in the final phase of writing by their critical interest and enthusiasm: I am grateful to them all for reading the typescript and for making many useful suggestions, and especially to Graham Ford for undertaking the onerous task of proof-reading the footnotes. My thanks also to Marjan Bhavsar for typing numerous earlier drafts of chapters, to Elvi Dobie for undertaking some of the later typing, and to Carol Haines for producing a clean and accurate final copy with exemplary speed and efficiency.

I owe more than I can say to Elín Hjaltadóttir, for her constant tolerance and support, both in the difficult early stages of research, when it was by no means certain what, if anything, was going to emerge from my sojourns in the archives, and in the later stages of writing, when it seemed at times as if the cholera epidemic had entered the household and was taking it over.

And the book could certainly not have been completed without the critical participation, sustained interest, moral support and repeated, generous hospitality of my many friends in Hamburg, past and present, who have done so much to make my work on this project enjoyable as well as rewarding, among them Michael Grüttner, Liz Harvey, Alan Kramer, Mary Lindemann, Tony and Willy McElligott, Helga Stachow and Volker Ullrich. To them, and many other denizens of Hamburg, as a small token of thanks, this book is dedicated.

R.J.E.

Norwich
July 1986

CONTENTS

LIST OF PLATES

LIST OF MAPS

LIST OF FIGURES

LIST OF TABLES

LIST OF ABBREVIATIONS

BA	Bundesarchiv
BD	Baudeputation
Bürgerschaft	*Sitzungen der Hamburger Bürgerschaft* (reports from *Hamburger Nachrichten*, in StA Hbg library)
FA	Familienarchiv
GStA	Geheimes Staatsarchiv
Hbg	Hamburg
MdB	*Mitglieder der Bürgerschaft* (biographical files in StA Hbg)
MK	Medizinalkollegium
MS	*Berichte des Medicinal-Inspectorats über die medicinische Statistik des Hamburgischen Staates*
PP	Politische Polizei
RT	*Stenographische Berichte über die Verhandlungen des Deutschen Reichstags*
SHS	*Statistik des Hamburgischen Staates*
StA	Staatsarchivs
ZHG	*Zeitschrift des Vereins für Hamburgische Geschichte*

I

The World the Merchants Made

a. Patricians and Politics

I

THE German Empire founded by Bismarck in 1871 has sometimes been described as a 'federation of monarchs',[1] but strictly speaking it was not. Certainly the Empire was a federation, with twenty-five member states combining in a 'perpetual union' under a German Emperor or *Kaiser*, and sovereign power being exercised by a Federal Council (or *Bundesrat*) in which all the states were represented.[2] But while twenty-two of the member states were indeed monarchies, ranging from the Kingdom of Prussia at one extreme to the hereditary principality of Schwarzburg-Rudolstadt at the other, three of them were republics. These were the cities of Hamburg, Bremen, and Lübeck, which had established their independence as part of the powerful Hanseatic League in the Middle Ages and by one means and another had managed to keep it ever since. Long before the middle of the nineteenth century, Hamburg, thanks largely to its advantageous situation on the River Elbe, through which traffic from a hinterland stretching as far as Berlin and Prague passed on its way to the North Sea a hundred kilometres or so downstream, had become the largest and most important of the Hanseatic towns. After Berlin it was by a long way the second largest city in the German Empire. In wealth, size, and importance it left such provincial capitals as Munich, Stuttgart, Leipzig, and Dresden far behind.[3]

Unlike all the other major cities in Germany apart from Bremen, Hamburg was not subject to outside control over its own affairs: it was a federated state in its own right. In recent years it has become commonplace to describe the German Empire as 'Greater Prussia',[4] and the widespread assumption of

---

[1] J. C. G. Röhl, 'Kaiser Wilhelm II., Grossherzog Friedrich I. und der "Königsmechanismus" im Kaiserreich. Unzeitgemässe Betrachtungen zu einer badischen Geschichtsquelle', *Historische Zeitschrift*, 236 (1983), 539–77, here p. 553. Röhl's remarks on the neglect by historians of the particularist elements in the Empire and their persistence to the turn of the century and beyond deserve underlining, however.

[2] For a guide to the constitutional structure of the Empire, see E. R. Huber, *Deutsche Verfassungsgeschichte seit 1789*, iv. *Struktur und Krisen des Kaiserreichs* (Stuttgart, 1969).

[3] G. Hohorst, J. Kocka, and G. A. Ritter, *Sozialgeschichtliches Arbeitsbuch II* (Munich, 1975), p. 45.

[4] H.-U. Wehler, *The German Empire 1871–1918* (Leamington Spa, 1985), p. 52.

the virtual identity between Prussia and the German Empire is frequently expressed through the use of the term 'Prusso-Germany' to denote the political entity created by Bismarck.[5] This too is at best a half-truth. Certainly the member states of the Empire were unable to pursue their own foreign policies, and the external affairs of the Empire were undoubtedly managed under Prussian control. Equally, the army, though nominally decentralized, was in reality run by the Prussians, above all when it counted, in wartime. Matters in the Federal Council, too, were so arranged that the Prussians could always secure a majority of the votes if they wanted to. But all this still left an enormous amount of power in the hands of the federated states. In many respects, they were free to run their own affairs as they pleased. Education, policing, law and order, health and social welfare, taxation, commercial and economic policy: these and a host of other matters were left largely to the discretion of the federated states by the constitution of 1871, as they had been by previous constitutions such as that of the much looser German Confederation in which the states had organized themselves from 1815 to 1866.[6]

All this meant in reality that what held good for Prussia by no means held good for the rest of Germany. Prussia itself was deeply divided, the newer territories of the Rhineland, acquired in 1815, having little in common with the rural hinterland of 'Old Prussia' east of the Elbe.[7] Even greater was the variety of traditions, institutions, and habits of mind that obtained in the rest of the Empire. Each state had its own peculiarities, its own way of doing things: and of no member state of the German Empire was this more true than of Hamburg. It has, indeed, been described by historians as 'a special case in the history of Germany',[8] 'a foreign body in Prusso-Germany',[9] and 'the most English city on the continent'.[10] An island of republicanism in a monarchical sea, a bastion of bourgeois rule in an Empire dominated by aristocratic forms, the city of Hamburg seems to confound almost every generalization historians have made about the German *Kaiserreich* in recent years. Of course, needless to say, Hamburg had always been obliged to pay heed to the wishes of the larger entities that surrounded it. One of the problems of analysing the relationships of state and society in nineteenth-century Germany has always been the need to recognize that the state existed on at

[5] Ibid., p. 235. Cf. V. R. Berghahn, *Germany and the Approach of War in 1914* (London, 1973), ch. 1, for a discussion of the 'Prusso-German' constitutional system.

[6] Huber, *Struktur*; for the German Confederation, see the previous volumes in the series, *Deutsche Verfassungsgeschichte seit 1789*, i. *Reform und Restauration 1789–1830* (2nd edn., Stuttgart, 1975), ii. *Der Kampf um Einheit und Freiheit 1830–1850* (2nd edn., Stuttgart, 1978).

[7] See, in general, T. Nipperdey, *Deutsche Geschichte 1800–1866* (Munich, 1983), p. 91.

[8] P. E. Schramm, *Hamburg. Ein Sonderfall in der Geschichte Deutschlands* (Hamburg, 1964).

[9] E. Böhm, 'Wirtschaft und Politik in Hamburg zur Zeit der Reichsgründung', *ZHG* 64 (1978), 52–3.

[10] H. Böhme, *Frankfurt und Hamburg. Des Deutschen Reiches Silber-und Goldloch und die aller-englischste Stadt des Kontinents* (Frankfurt, 1968).

least two separate though interrelated levels—national and regional. The decentralized structure of the German state gave a considerable measure of autonomy at a regional or local level. Correspondingly, however, the regional or local state could only operate within the constraints laid down by the state at a national level. These constraints became markedly more severe after the foundation of the North German Confederation in 1867 and above all after the establishment of the German Empire in 1871.

By its geographical location on the North German plain Hamburg fell into the orbit of Prussian power, especially after the territorial changes of 1815.[11] The city did, it is true, possess its own military force, in the shape of the Citizens' Militia (*Bürgermilitär*), but this was hardly capable of putting up any more than token resistance to the professional army of a Great Power, and in any case it was mainly intended as a means of maintaining order within the city. Traditionally, therefore, Hamburg's diplomacy rested on trying to play one side off against the other in times of Great Power conflicts, or, failing that, to back the stronger side in the hope of winning concessions. In 1804, for example, the Senate ordered all the outer fortifications of the city walls to be levelled as a gesture of peace and goodwill to all sides at a time when any one of half a dozen major armies might have invaded it. Already in 1801 Hamburg had been occupied briefly by the Danes; in 1806 it was the turn of the French. From 1807 to 1808, some 15,000 Spanish troops were quartered within the city walls, after which the French took over again. To prevent further disorder, the Senate requested admission to Napoleon's Confederation of the Rhine in 1810, but the next year the French Emperor incorporated the Lower Elbe into France as the *Département des Bouches de l'Elbe* and Hamburg became a 'bonne ville de l'Empire français'. Although the municipal administration was remodelled along French lines, most of its members were drawn from the ranks of the former Senate and the leading merchant families, and none of them, not even the *maire* Amandus Abendroth, seems to have suffered any opprobrium as a result. Abendroth, indeed, was made police chief in 1815 and continued to play a leading part in the city's affairs for years afterwards, becoming Burgomaster in 1831.

In 1813 the French were forced to withdraw, and Hamburg was occupied by Russian cossacks. Shortly afterwards it was reoccupied by the French, who imposed on the unfortunate citizens an enormous fine for having allowed themselves to be invaded by the Russians. The new French occupation, which destroyed what remaining autonomy the city possessed, thoroughly alienated the leading Hamburg families, and in 1814 the citizens gratefully restored the old constitution of 1712 as the last French troops left the city gates. Yet

[11] The following summary is based on E. Klessmann, *Geschichte der Stadt Hamburg* (Hamburg, 1981), pp. 317–18 and W. Jochmann and H.-D. Loose (eds.), *Hamburg. Geschichte der Stadt Hamburg und ihrer Bewohner*, i (Hamburg, 1982), ed. H.-D. Loose (cited below as Loose, *Hamburg*, i).

there was little nationalist enthusiasm to be found among the citizenry, as the historian Barthold Niebuhr complained.[12] What they wanted was the freedom to run their own affairs, not incorporation into a larger state. As the experience of the Napoleonic occupation showed, it was immaterial to them whether they were taken over by France or Germany, so long as they could retain a sufficient degree of autonomy. Indeed many of the great nineteenth-century Hamburg families were of non-German origin, from the Amsincks to the Chapeaurouges, the Godeffroys, the Slomans, and the O'Swalds. The Bavarian diplomat von Homayer complained in 1845 that 'I can find next to nothing that is German in Hamburg, apart from the language ... There can be no question of any German blood here.'[13]

This distance from German nationalism and nationality was increased by the common tendency of Hamburg's merchants to send their sons to serve their apprenticeship in one of the firm's agencies overseas. Characteristically, for example, the later merchant Senators Adolph Hertz, Charles Ami de Chapeaurouge, Max Hayn, and Johann Stahmer spent their youth respectively in East Africa, India, Mexico, and the West Indies. Most of the Amsinck family served their apprenticeships abroad; Martin Garlieb Amsinck (1831–1905) for example took part in the building of Brunel's ship the *Great Eastern* in Glasgow.[14] It was often said that the Hamburg merchants knew Peru or Zanzibar better than they knew their own country. There were, remarked Julius von Eckardt of his period as Senate Secretary during the 1870s, 'in Hamburg in those days dozens of older gentlemen who knew "every town on the Mississippi" from personal experience, and had been "twenty times in London", but had never visited Berlin at all'.[15] Particularly close were the connections to England. In the 1830s half the city's sea-borne trade was carried in English ships.[16] Many of the leading Hamburg firms had branches in London. The greatest merchant families cultivated a self-consciously 'English' style of life, employed English nannies, bought English clothes,[17] and frequently gave their children English names such as Percy, Henry, John, or William.[18]

All this meant that the nationalist aspects of the 1848 Revolution had little resonance in Hamburg. Only the Schleswig-Holstein issue aroused some

[12] Quoted in Loose, *Hamburg*, i. 429.

[13] Cited in R. Hauschild-Thiessen, 'Der Freiherr von Homayer und die Hamburger', *ZHG* 63 (1967), 55–6. Local resentment was stronger than nationalist enthusiasm in other parts of Germany too.

[14] Otto Hintze, *Die Niederländische und Hamburgische Familie Amsinck*, iii (Hamburg, 1932).

[15] J. von Eckardt, *Lebenserinnerungen* (2 vols.; Leipzig, 1910), ii. 12.

[16] Loose, *Hamburg*, i. 448.

[17] StA Hbg, FA Merck II 9 Konv. 4a, Heft II, pp. 2, 9, 16. The Mercks had an English nanny and purchased the children's clothes from Samuel Brothers in Ludgate Hill.

[18] Thus Percy Ernst Schramm, William Henry O'Swald, John Berenberg-Gossler; an exception was Charles Ami de Chapeaurouge, another Senator like O'Swald and Berenberg-Gossler (Schramm, the historian, was the son of a Senator). See entries in index for further details.

nationalist enthusiasm in the city, as much because it concerned a regional market and source of supplies, and because the province bordered on the lower Elbe, Hamburg's lifeline to the sea, as because the citizens were passionately convinced that Schleswig or Holstein should be German rather than Danish.[19] But the brief occupation of the city by Prussian troops in 1849, though encouraged by the Senate as a means of defeating the revolutionary opposition, indicated that Hamburg could not stand aside from national politics for ever, a point further underlined by the occupation of the city by Austrian troops in 1851.[20] Hamburg welcomed the German victory over the Danes in the war of 1864, and the consequent incorporation of Schleswig-Holstein into the Kingdom of Prussia, not least because this made for better relations with the province. In 1866, sympathies in the Senate were on the side of Austria, which—in contrast to Prussia—had helped the city with a generous loan during the economic crisis of 1857. The Senate had consistently fought against attempts to create an effective central authority in Germany, from the days of the Frankfurt Parliament of 1848 onwards. It was initially disinclined to give in to Prussia's demands in 1866, which included the placing of the Citizens' Militia at Prussia's disposal, largely because of Bismarck's intention to limit the city's autonomy by incorporating it into the newly formed North German Confederation, forerunner of the Empire of 1871.[21] However, the Senate, frightened by Bismarck's threat to reduce it to the role of a Prussian municipality, and reassured by his promise to respect Hamburg's status and take account of its trading interests in future economic policies, gave in—the last North German state to do so—and took the city into the new Confederation and, in 1871, the Reich.[22]

The unification of Germany (described by Burgomaster Martin Haller in 1870 as 'our contract with Prussia') brought about obvious changes in the daily life of the city. Like other member states of the German Confederation, Hamburg had its own weights and measures and its own postal service; these now disappeared as unitary systems were introduced throughout the North German Confederation and then the Reich. Hamburg's local currency—12 Pfennigs to the Schilling, 16 Schillings to the Mark Banco[23]—gave way to the new Imperial decimal coinage. Hamburg's ensign, a three-towered white castle on a red field, was replaced on Hamburg's ships by the Imperial black–white–red. The Citizens' Militia was abolished and the Second Hanseatic Infantry Regiment formed under Prussian command. Hamburg's diplomatic and consular service had to cease functioning. The citizens were also subject

[19] W. Schmidt, *Die Revolution von 1848–49 in Hamburg* (Ergebnisse, Heft 22, Hamburg, 1983).
[20] Loose, *Hamburg*, i. 481.
[21] Ibid., pp. 496–8.
[22] Von Eckardt, *Lebenserinnerungen*, i. 210.
[23] The Mark Banco (0.33 of a Banco-Thaler) was a standard unit of account used in bank transactions and valued at 1.25 Mark Courant (the unit of currency in circulation). In the 1870s one Mark Courant was valued at 1.20 Reichsmark.

to Imperial taxation, mild though this was. The Hanseatic judicial system had to be co-ordinated with that of the Reich; the constitutional changes of 1879, which separated the judiciary from the executive and the judges from the advocates, were largely consequent upon the introduction of the Imperial Criminal Code to replace Hamburg's own criminal law.[24]

None of this was welcomed by the vocal party of Old Hamburg Particularists in the Senate, which included Burgomasters Haller and Gossler and Senators Sieveking and Rücker, and was led by Burgomaster Gustav Heinrich Kirchenpauer (born 1808, and Senator since 1843) and Senate Syndic Carl Merck (born 1809, in office since 1847).[25] From 1867 to 1880 Kirchenpauer was Hamburg's representative on the Federal Council. He regarded its policy as 'imperialism in all directions', and described its constitution as a 'concoction' in which 'the Senates are downgraded to town councils'.[26] He was virtually the only member of the Federal Council who objected to Bismarck's constitutional proposals. He fought the Chancellor over the unitary ensign, over military service, and over other issues as well. Even Bremen and Lübeck refused to support him. Bismarck for his part complained that he encountered in Kirchenpauer the 'narrowest particularism, a clinging to peculiar institutions, a refusal to bear common burdens, such as I have not encountered in any of the princes'. He organized a press campaign against Hamburg and forced the Senate to give in, which it did under written protest.[27] Senate Syndic Merck, who with Kirchenpauer was responsible for Hamburg's foreign policy, was even more determinedly particularist in his sympathies. 'We make no secret', he wrote, 'of the fact that we want to remain Hamburgers, we fight tooth and nail against the ever-approaching danger, for what is the whole creation that Berlin is making except a gradual sucking dry of the other states?!' He considered emigrating in 1869 to escape what he regarded as a humiliating situation, and in 1870, in the middle of the Franco-Prussian War, he compared the local Prussian army commander in Hamburg with Marshal Davout, who had led the occupying French forces in their depredation of Hamburg during the Napoleonic War.[28]

The victory of Sedan of 1870 aroused a good deal of enthusiasm in Hamburg; but at least one Senator was heard to remark that any more quick

[24] Ibid., pp. 212–15; R. Hauschild-Thiessen, *Bürgerstolz und Kaisertreue. Hamburg und das Deutsche Reich von 1871* (Hamburg, 1979), p. 5.

[25] Loose, *Hamburg*, i. 498–9.

[26] H.-G. Schönhoff, *Hamburg im Bundesrat. Die Mitwirkung Hamburgs an der Bildung des Reichswillens 1867–1890* (Hamburg, 1967), p. 29.

[27] Ibid., p. 39.

[28] Loose, *Hamburg*, i. 501–2. See also von Eckardt, *Lebenserinnerungen*, ii. 8–11. Senate Secretary Otto Beneke, the city archivist, was even more extreme. He refused until the end of his life to attend any celebrations in honour of the Reich or the Kaiser, including the victory celebrations of 1870. See von Eckardt, op. cit., ii. 13–14; also Hauschild-Thiessen, *Bürgerstolz*, pp. 108–25. Von Eckardt, however (i. 217–21), reported widespread enthusiasm on the Exchange during the war of 1870–1.

Prussian victories in the war would endanger Hamburg's autonomy,[29] and in fact throughout the late 1860s and the 1870s Hamburg regarded the Federal Council solely in the light of its own particular interests. As the historian of the city's relations with the North German Confederation concluded,[30]

As the negotiations of the administrative laws, the industrial code, the apportionment of contributions to the Reich and the Supreme Commercial Court show, Hamburg consistently resisted these measures in order to preserve its particular characteristics and in order to avoid as far as possible being disturbed in its previous state practices by the new Confederation.

In some areas in which the city had no interest, such as the *Kulturkampf*, Hamburg followed the Prussian line; on other issues, such as the Anti-Socialist Law, it objected simply because an increase in the powers of central government was involved.[31] Most of these efforts had little success, although the Senate was able to play a part in the shaping of a new Banking Law.[32] But together with Bremen, Hamburg got its own way with regard to the question of German consulates, and usually successfully proposed its own nominees for these posts, which were so vital to Hanseatic trading interests.[33] None of this endeared the Hamburgers to the Prussians. 'The citizens of Hamburg', complained the German Ambassador in London in December 1879, 'are the worst Germans we have, and they use the imperial government only for their own purposes, if they can'.[34] The Senate, as another Prussian official remarked, would 'participate in questions of grand European diplomacy at most in so far as they affected business on the Exchange'.[35]

Already by this time, however, the Prussian party in the Senate was beginning to get the upper hand. Its leading figure, and the most important Senator in Hamburg throughout the last quarter of the nineteenth century, was Johannes Versmann.[36] Versmann's career repays close attention because it was in many ways characteristic of the personal history of many leading members of Germany's liberal bourgeoisie in this era, and also because he played a leading role in the events described later in this book. He was one of those rare outsiders who made his way in Hamburg politics by sheer ability and force of character. Born in St Pauli, outside the city boundaries, in 1820, he was the son of an apothecary. He was not related to the old Hamburg

[29] Von Eckardt, op. cit., i. 221.
[30] Schönhoff, *Bundesrat*, p. 71.
[31] Ibid.
[32] Von Eckardt, *Lebenserinnerungen*, ii. 47–8.
[33] Schönhoff, loc. cit.
[34] Quoted in F. Stern, *Gold and Iron. Bismarck, Bleichröder and the Building of the German Empire* (London, 1977), p. 399.
[35] Von Eckardt, *Lebenserinnerungen*, i. 191.
[36] Ibid., ii. 16–17. See Plate 3.

families, nor did he marry into one. His forebears came from Uelzen, a small town to the south of Hamburg. Versmann was a school friend of the later ancient historian and liberal politician Theodor Mommsen; both of them belonged to the same Science Club (*Wissenschaftlicher Verein*) in 1837–9. In 1839–40 Versmann attended the Johanneum High School in Hamburg before going to Jena to study medicine. He did not get along with the Jena medical school, however, so he moved to Göttingen in 1842, then to Heidelberg in 1843–4. His new subject was law, in which he qualified in 1844. Back in Hamburg, he joined a law firm, where he worked with Carl Petersen, subsequently his fellow Senator, on commercial cases. Soon he began to take an active role in politics. At university he had already moved in liberal circles and met the later radical Gustav Struve; in 1845 he joined the St Pauli Citizens' Club and in 1846 the Hamburg Lawyers' Club—both leading institutions in the liberal opposition that was beginning to form against the old Hamburg constitution at this time.[37]

It was the 1848 Revolution that first brought Versmann to prominence. He joined a volunteer force which marched against Denmark, and he was captured and imprisoned by the Danes on 9 April; but after the truce of Malmö he was released and made his way back to Hamburg, where he became a spokesman for the liberal-democratic opposition and was elected to the Constituent Assembly which met in 1849. By 14 March he had impressed the delegates so much that they elected him President. But the Senate's delaying tactics, supported by Prussian troops, nullified the work of the Assembly. Versmann's last speech before its dissolution could stand as a motto for his entire political career. 'No one can fight against the power of events,' he said: 'it is well for us, doubly so under such circumstances, that we can say, we have done our duty.' His efforts had been directed towards ensuring administrative continuity while sweeping away enough of the old institutions to satisfy popular demand. Defeated, he retired from public life and resumed his legal career, becoming President of the Commercial Court in 1859. The new constitution of 1860, however, brought Versmann's immediate election to the Citizens' Assembly, which proceeded without hesitation to install him as its President. His successful efforts to reach a final compromise with the Senate over the remaining details of the constitutional reform brought him further goodwill on all sides. In 1861 he became a Senator, a position he held without a break until his death in 1899.

In his early years in the Senate, Versmann was said to have been 'somewhat isolated', no doubt because of his humble background as well as because of his support for all kinds of unfashionable causes. He was, for example, an advocate of administrative reform; for over twenty years he tried unsuc-

---

[37] For the details of Versmann's life in this and following paragraphs, see A. Wohlwill, 'Johannes Versmann. Zur Geschichte seiner Jugendjahre und seiner späteren Wirksamkeit', *ZHG* 15 (1910), 166–252.

cessfully to persuade the Senate to delegate minor matters to a professional administration, and he urged the appointment of paid higher civil servants long before the Senate finally introduced them.[38] Although he was highly respected in the Senate, he was, unusually for a leading member of a body which depended heavily on informal social relations for its effectiveness, not well liked. Johann Georg Mönckeberg, who compiled private obituaries of most of his colleagues, had, exceptionally, no personal reminiscences to record of Versmann; he merely included a copy of the anodyne formal speech he delivered at the swearing in of Versmann's replacement. Versmann won his dominant position in the Senate partly through his hard-headed political realism, partly through the intellectual power with which he could argue a case, partly by his patience, persistence, and sometimes deviousness when fighting for a cause he believed in (Mönckeberg described him as 'stubborn'). More than anything else, however, Versmann was thorough. While other Senators continued to run their businesses, or simply relaxed in private, Versmann, a man of 'tireless industriousness', as a colleague described him,[39] worked long hours and mastered every subject he put his hand to. The result was that other, less energetic Senators, which is to say the great majority, simply could not compete. Max Hayn, for example, as the senior merchant Senator, was elected Burgomaster in 1887 to fill in for a few months between Kirchenpauer's death and the next election, but according to Mönckeberg, 'Hayn has scarcely functioned as Burgomaster, because Versmann took charge of all the business with the greatest zeal'.[40] Gloomy and pessimistic by nature, Versmann had a sharp eye for political reality, as he had already demonstrated in 1849—'that "sixth sense" ... which no politician can afford to lack: a feeling for what is possible and attainable'.[41] His biographer was forced to admit that 'Here and there one heard however complaints against his cool reticence or his all too derogatory judgments'.[42] Versmann was not a man to suffer fools gladly, a fact abundantly illustrated by even the most cursory glance at his voluminous diaries.

He worked influentially in the Senate to persuade the Old Hamburg Particularists of the necessity of giving in to Prussian pressure in 1866 and again in the 1870s, and did more than anyone else to secure the introduction of Reich laws and the reorganization of the school system in the city after unification. But it was in the question of the Customs Union that he gained his greatest triumph. Hamburg's merchant community regarded it as an article of faith that free trade was the foundation of mercantile prosperity. Not only did they fear that tariff barriers would hit trade; increasing numbers

[38] Von Eckardt, *Lebenserinnerungen*, ii. 7.
[39] Ibid., ii. 16.
[40] StA Hbg, FA Mönckeberg 21a, Bl. 259, 268–9.
[41] Von Eckardt, *Lebenserinnerungen*, ii. 16.
[42] Wohlwill, 'Johannes Versmann', p. 248; cf. von Eckardt, *Lebenserinnerungen*, ii. 55.

of them were also engaged in importing raw materials, processing them, and re-exporting them, an activity that could only be really profitable under a free trade regime. In consequence Hamburg steadfastly refused to join the German Customs Union (*Zollverein*), arguing as early as 1820 that 'The advantage of the German seaports required free trade. Where they got their wares from, and where they took them to, did not come into the picture.'[43] As early as 1845, Versmann had argued in favour of Hamburg joining the Customs Union, largely for nationalistic reasons.[44] But thirty years later, his wish had still not been fulfilled. Free trade was something of a dogma among the citizens of Hamburg. It was held to be the foundation not only of the city's prosperity but even of its whole way of life, a view summed up in the toast to the English free trader Richard Cobden on his visit to the city in 1847 by the President of the Commercial Deputation: 'The creator of every other freedom: freedom of trade!'[45] As the Prussian historian Treitschke later complained, the proponents of free trade in Hamburg had 'in German fashion made out of necessity not just a virtue but a theory'.[46]

Hamburg had managed to preserve its status as a customs-free port on joining the North German Confederation in 1866, and continued to remain aloof from the Customs Union even after the founding of the German Empire in 1871. As long as economic policy in the Reich was also dominated by free-trade thinking, there seemed little to worry about. But in 1878 Bismarck put an end to this period by demanding the introduction of import tariffs, partly to improve Reich finances, partly to confound the National Liberals, on whom he felt he had become too dependent, and partly to appease the landowners and industrialists who wanted protection against foreign competition. The new scheme demanded that Hamburg, Germany's biggest import centre, join the Customs Union. The Old Hamburg Particularists compared this prospect with the incorporation of the city into the Napoleonic Empire in 1808.[47] Kirchenpauer clashed with Bismarck in the Federal Council once again, and this time the pressure from the Chancellor was so great—including the threat of removing Hamburg's status as a free port by force—that Kirchenpauer felt obliged to hand over his position as Hanseatic representative on the Federal Council to Versmann, since in the long run the victory of Bismarck's policy seemed inevitable. The Senate and the merchant community were convulsed by a furious debate on the question of whether or not to join. Skilfully steering a middle course between the warring parties and the Chancellor, Versmann, aided by Senate Syndic Roeloffs, his *alter ego* and right-hand man,[48] and negotiating on some points without even informing the Senate of what he

[43] Quoted in Schmidt, *Die Revolution*, p. 121 n. 34.
[44] Wohlwill, loc. cit.
[45] Schmidt, op. cit., p. 14.
[46] Loose, *Hamburg*, i. 443.
[47] Hauschild-Thiessen, *Bürgerstolz*, p. 18.
[48] Von Eckardt, *Lebenserinnerungen*, ii. 59.

was doing, achieved an ingenious compromise. Indeed, he went so far as to organize public opposition to the Customs Union in Hamburg so as to extract enough concessions from Bismarck to make the policy acceptable to the free-trade majority in the Senate.[49] Finally, in 1881, the deal offered by Versmann was accepted. It created within the Hamburg harbour a very extensive new duty-free area, sealed off from the hinterland by new customs posts, a 'free port' in which export industries could function; Hamburg was allowed to control the customs arrangements itself, and was assured that they could be conducted in a relatively unbureaucratic manner.[50]

The opening of the new free port, and the entry of Hamburg into the Customs Union, which finally took place in 1888, had profound consequences for the city's economic and social life. More immediately, however, it marked the final demise of the Old Hamburg Particularists and the triumph of the pro-Prussian party. From the moment of his victory in 1881 until his death in 1899, Versmann, supported in the Senate by increasing numbers of his protégés such as Mönckeberg and Burchard, was the dominant figure in Hamburg politics. His only rival, Senator Carl Petersen, was already elderly (he was born in 1808) and in any case by this stage in his career he agreed with Versmann in most essentials. Symbolically enough, Versmann's own final appearance on the political stage, on 28 March 1899, was as President of the Hamburg branch of the Navy League, when he spoke in favour of the construction of a German battle fleet, a cause he had in fact actively espoused as early as 1861. A consistent liberal nationalist, he had thus travelled the long road from opposition in 1848 to support for the government's expansionist foreign policy at the turn of the century, along with most of the rest of the German bourgeoisie.[51]

Nationalist sentiment was by no means incompatible with a wish to preserve regional peculiarities, still less with a desire to secure the best possible political conditions for Hamburg's trade.[52] Just as historians have persistently underestimated the strength and vehemence of particularist sentiment in Germany in the second and third quarters of the nineteenth century, so too they have commonly overestimated the degree and extent of centralization and uniformity in the German Empire in the last quarter. Whatever they thought were the needs of the German Empire as a great power, the rulers of Hamburg remained firmly wedded to the principle that they, rather than the Prussians, were the best judges of what was good for Hamburg. 'May Hamburg', as one speaker in the Citizens' Assembly put it in 1892, 'retain the peculiarities which harm no one ... May we protect them as long as we

[49] H.-K. Stein, 'Interessenkonflikte zwischen Grosskaufleuten, Handelskammer und Senat in der Frage des Zollanschlusses an das Reich 1866–1881', *ZHG* 64 (1978), 55–89.
[50] For a brief account of the struggle over the Customs Union, see Loose, *Hamburg*, i. 514–17.
[51] Wohlwill, 'Johannes Versmann', p. 248.
[52] Cf. von Eckardt, *Lebenserinnerungen*, i. 209.

can.'[53] How far this was possible men such as Versmann, who kept a file on 'Notes concerning measures and demands on the occasion of the loss of Hamburg's autonomy'[54] clearly doubted. But that it was worth attempting, not even Versmann was moved to deny.

II

The pecularities of Hamburg began with its representative constitution. The provisions of the constitution were of a complexity that defies easy summary. During the first half of the nineteenth century, the city governed itself in all essentials according to the constitution (*Hauptrezess*) forced on it by the Holy Roman Emperor in an attempt to put an end to several years of violent struggles between the Council and the citizens in 1712. According to this constitution the city was ruled by a Council (*Rat*) or Senate (*Senat*) jointly with the Propertied Citizenry (*Erbgesessene Bürgerschaft*). No law could be passed without the approval of both, although in practice the Propertied Citizenry only possessed a blocking power. The Senate consisted of four Burgomasters (*Bürgermeister*)[55] and twenty-four Senators. It co-opted its members, who held office for life, and it wielded general executive powers. In the Senate there were also four non-voting members, also co-opted, called Syndics (*Syndici*), whose task it was to give the Senators legal advice and to carry out some of the more detailed administrative work. Finally, there were five Senate Secretaries, to complete the picture. The Propertied Citizenry consisted of all male citizens who possessed landed property within the city walls and could demonstrate possession of non-fixed assets in excess of 3,000 Marks; by 'citizen' (*Bürger*) was meant a man who had paid the citizenship fee (a substantial sum of money) and was a permanent inhabitant of the city.[56]

[53] *Bürgerschaft*; these bound newspaper reports are the only easily accessible accounts of the debates of the Citizens' Assembly until official stenographic reports began to be issued later in the 1890s; here the date is 3 Feb. 1892 and the speaker Amandus Gérard.

[54] StA Hbg, FA Versmann F4.

[55] For a convenient brief introduction to Hamburg's constitutional history, see H. W. Eckardt, *Privilegien und Parlament. Die Auseinandersetzungen um das allgemeine und gleiche Wahlrecht in Hamburg* (Hamburg, 1980), pp. 10–11. Further details in Schmidt, *Die Revolution*, pp. 20–2. The word *Bürgermeister* is conventionally translated as 'Mayor', but while this is reasonable enough for an ordinary German town, it completely fails to convey the significance of the office in Hamburg, which was both more important than that of a mayor, because Hamburg was a state as well as a city, and appointed in an entirely different way from the office of mayor in a Prussian municipality. The translation I use (Burgomaster) derives from an article on Hamburg in the *Illustrated London News*, 2797, 26 Nov. 1892 (copy in StA Hbg, FA Petersen D23).

[56] The translation of the word *Bürger* poses almost insoluble problems. To be consistent with the term 'Burgomaster' it should perhaps be translated as 'burgher', but in English this now possesses an antiquated, medieval significance that it did not have in 19th-century Germany ('the burghers of Calais'). I have chosen therefore to be inconsistent and use the term 'citizen', which conveys the centrality of political rights to the concept in a way that 'burgher' does not.

A new constitution came into force on 28 September 1860, just over a decade after the 1848 Revolution,[57] and introduced a stronger parliamentary element into the city's government. The elective principle was strengthened. The Senate was reduced to eighteen in number and was no longer self-perpetuating: Senators were elected jointly by the Senate and the Citizens' Assembly (*Bürgerschaft*) from a short list compiled by representatives of both; but once elected, they remained in office for life and could not be removed. The number of Syndics (non-voting legal advisers present at all Senate meetings) was reduced to two and there were four Senate Secretaries, of whom however only three attended Senate meetings, the fourth being *ex officio* city archivist. The Senators in office in 1860 continued to function, so that the new procedure only came into effect gradually as they retired or died.[58] The Senate and the Citizens' Assembly retained joint sovereignty and all legislation had to be approved by both. The new Citizens' Assembly (*Bürgerschaft*) consisted of 192 elected deputies. 84 of them were elected in the general elections by tax-paying citizens (who continued to have to pay a substantial citizens' fee). Another 60 were elected by the 'notables'—citizens occupying civic office (either in the courts or the Deputations[59])—while the rights of the property-owners were safeguarded by giving them 48 deputies to appoint in their own elections. The term of office of the deputies was six years; elections for half the seats in the general elections and those of the property-owners took place once every three years. This constitution remained in force in its essentials until 1918, but it underwent, as we shall see in the course of this book, a series of hotly contested and by no means unimportant amendments in the intervening years. The first of these took place in 1879–80, when the number of deputies was reduced to 160, with 80 being elected in the general election, and 40 each in the notables' and property-owners' elections. No more amendments were made until near the end of the century.[60]

The cumulative effect of the constitutional changes of 1860 and 1879–80 was to increase the power of the ordinary taxpaying citizen in the Citizens' Assembly, partly through making the Assembly a smaller body more easily responsive to his needs, partly by opening it up for discussion and debate, partly by reducing the representation of the notables and office-holders, and partly through subjecting Senators and deputies for the first time to the electoral process. By making the Senate into an elective body, the changes shifted the balance of power in the constitution slightly in favour of the citizenry since it could now block the appointment of Senators whose views or personalities it found objectionable. However, if the Senate was really set on electing someone, it usually got its way in the end: of the seven candidates

[57] For the following, see the works cited above, n. 55.
[58] Von Eckardt, *Lebenserinnerungen*, ii. 9.
[59] For a brief account of these, see below, pp. 26–7.
[60] Eckardt, *Privilegien und Parlament*, pp. 25–8, 31.

defeated in the Senatorial elections between Septembèr 1886 and February
1900, for example, four were elected at a second attempt, one at a third and
one, indeed, at the fourth try; one died soon after losing the election and only
one candidate was not put forward again.[61] These gradual reforms, the
element of continuity, and the principle of a property-owning parliamentary
system, albeit one with its own very distinctive features, all helped single
Hamburg out as an 'English' city. Yet the irremovability of the Senate was
an obvious 'German' feature in all this, paralleling the freedom of ministers
in the Reich from direct parliamentary censure and removal from office by
parliamentary vote, even though the Reich Ministers were appointed by the
Emperor, not elected, and could be dismissed by him. Moreover, merely to
describe the formal provisions of the constitution conveys little of the realities
of city government. Politics in Hamburg, as elsewhere, depended to a large
extent on informal structures and traditions, which breathed life into what
were only skeletal provisions in the constitution. Here too, as we shall now
see, Prussia and Prussianism seemed far away: for in looking at these informal
state structures, we enter the cosy world of the mercantile bourgeoisie made
famous by Thomas Mann's great novel *Buddenbrooks*.

Hamburg had never experienced a closed patriciate. In the eighteenth
century the great merchant houses rose and fell with a febrile instability that
reflected the risks as well as the rewards of a rapidly expanding mercantile
capitalism.[62] In the course of the nineteenth century, however, a number of
great families emerged to dominate the Senate, and beneath all the constitutional changes that took place, the city's government gradually became
oligarchical. The reforms of 1860 made little or no difference to the requirement—which the Senate could always insist on—that Senators should in the
main be chosen from the wealthiest and most socially prominent of the
merchant families.[63] This remained the case even after the turn of the century.
When Rudolf Martin compiled his *Yearbook of Hanseatic Millionaires*[64] on the
eve of the First World War, he was able to include no fewer than 12 out of
the 18 members of the Hamburg Senate on his list. The interrelationships of
the Hamburg Senators were so complex and many-layered that it would take
a professional genealogist to disentangle them all. They formed large clans
such as the Amsincks, who supplied not only one of Hamburg's leading
Senators, Burgomaster Wilhelm Amsinck (1752–1831) but also married into

[61] StA Hbg, FA Voigt B68 (newspaper clipping); see also ibid., FA Buehl 2c, p. 42.

[62] For Hamburg in the 18th century, see F. Kopitzsch, *Grundzüge einer Geschichte der Aufklärung
in Norddeutschland* (Hamburg, 1984), and J. Whaley, *Religious Toleration and Social Change in
Hamburg 1529–1819* (Cambridge, 1985).

[63] L. Lippmann, 'Mein Leben und meine amtliche Tätigkeit. Erinnerungen und ein Beitrag zur
Finanzgeschichte Hamburgs', p. 11 (typescript in StA Hbg, FA Lippmann A4). The memoirs were
subsequently published under the same title, edited by Werner Jochmann, in 1964.

[64] R. Martin, *Jahrbuch des Vermögens und Einkommens der Millionäre in den drei Hansestädten*
(Berlin, 1912).

a number of other senatorial families such as the Gosslers, the Sievekings, the Burchards, the Westphals, and the Mercks.[65] All these clans were owners of considerable wealth. The richest man in the city in the early twentieth century was said to be the shipowner Henry Sloman, worth 60 million Marks with an annual income of over 3 million.[66] He too was related to the Amsincks; one of Wilhelm Amsinck's numerous grandchildren married his relative Carl Brödermann-Sloman in 1900.[67] The Amsincks were only one of a score of such clans, all related in one way or another. At any one time several of the men who sat on the Senate were bound to be related. Four of the most prominent Burgomasters of the nineteenth century for instance, Petersen, Mönckeberg, Kirchenpauer, and Kellinghusen, were all related by marriage; between 1876 and 1879 all four of them were in the Senate together.[68] Those fortunate enough to find themselves at the centre of the web of intermarriage that linked Hamburg's great families could expect early advancement in politics, provided their abilities warranted it. Johann Heinrich Burchard, who not only belonged to a patrician family but also married into one through his wife Emily Amsinck, became a Senator at the early age of thirty-two. And even those who were not born into the patriciate were often co-opted into it by marriage. Johann Predöhl made his reputation very quickly as one of Hamburg's most brilliant lawyers; despite his relatively humble origins, this was in itself enough for him to be able to marry an Amsinck, and in due course to be elected to the Senate.[69] Throughout the nineteenth century and well into the twentieth, therefore, Hamburg's Senate consisted of members of a close-knit group of patrician families, not only related to one another by marriage, but also part of a much wider kinship network embracing the richest segment of the mercantile and financial community.

Yet although it is often said that Hamburg was ruled by merchants, the reality was not quite so simple. According to the constitution of 1712, 3 of the Burgomasters, 11 Senators and all 4 Syndics had to be lawyers, and 1 Burgomaster and 13 Senators merchants. This division of power was perpetuated in the constitution of 1860, according to which at least 9 of the 18 Senators and all 4 Syndics had to be lawyers. Some 7 places were reserved for merchants, though in practice they often occupied the remaining 2 seats as well. Only the lawyers among the Senators were traditionally entitled to function as Burgomaster or President of the Senate. At any one time after the reforms of 1860 there were two Burgomasters; each of the three longest-serving legal Senators served a year as Second Burgomaster, the following

---

[65] Hintze, *Die Familie Amsinck*, iii.

[66] Martin, op. cit.

[67] Hintze, op. cit.

[68] H. von Marchtaler, *Aus Alt-Hamburger Senatorenhäusern. Familienschicksale im 18. und 19. Jahrhundert* (Hamburg, 1958), genealogical table. Details of Senators' terms of office are taken from *MdB*.

[69] StA Hbg, FA Buehl 2c, pp. 75–7.

year as First Burgomaster, then took a year off before beginning the cycle again.[70] Thus the merchant Senators were excluded from the two most powerful and important posts after 1860; in practice they had played a relatively modest role in the executive even before. Moreover, serious merchants from large and important firms seldom entered the Senate, even though in theory they were entitled to continue their business after their election. Looking back on his long career as a Senator in 1902, Johann Georg Mönckeberg[71] recalled that

None of the five merchants who left the Senate during the last few years—Möring, de Chapeaurouge, Stahmer, Hertz, and Roosen—was an active merchant; Möring and Roosen, as far as I am aware, never had businesses of their own that amounted to anything, and the three others had long since withdrawn from commercial life. The same goes for Hayn, Grossmann, and von Melle.

Their importance did not therefore lie in the fact that they were active businessmen who represented the interests of the merchants of Hamburg in any direct sense; nor did the fact that most of them had spent part of their now distant youth working for Hamburg merchants abroad make much difference in this respect. Mönckeberg remarked that the Chamber of Commerce knew much better what the immediate needs and problems of the merchant community were than any of the so-called merchant Senators.

Not only were the merchant Senators usually not very active merchants, however, they were not very active Senators either. According to Mönckeberg 'It cannot be doubted that the mercantile gentlemen are less well-suited for the duties of the Senate than are the legal members'. With very rare exceptions such as Senator William O'Swald (born 1832, elected 1869, and, exceptionally, Burgomaster in 1908–9) the merchants in the Senate were in no way the equals of the lawyers. They lacked the proper training and experience for coping with modern administration, especially as it became more complex and more subject to legal controls. By the 1890s elaborate laws were having to be drawn up on all kinds of subjects, often involving technicalities which the merchants were unable to master. In earlier times, thought Mönckeberg, administration had been 'less constricted by laws' and the merchant Senator 'had thus been able to proceed with great self-reliance simply by following his own common sense'. It was increasingly unusual for them to be put in charge of major committees. Thus Senator Carl Möring (born 1818, elected 1861), though a conscientious Senator, was described by Mönckeberg in a

---

[70] Details of these provisions ibid.; in Eckardt, *Privilegien und Parlament*, p. 75; and in Schmidt, *Die Revolution*, p. 66 n. 122. A rare exception was made for Senator William Henry O'Swald, who, although a merchant Senator, played an important role in the Customs Union negotiations (see pp. 9–11, above) and was generally recognized as a figure of outstanding ability; even he, however, only became Second Burgomaster in the two years 1908–9, never First.

[71] The following account and quotations are taken from StA Hbg. FA Mönckeberg 21a: Erinnerungen von Johann Georg Mönckeberg (1854–1908), Bl. 276–8. See Plate 1.

favourite phrase as 'intellectually not a very outstanding man ... His views rarely made themselves known in the Senate, he spoke seldom, and usually voted with the Chairman.' His position was further weakened by the fact that he was a retiring individual who played little part in the social life of Hamburg's ruling class. 'He never took charge of the great, important departments of state.' Adolph Hertz and Rudolph Roosen, too, according to Mönckeberg, were 'intellectually not very outstanding men'. Hertz became notorious in the Senate for his long speeches, and his performance in administration was disastrous. 'He was never able to cope with the administration of the City Engineer's Department', declared Mönckeberg: 'he was quite incapable of discussing the difficult problems that occurred in the Tax Deputation.' As for Roosen, Mönckeberg declared roundly that 'he failed to find a role in the Senate'. Both indeed eventually resigned on grounds of ill health.

Even a more intelligent and well-liked merchant Senator such as Johann Stahmer (born 1819, elected 1875) was scarcely any more important in the Senate. His 'sharp wits' and his 'affable humour' were said by Mönckeberg to have won him 'general respect and affection' in the Senate. Yet as head of the Section for River and Harbour Buildings, not one of the central offices, he was not a success, and became involved in many quarrels with more important arms of government such as the Deputation for Trade and Shipping. In consequence, perhaps, he refused to take on any more major posts in later years; indeed, when he was once sent on a mission to Berlin he proved unable to cope with the Prussian bureaucrats with whom he was supposed to negotiate and returned home suffering from a diplomatic illness. Eventually he found his niche as the Senate's wine steward: 'When the Senate held a banquet, Stahmer had to check the menu and the wines.' He was also much in demand at these functions as an after-dinner speaker. All in all, therefore, the merchant Senators, if one is to believe Johann Georg Mönckeberg, did not contribute much of importance to the running of the city. 'So what then is their importance for the Senate?' asked Mönckeberg. He went on:

I would like to answer the question in the following sense, that according to the basic concept of the constitution, the government of Hamburg should reflect not only the legal or the technical and administrative point of view, but also the general point of view of the ordinary citizen, the standpoint of so-called common sense, an unprejudiced judgement such as can be expected from educated laymen in public affairs, and it reflects all this through the merchant Senators. This composition of the Senate makes it easier to reach agreement with the Citizens' Assembly, in which the lay element (in relation to administrative questions of all types) is predominant. It is also a result of the organization of our administration. When the departments of state consist to a large extent of laymen, it is only logical to elect proven members of the Deputations to the Senate as well.

Of course, 'common sense' here meant, as it usually does, a set of attitudes and prejudices whose limits were more or less narrowly defined. Only merchants from a specific social and political background were elected as Senators; and Mönckeberg seems to have considered that they were most useful when they were most in touch with the merchant community. He prized Senator Stahmer despite his disinclination for administrative work precisely because his contacts were particularly good:

Partly from his own experience—he had been active for a long time in a large merchant house in the West Indies—and partly through his social intercourse in various circles, he was well-informed on matters of current interest among the mercantile community; yet he often showed great confidence in his own judgement by taking a point of view opposite to that of the leading spirits of the Chamber of Commerce.

The Chamber of Commerce (*Handelskammer*) was in fact long dominated by middling and small overseas firms, and the great merchant families were thus forced to exert their influence more informally.[72] It was for this that the merchant Senators were especially important. In terms of day-to-day administration, there is no doubt that the actual work was done by the lawyers in the Senate. They were the people who exercised power in Hamburg, in the most direct and immediate sense of the word.

III

Law in nineteenth-century Hamburg meant in the first place commercial law. Liability, breach of contract, indebtedness, salvage, and a thousand other legal aspects of overseas trade were too technical for merchants to handle themselves. So most of the great merchant families maintained close contacts with legal partnerships and made sure that those of their offspring who seemed suitable embarked on a legal career. In every generation, for example, the Amsinck family had one lawyer: Wilhelm Amsinck (1752–1831), his second son Wilhelm (1793–1874), and his son Caesar (1849–1922) were all lawyers; the rest of this large clan were almost all merchants or shipowners, though a good number of them were also related to lawyers by marriage. Until 1879 the Hamburg legal system distinguished between barristers (*Prokuratoren*) and solicitors (*Advokaten*), but there was one court where solicitors were allowed to plead in person rather than appointing a barrister to represent them, and that was the Commercial Court (*Handelsgericht*), established in 1816 along French lines with verbal rather than written proceedings. Traditionally, ambitious lawyers preferred to be solicitors; from here it was common to advance to the position of a judge, and thence ultimately, if all

---

[72] Stein, 'Interessenkonflikte'. For a detailed study of a comparable ruling system in another autonomous city (until 1866), see R. Koch, *Grundlagen bürgerlicher Herrschaft. Verfassungs- und sozialgeschichtliche Studien zur bürgerlicher Gesellschaft in Frankfurt am Main (1612–1866)* (Wiesbaden, 1983).

went well, to the Senate.[73] The legal profession, or at least that part of it—the solicitors—that supplied the members of the Senate, was closely bound into the network of great merchant families. While the merchant Senators not infrequently came from second-rank mercantile houses, the legal Senators were largely drawn from the members of the most prominent patrician families. Indeed the pressures on a successful lawyer from a patrician family to join the Senate were overwhelming. A major scandal was caused in 1875 when Friedrich Sieveking, a prominent lawyer from one of the great Senatorial dynasties, refused election to the Senate and barred his door to the officials sent to bring him to the investiture. Two years later he gave in, with scarcely concealed bad grace, and accepted a second election, only to cause yet further disapproval when he resigned in 1879 to become a judge in the newly created High Court.[74] The legal Senators were almost consciously predestined to represent mercantile interests; and through their family connections they were subject to constant mercantile influence of an informal kind. Yet the legal Senators cannot simply be regarded as the creatures of the merchant community, without any separate identity of their own. To begin with, all of them received their legal training outside Hamburg, since the qualification was a university law degree and Hamburg did not have a university until after the First World War. Most of them studied at Heidelberg, Göttingen, or Bonn, and many were members of a student corporation, the *Corps Hanseatica*, specially reserved for natives of the Hanseatic towns.[75] Already as students, therefore, Hamburg lawyers had established patterns of sociability separate from those of the merchant community back home. These were strengthened when they returned to the city by the Heidelberg Club, where graduates of the university, mostly lawyers, met once a month in the company of friends and relations to reminisce about their student days.[76]

Unlike in Berlin and other Prussian towns, there was no social gulf between lawyers and judges. Until 1879 no one in Hamburg could become a judge before reaching the age of twenty-seven. Most passed their law finals at the age of twenty-three or twenty-four and so spent the intervening years in legal practice. In addition, there was a Hamburg Lawyers' Club (*Gesellschaft Hamburger Juristen*), which, as the lawyer and later Senator Carl August Schröder reported, 'had the explicit aim of encouraging collegial relations between judges and lawyers'.[77] Virtually all lawyers and judges in Hamburg belonged to the society. Both laywers and judges (or former judges) sat in the Citizens' Assembly and could be elected to the Senate. This network of informal ties survived the introduction of career judges on Prussian lines in

[73] W. Treue, 'Zur Geschichte einer Hamburgischen Anwaltssocietät 1812–1972', *Tradition*, 2 (1972), 48–83.
[74] Von Eckardt, *Lebenserinnerungen*, ii. 22–3.
[75] Ibid., i. p. 198.
[76] Ibid., ii. 10–11.
[77] For the following, see C. A. Schröder, *Aus Hamburgs Blütezeit* (Hamburg, 1921), pp. 59–62.

1879. It also served as a selection process, whereby radicals and dissenters in the legal profession could be uncovered and their way to political office blocked. As Schröder explained,

When I became a lawyer, the size of the legal profession was still quite small, and as soon as one was appointed, it was the custom to pay a call on the older and better-known lawyers and at least to make the acquaintance of the younger ones. In this way a collegial atmosphere emerged of its own accord, and since it was cultivated by almost everyone, it not only provided an agreeable social life, but also stood one in good stead in the conduct of business both in and out of court. That there were also a few personalities even in this relatively small circle, with whom a collegial relationship was excluded, is indeed understandable.[78]

At its beginnings in 1846, the Hamburg Lawyers' Club had been an oppositional force, as the legal profession sought to reduce the lay control exercised over judicial affairs in the city by the Senate (which functioned as an appeal court at the time) and to establish a separation of powers that would allow it more say in its own affairs. By the second half of the nineteenth century it had abandoned this opposition to the status quo. Nevertheless, by fostering an occupational consciousness among the lawyers alone, the Club also served to cut them off from the merchants and help them maintain a separate identity.

Carl August Schröder's immediate family background consisted entirely of lawyers. The lawyers in the Amsinck family, as we have seen, also came from one particular sub-branch.[79] Similarly, the Mönckebergs appeared to be founding a Senatorial dynasty too, cut short by the early death of Senator Otto Mönckeberg in 1893. Such clans as the Mönckebergs were large enough to evade the provisions of the constitution that a Senator could not be elected if he was the son, father, brother, uncle, nephew, or immediate in-law of a sitting Senator.[80] It seems at least possible that the great merchant families were becoming less interested in training their sons for the law and the Senate, confident perhaps in the strength of informal pressures and intermarriage networks to keep the legal dynasties in place. The social status of lawyers remained equal to that of even the greatest merchants. 'According to the prevalent view in Hamburg', as one observer complained, 'only merchants and lawyers were born to rule—two kinds of people who would be unthinkable without the possession of a substantial fortune to support them.' Nor had they any reason to be worried about their financial position. Coming from affluent families, they invariably made a great deal of money from their practices—if they did not, they were unlikely to be proposed for the Senate—and as Senators they received a substantial salary. This amounted to 4,000

---

[78] Ibid., p. 72; and for the following.
[79] See above, p. 18.
[80] StA Hbg, *MdB* entries; constitution of 1860, article 8 (reprinted in Eckardt, *Privilegien und Parlament*, p. 75).

Marks, and 11,000 for a Burgomaster, even in the 1840s.[81] By 1892 the Burgomasters' salaries stood at 30,000 and 28,000 Marks respectively, while the difference in status between the legal Senators and their merchant colleagues was marked by the fact that the former were paid 25,000 Marks a year each, the latter less than half as much, a mere 12,000 Marks each. Even the Senate Syndics got more than this (between 16,000 and 18,000 Marks a year each). Their education and professional life gave them a certain group consciousness, evident for example in Johan Georg Mönckeberg's negative judgements on his merchant Senator colleagues. Finally, the fact that they, rather than the merchant Senators, carried out most of the day-to-day administrative work on the Senate, and occupied the supreme executive position of Burgomaster, inevitably caused them to see things in a broader perspective than the merchant community was able to do. The very activity of governing predisposed them to take a number of different points of view into account. They were there not only to foster trade, but also to keep the peace and to maintain social order, and the consciousness of this duty sometimes led them to take a line other than that favoured by the merchants.

At the same time, the lawyers in the Senate could not afford to stray too far from the paths which the merchant community expected them to take. Not only were they constrained by the opinions of the merchant Senators, the Chamber of Commerce, and the lay element on powerful bodies such as the Finance Deputation and the Deputation for Trade, Shipping, and Industry, they were also subject to a whole range of informal pressures exerted by their families, friends, and neighbours. Particularly important were the 'gentlemen's dinners' (*Herrendiners*) to which Senators and above all wealthy merchants customarily invited the politically influential men of the city. These were substantial feasts with up to thirty guests who ate their way through six to eight courses in an evening, each accompanied by a different wine. 'At gentlemen's dinners', recalled Senate Syndic Buehl, 'one met the heads of the administration, leading officials, members of the Citizens' Assembly, great merchants, individual clergymen, and other representatives of the educated professions, artists, and so on. An advantage of this institution', he added, 'was that it often afforded the opportunity to deal with difficult official or political problems. These were much easier to decide at the dinner-table than they were at the committee table.'[82] These occasions, which took place with great frequency, were equally important in forming a climate of opinion, in defining for Hamburg's ruling circles what was sayable and thinkable, and

---

[81] Von Eckardt, *Lebenserinnerungen*, i. 200; *Entwurf zum Hamburgischen Staats-Budget für das Jahr 1892*, Art. 70, p. 66.

[82] StA Hbg. FA Buehl 2c, p. 55. See also ibid.: FA Merck II 9 Konv. 4a, Heft II, pp. 9–10; and Friederike Koch (ed.), 'Die Tagebuchaufzeichnungen Georg Kochs über die Hamburger Cholera-Epidemie des Jahres 1892', *Die Heimat. Monatsschrift zur Pflege der Natur- und Landeskunde in Schleswig-Holstein und Hamburg*, 80 (1973), 24. Koch's diaries consisted mainly of accounts of such dinners.

what was not. The legal Senators were even limited by their very legal training, for, as Julius von Eckardt, a Baltic German who became Senate Secretary in 1874, remarked,[83]

Because Hamburg needed from lawyers in the first instance a training in common law and a knowledge of the Commercial Law Code, it was considered as indisputable in ruling circles that a command over these two disciplines provided the key to unlock all the mysteries of policy-making and statecraft; and whatever was needed beyond this in the way of knowledge of economics or commerce was best obtained by mingling with the Hamburg merchants, who as practitioners of these things in a big way must surely know more about them than anyone else.

The amateurish approach to government which Eckardt identified was not simply peculiar to the Senate, but extended throughout the whole of Hamburg's administration.[84]

IV

The first and most obvious drawback of Hamburg's system of government lay in the irremovability of the executive. The constitution of 1860 did allow Senators who had reached the age of seventy to retire on full pay, and it was also open to any Senator to resign his office provided he had served for a minimum period of six years, though a pension was only payable if he had served for more than ten and was over the age of sixty.[85] And indeed, the system of election for life did not, contrary to what one might have expected, result in a gerontocracy. True, commentators were accustomed to refer to the Senators as 'the old gentlemen', and the absence of any obligation to retire meant that there was usually a sprinkling of Senators in their seventies and eighties. Burgomaster Bartels, for example, born in 1761, joined the Senate in 1798 and was still in office at the time of the 1848 Revolution. Burgomaster Petersen, similarly, died in office in 1892 at the age of eighty-three after thirty-seven years as a member of the Senate.[86] But such venerable figures were very much in a minority. With the state of medicine and health care that existed in the nineteenth century, even the wealthy could not expect to remain active into advanced old age except in a small number of cases. Moreover, legal Senators were often elected very young. Johann Georg Mönckeberg, for example, was thirty-seven when elected to the Senate; Johann Heinrich Burchard, as we have seen, was only thirty-two. This enabled them to become Burgomaster while still in their prime, because the office was tied to length of service, not to age.[87]

[83] Von Eckardt, *Lebenserinnerungen*, i. 198.
[84] Ibid.
[85] Article 10, in Eckardt, *Privilegien und Parlament*, p. 77.
[86] Schmidt, *Die Revolution*, p. 123 n. 68; StA Hbg, *MdB*.
[87] StA Hbg, *MdB*, and for the following analysis.

The average age at death of the forty Senators in office from October 1879 to the end of 1906 was seventy-two years four months. Some of them died too soon after their election to make any impact at all: Senator Eugen Braband, elected on 16 March 1857, died on 3 December the same year at the age of forty-four, for example, while Senator Dr Otto Mönckeberg, elected on 28 November 1892, died on 14 June the next year at the age of forty-nine. A good many Senators of more advanced age died in office, of course; but a surprisingly large number either retired or resigned. Of the forty Senators mentioned, excluding the six who were obliged to resign as a result of the Revolution of 1918–19, fifteen, or 44%, resigned, retired, or (in a couple of rare cases) were dismissed, rather than dying in office. There was strong pressure on Senators to resign if they became incapacitated through ill health. According to Johann Georg Mönckeberg, for example, Gustav Hertz resigned in 1904 when it was clear he had become 'feeble-minded', Charles Ami de Chapeaurouge resigned in November 1892 when chronic rheumatism had deprived him of the ability to walk, Georg Kuhnhardt retired in 1887 during a serious illness which resulted in the amputation of a leg and the virtual loss of his ability to speak, while Rudolph Roosen, already hard of hearing on his appointment at the age of sixty, resigned ten years later, in 1901, when his increasing deafness made it impossible for him to follow the Senate's proceedings at all. Only if a Senator was incapable of making a formal decision to retire was he forced to do so, as in the case of Octavio Schröder, who was made to resign on grounds of insanity in 1884, and of Adolph Hertz, 'dismissed on health grounds by joint decision of the Senate and Citizenry' in 1901. In four cases the retiring Senator resigned during what turned out to be a terminal illness and died before the year was out.[88]

For all this, however, there was no question of retirement for any Senator who was reasonably sound in mind and limb (Friedrich Sieveking, mentioned above, was a solitary, scandalous exception to this rule). This meant that, for a variety of reasons, a good many Senators did not play any very active part in government. Some simply lost interest, like Peter Grossmann, born in 1807 and elected in 1864. Johann Georg Mönckeberg recalled that by the late 1870s, Grossmann 'clung to the old days when Hamburg was smaller and in some respects more independent, when Berlin did not interfere in Hamburg's government and administration'. By 1880 he usually only appeared on ceremonial occasions, when he would spend hours regaling his colleagues with endless stories about the old days. Other Senators often proved unable to make the transition from legal practice to state administration. Johannes Lehmann, for example, elected Senator in 1889, had been a successful commercial lawyer in his time, a judge in the Commercial Court from 1858, and Vice-President of the Commercial Court from 1861 until his appointment.

[88] StA Hbg, FA Mönckeberg 21a, Bl. 258–75; and for the following accounts.

But he was not a success as a Senator. Although he was only sixty-five years old in 1892, he was already so mentally befuddled that he could scarcely be understood any more. His contributions to discussion, Mönckeberg complained, were 'long and boring', while his written reports and even the motions he put to Senate meetings were generally quite incomprehensible. Indeed when his turn came to be elected as Second Burgomaster in December 1893, there was considerable opposition from his colleagues, and only after a powerful appeal to tradition by the First Burgomaster did they relent. Once in office, Lehmann repaid their loyalty to established custom with disastrous speeches, notably one on the occasion of the Kaiser's birthday, which, said Mönckeberg, 'caused offence' and 'genuinely displeased' his colleagues. Another legal Senator, Gustav Hertz, was also sixty-five and according to-Mönckeberg was too old when he was elected to be able to adjust to the new role he had to play in the Senate. Hertz, indeed, had been active as a liberal in the 1848 Revolution and subsequently had a distinguished career as a judge. But in the Senate, noted Mönckeberg, 'he lacked the energy and flexibility needed to deal promptly with the mass of business involved in large departments of state. There were many complaints about him as Head of the Justice Department.' His colleague Friedrich Lappenberg, born in 1836 and elected in 1888, was hard-working, but despite his experience as a judge he was, Mönckeberg wrote, 'not an independent personality and did not make a strong impression' and was without influence.

The method of choosing the Senators, by election from the Citizens' Assembly with the assent of the Senate, thus involved something of a gamble. No one could predict how well they would do in administration on the basis of their performance as judges, lawyers, or merchants (and as we have seen, the most successful merchants generally declined to be elected anyway). The most obviously incompetent could be weeded out in the course of the services on voluntary bodies or in the Citizens' Assembly which all of them had to perform. But this still left plenty of room for error. The problem was not so much that the Senators were old; it was more that most of them, whatever their age, were incompetent, because incompetent Senators were never removed from office. Thus in practice the Senate was usually dominated by one or two outstanding individuals. Even they were unable to keep control over all the branches of administration, and inevitably substantial areas of business were left in the hands of Senators barely capable of carrying them out. Some Senators found it difficult to delegate, and tried to do everything themselves; others attempted to keep everything in their head, rather than make notes or keep files. As they grew older, they often failed to keep up with the current state of the law.[89] Moreover, as one of the Senate Secretaries noted in his memoirs,

[89] Ibid., pp. 276–80.

The work with which the Senate had to deal grew from year to year until it became, one might almost say, unmeasurable. It encompassed the multifarious tasks of a German federated government, including the work this involved in the Federal Council; further, the many-sided functions of the town council of the second largest city in the Empire, whose mighty harbour operations imposed particular burdens on it; and then the supervision of the whole administration, and of the religious congregations too.[90]

With the growing complexity of business in the second half of the nineteenth century, Senators, Syndics, and Secretaries, among whom the various areas of government were divided up to form the basis of papers submitted to the Senate for discussion, found it increasingly difficult to master their briefs.[91]

The sharing of legislative responsibility between the Senate and the Citizens' Assembly made it difficult to pass laws quickly. If the Senate decided on new legislation, a draft was sent to the Citizens' Assembly, which frequently appointed a subcommittee to examine it. Once it passed in second reading, the draft law was returned to the Senate for ratification, and there would be further delays if the Citizens' Assembly had inserted amendments which the Senators did not like. The whole procedure, as one official complained, was very time-consuming.[92] Moreover, from 1842 to 1896 the Senate met in rooms in the Admiralitätsstrasse, while the Citizens' Assembly met in the Patriotic Building, and the considerable distance between them was frequently a cause of further delays in negotiations between the two bodies.[93] Meetings of the Senate were conducted informally. Voting was carried out openly, in order along the rows of Senators, who were seated by seniority with the two Burgomasters ensconced in thrones at the top. There was no formal quorum for Senate meetings. It was understood that half the members—nine—should be present, but smaller numbers were not unknown.[94]

When the new Town Hall opened in 1897, a small room, the Senate Arcade (*Senatslaube*) was constructed next to the Senate Meeting Chamber, between the cloakrooms, and provided with large coloured windows and comfortable chairs. Here Senators could meet before a session, conduct specialized or private negotiations during a meeting, or withdraw when they found the matter under consideration too technical or boring. A cabinet was provided with decanters of red wine, sherry, cognac, soda water, and (in summer) lemonade, and there were also cakes and biscuits available. Frequently there were more Senators to be found here than in the Meeting Chamber, and the First Burgomaster had to send a discreet message to

[90] StA Hbg, FA Buehl 2c, p. 29. See also von Eckardt, *Lebenserinnerungen*, ii. 4.

[91] StA Hbg, FA Buehl 2c, p. 26. Buehl's memoirs cover much the same ground in Hamburg as Julius von Eckardt's, but for a period thirty years later.

[92] Ibid.

[93] Schröder, *Blütezeit*, p. 70.

[94] The following account is based on StA Hbg, FA Buehl 2c, pp. 1–15, 26; there are similar accounts in Lippmann, 'Mein Leben', and von Eckardt, op. cit., ii. 7, dealing with the 1870s.

summon them back for a vote or to make up the customary quorum. Senators did not require permission to leave town, but generally informed the First Burgomaster of the dates of their absence, which by convention was not supposed to be longer than a month. A general atmosphere of collegiality prevailed. The Senators conducted debates with ceremonious politeness. It was unheard of to lose one's temper or raise one's voice. Heated or even lively discussions were virtually unknown. Speeches tended to be very long, but no one ever urged a colleague to be brief or committed the *faux pas* of daring to interrupt him. The First Burgomaster virtually never intervened, except to bring back the debate to the subject in hand if it wandered off the point, or to urge in general terms that a conclusion be reached to 'a discussion which was losing its way in its interminability'.[95] On warm summer evenings, amid the endless speeches, as the atmosphere in the windowless Senate Chamber became ever stuffier, it was not unusual, a Senate Secretary observed, that 'among the venerable and distinguished heads that adorned the neighbourhood of the Chair, one after the other fell forward into a gentle slumber, interrupted only when the speech came to an end'.[96] Everybody voted; abstentions or requests to record dissenting opinions in the minutes were rare. Meetings were held only twice, sometimes thrice weekly. Everything was governed by unwritten and seldom-enforced convention: another respect in which Hamburg's constitution resembled its English counterpart, although undoubtedly the most English feature of the Senate's business was the secrecy with which it was conducted, a secrecy so profound that the majority of the Senators never became known individually to the public for their personalities or opinions.[97]

In sharp contrast to Prussia, which had been effectively governed since the eighteenth century by a full-time, professional bureaucracy, Hamburg possessed no paid higher civil servants until the very end of the nineteenth century. 'Only gradually', wrote Julius von Eckardt, Senate Secretary from 1874 to 1882, 'did the recognition of the dignity and importance of the civil service customary in the rest of the world find its place on the banks of the Elbe.' Almost until the end of the century, civil servants were regarded, as Eckardt complained, as 'serving-men'. The President of the Citizens' Assembly, Dr Otto Mönckeberg, celebrated in 1892 the fact 'that we have always remained free from stiff bureaucratic forms, and through this we have awakened a free public spirit (Bravo)'.[98] So far did this hostility to bureaucratic forms go that the Senators were not provided with offices but did all their paperwork at home in their private studies.[99] 'Up to the turn of the century',

[95] StA Hbg, FA Buehl 2c, pp. 1–15.
[96] Von Eckardt, op. cit., ii. 20.
[97] StA Hbg, FA Buehl 2c, pp. 1–15; von Eckardt, op. cit. ii. 3.
[98] Von Eckardt, op. cit., i. 200.
[99] StA Hbg, FA Merck II 9 Konv. 4a, Heft II, p. 8.

as one official later remembered,[100] 'almost all the higher administrative work was carried out by the Senators, the Syndics, and the Secretaries and the merchants who served in the Deputations in an honorary capacity.' These 'Deputations' were perhaps the most remarkable feature of Hamburg's administrative system in the nineteenth century. They embodied an ideal of amateurism and 'common sense' which, once more, seemed more English than German. Earlier in the century there had been thirty-four of these Deputations, each responsible for a particular aspect of government. They were led by members of the Senate, but they also included prominent members of the ordinary citizenry. In the constitutions of 1860 and 1879 it was the present and former members of these bodies who, along with the judges, formed the constituency for the notables' elections to the Citizens' Assembly. The lay members of the Deputations were nominated by the Citizens' Assembly, except for a minority who belonged *ex officio*, and they usually served for a fixed period. They were expected to carry out their duties without pay. Each Deputation was granted a budget by the Senate and had to answer to the Senate if it overspent. It could make proposals to the Senate relating to its area of competence, and was able to have a powerful influence on policy-making. In essence, however, the main task of the Deputations lay in day-to-day administration.[101]

The large number of these bodies and the administrative confusion to which this led had already resulted in widespread complaints in the 1840s. As a result, their number was eventually reduced. Some were transformed into voluntary associations, like the Commercial Deputation (*Commerz-Deputation*), for instance, which turned itself into the Chamber of Commerce. Others merged or disappeared. But the principle of lay administration remained intact. It represented a further check by the property-owning citizens on the independence of the Senate. By the end of the century a senior Senate official was forced to describe Hamburg's system of government as slow-moving (*schleppend*),[102] and indeed it had long since ceased to be able to respond effectively to sudden crises and disasters. The lack of competent Senators, the enormous growth of government business unaccompanied by any corresponding elaboration of the administrative machinery, the comfortable and slow-moving deliberations of the Senate, the cumbersome system of legislation, the absence of trained higher civil servants, the lay composition of the Deputations—all these features of Hamburg's government led to increasingly frequent breakdowns of the administration in the face of new challenges as the century progressed.

[100] Lippmann, 'Mein Leben', p. 3.
[101] Eckardt, *Privilegien und Parlament*, pp. 86–8.
[102] StA Hbg, FA Buehl 2c, p. 26.

b. *Fractions of Capital*

I

Hamburg's prosperity in the nineteenth century was founded on the expansion of world trade in the era of British 'free trade imperialism' following the victory over Napoleon. The city became the main port of exit for European grain, which the British were importing in ever-larger quantities to feed their growing population, and in return Hamburg became the main port of entry into Germany for the products of the British industrial revolution, leading to widespread complaints among German competitors. 'What of the German Barbary corsairs, the Hanseatic towns,' asked a pamphlet published in Württemberg in 1820, 'whose interests as English trading posts lie in the plundering of the rest of Germany and the destruction of its industry?'[1] The city was quick to take advantage of the opening up of the American continent to trade after the freeing of Latin America from Spanish and Portuguese rule in the 1820s, and from the 1830s firms such as Hertz and O'Swald began trading with Africa; by 1848 there were 37 Hanseatic firms operating in the Far East, and trade with China and Japan experienced a boom from the 1860s with the opening up of these countries, mainly under Anglo-American pressure, for imports. The Godeffroy company set up an agency in Samoa in 1856, and soon the Hamburg merchants were dealing widely in the South Seas as well. By 1846 there were already 162 Hanseatic consulates all over the world.[2]

In 1865 Hamburg imported British goods to the value of 334 million Marks Banco, a sum that far exceeded the worth of the city's trade with Africa, America, and the Far East. But with the growth of the guano industry and the increasing demand of German industries and consumers for raw materials ranging from petroleum and metal ore to coffee and tobacco, overseas trade grew with increasing rapidity. Growth was further accelerated by the rapid industrialization of Germany, with its increasing ability to export finished goods, by the growing internal demand for imported wheat and other foodstuffs as the population of Germany grew, and by the colonial acquisitions made by Bismarck in the 1880s. Colonial policy was initially unpopular in Hamburg because it was associated with protectionism. The Hamburg merchants feared annexations would provoke the British and French to seal off their own colonies from German trade. Colonial propaganda received almost no support in Hamburg, mainly for these reasons. The Senate rejected Bismarck's suggestion that it might take a part in governing the colonies; but

[1] Loose, *Hamburg*, i. 443–5.
[2] Ibid.

by the 1890s the benefits of an overseas Empire for Hamburg's trade were obvious, and it was largely for this reason that the campaign for a German navy found such resonance in the merchant community from the turn of the century.[3]

An idea of the scale of Hamburg's sea-borne trading activities can be gained from the number of the seagoing ships entering the harbour: 2,200 a year in 1816–20; 4,800 in 1856–60; over 7,000 by 1887; over 8,000 by 1890. All the time too, of course, their capacity was getting larger, so that whereas in 1816–20 the average annual tonnage of seagoing ships entering the port was 76,000, by 1856–60 it was 395,000, by 1885 it had increased tenfold again, to 3,700,000, and by 1890 it had reached the impressive figure of 5,200,000; it doubled again in the following fifteen years.[4] Hamburg was not only by far the largest seaport in Germany, it was the largest on the European continent and the fourth largest in the world after London, Liverpool, and New York. Its trade in terms of the capacity of incoming seagoing ships was three times greater than that of the second largest German port, Bremen, in the 1870s, and more than four times greater by the 1890s, and it also far outstripped Antwerp and Rotterdam, though the gap began to close after the turn of the century.[5] By the eve of the First World War, Hamburg was shipping a good fifth of Germany's industrial and agricultural exports, and importing huge quantities of coal and ore for German industry, and wheat, coffee, and tobacco for German consumers.

This massive expansion of sea-borne trade brought with it the rapid growth of the shipping business. As late as the 1870s, more than half of the tonnage entering Hamburg was provided by British ships, but by the turn of the century German companies made up more than half the total, reaching 60% by 1912. Hamburg's shipping activities were associated above all with the steamship era. Already in 1863 the tonnage of incoming steamships exceeded that of sailing ships; from 1880 onwards sail began to decline in absolute as well as relative terms. Among the major steamship lines based in Hamburg were the Hamburg–South America Steamship Line, founded in 1871, the third largest German shipping company; others included the African Steamship Company, the German East Africa Line, and the German–Australian Steamship Line. Often they were known by the name of their founder—the Woermann Line, the Sloman Line, the Carr Line, and so on. Greatest of all was the Hamburg–America Steamship Company, which under the directorship of Albert Ballin soon became the largest shipping line in the world. Its fortunes, and those of a number of other Hamburg shipping lines, were based on the

[3] Ibid., pp. 517–19; H. Washausen, *Hamburg und die Kolonialpolitik des Deutschen Reiches 1880–1890* (Hamburg, 1968); E. Böhm, *Überseehandel und Flottenbau. Hanseatische Kaufmannschaft und deutsche Seerüstung 1879–1902* (Düsseldorf, 1972).
[4] These figures have been rounded off. See Loose, *Hamburg*, i. 447.
[5] M. Grüttner, *Arbeitswelt an der Wasserkante. Sozialgeschichte der Hamburger Hafenarbeiter 1886–1914* (Göttingen, 1984), pp. 20, 29.

traffic in emigrants to the New World. In the 1840s a substantial proportion of the thousands of German immigrants leaving for America every year set sail from Hamburg. As German emigration began to cease with the growth of industrial employment in the last quarter of the century, its place was taken and even enlarged by the millions of migrants who began to stream across to America from Russia and Eastern Europe, embarking at Hamburg or Bremen. In 1892, for example, well over 100,000 emigrants left Hamburg for the United States.[6]

Hamburg's shipowners were able to combine human with material cargo, offering cheap passages on the outward trip, and using the profits to provide low freight fees on the return journey, and vice versa. By the early 1890s the Hamburg–America Steamship Company was recording profits of 10 million Marks a year from the migrant traffic alone.[7] In 1914 it possessed over 175 ocean-going ships with more than a million net registered tons capacity. The great ocean liners such as the *Deutschland* and the *Imperator* (at the time the biggest ship in the world) gained these companies national fame and world-wide prestige.[8] But conditions on many of the migrant ships were primitive in the extreme, as the shipowners sought to reduce costs to a minimum. Sloman's line was particularly notorious. On one of his ships, the *Howard*, 38 out of the 286 passengers died on the journey in 1858, probably of typhoid; another of his ships, the *Leibnitz*, landed in New York in 1868 with a hundred passengers dead. A contemporary report described the lower 'tween deck, in which those with the cheapest tickets were forced to travel, as a 'real plague-spot', badly ventilated, ill-lit, befouled by bilge-water and by urine and faeces seeping down from the upper decks. The 542 passengers who travelled on the ship had only six toilets at their disposal. There was no obligation to carry a doctor on such ships until 1887, although it was common practice by the mid-1870s. Similar conditions were present on other ships as well.[9]

The rapid growth of this lucrative business soon led to the emergence of a shipbuilding industry in Hamburg. There were of course many shipyards in the city already, but these specialized in sail and lacked the resources to construct ocean-going steamships. Most of them had their origins in artisan

---

[6] H. W. Kellenbenz, 'Die Hansestädte', in G. W. Sante (ed.), *Geschichte der deutschen Länder*, ii (Würzburg, 1971), pp. 633–4; H.-J. Teuteberg, 'Die Entstehung des modernen Hamburger Hafens (1886–1896)', *Tradition*, 17 (1972), 257–91; E. Wiskemann, *Hamburg und die Welthandelspolitik* (Hamburg, 1929); L. Cecil, *Albert Ballin. Business and Politics in Imperial Germany 1888–1918* (Princeton, 1971).

[7] M. Just, 'Hamburg als Transithafen für osteuropäische Auswanderer', in *'Nach Amerika!'* (Museum für Hamburgische Geschichte, Hamburg, 1976), pp. 49–54 (here p. 50).

[8] V. Plagemann (ed.), *Industriekultur in Hamburg. Des Deutschen Reiches Tor zur Welt* (Munich, 1984), pp. 69–71.

[9] B. Gelberg, *Auswanderung nach Übersee. Soziale Probleme der Auswandererbeförderung in Hamburg und Bremen von der Mitte des 19. Jahrhunderts bis zum Ersten Weltkrieg* (Hamburg, 1973), pp. 42–3, 46–9. See also P. Marschalck, *Deutsche Überseewanderung im 19. Jahrhundert* (Stuttgart, 1973); G. Moltmann (ed.), *Deutsche Amerikaauswanderung im 19. Jahrhundert* (Stuttgart, 1976); and Just, 'Hamburg als Transithafen'.

enterprises led by master shipbuilders. The transition from wooden to iron ships and then from sail to steam led to the growth of new limited companies which soon began to take over the supply of steamships from the British yards which had initially provided them. The Reiherstieg Shipyard, Stülcken's Shipyard, and other long-established enterprises that managed a successful transition into the new age were swiftly overtaken by new firms, above all Blohm and Voss, the greatest of the Hamburg shipyards in the thirty years before the First World War. From the turn of the century it played a major part in constructing the new German battle fleet. It was only from the 1880s, however, that shipbuilding became really significant in Hamburg. Here too, the economic expansion following Hamburg's entry into the Customs Union played an important role.[10]

Up to this point, industry had only been of relatively minor importance in the city's economy. Indeed, during the first half of the nineteenth century the mercantile interest had done its best to keep industrial growth within closely restricted bounds. In sharp contrast to its views on the freedom of trade, the Senate maintained the rights and privileges of the 38 Hamburg guilds as a guarantee of economic stability and social order. It was not until 1860 that the Senate ended the nightly shutting of the city gates, with all the inconvenience this had entailed for those who worked in the suburbs and lived in the city (or vice versa); and only in 1865 did Hamburg end the privileges of the guilds and introduce freedom of industrial enterprise.[11] In the 1840s there were only two factories in the city with over 100 workers, and only one that used steam power; warnings were issued all the same against an 'excessive extension of the factory system'.[12] Even when industries did begin to emerge in the city, they were strictly subordinate to trading interests. The most important branch of industry consisted of processing raw materials for import and re-export, above all foodstuffs such as corn, coffee, and chocolate, but also hides and furs, hardwood, mineral ores, guano, and the like. At the same time, of course, industries such as building and construction grew as the city grew, and a substantial service sector emerged to cater for the daily needs of its ever-increasing population. In 1879 there were said to be some 563 factories in Hamburg, employing just over 16,000 workers; by 1890, largely as a result of the Customs Union and the free port, these figures had almost doubled. The average annual rate of industrial growth in the city stood at about 5% in the years 1880–1900.[13]

None of this could compare with the importance of trade, but it did signify important changes in the nature of capitalist enterprise in the city. The great steamship and shipbuilding companies were only able to function by

[10] Plagemann, *Industriekultur*, pp. 60–1.
[11] Klessmann, *Geschichte*, p. 438.
[12] Schmidt, *Die Revolution*, pp. 14, 121 n. 47.
[13] Plagemann, *Industriekultur*, p. 53.

constituting themselves as limited companies and issuing shares to raise investment capital. Hamburg's leading merchant families acquired a substantial proportion of these share issues. The Amsinck family firm of Johannes Schuback and Sons had a considerable number of shares in the Hamburg–America Steamship Company, for instance; Heinrich Amsinck sat on the board of directors from 1854 to 1883.[14] His fellow directors included representatives of Ferdinand Laeisz and C. Woermann, two shipping companies which specialized respectively in sail-borne grain shipments and in the African trade, and Merck and Company and A. Godeffroy, two of the great Hamburg merchant banks. The city was not only a centre of trade, it was also a hub of finance. Banking houses such as Merck and Godeffroy, Baur, Donner, Berenberg, Gossler, Heine, and Warburg played a major part in the rise of shipping and industry in the late nineteenth century.[15] Typically such banks combined investments and loans with trade, shipping, and insurance—the last-named a major source of income with Hamburg firms underwriting nearly 500 million Marks Banco worth of sea-borne ships and goods by the 1860s.[16]

Thus Hamburg's economy experienced a growing concentration of capital from the 1870s at the latest. The new industrial firms and shipping lines were often very large, the Hamburg–America Steamship Company being perhaps the most obvious example. Almost all the major steamship lines had close relations with one another and purchased each other's shares. Albert Ballin, managing director of the Hamburg–America Line, sat for instance on the boards of the Woermann Line, the Kosmos Line, and the German Levant Line as well. Such connections were cemented by the personal relations and patterns of sociability of the leading Hamburg merchants and shipowners. Hermann Blohm, for example, may have been an outsider to start with, but before long he was married to a sister of Senator Otto Westphal, whose wife was an Amsinck and whose sister-in-law, another Amsinck, was half-sister to Burgomaster Burchard's wife.[17] Such informal connections doubtless helped the shipping companies to form an Association of Hamburger Shipowners (*Verein Hamburger Reeder*) in 1884 and to conclude price-fixing agreements with their rivals in Bremen as early as 1875. A similar process of concentration and organization took place in the shipbuilding industry, where more than 70 shipyards and components factories joined the Iron Industry Society (*Verband der Eisenindustrie*), led by the shipbuilder Hermann Blohm, on its foundation in 1888. In 1890, finally a whole range of firms in shipbuilding, metal processing, engineering, shipping, brewing, and other branches of

[14] Hintze, *Die Familie Amsinck*, iii, has an extended account of the ramifications of the Amsincks' involvement with the Hamburg–America Line and other shipping companies.

[15] Klessmann, *Geschichte*, p. 451.

[16] Loose, *Hamburg*, i. 448.

[17] Martin, *Jahrbuch*; Cecil, *Albert Ballin*, for details.

industry, employing a total of 50,000 workers, joined together to found the Employers' Association for Hamburg–Altona (*Arbeitgeberverband Hamburg–Altona*). Within a relatively short space of time, therefore, merchants, bankers, shipowners, and industrialists had created the most tightly-knit and highly organized concentration of capital in Germany.[18]

II

Throughout the nineteenth century, and even beyond, no one in the upper reaches of Hamburg society doubted that trade, and primarily overseas trade, was the foundation of the city's prosperity. No matter how important shipping, insurance, processing industries, banking, shipbuilding, and the rest became, they all remained ultimately dependent on the city's activity and reputation as a trading centre. Virtually everything was ruthlessly subordinated by the Senate and the administration to the interests of trade. This policy was justified by the Senate and the leading merchants in terms that remained essentially unaltered throughout the century. As Senator Heinrich Geffken put it in 1847,

Above all in Hamburg the interests of the merchant affect the interests of all other groups more deeply and coincide with them more closely than perhaps in any other place on earth. The great merchant passes on his merchandise to smaller merchants, if we disregard his foreign trading relations; the small merchant or retailer, perhaps lacking the capital to acquire important stocks, finds in the warehouses of the larger merchants the welcome opportunity to augment his stock at any time. When merchants are making profits, artisans get more orders, and these are not just limited to Hamburg, for the enterprises of the merchants open new sales opportunities to artisans outside the city too. Hamburg in general can only be sure to prosper and blossom through large-scale merchant enterprise.[19]

Such sentiments were repeated time and again in the following years.

The paramount importance of trade for the well-being of all Hamburg's inhabitants, whether or not they directly engaged in it, was the fundamental tenet of what one might call the official rhetoric or hegemonic ideology of Hamburg society in the nineteenth century. Another word for it was 'common sense', as used by men like Johann Georg Mönckeberg.[20] This ideology was often expressed in an open and explicit form, as in the passage by Heinrich Geffken quoted above; but it also went much further than this, informing the

---

[18] M. Cattaruzza, 'Das "Hamburgische Modell" der Beziehung zwischen Arbeit und Kapital. Organisationsprozesse und Konfliktverhalten auf den Werften 1890–1914', in A. Herzig, D. Langewiesche, and A. Sywottek (eds.), *Arbeiter in Hamburg. Unterschichten, Arbeiter und Arbeiterbewegung seit dem ausgehenden 18. Jahrhundert* (Hamburg, 1983), pp. 247–60, here pp. 248–9.

[19] Quoted in R. Hauschild-Thiessen, *150 Jahre Grundeigentümer-Verein in Hamburg von 1832 e. V. Ein Beitrag zur Geschichte der Freien und Hansestadt Hamburg* (Hamburg, 1982), pp. 75–6.

[20] See above, p. 17.

whole style of life and mental world in which the city's bourgeois inhabitants lived. As the author of the guidebook *A Walk Through Hamburg's City* (1897) told his readers, perhaps thinking of the irritation that an upper-class Prussian tourist might arouse if he tried to behave as if he were in Berlin,

The fact that there are no real status differences is an important element in the ease with which one can settle down here. Of course there are differences, and these also count for something in social life; but they rest—as one can understand in a merchant republic—on inherited and even more on acquired property. One asks in Hamburg, as in New York and London, how much is the man worth?[21]

Hamburg's inhabitants did not need titles; wealth itself was honour enough, for, as the guidebook went on to explain, 'it is assumed that property and wealth are the tangible expressions of energy and ability'.[22]

In order to maintain the integrity of what Burgomaster Petersen called in 1886 'one of the most splendid flowers in the garden of political culture, a free citizenry',[23] the Senate consistently refused to allow its members to accept titles awarded by foreign monarchs. When Syndic Sieveking received the insignia of a noble order from the Ottoman Sultan in 1840 for his services in negotiating a trade treaty, the Senate resolved to sell the diamonds they contained (for which it received 560 Marks Banco) and to deposit the rest of the insignia in the city archive. The money was given to the Senators' Widows Fund.[24] Gifts and presents, such as Senators often received, were another matter: however lavish they were, they could be accepted without fear of creating a relationship with a foreign monarch that could be seen 'as a theoretical humbling or submission, even if not as a direct subjection' in the way that acceptance of an order or title could.[25] For, as Burgomaster Weber declared in 1885,

We have the undeviating intention of maintaining a genuine republican civic spirit, and any suspicion—also on the part of the citizenry—that a member of the Senate might not discharge his office in a completely impartial manner, or feel that it was a genuinely 'honorary' position, out of desire for the favour of princes as outwardly signified by decorations, must, however unjustified, be avoided.[26]

So strictly did the Senate observe this principle that when former Senator Gustav Godeffroy accepted a high decoration from the Russian Tsar in 1878, his name was struck from the list of former Senators and he was banned from using the title of Senator or any of the privileges pertaining to it.[27]

[21] *Ein Spaziergang durch Hamburgs City* (Hamburg, 1897), pp. 23–4.
[22] Ibid., p. 24.
[23] StA Hbg, FA Petersen D23, copy of obituary of Burgomaster Carl Petersen by Burgomaster Johann Georg Mönckeberg, 5 Dec. 1892.
[24] Hauschild-Thiessen, *Bürgerstolz*, p. 103.
[25] Ibid., p. 104, citing Senate Secretary and city archivist Otto Beneke.
[26] Ibid., p. 99.
[27] Ibid., p. 105.

Under the rubric 'foreign monarch', of course, the Senate also included the King of Prussia and German Emperor. Great alarm was caused in 1885 when Kaiser Wilhelm I gave Burgomaster Buff of Bremen the Order of the Crown (Second Class): not because it was only a second-class decoration, though this of course aroused much adverse comment, but because it was seen in Hamburg as an attack on the 'worthy pride of republican simplicity' and an example of 'the Prussian tendency to degrade the Senators of the Hanseatic cities to the status of local town council officials' as Burgomaster Weber put it. However, the embarrassed Burgomaster of Bremen explained that he had felt unable to refuse the offer for fear of offending the monarch; and a joint approach to the Prussian ambassador by Hamburg and Lübeck, led by Burgomaster Carl Petersen, discovered that the award had indeed been made in the belief that 'altered political circumstances' justified a change of practice. Tactfully but firmly Petersen made it clear that such an attempt should not be made again. And it was not.[28] As Burgomaster Burchard remarked on one occasion, the Emperor might *give* a Hamburg merchant a *title*, but he could not *raise* him to the *nobility* (as it was conventionally described), for 'a Hamburg merchant cannot rise any further in status than he already is'.[29] Disdain for 'the tawdry splendour of a personal distinction and superiority over other citizens'[30] was more generally present in the patrician families and mercantile community. One of the most telling points made by the free traders against the protectionists in the argument over the Customs Union in 1880 was the accusation that several of them possessed titles and decorations. They included, for example, two ennobled landowners, a shipowner (Sloman) who had married into the Prussian nobility, and a *Kommerzienrat*, the last-named title of 'commercial councillor' being a distinction much sought after by businessmen in Prussia but generally disdained as worthless in Hamburg. That these individuals could be lumped together by the free traders with the Jews, the foreign consuls, and the religious deviants (one Calvinist and one Catholic) among the protectionists showed the kind of company to which traditionalists in the mercantile community thought such title-holders belonged.[31]

This disdain for honours and titles went hand in hand in Hamburg with a general contempt for the life of leisure and pleasure led by the court nobility in Berlin. Of all the bourgeois virtues present in Hamburg, none was more striking to outsiders than its industriousness. The Baltic German Julius von Eckardt, Senate Secretary from 1874 to 1882, remarked that the people of Hamburg 'saw ... work and the fulfilment of duty as the main preoccupations of life'.[32] Young men from even the most patrician of families were sent to

---

[28] Ibid., pp. 98–100.
[29] Ibid., p. 97.
[30] Ibid., pp. 105–6, citing Otto Beneke.
[31] Stein, 'Interessenkonflikte', pp. 68–9.
[32] Von Eckardt, *Lebenserinnerungen*, i. 204–5.

begin their careers as office juniors in other firms, so as not to become lazy or spoilt in the years before they took over their father's business.[33] Eckardt regarded 'passion for business and solidity of work' as two of the most universal characteristics of the Hamburg bourgeoisie.[34] Other obervers shared this view. 'Yes, Hamburg is a city of work', sighed the author of *A Walk through Hamburg's City* resignedly:

Everyone must stretch his mental and physical powers to the limit, in order to keep his position in this great workplace. The stranger immediately notices that there are no real walks in Hamburg, no promenades, no parks or resorts in the city, where one can always or at certain times see people go or gather ... No one has time to stroll or idle during the day, and after work everyone goes straight home and usually stays there.[35]

This lack of sights to see and things to do posed problems for the authors of guidebooks. There were, of course, as they were forced to note, 'public amusements ... in St Pauli', a district near the waterfront, but these were hardly suitable for 'the better class of people' for whom the travel guides were intended.[36] Moreover, the sober business sense of the city fathers had ensured that, as another guidebook, the *Guide to Hamburg* (1894) was obliged to inform its readers, 'Hamburg is poorly supplied with public monuments'.[37] This was only too true.

In 1802, the Senate ordered Hamburg's Gothic cathedral to be pulled down, a decision which aroused no serious opposition within the city and which was carried out between 1804 and 1807. The stones were sold off or used to reinforce the sea defences along the Elbe; the funerary sculpture and monuments were broken up and used in the reconstruction of the city's rudimentary sewage system. The Senate was partly motivated by the desire to rid the city of an extraterritorial institution, but it is more than possible that the rise in rents and the high demand for housing at the time also played a role. In any case the incident was typical of the celebrated philistinism of the Hamburg authorities. Five more medieval churches in the city were pulled down between 1807 and 1837. In 1788, indeed, the authorities had demanded the abolition of church music on the grounds that it was too expensive. Three-quarters of a century later, the composer Johannes Brahms, born in 1833 in Hamburg, was forced to leave the city for Vienna against his will because he was unable to find a decent job. Hamburg owed virtually all its cultural life, such as it was, to private initiative: there was no city art gallery until the construction (privately funded) of the *Kunsthalle* in 1868;

---

[33] Ibid.
[34] Ibid.
[35] *Ein Spaziergang*, p. 22.
[36] Ibid.
[37] *Führer durch Hamburg zum III. Allg. Deutschen Journalisten- und Schriftstellertage 1894* (Hamburg, 1894), p. 35.

the city's own art collection had been auctioned off by the Senate in 1789 to raise money for the city treasury. As a centre of artistic and musical life in the nineteenth and early twentieth centuries Hamburg was completely eclipsed by the much smaller Munich. The opera house and concert hall were built by private enterprise; even the zoo, the celebrated Hagenbeck's Tierpark, was and remains virtually the only privately financed zoo in Germany, built not for prestige but for profit. Nor did Hamburg's Senate consider it necessary to found a university in the city. There was no state schooling or obligatory primary education until 1871; even after this date, the merchant Senator in charge of the Education Board spent much of his time trying to replace Latin—necessary for university entrance—with English, on grounds of the greater commercial utility of the latter. 'The pleasure that a scholar takes in his subject for its own sake,' complained the theologian Johann Anton Fahrenkrüger in 1811, 'apart from the pecuniary advantages that accrue from his pursuit of it, is incomprehensible to the Hamburger ... The value of people and things is fixed by the merchant. Such is the Hamburger in the most complete possible sense.'[38]

Faced with the absence of public monuments, the authors of guidebooks to Hamburg recommended tourists to take the city as it was, and directed them elsewhere. A trip round the port (described in minute and enthusiastic detail) gave the visitor a graphic impression of the city's commercial and industrial power. But for a more intimate sampling of Hamburg life, the guidebooks suggested a visit to the Exchange (*Börse*), a large building in mock-Italian Renaissance style situated in the centre of the older part of the city. This housed not only a Stock Exchange but also a Shipping Exchange and an Insurance Exchange, and there were also special departments for dealing in corn, coffee, and sugar. On average some five to seven thousand people attended the Exchange every day in the early 1890s, all attired in the obligatory frock-coat and top hat. As a contemporary guidebook explained,

The Exchange is not just the centre of the mercantile business of Hamburg, for around midday (towards 1 o'clock) everyone who has anything to do with business life can be found there, for example the captains of the ships lying in the harbour, the bargees from the riverboats, the boatmen who own the craft that ply the canals, factory-owners and big industrialists, and even lawyers. Everything that excites Hamburg is talked over at the Exchange, from candidatures for Senatorial and Reichstag elections to sensational family events.[39]

The central importance of the Exchange to the city was underlined in the physical form of the new Town Hall, begun in 1886 and officially opened a decade later, in 1897. It was built next door, and linked to the Exchange by

---

[38] Klessmann, *Geschichte*, pp. 2, 370, 378–82, 489–90, 498, 563; von Eckardt, *Leben-serinnerungen*, ii. 12–13.

[39] *Führer durch Hamburg*, p. 48; see also StA Hbg, FA Merck 119 Konv. 4a, Heft II, p. 6.

connecting passages. This was a deliberate act, taken self-consciously to symbolize the links between capital and state in the city.

This close relationship of capital and state had a practical as well as a symbolic expression. In contrast to cities such as Rotterdam or New York, where harbour facilities were constructed by private enterprise and without any overall concept or plan, Hamburg placed the extension of its harbour in the hands of the state.[40] In the first half of the nineteenth century the ships simply dropped anchor in the river and wares were transported to and from the warehouses by small boats (*Ewer* or *Schuten*) which loaded and unloaded on the canals or fleets (*Fleeten*) which criss-crossed the city and along which the warehouses were built.[41] As the volume of traffic and the capacity of ships grew, the Senate decided on the construction of a new harbour, with a quayside, warehouses, and a railway connection. The new facility, the Sandgate Harbour (*Sandtorhafen*), opened in 1866, made possible a good deal of the expansion of Hamburg's trade in the following years. Since Hamburg remained a tidal harbour, loading and unloading in the river continued, but the warehouses on the fleets gradually fell into disuse. This process was greatly accelerated by the construction of the free port in the 1880s. Large new harbour facilities, extensive quays, and railway yards were built at public expense on the southern bank of the Elbe, across from the city. 40 million Marks were provided for this purpose by the Reich, but the total cost came to as much as 113 million. A major feature of the free port was the magnificent 'warehouse town' (*Speicherstadt*), which remains to this day the most striking complex of buildings in Hamburg. The land was provided by the Senate, which recouped some of its investments from the profits, while the building of the gigantic warehouse complex was financed by the North German Bank. Thus public funds were extensively used for the construction of harbour facilities, and were repeatedly invested as the port was further extended in the years up to the First World War.[42]

This generosity where the interests of trade were affected did not apply to most other forms of public expenditure. As Leo Lippmann, a leading official in the Finance Deputation, wrote in his memoirs,

Proposals for the voting of many millions to be spent on the harbour and Elbe were usually approved in the Finance Deputation almost without debate, whereas, up to the World War and after, proposals to spend a few thousand Marks on subterranean public conveniences or other 'superfluous modern luxuries' gave rise to long debates and often required the establishment of special subcommittees to discuss.[43]

[40] Grüttner, *Arbeitswelt*, p. 19.
[41] Plagemann, *Industriekultur*, pp. 57–8.
[42] Grüttner, *Arbeitswelt*, pp. 19, 25; see also Teuteberg, 'Die Entstehung des modernen Hamburger Hafens'.
[43] StA Hbg, FA Lippmann A4, pp. 10–12.

Another senior official confirmed that the Senate was 'very restrained' in matters of social expenditure.[44] It justified this attitude on the grounds that money spent on harbour facilities constituted, in effect, an investment that would bring a more than satisfactory return. Since trade was the foundation of the city's prosperity, it was the Senate's duty to do everything in its power to further its growth.

In other matters, however, the Senate followed a thoroughly Gladstonian financial policy. The aim was to avoid unnecessary expenditure, to hold down income tax, and to achieve a surplus on the state budget. Income was brought in by an inheritance tax, a land tax, and an income tax, as well as by various indirect taxes and smaller levies such as a fee payable on moving house and a fee collected from public amusements. These were administered by at least three quite separate bodies, co-ordinated only by the Senate. There were no properly trained officials in the tax office. Considerable administrative confusion was the result. The two most important taxes, the land tax, levied at 5% of the capital value of property (including rents), and the income tax, brought in about 8–9 million Marks a year each in the late 1880s. Income tax was levied at no more than $3\frac{1}{2}$% even on the highest income groups, and declined slightly in lower income groups, with those earning less than 600 Marks exempt. It was self-assessed.[45] This very low rate of income tax could naturally only be maintained by holding down public expenditure to an absolute minimum, except where the promise of a good return was offered. In this way, yet further room was created for the flourishing of private enterprise and individual initiative on which the well-being of the city was held to depend. The dominant ideology of Hamburg society, the common-sense dogma of the primacy of trade, was not only an engine of consent, it was also a very real influence on the distribution of wealth and resources among Hamburg's inhabitants.

III

The grand bourgeoisie which dominated the Senate and the institutions of government in Hamburg did not have everything its own way. As was apparent in the question of the Customs Union, the Chamber of Commerce, in which middling and smaller merchants possessed a strong numerical superiority over the great trading houses, could sometimes take a line strongly opposed to that of the biggest firms. Equally important, however, was the fact that the city's major representative institution, the Propertied Citizenry (after 1860, the Citizens' Assembly) was jointly sovereign with the Senate and could easily block any legislation of which it strongly disapproved. During

[44] StA Hbg, FA Buehl 2c, p. 20.
[45] Lippmann, 'Mein Leben', p. 55; *Statistisches Handbuch für den hamburgischen Staat 1891*, p. 310.

the first half of the century, the Propertied Citizenry became increasingly unrepresentative. On the eve of the 1848 Revolution, the population of the city and inner suburbs numbered about 150,000, including some 93,000 adults, of whom 27,000 were citizens. Only 3,000 or 4,000 of these, however, qualified as Propertied Citizens (*Erbgesessene Bürger*), because the qualification was tied to individual properties, of which there were only 7,000; persons owning more than one property still had only one vote, and women property-owners were excluded from the franchise. Even among this small minority, only 200 to 300 usually took part in the Convention in which the Citizenry met. Thus not only workers, apprentices, and journeymen were excluded, but also virtually the whole of the petty bourgeoisie and even large segments of the established middle classes.[46]

It was scarcely surprising, therefore, that pressure for change began to mount during the 1840s. The catalyst was the Great Fire which broke out in the city on 5 May 1842 at one in the morning and lasted until 8 a.m. on 8 May, devastating a large part of the city. 51 people were killed and 1,100 houses were destroyed along with 102 warehouses, 7 churches, 2 synagogues, and numerous public buildings. A good deal of the damage was done by the Senate, which caused numerous buildings to be blown up in order to create gaps across which the flames would be unable to leap. By contrast, gangs of heroic stockbrokers and merchant bankers worked tirelessly for hours on end to save the Exchange, with its irreplaceable financial records, from destruction. While the Exchange was saved, some 20,000 out of the city's 160,000 inhabitants were made homeless. The city's biggest insurance company was bankrupted, and thousands lost their property with little or no compensation. Crowds of the dispossessed roamed through the streets, looting buildings or falling upon the homeless and carrying off whatever possessions they had managed to rescue. St Jacob's Church, in which furniture from endangered houses was temporarily stored, was sacked by the crowd; and order was only restored with the aid of a battalion of Prussian infantry. To many of the disgruntled citizens it seemed only too fitting that one of the first public buildings to be destroyed had been the Town Hall. It was widely held that Hamburg's antiquated constitution was largely to blame for the catastrophe. The Senate, dominated by the great merchants, had proved manifestly incapable of co-ordinating the effort to fight the fire, nor indeed was there any professional fire brigade which they could have employed to do so. Worse still from the point of view of the majority of property-owners, the government of the city had shown itself utterly unable to maintain public order. If there was any one sight that moved the citizens of Hamburg to press for reforms, it was that of a crowd dividing the spoils of looting in public in the Goosemarket (*Gänsemarkt*), undisturbed by any

---

[46] Schmidt, *Die Revolution*, p. 22; Eckardt, *Privilegien und Parlament*, p. 18.

intrusion of the forces of order. Just as the city itself was now to be reconstructed along more rational lines, so too, it was widely argued, should its political constitution be reformed. Throughout the rest of the 1840s a number of clubs and societies (*Vereine*) were established, ranging from the Association for the Political and Social Interests of the Jews (1845) to the Hamburg Lawyers' Club (1846). All of them soon began to issue calls for constitutional reform.[47]

The most important of these associations were the Citizens' Clubs (*Bürgervereine*), three of which were established in the 1840s. They represented the economic and political interests of districts (or, as with the Citizens' Club of Non-Property-Owners, groups of people) not catered for by existing institutions. The first one was founded in St Pauli in 1843 and soon acquired political significance. St Pauli was a harbour district outside the city walls seriously underrepresented in the city's affairs. Only in 1833, indeed, largely as a result of the unrest stimulated by the French Revolution of 1830, had the right to sit in the Convention been extended to qualified citizens in the two inner suburbs of St Pauli and St Georg.[48] Later on, as the city continued to grow, new Citizens' Clubs were formed in the outer suburbs, and busied themselves with naming the streets, numbering the houses, and putting pressure on the Senate for proper sanitation, water-supplies, street lighting, paving, and other amenities. These were mainly propertied citizens, often of some means: in Eimsbüttel in the 1860s, for example, the Citizens' Club even raised the capital to form its own horse tram company. Subsequently the Citizens' Clubs also took on the role of organizing the district elections to the Citizens' Assembly, and became an essential part of the city's informal constitution: one was founded in the 1850s, three in the 1860s, thirteen in the 1870s, and twelve in the 1880s; by 1892 there were thirty-two altogether, most of them organized in a central committee. In the 1840s, however, the St Pauli Citizens' Club was a major centre of opposition to the existing system of government and the domination of the great merchant families over the self-perpetuating Senate. Even later on, since each Citizens' Club was supposed to contain all the citizens in a given district, the presence of a strong element of the middling and even the petty bourgeoisie in some districts gave at least some of the Clubs an oppositional slant. Indeed, tensions over elections to the Citizens' Assembly sometimes led to secessions and the founding of rival Clubs in the same district, while a few radical Clubs even included noncitizens and so were excluded from participation in the central committee.[49]

Of almost equal importance, but dating from a previous decade, was the

[47] Klessmann, *Geschichte*, pp. 395–406; Loose, *Hamburg*, i. 467.

[48] Loose, *Hamburg*, i. 460.

[49] A. Obst, *Geschichte der Hamburger Bürgervereine* (Hamburg, 1911), pp. 5–6, 15, 57–9, 84, 173–9.

Property-Owners' Association (*Grundeigentümerverein*),[50] founded in 1832. Like the other clubs, it represented social groups who thought themselves slighted by the Senate. It was basically a landlords' association, consisting of those who received all or a large part of their income from rents. In a big city such as Hamburg, this was a very important social group. Most of its leading members were master artisans and small tradesmen. The founding committee included a lawyer, two master masons, a tobacco dealer, a master pewterer, an ironmonger, two brokers, and three landlords. The Property-Owners' Association fought a war on two fronts. On the one hand, it aimed to protect its members against 'disadvantages which accrue to them because of the irresponsibility or ill will of tenants' such as 'moonlight flits, false receipts', illicit subletting, sale of the landlord's furniture, and so on; black lists of 'undesirable' tenants were circulated and standard rent contracts were issued to members. On the other hand, the Association also tried to protect its members against the state, for example by resisting rises in the land tax. It organized a massive campaign of protest against the compulsory purchase orders issued in the course of the city's reconstruction after the Great Fire of 1842, though to little effect. By 1847 its 360 members—'mostly people of the comfortably off *Mittelstand*: artisans, retailers, shopkeepers, also a few owners of small dwellings', as they were described in a police report—were thoroughly dissatisfied with their lack of effective representation in the city's organs of government. Like the St Pauli Citizens' Club, the Property-Owners' Association became a centre of opposition to the self-recruiting oligarchy of the Hamburg Senate in the 1840s.[51]

The eventual result of this widespread political mobilization of the petty bourgeoisie and the disfranchised sectors of the middle classes was, as we have seen, the constitution of 1860, which transformed Senate and Citizenry into elective bodies. While the Citizens' Clubs discovered a new role in organizing elections, and underwent a rapid growth in number, the Property-Owners' Association declined in importance after its active period of political pressure in the 1850s. It seemed to have been rendered more or less superfluous by the provision of 48 (from 1869: 60) seats in the Citizens' Assembly elected by those who were entitled to become its members. By 1868, only 88 people were left in the Association. Ten years later, however, it began to re-emerge as a force in city politics. This was partly because things were becoming difficult for landlords in the late 1870s and 1880s after the end of the long economic boom, and partly because new laws and regulations, consequent upon Hamburg's joining the Reich but also reflecting the results

---

[50] Literally Landowners' Association. But in English this sounds too much like a Country Gentleman's Association, and Landlords' Association is too reminiscent of the public house, so the translation preferred here renders *Grundeigentum* in terms of what estate agents like to call 'property'.

[51] Hauschild-Thiessen, *150 Jahre*, pp. 17–22, 29–30, 44–5, 71–4, 78–9.

of the growing size and complexity of the city, gave the Association a new role in providing legal advice and legal aid to its members. The new period of growth in the importance of the Property-Owners' Association was led by Dr Heinrich Gieschen (born 1843), a lawyer who was its Chairman from 1878 to his death in 1896. A devious, forceful, vigorous, cantankerous, and extremely talkative man, Gieschen not only restructured the Association so as to provide more comprehensive services for its members, he also acted as a watchful and often skilful advocate of their interests in the Citizens' Assembly. His efforts were rewarded by an increase in the membership of the Association from 300 to nearly 4,800 during his term of office.[52]

By organizing the landlords as an extra-parliamentary pressure group and by bringing into line behind it the 60 deputies in the Assembly who owed their seats to the property-owners' elections, Gieschen made the landlords of Hamburg a force to be reckoned with in the 1880s. At this time the membership of the Association was still predominantly petty bourgeois in character. In 1861 the executive committee consisted of an apothecary, a watchmaker, a secretary, an accounts clerk, a librarian, a baker, a master pewterer, a brewer, a sugar refiner, an estate agent, a manufacturer of sailors' clothing, and a bookbinder. Speculative builders and large landlords did not become members. The Association was first and foremost designed to represent the interests of the small-scale landlord, and most of its members were relatively modest in their style of life. In 1891, for example, there were 2,658 members in the Association, out of a total of 8,000 property-owners in Hamburg who rented out houses, apartments, or rooms. At about the same time, the number of property-owners in Hamburg as a whole stood at well over 15,000, but only 6,150 of these had obtained citizenship and voted in the property-owners' elections. The Association's animus against the grand bourgeoisie was unconcealed. It constantly complained 'that', as it declared in 1874, 'taxation policy as it has been exercised by the ruling circles in the state of Hamburg has always sought to heap as much of the burden as possible on the property-owners and the *Mittelstand* and to protect the merchant class'.[53]

Nevertheless, the property-owners were far from willing to attack the official rhetoric of the primacy of trade and the freedom of industrial enterprise that informed political discourse within the city. In 1885 Heinrich Gieschen tried to reconcile the sectional interests of the landlords with the overall demands of capital in a lengthy statement of the aims of the Property-Owners' Association:

We do not seek petty advantages for property-ownership, we want no special treatment or state support, nor do we want to limit the rights of our mortgagee or our

---

[52] Ibid., p. 149. See also Plate 4.
[53] Ibid., pp. 133, 157–8, 162, 232.

tenants. Our endeavours are far removed from any antagonism between property-ownership and mobile capital, or to put it bluntly, any 'property-agrarianism'. We believe that a biased state preference might temporarily help property-ownership, but will in the long run act to its detriment. Our view is that property-ownership in a state can only flourish and prosper if the state's trade and industry flourish and prosper at the same time.'[54]

Therefore, he went on, it was in the interests of the bankers and merchants who supplied the landlords with their mortgages 'that disadvantageous laws and regulations should be removed'. Profit for landlords was good for trade. From this point of view too, what ultimately mattered was that the interests of the different fractions of capital—'mobile and fixed capital', as trade and property were customarily referred to in Hamburg—should as far as possible be reconciled.

IV

The achievement of this goal was widely regarded as constituting the major function of the Citizens' Assembly. National political parties were unrepresented in this body in the nineteenth century. Instead, the deputies organized themselves loosely into three Caucuses (*Fraktionen*). The property-owners and other artisans, shopkeepers, and small business men mostly belonged to the Caucus of Leftists (*Fraktion der Linken*). In 1895 the Caucus included 26 'merchants' (some of them in fact estate agents), 18 master artisans, 3 doctors or apothecaries, 2 gentlemen of private means, 3 shopkeepers, a lawyer, an architect, an innkeeper, a teacher, and a white-collar worker. With its close links to the Property-Owners' Association, which actively campaigned for its candidates in the elections, the Caucus of Leftists was often referred to as the landlords' party and its deputies described *en bloc* as *Hausagrarier*, 'house agrarians', in a reference to the Prussian landowners, the Junkers, although their land of course was all built on and they owned houses rather than fields. In 1895, 38 out of the 56 members of the Caucus belonged to the Property-Owners' Association; 20 of its deputies had been elected in the property-owners' election. Its strongest support lay in the inner city.[55] There was a strong populist element in the Caucus of Leftists which lent it something of a radical air on occasion. Here also were gathered the handful of left-liberal 'democrats', often renegade members of the great bourgeois families, who constituted the only principled opposition to the Senate in the Citizens' Assembly.[56] Their most celebrated member was the lawyer Dr Eduard Banks

[54] Ibid., p. 150.
[55] A. Cord, 'Die soziale Schichtung der Hamburger Bürgerschaft von 1859 bis zum Jahre 1921. Ein Beitrag zur parlamentarischen Geschichte des Kaiserreichs' (Wiss. Prüfung für das Lehramt an Gymnasien, Hamburg, 1961; StA Hbg, Handschriftensammlung 1023), p. 44.
[56] Lippmann, 'Mein Leben', p. 41.

(1836–85),[57] son of a Senate Syndic and grandson of the legendary Burgo-master Bartels. Dr Banks lost no opportunity of attacking his fellow patricians in public. Men such as Banks, Gieschen, and Wex (a cousin of Senator Gerhard Hachmann) were expelled from Hamburg high society and generally shunned in institutions such as the Lawyers' Club. In national political terms they tended to be Left-Liberals in the 1870s and 1880s. A reputation as a radical often did no harm to one's legal practice, and so such 'democrats', although unwelcome guests at dinner, were nevertheless tolerated at the Exchange and the law courts. As one commentator remarked even in the eighteenth century, 'A friend is to the Hamburger anyone with whom he does business from which he himself hopes to profit.'[58]

The Senatorial party in the Citizens' Assembly was known as the Caucus of Rightists (*Fraktion der Rechten*). It consisted mainly of deputies elected by the notables; never less than 58% of its members were elected in this way. In 1895, 34 of its 43 deputies had been elected by the notables, 7 in the general elections, and 2 in the property-owners'. 22 were large-scale merchants, 13 lawyers, and the rest were pastors, doctors, apothecaries, and architects. Many of them belonged to the grand bourgeois families. Senators were almost invariably elected from this group.[59] Here too there were divisions, as some remained firmly wedded to Old Hamburg Particularism while others inclined more to the Prussian (or realist) party led by Johannes Versmann and Carl Petersen. They were generally united, however, in their support for whatever policy the Senate undertook. This was understandable given the fact that so many of them were present or former notables and therefore active in the Deputations which were partly responsible for the Senate's policies in the first place. In 1895 13 deputies in the Caucus also belonged to the Finance Deputation or the Deputation for Trade and Shipping, and 7 of them were members of the Chamber of Commerce. Their place in the governing system was underlined by the fact that 16 of them were related to other members of the Assembly (compared to only 6 in the Caucus of Leftists). It would be misleading to describe any of the Hamburg Caucuses in terms of national political parties, which played no role at all in the deliberations of the Citizens' Assembly; but when it came to elections for the Reichstag, it seems likely that the great majority of deputies in the Caucus of Rightists revealed themselves to be supporters of the National Liberal Party. It was noticeable, too, that at the end of the century 9 of them were members of the Navy League.[60]

A third Caucus on the Citizens' Assembly, the Left-Centre Caucus, (*Fraktion Linkes Zentrum*) occupied a rather indeterminate position. In social terms the deputies of the Left-Centre Caucus were clearly a notch lower down the ladder

[57] StA Hbg, *MdB*.
[58] Von Eckardt, *Lebenserinnerungen*, i. 201–2.
[59] Cord, 'Die soziale Schichtung', p. 42; Lippmann, 'Mein Leben', p. 41; Schröder, p. 66.
[60] Cord, op. cit., p. 42.

of prestige than the members of the Caucus of Rightists.[61] Very few of them owed their seats to the notables' elections. In 1895, 38 of their 61 members had won their seats in the general, 18 in the property-owners', and 5 in the notables' elections. They were particularly well supported in the suburbs and the rural districts outside the city boundary. Over half of them were merchants, but a noticeably high proportion of these had strong interests in industry as well as, or rather than, trade. In 1895 this Caucus numbered 35 merchants, 6 lawyers, 8 master artisans, 5 gentlemen of means, 2 teachers, 2 farmers, a doctor, a judge, and an architect. Over half of them also belonged to the Property-Owners' Association. In terms of national politics their allegiances were probably divided several ways, between the National Liberals, the Left-Liberals, and perhaps also the Conservatives.[62] The political origins of this Caucus lay in the late 1860s, when it was founded in an attempt to mediate between the 'democratic' Caucus of Leftists and the Senatorial Caucus of Rightists.[63] This uncertain political position, and its mixed social constituency, made the Left-Centre Caucus somewhat unpredictable, although as the largest of the three Caucuses it clearly held the balance of power. The fact that the Property-Owners' Association had members in two of the three Caucuses gave it a power in the Citizens' Assembly even greater than the allocation of 60 seats to the property-owners' elections would suggest. A good number of the Association's members in the Assembly achieved their position through the general rather than the property-owners' elections. In 1895, for instance, no fewer than 78 deputies were members of the Association. In a body of 160 which reached its decisions by majority vote, this gave them a virtual veto over any legislation of which they disapproved, the more so since they were likely to be better organized and more disciplined on such occasions than other groups in the Assembly, such as the Senatorial party.[64]

Such representation of interests across Caucus lines was possible because the Caucuses were not parties in the modern sense but simply loose, informal associations of deputies. There was no party discipline, no whipping-in system in the Assembly, and on many major issues voting cut right across party lines. The Caucuses had no connection with national political parties; of the two deputies who sat at one time or another in the period 1886–1905 as National Liberals in the Reichstag, one belonged to the Caucus of Rightists and the other to the Left-Centre Caucus. None of the Caucuses had a published programme, nor did they do anything to organize the elections to the Assembly, which lay in the hands of the Citizens' Clubs. In 1859 only 11% of the deputies belonged to the Clubs, but as the number of Clubs increased

[61] Lippmann, op. cit., p. 41.
[62] Cord, op. cit., p. 43.
[63] Schröder, op. cit., p. 66.
[64] Ibid., p. 45.

so too did their role in the elections. By 1895, 60% of the deputies were
Citizens' Club members. The Clubs, however, made no distinction between
the Caucuses: of this 60%, 46% belonged to the Caucus of Leftists, 39% to
the Left-Centre Caucus, and 15% to the Caucus of Rightists. This last figure
reflects the fact that the notables, of whom there were only 500 in 1880
(600 in 1890) organized their own elections. The clubs' main task was to
organize the general elections and the property-owners' elections.[65]

Once elected to the Assembly, a deputy was committed (in theory at least)
to attending two sessions a week for most of the year, excepting July, when
there was only one session a week, and August, when the Assembly was
prorogued for the summer holidays.[66] Sessions were held on Mondays and
Wednesdays from 7 p.m. until about 10 p.m., and were devoted to a colourful
mixture of topics varying from relations with the Reich through major pieces
of legislation such as constitutional reforms and taxation proposals, down to
the smallest minutiae of city government.[67] In the first few months of 1892,
for example, the Assembly debated the reform of the administrative system,
the extension of citizenship and voting rights to a wider section of the
population, and the reorganization of the Hamburg police force; but it also
considered an emergency motion for the removal of a wreck that was proving
a danger to shipping in the river, and a Senate proposal to introduce tough
new sanctions to deal with stray cats. Most of the Senate's proposals on minor
matters of city administration went through on the nod, but larger issues
frequently aroused lengthy debates.[68]

The atmosphere in the Assembly was formal and polite. As its President
Otto Mönckeberg remarked on 5 March 1892, 'As long as the real, true
Hamburg citizenry is represented here, there are no grounds for deep-seated
party struggles'. Impassioned debate, heckling, and even interruptions were
virtually unknown. No speaker was ever shouted down; but then, no speaker
ever gave a cause. With the possible exception of the handful of 'democrats'
in the Assembly, all the deputies were clear in their minds that their purpose
was to reach a satisfactory compromise between the interests of large and
small merchants, traders and industrialists, property-owners and bankers,
master artisans and grand bourgeoisie. Lip-service was paid to the interests
of the majority of the population unrepresented in the Assembly, but hardly
anybody thought of allowing them to speak directly for themselves. The vote
was confined to citizens of Hamburg, that is those who were born in the city
or had a permanent home there for a number of years, who had paid a fee
(*Bürgergeld*) of 30 Marks, and who earned enough to pay the local income
tax. Those who earned more than 3,600 Marks a year were legally obliged

[65] Ibid., p. 39.
[66] Ibid., pp. 62–6.
[67] Ibid., pp. 76–7.
[68] *Bürgerschaft*, Jan.–June 1892.

to become citizens. These conditions put the right of citizenship far beyond the means of the majority of inhabitants.[69]

In 1859, 1,916 people applied for citizenship; by 1870 the figure had sunk to 367. In 1875, only 8.7% of Hamburg's inhabitants were citizens—34,000 out of 390,000. By 1890 the number had fallen to 28,000, of whom 5,000 were debarred because they fell below the minimum voting age of 25. Further inequality was introduced by the fact that the property-owners (about 6,000 electors in 1890) had two votes each, since they were also citizens and could thus vote in the general elections. Most privileged of all was the position of the 600 or so notables, all of whom were also citizens and most of whom were property-owners as well. The great majority of the notables thus possessed three votes each, and, since the notables' elections were held some days after the property-owners' which in turn followed those of the ordinary citizens, the notables had three bites at the cherry, as it were, and frequently used their own elections to put into the Assembly candidates of their choice who had failed to get through in the other two elections: a privilege that was augmented by the fact that the notables' elections were held every three years, while the property-owners and the ordinary citizens could only vote in any given constituency once every six years.[70]

Restricted franchises were the norm in nineteenth-century Europe, even in the 1890s; in England, for example, despite the Reform Acts of 1832, 1867, and 1884, a very large part of the working class still failed to qualify for the vote, while in Italy, Austria–Hungary, and the Scandinavian countries the right to vote still depended to a large extent on property, income and status. Within Germany itself, the municipal suffrage in many cities and towns was similarly restricted. Even in small villages the right to vote for the village council (*Gemeinderat*) was confined to those who could satisfy a residential qualification of 10 years or more, a requirement which disfranchised large numbers of the geographically mobile proletariat at a stroke.[71] In Prussia the electorate was divided into three unequal classes by property and income, and other German states also possessed unequal electoral systems, even if this only consisted in the absence of a direct vote. The absence of national political parties from the Hamburg scene was more unusual, and a reflection of the stubborn force of local particularism; but here the true comparison is not with other federated states in the German empire, but with other municipalities, and when one looks at urban councils in the rest of Germany, there too one can see the persistence of what James Sheehan has called 'unpolitical politics' up to the end of the century and sometimes beyond. The

[69] Eckardt, *Privilegien und Parlament*, 30–3.
[70] Ibid.
[71] See R. J. Evans and W. R. Lee (eds.), *The German Peasantry. Conflict and Community in Rural Society from the 18th to the 20th Centuries* (London, 1986), especially the contributions by C. S. Catt and W. Kaschuba.

electoral strength of German liberalism all over Germany at this level depended on the persistence of a restricted franchise, and Hamburg's liberal bourgeoisie was no exception in wanting to see it continue.[72]

Property thus in a very real sense formed the foundation of direct political power in nineteenth-century Hamburg. Possession of capital alone was what enabled an inhabitant of the city to participate in the legislative and administrative decisions that shaped Hamburg's future. The grand bourgeoisie of the wealthiest and most established merchants, bankers, and lawyers, bound together by a tight web of familial and social ties that effectively excluded the rest of the population from their ranks, managed to reserve for itself the right to executive office; but from the 1840s onwards and above all after the reforms of 1859–60, the middling bourgeoisie of lesser (but still substantial) merchants, doctors, architects, apothecaries, teachers, and the like was able to make its voice heard through the Citizens' Assembly, the Chamber of Commerce, the Citizens' Clubs, the Deputations, and other informal institutions. More significantly still, those in this group who, with the better-off among the petty bourgeoisie, depended for a large part of their existence on the possession of fixed capital in the form of rented accommodation, were able to exert an increasingly significant degree of influence over legislation, so much so that after the reforms of 1859–60 they were effectively able to prevent the passage of almost any measure which they considered ran counter to their interests.

These were the dominant classes in Hamburg in the second half of the nineteenth century; and they were bound together by a powerful ideology which, however divergent the positions of the various fractions of capital on secondary issues, made it virtually inevitable in the last analysis that primacy should be accorded by all to the interests of trade. The sense of solidarity that this ideology expressed and furthered was one of the features of Hamburg life which outsiders found most striking. The Baltic German Julius von Eckardt, for example, found much to praise in the fact 'that the citizens of this great city, although it has in some respects become modern, felt themselves as parts of a *single* body, and were filled with a sense of solidarity that has long since vanished from most of today's middle-sized towns'.[73] This sense of solidarity among the dominant classes was more an unconscious reflex against threats from outside and below than a consciously worked out political theory. It was to find increasingly explicit expression as the century drew to its close.

---

[72] J. J. Sheehan, 'Liberalism and the City in 19th-century Germany', *Past and Present*, 51 (1971), 116–37.

[73] Von Eckardt, *Lebenserinnerungen*, i. 258.

c. *Standards of Living*

I

Contemporary observers in late nineteenth-century Hamburg were well aware that the style and substance of economic prosperity and political participation stretched relatively far down the social scale. As Julius von Eckardt, looking back on his period in Hamburg in the 1870s, remarked,

The generally comfortable style of life of the ruling stratum spilled over into the other levels of society in so great a measure that the remaining social distinctions seemed trivial. Right into the middle of the artisanate, people lived in a manner that suggested affluence and secure conditions of existence, and which contrasted sufficiently clearly with the frugal circumstances of other parts of Germany to make a real impression on strangers to the city.[1]

Nevertheless, an enormous gulf separated the patrician families and Senatorial dynasties at the top from the petty-bourgeois clerks, master artisans and tradespeople at the bottom of the dominant classes. On the eve of the 1848 Revolution, for example, the grand bourgeoisie, numbering about 1,000 heads of household in all, could count on capital assets well in excess of 50,000 Marks Banco each, and an annual income that was commensurate with this in scale. The top 600 or so, indeed, possessed on average 100,000 Marks Banco in capital per family. About 750 individuals recorded a taxable income of more than 4,500 Marks Courant a year, and all told there were about 4,500 people whose annual earnings exceeded 3,000 Marks—that is, not only the patricians but also the middling merchants and bankers, brokers and dealers of one kind and another, a few professionals such as junior lawyers, officials, and pastors, and the richest and most successful of the master artisans. All these people employed labour of one kind and another and can be counted as belonging to the grand or middling bourgeoisie. Below them came another 22,000 or so taxpayers earning between 500 and 3,000 Marks Courant a year, the bulk of the master artisans, innkeepers, retailers, small tradesmen, lower professionals, and clerks, who can be counted as belonging to the petty bourgeoisie. A wealthy merchant banker or Senator, therefore, could be earning ten times as much as a master artisan working on his own or a retailer running a small shop, and was likely to possess capital assets vastly greater in scope and scale.[2]

Yet these differences paled once more beside the chasm that existed between all these groups and the rest of the population. For the same investigation carried out in 1848 went on to show that almost 70% of those registered as

[1] Von Eckardt, *Lebenserinnerungen*, i. 207.

[2] Schmidt, *Die Revolution*, pp. 16–20; A. Kraus, *Die Unterschichten Hamburgs in der ersten Hälfte des 19. Jahrhunderts. Entstehung, Struktur, Lebensverhältnisse. Eine historisch-statistische Untersuchung* (Sozialwissenschaftliche Studien, 9; Stuttgart, 1965), p. 74.

employed in the city earned so little money that they fell below the tax threshold and so did not enter the statistics at all. Taking into account the fact that the better-off taxpayers generally had non-earning wives, we can estimate that perhaps 20% of the population lived a reasonably comfortable to very well-off style of life with the bread-winner bringing in over 1,000 Marks a year, while another 20%, dependent on 500–1,000 Marks a year, lived in modest or barely adequate circumstances and the rest—60%—fell below the poverty line.[3] These were in the first place the people who provided the muscle-power that kept the goods flowing through Hamburg's harbour: boatmen, sailors, porters, wagoners, shipyard workers, warehousemen, mechanics, and many others, down to the general labourer and the navvy. Perhaps 10,000 people worked in the harbour in the middle of the century,[4] while many more were employed in the trades and services necessary for the everyday life of a great trading city with a substantial middle class: tailors, shoemakers, carpenters and joiners, silversmiths, printers, cabinet-makers, messengers, domestic servants, washerwomen, needleworkers, cleaners, barmen, prostitutes. All in all, between two-thirds and three-quarters of those working in the city at mid-century earned less than 500 Marks a year. Small wonder, therefore, that so few of Hamburg's inhabitants were able to afford the 40-Mark fee required for registration as a citizen.[5]

During the first half of the nineteenth century manual labour came in theory under the control of the guilds, but in practice their ability to prevent non-guild labourers from working in the city was limited. The growth of Hamburg's economy acted as a magnet for the labour force in the surrounding countryside, and indeed even further afield. The Senate was unwilling to restrict the entry of these 'little people, who establish themselves here relying solely on their luck and the strength of their arms (and who we cannot do without in appropriately limited numbers)',[6] because this would lead to a rise in wages that would undoubtedly have an adverse effect on business. Thus the number of non-guild workers in 1847–8 was at least as great as the number organized within the guilds—about 13,000—even not counting a further 13,000 classified as servants and the like.[7] What the guilds were able to do, however, was to ensure that these people had a hard time of it, and that registered journeymen and apprentices had the first claim on the best work going. Not surprisingly, therefore, poverty and destitution were widespread even at the best of times. As the historian Antje Kraus has concluded, for the large proportion of the population that lived on the borderline of subsistence in the first half of the century, the problem lay in

---

[3] Kraus, *Die Unterschichten*, pp. 74–5.
[4] Schmidt, *Die Revolution*, p. 20.
[5] Kraus, *Die Unterschichten*, p. 74.
[6] Quoted ibid., p. 78.
[7] Schmidt, *Die Revolution*, p. 18.

The narrow margin between income from paid labour—which in the city could not be augmented by the secondary income from the collection or cultivation of natural products—and the fixed part of the costs of living. Age, sickness, death of the main bread-winner or other exceptional burdens on income thus usually led to a transition across the margin into destitution.[8]

From the middle of the nineteenth century onwards, Hamburg's social structure began to undergo a process of rapid change. The ending of the nightly shutting of the city gates in 1860 made it easier for workers to live outside the city walls and led to a rapid expansion of the suburbs. This was accelerated by the abolition of guild controls in 1865 and the opening of the new Sandgate Harbour in 1866. The quickening of the pace of economic growth, pushed on by Germany's industrialization, brought ever-increasing numbers of workers to the city in search of a job. The opening of the free port in 1888 and the rapid expansion of ancillary and processing industries added to the demand for labour. Hamburg's harbour, and the employment it offered, became, it was said in 1895, 'the last lifebuoy for those labourers and small artisans who had suffered shipwreck in their trade. Everyone who no longer had any hope of finding work elsewhere went to the harbour in order to find some remaining work there if possible.'[9] Already by the 1870s, less than 60% of Hamburg's inhabitants had been born in the city.[10] Before long Hamburg's population, which had increased by less than 20% between 1817 and 1850, had doubled in size;[11] by 1880, as Figure 1 shows, it was pushing towards the half-million mark; by 1890 it stood at 623,000. Well before the First World War it had passed a million without showing any signs of levelling off.[12] Despite the growing diversification of industry within the city, the harbour became, if anything, even more dominant than before. Trade and transport (which in Hamburg meant above all shipping and river or harbour work) occupied 30% of the economically active population in 1871 and 38% in 1895, the highest proportion in any German city. Of the 35% occupied in industry in 1882, a substantial proportion were employed in jobs such as shipbuilding and ship repairs. Nevertheless, the rise of ancillary and processing industries, and the construction boom that accompanied the physical expansion of the city in this period, did offer an increasing variety of jobs outside the free port and the harbour area as well as within.[13]

   [8] A. Kraus, 'Unterschichten und Sozialpolitik in Hamburg, 1815–1848', in Herzig, *et al.*, *Arbeiter in Hamburg*, pp. 71–7, here p. 76.
   [9] Quoted in Grüttner, *Arbeitswelt*, p. 81.
   [10] C. Wischermann, *Wohnen in Hamburg vor dem Ersten Weltkrieg* (Münster, 1983), p. 57.
   [11] Kraus, *Die Unterschichten*, p. 31.
   [12] The discrepancy between the state and the city is accounted for by the population of rural areas and exclaves such as the Ritzebüttel demesne (including Cuxhaven) at the mouth of the Elbe.
   [13] Dieter Langewiesche, 'Die Zeit des Kaiserreichs', in Herzig *et al.*, *Arbeiter in Hamburg*, p. 16; H. Kutz-Bauer, 'Arbeiterschaft und Sozialdemokratie in Hamburg vom Gründerkrach bis zum Ende des Sozialistengesetzes', ibid., pp. 179–92, here p. 180.

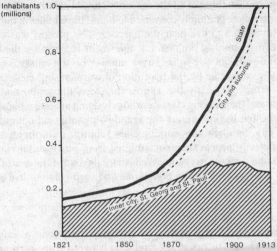

Source: Werner Matti, 'Bevölkerungsvorgänge in den Hansestädten ...', *ZHG*, 69 (1983), 114

FIG. 1. Population growth in Hamburg, 1821–1913

One of the major consequences of economic expansion in the second half of the nineteenth century was the formation, from the 1860s, of a wage-earning proletariat, as a new working class emerged from the shadow of the guilds and began to establish its own institutions and ways of life: the more substantial masters—some of whom were employing up to 100 men by mid-century[14]—rose into the ranks of the politically enfranchised petty bourgeoisie, while the mass of small single masters and journeymen slowly merged into a new proletariat. The growth of a working class was perhaps most obvious in the residential segregation of the different classes which took place as the city grew. In the early part of the century, as the majority of the city's inhabitants lived cheek by jowl in the close confinement of the city walls, rich and poor, even if they lived in different houses, could hardly avoid confronting one another in the daily round. Traditional in Hamburg was the 'old unity of living-quarters, office, and warehouse' in the same building,[15] but with the growth of trade, the merchants began to move out to larger, more comfortable houses outside the city walls. In 1861, for example, 12 Senators, Syndics, and Secretaries still lived in the Altstadt and 17 in the Neustadt; by 1911, however, only one still lived in the inner city, and that was the Police Chief, whose official residence lay there; his private home was

[14] Arno Herzig, 'Vom ausgehenden 18. Jahrhundert bis zu den 1860er Jahren', ibid., p. 10.
[15] P. E. Schramm, *Hamburg, Deutschland und die Welt. Leistung und Grenzen hanseatischen Bürgertums in der Zeit zwischen Napoleon I. und Bismarck. Ein Kapitel deutscher Geschichte* (Munich, 1943), p. 348.

in the suburbs, like those of all the others.[16] The old merchant habitations in the city centre were gradually converted to house the families of the labouring classes who needed to live near the harbour. This process was accelerated with the construction of multi-storey apartment blocks after the Great Fire of 1842 and subsequently in far larger number on the outskirts of the city, and virtually completed by the relocation of warehousing facilities into the free port in the 1880s. By the 1890s, therefore, the grand and middling bourgeoisie and the working class were largely living in quite separate districts of the city. Often the children of the grand bourgeoisie did not even go into the inner city, let alone the working-class suburbs, until they were grown up, and the only people they encountered from other social classes were tradesmen and domestic servants. Well before the end of the century, indeed, the grand bourgeoisie and the proletariat had each come to live in a world of its own.[17]

II

The process of social segregation by residence had gone a long way in Hamburg by 1892. The negative correlation between wage-earning manual labourers and economically independent occupied persons by district was as high as -0.92 by this time; for manual and white-collar workers the negative correlation, at -0.83 was scarcely less impressive. The process of class segregation can be clearly seen from Maps 1–10.[18] They show that the twenty residential districts of the city at the end of the nineteenth century fell roughly into four groups. First, the four densely populated districts of the inner city, the Altstadt Nord and Süd and the Neustadt Nord and Süd. With the exception of the Altstadt Süd, which contained extensive harbour facilities and a number of offices and public buildings, these were mostly covered in old, frequently half-timbered houses and criss-crossed by a maze of narrow alley-

[16] StA Hbg, FA Voigt B68; J.F. Voigt, 'MS. über die Wohnungen hamburgischer Senatsmitglieder 1712–1911'.

[17] StA Hbg, FA Merck II 9 Konv. 4a, Heft II, p. 16.

[18] See the Statistical Appendix for a discussion of the principles on which the maps have been drawn. For statistical evidence, see Table 15. For Senatorial families in Harvestehude (p. 56), see *Jahresbericht des Armenpflegevereins zu Harvestehude für das Jahr 1897* (list of donors). There is a very careful and thorough study of residential segregation in Wischermann, *Wohnen in Hamburg*, pp. 266–399. Wischermann carefully avoids using the concept of class and points out the problems of squaring administrative districts with socially-defined areas. However, by using qualitative evidence it is possible to take account of this difficulty, and evidence of class consciousness can be provided (with all due reservations) by electoral statistics (see Maps 13–15 below). Wischermann is properly cautious, however, in his reservations about Bruno Fritzsche's claim 'that the location of living-quarters plays a more decisive role in the formation of the labour movement in general and class consciousness in particular, than the workplace' (B. Fritzsche, 'Das Quartier als Lebensraum', in W. Conze and U. Engelhardt (eds.), *Arbeiterexistenz im 19. Jahrhundert* (Stuttgart, 1981), pp. 92–113, here p. 104; discussed in Wischermann, op. cit., pp. 398–9). For another study of residential class segregation see I. Fischer, *Industrialisierung, sozialer Konflikt und politische Willensbildung in der Stadtgemeinde. Ein Beitrag zur Sozialgeschichte Augsburgs 1840–1914* (Augsburg, 1977), pp. 107–13.

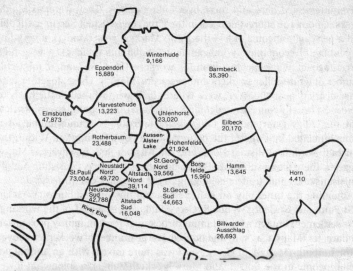

Source: MS *1893*, Plate I

MAP I. Hamburg in December 1892: the districts (*Bezirke*) and their population

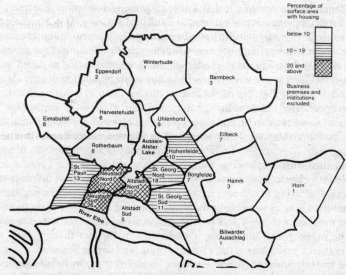

Source: SHS 21 (1903), Table 4. Business premises and institutions excluded

MAP 2. Percentage of surface area with housing, by district, Hamburg 1896

ways, intersected here and there by winding canals. They were, as Map 4 shows, among the poorest districts in the city. The Neustadt Süd in particular had a per capita income of less than 400 Marks a year (Map 4), a very low percentage of economically independent inhabitants (Map 5), a very high percentage of wage-earning manual workers (Map 6), and a miniscule number of white-collar workers and overseers (Map 7). These, together with other districts near the river, were where those who worked in the harbour were most heavily concentrated (Map 8). It was in these four inner-city districts that the 'Alley Quarters' (or *Gängeviertel*) were to be found; tumbledown slums inhabited by some of the poorest of the city's population. Within the Neustadt Nord, the Altstadt Nord, and the Altstadt Süd, however, as Map 5 suggests, there was a substantial petty-bourgeois presence, consisting mainly of artisans and small traders belonging to the so-called 'old *Mittelstand*'.

Adjoining the inner city on either side were the inner suburbs (*Vorstadt*) of St Pauli and St Georg. While St Georg Süd, covering part of the working-class settlement known as the Hammerbrook, was predominantly proletarian in character (Maps 3, 4, 5, 6) and housed a large number of workers employed in the harbour (Map 8), St Georg Nord was more mixed, with an annual per capita income in the 800–1,200 Mark bracket (Map 4), a somewhat lower percentage of wage-earners (Map 6), and a fairly substantial proportion of white-collar employees (Map 7). St Pauli, increasingly shaped as the century progressed by its role as a centre of entertainment and prostitution, mainly for sailors, had a similarly mixed, but slightly more proletarian character.

Thirdly, moving northward from St Pauli and St Georg, Map 4 reveals an inner circle of better-off districts surrounding the Aussen-Alster, the large lake which forms perhaps the most attractive physical feature of the present-day city. On the left bank, Harvestehude and Rotherbaum, the so-called 'villa quarter' (*Villenviertel*), were characterized by a low population density (Maps 2 and 3), a very high per capita annual income (Map 4), a high percentage of economically independent inhabitants (Map 5), a small percentage of manual workers (Map 6), and a low proportion of people working in industry and building (Map 9). Here, above all in Harvestehude, lived the grand bourgeoisie, in enormous *Gründerzeit* villas (many of which can still be seen in all their vulgar splendour today), surrounded by spacious gardens and cared for by hordes of servants. Over half the households in these two districts, indeed, had living-in servants in the 1890s (Map 10). Those who registered themselves here as working in trade and transport were most likely to have been merchants (Maps 5 and 8). The persistence of these districts as centres of the ruling grand bourgeoisie is underlined by the fact that in 1897 no fewer than 13 members of the 18-man Senate (and former Senators' widows) lived in Harvestehude. Active Senators domiciled there included Johannes Versmann, Johann Georg Mönckeberg, and Johann Heinrich Burchard. Their neighbours ranged from Albert Ballin of the Hamburg–America Line and

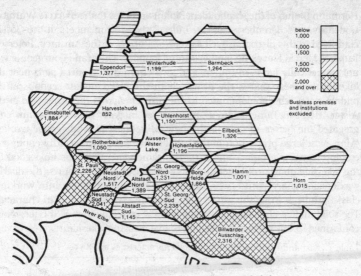

Source: SHS 16 (1894), 18. Business premises and institutions excluded

MAP 3. Inhabitants per hectare of built-up land, by district, Hamburg 1892

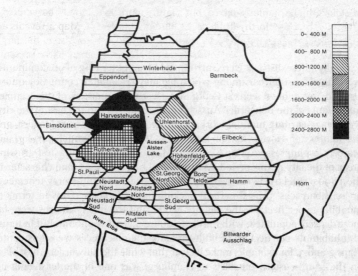

Source: MS 1893, Plate 1 (based on tax returns)

MAP 4. Annual per capita income, by district, Hamburg 1892

Hermann Blohm of the shipbuilders Blohm and Voss to the bankers Warburg, Godeffroy, and Berenberg-Gossler. Indeed, six adult members of the Gossler clan lived in this district as well as representatives of the Amsinck, Petersen, Ruperti, Merck, Sieveking, and Westphal families. The grand bourgeoisie was not numerically large, of course, and away from the favoured plots near the lake its members shared the district with the more modest sections of the middle class, who predominated in the districts across the other side of the Alster. Here, in Hohenfelde, as to a degree in parts of Rotherbaum, congregated the better-off among the new *Mittelstand* of white-collar workers (Map 7); a large proportion of the inhabitants were also wealthy enough to employ servants (Maps 4 and 10). The same generalizations hold good for the lake-side quarter of Uhlenhorst as well; for as Table 1 shows, the district was divided sharply into two, the eastern side running over into working-class Barmbeck while the western side was clearly middle class in character. The solid middle-class element in the socially mixed district of St Georg Nord conformed to this pattern by tending to live near the lakeside.

Table 1. East and West Uhlenhorst: social characteristics in 1895

Sub-district	Percentage of occupied persons, in following categories:				
	Industry and Building	Trade and Transport	Economically Independent	White-collar, overseers	Wage earners
East	52	25	22	12	66
West	32	29	38	12	50

Source: SHS 18 (1898), p. 12.

Finally, these districts were surrounded by an outer ring of predominantly working-class suburbs, among which we may reasonably count Uhlenhorst Ost and, as we have seen, St Georg Süd. Over three-quarters of the occupied inhabitants of the Billwärder Ausschlag, near the river to the east of the city, were wage-earning manual workers, at the bottom of the social ladder, and the figures for Horn, Hamm, Barmbeck, Winterhude, and Eppendorf are scarcely less impressive (Map 6). These outer suburbs were the fastest-growing areas of the city at this period (Map 1). They had a curious dual character in the 1890s: still largely rural, but with areas of dense multi-storey tenements or 'rent barracks' (*Mietskasernen*) backing onto the fields. Thus in terms of inhabitants per hectare, the old city centre and the inner suburbs were far more densely populated, with hardly a square metre left unbuilt. But in terms of inhabitants per hectare of built-up land, the differences were less acute. Maps 2 and 3, for example, make it clear that while the Billwärder Ausschlag, on the south-eastern outskirts of Hamburg, was one of the least built-up areas, with only 1.3% of its land occupied by houses, it was also one of the most densely populated, with 2,316 inhabitants per hectare of built-up land,

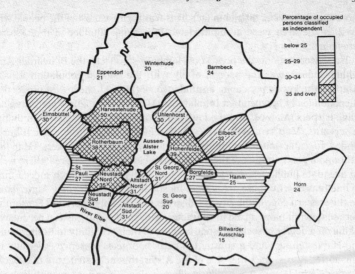

Source: SHS 18 (1898), 12

MAP 5. Economically independent occupied persons, by district, Hamburg 1895

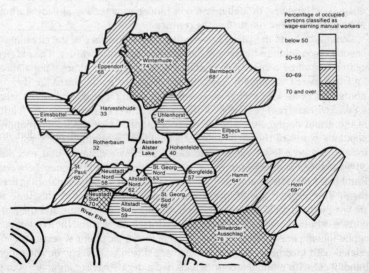

Source: SHS 18 (1898), 12

MAP 6. Wage-earning manual workers, by district, Hamburg 1895

more than any other district in fact. This was because most of the people who lived in the area were accommodated in a small number of multi-storey tenements.

These were among the poorest of Hamburg's districts: the Billwärder Aus-schlag, indeed, was the poorest of all, with the highest population density (Map 3), the lowest per capita annual income (Map 4), the lowest proportion of economically independent inhabitants (Map 5), the highest percentage of wage-earners (Map 6), and the lowest proportion of households with living-in servants (Map 10). With the exception of this district, the outer suburbs tended to cater more for industrial than for harbour workers (Map 8), although a good number of them still worked in the harbour area; there were no adequate public transport facilities to the city centre, which indeed may be one reason why these areas were mostly avoided by the new *Mittelstand*. On the western edge of the city, the districts such as Eppendorf and Eimsbüttel were somewhat more mixed in character, with their south-eastern perimeters taking on a degree of social prestige because of their proximity to Rotherbaum and Harvestehude, and a substantial petty-bourgeois presence especially in Eimsbüttel. Across the other side of the Alster, the social structure of Eilbeck, Borgfelde, and Hamm was similarly affected along their borders with Hohen-felde, the third most prestigious of the city's residential areas. Finally, the most easterly district of all, Horn, still possessed an almost wholly rural character at this time, which marked it off to a degree from all the other districts of Hamburg, though here too its inner perimeter was already starting to be built on before the turn of the century.

Commercial and industrial growth thus altered the face of the city almost beyond recognition in the second half of the nineteenth century. The old city centre contained a rapidly decreasing proportion of Hamburg's population and underwent an equally rapid deterioration in social status. A ring of grand-bourgeois and middle-class suburbs sprang up around the Alster, flanked by new 'rent barracks' for the industrial working class. To the world of the grand bourgeoisie, already described, was added the infinitely more populous world of the petty bourgeoisie and the working class, separated from it and, to a lesser extent from each other, by a distance that was not only economic and social but geographical as well. These differences between Hamburg's districts enable us to compare different social indicators across them. The decisive importance of economic independence at this time is shown by the high positive correlations between this indicator and the pro-portion of households with servants (0.87) in each district, and the average per capita income in each district (0.82), while the employment of servants cor-related with income levels very closely indeed (0.95). Poverty, on the other hand, went with manual labour (which had a negative correlation of −0.84 with income levels). We turn now, therefore, to examine how the realities of poverty and deprivation were experienced by those who suffered under them.

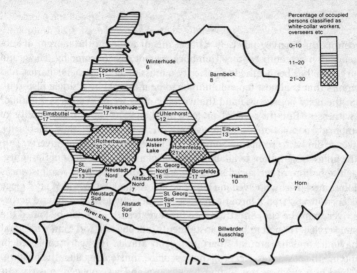

Eppendorf 11

Winterhude 6

Barmbeck 8

Harvestehude 17

Eimsbuttel 17

Uhlenhorst 12

Eilbeck 13

Rotherbaum 30

Aussen-Alster Lake

Hohenfelde 21

St. Pauli 13

Neustadt Nord 7

St. Georg Nord 16

Borgfelde 17

Hamm 10

Horn 7

Altstadt Nord 7

Neustadt Sud 5

Altstadt Sud 10

St. Georg Sud 13

River Elbe

Billwarder Ausschlag 10

Percentage of occupied persons classified as white-collar workers, overseers etc

0–10

11–20

21–30

Source: SHS 18 (1898), 12

MAP 7. White-collar workers and overseers, by district, Hamburg 1895

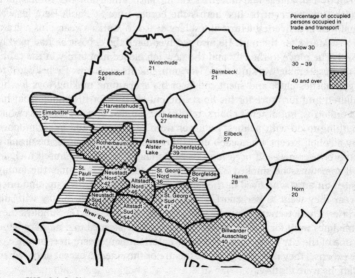

Eppendorf 24

Winterhude 21

Barmbeck 21

Harvestehude 37

Eimsbuttel 30

Uhlenhorst 27

Eilbeck 27

Rotherbaum 41

Aussen-Alster Lake

Hohenfelde 39

St. Pauli 38

Neustadt Nord 42

Altstadt Nord 46

St. Georg Nord 36

Borgfelde 32

Hamm 28

Horn 20

Neustadt Sud 42

Altstadt Sud 54

St. Georg Sud 47

River Elbe

Billwarder Ausschlag 40

Percentage of occupied persons occupied in trade and transport

below 30

30 – 39

40 and over

Source: SHS 18 (1898), 12

MAP 8. Persons occupied in trade and transport, by district, Hamburg 1895

III

Accounts that convey precisely what it meant to be on the margin of subsistence in nineteenth-century Hamburg are not easy to come by. The grand bourgeoisie has bequeathed to posterity a mass of family papers, diaries, and memoirs that is almost too voluminous to be mastered by a single historian; from the petty bourgeoisie and the working class we only possess a handful of witnesses. But they afford at least a glimpse of how the majority of Hamburg's population came to terms with their lot, and they enable us, however dimly, to recapture some of the subjective aspects of poverty. One of the fullest descriptions available of the life of a poor inhabitant of Hamburg, near the bottom of the social scale, is derived from the family reminiscences of Johannes Fiege, who lived in Hamburg before the First World War.[19] Fiege was born in 1871 on a farm near Stade, a little way downstream and across the river from the city. Shortly before his seventeenth birthday he joined the postal service. He had to pay in instalments a deposit of 200 Marks for good behaviour, and his annual salary was 390 Marks. His work consisted in emptying the postboxes, cleaning the post office, and looking after the heating. He lived in a room in the postmaster's house and was obliged to carry out numerous small unpaid jobs for the postmaster and his wife. This menial position lasted for some three years.

But by 1899 Fiege had moved to Altona, part of the Hamburg conurbation under Prussian control, just across the border from St Pauli. Here he was employed in delivering letters at a salary of 1,050 Marks a year, plus a grant of 240 Marks for the rent. He also received back the deposit he had paid in 1888. The move to the city and the new job placed him firmly in the ranks of the respectable working class. His amusements were few. He belonged to a gymnastics club, and spent much of his spare time making toys for his children and furniture for his home. He cut slippers for his family from his old uniforms, upholstered chairs, resoled the family's shoes. Fiege never had anything to do with politics, he never went to the pub, and never touched any alcohol, except when each of his three sons was confirmed; he drank a bottle of beer on each occasion. Every Sunday he allowed himself a cigar, and sometimes he smoked a pipe. Once a year, at Easter time, the family visited an aunt who lived in the farm where Fiege had grown up, and once a year they went to Bergedorf, also just outside Hamburg, to stay with his in-laws. These were the only holidays the family ever had. On Sundays they sometimes went for a walk, visited a museum, or listened to a military band in one of the city's few parks. All these entertainments were free; because of the expense, they never went to the theatre or the cinema, except once, when relations were visiting.

[19] For the following, see H. Fiege, 'Aus dem Leben eines unteren Postbeamten vor dem Ersten Weltkrieg', *Hamburgische Geschichts- und Heimatblätter*, 10. 5 (1978), 119–32.

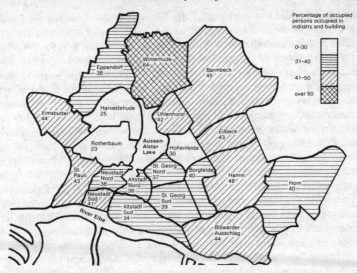

Source: SHS 18 (1898), 12

MAP 9. Persons occupied in industry and building, by district, Hamburg 1895

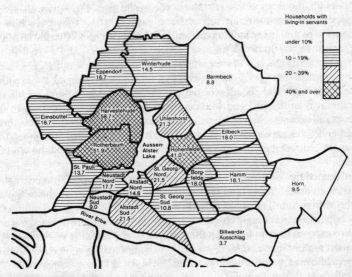

Source: calculated from *SHS* 19 (1900), 165

MAP 10. Percentage of households with living-in servants, by district, Hamburg 1890

Fiege's wife did not work outside the house, but she made her sons sailor suits from his old uniforms, which were supplied free of charge by the Post Office, and she made her own clothes as well. She bought food for the family at the Civil Servants' Union shop. Fiege rented an allotment where he grew potatoes and vegetables for the family and flowers for his wife. He fertilized the ground with compost made from dung and offal obtained from a nearby slaughterhouse, mixed with dead leaves gathered from the churchyard in Ottensen and vegetable waste from the allotment itself. In the summer and autumn the family often went for walks in the woods to collect wild berries and fruits, some of which they used for home-made teas. With all this economizing, Fiege managed to save enough money with the Altona Savings and Housing Society to acquire a newly built apartment in 1905 for an annual rent of 260 Marks. By 1908 Fiege was earning 1,640 Marks a year at the Main Post Office. Even so, whenever there was a serious illness in the family, problems began to occur. In 1911 Fiege's wife had a difficult time giving birth to their third son, and a doctor and nurse had to be called to the house; in 1912 all three children had serious tonsilitis and had to be seen by a specialist, and finally the new baby had rheumatism and had to receive medical treatment for three months and undergo an operation. The birth cost Fiege a total of 15 Marks for the doctor, 15 Marks for the midwife, and 42 Marks for the nurse, while the children's illnesses in 1911–12 cost him 108 Marks for the doctors and 17 Marks for medication. Fiege was obliged to apply to his employers for support, and early in 1913 they gave him 60 Marks to pay off his remaining medical debts. This left him still with 10 Marks a month to pay into the Housing Society for another year, as well as the usual rent and the cost of supporting the family. Yet his was a success story; he had made his way from the country to the city, obtained a job with a steady income and security of tenure, earned promotion, and acquired a home in a light, airy, and well-constructed new building. His sons in due course all became schoolteachers; one of them eventually obtained a doctorate and ended his career as a professor. Fiege's story illustrates how precarious was the existence even of the most solid and thrifty sections of the working class.

Others were not so fortunate. One of the few working-class autobiographies that we possess from Hamburg in this period, written by Wilhelm Kaisen, who was born in Eppendorf in 1887, describes a life equally unremitting in its harshness and equally obsessive in its thrift, but far more directed towards mere survival than to founding the basis for escape from the working-class.[20] Kaisen's father was a building worker who helped in a slaughterhouse during the cold winter months when work on the building sites was impossible. The family was fortunate enough, shortly after Kaisen's birth, to move into the

---

[20] W. Kaisen, *Meine Arbeit, Mein Leben* (Munich, 1967).

countryside; they lived in Alsterdorf, a rural dependency of Hamburg just to the north-east of the city boundary. Here they rented a four-room dwelling in a terrace for 20 Marks a month. This accommodation had to house not only Kaisen and his parents but also three elder sisters and a brother as well. But it was far cheaper than anything that could be found in the town. The family also had the use of a garden and was able to rent a small plot of land, on which it kept a pig for fattening and two goats for their milk. Every member of the family had to contribute in one way or another to the joint income.

My mother 'did' for a bourgeois household every morning and got first six then finally ten Marks a month for this, i.e. half the rent. I myself did a delivery round for a Hamburg newspaper ... [and] got ... three Marks a month for this ... which also went straight into the rentbox, in its entirety. My brother helped out in a bakery, carrying wood for the ovens or running errands. My three sisters tried to make themselves useful around the house and in the garden.

Kaisen himself was charged with finding food for the goats. His parents taught him which wild plants were good for them to eat and which were poisonous. In summer the children gathered wood and sticks from the hedgerows for the fire. The family lived with a simplicity even more extreme than that of the Fieges. The children's clothes were made by their mother, or repaired by her so frequently and so extensively that it came to the same thing. They only wore shoes on special occasions; normally they went barefoot. The house had no electric light or running water, no carpet, no bath, no toilet. There was enough crockery for all the family, but no more. Meat was a rarity at table; fruit was seldom seen, despite the fact that they lived surrounded by countryside. The family generally ate fried potatoes for lunch, and milk soup 'with flour dumplings' for dinner, 'or potatoes and vegetables with a piece of smoked bacon fat as a stew'.

Opportunities for supplementing income and diet and gathering fuel in these ways were also open to some extent to those working-class families who lived on the borders of Hamburg, in Barmbeck or Winterhude; but they were almost wholly denied to the many thousands who lived in the inner city. An example of one such family is provided by Ernst Neddermeyer, who worked in a tannery for 18 Marks a week and as a sailor on his employer's cargo boat in the summer. He lived in the late 1880s and early 1890s in a two-room Hamburg apartment with a kitchen, for which he paid 24 Marks rent a month, or 30% of his wages. In this sparse accommodation, which was without electricity or gas or a proper toilet, lived not only Neddermeyer and his wife but also five children, and a lodger who brought in 2 Marks 50 a week. The five children slept in a single bed, the couple in the main bedroom and the lodger in the parlour (*gute Stube*), a room otherwise reserved for festive occasions and receiving visitors. The main item in the family's diet was bread smeared with 'an indefinable kind of dripping' known as 'American ape-fat'. On Saturdays an oatmeal 'sausage' was consumed to vary the diet.

Four of the children were chronically ill, and the family's situation only began to improve when it moved to Ottensen, in Altona, in 1896, and the mother opened a small grocer's shop with 100 Marks lent by the lodger. By keeping it open until midnight and granting credit she acquired an increasing number of customers, especially railwaymen, postmen, and others unable to shop during normal working hours. The father's situation also improved as he left his old job and went to work in the harbour. Change and improvement, therefore, were always possible; but so too was illness and disaster.[21]

An even more graphic and detailed example of how a working-class family in Hamburg spent its income was provided by a harbour worker's wife, who was persuaded to write down details of all the family's outgoings over a period of 18 weeks in 1898.[22] Her husband had a regular job in the harbour and brought in an average of 24 Marks a week, from which 15 Pfennigs was regularly deducted by his employer to meet insurance costs.[23] His wife also worked part-time in a clothing shop. She was not paid any wages for this job, but was allowed instead to take home underwear and clothes for her children. This mode of payment was not to be sneered at in a family which consisted of no fewer than 8 children, 3 boys and 5 girls, between the ages of 18 months and 13 years. The oldest girl worked afternoons, but only brought in 1 Mark a week. So the family's annual money income stood at just over 1,290 Marks a year. The father was a high-earning port worker, and the fact that he could count on a regular income, rather than depending on casual work, also placed him among the upper reaches of the working class. Yet the family lived in a four-room apartment for which they paid 170 Marks a year, or just over 20% of the annual income. The wife had charge of the finances and gave her husband 1 Mark 50 a week pocket-money. However, this was not beer money, but lunch money, since his wife did not give him any food to take with him to work. The family spent nothing on leisure activities; indeed, they hardly seemed to have had any. They were well placed for the children's clothes, but whenever shoes had to be bought, or the husband and wife needed clothes for themselves, the money could only be raised by pawning some of the furniture. Additional unavoidable running costs of the household included soap, wool for clothing repairs, matches, petroleum and fuel for fires and lamps, soda for doing the washing, school books for the children, shoe repairs, writing paper and stamps.

This still left the bulk of the family's income to be spent on food. But with 10 mouths to feed there was not much room for manœuvre. Meat was only really possible on Sundays, though occasionally the family also consumed a

[21] R. Neddermeyer, *Es begann in Hamburg ... Ein deutscher Kommunist erzählt aus seinem Leben* (East Berlin, 1980), pp. 10–19.

[22] 'Ein Blick in die Haushaltung einer Hamburger Arbeiterfamilie', *Mitteilungen aus der Arbeit der Hamburger Stadtmission*, 20 (1899), 77–85.

[23] For further information on wage levels among port workers, see Grüttner, *Arbeitswelt*, 48–56.

'beefsteak' made out of cheap minced horsemeat, no doubt with a high proportion of fat, on weekdays. Most of the time they lived off potatoes, bread, and coffee, with fish, fruit, oats, and milk as additional extras. On Monday 17 October, for example, they ate a lunch of potatoes, quaker oats, fish, black bread with margarine, and plums with sugar. This was followed by an evening meal of coffee and bread. The next day the family's lunch consisted of bones, pot-barley, potatoes, bread, and margarine; dinner consisted of sausages, potatoes, and coffee. Variations on this diet during the rest of the week included half a pound of fat consumed on Thursday evening, turnips, gruel, rice, and skimmed milk. The 'bones' turned up on two more occasions. The memory of the grand Sunday lunch on 16 October, with beef (*Ochsenfleisch*), eggs, and cheese, had to last them for the rest of the week, and the following Sunday they had to make do with a horsemeat 'beefsteak' and potatoes. The Sunday joint never weighed over a pound, which must have given the children scarcely more than a mouthful each. Clearly the wife was doing her best to vary the family's fare within the very strict limits which financial constraints imposed on her. Yet these constraints in the end forced upon the family a monotonous carbohydrate diet of bread and potatoes, and even here the quantities consumed were hardly enough to satisfy ten people. Potatoes were eaten in quantities of between 2 and 4 kilos per meal, giving each member of the family between two and four medium-sized potatoes each. Bread was in fact the basis of this family's diet. It regularly constituted the most expensive item in the food budget, which meant that it must have been purchased and consumed in more considerable quantities than any other item.[24]

This particular family was nevertheless fortunate in more ways than one. Not only did it have a regular income, but it also, rather unusually,[25] enjoyed good connections with the church, to whom indeed the details of its budget were supplied. The family's piety enabled it to benefit from the charity of the wealthier parishioners, who occasionally donated money or expensive necessities such as shoes for the children. Over the 18 weeks covered by the budget, income from this source totalled no less than 31 Marks, compared to 455 Marks 15 net brought in by the husband and 11 Marks 20 by the daughter. The budget also covered the summer months, when harbour work was at its most remunerative and food prices at their cheapest. Even so, by the end of the third week the family, having started without any debts, was beginning to get into the red, and by the end of the whole period it owed some 20 Marks unpaid on the rent. The family was also lucky that all its members were in good health during the weeks of the survey. Any extra outlay, such as medical treatment, would have plunged it into a deep financial crisis. In the longer term, however, illnesses were bound to occur: indeed, an

[24] See Chapter 2d for further discussion of nutrition.
[25] For religion and the church, see pp. 100–3 below.

item of 1 Mark 25 for 'a bottle of herbal medicine for a child' on 23 August
suggests that it was already present, though not perhaps in a serious form.
The long-term effects of a meagre and protein-deficient diet were bound to
include weakened resistance to infection and disease.

IV

Despite the obvious difficulties of reaching any firm conclusions about the
changes that took place in income differentials and living standards in the
course of the nineteenth century, there is at least enough material available
for the historian of Hamburg to make an educated guess. The two main
constituents in the daily expenditure of the propertyless and the poor were
housing and food. Of these two items, housing made up about a quarter of
average expenditure in the subordinate classes, and was by far the more
difficult to adjust. In the first half of the century, the demand for housing was
concentrated within the city walls, and extra accommodation for the city's
growing population could only be found by adding more storeys to existing
houses, or by converting cellars to living quarters. In this way a good deal of
the extra demand could be catered for. In 1817, for example, only 44% of
dwellings in Hamburg were situated on the upper floors of buildings; by 1865
the figure had increased to 65%, and in addition there were nearly 9,000
Etagen, upper-storey apartments of a new type, with separate ground floor
entrances, in the city, whereas there had been none at all at the beginning
of the 1840s. Similarly, the number of cellar apartments grew by 60%
between 1817 and 1866.[26] In this situation, rents fluctuated considerably,
falling when demand for housing fell (for example in the epidemic years of
the early 1830s and the late 1840s) and rising when population growth was
high or when the housing stock decreased, as in the years immediately after
the Great Fire of 1842. In the 1850s, they levelled off once more. Throughout
the first half of the century, therefore, there were periods of acute housing
shortage and abnormally high rents, with remissions in between. More seriously, perhaps, overcrowding became steadily worse, with the number of
people per dwelling rising to an average of 5 in the late 1820s, and again to
5.2 after the Great Fire of 1842, although the high mortality of the early
1830s and late 1840s led to a fall in the number of persons per dwelling to
4.7 and just over 4.3 respectively.[27]

The opening of the city gates in 1860 and the rapid expansion of the
working-class suburbs in the following decades might perhaps have been
expected to ease the situation. But it did not. In the first place, there were no
public transport facilities from the new outer suburbs to the harbour. The

[26] Wischermann, *Wohnen in Hamburg*, pp. 39–40.
[27] Ibid., pp. 43–4.

bulk of work in the port remained casual, so harbour workers had to be constantly on hand to find employment at a moment's notice. Above all, from the early 1880s, when Hamburg decided to join the Customs Union, the authorities began to pull down houses at the southern end of the Altstadt to make room for the construction of the free port opened in 1888. Some 24,000 people were driven from their homes, and no attempt was made to find them accommodation elsewhere. These unfortunate people were almost entirely dependent on harbour work. 8,000 of them took up residence in the inner city, and the rest mainly went to live in the Billwärder Ausschlag, St Pauli, and the Hammerbrook (mostly in St Georg Süd).[28]

The result of these developments was a rapid rise in rents from the late 1850s onwards. The average rent of a small apartment in the cheapest areas of the Altstadt and the Alley Quarters rose by 33% between 1855 and 1870. Rents seem to have levelled off during the 1870s and early 1880s, but then they rose sharply up to the early 1890s as the families evicted from the free port area came onto the housing market looking for dwellings near the harbour. Thus by 1890 rents for small apartments in the inner city were 50% higher than those in outer suburbs such as Barmbeck, even though the quality and size of the housing was no better and in some respects even worse. As Map 11 indicates, cheap accommodation was easiest to obtain in the outlying districts on the east of the city, and rather more difficult in the inner city as a whole. In order to try and pay these high rents, the inhabitants of the inner city districts took in lodgers, young single men who came to the Hamburg docks looking for work. Map 12 shows that almost a third of the households in the inner city and inner suburbs had lodgers at the beginning of the 1890s; in the Neustadt Nord, indeed, over a third. Given the probability that many households refused to declare the presence of lodgers, it seems likely that the real figures were even higher. In the newer districts on the periphery, by contrast, where rents were lower and the possibility of supplementing income and diet by gardening, keeping a pig, or gathering wild berries were greater, fewer households took in lodgers, though the proportion was still by no means negligible. This further increased the overcrowding already noticeable in the inner city dwellings; indeed, the average number of persons per dwelling in the city as a whole increased from 4.5 at the end of the 1870s to 4.8 by 1890.

Not only did the rise in rents from the end of the 1850s to the beginning of the 1890s exacerbate the overcrowding problem, it also meant that many of the poorer sections of the population had to spend an increasingly significant proportion of their income on housing. Between 1868 and 1891, for example, the proportion of income spent on rent by an average taxpayer in Hamburg

---

[28] Ibid., p. 67; and Kutz-Bauer, 'Arbeiterschaft', p. 182. See also Plate 13.

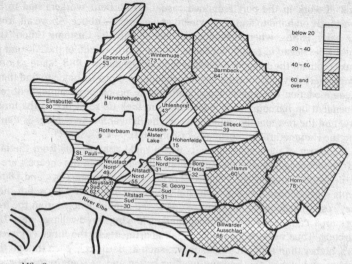

Source: MS 1892, 39

MAP 11. Percentage of accommodation rented for below 300 Marks a year, by district, Hamburg 1892

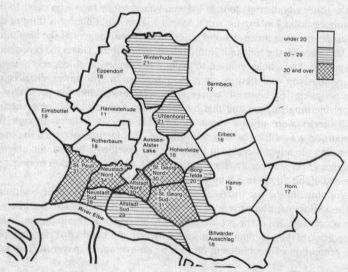

Source: SHS 16 (1894), 84

MAP 12. Percentage of households with lodgers, by district, Hamburg 1890

earning between 900 and 1,200 Marks a year rose from 19.8% to 24.1%.[29] These global figures conceal substantial variations between different types of housing and different districts of the city. The average rent of the commonest type of working-class dwelling, with a single heated room among perhaps 3 rooms in all, rose from 192 Marks a year in 1885 to 222 Marks a year in 1890.[30] The rent rise in the harbour district was particularly steep. In the years 1850 to 1880, for example, the cost of renting a dwelling in the Steinstrasse (Altstadt Nord) or Eichholz (Neustadt Süd) almost doubled, and by 1890 it had reached on average at least 230% of its level in 1845.[31] The rent paid by an average worker in H. C. Meyer's walking-stick factory[32] for the same three-room dwelling, inhabited by the same family over a period of 35 years, more than doubled from 1840 to 1875, from 89 Marks a year to 179 Marks a year, rising steadily all the time. For those workers who lived in the same type of apartment from 1850 to 1875, rents rose on average by 60%, from 102 Marks to 164 Marks a year, and this was even before the massive rent rises of the 1880s.[33]

The rise in rents left less money to spend on food. Food prices rose little overall in the first half of the nineteenth century apart from during the period of the Continental System under Napoleon and the potato shortage of the late 1840s.[34] 50 kilos of potatoes, for example, cost 2 Marks 92 in an average year in 1846–50, compared to 1 Mark 82 in an average year in the first half of the 1840s, while the price of rye bread increased only slightly in the same period, from 7 Marks 26 to 7 Marks 34 for 50 kilos. Rye bread and potatoes continued to rise in price, reaching 8 Marks 91 and 3 Marks 10 for 50 kilos respectively in 1851–5, thereafter declining and stabilizing in the period 1856–70 at their lowest level since the early 1840s.[35] From the beginning of the depression which followed the financial crash of 1873, food began to become more expensive again, and prices rose steadily until 1880.[36] Rye bread cost 8 Marks 74 for 50 kilos on average in 1871–5 and potatoes 3 Marks 32 for 50 kilos. From 1881 to 1887 prices fell once more, but in 1888 Hamburg's entry into the Customs Union brought a dramatic jump in the cost of food, as import tariffs on grain and other foodstuffs became operative.

[29] *SHS* 17 (1904), 39. Conclusions about the average cost of housing to income groups above the very lowest levels are vitiated by the increasing proportion of home-ownership as income rises; in upper income levels they are meaningless unless mortgage rates are taken into account. This would appear to render the discussion in Wischermann, *Wohnen in Hamburg*, pp. 201–3 highly problematical.

[30] Grüttner, *Arbeitswelt*, p. 105.

[31] G. Koch, *Beiträge zur Statistik der Löhne und Preise in Hamburg* (Hamburg, 1891), p. 11.

[32] J. C. F. Nessmann, *Ein Beitrag zur Statistik der Löhne und Preise* (Hamburg, 1876), pp. 3–4.

[33] Wischermann, *Wohnen in Hamburg*, 191–213, provides average figures that are of little help in this context.

[34] Kraus, *Die Unterschichten*, pp. 60–7.

[35] Nessmann, *Ein Beitrag zur Statistik*, p. 4.

[36] Ibid.

Many retailers and street traders, according to contemporary reports, used the opportunity of public confusion over the proper price of food to increase their profits by putting up prices higher than was necessary to cover the extra cost caused by the import duties. In 1888 alone the price of rye bread jumped from 8 to 9 Marks for 50 kilos after the opening of the free port, and the price of other foodstuffs such as green peas, rice, coffee, tea, and butter also rose by up to 50%. Meat prices, which had declined from the high levels of the early 1880s, rose again (pork by 17% in 1888, for example). Food prices soon reached record heights. 50 kilos of rye bread, for example, cost 10 Marks in 1890, compared to a mere 8 Marks in 1887, and 50 kilos of potatoes cost more in 1888 than at any time since mid-century. Thus while rents for small dwellings in the inner city were rising steadily throughout the second half of the century, the prices of the staple foodstuffs of the working class tended to fluctuate, but rose particularly sharply from the mid-1840s to the mid-1850s, 1873–80, and 1887–90. At these periods in particular, therefore, it is likely that many working-class families were forced to cut back on their consumption of food and reduce the overall quality of their diet.[37]

Such a conclusion would not be justified, of course, if wage levels had risen sufficiently to cover the extra cost of food and rent. Here average levels are of little value, since the changing structure of the labour market was reflected in strong and constantly changing wage differentials between different sectors and different trades.[38] The growth of ancillary and processing industries in particular meant the gradual emergence of an upper level of the working class, with relatively steady employment and relatively high wages. On the other hand, the expansion of the harbour also brought an increase in the employment of unskilled casual dock labour, warehousing work, and the like, where wages not only remained static but employment was seasonally conditioned (particularly by the annual freezing-over of the Elbe in the winter) and intermittent even at the best of times. And the general employment situation was made considerably worse by periodic economic crises with corresponding high levels of unemployment; significantly, one such downturn began in 1890 and continued for most of the earlier part of the decade. The number of taxpayers earning less than 1,000 Marks a year more than doubled between 1868 and 1882; while that of the better-off sections of the working class, earning between 1,000 and 1,800 Marks a year, only increased by one and three-quarters. By 1891, the increase in the higher group had overtaken that in the lower; it stood at a level of 32.9% compared to that of 1868, whereas the rise in the number of taxpayers in the lowest bracket was only

---

[37] Kutz-Bauer, 'Arbeiterschaft', p. 182; Grüttner, *Arbeitswelt*, p. 52; Koch, *Beiträge zur Statistik*, pp. 16–18, 24. The priority of rent in expenditure patterns is reflected in the high correlations between the proportion of households in each district of Hamburg paying less than 300 Marks a year rent, and the percentage of manual labourers (0.88) and white-collar workers (−0.83) in the occupied population (see Table 15).

[38] Koch, op. cit., for details.

27.6%. However, 28% of the occupied population of Hamburg in 1890 earned less than 600 Marks a year and so fell outside the tax system altogether, while another 29% earned only 600–800 Marks a year. These 57% of the occupied population constituted the bulk of Hamburg's working class. Above the level of 800 Marks a year, the numbers rapidly began to thin out. 12% of occupied persons in Hamburg earned between 800 and 1,000 Marks in 1890, 6% between 1,000 and 1,200 Marks, and 5% between 1,000 and 1,500 Marks.[39]

Here, however, we are at the top end of the working class, for these wage levels were attained only by skilled workers such as crane operators, artisans (*Handwerker*) such as those employed in the city waterworks, or the élite of permanently employed workers on the city quays (*Kaiverwaltung*).[40] As we saw in the case of the postman Johannes Fiege, these wage levels were already high enough to include some workers whose aspirations and style of life had a discernible element of the petty bourgeois in them.[41] Below this level, as the examples of Kaisen and Neddermeyer suggest, earnings had to be supplemented by paid work carried out by the rest of the family. In 1887, just before the sharp rise in rents and food prices of the late 1880s, the minimum income necessary for the maintenance of a family of 5 in the Hamburg conurbation was estimated at 1,340 Marks a year; the historian Lothar Schneider put the figure more generally at 1,040 Marks for 1888.[42] Taking the more conservative estimate of Schneider—an estimate confirmed in the early 1890s by the raising of the lowest tax threshold in Hamburg from 600 Marks to 900 Marks a year—it seems then that almost 70% of the occupied population of Hamburg fell below the poverty line, or in other words the same proportion as at the end of the 1840s.

V

In March 1848, the Hamburg city archivist Dr Johann Martin Lappenberg, in a report on wage labour in the city, declared that 'Pauperism, in such a lamentable form as it assumes in most large cities, has so far remained unknown in Hamburg'.[43] Lappenberg's view, which can be taken as representative of that of the grand bourgeoisie, was that trade offered everyone who sought it 'an easier, more lucrative, and more respected source of earnings than any other'. The policy of the Senate, declared Lappenberg, was that the remedy for poverty lay in the increase of employment through the

[39] Wischermann, *Wohnen in Hamburg*, pp. 202–3; Kutz-Bauer, 'Arbeiterschaft', p. 180; *SHS* 17 (1904), 30. The figures listed by Wischermann (p. 203) are insufficiently differentiated at the bottom of the scale and take no account of those who fell below the tax threshold.

[40] Koch, *Beiträge zur Statistik*, pp. 27–31.

[41] See above, pp. 62–4.

[42] Kutz-Bauer, 'Arbeiterschaft', pp. 189 nn. 12 and 14.

[43] Kraus, 'Unterschichten', p. 75.

growth of trade, and above all, 'as long as there are no complaints or momentary nuisances, not to restrict the freedom of the individual through legislation, above all not to allow itself to be led astray by any theory, however brilliant, into experiments which might in any way have an adverse effect on the prosperity of individuals, especially in the merchant community'. Thus the state did relatively little in the first half of the nineteenth century to tackle the problem of poverty in Hamburg. The only legislative actions it undertook in this direction were to undertake police purges against begging, which was forbidden by law on numerous occasions in the early part of the century; to ban unmarried men and women from living together in concubinage, which was said in a law of 1833 to be 'a pernicious influence ... on public security and also in particular on the upbringing of children';[44] and to bring to book journeymen and labourers who had evaded their duty of registering their presence in the city with the authorities.

In 1788, to be sure, a new Poor Law had been passed in Hamburg, largely on the initiative of a number of merchants and private citizens. Acting on 'enlightened' principles, they had secured the secularization of poor relief in the form of the General Poor Law Board (*Allgemeine Armenanstalt*), which soon achieved a wide enough reputation to find imitators in some twenty other towns. In contrast to the relatively indiscriminate charitable activities of the religious foundations, the General Poor Law Board aimed to encompass all the paupers in the city, to direct the able-bodied towards labour and to encourage them to work by providing them with poor relief well under subsistence level. It sought to restrict direct support only to those deemed physically incapable of supporting themselves. Its fundamental thrust, to educate the poor to work, was thus all of a piece with the moralizing police measures directed at begging and concubinage. The General Poor Law Board was a characteristic Hamburg institution: founded on private initiative, it was intended to subsist solely on private donations; yet on its governing body at least five seats were reserved for members of the Senate, so that the state remained in overall control.[45]

As time passed it proved progressively more difficult to raise money for this purpose from private sources, perhaps as a result of the fading memory of the appalling pauperism of the Napoleonic years and the growth of assumptions such as those revealed by Lappenberg at the beginning of this section. In 1789 over 80% of the Board's income came from private sources; by the early 1830s it had dropped to just over 20%.[46] Wealthy citizens were beginning to regard the Board as a state institution and their contributions as a form of

  [44] Ibid., p. 72.
  [45] A. Herzig, 'Vom "Hamburger Modell" zum "Elberfelder System"', in B. Mehnke, *Armut und Elend in Hamburg. Eine Untersuchung über des öffentliche Armenwesen in der ersten Hälfte des 19. Jahrhunderts* (Ergebnisse, Heft 17; Hamburg, 1982), p. iv.
  [46] Mehnke, op. cit., pp. 63, 160.

tax, and they were channelling an increasing proportion of their charitable efforts into private foundations (*milde Stiftungen*) such as the Magdalen Foundation for Fallen Girls (*Magdalenenstift*) (1821), the Institutions for the Deaf and Dumb (*Taubstumnenanstalt*) (1827) and Blind (*Blindenanstalt*) (1827), or the famous *Rauhes Haus* ('rugged house') for 'neglected children' (1833). These could all be presented as deserving causes, while the General Poor Law Board, particularly after its reorganization in 1814, when paupers were no longer directed to work, but merely given support, came to be regarded as caring largely for the undeserving poor. These included not only the ablebodied who accounted for the bulk of the Board's outlay, but also the sick: 'How many sick people must we treat', asked the Board in 1818, 'who got their dropsy in the pub, their consumption in the dance-hall, or their first infection in some other type of life of debauchery?'

The state responded to the growing need for subventions to the General Poor Law Board by levying an excise duty (*Akzise*) on foodstuffs. As the Board itself pointed out in 1829, this meant 'that even the poorest person is compelled to contribute to the alms that he himself receives, by paying excise and the other duties from which the grant for the General Poor Law Board is drawn'.[47] On average some 2,600 or so people received support every year through the period 1821–50. The vast majority of these were elderly or old— over half were above the age of 60—and many of them (well over 40%) were single women, either spinsters or widows. The Board also ran Poor Law Schools for about 4,300 children by the middle of the century, placed up to 500 children of poor families in foster care, and paid for the medical treatment (at home) of about 14,000 people a year. Finally, it granted single payments, usually of food, clothing, or heating materials, to some 20,000 people a year. The extent of the sums involved in normal times were not very great. In the first half of the 1820s, the state subvention for the General Poor Law Board made up on average just over 55% of the annual stipends paid to the Senators and the parish representatives in the legislature.[48]

These figures suggest that the rosy picture painted by Lappenberg of the standard of living of the inhabitants of Hamburg was far from the truth. Lappenberg himself estimated that the average wage of an unskilled labourer around mid-century was 400 Marks a year,[49] which, as we have seen, was well below the bottom tax threshold in 1848. By the 1830s the General Poor Law Board was supporting 16.4% of the population every year on average with single donations; in the crisis year of 1848 the proportion actually exceeded 25%, or one in four of the entire population of the city and the inner suburbs. While the dimensions of the problem of poverty are starkly demonstrated by these statistics, it should not be supposed that the individual

---

[47] Ibid., p. 138.
[48] Ibid., pp. 62–3; 62 n. 2, 130.
[49] Kraus, *Die Unterschichten*, p. 64.

pauper benefited very much from the meagre amount of assistance which the General Poor Law Board was able to afford. Indeed, the larger the number of paupers, the smaller the amount of support that each received. In 1847, for example, the average rate of support per family was little over 1 Mark a week, the maximum 3 Marks, while the generally agreed minimum necessary to support an individual worker even in a normal year was 5 to 7 Marks, and the comparable figure for a family 10 Marks or more. This was even less than the level allowed for in the regulations of 1788.[50]

Given the complacency of the views expressed by Lappenberg, and the failure of the 1848 Revolution to bring about any immediate change in the city's constitution, it is perhaps not surprising that the dominant classes in Hamburg made little or no attempt to reform the system of poor relief during the following decades. As a consequence of the Constitution of 1860, private charities were placed under state supervision; but no real attempt was made to co-ordinate their activities, or even to find out how many there were and what they did, until ten years later. It appears that there were perhaps 460 different charities in Hamburg around 1870, including over 100 within the Jewish community alone. In a city without a state education system, it is not surprising that many of these—over 150—were for scholarships and school grants. A further 170 were for general support of the poor. The rest were for more specialized purposes. The money they received in donations and wills fluctuated considerably from year to year, but in an average year in the 1860s it seems to have come to not far off a million Marks. Much of this was invested to provide capital for recurrent expenditure from the accruing interest, but the figure still provided impressive evidence of what an official report described as the influence of 'the free, uncontrolled private phil-anthropy of the individual citizen on the raising of the money needed for the fight against poverty and social indigence'.[51] By the late 1870s the 500-odd private charities in Hamburg were paying out over 600,000 Marks a year to a total of over 40,000 people.[52] Much of this was in the form of food, clothing, and fuel; in addition a substantial proportion was paid in the form of rent support and free housing, which over 1,000 people a year were receiving in one form or another from private charities in the late 1870s. The rent was usually paid directly to the landlord. Even if a large amount of these private funds went to provide scholarships and similar support for those whose circumstances were modest rather than desperate, private charity—which was also one of the few areas of public life where middle-class women could play an active role—was still of major importance in relieving poverty in mid-nineteenth-century Hamburg.[53]

[50] Mehnke, *Armut und Elend*, pp. 137, 152.

[51] *SHS* 3 (1871), 103.

[52] *Statistisches Handbuch für den Hamburgischen Staat* (1891), p. 296.

[53] See also Hermann Joachim, *Handbuch der Wohltätigkeit in Hamburg* (2nd edn., Hamburg, 1909).

The deterioration of working-class living standards in the 1880s was clearly reflected in the activities of these charities, as their expenditure rapidly rose to the level of a million Marks a year. But it was the state system of poor relief that registered the most startling increase. The amount spent by the General Poor Law Board each year rose from 330,000 Marks in the 1820s to 460,000 Marks in the 1840s, 580,000 Marks in the 1860s, and over 800,000 Marks a year in the second half of the 1870s. Then it jumped to one and a half million Marks a year in the first half of the 1880s.[54] In 1885 the authorities were forced to report that 'Hamburg, despite the relatively favourable position of its labouring population'—here the views expressed by Lappenberg almost forty years earlier clearly found renewed expression despite all the evidence to the contrary—'and despite a very high level of private charitable activity, is obliged to record the relatively highest number of state supported paupers and the highest gross expenditure on poor relief of any German city'.[55] Hamburg, it was calculated, was spending over 9 Marks per inhabitant on poor relief, compared to less than 6 in Berlin, less than 5 in Frankfurt, and less than 3 in Breslau. 13% of the city's population were in receipt of poor relief, almost twice the figure for Berlin, Leipzig, or Frankfurt. Despite these startling figures, Hamburg recorded a very low ratio of poor-law overseers (*Armenpfleger*) to those receiving relief: 1 to 58, compared with 1 to 11 in Dresden, and 1 to 6 in Frankfurt and Leipzig. There were, indeed, only 291 poor-law workers in the whole of Hamburg in 1885, so it seems likely that a great deal of poverty in the city went unrecorded. Altogether over 30,000 people in Hamburg were receiving state poor relief in 1885, at a cost to the exchequer of 2,147,000 Marks.[56] These figures provide graphic evidence for the extent of poverty in Hamburg in the second half of the nineteenth century, and the deterioration of working-class living standards that took place in the 1880s. Yet when they were presented to the Hamburg Senate, the response they elicited was not that Hamburg had a particularly severe poverty problem—for as we have seen, it was still generally believed that Hamburg's working class was unusually well off—but that Hamburg's system of poor relief was too extravagant.[57]

The history of poor relief in Hamburg underlines how misleading it is to speak of a general improvement in the living standards of all sectors of the population in the course of the nineteenth century.[58] The global averages with which the proponents of this argument customarily operate conceal wide variations between different social classes. This was particularly true in

[54] *Statistisches Handbuch für den Hamburgischen Staat* (1885), p. 210, ibid. (1891), p. 285.

[55] Ibid. (1891), p. 285.

[56] *Das öffentliche Armenwesen in Hamburg während der Jahre 1893–1903. Darstellung seiner Reorganisation und weiterer Entwickelung, herausgegeben vom Armenkollegium* (Hamburg, 1903), pp. 7–8.

[57] Ibid.

[58] See also the remarks in Wischermann, *Wohnen in Hamburg*, p. 213.

Hamburg, where the centrality of trade, commerce, and banking to the city's economy meant that there were unusually large numbers not only of well-off bourgeois but also of clerks and white-collar workers among the city's occupied population. By 1907, for example, nearly 15% of Hamburg's economically active population counted as white-collar workers (*Angestellte*) compared with 5% in Berlin.[59] Most of these members of the 'new *Mittelstand*' were concentrated in the trade and transport sector of the economy. In 1895, a third of the occupied population in this sector were self-employed; these included substantial numbers of shopkeepers and small traders as well as the bulk of the more substantial merchants. Hamburg's population, in other words, contained a smaller than average proportion of wage-earners (62% in 1907 compared to 73% in the Reich as a whole). The working class was confronted not only with a wealthy grand bourgeoisie but also with a large middling and a substantial petty-bourgeois class as well. While this obviously had a powerful effect on average income levels and expenditure patterns across the whole population, income differentials remained extreme throughout the period. From 1868 to 1891, for example,[60] the numbers of those recording earnings of over 30,000 Marks a year increased by 320% while those with an income of between 3,000 and 30,000 a year rose only by 246%; but the comparable figure for the petty-bourgeois taxpayers earning 1,800 to 3,000 Marks a year was 318%; and there is no doubt that the existence in the city of a large petty bourgeoisie was an important element not only in Hamburg's social structure but also in its political life as well. Hamburg was not a city in which a tiny stratum of big employers confronted a vast mass of wage-earning labourers with only the thinnest layer of managers, white-collar workers, and traders in between, like the company towns of coal-mining areas such as the Ruhr:[61] as a great commercial centre it had a more complex and varied social structure, and this had a discernible effect on the style of politics dominant in the city as well.

d. *The Threat from Below*

I

The complacency with which the dominant classes in Hamburg contemplated the question of pauperism for most of the first half of the nineteenth century was to some extent a reflection of the relative lack of serious popular disturbances in the city. 'An uprising or even a disturbance among the lower class of the people, in order to obtain easier subsistence', noted Dr Lappenberg

[59] Kutz-Bauer, 'Arbeiterschaft', p. 180.
[60] Wischermann, op. cit., p. 203.
[61] Cf. D. F. Crew, *Town in the Ruhr. A Social History of Bochum 1860–1914* (New York, 1979); E. Lucas, *Arbeiterradikalismus: Zwei Formen von Radikalismus in der deutschen Arbeiterbewegung* (Frankfurt, 1976).

in March 1848, 'has never happened here, with the exception of the disturbances which occurred in 1847 at the time of the potato famine and the increase in bread prices in Germany and other European countries.'[1] The city had been the scene of numerous minor disorders since the end of the Napoleonic Wars, but none of them seems to have borne comparison with the mass rioting common in other German towns; nor did the series of popular disturbances that began just as Lappenberg was completing his report and continued for most of the summer of the revolutionary year 1848 even begin to approach the scale and seriousness of the great popular uprisings that took place in Berlin or Vienna at around the same time. The political struggles of the 1840s centred in Hamburg mainly on the demand of the petty bourgeoisie and parts of the middling bourgeoisie for greater participation in the exercise of political power, which they eventually achieved, as we have seen, through the constitution of 1860. Attempts at regulating and disciplining the poor were frequently made, as the history of poor-law legislation indicates. But there seem to have been few grounds for a serious panic about the problem of public order on the part of the dominant classes. Even the most serious disturbances, such as those accompanying the Great Fire of 1842, clearly lacked any real political direction, and exhausted themselves in assaults on symbolic targets—in this case the English, who were widely held responsible by popular opinion for starting the fire. The 'potato riot' of 1847, for its part, was directed at restoring the 'moral economy' of the food market, disturbed by sudden and massive rises in the price of potatoes; it too lacked any wider political significance.[2]

It was only in the 1860s that this situation began to change. The opening of the gates, the ending of the power of the guilds, the building of the Sandgate Harbour, the quickening pace of economic growth: all accelerated the process of the formation of Hamburg's working class in this decade. This found its expression in the beginnings of an organized labour movement. Already in 1844 radical journeymen had founded the Educational Association for Workers (*Arbeiter-Bildungsverein*). It was led by Joachim Friedrich Martens, who had come into contact with early socialist ideas in London, Paris, and elsewhere. Martens was a personal acquaintance of Wilhelm Weitling and belonged to the League of the Just and (during the Revolution) the League of Communists, for which Marx and Engels wrote the *Communist Manifesto*. The Educational Association represented the specific aspirations of the journeymen as much as it acted as the proponent of a socialist revolution, and in the reaction following the Revolution it gradually assimilated itself to the

---

[1] Kraus, 'Unterschichten', pp. 71–7, here p. 75. The alarmist sentiments cited by Herzig ('Im Hamburger Pöbel steckt ein wildes Thier', F. Sass, 1842) in his essay 'Vom "Hamburger Modell" zum "Elberfelder System"' (Introduction, Mehnke, *Armut und Elend*, p. viii), come from a book published in Leipzig and do not appear to reflect the views of the Hamburg grand bourgeoisie.

[2] See A. Herzig, 'Organisationsformen und Bewusstseinsprozesse Hamburger Handwerker und Arbeiter in der Zeit 1790–1848', in Herzig *et al.*, *Arbeiter in Hamburg*, pp. 95–108, here p. 103.

petty-bourgeois democratic movement that dominated the political opposition in mid-nineteenth century Hamburg. Although the Association was unusual in its continuity of existence and, to some extent, personnel, from the 1840s through to the 1860s, by the latter decade Martens had become a comparatively well-off man and many of the radical ideas debated by the Association in earlier years had silently been dropped.[3]

It was at this point—in 1863—that Lassalle's General German Workers' Association (*Allgemeiner Deutscher Arbeiterverein*) was founded, as an explicitly socialist alternative to Martens's organization. Amid a good deal of mutual recrimination, the Hamburg branch of Lassalle's Association soon established itself not only as more active and more popular than its rival, but also as by far the most important element in the Lassallean movement as a whole. The Lassallean movement in Hamburg incorporated many guild customs and forms in its activities. Yet it was dominated not by old-style artisans but far more by workers in trades which already had a high degree of capitalist organization, and its leaders and members consisted above all of wage-labourers. By combining guild forms with a broad appeal, the Lassalleans quickly gained support in Hamburg, but after Lassalle's death, as his successor Schweitzer revoked the Association's democratic constitution, the Hamburg branch broke up. Although it revived somewhat during the 1870s, the running was now made by the Social Democratic Workers' Party, founded by the dissidents in Hamburg and elsewhere, in Eisenach in 1869. From 1871 to 1878 the permanent seat of the party—renamed Socialist Workers' Party of Germany on its union with the remainder of the Lassalleans at the Gotha Congress in 1875—was in Hamburg, in recognition of the strength of its support in the city. In 1875, indeed, the party's leader August Bebel described Hamburg as 'the capital city of German socialism'.[4]

The rise of the socialist labour movement was not a local phenomenon but a national one. The Social Democrats scarcely began to consider how socialism might be implemented at a community level until the 1890s, and they remained remarkably uninterested in local political issues right until the First World War. Restrictive local franchises all over Germany, including Hamburg, reserved participation in city politics for the small élite of property-owners; the working class was excluded from the vote almost everywhere.[5]

[3] See J. Breuilly and W. Sachse, *Joachim Friedrich Martens und die deutsche Arbeiterbewegung* (Göttingen, 1984) and more generally the classic by H. Laufenberg, *Geschichte der Arbeiterbewegung in Hamburg-Altona und Umgegend* (2 vols; Hamburg, 1911–31).

[4] A. Herzig, 'Vom ausgehenden 18. Jahrhundert bis zu den 1860er Jahren', in Herzig *et al.*, *Arbeiter in Hamburg*, pp. 9–16, here pp. 15–16. To avoid confusion the party is described throughout this book as the Social Democratic Party.

[5] See Fischer, *Industrialisierung*, pp. 107–13, 223, and 378–9; A. von Saldern, *Vom Einwohner zum Bürger. Zur Emanzipation der städtischen Unterschicht Göttingens 1890–1920. Eine sozial- und kommunalhistorische Untersuchung* (Berlin, 1973), pp. 422–4; and K. Jasper, *Der Urbanisierungsprozess dargestellt am Beispiel der Stadt Köln* (Cologne, 1977), pp. 252–4, for similar examples of the influence of restricted local franchises and the lack of Social Democratic interest in local affairs.

Socialism promised the collapse of the capitalist system and the coming of a revolution that would put an end to exploitation and inequality. It sought political democracy and common ownership of the means of production. It was confident in the ability of the state to control economy and society in the interests of all once the revolution had been achieved. It constantly attacked the evils and absurdities of every aspect of the social, economic, and political system of Imperial Germany. It offered the working class a nationally oriented ideology which, among other things, held out the promise of a participation in local affairs to be achieved by nationwide revolution rather than local pressure. The Social Democrats thus broke decisively with virtually all the dominant traditions of politics in Hamburg, from the primacy of privilege and particularism to the centrality of *laissez-faire*, mercantile interests, and liberal individualism. The Social Democrats, of course, stood no chance under Hamburg's constitution of 1860 of getting any of their representatives elected to the Citizens' Assembly. The cost of the Citizens' Fee was beyond all but a very few among the working class. But they did possess one important means of expressing their views. These were the elections to the Reichstag, held on the basis of universal manhood suffrage, introduced by Bismarck for the North German Confederation and then for the German Empire as a whole in the belief that the rural masses would vote Conservative. As election succeeded election the scale of Bismarck's miscalculation became steadily more apparent. Initially, relatively few among the working class troubled to vote. But the percentage poll in Hamburg rose steadily from 28% in 1871 to just over 40% in 1874 and 69% in 1877. After fluctuating within fairly narrow limits during the subsequent three elections it reached 80% in 1887 and 83% in 1890. These figures indicate the steady spread of a national political consciousness through the Hamburg working class. It found expression in steadily rising support for the Social Democrats.

Initially the three Reichstag seats in Hamburg had been virtually monopolized by the mercantile interest and leading figures from the Caucus of Rightists in the Citizens' Assembly. It was characteristic of the primacy of local interests that the deputies elected in the 1860s and 1870s did not regard their membership of the Reichstag as an object in itself, and that none of them embarked on any kind of national political career. Thus they tended to serve for relatively short periods of time before returning to local politics, where their real interests lay. Although the seats were almost invariably won by National Liberal candidates, only one of them was elected four times (Dr Isaac Wolffson, 1871–81, a prominent figure in the Caucus of Rightists in the Citizens' Assembly), one three times (Rudolf Möring, 1874–81), and three twice, including one Left-Liberal. Adolph Woermann (1884–90), the last National Liberal deputy in Hamburg, was also elected twice. The other seven 'national' or National Liberal deputies, and two Left-Liberals were each elected only once. They included the shipping magnate Robert Sloman and the later

Senators Charles Ami de Chapeaurouge and Emil von Melle; of the total of fifteen deputies who sat for the liberals and National Liberals, seven were merchants, and the rest were a mixture, including two lawyers but also two master artisans. They were thus a fair reflection of the composition of the dominant classes in Hamburg from the 1860s. Already in 1880, shortly after the passage of the Anti-Socialist Law, the second Hamburg Reichstag constituency fell to the Social Democrats; in 1883 Bebel himself won the first; and in 1890 the third fell, to Friedrich Wilhelm Metzger. Of the three Social Democratic Reichstag deputies elected for Hamburg in 1890, it was significant that only one—Metzger—actually had anything to do with the city; of the other two, August Bebel, the party leader, lived near Dresden, and Johann Heinrich Wilhelm Dietz, the party publisher, lived in Stuttgart. Neither visited Hamburg very often, not even during the election campaigns. The national, rather than local, orientation of Social Democrats could hardly require any clearer or more concrete demonstration than this.

The class basis of the changing Reichstag vote in Hamburg can be illustrated by the example of the 1890 election. Map 13, when compared with Map 4 above, shows that the established party of the grand bourgeoisie, the National Liberals, gained most votes in the richest districts around the Alster, and fewest in the poorest districts, in the Neustadt, Barmbeck and Winterhude, St Pauli, and Billwärder Ausschlag. In the three wealthiest districts they still scored more than 50%, while in the two poorest they had fallen to single figures. Map 14 shows that the Left-Liberals, the party associated most closely with the Hamburg 'democrats', scored even worse in the poorer outlying districts but picked up rather more in the inner city and St Pauli, where they could still rely on a tradition of petty-bourgeois support dating back to 1848. A substantial middle-class element voted for them in the comfortable villa quarters of Harvestehude and Rotherbaum, but on the other side of the Alster, where the threat from encroaching tenements was greater and the overall social tone not quite so high, they had clearly lost out to the National Liberals, who by this time offered by far the better chance of defeating the Social Democrats. As for the Social Democrats, Map 15 shows that their support in the poorest areas was overwhelming. Looking at Map 6 we can see that the Social Democratic vote coincided almost exactly with the proportion of wage-earning manual labourers in any one district, except for part of the deferential servant vote in Harvestehude and Rotherbaum, and perhaps a comparable element among state employees in the Altstadt Süd. The maps underline once more the mixed social composition of areas such as St Georg Nord and the Altstadt Süd, and the divided pattern of occupation in a few of the outer suburbs such as Eilbeck or Eimsbüttel.

The conquest of the three Hamburg Reichstag constituencies by the Social

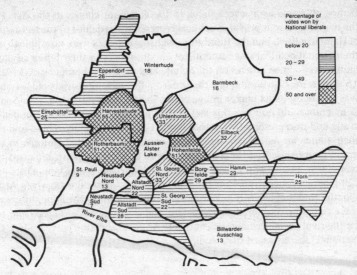

Percentage of
votes won by
National liberals

below 20

20 – 29

30 – 49

50 and over

Source: SHS 20 (1902), 92

MAP 13. National Liberal vote, by district, Hamburg, Reichstag election 1890

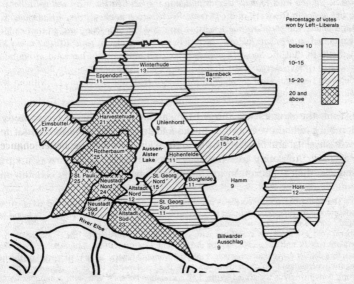

Percentage of votes
won by Left–Liberals

below 10

10–15

15–20

20 and
above

Source: SHS 20 (1902), 92

MAP 14. Left-Liberal vote, by district, Hamburg, Reichstag election 1890

Democrats came as a severe shock to the dominant classes in the city. For the working class, it provided political representation denied in the legislature of Hamburg itself, and the Hamburg Reichstag deputies were now able to use the national political stage to criticize circumstances in their home city and launch well-aimed attacks on the Senate and the grand bourgeoisie. As Map 16 shows, the distribution of citizens across the various districts of Hamburg was an almost exact mirror image of the Social Democratic vote.[6] The Social Democrats could now use this fact, if they wished, to point out the undemocratic and unrepresentative nature of the Citizens' Assembly. This—and not their stance on national issues, which were only of limited concern to the grand bourgeoisie and the middle classes in the city—was what caused the real alarm. In the 1893 elections, indeed, while the Social Democrats and Left-Liberals concentrated on the issue of Reich Chancellor Caprivi's Army Bill, the National Liberals in Hamburg barely mentioned the issue. In urging the electors to vote for their candidate, the shipowner Carl Laeisz, and not for the rival Social Democratic candidate August Bebel (the party leader), the National Liberals asked their audience

if you want to *support* men, who
1) do not *live* in *Hamburg*,
2) who thus have *no* feeling for the life and activities of *Hamburg*,
3) and *no idea at all* of what *Hamburg*, as the *foremost trading-place* on the Continent needs . . . if you want to make a contribution to the fact that Hamburg will not collaborate or give advice in the work of the German Reichstag for a full 5 years, if Hammonia is to stand before the portals of the Reichstag as a goddess abandoned and scorned—indeed abandoned by her own children—merely in order to suffer in patient silence every kick in the teeth that the Social Democrats, above all, mete out to her, and in boundless misery to receive every blunder that is made inside the Reichstag with disadvantageous effects on Germany's and above all on Hamburg's trade and development, without being able to raise her voice in warning?

Instead, the electors were urged to vote for men who knew and lived in Hamburg 'who have *grown up* in the middle of the *grand hustle and bustle* of *trade, shipping,* and *industry* and who have *also achieved something in their own profession*'. Appealing to what they evidently still imagined was a strong element of local patriotism in Hamburg's working class, and echoing once

[6] The Social Democratic vote was negatively correlated with white-collar workers (-0.80), economically independent occupied persons (-0.87) and citizens (-0.74) by district, and very highly correlated with the percentage of manual workers (0.95) by district; and the National Liberal vote was positively correlated with white-collar workers (0.76), the economically independent (0.74), and citizens (0.71), by district. The extent to which a high Social Democratic vote in a district drove bourgeois voters into the National Liberal camp is suggested by the high negative correlation (-0.92) between the two. The Left-Liberals' inability to capture any single group convincingly is illustrated by the low correlations of their vote with economically independent persons (0.50) and white-collar workers (0.25) by district (Pearson's product-movement coefficient of correlation for 20 districts, maps 5, 6, 7, 13, 14, 15, 16).

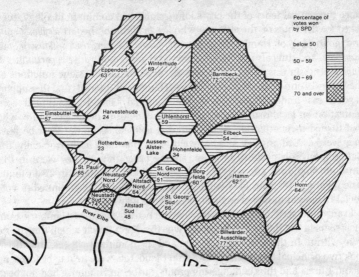

Source: SHS 20 (1902), 92

MAP 15. Social Democratic vote, by district, Hamburg, Reichstag election 1890

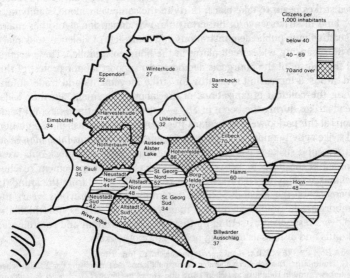

Source: SHS 22 (1904), 8

MAP 16. Citizens per thousand inhabitants, by district, Hamburg 1892

more the central tenet of the city's long-established dominant ideology, they asked for the votes of 'those of you who are *in favour* of the *further blossoming* and *flourishing* of Hamburg, and so *in favour* of her *trade, industry, and transport*, and thus also in favour of *increased and remunerative opportunities of employment*'. In this view, the Reichstag served much the same functions as the Federal Council: the representation of Hamburg's interests and the support of overseas trade. Unfortunately the National Liberals' continued concentration on local issues cut no ice with the majority of the electorate, who had turned their attention to the national political scene not least because they were denied any say in what went on in Hamburg itself. Ironically, the National Liberals declined because, among other things, they were in this sense not 'national' enough. Their appeal to local sentiment in 1893 found little favour in the eyes of Hamburg's working class, who continued to vote Social Democrat in increasing numbers all the way up to 1914.[7]

Even more serious than the threat which they posed to Hamburg from their seats in the Reichstag, however, was the direct threat which they posed from within. In the eyes of the Senate and the dominant classes, this threat took two principal forms. First, the Social Democrats were held to be fostering labour unrest and thus endangering profits. Strikes in Hamburg had not been unknown in the previous decades, but they were mainly concerned to assert the interests of journeymen against not only masters but also non-guild labour. Only with the ending of guild privileges in 1865 did more broadly based strikes begin to take place: thirty in the same year alone, signifying a new kind of strike wave of hitherto unknown dimensions. Another major strike, involving public demonstrations and some acts of violence, took place in 1869, causing widespread alarm in the bourgeois public.[8] These events, and the refusal of the bourgeois democrats to support labour protest of this kind, aroused increasing sympathy for strike movements and trade unions among the political organizations of the labour movement. Further widespread strikes during the boom of 1871–3 strengthened these ties. Yet trade unions at this period were often short-lived, and after the crash of 1873 union and strike activity underwent a drastic decline. It was not until the late 1880s that a second strike wave broke out. Over thirty strikes and lock-outs were recorded in the harbour between 1888 and 1890. The movement reached its climax on May Day 1890, when in response to a call from the founding conference of the Second Socialist International the previous year, the Hamburg trade unions planned a massive series of strikes, to which the employers responded by setting up their own organization and co-ordinated lock-outs and dismissals affecting nearly 20,000 workers.[9]

[7] StA Hbg, PP S3625 Bd. 5: *Hamburger Fremdenblatt*, 14 June 1893.

[8] G. Trautmann, 'Das Scheitern liberaler Vereinspolitik und die Entstehung der sozialistischen Arbeiterbewegung in Hamburg zwischen 1862 und 1871', in Herzig *et al.*, *Arbeiter in Hamburg*, pp. 163–76, here pp. 170–3; and Herzig, 'Vom ausgehenden 18. Jahrhundert', ibid., p. 12.

[9] Grüttner, *Arbeitswelt*, p. 135.

Even though May Day 1890 ended as a victory for the employers, the great strike wave that preceded it, even more than the strike waves of the 1860s and early 1870s, created serious alarm among the mercantile and industrial community and correspondingly also in the Senate and Deputations. Trade had already been seriously disrupted, and unless something could be done, the unsettling prospect opened up of a seemingly endless series of similar, perhaps increasingly widespread disruptions in years to come. Even more alarming was a second threat which the labour movement posed: the threat of violent revolution. The change in the attitude of mind of the Senate and administration towards the possibility of a serious challenge to their authority from the mass of the people that had taken place since the complacent decades before the 1880s was clearly conveyed by an official report compiled in April 1890, which referred pessimistically to the coincidence of the Reichstag elections and the end of the Anti-Socialist Law in the following terms:

An inclination to indulge in excesses has not so far been observable among the working people here, but the electoral successes and the present social and political atmosphere, favourable as it is to the labouring people, have roused their self-esteem to a considerable degree and led them to think that the existing order of state and society will soon collapse and be replaced by a socialist state.[10]

This view seemed confirmed by the serious rioting that broke out in May in the Alley Quarter of the Altstadt, which the prosecution in the subsequent trial of the alleged leaders of the rioters described as a 'riot bordering on a revolution' caused by years of 'Social Democratic agitation'.[11] It was indeed the most serious popular disturbance in the city since the violence that had accompanied the strike of 1869. When taken together with the other developments that had taken place since the middle of the 1880s, it seemed to provide yet another piece of evidence that the long-established dominance of the patrician families in alliance with the commercial and professional middle class and the upper segments of the petty bourgeoisie was now faced with its first serious threat from below.

II

The changing attitude of the dominant classes to the threat—or lack of threat—from below, was not merely expressed in the degree of their use of alarmist rhetoric. It also found a very practical, physical expression in the arrangements they made for law and order. At exceptional times, notably in 1849, they were prepared to call in the Prussian army to overcome a threat to their hegemony of a really serious kind. But while this seemed a safe

---

[10] Quoted ibid., p. 135.
[11] Quoted ibid., p. 145.

enough policy under the German Confederation, it was clearly far more dangerous once Hamburg joined the German Empire, for the pressures to terminate the city's autonomy and transform it into a Prussian municipality would then have been overwhelming, especially if a comparable degree of disorder was not evident elsewhere. From the mid-1860s onwards, therefore, Hamburg thought it prudent to try and prevent social unrest and political revolution as far as possible with its own resources. Even before this time, of course, in normal periods the city had had no need of assistance from outside.

Ideals of liberty and freedom were very prominent in Hamburg's official rhetoric. They were encapsulated in the legend set in letters of gold above the entrance to the new Town Hall constructed in the 1890s: *Libertatem, quam peperere maiores, digne studeat servare posteritas* ('may posterity strive worthily to preserve that liberty which our ancestors achieved').[12] But they did not apply to those who were denied the rights of citizenship—which is to say, the great majority of the city's population. If trade was to flourish, law and order had to be maintained. If the liberal state considered it a duty to withdraw from the market place so as to allow the free interplay of market forces, it also considered it a duty to ensure that those forces were not undermined or called into question. Strikes and revolutionary uprisings may not have loomed very large in the consciousness of the dominant classes until the latter part of the century, but the maintenance of social order and discipline, the creation of a society in which business could be carried on in peace and the fruits of merchant capital enjoyed without fear of robbery or theft, was another matter.

While Hamburg ensured, therefore, that its Commercial Court conducted its business openly and according to the principles of open, adversarial justice and fair play, it was far less concerned to apply these principles to the maintenance of everyday order on the streets. In the first half of the nineteenth century, criminal justice was essentially part of the executive. One of the Senators functioned as Police Chief and at the same time the Senate acted as a court of appeal. The police could levy summary fines and short terms of imprisonment (up to 2 months) on minor offences including 'petty theft and deception, minor cases of assault, acts of violence, trivial cases of resisting officials, and other similar crimes'.[13] They also enforced municipal regulations relating to traffic, clearing the streets of ice and snow in the winter, and so on, and controlled the presence of journeymen and non-guild labourers in the city. In the 1830s the Police Chief, Senator Hudtwalcker, decided perhaps four to five thousand cases each year in daily sessions held at his office.

[12] J. Berlin (ed.), *Das andere Hamburg. Freiheitliche und demokratische Bestrebungen in der Hansestadt seit dem Spätmittelalter* (Hamburg, 1981), p. 7.

[13] A. Lessat, 'Vom "Corps der Nachtwache" zur modernen Schutzpolizei. Aus der 150jährigen Geschichte der Polizeibehörde Hamburg', in *Hundertfünfzig Jahre Hamburger Polizei (1814–1964)* (Hamburg, 1964), p. 17. The date of the quotation is 1826.

Among these were also civil cases, such as marital disputes. Thus police, prosecution, court of judgment, and court of appeal were not separated from one another, and civil cases were mixed up with criminal ones. Trials were not held in public, and justice was not only summary, but, given the number of cases with which the Police Chief regularly dealt, inevitably often very rough as well.[14]

That the police were notoriously inefficient may have made this system of criminal justice less intrusive, but it also made it more arbitrary. Police powers were divided between the Citizens' Militia (*Bürgermilitär*), the Alley Officers (*Gassenoffizianten*), and the Corps of Night-watchmen (*Nachtwächtercorps*), and quarrels between these different institutions were far from unknown. This was not least because of the custom of *Sporteln*, a fine of 5 Marks Courant and 14 Schillings payable to the Police Chief as *Losgeld* (freedom money), usually the day after arrest. A portion of this fine was paid to the arresting officer, and formed an important part of a policeman's income. Not only did this encourage arbitrary arrests and quarrels over possession of the unfortunate victim, it also led to widespread corruption as a sum less than the *Losgeld* but more than the policeman's portion of it could be paid to the arresting officer as a bribe by those who could afford it. Bribes paid to night-watchmen by prostitutes were said to amount virtually to a regular income. None the less, the officers' pay was notoriously low—a mere 168 Marks a year in the 1820s—and many night-watchmen took daytime jobs as well; as a result, they were often observed fast asleep at their posts. In their waking moments, they earned extra money by leaving their posts and showing late-night revellers or visitors to the city the way to their home or hotel, a practice uncovered when Police Chief Abendroth posed as a Frenchman and asked a night-watchman to do this early in the 1820s.[15]

The night-watchmen were also said to be notorious drunkards. Police Chief Hudtwalcker noted in 1834 'that the vice of drunkenness is becoming ever more evident among the corps of night-watchmen',[16] but his order to them to stay sober on duty was widely resented. None of the night-watchmen joined the temperance movement, despite his encouragement, and, indeed, when, in a famous incident in 1841, the drinkers of Hamburg sacked the headquarters of the recently founded temperance club, the night-watchmen were said to have stood by and turned a blind eye. By the 1840s the Corps of Night-watchmen contained so few locally born officers that the practice of calling out the hour in Low German had to be abandoned because so few of them could speak it. The force was described even by Police Chief Binder as

[14] *150 Jahre Hamburger Polizei* (Hamburg, 1964); this is a different, shorter publication than the one cited in n. 13 above; but it also appears to rest on quite a solid base of archival research.
[15] Ibid.; and W. Henze, ' "Dem Nachtwächter wird hiemit anbefohlen ...": aus "Reglements", "Instructionen", alten Dienstvorschriften und über Organisationsformen der Hamburger Polizei', in *Hundertfünfzig Jahre Hamburger Polizei (1814–1964)* (n. 13, above), p. 104.
[16] Lessat, 'Vom "Corps der Nachtwache" ', p. 25.

an 'asylum for a local and foreign pack of ruffians'. The Citizens' Militia, where the practice had been established by unwilling citizens of paying substitutes taken from the local gaol to carry out their duties for them, with results that can be imagined, was if possible even worse. Nor was the numerical strength of the night-watch, at less than 50, in any way adequate to maintain order in a city of over 200,000 inhabitants. Not surprisingly, the disturbances accompanying the Great Fire of 1842 led to widespread calls for a reform. But the panic quickly died down, and when proposals were eventually produced by the Senate in 1847 they were soon overtaken by the Revolution and nothing was done. As in other parts of Germany, however, the post-Revolutionary reaction brought a reform of the police in 1851–2. Characteristically for Hamburg, it concentrated on reducing expenses. The Senate found that 'existing weapons, uniforms, parades, and exercises of the night-watchmen are a superfluous luxury. Police officers do not need such accoutrements at all.' So the Corps of Night-watchmen were transformed into a police force with over 300 officers and a new, more bureaucratic organization, but cheaper, less military uniforms and equipment. Otherwise, however, the system of law enforcement and criminal justice suffered few alterations, and although the ordinary policeman was now better paid than before, at 450 Marks a year, he still received less than a living wage, and the custom of *Sporteln* continued unchanged.[17]

Hamburg's policing system in the 1850s and 1860s was in many ways based on the English model of a non-military force; in constructing it in the wake of the Napoleonic Wars, the Senate had been concerned that 'nothing at all could happen that might (limit) civil freedom ... more than is necessary for the maintenance of public security and order'.[18] Indeed, the Propertied Citizenry was canny enough to insist that the police law be approved and renewed for fixed periods only, just in case it failed to fulfil this promise. As Senator Hudtwalcker remarked, 'In a state such as England, it is believed that where there is too much government, men become machines.'[19] Correspondingly, while the mass of ordinary offenders were subjected to arbitrary arrest and summary justice, the educated critic or reformer could expect to enjoy a wide degree of tolerance and freedom in the city. Censorship did indeed exist, as Hamburg had been forced to carry out the repressive provisions of Metternich's Karlsbad Decrees (1819); but it was extremely lax, especially where books rather than newspapers were concerned, and Hamburg became something of a centre for the publication of books that were banned in Prussia and elsewhere, perhaps the best-known being the works of Heinrich Heine; his publishers, the Hamburg house of Hoffman and Campe, were subject to

---

[17] Ibid., p. 27; Henze, ' "Dem Nachtwächter ..." ', p. 107.
[18] *150 Jahre* (n. 14, above).
[19] Ibid.

a total ban on all their publications by the Prussians in 1841.[20] In the period of reaction after the 1848 Revolution, the Prussians considered the Hamburg authorities so ineffectual that they actually sent their own agents into the city to gather information on organizations such as the Educational Association for Workers. While the Prussians placed the Senate under heavy pressure to ban the Association and other, smaller workers' clubs, Police Chief Senator Gossler argued that by banning them, 'revolutionary beliefs will not so much be exterminated as strengthened by driving those who hold them closer together'. Instead these organizations were encouraged by Gossler to develop along non-political lines.[21]

A similar stance was taken by the Hamburg authorities in the next great wave of repression that rolled over Germany following two unsuccessful attempts on the life of Emperor Wilhelm I in 1878. The intervening period had seen significant changes in the system of justice and law enforcement in the city. The constitution of 1860 led to a series of legal reforms in 1869, separating the executive and ending the system of summary police justice administered by a Senator and introducing new rules governing court procedures and police competence—including the abolition of *Sporteln*. The constitutional changes of 1879 completed this process by introducing a professional judiciary, a state prosecutor, and a new court system entirely independent from the Senate. In 1868, the dissolution of the Citizens' Militia meant that the main weight of maintaining order now fell on the police; and in 1876, in consequence, the old night-watch and police force were wound up and replaced by a Constabulary (*Constablercorps*) responsible for maintaining order by day and night alike. Dressed in uniforms of navy blue, the constables resembled nothing so much as London bobbies, especially since they wore helmets identical to those in use across the North Sea. It was with this force, numbering some 650 constables and 165 sergeants and senior officials, that the Hamburg Senate was supposed to effect the Law against the Generally Dangerous Activities of Social Democracy (*Gesetz gegen die gemeingefährlichen Bestrebungen der Sozialdemokratie*) that came into effect in the whole of the German Empire in 1878.[22]

The Anti-Socialist Law did not affect the electoral activities of the Social Democrats, but it did make things very difficult for them in every other respect. Membership in the party was now illegal, meetings were banned, publications forbidden. The party established its headquarters in Switzerland and smuggled newspapers and journals across the border by the 'red field-post'. Meetings were held illegally, Social Democratic organizations given

[20] Klessmann, *Geschichte*, p. 425.
[21] T. Offermann, 'Arbeiterbewegung, Bürgertum und Staat in Hamburg 1850–1862/63', in Herzig *et al.*, *Arbeiter in Hamburg*, pp. 121–37, here p. 128.
[22] *150 Jahre* (n. 14, above); A. Lessat, 'Alte Kameraden ... Aus der Geschichte Hamburger Polizeiuniformen', in *Hundertfünfzig Jahre Hamburger Polizei (1814–1964)* (n. 13, above), p. 84.

harmless-sounding names. The ultimate effect of the Law was simply to increase working-class support for the party at election time and drive the party leadership to adopt a more explicitly Marxist ideology, embodied in its Erfurt Programme of 1891. But the extent and severity of the repression was very considerable. Except in Hamburg, that is: already in 1876 the local police had begun to investigate the socialist movement, but found that one leading figure, August Geib, had a 'disinclination for excesses', and another, Georg Hartmann, 'enjoyed bourgeois respectability', while the party's local newspaper, it reported, adopted an 'incomparably more moderate' tone than the Social Democratic press elsewhere. Indeed, at least one senior Hamburg official was accustomed to use the local Social Democratic press for the publication of his unsigned articles attacking the city's proposed entry into the Customs Union. Consequently the Senate resisted Prussian attempts to get it to ban the party and its activities in 1876–7 and the semi-official daily, the *Hamburgischer Correspondent*, published sharp attacks on the Anti-Socialist Law, which was seen as a Prussianizing measure on the lines of the proposal to bring Hamburg into the Customs Union.[23]

Nevertheless, the 'excessively lax proceedings' of the Hamburg police against the outlawed party, as the police chief of the neighbouring Prussian town of Altona termed it, brought increasing pressure on the Senate from Berlin. In 1880 the city was put under a 'minor state of siege', which lasted for the rest of the decade; there were numerous arrests, and 75 Social Democrats were expelled from Hamburg and Altona. Prominent merchants gave them donations as a form of protest against what they regarded as an act of Prussian militarism. Sympathy for them among the working class was widespread and deeply felt and undoubtedly contributed to the party's electoral victories during the decade. The common 'trust in the Hamburg Senate' that it would not enforce the Law was severely disappointed. Despite continued arrests and prosecutions, however, the Prussians continued to accuse Hamburg of laxity in carrying out the Anti-Socialist Law. Police Chief Kuhnardt commonly granted repeated postponements of expulsion orders; his conduct was the subject of repeated complaints from Berlin. Indeed, the contrast between policing styles at this period in Hamburg and Prussia could be observed as an aspect of everyday life. In the 1880s, street fights formed a common popular amusement in the harbour quarter on the border between St Pauli and Prussian Altona. 'The good-natured Hamburg constables', remembered one witness, 'armed with their nickel buttons and broad, curved sabres let the people roister about unhindered, in their generous Hanseatic way, while the notoriously "mean" Prussians did not hesitate long' before stepping in. When the 'spiked helmets' in Altona tried to stop these fights, the combatants simply ran over the border into Hamburg: 'to the applause of the onlookers

[23] Kutz-Bauer, 'Arbeiterschaft', pp. 179–92, here pp. 184–5.

on both sides they could now abuse their impotent pursuers at the distance of a few paces from enemy territory without fear of punishment, protected there by the malicious smiles of the local force'. When Police Chief Senator Kuhnardt fell seriously ill in 1886 he was replaced by Senator Gerhard Hachmann, and a much harsher era of repression now began. Hachmann lacked the ability to stand up to pressure, and it may be that his tough policy was a response to repeated injunctions from Berlin. But labour unrest began to take on unprecedented dimensions in the same year, as we have seen, and the new harshness of the police probably reflected a new level of anxiety among the governing fraction of the bourgeoisie as well.[24] At any rate, the total length of imprisonment for offences against the Anti-Socialist Law in Hamburg rose from ten and a half years in the period 1879–83 to some forty-two years in the period 1886–8.[25] Since the middle of the 1880s, the relationship between the dominant classes and the proletariat in the city had undergone a dramatic deterioration. While the anger and disillusion of the working class was expressed in massively increased votes for the Social Democrats, the rapidly growing fear of the mob among the ruling fraction was expressed in a further, and this time drastic reorganization of the police. Already in 1888 the number of constables in the force was increased from 650 to 1,022, and another 92 sergeants and senior officials were added to the 165 already in service. The mounted police division, hitherto used for service in outlying rural districts, was reorganized and transformed into a city force for use against 'riotous assemblies'. The police force was professionalized, and it was forbidden for a policeman to carry on a second business or trade. Pay was raised to the respectable sum of 1,350 Marks for a constable and 1,500 to 2,250 Marks for the ranks immediately above.[26]

Most important of all, the constabulary was militarized. Even before the late 1880s, of course, it had been distinguished from the English police by the variety of weapons—notably sabres—which the constables carried. But voices were raised in 1887 complaining that 'a larger part of the constables have a poor, almost bowed physical posture by the time they are 48 or 50, suffer from rheumatism and have lost all traces of the military in their appearance'. The hours of work were reduced and attempts made to realize the 'promotion of military erectness and a strong commitment to service'.[27] In 1888 recruitment of the local artisans and workers who had previously supplied the bulk of the police force ceased, and a law was introduced whereby

[24] Ibid., p. 185 and nn. 69, 80. For an account of Hachmann's character, see below, pp. 308–9.
[25] Kutz-Bauer, 'Arbeiterschaft', p. 185. For the account of pugilistic customs on the Hamburg–Altona boundary, see H. Reuss-Löwenstein, *Kreuzfahrt meines Lebens. Erinnerungen* (Hamburg, 1962), p. 4.
[26] Lessat, 'Vom "Corps der Nachtwache"', pp. 38, 41; Henze, '"Dem Nachtwächter ..."', p. 113.
[27] Lessat, op. cit., p. 38.

applicants had to have served at least 9 years in the army and to have reached the rank of non-commissioned officer.[28] In 1889, the Senate began to prepare a reorganization of the police along Prussian lines. Since this involved the appointment of permanent paid higher civil servants to head the police department (under the continuing chairmanship of the responsible Senator, of course), it is not surprising that it took some time to get through the Citizens' Assembly. However, in 1892 the measure finally passed into law, with effect from 1 January 1893. It transformed the Constabulary into a Prussian-style police force (*Schutzmannschaft*) with—as the senior active officer of the force, Major Gestefeld, described it—an 'NCO's uniform like that worn in the army' for the constables and Prussian titles for all ranks, 'whereby once more expression will be given to the force's equality of value and status with the army'. Military discipline was introduced, based on that of the Prussian army. The change was most graphically symbolized by the abandonment of the top hats, flat caps, and bobbies' headgear worn by the various grades of the old constabulary and their replacement by the symbol *par excellence* of Prussian militarism, the spiked helmet.[29]

The reforms of the years 1888–93 were both a recognition and a further development of the distance which had grown up between the police and the people under the Anti-Socialist Law in its harsher phase during the late 1880s. However arbitrary the conduct of the former Constabulary, it had at least recruited its members from the local civilian population, and by social background, economic circumstances, and even appearance, the constables had to some extent belonged to the local working class. By 1893, however, the Hamburg police force had been transformed into something like an occupying army, removed from the mass of the population in every respect. Moreover, the same period saw the construction of an extensive network of political spies and informers as an integral part of the force. Hamburg's Combination Law (*Vereinsgesetz*) was much more liberal than Prussia's in more than one respect—for instance in the freedom it gave women to attend political meetings—but one thing at least it did have in common, and that was the obligation it laid on the organizers of public political meetings to obtain police permission in advance and to tolerate the presence of a uniformed policeman on the tribune, next to the chairman, with powers to dissolve the meeting if it went against the law and instructions to give a detailed report of its proceedings to his superiors. The political police sent plain-clothes agents to meetings that were not open to the public and built up an elaborate system of secret surveillance over bars and pubs known to be the haunt of Social Democrats and other radicals. It backed up the information it acquired in this way with a systematic monitoring of the local and

---

[28] Henze, op. cit., p. 113.

[29] Ibid., p. 42; the changes in title were *Oberwachtmeister* for *Sergeant*, *Wachtmeister* for *Offiziant*, and *Schutzmann* for *Constabler*.

national press. The head of the political police reported regularly to the Senator in charge of the police force on the state of working-class opinion in the city. By the early 1890s this system of surveillance had reached an extraordinary pitch of thoroughness and sophistication, easily outdoing in these respects the achievements of its counterpart in Berlin. The authorities in Hamburg thus entered the 1890s not only seriously alarmed by the threat from below, but also unusually well informed about it as well.[30]

III

In its efforts to secure the allegiance, or at least the quiescence, of the working class, the grand bourgeoisie did not content itself with coercive measures alone. Powerful instruments of rule though they might be, a militarized police and an aggressive and well-organized employers' association were not going to win the hearts and minds of the people. The appeal of the ideology of the primacy of trading interests had faded during the labour struggles of the 1880s, though it was always invoked by the employers, the authorities, and the candidates of the National Liberal Party at moments of particular tension such as harbour strikes or Reichstag elections. This ideological thrust was directed, however, mainly at people's intellect and alleged self-interest. Just as important, if not more so, were less overtly rationalistic appeals to the popular mentality. The Senate's strict republicanism and rejection of titles, for instance, embodied an attempt to preserve the fiction that the city was governed by ordinary citizens who were in no way above their fellows in dignity or station. Swearing in new citizens before every Senate meeting to some extent managed to preserve the face-to-face relationship between Senate and citizen of former times. A patriarchal conception of government was also expressed in the notion, which nothing was done to discourage, that the Burgomasters and Senate were directly available to the citizenry for consultation and advice, so that the volume of petitions to the Senate from the public had reached considerable proportions by the 1890s.[31]

But these aspects of the presentation of authority were mainly confined to the relationship of the Senate with the small minority of qualified citizens. In the face which it traditionally presented to the mass of the disenfranchized, the Senate had customarily abandoned all pretence of equality. A characteristic example of this was the relationship between the Senate and the inhabitants of the rural exclaves such as the demesne of Ritzebüttel, at the mouth of the Elbe, or Volksdorf and Bergedorf, inland from Hamburg, which the city had acquired over the course of the centuries. These people had no rights in Hamburg itself, and were treated like feudal subjects long after the formal

[30] See J. Jensen, *Presse und politische Polizei. Hamburgs Zeitungen unter dem Sozialistengesetz 1878–1890* (Hanover, 1966).

[31] StA Hbg, FA Buehl 2c, p. 24.

feudal aspects of their relationship to the city had ceased to exist.[32] Twice every year, until 1918, the Finance Deputation, led by the senior Senators, went on a progress of the state buildings, farmlands, and woods in these areas, travelling in a number of carriages and accompanied by servants and attendants. As the procession approached each of the villages on its route, it was met by the local brass band, by peasant dances, by a turn-out of the local voluntary fire brigade, by a speech in Low German from the chairman of the village council, or, if it was evening, by the accompaniment of a torchlight parade.

These tours of inspection had long since ceased to have any real function by the late nineteenth century, and the members of the Finance Deputation treated them generally as a kind of company outing. The high point of the progress was invariably its arrival at the manor-house in Wohldorf, once, appropriately enough, the seat of a medieval robber baron. Here conditions had a simplicity which the older Senators treated as a solemn reminder of the legendary frugality of the Protestant merchant class from which they were descended. Even in the 1890s there was no electric light, water had to be fetched from a bakery 200 metres down the road, and the sanitary arrangements, as one member complained, were reminiscent of an age that had long since passed into history. Only when the Social Democrats took over the city government in 1918 were modern conveniences introduced. While the President (*Präses*) of the Finance Deputation had a room to himself, other members had to share, and if—as some were already beginning to in the years immediately before the First World War—anyone chose rather to sleep in more comfortable circumstances at the local inn, he was sure to be met with disapproving glances the next morning. Nevertheless, despite these simple surroundings, the gentlemen did not stint themselves when it came to eating; indeed the progress was as much a gastronomic as a ceremonial event:

An exceedingly rich and elegant meal was consumed in the old manor house, following on a really substantial breakfast early in the morning at the Senior Forester's house in Volksdorf and a by no means frugal tea at the country residence of a member of the Finance Deputation, Henry Lütgens, in Gross Hansdorf ... Next morning, a heavily laden breakfast-table, embellished above all by a cold plum pudding, ensured that no one would suffer from starvation ... At midday yet another solemn, heavy meal was eaten.

After dinner, the senior members of the Deputation delivered light-hearted speeches, some of them, as Senator Mönckeberg reported disapprovingly, 'somewhat daring and not suitable for ladies'. In between times, the chief event was a walk in the state woods, where two members of the Deputation, nominated as 'Lords in the Wood' (*Herren am Walde*), each carrying a large

[32] See briefly Eckardt, *Privilegien und Parlament*, p. 17, for this point.

ceremonial hammer, formally tapped the trees which the forester had designated for felling. Otherwise the members stayed in the manor-house and
played *Skat*, a popular card-game, for stakes of half a Pfennig.[33]

Within the city itself, however, little attention was paid to ceremonial
presentations of authority for most of the nineteenth century. Before 1800,
it is true, public processions had been commonplace, namely at funerals,
where the cortège had reached an unparalleled elaboration and grandiosity.[34]
Since private citizens could hire the Burgomasters and Senate for these
processions—on payment of a suitably extravagant fee—they frequently
became, through their composition, carefully ordered by rank and degree,
symbolic expressions of the structure of social and political power in the
city.[35] By the nineteenth century they had disappeared. Other open representations of authority, such as public executions and punishments, became
extremely rare, and ceased to exist after mid-century. The official dress of the
Hamburg Senate, known as the *Habit*, *Ornat*, or *Stalt*, a late sixteenth-century
Spanish-Dutch merchant costume such as can be seen in the paintings of
Rembrandt, had been worn on all official occasions before the incorporation
of the city into the Napoleonic Empire in 1810, and in numerous private
ceremonies as well; but after the end of the Napoleonic Wars it was seldom
used, and then mainly by the Burgomasters. After Burgomaster Benecke was
insulted by a crowd while returning home in the costume at the end of
1848, the Burgomasters too abandoned the *Habit* and adopted the by now
conventional frock-coat and white cravat (black for the Chief of Police). From
1857 the Senators were no longer obliged to appear in the costume at church
except on major festivals, and even this rule was dropped in 1866. The
appearance of the Senate in full dress was now confined to occasions and
institutions deriving from the *Hauptrezess* of 1712, but this too ceased after
the introduction of the new constitution in 1860.[36]

With the incorporation of Hamburg into the North German Confederation
and then the Empire, however, as Senator Versmann noted sourly in his
diary, the 'masquerade' of the *Habit* was 'now to be forced into the light
again', a policy which he thought showed 'how much the adherents of the
old order are getting the upper hand again'. Much to Versmann's disgust,
the Senate voted to appear *in pontificalibus*, as the phrase went, on the
Emperor's birthday on 22 March 1871 and on the occasion of the return of
the Hanseatic Regiment from France on 17 June. Since few Senators now
possessed the full costume, and those who did had long since grown too
plump for it, the *Habit* had to be redesigned. The new costume was more

[33] Von Eckardt, *Lebenserinnerungen*, ii. 15; StA Hbg, FA Buehl 2c, pp. 52–3; ibid., FA Lippmann
A4, Bd. 2, Teil 1, pp. 5–9; ibid., FA Mönckeberg 21a, p. 277.

[34] J. Whaley, *Toleration and Society in Hamburg 1529–1819* (Cambridge, 1985).

[35] Klessmann, *Geschichte*, p. 433.

[36] The account of the *Habitfrage* here and in the following paragraphs is taken from Hauschild-
Thiessen, *Bürgerstolz*, pp. 33–46. See also Plates 1 and 2.

ornate than the old one, and was 'improved' by the addition of a sword. It consisted of an elaborately embroidered black gown, adorned with fur in winter, a large round white ruff, black breeches, stockings and buckled shoes, an enormous black hat (designed originally to fit over a sixteenth-century wig), and various other invisible but no less antiquated items worn underneath this curious assemblage. The Senate now wore the costume on most ceremonial occasions; and in 1888, indeed, Versmann himself caused a sensation in Berlin by wearing it at the opening of the Reichstag by Emperor Wilhelm II. From now on it became customary to appear in it at all court functions in the capital city. Here it was clearly intended to emphasize Hamburg's continuing claims to autonomy, to conceal as far as possible the city's loss of independence, and also to act as a reminder that the city was a federated state, not merely another municipality. In Hamburg itself the Senate now donned this grotesque costume whenever it appeared collectively before the public, including on the occasion of Senatorial elections: and here the *Ornat* served equally important legitimating functions.

In the old days, as Heinrich Merck noted, everyone had agreed that 'Hamburg means refinement, dignity, and—even where there is considerable wealth—simplicity'.[37] The Senate had found it very difficult to hold formal ceremonies after the destruction of the Town Hall in 1842. As Senate Syndic Merck remarked in 1868, it was unable even to give a formal dinner, since it possessed 'no premises, no dinner service, no silver, in short, nothing to meet even the most moderate requirements'.[38] With the building of the new Town Hall, all this was to change. The foundation stone was laid, significantly, in 1885, and the new building, opened in 1897 and still standing today, was grandiose in the extreme: a huge, elaborate edifice, one of the major features of which is a suite of richly decorated reception rooms and a grand dining-room for state occasions. Seen from the outside, its spire reaching up to rival those of Hamburg's five inner-city parish churches, it was a potent physical symbol of the power and wealth of the city's government. Even before it was formally opened, the Senate had adopted an increasingly 'grand style'. Receptions and formal occasions proliferated, and pomp and ceremony took the place of the old quiet way of doing things.[39] As Senate Secretary Julius von Eckardt wrote, 'while the city filled more and more with people who were complete strangers to the traditions and peculiarities of life in Hamburg, and scarcely knew that Hamburg was also a state in its own right, this state burst externally into bloom'.[40] The tendency von Eckardt observed with such disapproval was not merely an historical irony; it also served a very real and obvious political purpose.

---

[37] StA Hbg, FA Merck II 9 Konv. 4a, Heft II, p. 9.
[38] Hauschild-Thiessen, *Bürgerstolz*, p. 7.
[39] StA Hbg, FA Merck II 9 Konv. 4a, Heft II, p. 11.
[40] Von Eckardt, *Lebenserinnerungen*, ii. 48.

Familiarizing the majority of the city's inhabitants with the city's institutions through administering them with increasing dosages of pomp and circumstance was intended to promote acceptance of the governing system's legitimacy. Such invented, or reinvented, traditions as the Hamburg Senate adopted in the late nineteenth century were calculated to awaken in the popular mind feelings of respect, even awe, for a system of rule apparently centuries old.[41] The sixteenth-century costume of the city's rulers symbolized a system of government hallowed by the passing of time, steeped in the experience of past ages, rooted in the past and therefore irremovable in the future. Pride in Hamburg's heritage and pride in belonging to a city-state with its own distinct traditions and way of life was an essential element in the local patriotism to which the grand bourgeoisie appealed in its struggle to prevent the growing support of Hamburg's working class for the 'anti-Hamburg' Social Democrats.

IV

At the same time as it overhauled its system of policing and elaborated the public presentation of its own authority, the Hamburg Senate also embarked upon a fresh moralizing offensive against the poor. A central aspect of this was the introduction of the Elberfeld system of poor relief in 1892–3, resolved upon once the Senate had decided to abandon the existing system in 1885. The introduction of the new system in Elberfeld itself had taken place as a reaction to popular unrest and political radicalism in the town—the home of Friedrich Engels—in the 1840s, and similar considerations played a role in Hamburg too. Apart from its financial promise, the system also held out the possibility of a greatly intensified supervision and control over the poor. The number of overseers (*Armenpfleger*) was increased from 440 to 1,565 under the new system. This was so that each could come into 'continual direct contact with the paupers'. The overseer was obliged by his terms of contract to become 'the paupers' truest friend and adviser. He has to know the paupers assigned to him', he was told, 'like his own family, their dwellings like his own house'. He was to visit them regularly to report on their circumstances and recommend a suitable level of support. He was to convince himself by personal observation that this support was being wisely used; 'he shall', as the instructions said 'censure disorder and bad habits, and if necessary report them, and admonish the paupers to adopt an honourable mode of life'. In particular he was to ensure 'that the children of the paupers assigned to his care are not physically and morally put at risk by excessive demands on them to undertake paid employment'. At the earliest possible opportunity the

---

[41] Cf. D. Cannadine, 'The Context, Performance and Meaning of Ritual: The British Monarchy and the "Invention of Tradition", *c.* 1820–1977', in E. Hobsbawm and T. Ranger (eds.), *The Invention of Tradition* (Cambridge, 1983), pp. 101–64.

overseer was to find the pauper a job, which had to be accepted, no matter how badly it was paid, on pain of being deprived of poor-law support.[42]

As the historian Bernd Weisbrod has remarked, the transition from the relatively indiscriminate support provided before this point to this new system amounted in effect to 'a modern, bureaucratic form of social disciplining',[43] in which the pauper was placed in direct personal dependence on the overseer; paupers were expected to show gratitude for the support they received, and to express it by conforming as far as possible to bourgeois behavioural norms. Drink, politics, and other pleasures were to be avoided, and the children were to be sent regularly to school instead of supporting the family by working (although in the case of poor families such as the Kaisens and the Neddermeyers, as we have seen, such support was vitally necessary). The direct subjection of the pauper to the symbolic violence exerted by the overseer was also a direct subjection of the proletarian to the bourgeois; for as usual in Hamburg, the poor-law overseers were not paid officials but propertied citizens acting in an honorary capacity.[44] In Hamburg in 1902 the 108 chairmen of the Poor Law Districts included a broad cross-section of the city's dominant classes, from merchants (including industrialists and brokers) (22) and professionals such as pastors, lawyers, doctors, civil servants, and teachers (26) to small tradesmen (23) and master artisans (20). Among the 1,563 overseers, the merchants and professionals were less prominent, with 253 and 254 respectively, while the petty-bourgeois element was much more in evidence: no fewer than 528 of the overseers were master artisans and 231 small tradesmen. The overwhelming majority of these men are also likely to have been active members of their local Citizens' Club, with which the district poor-law committees stood in close though informal contact.[45]

The moral control exercised by the poor law system over the poor was to some extent a substitute for another form of moral supervision which had largely ceased to be effective in Hamburg by the 1890s: religion. Hamburg was an almost exclusively Protestant city (92% in 1890), and for centuries the Lutheran church had been the official state religion. Up to 1860 the parish was the fundamental basis on which public life was organized at a local level in Hamburg, and the absence of a state education system devolved the responsibility for schooling onto the church. The Senate functioned as the church's governing body and exercised a close control over ecclesiastical affairs, all the way down to the appointment of pastors. Following on the promulgation of the constitution of 1860, a series of lengthy negotiations led

[42] *Das öffentliche Armenwesen*, pp. 9, 15–17.

[43] B. Weisbrod, 'Wohltätigkeit und symbolische Gewalt in der Frühindustrialisierung. Städtische Armut und Armenpolitik im Wuppertal', in H. Mommsen and W. Schulze, *Vom Elend der Handarbeit. Probleme historischer Unterschichtenforschung* (Stuttgart, 1981), pp. 334–57, here p. 355.

[44] See above, pp. 26–7, 74–7.

[45] *Das öffentliche Armenwesen*, p. 18.

to the formal separation of church and state ten years later. However, the Senate's collective authority over the church was replaced by the provision that individual Senators should act as 'patrons' of the five city parishes, a measure intended originally to provide a counterweight to the representative organs of the parish. The *Patronat* had the right to confirm the appointment of pastors and to endorse or reject ecclesiastical laws. Although the church's affairs were now governed by church bodies, the Church Council (*Kirchenrat*), and the Synod, two Senators sat on each of these bodies, and one of them customarily took the chair. Similarly, two Senators sat on every parish council (*Kirchenvorstand*) as 'First and Second Parish Lord' (*Kirchspielherr*). The church remained to a considerable extent financially dependent on the state. In practice, therefore, the Senate continued to exercise supervision over the church at every level.[46]

Most of the Senators seem to have been active Christians. As Senate Syndic Dr Buehl remarked, 'many Senators showed a lively interest in ecclesiastical affairs and devoted themselves to church business with particular partiality'. Burgomasters Johann Georg Mönckeberg and Johannes Heinrich Burchard were both described by Buehl as 'pious'; and Carl August Schröder, who became a Senator in 1899, had long been an active lay member of his parish and wrote in his memoirs that 'I have always been interested in church affairs and questions of ecclesiastical policy'.[47] Schröder's own career had been helped in no small measure by his election to the parish council in Eppendorf in 1892, in which capacity he was able to cultivate friendly relations with the chairman of the council, Senator Kähler. Here was yet another of the complex network of informal institutions which bound the dominant classes of Hamburg together. It was possible for a pastor to be on close personal terms with the patrician families; Pastor Faass, for instance, of the Eppendorf church, was Schröder's uncle by marriage.[48] Pastor Christian Behrmann and his wife and children frequently stayed in the summer homes of the Gosslers and Petersens, and he described in his memoirs long walks which the families took together in the countryside. Behrmann himself came from a humble background; he had been brought up by his uncle, a master artisan; nevertheless he had a highly successful career, becoming the Senior Pastor of the Hamburg Church in 1884, and serving in this capacity, as it were, as the house preacher of the grand bourgeoisie. But normally, unless they were close relations, pastors could not expect to move in such rarified social circles, and even Behrmann did so only on relatively rare occasions. The very few daughters of leading families who married pastors were, as Thomas Mann's *Buddenbrooks* suggests, somewhat looked down upon by the rest of the clan,

---

[46] H. G. Bergemann, *Staat und Kirche in Hamburg während des 19. Jahrhunderts* (Hamburg, 1958), p. 83. Separate arrangements were made for the small communities of Catholics and Jews.

[47] StA Hbg, FA Buehl 2c, pp. 35, 75–8; Schröder, *Blütezeit*, p. 75.

[48] Schröder, loc. cit.

since their marriage broke the magic circle of business and family connections on which much of the merchants' prosperity depended. Unless they had private means, pastors were no more than moderately well-off, with a stipend fixed at 5,000 Marks by the reform of 1860. In the great majority of the informal institutions of the city's ruling system, from the grand gentlemen's dinners to family and kinship networks, they were subordinates.[49]

To the Senate, the precise nature of their theological position was more or less a matter of indifference: as Senator Burchard, who did not entirely approve of this attitude, said in 1894, 'We in Hamburg perhaps allow the individual a greater degree of individual independence in the field of theology than is the case elsewhere'.[50] This latitudinarian stance meant that sometimes pastors were appointed who were, theologically speaking, quite radical. But this did not unduly concern the Senators.[51] What mattered was that the church should convey to the mass of the people the Pietist message of patience in suffering and the Lutheran dogma of submission to authority. In order to further this cause, indeed, a massive church-building programme, partly subsidized by private donations, was embarked upon in the 1880s. As Senior Christian Behrmann noted, although the need for new churches to cater for the increase in population, above all in the suburbs, had long been evident, 'up to 1880 hardly any progress was made towards solving this task'. By the early 1900s, when Behrmann wrote his memoirs, the number of churches in Eppendorf had increased from 1 to 4 and the number of preachers from 2 to 13, while in St Georg there had been a similar increase from 1 church to 5 and 2 pastors to 15. If a decline in religion and morality in the working class was held responsible for the growth of social and political unrest, then clearly a response on the part of the church could expect a wide measure of support from the bourgeois laity.[52]

But it was in reality already too late to rescue the working class of Hamburg for the Christian religion. Already in 1849 Senator Martin Hudtwalcker noted that hardly anyone over school age went to church any more. Senior Behrmann wrote of his early days in Hamburg in the 1880s, that 'Only a very small part of the *Mittelstand* and the so-called humble people went to church'.[53] In the years 1880–4 fewer than 10% of the Protestant population of Hamburg attended communion, the lowest proportion in Germany. Even Berlin managed to produce a figure of 15%, while in rural Schaumburg-Lippe the proportion exceeded 80%. The relatively small number of churches compared to the population—one for every 10,000 in 1881—and the identification of the church with the state were among the causes of secularization;

[49] C. K. G. Behrmann, *Erinnerungen* (Berlin, 1904), pp. 268–9; Bergemann, *Staat und Kirche*, p. 62.
[50] Behrmann, op. cit., p. 389.
[51] Schröder, *Blütezeit*, p. 75.
[52] Behrmann, op. cit., p. 238.
[53] Bergemann, op. cit., p. 83; Behrmann, op. cit., p. 238.

more generally, too, the role to be played by religion in daily life was less obvious in urban society than in rural, and with its accent on discipline and morality the Lutheran Church did little to make itself attractive to the working class.[54]

Many poor people did not see why they should give the pastor his customary Taler for carrying out duties such as baptism, confirmation, or marriage.[55] In the 1870s, as Senior Pastor Behrmann remembered, these rites of passage were 'almost without exception also requested by those who otherwise had nothing to do with the church'. They had little effect on working-class consciousness. Behrmann even recalled being asked to a working-class home to baptize an infant girl 'Lassaline'. It was in fact traditional in Hamburg for baptisms and weddings to be held at home rather than in church, and this custom brought the pastors, as Behrmann's recollections vividly show, into close contact with aspects of poverty and working-class life which they might not otherwise have seen. Long before the turn of the century, however, this tradition had become a thing of the past, and baptisms and weddings were generally held in church or in the pastor's own house: a symbol of the decay of the earlier patriarchal relationship of the pastor with his flock and the growing distance between the pastorate and the people.[56] By the same time, too, preaching, with its accent on a rather literary form of High German, had little appeal to a working population whose customary form of expressing themselves was still often in Low German dialect. To speak High German in Hamburg was to speak the language of authority;[57] and whatever degree of deference might have persuaded masters and journeymen to listen to it in church in the past was no longer present in the working class that formed itself in the city after the middle of the nineteenth century. Nor was there any tradition of Protestant sectarianism to which the working class could turn, as it could in England.

At the same time, Hamburg's educational system also underwent significant changes. The Johanneum, for many years the city's only high school, was transformed into a modern grammar school along Prussian lines, and joined by a second grammar school in 1881. There were no more such foundations before the First World War. Learning was reserved, in other words, for a tiny élite.[58] For those who did well in primary school a special class, the *Selekta*, was instituted in which outstanding pupils from the top classes of a number of primary schools were admitted to be trained for clerical

---

[54] See H. McLeod, 'Protestantism and the Working Class in Imperial Germany', *European Studies Review*, 12 (1982), 323–44.

[55] Kaisen, *Meine Arbeit*, p. 213.

[56] Behrmann, *Erinnerungen*, pp. 174, 233.

[57] Cf. K. Schlegel, 'Mistress and Servant in Nineteenth-Century Hamburg', *History Workshop Journal*, 15 (1983), 60–77.

[58] Plagemann, *Industriekultur*, p. 225.

work in Hamburg's great merchant houses.[59] While creaming off the most able pupils from humble backgrounds into the new *Mittelstand* of white-collar workers and clerks, the system subjected the vast majority of those who remained to an increasing degree of moral training and political indoctrination. It was only in 1871 that elementary education became compulsory in Hamburg and that a state school system was finally established. The resulting improvements in the educational attainments of the working class clearly demanded an ever-increasing effort on the part of the teachers and the School Board—the latter of course under the direct control of the Senate— to prevent the Social Democrats from reaping the benefits. These efforts met with little success, however; and the rapidly rising standards of literacy and education among the working class that followed from the introduction of universal primary education in 1871 were already beginning to make themselves felt as the first generations of children to benefit from them reached adulthood fifteen years or so later. Pride in knowledge and belief in the benefits of science were two of the most outstanding features of labour movement culture in the late nineteenth century, and they too played their part in the growing resentment of Hamburg's working class against its exclusion from economic prosperity and political power.

Throughout the nineteenth century, Hamburg's grand bourgeoisie remained convinced that poverty was in the first place an outcome of moral laxity. Drink, sexual excess, irreligion, frivolity, lack of foresight, and a host of other moral failings that could be summed up in terms of a refusal to adhere to the dominant ideals of thrift and hard work, were made responsible for almost every aspect of poverty, from unemployment to sickness, disease, and early death. Since poverty was an expression of immorality, it was understandable if not excusable that poor people also fell victim to the lure of Social Democracy. In the struggle against the labour movement, therefore, the grand bourgeoisie enlisted the aid not just of the police and the forces of coercion, but also of a whole battery of moralizing institutions, from the prison and the primary school to the Elberfeld system and the Lutheran church. There is little convincing evidence to suggest that these efforts met with any real degree of success.[60] The Social Democrats continued to gain more votes, and their demands for a reform of the existing system of government in Hamburg grew ever louder and more insistent. Beyond the organized labour movement, in the alleys and passages of the inner city, the threat from the 'dangerous' sector of the working class was growing, as the events of 1890 seemed to show. The final loss of all three Hamburg Reichstag seats to the Social Democrats in the same year, with a high proportion of the support for the party coming from the inner city, seemed to underline the connection

[59] H. Naumann, *Wilhelm Koenen* (Halle, 1973), p. 8.
[60] For the general background to this argument, see R. J. Evans (ed.), *The German Working Class 1888–1933: The Politics of Everyday Life* (London, 1982).

between the two processes. As they entered the last decade of the nineteenth century, Hamburg's dominant classes may well have felt for the first time since 1848 that their hold on power was beginning to slip.

V

If at times this account of the world the merchants made has seemed perilously reminiscent of vulgar Marxism at its most economistic, then this is not least because, as Michael Grüttner has remarked, 'In a much more direct, or at least more obvious way, than elsewhere, economic power in Hamburg was also political power'.[61] The dominance of trade and capitalist enterprise was undisguised. Untroubled by the existence of a large and powerful bureaucracy or a mighty class of aristocratic landowners such as existed in Prussia, Hamburg's grand bourgeoisie, in alliance from the middle of the century with the city's substantial middle class and parts of the petty bourgeoisie, could arrange the city's political system to a greater degree than might have been possible elsewhere to serve its own interests. Not only did they make no secret about the primacy of trade, they even erected it into an ideology, symbolized by the union in 1897 of Town Hall and Exchange in the same complex of buildings in the city centre.

Nevertheless, the state in nineteenth-century Hamburg cannot be reduced to a simple instrument of the mercantile interest. To begin with, as we have seen over issues such as the Customs Union, that interest was itself divided. Formal and informal state institutions, from the Senate at the centre of the state structure to the Chamber of Commerce on the outer periphery, took part in, and to some extent also formed the scene of, struggles between large merchants and middling merchants, those whose businesses focused on processing imported goods for re-export and those who were mainly involved in bringing in goods from overseas for distribution to the German hinterland, those with heavy investments in inland industry and those with none. In the last instance the wishes of the great merchant houses were usually decisive, but only after a number of important concessions had been made to the wishes of others. Secondly, the executive arm of the state was dominated by lawyers who, despite their personal ties to the leading merchant families, were liable by virtue of their training, their patterns of sociability, and their role in government, to take a line that was less than entirely in accordance with the wishes of the grand bourgeois houses. Thirdly, the class compromise arrived at in mid-century incorporated into the legislative branch of the state a built-in representation of the interests of middling and petty-bourgeois landlords which often ran counter to those of the mercantile community.

---

[61] Grüttner, *Arbeitswelt*, p. 21.

Two further constraints on the freedom of action of Hamburg's merchants to shape the state as they wished became increasingly stronger as the century went on. One, the most obvious, was the external constraint of membership in the German Empire and, before that, in the North German Confederation. The city, of course, had always had to pay heed to its more powerful neighbours, and as the introduction of the Karlsbad Decrees in 1819 or the occupation of Hamburg by the Prussians thirty years later clearly demonstrated, there were obvious limits beyond which, even in the easy-going atmosphere of the German Confederation, the city would never have been able to go. But until 1867 it had at least been able to retain its own peculiar institutions more or less intact. From now on, however, these were increasingly harmonized with those of the rest of the Empire, beginning with the currency and the system of weights and measures in 1867 and moving on through the church reform in 1870, the educational system in 1871, the legal system in 1879, the tariff laws in 1888, the poor law in 1892, and the police force in 1893. Hamburg was also increasingly subject to Reich laws which it might not have wanted to introduce had it been left to itself to decide, most notably the Anti-Socialist Law of 1878–90. The defeat of the Old Hamburg Particularists and the victory of the Prussian party in the Senate, led by Johannes Versmann, merely set the seal on Hamburg's transition from a self-governing city to an autonomous but clearly subordinate member state of the German Empire.

However, two important reservations must be made about this process of incipient Prussianization. The first is that the Senate and the dominant classes were frequently able either to manipulate Imperial institutions to suit their own interests, as in the creation of the free port on the city's entry into the Customs Union, or the Hanseatic cities' domination of the Imperial consular service, or to pay lip-service to Imperial legislation while putting their own interpretation on it in practice, as in the case of the Anti-Socialist Law during the first eight of its twelve years of operation. In other ways, too, it was possible by minor adjustments to affect the operation of Prussian-style institutions in a direction favourable to the particular needs of the mercantile interest, as with the creation of the *Selekta* class in the elementary school system. The second reservation about the process of Prussianization is that a substantial part of it happened not least because it was in the interests of Hamburg's dominant classes that it should. There was no external pressure on the Senate in the 1880s to introduce the Elberfeld system of poor relief or to militarize the local police; Hamburg adapted itself to common German practice in both these areas largely because it seemed the most effective way of solving problems that affected it from within.

This brings us to the final and in some ways most important of the constraints on the state's role as an instrument of the merchants' interests, which was, ironically, the very economic success which the merchants of

Hamburg themselves achieved. The rapid growth of overseas trade which the merchants did so much to foster and to exploit led to a tremendous, only occasionally interrupted increase in their wealth. Germany's industrial revolution and Europe's streams of migrants to the New World brought the growth of major ancillary industries and huge shipping and shipbuilding firms as well as a further massive expansion of trade. Merchant capital was transformed into mercantile-industrial and finance capital and concentrated in business enterprises of very substantial dimensions, including some of the largest companies in their particular branches anywhere in the world. The concentration of capital enabled Hamburg firms to organize themselves into powerful associations and cartels in the late 1880s and early 1890s. But it also led inexorably to the growth of a substantial and well-organized working class. Already by the 1870s Hamburg was the major centre of German socialism, as August Bebel described it. Socialist trade unions began to organize successfully in the harbour and the shipyards, while the local Social Democratic Party swiftly conquered all three local Reichstag constituencies and showed its power by organizing impressive mass demonstrations and parades.

The growth of Social Democratic strength and labour militancy in the 1880s stimulated an increased mobilization of the coercive and disciplining forces of the state, which found its expression not merely in the enlarged strength and transformed character of the police but also in the reform of the poor law through the introduction of the Elberfeld system at the same time. But this process of increased state activity also had its limits. Hamburg continued to be in all essentials an outpost of the night-watchman state: the number of the night-watchmen might have been increased and their equipment strengthened, as it were, but in other respects things remained as before. State intervention was still avoided where it was thought to involve unnecessary expenditure—which meant on most counts, except for the furtherance of trade and the maintenance of an orderly society in which trade could flourish. In this respect, above all others, the Manchesterite ideology of the dominant classes lived on well into the period of increased class conflict that began in the middle of the 1880s.

The structures of politics and habits of mind that dominated the administration of Hamburg in the second half of the nineteenth century were ill-suited to the circumstances of a major European city. Rapid urban growth of the kind experienced by Hamburg in this period posed challenges which would have taxed the energy and imagination even of the most dedicated and efficient urban administrators. As thousands of migrants continued to settle in the city every year, swelling its numbers to half a million and more by 1890, the Senate and the Citizens' Assembly were confronted with the problem of how the city's growing population was to be supplied with fresh water and hygienic food, how it was to be housed, how the rubbish and waste matter generated by its presence was to be disposed of. Urban growth meant massive changes in the urban environment. We turn now to see how well the rulers of Hamburg managed to cope with them.

2

The Urban Environment

a. Soap and Civilization

I

THE concept of environmental pollution—indeed the concept of the environment itself, in the sense of the physical constituents of the natural world in which human society is situated—is a relatively new one. The damage which advanced industrial society is inflicting upon the air we breathe, the water we drink, the food we eat, the woods, fields, and rivers which surround us, has only become a major object of public attention in the last few decades; its place in political debate had been recognized for an even shorter period, perhaps as little as five or ten years.[1] A decade ago, it would not have been easy to see these things as being connected with one another, or with more than the general structure and development of society and politics in the past. But the newly acquired sensitivity to the environment in our own day has alerted historians to the role played by the environment in former times.[2] The growing interest in demographic history and the study of disease and mortality in the past has led to questions about the influence of environment on population patterns in previous centuries.[3] Finally, in England at least, the history of sanitary reform is relatively familiar because of the place it occupied in the political changes of the 1830s;[4] and more recently, the influence of Michel Foucault has led to a revival of interest in the subject as an aspect of the history of the social disciplining of the working class.[5]

As with many other aspects of social reform in the nineteenth century, so with sanitary reform—the 'great clean-up'—there has been an understandable tendency in the older literature simply to treat the subject as a

[1] For a résumé of the debate and its historical development, see E. Schramm, Ökologie-Lesebuch. Ausgewählte Texte zur Entwicklung ökologischen Denkens (Frankfurt, 1984).

[2] See W. Stenz et al., 'Zu den Beziehungen zwischen Gesellschaft und Umwelt von der Industriellen Revolution bis zum Übergang zum Imperialismus', Jahrbuch für Wirtschaftsgeschichte, I (1984) 81–132, for a first, though rather schematic, attempt at an overall account. See also K. G. Wey, Umweltpolitik in Deutschland. Kurze Geschichte des Umweltschutzes in Deutschland seit 1900 (Opladen, 1982).

[3] A powerful influence has also been exerted by the tradition established by F. Braudel, The Mediterranean and the Mediterranean World in the Age of Phillip II (2 vols.; London, 1972).

[4] Much of this is summed up, and carried further, in A. S. Wohl, Endangered Lives: Public Health in Victorian Britain (London, 1983).

[5] See especially A. Corbin, Pesthauch und Blütenduft. Eine Geschichte des Geruchs (Berlin, 1984).

history of steady progess and growing rationality in the conquest of evils belonging to an ignorant and barbarous past: sanitary reform enshrined as the centre-piece of the altar of social progress. This has led too easily to the kind of cliché, long since banished from the history of politics, in which small bands of enlightened reformers are pictured as battling against evil forces of indifference and tradition.[6] Quite apart from its intellectual poverty, this way of looking at the past prevents us from discovering why sanitary reform was implemented in different places at different times in any terms other than the presence or absence of reform-minded individuals. In a story such as the present one, such individuals, as we shall see, do play a role.[7] But the scene against which the action was played out was set by wider, more impersonal forces. Sanitary reform, like other aspects of urban reform, stood at the centre of a complex interplay of economic, political, and ideological forces. It is the exploration of these forces, and their relationships with one another, that forms the principal justification for its study.

The urban environment of the nineteenth century was already in obvious and fundamental respects quite different from that of past ages. The sheer size of towns such as Hamburg dwarfed by comparison almost anything previously experienced in human history, but far more important was the extreme rapidity with which the population, and to a lesser extent the geographical area, of towns in nineteenth-century Britain and Europe began to grow with the onset of industrialization. In many respects, urban life continued much as it had done in the past,[8] but what was bearable or imperceptible in the small town of the pre-industrial era quickly became obnoxious when multiplied a thousand times in the rapidly expanding urban centres of the industrial age. While the urban environment deteriorated initially through the exaggeration of pre-existing problems, it soon began to experience fresh sources of pollution from the innovations which the process of industrialization was beginning to introduce.[9] When all these forces coincided, the consequences for everyday life in the city could be very severe.

Environmental pollution in the nineteenth century did not affect all people equally, any more than it does today. Different social classes not only suffered in different ways and degrees, they also perceived the problem differently and drew different conclusions from what they perceived. In a city where political power and social goods were as unevenly distributed as in Hamburg, such

---

[6] There are still traces of this approach in Wohl, *Endangered Lives*; however, the German literature on this subject, such as it is, takes a markedly more pessimistic view (cf. Wey, *Umweltpolik*, and G. Spelsberg, *Rauchplage: Hundert Jahre Saurer Regen* (Aachen, 1984).) The question of gains and losses in terms of environmental reform will occupy us again in Chapter 6 below.

[7] Notably William Lindley and Franz Andreas Meyer (cf. Chapter 2c).

[8] For examples of environmental pollution in the pre-industrial town, see Spelsberg, *Rauchplage*, pp. 17–20.

[9] R. D. Sieferle, *Der unterirdische Wald. Energiekrise und industrielle Revolution* (Munich, 1982).

experiences and perceptions were particularly diverse. Environmental pollution was an aspect of social inequality. Its history, and the history of how
it was perceived and tackled, was closely enmeshed with the history of
class relations. Mercantile success and prosperity and the expansion and
concentration of capital which accompanied it had consequences for the
physical world as well as for the people who lived in it. In Chapter 1 of this
book we have already seen how economic growth in the context of a classic
bourgeois liberal state structure brought about severe problems for the dominant classes by the 1880s.[10] The physical, environmental problems which it
caused were no less severe, and their consequences were fundamental for the
further development of class relations in the city during the 1890s. In Chapter
2, therefore, we turn to the question of environmental pollution, and follow
the separate strands of its history through the century up to the eve of the
catastrophe in 1892 which it did so much to bring about.

II

The first, and to the casual observer of the everyday street scene, the most
obvious problem caused by rapid urban growth was the tremendous increase
it brought in the number of animals inhabiting or moving through the city.
To an extent that would be inconceivable in a great urban centre of today,
the citizens of nineteenth-century Hamburg lived in close proximity to a large
variety of animals, big and small. This was, of course, a horse-drawn society:
not only omnibuses, but also hansom cabs, trams, carriages, carts, and
wagons of all kinds were pulled by horses well after the turn of the century,
and horse-riding was a standard accomplishment among wide sectors of the
population.[11] The movement of goods to and from the harbour and along the
waterfront was also made possible by horses, though the quayside railway
lines began to have an increasingly important function from the 1860s. In
1892 no fewer than 12,000 horses were stabled in the inner city and suburbs;
7,000 of them were used as draught commercial animals, and almost 5,000
were kept for transport and domestic purposes.[12] Two decades previously, in
1873, the inhabitants and commercial enterprises of the Altstadt and Neustadt had stabled nearly 2,500 horses in the area, and there had been nearly
1,500 more in St Pauli and St Georg. The ratio of equine to human inhabitants
of the inner city at that time was one to sixty-six. Numerous horses also came
in from outlying areas every day, pulling carriages and wagons with people
or goods destined for the harbour or the city. Horses in large numbers were
thus an everyday part of the Hamburg street scene; and as the fleets or canals

---

[10] See Chapter 1d.

[11] For some ideas on the importance of horses in 19th-century society, see F. M. L. Thompson,
Victorian England: the Horse-drawn Society (London, 1970).

[12] *SHS* 15 (1894), 150–66. The distinction is between *Lastpferde* and *Personenpferde*.

gradually fell into disuse and were replaced from the mid-1860s, still more from 1888, by new harbour facilities, horse-drawn wagons to some extent replaced boats as means of transporting goods into the city.

Not only horses but also many other kinds of animals shared the streets and courtyards of Hamburg with the human population. The animal census (*Viehzählung*) of 1873 revealed that the Altstadt and Neustadt housed between them a total of 2,171 chickens, 77 ducks, 43 goats, 32 head of cattle, 17 pigs, 7 sheep, 6 geese, one donkey, and a turkey.[13] Some of these animals were of course counted at the slaughterhouse, caught by the census-taker at the arbitrary moment of the last day of their existence. On the other hand, the thousands of cattle and pigs regularly driven through the streets to the slaughterhouse, like the horses and other animals sold on the markets, were not included in this enumeration. Many animals were in the permanent possession of private inhabitants of the city, and served as a means of adding to their modest income and unvaried diet. It had long been the custom for families or groups of families in the city to keep a cow for milking. Some milk dealers kept as many as 25 cows on their premises in the Altstadt in the 1820s. An investigation carried out in 1827, for example, revealed that no less than 576 head of cattle were stalled in the city. They were kept by a total of 139 people; 75 had only one cow each, 15 had over ten, and the rest had a number somewhere in between. Among the inhabitants of the inner city recorded as keeping cows on the premises in 1827 were two Senators and several of the richest merchants. This custom became less popular as time went on, but there were still 3 households in the Altstadt or Neustadt recorded as keeping cattle as late as 1900.[14] Some 29 beehives were maintained in the courtyards of the Altstadt and Neustadt in 1873, too, and the breeding of rabbits for food was also very popular. As late at the 1880s it was not uncommon for poor people to keep chickens in their homes. Wilhelm Wachendorf, for example, remembered how as an infant in the Altstadt Süd he was left alone in a neighbour's house every morning by his working mother until the older children finished school. The neighbour kept hens in her living-room—they roosted at night on two wooden bars placed over the stove—because 'the rich liked to buy fresh eggs from her', and so she could supplement her meagre income, mostly earned from fruit-selling, to look after her tubercular daughter. 'I crawled around among the hens on the tiled floor all morning,' remembered Wachendorf; 'as time went by, the hens and I got used to each other. Of course they pecked me sometimes and made me dirty, but I didn't know any better.'[15] Hens and other animals were maintained in even larger quantites in the inner suburbs. In 1873, the census counted some

[13] *SHS* 6 (1873), 1–30; also for the figures in the previous paragraph.

[14] StA Hbg, MK II A 3a Bd. 1, Bl. 120: *Hamburgischer Correspondent*, 13 Feb. 1906.

[15] H. Wachendorf, 'Im Gängeviertel stand meines Vaters Wiege' (typescript, copy in StA Hbg), p. 14.

1,940 chickens in St Georg and another 1,268 in St Pauli. Two decades later in 1892 the authorities noted the presence of 35 cows and 16 pigs in St Georg Süd, as well as a total of 3,059 pigs, 1,735 head of cattle, and 859 sheep in the city and its suburbs as a whole.[16] Certainly, once more, many of these were counted in the central slaughterhouse of St Pauli; but in the suburbs at least, a good number were also kept on a more permanent basis.

Naturally enough, the Senate had long been aware of the disadvantages of the long-term presence of the larger animals in the Altstadt and the Neustadt. On 26 September 1818 it had given all pigs eight days to leave the city, after which they were permanently banned from entering the Altstadt and Neustadt except to be slaughtered. In 1869 this ban was extended to St Georg as well.[17] In this respect, Hamburg was well in advance of most other nineteenth-century towns.[18] In Gateshead, in the north-east of England, pigs roamed freely around the streets as late as the 1840s; in 1856 the 40,000 inhabitants of another English town, Dudley, staged public protests against a decision of the Local Board of Health to ban pigs within the city limits. The historian F. B. Smith has described pigs as 'efficient, reasonably healthy disposers of wastes' which 'gave good value in cash and calories ... In the short run', he has claimed, ' ... pigs probably curbed the death rate more than reformers.'[19] But in Hamburg these advantages were reduced because pigs were not allowed in the inner city. Further out, they became a nuisance. As the built-up area of the city expanded into the suburbs, where pigs were still allowed, a continuous stream of complaints about them began to flow into the offices of the city authorities. In June 1894, when the suburbs and St Pauli were legally united with the city, the ban on pigs was automatically extended to cover the whole area. But by December 1894 the pig-owners of Hamburg had successfully obtained an effective exemption from this rule so long as the pigs were housed outside the inner city.[20]

Predictably enough, it was in the poorest areas that the nuisance was greatest. There were over 1,000 pigs in Barmbeck in 1892, for example, and complaints were made by the working-class inhabitants of the areas about the 'stink' of the large piggeries which clustered around the state tannery and knacker's yard. In the 1870s, the Citizens' Club in Pöseldorf, an area constituting an enclave of relative poverty in the wealthy district of Harvestehude, was much exercised by the problem of 'keeping of animals, especially for example, pigs in bath-tubs'. The Social Democratic *Hamburger Echo* noted in 1894 that many workers who had access to a garden 'are accustomed to keep a pig, which is generally purchased young at the annual

---

[16] *SHS* 6 (1873), 1–30, 15 (1894), pp 150–66.
[17] StA Hbg, MK II G 6 Bd. 1, Bl. 65 ff.
[18] C. Rosenberg, *The Cholera Years, The United States in 1832, 1849 and 1866* (Chicago, 1968).
[19] F. B. Smith, *The People's Health 1830–1910* (London, 1979), pp. 197–8.
[20] StA Hbg, MK II G 6 Bd. 1, Bl. 65 ff.

fair and "fattened up" during the year, then to be slaughtered and used for subsistence'.[21] As late as 1908, pigs were still being kept in the Borstellmansweg, a working-class street in the suburb of Hamm, by a milk trader who lived in the cellar of Number 4. At the same time, some 1,500 pigs were being maintained in the Billwärder Ausschlag, The local branch of the Property-Owners' Association and the local Citizens' Club had both sent in numerous complaints about them.[22] One irate inhabitant wrote in April 1908 that 'the main centre of miasmas, the source of penetrating repulsive smells on hot summer days, the breeding-place of rats, is and remains the pigsty, especially it if is inadequately cemented, dilapidated and, as it very often is, connected with a closet and sleeping-place of the obscurest kind.'[23] Apart from the smell, the main objection to pigsties was the encouragement they gave to rats. As another inhabitant put it, 'We inhabitants and associations of the Billwärder Ausschlag have long been fighting against rats and mice in this suburb. It is impossible to remove or exterminate these animals so long as the maintenance of pigs is not forbidden.'[24] An official inspection revealed that rats had gnawed through the floorboards of houses in the area.[25] Poison had been laid down but to little effect because 'under the floors there are defective sewage pipes, out of which fresh rats are perpetually emerging'.[26]

Rats were a particular problem in a port such as Hamburg, where they regularly arrived on ships coming from all corners of the globe and disembarked to find rich nourishment in the warehouses and stores on the quayside and along the canals. The human inhabitants of the city seem to have accepted them as the inevitable accompaniment to life in a harbour town, and little was done to combat them other than to engage dogs and cats known for their ratting abilities. In 1899, however, as a new pandemic of bubonic plague was sweeping the globe, the Imperial Health Office in Berlin awoke to the possibility that immigrant rats might bring the disease with them when they landed. Instructions duly went out to all German ports to take measures to curb the sea-borne inflow of rodents. The Hamburg authorities were forced to admit 'there are also very many rats in the city, namely in the warehouses situated along the canals and in many dwellings'. According to one local newspaper, indeed, there was currently a veritable 'Rat War' raging in St Georg.[27] In order to try and reduce the numbers of rats landing in the port, anti-rat devices were fitted to mooring ropes, ship's

[21] *SHS* 15 (1894), 150–66; A. Obst, *Geschichte der Hamburger Bürgervereine* (Hamburg, 1911), p. 77; StA Hbg, PP S3496 Bd. 1: *Hamburger Echo*, 12 July 1894.

[22] *SHS* 15 (1894), 150–66; StA Hbg, MK II G 6 Bd. 2, Bl. 56a, 59.

[23] Ibid. Bl. 45: *Neue Hamburger Zeitung*, 30 Apr. 1908.

[24] Ibid. Bl. 40h: *Hamburger Fremdenblatt*, 16 Aug. 1908.

[25] Ibid. Bl. 40n.

[26] Ibid. : *Hamburger Fremdenblatt*, 28 Aug. 1908.

[27] StA Hbg, MK III C 2 Bd. 1, Bl. 30: Bericht über eine Beratung, betreffend Massnahmen zur Verhüthung der Einschleppung der Pest durch *Ratten* in Hamburg, 10 Oct. 1899; ibid., Bl. 47: *Hamburgischer Correspondent*, 4 Nov. 1899.

gangways were removed at night, and rat poison was laid down on board all incoming ships. The police offered a reward of 5 Pfennigs for every dead rat delivered to them, and soon the 'Hamburg Rat War' (*Hamburger Rattenkrieg*) was being discussed in all the daily newspapers. But it was not a great success. The 'result' as one newspaper reported on 16 February, 'was a very poor one'.[28] A 'Survey of Rats Brought in' was compiled by the police and showed that when the 'Rat War' was declared officially over, only 2,616 rodents had been collected. This was a miserable result, especially when it is remembered that 5 Pfennigs was far from negligible a sum; 75 rats would bring in the rough equivalent of a day's wages for an unskilled labourer on a 12-hour shift. In reality the Rat War was doomed from the start because, as Dr Arnold Versmann explained, 'This reward of 5 Pfennigs for every dead rat brought in was only offered for a period of three weeks, so as not to make it possible for industrious individuals to breed rats and offer the young ones for the reward, and also to prevent the possibility of dead rats being imported'. Thus too little time was available for a really thorough campaign to be waged, and Versmann was forced to confess that the many buildings still 'infested with rats' at the end of the Rat War included not only the Customs Offices and the City Engineer's Department but also the harbour police station itself. In addition, while he was on the subject, he pointed out that the railway dyke intended to prevent the flooding of the river Bille 'serves as a dwelling-place for innumerable mice, so that the turf has died off and the security of the dyke has been endangered'.[29] Disappointed with the results of the 'Rat War', the Senate went on to appoint two official rat-catchers for the quayside.[30] Most people, however, were content to keep the rodents at bay with one of the many proprietory brands of rat poison on offer in the city, such as 'Apothecary E. Hammerschmidt's *rat sausages* with scent',[31] and no more was heard of official efforts to deal with the problem.

Rats, notoriously, brought with them swarms of fleas and lice, which were also encouraged by the presence of other animals in the city. In the early years of the poor-law regime instituted in 1788, investigations had revealed 'whole courtyards full of the lowest creatures' including '2,000 children of these poor people ... dressed in rags and covered in vermin', and a special hospital, the Scabies House (*Krätzehaus*), was temporarily constructed to try to eradicate the widespread infection of scabies in these quarters. Little seems to have changed in the century following these revelations. The Housing Inspection Law (*Wohnungspflegegesetz*) of 1898, which instituted for the first time a regular inspection of sanitary and health conditions in the houses of

[28] Ibid., Bl. 134: *Hamburger Neueste Nachrichten*, 16 Feb. 1900.

[29] BA Koblenz R86/954, Bd. 1, Zusammenstellung der in Hamburg bestehenden Anordnungen zur Durchführung des Reichsgesetzes (etc.), Dec. 1902, Anlage 8: A. Versmann, 'Massnahmen zur Vernichtung der Ratten im Hamburgischen Staate', pp. 6–8.

[30] Ibid., Bl. 148 (report of 26 Feb. 1900).

[31] Ibid., Bl. 168.

the poor, revealed a widespread infestation of the Alley Quarters and other working-class areas with vermin and parasites of various kinds, above all fleas, mites, bedbugs, lice, and beetles. These often proved very difficult to eradicate. There was no effective chemical means of disposing of mites until 1911, for example.[32] The childhood experience of Wilhelm Wachendorf, whose parents were forced to move into rooms in a courtyard off the Fuhlen-twiete, round the corner from the Niedernstrasse, when their old house was demolished in the 1880s to make way for the new harbour facilities, was probably far from untypical:

The apartment was completely bug-ridden. Moreover the kitchen was swarming with cockroaches, so-called firebugs ... All our furniture was infested with bugs, especially the beds. Things were particularly lively around the pictures that were hanging on the walls, for there were whole nests of bugs sitting underneath the wallpaper. ... [On] Sunday the fire was lit early in the kitchen, so that boiling water would be at hand. Then my parents placed the furniture in the middle of the room and tore the paper off the walls and burnt it straightaway. The bugs vanished in wild panic into cracks in the walls and floorboards. Next my parents poured hot water over the walls and floors. I did the same in the bedroom. Here the beds were taken apart and treated with soap and water ... [The] kitchen was completely cleared, then we carefully poured paraffin over the floor and ignited it. Thousands of firebugs were incinerated with a loud cracking noise, but many hid themselves in the cracks. For months my parents had to repeat this laborious process every Sunday, just to get the vermin to some extent under control. However, we never got rid of them entirely, for the apartment beneath us was an ideal breeding-place for these animals. A married couple lived there; the wife was blind and did not notice the firebugs even when they fell into the saucepan while she was cooking. The couple didn't mind fishing the vermin out of the food. Both of them were well-nourished and they had simply got used to the bugs.[33]

As late as 1911, there were complaints in Hamburg about 'the enormous extent of scabies infestation, mostly combined with lice in the clothes and hair. 1,198 male and 415 female patients have been treated for scabies in St Georg alone.'[34] By this time, measures to uncover and deal with these prob-lems had been in operation for some years: two decades before, such infes-tations were probably more widespread, and more generally tolerated.

III

Vermin and parasites afflicted the poor not least because few of them ever had the opportunity to take a bath. The great majority of houses in the older,

---

[32] StA Hbg, MK II G 15 Bd. 1, Bl. 60; B. Mehnke, *Armut und Elend in Hamburg* (Ergebnisse, Heft 17; Hamburg, 1982), pp. 20–1, 73.

[33] Wachendorf, 'Im Gängeviertel', pp. 19–20.

[34] StA Hbg, MK III H 12 Bd. 1, Bl. 10: Sitzung, betr. Bekämpfung der Krätze, 25 Feb. 1911.

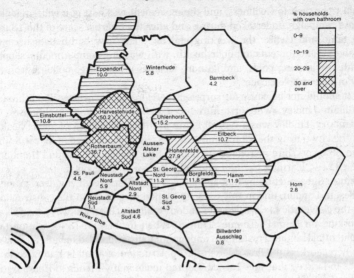

Eppendorf
10.0

Winterhude
5.8

Barmbeck
4.2

Eimsbuttel
10.8

Harvestehude
50.2

Uhlenhorst
15.2

Eilbeck
10.7

Rotherbaum
36.7

Aussen-
Alster
Lake

Hohenfelde
27.9

St. Pauli
4.5

Neustadt
Nord
5.9

Altstadt
Nord
2.9

St. Georg
Nord
11.3

Borgfelde
11.8

Hamm
11.9

Horn
2.8

Neustadt
Süd
1.1

Altstadt
Süd 4.6

St. Georg
Süd
4.3

Billwärder
Ausschlag
0.8

River Elbe

% households
with own bathroom

0–9

10–19

20–29

30 and
over

Source: SHS 20 (1902), Table 53g

MAP 17. Percentage of households with own bathroom, by district, Hamburg 1892

poorer districts were without bathing facilities, as Map 17 clearly shows. While the majority of households in Harvestehude, the richest district in the city, had their own bathroom, the figure in the poorest districts was generally less than 5%. The proportion of households with their own bathroom correlated by district with average per capita income at the level of 0.96, and with the proportion of manual workers in the occupied population (negatively) at the level of −0.89. The newer tenement blocks were usually provided with communal bathrooms but in the older parts of the city such as the Alley Quarters, water usually had to be carried into the apartment from a common tap in the courtyard. In earlier centuries there had been a number of public baths in the city, where haircutting, manicure, and even minor surgical operations had been carried out. But these had been closed down in the course of the eighteenth century because they were thought to spread disease. The modern public bathhouse was pioneered in England, where a growing movement, spearheaded by the Association for the Establishment of Baths and Washhouses for the Labouring Poor (1846), brought about the provision of communal bathing facilities in Liverpool, London, and many other cities by the 1850s.[35] Cleanliness, to the British, was popularly

[35] A. S. Wohl, *Endangered Lives*, pp. 72–6; for the correlations, see Table 15, p. 593 below.

said to be next to Godliness, and the movement was part of a wider middle-class campaign undertaken during and after the Chartist scare of the 1840s to tame and civilize the working classes.[36] The new bathhouses became elaborate monuments to public health, with washing compartments, slipper baths, swimming pools, and laundry facilities in one large building fronted by ornate marble façades.

It should not be cause for surprise, therefore, that it was an Englishman, William Lindley, who first introduced public bath- and washhouses to Hamburg. Lindley was a central figure in the improvement of public health in the city during the 1840s and early 1850s. Born in London in 1808, the son of a Yorkshire merchant, he had spent a year in and around Hamburg in 1824–5 learning German and breaking away from his mother's apron-strings. Subsequently he had apprenticed himself to a civil engineer, Francis Giles, in London, and in this capacity he had taken part in the construction of the Newcastle to Carlisle and London to Birmingham Railways, as well as working on Brunel's Thames Tunnel. When in the mid-1830s a group of influential Hamburg merchants and manufacturers decided to build a railway to Bergedorf, as the first stage in the construction of a rail link to Lübeck, it was to Lindley that they turned. He had made many friends in Hamburg in 1824–5, he spoke German, and he was personally recommended by the great Isambard Kingdom Brunel himself. The first railways to be built on the Continent were virually all designed and constructed by Englishmen, with English labour and materials. Lindley came over to Hamburg in 1838 and the railway was successfully completed under his supervision in 1842. By this time, however, he had won a much wider reputation in Hamburg, and he stayed in the city through the 1840s to supervise its reconstruction after the Great Fire in 1842.[37] Lindley was a disciple and acquaintance of the great English sanitary reformer Edwin Chadwick, and one of his most passionately advocated causes was the provision of public bathing and washing facilities. Like Chadwick, Lindley believed that improvements in cleanliness would have far-reaching effects on public order and social peace. His arguments were particularly relevant in the period immediately following the popular agitation and disturbances of the Revolution in 1848. The appeal to the interest of Hamburg's rulers in restoring social harmony and preventing a repetition of the revolutionary outbursts of the 1840s was obvious:

Lack of bodily cleanliness soon leads to lack of self-respect, roughness, and vice. Experience demonstrates that those who have dirty clothing avoid respectable places and therefore have the lowest kind of public house as their haunts. If they can employ an hour or so of their leisure time in taking a bath, then in most cases this will put them off going to the pub ... An unclean population will suffer comparatively high

[36] Wohl, *Endangered Lives*, p. 72.

[37] G. Leo, *William Lindley: Ein Pionier der Technischen Hygiene* (Hamburg, 1969), pp. 13–28. See also Plate 11.

rates of sickness and death, and since the poorer inhabitants of the city will be thrown onto the state finances to cover the costs in all such cases, this tax burden will for the most correspond to the cleanliness of the population. A dirty population degenerates and so commits all the more offences against the laws of the state, thus contributing to the continued need and expansion of our costly prisons ... Lack of cleanliness makes the population all the more receptive to devastating epidemics such as cholera, smallpox, fever, etc., and encourages such diseases to become endemic or to return again. Experience shows that when these epidemics have reached a certain degree of severity they also reach the dwellings of the well-off.[38]

Lindley was thus appealing to the merchant's pockets as well as to their fear of social disorder and disease. The argument that state investment in public health improvement would save money in the long run, expressed here in classic form, was to recur throughout the century and find its supreme justification in the cholera epidemic of 1892. Above all, however, concluded Lindley enthusiastically, 'personal cleanliness also leads to cleanliness in clothing and in the dwelling, and thus in various ways contributes to the increase of well-being and good behaviour'. This was important, he argued, in a reference to the popular disturbances of 1842, because 'lack of well-being encourages the pathological lust for destruction which, given the opportunity (e.g. during the Great Fire) turns against the possessions of the better-off'.[39]

Lindley therefore proposed to erect, at state expense, a public bath and washhouse with facilities for laundering, wringing, drying, and ironing bed linen and clothing. Slipper baths and showers were to be provided for sixty people. 'There must', he insisted, 'be completely separate entries and exits for the two sexes, preferably in two different streets.' There was, in other words, to be no repetition of the immorality for which the bathhouses of early modern Hamburg had been notorious. There should be two classes, 'the first class for so-called humble citizens, the second class for journeymen, workers etc'. Bathing and washing would thus no longer be a luxury. Soap and towels would be provided. The facilities would, of course, he added reassuringly, be 'so simple that as far as possible there will be no competition for the private bathhouses'.[40] These proposals found general support and were soon translated into action. In 1855 the city formally celebrated the official opening of 'the washing and bathing establishment on the Schweinemarkt, constructed along English lines and the first of its kind on the Continent'.[41] By taking this step, Hamburg was even in advance of a number of substantial British towns: ten years later, for example, there were still no public bathing facilities in

---

[38] W. Lindley, *Oeffentliche Wasch- und Bade-Häuser* (Hamburg, 1851), pp. 16–17. I have removed the numbers which appeared before each sentence in the original.
[39] Ibid.
[40] Ibid., pp. 9–10.
[41] *Die Gesundheitsverhältnisse Hamburgs im 19. Jahrhundert* (Hamburg, 1901), p. 73.

Manchester, and as late as 1875 a medical officer of health in East Anglia was still complaining that 'the inhabitants of Ipswich have no means of indulging in the luxury of immersing the whole body in water'.[42] In 1880 a second public bathhouse was erected in Hamburg, the *Hansabad* in the Theaterstrasse, to be followed in 1881 by a third, constructed along similar lines. But three such establishments were hardly sufficient for a city of over half a million. Much of the harbour work that provided the main source of employment in Hamburg was extremely dirty. One contemporary remembered for example how 'in the evening the "green men" could be seen here and there. They came from ships that had been loaded with green rye meal. They had to go home dirty after work because there were as yet no washing facilities in the harbour. So they went around like green devils, hair, face, clothes, and boots all covered in a thick layer of green rye meal.' This was in the 1880s. Many other workers must have encountered similar conditions. Nor can it have been easy to keep clean when so many dwellings, especially in the Alley Quarters, had no running water.[43] William Lindley in his day thought that one public bathhouse was needed for every 50,000 inhabitants. At that rate there should have been a dozen in Hamburg by the 1890s.[44] The great majority of the population continued to deserve the sobriquet 'the Great Unwashed'. This was a British term for the poor; in Germany it was unknown. The nationalist historian Heinrich von Treitschke once complained that the British confused soap with civilization;[45] but he might also have paused to consider the light which this statement cast on the state of public health and private cleanliness among his own compatriots.

IV

The industrialization that changed the structure of Hamburg's population with such speed and intensity in the second half of the nineteenth century also had a profound effect on the environment in which that population lived. No one would wish to underestimate the squalor of the early modern town, but as we have already seen, the simple increase in size of towns in the century aggravated traditional nuisances and made them harder to deal with and more serious in their effects. To old-established and only slowly eradicated sources of filth and disease were added as the century progressed new and more serious environmental problems brought on by the growth of industry and the rapid increase in the urban population. As the supply of coal from English and German coal-mines became cheaper and more plentiful, the

[42] Wohl, *Endangered Lives*, p. 74.

[43] *Die Gesundheitsverhältnisse*, p. 73; Wachendorf, 'Im Gängeviertel', p. 15.

[44] Lindley, *Oeffentliche Wasch- und Bade-Häuser*, p. 9.

[45] Cited in D. Blackbourn and G. Eley, *The Peculiarities of German History: Bourgeois Society and Politics in Nineteenth-century Germany* (Oxford, 1984), p. 219.

opportunities for gathering fuel from the wild declined with the growing size of towns, and the price of wood began to soar, so people started to switch from wood or peat to coal as their principal means of domestic heating, above all from mid-century onwards. Each newly built housing block with its coal-burning domestic fires and serried ranks of chimneys added to the clouds of unpurified smoke that daily poured into the skies above the city. Greater still was the atmospheric pollution caused by the factories that began to spring up everywhere in the last quarter of the century. Chemical works, glue and candle factories, breweries, guano-processing plants, slaughterhouses, shipbuilding and engineering yards, bleaching, dyeing, and cleaning establishments, jam and pickle factories, tar works, and a host of other plants in the manufacturing, processing, and servicing industries[46] multiplied with extraordinary rapidity in Hamburg, above all after the city joined the Customs Union in 1888. By 1890 all of them were belching vast quantities of noxious vapours into the atmosphere every day, and members of the Citizens' Assembly were complaining 'that the smoke nuisance in Hamburg has already assumed massive dimensions and is still continuing to increase, thereby most seriously affecting the life and health of its inhabitants'.[47] As early as the 1870s, when the effects of air pollution were first becoming generally visible in German cities, Karl Scheffler wrote that the visitor to Hamburg saw 'everything as if through a veil, for the smoke from a thousand chimneys spread over everything like a drifting mist and ran together with the atmosphere of the grey, wet day'.[48] Hamburg indeed was almost as foggy as London. 'The smoke nuisance', noted a newspaper reporter in 1899, 'is well known to be very considerable for us in Hamburg particularly when the air is humid and oppressive and when—as so often—there is fog.'[49] In fact, heavy air pollution actually created more fog, as water condensed around the particles of soot and ash floating through the air. Between 1877 and 1885 Hamburg counted an average of 130 foggy days a year, and enjoyed some 500 fewer hours of sun each year than Heligoland. It was described as 'one of the greatest sooty cities of Germany', and a committee noted in 1899 that 'the masses of smoke that are permanently situated over our cities' gave 'a gloomy and unpleasant appearance ... to whole areas of the city' and 'encourage the creation of dirty fog'.[50] And for travellers coming towards

[46] Wohl, *Endangered Lives*, pp. 205–32, gives some idea of the variety of noxious fumes created by 19th-century industry.

[47] *Bürgerschaft* 29 Dec. 1890.

[48] K. Scheffler, *Der junge Tobias. Eine Jugend und ihre Umwelt* (Hamburg and Munich, 1962), p. 21.

[49] StA Hbg, MK II E 6 Bd. 1: *Neue Hamburger Zeitung*, 25 Jan. 1899.

[50] G. Spelsberg, *Rauchplage*, p. 77, citing A. Reich, *Leitfaden für die Russ- und Rauchfrage* (Berlin and Munich, 1917). Spelsberg, loc. cit., notes that there were on average 59 foggy days a year in Munich from 1877 to 1895 and 80 from 1895 to 1905, as an example of the effects of air pollution on the weather. For the 1899 quotations, see StA Hbg, MK II E 6 Bd. 1: Bericht des ... Ausschusses ... betr. die Beseitigung von Rauch und Russ (Bürgerschafts-Drucksache Nr. 39, Oct. 1899).

Hamburg, the first sign that they were nearing their goal was when they 'saw from afar the layer of black air that always hangs over the city'.[51]

Air pollution controls, though they were not very effective, had been in force in Britain and France since the early 1850s, and it was not long before they were adopted by Berlin, Stuttgart, Munich, and other major German cities as well. Characteristically, however, it was many years before Hamburg followed suit. The city's building regulations had nothing to say on the subject apart from obliging factories to discharge their smoke through chimneys higher than the surrounding buildings. This was hardly calculated to overcome the problem, since on still days the soot simply fell straight down to earth. In the poor district of the Billwärder Ausschlag, for example, the factories' 'emissions expel such an amount of fine dust into the air that the inhabitants get attacks of breathlessness when they are asleep at night'.[52] Nearer the centre of the city the inhabitants of the Grosse Theaterstrasse, the Neuer Jungfernstieg, and neighbouring streets complained in 1882 about the 'soot which the chimney of the Public Baths Company ... emits': institutions that brought cleanliness to some evidently brought dirt and pollution to others: or perhaps we are dealing with an early example of artificially created demand. They were 'uncommonly inconvenienced' by the soot, they said, 'so that it is almost impossible to allow the absolutely undoubted necessity of fresh air into our dwellings by opening the windows. As for sitting in our admittedly modest gardens', they added, 'that is quite out of the question.'[53] Nevertheless, as the authorities soon established, the factory chimney, 34 metres high, was clearly in conformity with building regulations. 'In my opinion', observed the responsible official, 'the cause of the nuisance is to be sought less in factory chimneys than in the many surrounding chimneys in general.' The complaint was rejected.[54]

The medical authorities in Hamburg were certainly aware of the dangers to health posed by the clouds of sooty fumes that regularly billowed across the city. 'It cannot ... be denied', wrote Chief Medical Officer Dr Kraus in December 1882, 'that smoke causes a variety of nuisances in this city.' Kraus thought 'that it would be desirable in the interests of public health to improve the situation by means of smoke purification devices', but as he was forced to admit, 'on the other hand there are no legal means by which we can secure

---

[51] C. K. G. Behrmann, *Erinnerungen* (Berlin, 1904), p. 278.

[52] See the relevant motion in *Bürgerschaft* 29 Dec. 1890; and E. Müller, *Kleine Beiträge zur Geschichte des Billwärder Ausschlags* (Hamburg, 1902), p. 24.

[53] The growing street noise in parts of the city in the late 19th century was probably a contributory factor in the shutting of windows and reduction of ventilation. See O. Pelc, ' " ... Geräuschloses Pflaster wäre wünschenswert". Die Bemühungen einer Hamburger Schule um Lärmschutz zu Beginn dieses Jahrhunderts', *Hamburgische Geschichts- und Heimatblätter*, 11. 1 (1982), 13–24.

[54] StA Hbg. MK II E 6, Bd. 1, Bl. 22, 25.

the general introduction of smoke purifying systems'.[55] The problem was that purification devices available at the time were extremely inefficient. Buildings Inspector Olshausen noted that the public trials of the products of 'Schornburg's Patent Soot and Spark-Catcher Factory, Berlin' in 1882 had been 'not very good'. The 'whole structure' he declared, was 'very primitive'.[56] Little had changed by the time the *Hamburger Fremdenblatt* came to consider the problem in 1898:

Since 1890 the Building Control Office has issued permission for the construction of factories only on condition that care will be taken to provide soot-free power generation. Although this order was made in the interests of the population's health, little could be observed by way of its implementation. The by-law seemed to exist only on paper, a fact to which the inhabitants of those parts of the city that are blessed with industrial estates can certainly bear witness. Some of them have suffered so much from falling soot that they have not been able to open their windows at times.[57]

The new measures taken in 1890, even if they were for the moment a dead letter, reflected a more general feeling that something had to be done. On 29 December the same year, the Citizens' Assembly actually set up a special committee to investigate the problem.[58] It proceeded, however, at a pace that was leisurely even by Hamburg standards: its first report did not appear until almost a whole decade had passed, in 1899.

The reason why the problem of air pollution proved so intractable was because, like so many other public health issues it became the object of a clash of interests between the different fractions of capital in the city. Soot and smoke affected first and foremost the profitability of landlordism. Tenants were unwilling to pay high rents for apartments made dirty and unpleasant to live in by smoke and soot from nearby factories. Even the fabric of the houses themselves was at risk; as the local branch of the German Engineers' Association noted in 1882,

Soot is the most unpleasant part of smoke for all of us, and this is not only because of its dirtiness. It also damages and destroys our property, such as fabrics, furniture, carpets, etc. Moreover it is well known that it has a destructive effect on zinc roofing, because the fall of soot mixes with the humidity of the atmosphere and as a result of the combination, a sulphuric acid compound is formed, which comes from the burning of coal with its sulphurous content, and so creates the galvanic cell.[59]

Nearly two decades later, in 1899, a committee declared that it was clear 'that the smoke nuisance brings with it considerable damage to property

[55] Ibid., Bl. 26, report of Kraus, 29 Dec. 1882.
[56] Ibid., Bl. 25. For the general background, see Spelsberg, *Rauchplage*, pp. 92–104.
[57] StA Hbg, MK II E 6, Bd. 1, Bl. 104: *Hamburger Fremdenblatt*, 7 Oct. 1899.
[58] *Bürgerschaft*, 29 Dec. 1890.
[59] StA Hbg, MK II E 6, Bd. 1: Bezirksverein deutscher Ingenieure zu Hamburg: Aus der Versammlung am 5. December 1882.

through the dirt that forms on public and private buildings, monuments and statues, people's clothes, and the wares displayed in open stores or windows'.[60] In fact the great bulk of smoke and soot in the city was probably caused by domestic fires.[61] 'Experts maintain', as one newspaper reported in 1898, '... that the soot which is permanently flying around makes it virtually impossible to open any windows in the whole city at times. Apart from unsatisfactory coal heating, it is the chimneys and fireplaces of private houses that are to blame.'[62] But landlords were unwilling to support legislation to enforce or encourage the use of smokeless fuel or even to improve the standard and frequency of chimney-sweeping because the resulting expense would either reduce the margin of profit in rents, or affect the ability of tenants to pay, or both.[63] And, as the *Neue Hamburger Zeitung* noted in January 1899, 'The situation with regard to chimney-sweeping is not always optimal because of the completely free competition that obtains here in the chimney-sweeping trade'.[64]

What the Property-Owners' Association wanted, therefore, was the imposition of restrictions on air pollution caused by industrial rather than by domestic sources. Most of the deputies whose motion caused the Citizens' Assembly to set up the committee on smoke and soot in 1890 were prominent in the Property-Owners' Association, and the resolution which they succeeded in passing charged the committee with considering 'what legal requirements or institutions should be considered necessary in Hamburg from the point of view of hygiene, in order to secure the removal of smoke and soot, namely in industrial enterprises'.[65] When the committee reported in 1899 it re-emphasized the fact that 'As far ... as the origin of the smoke and soot problem is concerned, public opinion is inclined, as everybody knows, to seek it in factories and industrial enterprises'.[66] It recommended tougher measures against factories that persistently emitted sooty smoke, and the adoption of a requirement for factories to use smokeless fuel.[67] Not surprisingly, those close to the factory owners complained that these recommendations were 'exclusively directed against industrial power generation, while ordinary households are permitted to discharge their smoke and soot into their environs'.[68] 'Industry', said one speaker in the Citizens' Assembly, 'is not the main culprit, for industry saves fuel where it can; the blame lies with faulty heating

[60] Ibid., Bl. 117a: Bericht des ... Ausschusses ... betr. die Beseitigung von Rauch und Russ (Bürgerschafts-Drucksache, Nr. 39, Oct. 1899).

[61] Cf. Wohl, *Endangered Lives*, pp. 205–32.

[62] StA Hbg, MK II E 6 Bd. 1, Bl. 104: *Hamburger Fremdenblatt*, 7 Oct. 1898.

[63] Ibid., Bl. 117a: *Hamburgischer Correspondent*, 2 Nov. 1899, speech of P. Müller. Cf. ibid., Bericht ... (Oct. 1899), p. 3.

[64] StA Hbg, MK II E 6 Bd. 1, Bl. 106.

[65] *Bürgerschaft*, 29 Dec. 1890.

[66] StA Hbg, MK II E 6 Bd. 1, Bl. 117a: Bericht ... (Oct. 1899).

[67] Ibid., Bl. 117a : *Hamburgischer Correspondent*, 2 Nov. 1899.

[68] Ibid., Bl. 118: *Hamburger Nachrichten*, 21 Oct. 1899.

in households.' The measures recommended by the committee would place 'a great burden on industry'.[69] A similar clash of interests occurred in 1896 when a number of inhabitants and businesses in the harbour area complained that the burning of cheap coal by floating winches, tugs, and steamboats 'creates a pall of smoke that often darkens the light of day, stops the opening of windows in offices and storerooms, and causes considerable damage among the goods kept in the warehouses'. Although the interests of the merchants were affected by this nuisance, an attempt by the Senate to force the boatmen to use coke ran into 'the greatest opposition'.[70]

In the end, a characteristically voluntaristic compromise was reached. All concerned agreed in putting most of the blame for the pollution of the air by factories and steam tugs on ignorant and untrained stokers. Steps were taken to improve the training of these workers.[71] Prosecutions against factory owners for air pollution ceased; in any case, they had mostly been unsuccessful or had been overturned on appeal.[72] Instead, the Senate encouraged the formation of an Association for Boiler Maintenance and Smoke Reduction, which it supported with an annual grant of 10,000 Marks as a sort of block subscription for all the relevant state installations such as the incineration plant and the slaughterhouse. The Association, which was called into being by the Industrial Commission of the Chamber of Commerce, experimented with new smoke purification devices and new kinds of smokeless fuel.[73] It was hoped that in this way the problem of air pollution would be overcome by voluntary means. This hope, of course, was in the end sadly misplaced. The financial interests at stake were too great for voluntary action to have any great effect.

The problem of smoke and soot does not seem to have become serious in Hamburg until the 1880s, at least to judge from the sources. By this stage not only was the use of coal very widespread in domestic heating, but the creation of the free port was also beginning to cause a massive expansion of ancillary industries. The chronology and spread of traditional environmental pollution from animal sources was different. While cows and pigs more or less disappeared from the inner city early in the century, increasing overcrowding and population density probably led to a growth in verminous infestation that was only partly counteracted by the opening of public baths and not at all by private washing facilities, which probably deteriorated, especially in the Alley Quarters. The increase in trade brought more rats to the city; the expansion of the city brought more pigs and their associated nuisances in the suburbs. Environmental pollution of these kinds was easier

---

[69] Ibid., Bl. 117a: *Hamburgischer Correspondent*, 2 Nov. 1899.
[70] Ibid., Bl. 127: Mitteilung des Senats an die Bürgerschaft, No. 83 (6 May 1901), p. 1.
[71] Ibid. p. 6.
[72] Ibid., Bl. 107: *Hamburger Fremdenblatt*, 7 Oct. 1898.
[73] Ibid., Bl. 162–3. See Spelsberg, *Rauchplage*, for a similar failure of controls elsewhere.

for the well-off to escape than the poor. The richest, as we saw in Chapter 1, began to move out of the city, first to the suburbs, then even further away, to villas built along the River Elbe across the Prussian border, as soon as conditions began to become cramped and unhealthy, above all between the 1860s and the turn of the century. The long-established custom of maintaining a summer house in the countryside, and the gradual move to wealthy downriver suburbs, was not simply a sign of nostalgia for rural life; still less can it be seen as a sign of the incipient 'feudalization' of the Hamburg bourgeoisie. In truth, Hamburg's rich fled the inner city in the summer for health reasons, much as the rulers of the British Raj departed for the hill stations as soon as the hot season set in. As Heinrich Merck later recalled, this custom went back even to the days when the merchants lived in the inner city. At that time,

the provision of light and air must have been less than optimal, because the individual plots of land ... were narrow, built wall to wall, and backed on to the undoubtedly often evil-smelling canals. So it is understandable that those Hamburgers who could afford it had already begun generations before to live in the city only during the winter, and to establish a country retreat for themselves in the hinterland during the summer.[74]

18 Senators owned summer villas outside the city in 1842, and 14 in 1861, although the great majority of them had their permanent residence in the inner city.[75] Virtually all the nuisances which afflicted Hamburg, from rotten food and sour milk, smoke and dust, animal smells and ordure, vermin, parasites, and rats, were at their most unbearable in the summer months. The wealthiest taxpayers did little to improve the city's environment until they were forced to, because they could always escape from it when it became unbearable. Those who remained—the great mass of the poor and the impecunious—had to bear the brunt of conditions that steadily worsened as the century went on.

b. *The Politics of Pollution*

I

The world the merchants made in nineteenth-century Hamburg was a dirty world. Almost the first thing that a visitor would see on entering the city was the filth that littered the streets, above all away from the main thoroughfares. The 'loamy soil' on which most of Hamburg was built had the effect, as a report issued in 1879 noted,

[74] StA Hbg, FA Merck II 9 Konv. 4a, Heft II, p. 2.
[75] Ibid., FA Voigt B 68.

that any more considerable burden of traffic immediately forces a tough, greasy dirt up through the gaps in the cobbles; in the short dry season this becomes dust, in the much longer period of fine, dustlike rain it is formed into that well-known mass of filth that resists all attempts to clear it away and always calls forth general complaints when it lasts for any length of time.[1]

The streets were befouled not only, as today, by dogs, of which there were said to be an 'enormous number', perhaps as many as 25,000, in the city as early as 1810, but also by the thousands of horses that provided almost the only means of transport. Numerous cattle, pigs, sheep, goats, hens, ducks, and geese were driven through the streets daily on their way to the market or the slaughterhouse and added their contribution to the already considerable accumulation of filth in the streets. In 1888 it was estimated that over 190,000 cubic metres of rubbish and 100,000 cartloads of dung were annually removed from the streets of Berlin, while some 20,000 cubic metres of dung and other refuse were taken away every year from the streets of the much smaller town of Bremen. Horses and other animals thus probably dropped about 7,200,000 kilos or just over 7,000 tons of dung on to the streets of Hamburg every year.[2] The daily accumulation of ordure on the streets of Hamburg created serious problems at every season. When it rained it turned to mud and made it difficult to walk untainted through the streets. In winter, despite frequent warnings and fines, the inhabitants generally took little notice of police orders to clear away the snow from the area around their houses[3]; the result was, as one commentator noticed early in the century, that

the trodden-down snow thus turns to ice, and these masses of ice are made still higher by the daily loads of washing-up water that are poured over them and by the snow shovelled onto them from the courtyards, so that finally they become so hilly that one takes one's life in one's hands if one enters the streets where the poor live.[4]

[1] StA Hbg, Senat, Cl. VII, Lit. Cc, No. 3b, Vol. 54: Bericht des von der Bürgerschaft am 27. März 1878 niedergesetzten Ausschusses zur Berathung von Massregeln betreffend Verbesserung der Gassenreinigung und Abfuhr in Stadt und Vororten, p. 385; J. H. Scholz, *Freimüthige und bescheidene Rügen einer hamburgischen Polizei-Mängel nebst unmassgeblichen Vorschlägen zu ihrer Abstellung. Eine patriotische Schrift zur Beherzigung für Gesetz-Geber und Gesetz-Pflichtige* (Hamburg, 1810), pp. 38–9.
[2] StA Hbg, Senat, Cl. VII, Lit. Cc, No. 3b, Vol. 61: M. Knauff, 'Behandlung fester Stadtabfälle', *Gläser's Annalen für Gewerbe und Bauwesen*, No. 263 (1 June 1888), p. 219; calculation for Hamburg on the basis of Knauff's estimates for a city of 100,000 inhabitants. This compares with a contemporary estimate that 20,000 tons of manure were deposited on the streets of London every year in the 1850s (Wohl, *Endangered Lives*), p. 81. See also Corbin, *Pesthauch*, pp. 154–6.
[3] See StA Hbg, BD B1550, report by Ingenieur Westphalen (Bl. 9; 14 Jan. 1847).
[4] J. J. Rambach, *Versuch einer physisch-medizinischen Beschreibung von Hamburg* (Hamburg, 1801), pp. 29–30.

By contrast, of course, the streets of the rich were seldom allowed to get into such a parlous state: all they had to do was to have the snow cleared away by their servants.

If snow, mixed with dirt and filth from the street, was a problem in winter, then dust was the major nuisance in the summer. The human and animal ordure in the courtyards and on the streets mingled with ashes removed from domestic fires to form a fine, choking dust that dirtied people's clothes and made it difficult to breathe. By long-hallowed tradition the Senate sent water wagons round on these days to sprinkle their contents on to the streets and so damp down the dust. The problem with the sprinkling was that most of it had to be paid for by the inhabitants of the streets in question.[5] A series of petitions from the Central Committee of the Citizens' Clubs in May 1889 put this point with particular clarity:

As is well known, at present a small number of streets in the inner city and some of the better-frequented turnpikes such as 'an der Alster' etc., are sprinkled with water at public expense; however, in the great majority of streets the cost of sprinkling by the state waterworks must be provided by private collection; finally a third part of our city, where nobody will take the trouble or bear the rejections encountered in such collecting activities, or where there is less traffic and so less of a nuisance to be felt as a result of insufficient dampening of the street dust, does without the water-sprinklers altogether, even in the hottest weeks of the year!

'This system', concluded the petition, 'which is hardly worthy of the name, conceals within it a considerable health hazard.'[6] This view was very widespread. 'The conditions which obtain in Hamburg in respect of street cleaning are absolutely unworthy of a great city', declared a committee of the Citizens' Assembly in 1885: 'they approach those which obtain in isolated provincial towns that lie off the main roads, and which may well be appropriate in such places.'[7]

The only really effective method of cleaning the accumulated refuse off the streets, indeed, was by a really heavy and lengthy rainstorm. Most streets had a gutter in the middle, and along this flowed the used cleaning, cooking, or washing-up water from the houses on either side. These gutters were not always effective: in 1871, for example, an inspection revealed that many of the smaller streets in the Altstadt were badly plastered, 'the gutters unsatisfactory', and 'heaps of dirt in many places'[8] But sooner or later most of the

---

[5] StA Hbg, BD B1553, *passim*. For reminiscences of the dust and the water-sprinklers, see StA Hbg, FA Merck II 9 Konv. 4a, Heft II, pp. 2–4.

[6] StA Hbg, Senat Cl. VII, Lit. Cc, No. 3b, Vol. 59.

[7] Ibid., Drucksache Nr. 17: Zweiter Bericht des von der Bürgerschaft am 14. Mai 1884 niedergesetzten Ausschusses über den Antrag von Dr. Gerson, betreffend Abänderung des Regulativs der Stadtwasserkunst, p. 3.

[8] StA Hbg, MK II G4 Bd. 1: Bericht über die Ergebnisse der Sanitäts-Revision im I. Physicatsbezirk von 5. September bis 10. October 1871.

water found its way into one of the fleets (*Fleete, Flethe*, or canals), that criss-crossed the city, above all in the Altstadt. Many houses backing onto the fleets actually had lavatories attached to their outer walls, from which the excrement simply fell into the canal below. As an observer noted early in the century,

Those who live on the fleets can make them without embarrassment the recipients of their bestial evacuations, and indeed this is done by everyone. Moreover a multitude of chamber-pots are emptied into them from the bridges every night, and with such carelessness, that a large part of their disgusting contents is left lying on the bridge itself.[9]

Alongside a few of the broader streets, and by the Horsemarket (*Pferdemarkt*), there also ran low open ditches, called *Haasenmoore*, filled with 'a perpetual slime'. 'When a thunderstorm follows a long drought', it was reported, 'the whole mass rises with a dreadful stink, and flows into the Alster, the Elbe, or a fleet.'[10]

Hamburg's human and animal wastes were mainly disposed of, as in other German towns, by carting them away. Ashes, kitchen waste, and general rubbish were carried off by private enterpreneurs. Until the 1840s these private undertakings also provided the only means, apart from ditches and canals, of removing the excrement from the city. The authorities issued concessions for street cleaning and waste disposal to the individuals or firms offering the lowest tender.[11] They in turn were supposed to send round street-cleaning carts (*Gassenkummerwagen*) daily to every street, but given the basis on which the concessions were offered it is not surprising that the service provided was less than perfect. At the beginning of the century Dr Johann Rambach reported that

The carts certainly do not come every day into every street ... They are so leaky that they lose a good part of their loathsome contents again, and they are uncovered. So whenever there is even the slightest breeze, they are surrounded by a cloud of ashes that almost takes the breath away from passers-by. For this reason they sometimes also spread a horrible smell around them, particularly in narrow streets and alleys where one can barely get out of their way.

'In front of the entrance to the courtyards and alleyways', reported another observer in 1810 of a walk through the Neustadt, 'lay upturned chamber-pots, heaps of straw, and other heaped-up rubbish', despite the existence of wagons that were supposed to carry this mess away.[12] Moreover, the street-

[9] Rambach, *Versuch*, pp. 47–8.
[10] Ibid., p. 50.
[11] *Die Gesundheitsverhältnisse*, useful brief account of these arrangements (p. 42); but see also below, n. 65. The experience of Hamburg, discussed below, indicates that this business was by no means as lucrative as the material which forms the basis for Dickens's novel *Our Mutual Friend*, whose plot turns on the inheritance of a dustheap in London, would suggest.
[12] Rambach, *Versuch*, p. 28; Scholz, *Freimüthige und bescheidene Rügen*, p. 19.

cleaning carts were not obliged to cart off dead animals, which was the job of the city knacker (*Abdecker*). In the early nineteenth century animal corpses often lay in the streets for days. In 1810 one observer noted that 'In one passage through the Neustadt we counted nineteen dead dogs and cats rotting away here and there in the alley-ways'. This was said to be particularly bad in St Georg, where Dr Rambach reported that he had 'seen dead pigs and dogs lying around for months on end, gnawed at by thousands of the most revolting maggots and continuing to insult the sense of smell of the passer-by until they were completely reduced to skeletons by that army of anatomists'.[13]

The first tentative steps to improve the situation were taken in 1819, when it was reported that the current holder of the concession had only 'kept 22 carts, which is obviously too small a number for the whole city; thus the street-cleaning operation, as is notorious, has been extremely unsatisfactory'. It was thought that a minimum of 35 carts was necessary if the city were to be properly cleaned every day. After lengthy calculations about the possible cost, it was decided to renegotiate the contract and provide new, tougher conditions to which the concessionary had to adhere.[14] Thus the Senate hoped that 'complaints about the extraordinary filthiness of the alley-ways will cease'. At the same time it re-issued a decree of 1814 according to which

1. Nobody may pour or throw impurities from his house on to the street or on to public places, on pain of a fine of 1 Reichstaler for every contravention ...
2. The same fine shall also be levied on those who relieve themselves of their impurities by day or night from the walls or quays, and parents are reminded to forbid their children from indulging in such filthy habits, otherwise they themselves will be held responsible.
3. No one may throw straw or other rubbish into the fleets and canals, on pain of a fine of 2 Reichstalers.[15]

By the 1830s, however, these decrees were being widely disregarded. In February 1831, for instance, the concessionary was reprimanded because 'a great deal of rubbish which should have been cleared away by you has been left behind on many streets in the Neustadt, which is now free of snow and ice; namely there have been complaints that ... such rubbish is lying in heaps as well as spread around over the cobbles'.[16] There were further complaints in 1836,[17] while in 1852 it was noted that the concessionary's wagons were still spilling their load onto the streets after the manner described so graphically by Dr Rambach half a century earlier.[18]

In 1850 things actually got worse, as the Senate went over from offering

[13] Scholz, op. cit., p. 19; Rambach, op. cit., p. 28.
[14] StA Hbg. Senat, Cl. VII, Lit. Cc, No. 3b, Vol. 32, Bl. 1, 5 (p. 8).
[15] Ibid.: Bekanntmachung 1 Dec. 1819.
[16] StA Hbg, BD B1547, notice of 10 Feb. 1831.
[17] Ibid., Notice of 24 July 1839; StA Hbg, BD B1549, notice of 2 Aug. 1836.
[18] StA Hbg, BD B1548, *passim*.

the contract to the lowest tender to offering it to the highest bidder. This extraordinary situation, in which the concessionary now had to pay the state for the right to cart off rubbish, dung, and human excrement from the streets and courtyards of the city, lasted until 1869. In 1855 the Senate received 14,925 Marks Courant from this source.[19] The move was made because the Senate noticed that the concessionaries were earning considerable sums of money from selling what they collected to farmers. In 1831, for example, the concessionary was regularly transporting the dung and excrement to Pinneberg, across the Danish border, where, as he explained, the 'neighbouring localities ... have for ... years based their animal stock and their whole economy on fertilizing their fields with the street dung they buy from me'.[20] It was still being sold to farmers in Holstein and market gardeners in the nearby Vierlande in 1874.[21] The custom of spreading household rubbish and human and animal excrement collected from the city on to the nearby fields provided an important service for the rural and suburban poor. As Wilhelm Kaisen, who grew up in Alsterdorf, just outside Hamburg, as one of the children of a building worker in the 1880s and 1890s, noted,

The light sandy soil of the fields was fertilized with this rubbish in order to improve the meagre crop yield. Since Hamburg's households were all still dependent on coal or coke for their heating, one could still find usable left-over pieces of coal or coke among the rough masses of ash that found their way onto the fields of Alsterdorf. That was a real treasure-house for us children. In autumn we often gathered virtually the whole of our winter fuel from these refuse-strewn fields.[22]

It is doubtful whether the Hamburg Senate had such activities as these in mind when it decided that the city's rubbish could be used with profit by the inhabitants of the surrounding countryside.

The belief that sewage could be profitable was very widespread in nineteenth-century Germany. An official Prussian report compiled in 1865 concluded that 'neither the national economy nor agriculture can for a moment have any doubt that they must demand, with all possible emphasis, the retention of the dung that gathers in the cities'.[23] In Karlsruhe, the local

[19] StA Hbg, Senat, Cl. VII, Lit. Cc, No. 3b, Vol. 54: Bericht des von der Bürgerschaft am 27. März 1878 niedergesetzten Ausschusses zur Berathung von Massregeln betreffend Verbesserung der Gassenreiningung und Abfuhr in Stadt und Vororte (Drucksache Nr. 61, October 1879), p. 383.

[20] Ibid., Vol. 32, Bl. 8.

[21] Ibid., Vol. 48, Bl. 26: Protocolle über die Berathungen der von der Commission zur Berathung verbesserter Einrichtungen für die Gassenreinigung u. w. d. a. eingesetzten Subkommission 5. Febr. – 1. April 1874, p. 2.

[22] W. Kaisen, *Meine Arbeit, Mein Leben* (Munich, 1967), p. 13.

[23] H. Eichhorn, O. Roeder, and C. v. Salviati, *Die Abfuhr und Verwerthung der Dungstoffe in verschiedenen deutschen und ausserdeutschen Städten und darauf bezügliche Vorschläge für Berlin* (Berlin, 1865), pp. 93 ff., quoted in P. Gleichmann, 'Die Verhäuslichung körperlicher Verrichtungen', in P. Gleichmann, J. Goudsblom, and H. Korte (eds.), *Materialien zu Norbert Elias' Zivilisationstheorie* (Frankfurt, 1977), p. 264.

Property-Owners' Association even possessed a 'guano factory' where the dung was processed.[24] In 1871, Professor Bockendahl, a well-known propagandist for public health, in advocating the use of that great British institution, the water-closet, was forced to complain

that every improvement in this connection, every attempt to deal with this subject, encounters among us the narrowest self-interest; that immediately that property which was formerly despised and treated without care or attention is now zealously defended against encroachments in the common interest; that everyone wants to be and remain king of his own muck-heap, and regards the claim that his muck-heap will harm his neighbours as an amazing fantasy, which will seriously insult him in the end if it is persisted in.[25]

Thus attempts to clean up Germany's towns through state action, he concluded, were constantly frustrated. England was more advanced in this respect than Germany, not least because by the middle of the nineteenth century English towns were producing far more waste than English agriculture could use, and the use of sewage farms to treat waste matter was general by the 1880s.[26] In Germany, the import of large quantities of guano from South America from the 1850s, followed by the growth of the chemical fertilizer industry in Germany itself, began to offer farmers a cheaper and more effective way of improving their crop yields than the purchase of human and animal wastes from towns. The cost of removing the excrement grew rapidly as the towns themselves grew in size. Sewage became an increasingly attractive alternative; efficient, regular, effortless, and not that much more expensive than the old methods.[27] But it was not until the late 1870s that the capital city of Prussia and the German Empire began to acquire a comprehensive sewage system with underground pipes connected to water-closets. Until this point, Berlin's human waste products had been disposed of by open gutters in the streets, washed continuously by water from the central waterworks and discharging their untreated effluvia directly into the river. Over 90% of new buildings in the capital were provided with sewers in the first half of the 1880s and by 1890 most of Berlin's houses seem to have been connected. In smaller towns, progress was slower. In 1883, some 9.7 million Prussians lived in towns with more than 2,000 inhabitants, but those municipalities which boasted a sewage system housed only a quarter of this population, and not all of these lived in houses which were connected. As late as 1907, nearly twenty million people in the Prussian countryside possessed no sewage disposal facilities or water-closets at all. All over Germany, therefore,

[24] Ibid., p. 266. For similar evidence on French schemes to turn excrement into profit, see Corbin, *Pesthauch*, p. 155.
[25] Ibid., p. 269, quoting J. Bockendahl, *Das Erd-, Gruben-, Eimer- und modificirte Wasser-Closet in England* (Kiel, 1871).
[26] Wohl, *Endangered Lives*, pp. 100–11.
[27] Gleichmann, 'Die Verhäuslichung', pp. 254–8.

people continued to use privy middens, cesspits, ash closets, and other means of ridding themselves of their excrement right up to the turn of the century and beyond.[28]

II

The situation of Hamburg's waste disposal facilities was different from that of most other German towns in a number of ways. In the first place, the fact that until 1850 at least its excrement and dung was removed at public expense meant that there were relatively few vested interests in blocking the introduction of a sewage system. Secondly, as in so many other respects, the Great Fire of 1842 provided an unusual opportunity for the installation of such a system with the minimum disturbance. Indeed, but for the occurrence of the Great Fire, it is doubtful whether much would have been done in Hamburg in the way of sanitary reform. The city owed its reputation in this field to a chance occurrence. The conditions for a full-scale and influential sanitary reform movement such as existed in England simply were not present in Germany at this time.[29] Beyond this, too, the Great Fire created an atmosphere that was generally favourable to sanitary reform. The man responsible for the introduction of an underground sewage system in Hamburg was the English engineer, William Lindley, to whom, as we have seen, the city also owed its status as the pioneer of the public bath- and washhouse on the continent. After the Great Fire of 1842 Lindley put forward elaborate proposals for the reconstruction of the city along the lines of the latest sanitary developments in his native land. Just as he had explicitly used Liverpool as his model for the public bathhouse, so Lindley used London as a model for the proposed new sewage system. In November 1842 he travelled to London to discuss the city's sewage system with Edwin Chadwick and to inspect the progress so far made. On his return to Hamburg, Lindley set to work adapting the London system to the local peculiarities of the German town. In March 1843, at the behest of the city authorities, he produced a carefully worked out plan, aimed, as he wrote in a series of additions and explanations added to it in July, to bring about the 'removal of the earlier nuisances caused by the outflow of dirty sewage water into the Inner Alster, the little Alster, the Bleichenfleth, and other small canals'. He bolstered his case with public letters of support from Edwin Chadwick. Lindley included a suggestion, which quickly turned out to be wholly unpractical, that some of the costs might be recouped by selling off sewage to farmers as a fertilizer. The main feature of his scheme, however, was that it offered the city a centralized sewage

---

[28] R. Spree, *Soziale Ungleichheit vor Krankheit und Tod: Zur Sozialgeschichte des Gesundheitsbereichs im Deutschen Kaiserreich* (Göttingen, 1981), pp. 125–8.

[29] G. Göckenjan, *Kurieren und Staat machen. Gesundheit und Medizin in der bürgerlichen Welt* (Frankfurt, 1985), p. 111.

collection system with a single outlet into the river. It was thus, not surprisingly, very expensive to construct.[30]

Lindley's scheme quickly ran into fierce opposition. This was mainly on the grounds of its cost; there is no evidence that people in Hamburg considered it the equivalent of a state expropriation of their personal property in their own excrement. The city's chief water engineer, Heinrich Hübbe, considering it his duty to keep down expenditure wherever possible, put forward a counter-proposal for a much cheaper, decentralized system, with each block of houses having its own separate outlet into the Alster or the fleets. After Lindley had defeated him in committee in May 1843, Hübbe took his case to the public. A huge controversy followed, with pamphlets and accusations flying in all directions. Hübbe and his supporters were able to enlist the support of oppositional elements in the Propertied Citizenry who argued that the authorities had no right to construct such a system without obtaining the Citizenry's approval first. It thus became entangled in the constitutional struggles of the period leading up to the 1848 Revolution. Eventually the case was indeed brought to the Citizenry. Here, however, Lindley's plans were now approved, with the qualification that money should be saved by placing the outlet in the harbour instead of downstream on the border with Altona.[31] Construction soon began, at an initial cost of 1.2 million Marks for 11 kilometres of sewage pipes. Severe technical problems, including the digging of Hamburg's first subterranean tunnel, had to be overcome before the system came into operation in 1853. In 1859 St Pauli began to be connected and by 1860 there were some 48 kilometres of sewage pipes in the city.[32] In 1865 the Senate and the Citizens' Assembly decided to set up a commission to make recommendations for the improvement of the system, which was still discharging its effluvia directly into the harbour. As a result, the system was further centralized and a new outlet was built downriver, on the border with Altona, thus removing it as far as possible from the city itself. In the 1870s the outer suburbs were connected and a series of ordinances and by-laws put heavy pressure on the city's inhabitants to have their dwellings connected. This legislative activity culminated in the Sewage Law (*Sielgesetz*) of 1875, which banned the use of the open lavatories on the houses above the fleets. By the early 1890s the authorities were claiming that every house in the city was connected to the central sewage system.[33]

[30] Leo, *William Lindley*, pp. 37–44; Lindley, *Bericht über die Anlage eines neuen Siel-Systems zur Entwässerung der Stadt Hamburg* (Hamburg, March 1843); id., *Erläuterungen zu seinem Berichte über die Anlage eines neuen Sielsystems zur Entwässerung der Stadt Hamburg* (Hamburg, July 1843).

[31] Leo, *William Lindley*, pp. 37–44. See also Plate 12.

[32] Ibid., p. 60.

[33] StA Hbg, Senat, Cl. VII, Lit. Ta, Pars 2, Vol. 11, Fasc., 17, Inv. 1a, *passim*; cf. *Die Gesundheitsverhältnisse*, p. 42. For a study of the technical aspects of the system and a comparison with other sewage systems of the same period, see J. von Simson, *Kanalisation und Städtehygiene im 19. Jahrhundert* (Düsseldorf, 1983).

The gradual extension of the sewage system through the 1850s and 1860s progressively reduced the quantity of dung that the street-cleaning concessionaries could sell to the farmers. At the same time, the rapid growth in the city's population placed an increasing burden on them with respect to the removal of other, less profitable types of garbage. The result was that they became less and less willing to offer the Senate money for the right to clean the streets and cart off the rubbish, while their declining profits forced them to adopt ever more stringent economies in the conduct of their business itself. At this time, for example, the concessionary paid his employees no wages at all; they depended entirely on tips from householders. By the late 1860s even the highest bidder was offering the state 'almost nothing any more' for the concession because, as an official report noted, 'the value of the dung has now been definitively removed almost everywhere because of the spread of the sewage system, and exploitation of the rubbish cannot be brought into the account any more'. In 1869 the Senate returned therefore to the lowest tender system.[34] But by this time the damage had been done. Such was the neglect into which the concessionaries had allowed their business to fall that the police felt obliged in 1870 to issue an official 'notice to the street-cleaning contractors to improve the cleaning of the districts in their charge'. The concessionaries of course replied claiming that they had 'taken excellent care of everything' and could 'not understand ... where the complaints were coming from'. But they had none the less to accept official supervision by the police from this point onwards.[35]

By this time the Senate was having once more to pay out substantial sums of money for street cleaning. The tender accepted for the inner city and the inner suburbs in 1873 stood at no less than 116,000 Marks Courant.[36] Not surprisingly, therefore, the authorities were continually investigating proposals to recoup some of these losses, for example by processing the sewage before it reached the outlet. None of these schemes proved in any way practicable.[37] The only marketable element in the whole waste-disposal system was the horse and other animal dung which was deposited on the streets in ever-increasing quantities.[38] It was not surprising, therefore, that the street-cleaning concessionaries' 'work was set up so that more attention was paid to getting hold of the dung than to cleaning the streets'.[39] Thus complaints continued through the 1870s. In 1874 Senate Syndic Dr Behn

[34] StA Hbg, Senat, Cl. VII, Lit. Cc, No. 3b, Vol. 54: Bericht ... (op. cit., Oct. 1879, n. 19 above) p. 383.
[35] StA Hbg, Polizeibehörde I 44: 'Fernerer Bericht', 24 Jan. 1870.
[36] Ibid.
[37] StA Hbg, BD B1748, *passim*.
[38] C. Kaiser, *Zur Frage der Strassen-Reinigung* (Stuttgart, 1884), p. 29 (copy in StA Hbg, Senat Cl. VII, Lit. Cc, Vol. 56).
[39] StA Hbg, Senat, Cl. VII, Lit. Cc, No. 3b, Vol. 54: Bericht ... (op. cit., Oct. 1879, n. 19 above), p. 383.

admitted that 'the situation is not really any better than it was before', though he added in the same breath that 'it is no worse than in other large cities'.[40] For their part the concessionaries readily admitted that there were too few street-sweepers: in fact it appeared that the street-sweepers were the same men as those who drove the rubbish carts, doing a hasty bit of brushing, mainly for form's sake, between trips.[41] Finally the Chief of Police, Senator Carl Petersen, willingly conceded that 'the checks are not carried out everywhere by his officers as perhaps they should be'.[42]

The situation was, if possible, even worse in the outer suburbs of the city, which were being rapidly built over in the 1870s and 1880s. The urbanization of districts such as Barmbeck and the Billwärder Ausschlag proceeded at a pace far too rapid for the street-cleaning and waste-disposal services to be able to keep up with it. Here too the business was becoming steadily less profitable and more expensive. In 1875, for example, it was reported that Heinrich Schlemann, the concessionary for the Billwärder Ausschlag, received a mere 300 Marks for his services every year. 'The above-mentioned', it was added, 'will probably raise his demands, and indeed not without reason, in so far as a smaller quantity of dung is reaching the carts as a result of the construction of water-closets.'[43] Economies led to complaints that the street-cleaning concessionary 'is neglecting his duties here in the grossest manner!' as the Citizens' Club for the Billwärder Ausschlag was moved to protest in 1880. At least one of the major streets, the Club declared, 'is in such a neglected state that it defies all description. It is covered inches deep in muck and those who are compelled to pass along it literally have to wade through a morass'.[44] Similar protests continued for several years. In 1882 the police noted that in many streets 'filth is lying really deep in the gutter in places'.[45] So numerous were the complaints, indeed, that the concession for the district was eventually withdrawn from the holder in 1884.[46] In Borgfelde it was said in 1882 that some streets were not visited by the garbage carts at all.[47] Nor had matters improved very much in the inner suburbs and city by this time, despite the discussions of the previous decade; in 1882, for example, the 70 men engaged by the concessionary Roggenbau from Eppendorf to remove the garbage and clean the streets in the inner city overnight were also employed by him as farm labourers during the daytime. Not surprisingly, they were said to be carrying out their duties in a semi-comatose state.[48] As

[40] Ibid., Vol. 48: Protocolle ... 1874 (as in n. 21, above).

[41] Ibid., 26 Mar. 1874.

[42] Ibid., Bl. 32: Versammlung der Commission zur Berathung der Reorganisation der Gassenreinigung u. w. d. a. im Rathause am Montage den 20. April 1874.

[43] StA Hbg, Polizeibehörde I 60: Landherrenschaft der Marschlande, Dec. 1875.

[44] Ibid., Bürgerverein Billwärder Ausschlag to Finanzdeputation, 14 Nov. 1880.

[45] Ibid., Polizeibericht, 2 July 1882 (Bericht 2660).

[46] Ibid., report of 29 Mar. 1884.

[47] Ibid., 4 Jan. 1882 for these complaints.

[48] StA Hbg, Polizeibehörde I 44: 'N.N.', 20 Sept. 1882.

a result, the police noted that 'the street-cleaning system is in a poor, indeed a very poor condition'. Heaps of horse dung were lying on the street by the hansom cab stands, and 'very many offences' were reported, most of which went unpunished by the police. There were only four dustmen and street cleaners for the whole of the Hammerbrook, which was rapidly being urbanized at this period.[49] For his part, Roggenbau, the concessionary, protested that he was being persecuted by over-zealous constables ignorant of the true situation; he put much of the blame on the dirty habits of the population.[50] But his protests were hardly convincing in view of the complaints that were now pouring in from all quarters.

Over half a century of experience had thus amply demonstrated the inadequacies of the existing system of street cleaning and garbage disposal. The Senate had made a gesture towards improving matters by tightening up the contract and imposing police checks and controls on the workers.[51] But because it was easier for private contractors to sell the dung than it would be for the state, the Senate continued to insist that a full state take-over of these services would 'demand the most exorbitant financial commitments'.[52] After lengthy discussions, a committee of the Citizens' Assembly was set up in 1878 to investigate the whole question. It recommended the introduction of a state street-cleaning and garbage-collection service, on the grounds that only a co-ordinated operation of the two under state supervision would yield satisfactory results.[53] The Senate, while admitting the principle, turned this proposal down on grounds of expense.[54] The Property-Owners' Association had its doubts too. 'A state-run system', remarked the Association's President, Dr Heinrich Gieschen, in the Citizens' Assembly on 9 March 1881, 'is the worst and the most expensive.'[55] The property-owners were concerned to avoid a state take-over of the garbage-disposal service not only because it would have meant the state's agents entering their courtyards and compulsorily removing their property, but also because it would undoubtedly have been paid for in the end through an increase in the property tax.[56] It was much easier to argue, by contrast, that the state had the duty to remove public waste from the open street, and that the costs should be met by a general tax. Accordingly the Senate and the Citizens' Assembly finally agreed to the state take-over of the street-cleaning services in 1886. 'Hamburg', as a satisfied citizen wrote in January 1886, 'now enters the lists as the second

[49] Ibid., report 20806 Ia, 22 Oct. 1882.
[50] Ibid., Roggenbau to Kuhnardt, 6 Nov. 1882.
[51] StA Hbg, Senat Cl. VII, Lit. Cc, No. 3b, Vol. 48, Bl. 1: Mitteilung des Senats an die Bürgerschaft, Nr.117(15 Sept. 1873).
[52] Ibid.; Bl. 40: Mitteilung des Senats an die Bürgerschaft, Nr. 54 (1 May 1874).
[53] StA Hbg, Senat, Cl. VII, Lit. Cc, No. 3b, Vol. 54: Bericht ... (Oct. 1879).
[54] Mitteilung des Senats an die Bürgerschaft, Nr. 74, 5 July 1882.
[55] Report of the debate in StA Hbg, Senat, Cl. VII, Lit. Cc, No. 3b, Vol. 54.
[56] Ibid.: Bericht ... (Oct. 1879), pp. 389–90.

city in Germany with a good street-cleaning system, since up to now only Berlin has really carried out this task properly and in a manner fully befitting a great city.' Others were not so sure, however. Several months later, more critical voices were still attacking 'the miserable garbage-collection system, which is present in a more pitiable incarnation than in any other German town'.[57]

III

'Hamburg', proclaimed Heinrich Gieschen proudly in 1885, 'must be the cleanest city in the world with its water-supply and sewage system.'[58] But in reality the situation was by no means as healthy as he liked to imagine. In 1882, the Senate decided to prepare a 'Refuse Collection Ordinance' laying down regulations for the removal of human waste products from dwellings not connected to the sewage system. This was formally proposed on 14 November 1884, but it was suspended on 19 February 1886 when the Senate decided to investigate how many properties would be covered by the regulations; on the answer would depend the extent, and thus the cost, of the arrangements to be made.[59] The delay was perhaps not unconnected with the fact that the regulations laid the financial burden of these arrangements on the house-owner concerned.[60] The result of these investigations, reported on 17 December 1887, was a surprising one. A total of 4,945 lavatories in the city and suburbs were still not connected to the sewage system. 'About 400 privies', noted the report, 'are situated in the Altstadt Süd, for the most part on the Wandrahm and the Holländischer Brook, and discharge their effluvia into the canal there.' The report concluded, however, that the number of such lavatories was not sufficient to justify the introduction of special regulations, and so the proposal was dropped.[61] Thus there were no sanitary precautions covering the cleaning and disinfection of earth closets and no regulations about the kind of receptacle used. In 1871 there were still numerous bucket-closets in the courtyards of the Neustadt, and complaints were lodged about 'the dung-barrels commonly used in the area of the Niedernstrasse and Steinstrasse. They are without lids, and quite often excrement can be seen lying in them quite open to the light of day'.[62] As a further report

[57] Cf. Kaiser, *Strassen-Reinigung*; the quotations are from the *Hamburgischer Correspondent*, 10 Jan. 1886 (clipping in StA Hbg, Senat Cl. VII, Lit. Cc, No. 3b, Vol. 56) and StA Hbg, PP V164: Versammlungsbericht 21 July 1886 (W. Metzger).

[58] *Bürgerschaft*, 25 Nov. 1885 (report in StA Hbg, Senat Cl. VII, Lit. Cc, No. 3b, Vol. 56).

[59] StA Hbg, Senat Cl. VII, Lit. Cc, No. 3b, Vol. 58a, Fasc. 2, Bl. 1: Baudeputation—Bericht betr. Abfuhr-Ordnung (30 Dec. 1892).

[60] Cf. ibid., Fasc. 3: Auszug aus dem Protocolle über die Senats-Sitzung vom 5. Mai 1897; see also ibid., Fasc. 1, Bl. 4.

[61] Ibid., Fasc. 2, Bl. 1: Baudeputation—Bericht betr. Abfuhr-Ordnung (30 Dec. 1892).

[62] StA Hbg, MK II G 4 Bd. 1: Bericht über die Ergebnisse der Sanitäts-Revision im I. Physicats-Bezirk von 5. Sept. bis 10. Oct. 1871; ibid., III, Physicats-Bezirk.

pointed out in 1892, 5,000 lavatories were as many as existed in the whole of Kiel, and their numbers had certainly not diminished since 1887. Complaints were heard

that the bucket-closets were in part in a very neglected condition, partly also inappropriately and unhygenically situated in bedrooms and kitchens. There were also many complaints that full, uncovered buckets were standing on the streets at night and empty but uncleaned and undisinfected buckets in the morning, offending the eyes and noses of passers-by.[63]

The 'stinking pissoirs' on the waterfront and 'primitive privies' under many of the bridges were still discharging their wastes directly into the harbour in 1892.[64] Even as late as 1898, 900 buildings with over 2,000 lavatories were not connected to the sewage system, and it was estimated 'that the number of those persons whose excreta must be removed by some means other than the sewage system amounts even today to scarely less than 20,000'. Regulations covering the removal and disposal of this excrement were not finally introduced until 1899.[65]

In older areas such as the Alley Quarters, the lavatories, where they were installed, tended to be situated in the courtyard and shared by all the people living in the surrounding apartments. In the Pelikanhof, a courtyard off the Steinstrasse, in the Altstadt Nord, as one inhabitant later recalled, 'the toilet was underneath the staircase. The room was so cramped that one could hardly sit down in it. It was dark, and had neither a window nor a ventilation hole. Since the bucket was emptied once a week, the smell was almost unbearable.'[66] But it was not only in the Alley Quarters that unhygienic conditions were to be found. New, often cheaply built housing blocks for the working classes, in Barmbeck and other outlying areas of the city, often boasted about one water-closet on every floor, to be shared by even more people than its counterpart in the Alley Quarters. These common privies introduced even greater possibilities of infection than existed under the old system. Much of the progress that had taken place had in fact consisted of the mere removal of human excrement from public view. As late as the 1860s

[63] StA Hbg, Senat, Cl. VII, Lit. Cc, No. 3b, Vol. 58a, Fasc. 2, Bl. 1: Baudeputation—Bericht betr. Abfuhr-Ordnung (30 Dec. 1892).

[64] StA Hbg, MK II G 4 Bd. 1: Bericht über die Ergebnisse der Sanitäts-Revision im I. Physicats-Bezirk von 5. Sept. bis 10. Oct. 1871.

[65] StA Hbg, Senat, Cl. VII, Lit. Cc, No. 3b, Vol. 58a, Fasc. 4, Bl. 2: Mitteilung des Senats an die Bürgerschaft, Nr. 66, 18 Apr. 1898; *Amtsblatt der Freien und Hansestadt Hamburg*, No. 85 (1899). The account given of late 19th-century sewage, sanitation, and water-supply in *Die Gesundheitsverhältnisse* is highly unreliable. The desire to demonstrate that the city was clean and well managed in questions of sanitation was particularly strong in such documents after the cholera epidemic of 1892 and led to numerous inaccuracies. Thus a recent study such as C. Wischermann's *Wohnen in Hamburg vor dem Ersten Weltkrieg* (Münster, 1983), relying on this source, gives the entirely erroneous impression that all toilets in the city were connected to the sewage system by 1888 (p. 333). See also Plate 10.

[66] Wachendorf, 'Im Gängeviertel', p. 20.

people seem to have had few qualms about urinating or defecating in the presence of others.[67] In 1886 a discussion of working-class housing in Strasburg noted that 'it was possible for the great mass of the town's inhabitants and in particular for country-dwellers to perform their natural functions at any time and anywhere'.[68] But growing middle-class feelings of shame and modesty accompanied and furthered the removal of excretion and excrement from public view, verbal euphemisms came to replace the old plain descriptions of bodily functions, and open lavatories such as still existed in the Alley Quarters were now photographed and exhibited as evidence of the degeneracy of the area's inhabitants.

Even so, the people of Hamburg were by no means safe from the sight, smell, and public presence of human excrement in the 1890s. Several factors combined to reduce the effectiveness of the sewage system introduced in the decades after the Great Fire. The first was the lack of any kind of treatment. The sewage was simply poured, as it was, directly into the river. Moreover, because it was discharged at only one point, on the border with Altona, 'the dirty water ... flows with the ebb-tide along the northern bank of the river without really mixing with the river water. Only with the onset of the flood-tide does a greater mixing occur.' In Hamburg, a number of voluntary associations complained in 1893 'that pestilential vapours rise up when the water is low during the hot summer months (when, as the popular saying goes, "the water blossoms"), and that every large ship's screw churns up the filth from the sewage outlet at the St Pauli landing stage in the most disgusting manner'. It was not until the turn of the century that 'an installation was built to catch the floating refuse and the largest pieces of heavy rubbish' at the sewage outlet by Altona.[69] Thus the flood-tide often swept the untreated sewage upstream into the harbour, while, after a drought, when the river was low, it simply accumulated around the outlet in an ever-growing pool of excrement. This became really unpleasant when there was a major 'storm-flood', such as occurred about once every two or three years. During such floods, the low-lying parts of the Neustadt disappeared under several feet of water and many people had to leave their homes or seek refuge upstairs. After one such occasion, in December 1894, the Citizens' Club of the Neustadt Süd (1884) complained that 'a large number of lower ground-floor apartments and cellars' had been flooded for 'four whole days and nights'. Worse still, 'the water has come out of the sewage pipes and got into the cellars etc. This problem has got considerably worse since all the dwellings were connected to the main sewage pipe for in earlier years it was only pure Elbe water that flowed into the cellars, while nowadays it is filled with

---

[67] Gleichmann, 'Die Verhäuslichung', p. 257.

[68] Ibid., pp. 254–5.

[69] *Die Gesundheitsverhältnisse*, pp. 44–5; for the complaint of the 22 *Vereine*, see StA Hbg, BD B1748, *Hamburger Fremdenblatt*, 28 Oct. 1893.

repulsive sewage ...' This, complained the Citizens' Club, had happened 'repeatedly in earlier years and especially last year', and it happened again in 1896.[70] Similar calamities often befell the inhabitants of other districts of the city. Before the construction of the free port in the 1880s, the southern extremity of the Altstadt was also subject to flooding at high tide. 'Chairs and tables swam about in people's homes', remembered one former inhabitant, 'and sometimes even knocked against the ceilings ... Every flood meant a lot of work for the people who were affected. When the floodwaters had retreated, they had to clean up the courtyards and ground-floor flats, for everything was covered in a thick layer of slime.'[71] There was also frequent flooding in the working-class areas of Eilbeck and Barmbeck because, as a deputy complained in the Citizens' Assembly in 1896, 'the sewage pipes in the suburbs are too small for the great terraces and housing blocks and every substantial rainstorm causes them to overflow.'[72]

Another influence which severely reduced the impact of the new sewage system on public health in Hamburg was the continued use of the canals as dumping-grounds for all kinds of rubbish, including human ordure from chamber-pots. The number of properly constructed public lavatories in Hamburg was limited. There were thirty in 1850, but many were not connected to the sewage system, and in 1882–5 a fresh effort was made to improve facilities in this area by approving a concession to a private company to construct and run some more.[73] Many people simply seem to have used the canals. Although they were washed by the tide twice a day, 'the fleets', it was reported early in the nineteenth century, 'receive such a mass of filth from the alley-ways and houses that it cannot all be washed out with the ebb-tide, and if the water level is continually low, it all remains there and pollutes the air'. It had long been forbidden to throw 'dead dogs, stones, refuse, dung' and the like into the canals. But people did, and when the spring thaw came, sand, stones and ashes were washed into them with the melting ice. Over the century the fleets gradually silted up, until many of them were only under water at high tide.[74] The fleets, wrote two doctors and an engineer who carried out an officially sponsored sanitary inspection in the autumn of 1871, should 'more properly be described as sewers'.[75] Many if not most of the fleets in the Altstadt were filled with all kinds of rubbish which became clearly visible at low tide. All of them required dredging, and the removal of 'the heaps of filth that gather everywhere along the sides near the houses

[70] StA Hbg, MK II H 12, Bl. 21: Bürgerverein Neustadt-Süd von 1884 to Senat, 14 Dec. 1894, *et seq.* See also Plate 6.

[71] Wachendorf, 'Im Gängeviertel', pp. 16–17.

[72] StA Hbg, MK II O 1 Bd. 2, Bl. 19: 22. *Sitzung der Bürgerschaft am 12. Juni 1896*.

[73] StA Hbg, BD B513, *passim*.

[74] Rambach, *Versuch*, pp. 47–9. See also Plate 5.

[75] StA Hbg, MK II G 4 Bd. 1: Bericht über die Ergebnisse der Sanitäts-Revision im I. Physicats-Bezirk von 5. Sept. bis 10. Oct. 1871.

and dams.'[76] The *Haasenmoore* and the old cesspits under some of the houses were in a 'very dubious condition', filled with slime and rubbish.[77] 'Complaints about the generally dangerous vapours that emanate from such cesspits', it was noted in 1865, 'have long been common', and the 'city's fleets and canals' were 'disgustingly polluted'.[78] But the Senate was clearly unwilling to spend large sums of money on dredging and cleaning up these waterways. To be sure, the city had for many years paid so-called 'fleet-watchers' (*Flethenkieker*) to inspect the canals and remove illegally deposited rubbish.[79] But while these men were able to take away the most obvious obstructions as they waded through the canals at low tide, they were unable to stop the steady, almost imperceptible accumulation of sand and silt that by 1890 had rendered the majority of the fleets canals in name only.

Finally, whatever improvements Hamburg managed to make in the disposal of its own wastes were bound to be limited in their effects as long as the Senate had no control over the activities of Prussian municipalities further upriver. Many of these were growing rapidly in the late nineteenth and early twentieth century, and Hamburg soon began to feel the effects. The Alster, the lake in the centre of modern Hamburg, was dredged in 1884 after it had become unbearably dirty, and sewage pipes were laid round it and along the rivers that flowed into it on their way to the inner city and the harbour. These rapidly became polluted, however, by untreated sewage poured into them further upstream, in Prussian territory.[80] The Osterbeck in Barmbeck was said in 1894 to smell 'remarkably like alcoholic dregs', and its water was opaque and yellow-white. In the same year the Eilbeck, where it flowed into Hamburg across the Prussian border, smelt 'strongly of faeces' and was black and foamy. A bacteriological investigation revealed it to contain an average of 210,000 bacteria per cubic centimetre of water—a vast quantity by normal standards. In 1896 there was a public outcry about 'the pestilential vapours of the completely stagnant water of the canal in Eimsbüttel ... In the present hot weather', as the 'inhabitants of the Bismarckstrasse in Eimsbüttel' complained, 'the stink (for one cannot call it a smell any more) is unbearable ... '. The Isebeck was said to have been a 'dirty, evil-smelling ditch for its whole length in Hamburg' until 1882, and even after sewers had been laid and the rivers cleaned up, complaints continued to pour in. As late as 1903 the inhabitants of nearby houses concluded that 'the new sewage system ... does not seem to have met with the desired success'.[81] A special commission of the Senate reported in December 1896 on the pollution of

[76] Ibid.

[77] Ibid.

[78] StA Hbg, BD B1745: Matthias Graht, report of 5 Jan. 1865.

[79] Rambach, *Versuch*, pp. 47–9.

[80] For pollution of the Alster and tributaries by waste matter and sewage from Hamburg itself—a problem largely solved by 1870—see StA Hbg, BD B1745, *passim*.

[81] StA Hbg, MK II O 1 Bd. 1, Bl. 89a, Bl. 169–73 (Berichte des Hygienischen Instituts).

these rivers, and warned that their effluvia would soon have a serious effect on the Alster 'and become a calamity for the whole city'. Negotiations with the Prussian municipality of Wandsbeck, which was responsible for a good deal of this pollution, dragged on for several years and it was not until well after the turn of the century that matters began to improve.[82]

Conditions were hardly better in the River Bille, which flows into the Elbe through Hamburg's eastern suburbs. Complaints about pollution began to be received by the authorities in the 1880s, and a serious investigation was undertaken in 1891. Nothing came of this, however, and the complaints were renewed in 1894. Clearly the inhabitants of the districts through which it passed, most notably the Billwärder Ausschlag, were accustomed to use it for domestic purposes. As they wrote indignantly:

The water of the Bille is becoming ever more polluted by the admixture of harmful substances. It has by now begun to smell so bad that one simply has to call it 'stinking', so that it has become impossible to use it without running a serious health risk. If one follows the path from the Blue Bridge through the Billwärder Ausschlag, one's nose is led to the cause of this horrible nuisance, which must be removed as soon as possible. The complaints of those who live near the Bille are growing louder every day ... [83]

Once again, the impurities in the water were coming from upstream, across the Prussian border, this time from Regenbach and Bergedorf. There 'the urine from some 300 workers of the Bergedorf Ironworks flows into the Bille', it was reported in 1896.[84] By 1909 the untreated excrement of 1,500 of these workers was reaching the Bille; various attempts to remove the impurities had 'met with no success yet despite lengthy negotiations'.[85] The inhabitants of the areas through which it passed, noted the medical authorities somewhat complacently in 1909, were not particularly disturbed by the noxious vapours emanating from the river, because they lived 'in a district where large areas of land are often fertilized with rotten fish'.[86] This did not stop them complaining, as we have seen. But nothing was done.

With filth and excrement pouring in from all these sources at least from the 1880s if not earlier, it was hardly surprising that the River Elbe itself soon began to suffer a similar fate. Already in 1867, the 'silting-up of the river-bed' in the harbour had increased 'to such an extent ... that it was impossible for workers to use underwater diving-bells, since the lights were

[82] Ibid., Bl. 126–7 (*Hamburger Fremdenblatt*, 11 July 1896; Bericht der Senatskommission betr. die Verunreinigung der Alster, 15 Dec. 1896); ibid., Bd. 4, Bl. 17 (*Hamburger Fremdenblatt*, 28 June 1903); ibid., Bd. 5, Bl. 57 (*Hamburger Fremdenblatt*, 16 Apr. 1908).

[83] StA Hbg, MK II O 2 Bd. 1, Bl. 25, submission of 10 May 1894.

[84] Ibid., Bl. 32: Bericht des Hygienischen Instituts betr. die Verunreinigung der Bille und ihren Zuflüsse, 11 Dec. 1896.

[85] Ibid., Bl. 99, Bericht des Hygienischen Instituts ... 30 Jan. 1909.

[86] Ibid.

extinguished despite the substantial amounts of air supplied from above, and it became really difficult to breathe'.[87] While molluscs and shellfish were increasing in number, especially around the sewage outlets and in the canals,[88] fishermen were complaining by the turn of the century that catches of 'sturgeon, plaice, eel-pouts, smelt, and above all salmon' in the Elbe had 'decreased'. The salmon in particular no longer swam upstream through Hamburg's harbour because 'the evil-smelling, polluted water repels them'. The fishermen usually held their catch in nets in the water until the last moment before landing it; this was virtually the only way of keeping it fresh in the days before refrigeration. Now, however, they were losing half the catch because it was killed by the foul water in the harbour.[89] The attitude of the Hamburg Senate to any improvement was consistently obstructionist. Yet in 1874 it was still being reported that 'the water of the Elbe, which is polluted by virtually all the excreta and rubbish of the great cities of Hamburg and Altona, is widely drunk by boatmen and sailors'.[90] and this habit continued well into the early 1890s, when housewives were reported to be taking water for domestic use from the fleets when pressure in the taps was low.[91] And to the numerous and repeated complaints of the 1890s and 1900s about untreated sewage being washed up on shore, 'evil vapours ... faeces and masses of paper floating in the river' and so on, they merely pointed out that thousands of people still considered the water healthy enough to bathe in; the critics were exaggerating their case; Hamburg was 'one of the healthiest of cities' and there was no need at all to construct a sewage treatment plant.[92] Other towns and municipalities upstream thought likewise. The cumulative effect of all these various sources of pollution was obvious in Hamburg's harbour well before the 1890s. Just how dangerous it was for the city's inhabitants was soon to become apparent.[93]

c. *Troubled Waters*

I

With the increasing pollution of the Elbe and its tributaries and the ever-growing population of Hamburg in the nineteenth century, the problem of

[87] StA Hbg, MK II O 3 Bd. 5, Bl. 75: 3. Bericht des Hygienischen Instituts betr. die Beschaffenheit des Elbwassers ..., p. 6.

[88] Ibid., Bd. 4: *Hamburgischer Correspondent*, 13 Sept. 1903.

[89] Ibid., Bl. 62–3, submission of Finkenwerder and Altenwerder Fishermen to Reichsgesundheitsamt 12 Aug. 1904; and ibid., Bd. 2: *Hamburger Echo*, 22 July 1900.

[90] StA Hbg, Mk II 2 Bd. 2, Bl. 87: Beilage zu No. 91 des Altonaer Mercur-Sonntag, den 17 April 1874.

[91] *Bürgerschaft* 31 May 1893 (Dageför).

[92] StA Hbg O 3 Bd. 4, Bl. 8, 231–2.

[93] For a brief account of river pollution, see J. von Simson, 'Die Flussverunreinigungsfrage im 19. Jahrhundert', *Vierteljahrschrift für Sozial- und Wirtschaftsgeschichte*, 65 (1978), 370–90.

supplying the city's inhabitants with adequate quantities of fresh water for drinking, cooking, and washing became steadily more acute. In the early decades of the century, most people depended on either wells or on water taken directly from the harbour or the canals. They could also purchase it on the streets from water-carriers, and by the 1830s, if they were able to afford it, they could contract to have their houses supplied by a water company. One of these companies was exclusively used by the local breweries, which left three to choose from. None of them actually filtered its water before piping it into the houses, but the English firm of Smith's Waterworks, founded in 1839, took its supplies from the Elbe, which at this time was a good deal less polluted than the Alster, on which the other companies relied. All the Alster water companies were destroyed in the Great Fire of 1842 and Smith was now able to start expanding his business to take their place. Meanwhile, however, the ubiquitous William Lindley had come forward with a far more ambitious plan, drawn up in consultation with William Chadwell Mylne, the chief engineer of the New River Waterworks in London. Lindley and Mylne argued that a state-controlled, central water-supply system was necessary to meet Hamburg's future needs. It was also, they suggested, the only way of ensuring quantities of water in all parts of the city large enough to douse any small blazes that might occur, and so prevent any repetition of the Great Fire. In 1844 their plan, costing 1.7 million Marks, was formally approved by the Citizens' Assembly.[1]

The new system took the city's water-supply from a single inlet 2 kilometres above the city, in Rothenburgsort. As Lindley noted, 'It is a simple principle, which must be clear to everyone, that impure outflows must be discharged into rivers *below* towns, and waterworks on the other hand take their water from the same through inflows *above* towns, and not the other way round.'[2] The water was pumped through an 800-metre-long walled canal into three large reservoirs (*Klärbassins*) where it was allowed to settle. Then 'it was taken through covered channels to the pumping-wells underneath the machines, passing through a sluice-gate on the way'. A number of powerful steam pumps then directed it via a massive water-tower into pipes which carried it towards the city in different directions.[3] The pressure was not strong enough to pump the water regularly into upper-storey dwellings, so for two hours every night it was raised, and the water flowed into tanks (*Wasserkasten*) in the roofs of many houses, where it was stored for use during the following day.[4] Like all Lindley's projects, the city waterworks ran into considerable opposition from interested parties. The Property-Owners' Association was particularly active in the struggle. It regarded the plan as extravagant and

[1] Leo, *William Lindley*, pp. 45–53.
[2] Ibid., p. 47.
[3] See *Hamburg und seine Bauten* (Hamburg, 1913), for a detailed description.
[4] *Die Gesundheitsverhältnisse*, p. 49.

likely to lead to an increase in the land tax (*Grundsteuer*). As a result of this pressure, the Propertied Citizenry, having voted the initial finding of the project three years before, suddenly refused in 1846 to approve the funds necessary for its completion. After fresh quarrels, however, the funds were finally voted and the waterworks came into operation in 1848. By the end of 1850 some 4,000 out of 11,500 houses in the city had been connected. In 1860 daily consumption reached 70,000 cubic metres. By 1890 there were over 400 kilometres of pipes and nearly every house in the city had at least one tap either inside or in the courtyard.[5]

In many ways the city was justified in the evident pride it took in the elaboration and comprehensiveness of its water-supply system. As late as 1895, for example, only 42% of Prussian urban communities with over 2,000 inhabitants were serviced by mains water; the other 58% were dependent on wells, springs, river-water, or rain-water. Rural communities were even less well-off. Still, some 87% of German towns with over 10,000 inhabitants did possess a central water-supply by 1895. Most of these systems had been constructed, like Hamburg's, from the mid-nineteenth century onwards. These towns contained only a minority of the inhabitants of the German Empire,[6] but they did include virtually all the biggest cities. Berlin had mains water as early as 1856, though initially it was only used for washing down the open gutters that carried much of the capital city's sewage through the streets. The capacity of the waterworks was small; they were only capable of supplying some 54% of the new houses built in Berlin between 1856 and 1873. Older buildings only began to be connected after the construction of a new, much larger waterworks in the late 1870s. In 1875 only 43% of all houses in Berlin were connected; but by 1885 the figure had virtually doubled, to 85%. By 1890 some 93% of houses in the capital were supplied.[7]

Hamburg, therefore, was by no means backward in its construction and extension of a central municipal water-supply. Yet there was one crucial respect in which Hamburg in reality lagged far behind the capital city. From the very beginning, in 1856, Berlin's water had been purified by the sand-filtration method. After being taken from the River Spree upstream from the city, it was stored in a series of filter-beds, in which the water seeped through several layers of fine sand, to be collected by a system of underdrains and thence carried into the pipes. This system effectively destroyed harmful micro-organisms by introducing into the water bacteria hostile to their existence. Reinhard Spree has recently suggested that Berlin's water was unhygienic because it was taken from the river; but in fact, the sand-filtration plant actually succeeded in rendering it incapable of transmitting infectious

[5] Leo, *William Lindley*; see also R. Hauschild-Thiessen, *150 Jahre Hamburger Grun-deigentümerverein* (Hamburg, 1982), for the Association's repeated involvement in this question.
[6] Spree, *Soziale Ungleichheit*, pp. 118–21.
[7] Ibid., pp. 124–5.

diseases.[8] Not the source of the supply, but the treatment which it received, was the decisive factor. By contrast, Hamburg's central water-supply was equipped with no such effective filtration system. The water, as we have seen, was taken directly from the River Elbe above Hamburg and stored in large reservoirs before being pumped into the city. The head engineer of the State Waterworks, Samuel Samuelson, believed in 1880 that these reservoirs would surely remove any impurities that might come into the system from the river:

As soon as the water is taken from the flowing river, which carries along with it matter heavier than water as well as other, floating impurities, the lighter flotsam separates from the heavier matter. The flotsam, consisting of foam, corks, pieces of wood, etc., now and again dead fish or other corpses, if it manages to reach the reservoir in question, is driven to one or other of the banks of the reservoir according to the direction of the wind; the heavier matter sinks to the reservoir bed. If the water is taken from the reservoir at the right level and in the right way, it can avoid taking either kind of impurity with it. The foam and its contents can easily be removed by hand.[9]

According to Samuelson, therefore, a sand-filtration plant was not really necessary, since the water was pure enough already.

However, the reservoir system was unable to prevent a variety of small living creatures from entering the pipes of the distribution system from the river. Chief Engineer Meyer noted, indeed, that 'the Hamburg waterpipes, about 150 miles long, are covered with slime and shells, and small fish and other live animals are found in the water, because the Elbe-water passes unfiltered into the pipes'.[10] In 1885 a professional zoologist actually published an article called *The Fauna of the Hamburg Water-Mains* which reported that samples taken from underground water-supply pipes had found 'a chaotic jumble of the most varied life-forms'. The denizens of the water-mains numbered no less than 60 different species of 'vertebrates, insects, spiders, snails, mussels, shrimps, molluscs, ringworms, roundworms, flatworms, and protozoa'. They included no fewer than eight different varieties of snails and four different kinds of mussels. The zoologist responsible for the investigation concluded, reasonably enough, that 'they are undoubtedly lower forms of detritus-eaters, on whose existence the whole food chain of the higher animals is built.' They were fed by a constant supply of plant and animal food washed down from the reservoirs. Reassuringly, however, he added that

one cannot claim that the presence of living organisms in the water-pipes is a serious evil, and certainly not that it is generally felt to be an unbearable calamity. For water intended for drinking or for preparing food is usually purified by filtration in the

[8] Ibid.
[9] StA Hbg, FA Meyer B11: 'Stellungnahme zu dem Bericht von Dr Gerson: In welcher Weise ist eine verbesserte Wasservorsorgung Hamburgs herzustellen', pp. 14–15.
[10] StA Hbg, FA Meyer B6, Notizbuch, Frage 10.

house, and on the other hand water that is not filtered leaves behind a good deal of its organic impurities, living and dead, in the big water-tanks in the roofs of the houses, the so-called *Wasserkasten*. Also, most of the animals that live in the pipes should possess enough strength to resist being carried up out of the broader horizontal channel system under the streets into the narrow vertical pipes that lead into the houses.[11]

Others agreed with this assessment. The conservative Hamburg lawyer Carl August Schröder (Senator from 1899 to 1918), claimed in his memoirs that

precisely because it was not purified and frequently contained parts of algae and small fishes, indeed even thin eels, the mains water was not really used for drinking by anybody, or, as happened in private houses, was thoroughly cleaned by small filters beforehand. People regularly drank water from pumps and wells; it was carried though the whole city in numerous water-carts.[12]

According to Schröder, therefore, the water-supply posed no real danger to public health.

This complacency was shared by the great majority of the medical profession in the city. The director of the New General Hospital in Eppendorf, Theodor Rumpf, reported in his memoirs that just after his arrival in Hamburg early in 1892, at a convivial evening in the home of Dr Gläser, the senior doctor at the hospital, he asked where Hamburg got its drinking-water from. The reply was

'from the Elbe, after it has deposited its dirt in some big reservoirs'. As I replied that this was an antediluvian scandal, I was fallen upon by everyone present. 'Elbe water is the healthiest of drinks'. they cried back at me. 'All the big ocean liners take Elbe water on board off Blankenese, because it keeps perfectly.' I was also told that a chemical investigation had yielded an excellent result. Head Physician Gläser thought nothing of bacteriology. I was naturally unable to alter my point of view, but as a non-Hamburger, I was sympathetically excused for my heresies.[13]

Indeed the Elbe water continued to enjoy a good reputation, as this exchange suggests, right up to 1892. Sailors and harbour workers regularly refreshed themselves by drinking directly from the river in hot weather, even in the middle of Hamburg's busy harbour. As the official spokesman for the Medical Board declared in 1873, during the last cholera epidemic before 1892, 'among the public the most general satisfaction prevails with regard to the condition of the water'.[14]

Yet by 1892, in reality, the waters of the Elbe had long since ceased to deserve their reputation for purity. The many creatures that inhabited the

[11] K. Kraeplin, *Die Fauna der Hamburger Wasserleitung* (Separatabdruck aus dem IX. Band der Abhandlungen des Naturwissenschaftlichen Vereins in Hamburg; Hamburg, 1885).

[12] C. A. Schröder, *Aus Hamburgs Blütezeit* (Hamburg, 1921), p. 82.

[13] T. Rumpf, *Lebenserinnerungen* (Gotha, 1925), p. 42.

[14] Dr Buek, in *Bürgerschaft* 9 Sept. 1873.

pipes of the water-supply frequently managed to get further, whatever the author of *The Fauna of the Hamburg Water-Mains* might say. Heinrich Merck, a scion of one of Hamburg's leading families, recalled later that 'at our house in the Papenhuderstrasse a small, delicate, living eel was once taken from the tap in the wash-basin'; and Leo Lippmann, who grew up in a well-to-do Jewish family in Hamburg, recorded in his memoirs 'the recollection of a big eel, which was fished out of the water-tank of our house by a mechanic shortly before the cholera epidemic, to the jubilation of us children'.[15] So frequent were such occurrences that collecting animals found in the water-supply was a popular hobby among Hamburg's children. As Johannes Schult, who grew up in a working-class quarter of Hamburg in this period, reported,

In summer the boys liked to gather in the streets around the water-sprinkling carts. When the tank had been filled with the aid of a hydrant, a bell was rung and the driver turned the water off. He unscrewed the pipe and let the extra water run onto the street. To the boys' delight this water often contained eels and little fish, which were then carried off home in triumph.[16]

On other occasions these creatures blocked the water pipes in people's homes. It was also not unknown for dead mice and other corpses of small animals to be washed along the pipes from the reservoir, frequently fouling the tap-water and stopping the supply.

Even the author of *The Fauna of the Hamburg Water-Mains* was forced to admit that 'isolated woodlice and flea-crabs are nothing unusual in kitchen and household water and indeed the inlets and outlets of the water-tanks in the roofs are frequently enough blocked by eels, "water-moss" and the like'; and although fresh spring-water was regularly offered for sale on the streets, only the well-off could afford it. Fishwives on the streets were known to vary their cries advertising their wares with 'Eels! Eels! Fresh from Lindley's water-mains!' in the latter part of the century. A poem in a local newspaper summed up the widespread and growing disquiet of the bourgeois inhabitants of the city at this state of affairs:

> Of beasts in Hamburg's waterpipes
> There can be found some sixteen types:
> The lamprey, eel, and stickleback,
> Of worms—three kinds—there is no lack,
> Mussels three, slow snails the same
> With jolly woodlice frisk and game,
> A sponge, some algae, and a polyp,
> through the sieve they jump and frolic.

[15] StA Hbg, FA Lippmann A4 Bd. I, p. 32.
[16] J. Schult, *Geschichte der Hamburger Arbeiter 1890–1919* (Hanover, 1968), p. 41.

> As corpses in the pipes are found
> The mouse, the cat, also the hound;
> Unfortunately lacking yet—
> The engineer and architect![17]

Far worse than eels and mice, however, were the less spectacular but potentially more dangerous pollutants that no amount of storage tanks or metal grilles in people's houses could remove from the water. These were particularly noticeable in the spring, when dirty melting snow rendered the tap water 'totally milk-coloured [and] opaque'.[18] The sewage outlets were, it is true, several kilometres downriver from the water-supply intake. But the barges and inland shipping that passed up and down the river between Hamburg and towns upstream as far as Berlin and Dresden regularly discharged the excreta of their crews directly into the river. Moreover, there were many primitive lavatories on the waterfront in Hamburg with outlets that led straight into the river much further upstream than the main sewage outlet.[19] It was also, as we have seen, the habit of at least some of the inhabitants bordering on the fleets that criss-crossed the city to empty chamber-pots straight into these waterways.[20] Hamburg's water supply was thus polluted by a variety of sources in the late nineteenth century. Private wells were an alternative only for a tiny section of the population. Nor was there any escape to be had through going over to mineral water instead of tap-water. As a report of 1878 noted,

The pollution of the soil and of waterways in large cities by decomposing organic substances and the resulting, daily increasing deterioration of the drinking-water, has encouraged the development of the so-called 'mineral water' industry. Many people use this artificial mineral water, for they believe that they can protect themselves in this way against diseases which are conditioned by the consumption of bad drinking-water. But this protection is illusory.[21]

As the report went on to explain, most manufacturers of mineral water took water straight from the nearest river and simply added carbon dioxide to it. Not infrequently the chemicals used to produce carbon dioxide (including sulphuric acid) contained arsenic compounds which found their way into the finished product along with copper and lead particles from the pipes of the manufacturer's machines.[22] On balance, perhaps, it was better to stick to tap-water.

Yet the tap-water, as we have seen, was by no means free from contami-

[17] Kraeplin, *Die Fauna*, p. 8; StA Hbg, FA Merck, II 9, Konv. 4a, Heft II, p.3; W. Melhop, *Alt-Hamburgisches Dasein* (Hamburg, 1899), p. 56.

[18] *Die Gesundheitsverhältnisse*, p. 50.

[19] See above, p. 139.

[20] See above, pp. 130, 141–2.

[21] StA Hbg, MK II A 1 Bd. 1, Bl. 2: Bundesrat, Drucksache, Nr. 25, 9 Feb. 1878, p. 75.

[22] Ibid.

nation. The provision of a central sewage outlet on the boundary with Altona was certainly no guarantee against the infection of Hamburg's water-mains with human excreta and the bacteria they contained. Indeed, by the late 1890s the polluted harbour water was washed upriver to the water-supply inlet with such regularity that the inlet was turned off at every flood tide. Even so, a bacteriological investigation carried out in the middle of the decade revealed the river to contain over 3,000 bacteria per cubic centimetre at the inlet point.[23] The reservoirs described by Samuelson may have stopped the corpses of large dead animals getting into the system. But they had no impact on the micro-organisms that bred in them. Nor could they destroy the bacteria carried in the human excrement which also reached the reservoirs from the river, in however diluted a form. Only the provision of a sand-filtration system could achieve this effect.

II

A sand-filtration plant had in fact been introduced in Altona as early as 1859. The neighbouring town had to take its water from the Elbe below Hamburg and so it recognized the need for an efficient purification system. At the same time, the creator of the Hamburg Waterworks, William Lindley, had also attempted in 1853 to convert one of the reservoirs in Rothenburgsort into a filter-bed. The Citizens' Assembly had voted the money for the project, but Lindley spent it instead on constructing a fourth, unfiltered reservoir, completed in 1860. Demand was growing so rapidly that the additional reservoir had been urgent, while a single filter-bed was by now quite insufficient to purify the vast quantities of water consumed every day. Moreover, land prices in the area were rising so sharply that Lindley thought it prudent to buy the land for the fourth reservoir without delay, rather than waiting several years for the money to be voted by the Assembly. Lindley declared his intention in 1860 of going over to a filtration system at a later date. But in the same year, the Citizens' Assembly rejected the Senate's proposal to appoint him Chief Engineer as part of a general plan to co-ordinate and rationalize the City Engineer's Department (*Baubehörde*). Lindley had never held any official position in the city. In characteristic Hamburg fashion, he had merely been retained as an 'adviser', dependent on his connections with leading merchants and powerful men in the city. Many of his old allies had retired or died by now, while the increased power which the constitution of 1860 gave to the Citizens' Assembly allowed his opponents at last to get the upper hand. In the intervening years Lindley had made fresh enemies by his plans to create a new town by draining the Hammerbrook, in St Georg, and by his project for the extension of the harbour. Both of these schemes involved the compulsory purchase of substantial quantities of land and so aroused the wrath, once more, of the Property-Owners' Association. The Association and its allies in the Assembly now seized the opportunity and voted, in effect, for his departure.[24]

Lindley accordingly left Hamburg in 1860 and subsequently enjoyed an active and distinguished career in other parts of Europe. He designed and constructed water-supply systems in Düsseldorf, Chemnitz, Krefeld, Elberfeld, and Basle, and, with his three sons, who were also engineers, he built similar systems in Budapest, Warsaw, and St Petersburg. After his experience in Hamburg, Lindley was always careful to obtain an official post where his presence was demanded to carry out elaborate sanitary engineering projects. When he was charged with the design and construction of a sewage system in Frankfurt in 1865, he made it a condition of his work that he was appointed City Construction Officer (*Stadtbaurat*) with wide-ranging powers. 'I would not bear again', he declared, 'the stupid and malicious opposition which so long delayed our progress in Hamburg.' He even took care that his son was installed as *Stadtbaurat* on his own retirement from the Frankfurt post; the younger man occupied the position from 1879 to 1896 before returning to England, where he was eventually knighted for his services to engineering. William Lindley senior retired to England in 1879 and died in Blackheath in 1900, aged 91.[25] His career is remarkable evidence for the broad European influence and activities of British engineers in the heyday of British industrial hegemony. His departure from Hamburg in 1860 was a severe blow to the further development of the sanitary projects he had so energetically begun. His plans to convert the fourth water reservoir into a filter-bed gathered dust for the rest of the decade, and the remaining engineers in the city regarded the achievements of the Lindley era with complacency instead of using them as a basis for further improvement. It was not until the 1870s that a number of new developments gave a fresh impetus to the cause of sanitary reform in the city. In the meantime Hamburg lived on the considerable reputation for sanitary reform which it had acquired in the aftermath of the Great Fire thirty years earlier.

In 1872 the Hamburg Medical Board, encouraged perhaps by the city's new Chief Engineer, Franz Andreas Meyer, initiated a scientific study of the water-supply. The study indicated that it was not as pure as it was popularly held to be. The Medical Board pressed for the construction of filter-beds after the cholera epidemic of 1873, and the director of the State Waterworks presented plans along these lines to the Senate in the same year. 'These proposals', he reported later, 'did not meet with the approval of the Finance Deputation, however, or of the Senate; on the contrary, negotiations now

[24] Leo, *William Lindley*, pp. 66–100.
[25] Ibid. The quotation is on p. 100 n. 43.

became protracted.'[26] Eventually in 1875 a joint commission of the Senate and the Citizens' Assembly was set up to pursue the matter further. The Citizens' Assembly rejected the Senate's application to provide the commission with a budget of some 2,000 Marks, and forced it to work with only 1,000. However, this was enough to send a small group of officials, including Dr Johann Caspar Kraus, head of the medical office, and Dr Franz Andreas Meyer, the city's Chief Engineer, to Paris and London, to see how those cities managed their water-filtration systems.[27]

At this point, the project began to suffer further delays because of a growing animosity between the two main technical experts seconded to the commission, Chief Engineer Meyer and the Director of the State Waterworks, Samuelson. Chief Engineer Franz Andreas Meyer (1837–1901) was a powerful and influential figure in late nineteenth-century Hamburg. Those who knew him well spoke with some awe of 'the whole force of his personality', of his stormy character, his frequent 'tirades' and his 'extraordinary energy'.[28] By birth and upbringing he clearly belonged to Hamburg's governing circles. The son of a merchant, he was born in Hamburg in 1837 and attended the school where all the sons of Hamburg's leading families went, the Johanneum. His school fellows included Johann Georg Mönckeberg and Gerhard Hachmann, two of the most prominent members of the Senate at the time of the cholera epidemic in 1892; indeed he remained on intimate personal terms with Hachmann for the rest of his life.[29] From there, however, Meyer followed an unconventional course, attending the Polytechnic College in Hanover, then taking up a post in Bremen, working on the construction of the main railway station. In 1866 he returned to Hamburg to work on the water-supply. From this point onwards his promotion was rapid, helped perhaps by his marriage to the granddaughter of Senator Johann Heinrich Gossler. In 1869 he became District Engineer for the Inner City, and four years later, Chief Engineer of the Construction Deputation and City Waterworks. He held this post for over thirty years. It enabled him to play a central role in the rebuilding of Hamburg in the late nineteenth century. The monuments of his work can still be seen in many parts of the city. They included bridges (most notably the Trostbrücke), landscaped open spaces such as the park between Dammtor and Holstentor, and above all the gigantic new harbour facilities built in the 1880s, including the spectacular 'warehouse city' (*Speicherstadt*).

---

[26] StA Hbg, FA Meyer B11, pp. 3–4. According to the *Hamburger Tageblatt* it was the Citizens' Assembly that was to blame for the delay in 1873–5. Other sources blame the Senate. As this quotation suggests, the blame was probably shared between the two (StA Hbg, Senat Cl. VII, Lit. Ta, Pars 2, Vol. 11, Fasc. 17, Inv 1a: *Hamburger Tageblatt*, 277, 11 Nov. 1892).

[27] StA Hbg, FA Meyer, B11, for these events. Meyer's 'Notizbuch' (FA Meyer B6) contains a series of questions, drawn up in a comically Teutonic version of English, which he wanted to put to the London engineers.

[28] The following account is drawn from the obituaries in StA Hbg, FA Meyer B7a and B7b.

[29] See the letter from Meyer to Hachmann using the intimate *Du* form of address, in: StA Hbg, Senat, Cl. VII, Lit. Cc, No. 3b, Vol. 58a, Fasc. 2, Bl. 38 (22 Nov. 1896).

His inexhaustible energy, as well as his personal friendship with leading members of the ruling fraction of Hamburg's bourgeoisie, was attested by the head of Hamburg's Statistical Bureau, Dr Georg Koch, who recorded in his diary for 3 July 1893 his attendance at a 'fine gentlemen's dinner' for thirty, after which Meyer personally rowed six of the guests across the Aussen-Alster Lake at two in the morning.[30] Such was the force of his personality and the extent of his influence that the refusal of the Citizens' Assembly to allow city officials to be elected to it was ascribed not least to fear of the power that Meyer would undoubtedly wield if he succeeded in becoming a deputy. 'There is a Pope in Rome', said one of his critics bitterly in 1893, 'and a Pope in Hamburg', because it was clear 'that everything that Chief Engineer Meyer wills, comes to pass.' By the 1890s, therefore, Meyer was a well-known figure in the city; and when he died in 1901 he was accorded a grand state funeral.[31]

If Meyer had a fault, it was that he did not suffer fools gladly. In particular he made abundantly clear his contempt for his subordinate the Chief Engineer of the State Waterworks Samuel Samuelson. When Samuelson produced a draft report on the filtration of the water-supply, following on their expedition to Paris and London in 1875, Meyer immediately condemned it as 'superficial'. It contained, he claimed, 'erroneous data'. So without consulting his colleagues, he redrafted it. At this stage of his career, however, Meyer's appointment as Chief Engineer was still quite recent, and older-established officials were still capable of standing up to him. On receipt of the new draft, as he later complained, 'Samuelson denounced me'.[32] A flood of mutual recriminations now followed. They went on for several years. It was not until 1878 that the commission was able to submit its report. It largely reflected the views of Chief Engineer Meyer: clearly he had worn down the objections of his colleagues in the intervening period. Samuelson, indeed, complained that there were 'some very important points in the project' that had been 'included against my wishes and in opposition to my views'. He promptly set about blackguarding the report to anyone who would listen.

III

Samuelson's arguments against Meyer's project were couched in terms that found a ready audience in the Senate and the Citizens' Assembly. He thought it was too expensive. Meyer wanted new reservoirs to be constructed above the level of the new filter, but Samuelson thought this was unnecessary and

[30] F. Koch (ed.), 'Die Tagebuchaufzeichnungen Georg Kochs über die Hamburger Cholera-Epidemie des Jahres 1892', *Die Heimat. Monatsschrift zur Pflege der Natur- und Landeskunde in Schleswig-Holstein und Hamburg*, 80 (1973), 23–4.

[31] StA Hbg, FA Meyer B7a, B7b; *Bürgerschaft* 12 July 1893 (Langthimm); O. Beselin, *Franz Andreas Meyer* (Hamburg, 1974).

[32] StA Hbg, FA Meyer, B11, p. 5.

would cost far too much money. As we have already seen, he continued as late as 1880 to defend the existing system of storage reservoirs, in a report which Meyer covered in marginalia such as 'nonsense!' and 'outrageous!' and finally condemned as 'absolutely mistaken and useless'.[33] The only way that Samuelson could see of paying for the new project was to increase the water rate and install a water meter in every household. This, however, was not to the liking of the Citizens' Assembly, which sat on the matter for another three years while it was being discussed by yet another commission. After obtaining reports on the project from a number of outside experts, the Citizens' Assembly commission, appointed on 16 September 1878, finally reported in March 1881. On 29 June 1881 the project was approved in principle subject to a number of modifications. After eight years, the matter finally seemed to be settled. Once more, Meyer's arguments seemed to have won the day.[34]

In reality, however, the demand for modifications proved to be yet another source of delay. They took another four years to work out, and it was not until 16 May 1885 that the final project was submitted to the Senate. By this time the filtration of the water-supply had become entangled with two other issues, namely who was to bear the cost and what services were being paid for. The Senate wanted a flat-rate water tax to be imposed on every household, and to levy a limited amount in additional charges based on the quantity of water used. This would be calculated by a water meter installed at the mains tap in every household. Finally, it wanted the sprinkling of the streets in the summer—which of course would also use substantial quantities of the new mains water—to be paid for by the owners of the adjoining properties. Through this package of charges the Senate, led by the Finance Deputation, hoped to limit as far as possible the already considerable expense that the filtration scheme would involve. The Property-Owners' Association and its representatives in the Citizens' Assembly, led by Dr Heinrich Gieschen, took strong exception to these conditions, which they felt amounted to an attempt to introduce a filtration system largely at their expense. As Gieschen declared in 1885, 'we cannot approve the state's acquiring so much income from the most indispensable of nourishments, which nobody can do without'.[35]

Thus the filtration of the water-supply had become yet another object of dispute between the different fractions of capital within the city. The dispute had in fact been inherent in the issue from the very beginning, but by the middle of the 1880s it was beginning to take on epic proportions. The

[33] Ibid., pp. 14–15 (see n. 9. above).
[34] The account in this and succeeding paragraphs is based on a series of articles on the question in the *Hamburger Tageblatt* published in Nov. 1892 (copies in StA Hbg, Senat Cl. VII, Lit. Ta, Pars 2, Vol. 11, Fasc. 17, Inv. 1a), checked against the reports of the relevant Citizens' Assembly meetings (*Bürgerschaft*).
[35] StA Hbg, Senat, Cl. VII, Lit. Cc, No. 3b, Vol. 59: Zweiter Bericht des von der Bürgerschaft am 1884 niedergesetzten Ausschusses über den Antrag von Dr Gerson betreffend Abänderung des Regulativs der Stadtwasserkunst.

Property-Owners' Association now dug in its heels on four major demands. The first was that the water tax should be paid by the tenants, not by their landlords. In 1884 the Association proposed that the State Waterworks should conclude a separate contract with each individual consumer instead of merely with each house-owner. The Senate replied that there were already 14,000 separate contracts lodged with the Waterworks: the proposal of the Property-Owners' Association would increase the number of contracts to such a degree that a small army of officials would have to be employed to deal with them, resulting in further administrative costs that would inevitably be passed on to the house-owners in the form of higher taxes. For its part, the Property-Owners' Association was clearly afraid that defaulting or absconding tenants would oblige landlords to pay out of their own pockets a substantial part of the tax on the water they used. The Senate's reply to this was to allege that tenants would simply use communal taps or water-supplies in other, nearby buildings if they had to pay the water tax themselves.

Secondly, the Property-Owners' Association rejected the idea of a flat-rate water tax and argued for a sliding scale of charges according to the rental value of the dwelling, or in other words the ability of the tenant to pay; clearly, although landlords were anxious to pass on the costs of water consumption to their tenants, they did not want to do so to such an extent that the tenants' ability to pay the rent was endangered. These demands were not without a degree of justification. As early as 1852, indeed, the Property-Owners' Association had demanded a lowering of the water tax. Its repeated insistence on this point was based on the knowledge that the artisans, shopkeepers, and small tradespeople and businessmen whom it represented—and still more, the tenants whom it wanted to pay the tax—would always be charged more per gallon of water used than were the wealthy merchants and householders to whose ranks the Senators belonged. As Gieschen pointed out, his demands were 'all the more justified, since the individual rooms in the dwellings that are rented cheaply are much smaller than those in expensive dwellings. The former thus need smaller quantities of water to clean them than the grand rooms in the homes of the well-off.'[36] The wealthy were more likely to have water-closets and bathrooms; they lived in houses with gardens which they regularly watered in the summer; they stabled horses for business or pleasure purposes, and the average horse drank up to twelve gallons of water a day, and needed another four for grooming, while even greater quantities were used for washing out the stables.[37] Per capita, therefore, the comfortable classes consumed far more water than the less well-off. No wonder the Senate tried to set a flat-rate minimum payment of the water-tax; no wonder that the 'small men' of the Property-Owners' Association were so stubborn in their

[36] Ibid.
[37] Smith, *The People's Health*, pp. 215–23, has parallel English examples to the Hamburg quarrels over the water supply.

fight against its introduction and in their battle to frustrate the grandiose schemes of Lindley, Meyer, and their allies.

The third demand of the Property-Owners' Association, and one which followed naturally from the other two, was for the Senate to drop its insistence on the official installation of a water meter in every house. Of all the issues through which the battle over the water-supply was fought, this was the one that aroused the most passion. Indeed it has even been claimed that the water meter question was the main issue in all local Hamburg elections from the 1880s to the turn of the century. In time, the water meter became a symbol of the inequalities which the Senate was seeking to impose on Hamburg's inhabitants in their incarnation as water consumers. It eventually became somewhat detached from the realities of the question, as all symbols do. The Property-Owners' Association either wanted no water meters at all, or the right to install their own; what they did not want was standardized water meters installed by the state. The clearest summary of their importance was given by a hostile witness in 1896, during a debate in which the issue of water meters led to that rarest of spectacles, the Hamburg Citizens' Assembly in a state of uproar:

It has been said that the instruments are useless, or the state's finances will suffer, but the real reason for rejection is only the fact that the property-owners are afraid of the burden that will fall on them. If it had been proposed to collect the water-rate from the tenants, the same people would have hailed the water meters as a great discovery and voted for their introduction (Commotion in the Chamber).[38]

The property-owners feared the intrusion of state water inspectors into their private domain; and felt that if they themselves were charged a water tax according to the amount used, they would be put at the mercy of thirsty tenants, since the state had declared itself unwilling to install a meter in each individual dwelling. The landlord would thus have no means of apportioning the water charge equitably among his tenants unless he went to the considerable expense of installing separate meters himself—which, of course, the Property-Owners' Association was more than anxious to avoid. That the landlords held out for the right to install their own water meter for the whole house speaks not only for their fear that the state would manipulate its water meters to their disadvantage, but also perhaps for the hope that they could manipulate their own with the opposite effect.

The final issue around which the debate on the filtration of the water-supply revolved was the question of the sprinkling of the streets in the hot summer months. Up to 1885, as we have seen, this service was largely paid

[38] *Bürgerschaft*, 1896, p. 119, session of 30 Sept. 1896, speech of deputy Levy. The session became progressively more unruly. Speeches in favour of the meters were greeted with *Gelächter* ('cackles of laughter'). For water meters as an electoral issue, see E. Baasch, *Geschichte Hamburgs 1814–1918* (Gotha and Stuttgart, 1925), ii. 13.

for by the house-owners. Gieschen and his allies, however, now argued that it should be paid for exclusively by the state. If the state was going to gain a surplus by charging a water tax, they argued, then 'it is a simple demand of equity that a very small part of this surplus should be used to ease the situation of those who need it most'.[39] The Senate countered with a demand that the owners of land adjoining the streets sprinkled by the state should pay 50 Pfennigs per metre of sprinkled street in front of their property. The Citizens' Assembly, however, argued that the property-owners' interest was also that of the majority of the population:

The dust that is whipped up in the streets when the wind is strong—as happens more in Hamburg than in inland towns—not only offends passers-by and house-dwellers, it is also in the highest degree dangerous to health. Dust is an excellent carrier of numerous infectious diseases, and it is far from unlikely that these diseases are spread by the fact that the city does not bother to sprinkle the streets but leaves it to well-intentioned private persons to do the necessary in this respect.

'If the inactivity of the state, namely of city authorities with regard to this important sanitary arrangement, is unworthy', concluded the committee reporting to the Citizens' Assembly on the subject in 1885, 'the activity of private individuals is nothing short of risible.'[40] Citizens, it maintained, should not have to go from door to door, cap in hand, begging for money to hire a wagon to sprinkle the streets. The Senate continued to insist, however, on the 50 Pfennig charge. 'Finally', it argued, 'one may say with some justification of every similar measure of the state—even more for example of that of water filtration—that it serves the public good, without it thereby being right to devolve all the costs of such a particular measure from those immediately and directly affected on to the community as a whole.'[41]

These four main issues were debated with increasing passion on both sides throughout the second half of the 1880s. So great were the fears of the Property-Owners' Association that its representatives in the Citizens' Assembly or more than one occasion tried to call the whole filtration project into question. Thus when Meyer's scheme was debated by the Citizens' Assembly on 28 September 1887, Heinrich Gieschen sought to demonstrate that the project was badly worked out and alleged that the point from which the water was to be taken was too far downriver. He succeeded in persuading the Citizens' Assembly to set up another commission to examine the whole question all over again. Here, as one member later remarked, 'all the proposals to supply water from springs or artesian wells, that had already been rejected by the Joint Commission in 1878 as completely impracticable, were once more ventilated'. Expert testimony was able this time to dispose of all the

[39] StA Hbg. Senat, Cl. VII, Lit. Cc, No. 3b, Vol. 59: Zweiter Bericht ... (cf. n. 35, above).
[40] Ibid., Drucksache Nr. 17, Bericht des Bürgerschafts-Ausschusses ... März 1885.
[41] Ibid.: Mitteilung des Senats an die Bürgerschaft No 27, 19 März 1888.

technical objections quite rapidly. These objections had after all been disposed of at length once before. The Citizens' Assembly resigned itself to having to accept the project, and voted the money on 6 June 1888 by 65 votes to 60. But at the same time, it voted down the Senate's proposal that property-owners should pay at least three-quarters of the new water rate, however much water was used, and it approved a motion that property-owners should be able to install any kind of water meter, without interference from the state. The Senate was unwilling to accept these suggestions. It evidently felt that the house-owners could not be trusted to install water meters that would work properly. It was unwilling to go ahead unless the project was securely financed. So it rejected the Citizens' Assembly vote.[42]

Thus stalemate had once more been reached. Another eighteen months followed, in which the Senate and the Citizens' Assembly tried to agree on the financing of the new water-supply. At length, the matter was debated in the Citizens' Assembly on 22 January 1890. In this debate, the Senate, represented by Senator Lehmann, offered to take over the costs of the traditional service of sprinkling water on the streets in hot weather, but continued to reject the idea that tenants should pay the water rate. This, Lehmann argued, would cause 'a most uncommon increase in the work of the whole administration ... that will bring no direct benefits at all'. Nor would the Senate budge from its insistence on the installation of standardized water meters by the authorities. In reply, Heinrich Gieschen, speaking for the house-owners, put the whole principle of filtration in question yet again. It would, he declared, have no influence on bacteria, and the whole operation was a waste of money that would not bring about any improvement in the quality of the water. 'Let the existing system stay as it is', he urged. Gieschen continued to insist that the water rate should be paid by the tenants and he continued to argue that the amount charged should correspond to the amount used. Chief Engineer Meyer, speaking for the Senate, argued that meters were necessary to check excessive waste, and Dr Johann Julius Reincke, for the medical profession, spoke out in favour of filtration as a general principle. But the Citizens' Assembly took Gieschen's view and postponed a final decision once more.

Not content with these manœuvres, the property-owners' representatives also proposed that the Citizens' Assembly should vote for a substantial reduction of the annual water tax. 'Such substantial concessions have been made to the Senate in this matter', they opined, 'that it would now be a serious injustice to saddle our fellow-inhabitants with this burden, since the finances of the Waterworks are in such a healthy state.' The Senate's supporters suggested that enough had surely been said on the subject by now, but the view that the tax 'hits the *Mittelstand*' was accepted and the Assembly

---

[42] The account in this and the following paragraphs follows the sources listed in n. 34 above.

voted for the lower rate. In July 1890, however, the Senate discovered an unexpected budgetary surplus and, tired of the endless disruption, not only reaffirmed its willingness to take over the street-sprinkling without levying a charge on the house-owners, but also agreed to a lower water tax with a sliding scale according to rental value, with special charges for expensive houses and apartments.[43] It was thus able to inform the Citizens' Assembly on 9 July that the filtration of the water-supply would now go ahead. The decision was greeted 'with a loud bravo'.

The whole debate was a classic example of the balancing of interests between the different fractions of capital which was the major function of representative institutions in Hamburg. It also illustrated the delays to which the legislative system inevitably subjected expensive social and sanitary reforms. The compromise eventually reached in July 1890 was achieved at a cost that was ultimately to prove extremely high. Between the initial proposal, following on the cholera epidemic of 1873, and the final decision to construct a new, properly filtered water-supply for the city, had elapsed the astonishing period of seventeen years. A number of reasons were responsible for this extraordinary delay. Some of them, such as the quarrel between Meyer and Samuelson, were only relatively short-term in effect. Others, such as the absence of any really persistent pressure from the medical profession, were more negative than positive in character. More important was the fact that the period, which this project was under consideration also saw the immensely expensive and time-consuming construction of the new harbour facilities built for Hamburg's entry into the Customs Union in 1888. For most of the 1880s the energies of the Chief Engineer, the Senate, and the Citizens' Assembly were taken up by this project, which cost something in the region of 113 million Marks. Compared to this, the filtration of the water-supply appeared a measure of relatively low priority and—what was more important—no potential profitability. Moreover, the property-owners supported the construction of the free port because they thought that it would lead to a rise in land prices and an increase in rents as the housing stock was reduced with the demolition of the dwellings which stood in the designated free port area.[44] If the Senate and the Assembly did agree on major expenditure in a non-profit making area, then they were more likely to agree on a prestige project such as the building of the new Town Hall, a grandiose 'Renaissance' edifice designed, like so much in those years, to provide a symbolic reaffirmation of the waning power of the City Fathers. Faced with a choice between spending 6.75 million Marks on the Town Hall, and a little more on an unglamorous and unpretentious scheme such as the filtration of the water-supply, there

[43] Ibid: Drucksache für die Senatssitzung Nr 122, 8 July 1890. The water-meter question remained unsolved, despite almost uninterrupted debate, until 1906.

[44] H. K. Stein, 'Interessenkonflikte zwischen Grosskaufleuten, Handelskammer und Senat in der Frage des Zollanschlusses an das Reich, 1866–1881', *ZHG* 64 (1978), 68.

was no doubt which way Hamburg would turn. In June 1885, a month after the Senate had forwarded the waterworks project to the Finance Deputation, where it languished for another two years before returning, Senate and Citizens' Assembly gave their final approval to the Town Hall project. A grand ceremonial occasion was organized to mark the formal laying of the foundation stone. No such festivities were to mark the construction of the waterworks, when it eventually began. Moreover, work on the filtration plant proceeded at a less than urgent pace, not least perhaps to spread the cost over several years and avoid too great a burden on the city budget. In mid-August 1892 there were said to be only fourteen people working on the site, even though this was a good time for construction work; and the project was still generally estimated to need at least another year to be completed.[45]

d. *A Varied Diet*

I

The environmental pollution that afflicted nineteenth-century Hamburg did not exhaust itself in the foulness of the water, the smokiness of the atmosphere, and the filthiness of the streets, rivers, and canals. It also had a profound effect on the food that people ate and the beverages they drank. The quality of nutrition is perhaps one of the less obvious aspects of the state of the environment, but it is clearly one of the most important. If the environment is regarded as consisting of those aspects of the physical world necessary for the maintenance of human life, then food is clearly one of them, along with water and air: and the same holds good if we expand the definition of the environment, more satisfactorily perhaps, to include the physical world at large, not only earth, water, and air but also animal and plant life, which forms the essential basis of the food on which we depend.

Hamburg enjoyed throughout most of Germany a strong reputation as a centre of gastronomy. The people of Hamburg were generally believed to eat well. 'The Hamburger', wrote Johann Jakob Rambach, a local doctor, in 1801, 'likes above all nutritious foods. Most dishes are boiled in meat broth and with a lot of fat, and are little salted, but much spiced ...' Rambach found it remarkable that, as he said, 'very little bread is eaten with these dishes'. But, he went on, 'beef is a particular favourite dish of the people of Hamburg'. Indeed, he wrote, 'there is no lack of people here who eat beef every day'.[1] Not only meat, but all kinds of vegetables were consumed in early nineteenth-century Hamburg, and herrings and other fish were also very

---

[45] StA Hbg, PP S3490 Bd. 1: *Vorwärts*, 15 Oct. 1892.

[1] Rambach, *Versuch*, pp. 92–123, quoted in H. J. Teuteberg and G. Wiegelmann, *Der Wandel der Nahrungsgewohnheiten unter dem Einfluss der Industrialisierung* (Göttingen, 1972), pp. 243–4.

popular, though not as widely available as they had been some years before. Especially prized were 'strawberries, a favourite food of the Hamburg people'. During the summer season, wrote Rambach, 'almost every Hamburger eats them every day at least once, pulped, as a cold dish, with wine and milk'. During the day, he observed, people ate moderate meals, which 'are also mostly eaten quickly as well, because business awaits the active Hamburger again right after the meal'. But for grand dinners, which occurred with considerable frequency, the citizens enjoyed 'the refinements of the chefs of every nation, there are ragouts, puddings, stuffings, pies, and vol-au-vents with fillings from the four corners of the earth, pheasants from Bohemia and roast venison from the Harz with their accompaniments . . .' These 'armies of dishes', he continued enthusiastically, were followed by 'an almost equally lengthy tail of tarts, confectionery, creams, jellies, meringues, and ices'. All of course washed down by 'a swarm of fine wines'.[2] Such grand dinners played an important role in the informal mechanisms of rule in Hamburg in the nineteenth century, as we have seen, and leading Senators and city officials were likely to attend several every month. Rambach was aware, of course, that this standard of luxury was beyond the means of most of the city's inhabitants. They were, he reported, unable to afford most kinds of fish—the herrings of 1800 being something of an exception—and the common people tended to eat a lot of black rye bread and dumplings. Fresh vegetables were also too expensive for many when bad weather reduced supplies. But Rambach still maintained that many of the better-off working people ate meat daily, and that despite their simpler diet 'our poorer class of people still does very well and is bursting with health'.[3] If this was the situation in 1800, then, what was it like a century later? Had it improved or deteriorated? Could the poor still afford meat every day? Or had a century of urban growth and industrialization made things worse?

Hans-Jürgen Teuteberg, who is virtually the only German historian to have turned his attention to the problem of food consumption, has argued that 'a rapid improvement of the standard of living in the nineteenth century' brought with it a general improvement in nutrition.[4] People gradually came to enjoy a more varied diet, and better-prepared meals. Teuteberg estimated 'that energy supplies increased in a long trend through the nineteenth century'.[5] 'Since the turn of the century and thus since the beginning of the period of high industrialization in Germany, the average annual per capita value of nutrition in Germany has basically remained at the same level.' By 1900, industrialization had brought nutrition in Germany to its 'optimum' level in terms of quantity at least, even if it has continued since then to

[2] Ibid.
[3] Ibid.
[4] Ibid., p. 66.
[5] Ibid., p. 67.

improve in variety and taste. Teuteberg realized, of course, that there were differences in food consumption between rich and poor, and he conceded that the minimal diet offered, for example, to the inmates of institutions such as workhouses, was deficient in some respects. Nevertheless, he argued, the lower classes also benefited from the general improvement in nutritional standards during the nineteenth century. The periodic famines of earlier times disappeared as communications improved, and in the later stages of the century the food of the masses gained in variety as well as protein and calorific content.[6] Social investigators and propagandists educated the general public in the proper preparation of food, and traditional local and social dietary peculiarities disappeared. In particular, meat, and above all, pork consumption doubled between 1830 and 1900, largely because the lower classes were increasingly able to afford it.[7]

These arguments have been widely accepted by German historians. Reinhard Spree, for example, accords them a central place in his recent work on the decline of the death rate.[8] They are supported by a number of other statistical investigations into living standards carried out by historians such as Walther Hoffmann.[9] And yet Teuteberg's work is unsatisfactory in a number of respects. There is a remarkable circularity about an argument that uses indices of rising real wages to demonstrate an improvement in nutrition and then explains the improvement in nutrition by a rise in real wages. Moreover, attempts such as Hoffmann's to convert food consumption into calorific and protein values have run into severe criticism and must be regarded as unreliable.[10] The argument is also weak on a number of points of detail. Increased sales of pork, for example—one basis of Teuteberg's calculation—may merely have reflected a relative decline in the practice (which was probably largely unrecorded earlier in the century) of keeping pigs for private consumption. Even more serious is Teuteberg's failure to take account of the quality of the food consumed. Figures showing an increased consumption of food mean little or nothing if that food was simultaneously becoming poorer, less hygienic, and more liable to adulteration.[11] Above all, Teuteberg made no real attempt to differentiate between social classes. His assumption that the general increase in food consumption was so great as to have been impossible without the lower classes having taken some part in it

---

[6] Ibid., pp. 68–9.

[7] Ibid., pp. 130–2.

[8] Spree, *Soziale Ungleichheit*, p. 130.

[9] W. G. Hoffmann, *Das Wachstum der deutschen Wirtschaft seit der Mitte des 19. Jahrhunderts* (Berlin, Heidelberg, and New York, 1965), p. 659.

[10] R. A. Dickler, 'Labor Market Pressure—Aspects of Agricultural Growth in the Eastern Region of Prussia, 1840–1914. A Case Study of Economic-Demographic Transition', Ph.D. thesis (University of Pennsylvania, 1975), p. 179.

[11] See below, pp. 166–76.

remains no more than an assumption.[12] For, as John Burnett has remarked, in a study of nineteenth-century English nutrition that urgently needs replicating for Germany,

To discuss 'average' consumption is to ignore the really important economic results which industrialization did produce—improvement for some categories of labour and deterioration for others. Moreover, it neglects the fact that the first half of the nineteenth century saw the rise of a whole new social class whose consumption habits, in food at least, matched those of the landed gentry. Though still numerically small, the middle class of 1850, with its large families and armies of domestic servants, accounted for a much greater proportion of total food consumption than its numbers would suggest.[13]

This observation is particularly applicable to Hamburg, with its substantial middle class. Teuteberg's failure to take account of the extensive social differentiation produced by industrial capitalism, and his tendency to divide German society into a 'relatively thin upper crust'[14] and the rest, render his overall conclusions virtually worthless in concrete historical terms.

Nutritional standards among the working class in nineteenth-century Germany depended on a wide range of factors. It would be quite wrong to suppose that income level was the only determining influence: we cannot jump without further ado from evidence that money wages were increasing to the conclusion that people were eating better.[15] Food was only one item of expenditure among many, even for the working class, who spent well over half their income on it. As we have seen, the level of rent was more fundamental to the distribution of working-class expenditure, and workers adjusted their outgoings on food to their expenditure on accommodation, and not the

[12] For further work by Teuteberg, which has concentrated on working-class food consumption, but employs basically the same arguments and procedures and often the same material, see his 'Die Nahrung der sozialen Unterschichten im späten 19. Jahrhundert', in E. Heischkel-Artelt (ed.), *Ernährung und Ernährungslehre im 19. Jahrhundert* (Göttingen, 1976), pp. 205–87; 'Der Verzehr von Nahrungsmitteln in Deutschland pro Kopf und Jahr seit Beginn der Industrialisierung (1850–1975). Versuch einer quantitativen Langzeitanalyse', *Archiv für Sozialgeschichte*, 19 (1979), 331–88; 'Wie ernährten sich Arbeiter im Kaiserreich?', in W. Conze (ed.), *Arbeiterexistenz im 19. Jahrhundert* (Stuttgart, 1981), pp. 57–73; H. J. Teuteberg and A. Bernhard, 'Wandel der Kindernahrung in der Zeit der Industrialisierung', in J. Reulecke and W. Weber (eds.), *Fabrik, Familie, Feierabend. Beiträge zur Sozialgeschichte des Alltags im Industriezeitalter* (Wuppertal, 1978), pp. 183–97.

[13] J. Burnett, *Plenty and Want. A Social History of Diet in England from 1815 to the Present Day* (Harmondsworth, 1968), p. 50.

[14] Teuteberg and Wiegelmann, *Der Wandel*, p. 130.

[15] W. R. Lee, 'A commentary on Reinhard Spree: Determinanten des Sterblichkeitsrückgangs in Deutschland seit der Mitte des 19. Jahrhunderts', typescript, conference on 'Neuere Ergebnisse und Entwicklung einer Sozialgeschichte der Medizin und des Gesundheitswesens' (Bielefeld, Feb. 1982), for these points. In England higher wages could lead for example to higher consumption of less nutritious foods like white bread. For further critical observations on Teuteberg's work, see A. Lüdtke, 'Hunger, Essens- "Genuss" und Politik bei Fabrikarbeitern und Arbeiterfrauen. Beispiele aus dem rheinisch-westfälischen Industriegebiet 1910–1940', *Sozialwissenschaftliche Informationen*, 14 (1985), 118–26.

other way round. A lot also depended on the size of the worker's family and the age of his children. The more children he had, the less he could afford to spend on each. Children who were still too young to work, but old enough to need substantial quantities of food, were probably the greatest burden on the worker's pocket. Moreover, further inequalities were introduced by the fact that infants and children to some extent ate different food from their parents (more milk, for example), and that the largest portion may well have gone as a matter of course to the father of the family. The type and cost of food itself also has to be taken into consideration. The price of food, especially of basic items such as bread, varied considerably over time, and just as important, the worker's pattern of expenditure could be affected by local, culturally-determined peculiarities of habit and taste—for example, the preference of Hamburg's inhabitants for coffee rather than tea, beer rather than wine, or potatoes rather than noodles.

But by far the most important aspect of nutrition lay in the quality of the food consumed. A decline in quality could easily nullify an increase in quantity, so it is surprising that Teuteberg's numerous publications on the history of nutrition leave the quality of food almost entirely out of account. This is particularly significant in view of the fact that the nineteenth century saw a serious decline in the quality of many foodstuffs, due partly to problems of hygiene but above all resulting from the growing practice of adulteration. Difficult in the extreme when people produced it themselves, the adulteration of food was almost as difficult in a small-town environment where the grocer, brewer, or butcher still lived in close proximity to his customers. A big city such as Hamburg, however, offered an almost ideal environment for nutritional fraud. Old-established controls on the quality of food products were difficult to enforce in this environment, and in any case they were rendered increasingly inoperative by the doctrines of free competition. Whole classes of middlemen grew up. Bakers no longer milled their own flour, nor did publicans brew their own beer: in a large city such as Hamburg, they bought it from commercial millers or breweries, just as grocers depended increasingly on wholesalers for their supplies. Farmers also sold their milk, butter, and other produce through middlemen. All this increased the possibility of adulteration and made it more difficult to trace fraud back to its source.

At the same time, competition between retailers of one kind and another grew in the second half of the nineteenth century as people scrambled to make a living from supplying the inhabitants of the burgeoning cities with the necessities of life. Contemporary economists estimated that while there was one retail or wholesale trader for every 83 inhabitants of Germany in 1861, there was one for only every 54 in 1882 and one for every 30 in 1907. These varied of course from single-person small shops to larger wholesale firms employing over 50 workers apiece, but all had to exist in an atmosphere of cut-throat competition. The squeeze on profits was made worse by taxation and import duties from the end of the 1870s.[16] In this situation, as bakers, milkmen, grocers, and butchers struggled to undercut each other's retail prices, the temptation to make their wares go further, by reducing their strength, or including substitutes, was almost impossible to resist. At the same time, the growth of the chemical industry provided new means of adulterating food which were eagerly seized on by retailers as soon as they became available. All these influences combined to produce a veritable explosion of adulterative pratices in the nineteenth century. John Burnett has estimated that almost all the food and drinks sold in industrializing Britain were more or less heavily adulterated[17]; and there is no reason to suppose that the situation in industrializing Germany was any different. Most towns did of course possess regulations governing the quality of food; these were often, indeed, of great antiquity. But in the absence of random checks and proper chemical investigation they were mostly a dead letter, and adulteration and falsification of food spread unchecked.[18]

Hamburg was already large enough by the early nineteenth century for such practices to be commonplace. In 1810 J.H. Scholz complained of the almost complete absence of hygienic checks and controls on the sale of food:

If one goes through Hamburg's alley-ways, one often finds an opportunity to observe the lack of exact and active controls on this point. Bad lemons and oranges, rotten almonds, figs, and plums, stinking cheese swarming with maggots, unripe and half-putrefied fruit, bloaters, and herrings, boiled crabs and smoked eels are offered for sale with shouts and cries on barrows at street-corners, and are often bought by the poorer class of people because of their cheapness, which must have the most damaging effects on health. When seafish are sold, their gills are smeared with cows' blood to deceive the public as to their freshness, without any attempt being made to keep this 'industry' secret. Wine and beer adulteration is as well-known among small traders as it is among distillers ... Finally we can also count in butter, milk, bread, spice, flour, schnapps, and coffee adulteration, all of which is more or less in operation here and is not called to order by any high authority.[19]

Not only were no effective controls introduced, but the situation actually became worse as time went on. As cities and industrial conurbations grew in size, so it became progressively more difficult to keep food free from impurities. Even quite small towns were affected. 'Here in Kiel too', complained a local newspaper in 1877 for example, 'which has otherwise been considered such a solid town, there are often serious complaints to be made about the falsification of beer, butter, milk, etc.'[20] The reason for the fact that

[16] R. Gellately, *The Politics of Economic Despair: Shopkeepers and German Politics 1890–1914* (London, 1974), pp. 30–3.
[17] Burnett, *Plenty and Want*, p. 102.
[18] BA Koblenz R86/2104 Bd. 1–2 gives a survey of these regulations.
[19] Scholz, *Freimüthige und bescheidene Rügen*.
[20] BA Koblenz R86/2068 Bd. 1: *Kieler Zeitung*, No. 5902, 24 Aug. 1877.

'complaints about food adulteration' had 'become very general and urgent', according to another paper, was that the 'individualism that is the order of the day emerges in social life as crass self-interest, which subordinates the demands of honour and conscience to the lust for money-making and seeks to overcome competition through a greater deception of the public'.[21] These tendencies were above all encouraged by the economic depression which began in 1873 and which severely reduced profits for manufacturers, wholesalers, and retailers of food and food products. By 1878, as an official report presented to the Federal Council noted, 'complaints about the falsification of foodstuffs and consumables offered for sale have become louder year by year'.[22] The numerous articles published on the subject in 1877–8 bear all the hallmarks of an organized press campaign inspired by the government in an early stage of its turn to a more conservative social and political stance at this period. But there is no reason to doubt that they had a basis in reality. Even the liberal press joined in the campaign, and as we shall see, the facts which were now uncovered were indeed sufficiently alarming to take the issue far beyond the reach of party politics.

The methods and means of adulteration detailed in the 1878 report were staggering in their variety and ingenuity. Barite, gypsum, chalk, and other substances were added to flour, increasing its weight by up to 20 or 30%. Infusoria ore was also added for the same purpose 'in larger cities, namely in Hamburg, Altona, etc.',[23] while ground dried peas, lentils, beans, lupins, maize, potatoes, and other vegetable matter frequently serves as alternatives. Flour that was damp, musty, and sour was 'revived' with alum, blue vitriol (cupric sulphate), or even zinc sulphate to make the dough easier to knead and to give it a white colour.[24] Bread, as we have seen, was the staple diet of the working class. The poor depended on it for a very large proportion of their energy. It is quite possible that German bread was less prone to adulteration than its English counterpart. A good deal of the fraudulent treatment of English flour was designed to pass it off as first-grade flour necessary to produce the universally consumed white bread. In Germany, by contrast, brown or black rye bread was more common, and white bread was not so much in demand. This fact caused some astonishment in England, where it was attributed to the high cost of German wheat by politicians anxious to discredit the German tariff laws. A delegation of English workers sent to Germany in 1910 to investigate the effects of the import tariff on the working man's diet tried some black rye bread and found it quite palatable. They were forced to admit that the Germans ate it out of choice.[25] Even rye bread,

[21] Ibid.: *Norddeutsche Allgemeine Zeitung*, 18 and 25 Aug. 1877.
[22] StA Hbg, MK II A 2 Bd. 1, Bl. 2: Bundesrats-Drucksache 25, 9 Feb. 1878.
[23] Ibid.: *Berliner Tageblatt*, 13 Sept. 1877, on the 'increasing adulteration of food'.
[24] Ibid.
[25] *Report on Labour and Social Conditions in Germany: Working Men's Tours*, III, 3 (1910–11).

however, could be made more cheaply with poor quality flour or substitutes such as potatoes, or—if it was mixed rye and wheat bread—diluted with gypsum or chalk. Given the centrality of bread to the workers' diet, it only required a relatively small amount of adulteration to have quite a serious effect. And if they wished to spread butter on it, they were more than likely to get something else mixed in with it: in 1889, 72 out of 122 samples of butter (over 60%) investigated in Hamburg were found to be adulterated, mostly with margarine, and although the campaign to improve the quality of butter which began that year did meet with some success (the number of adulterated samples found fell sharply to 12% by 1892),[26] the inhabitants of Hamburg were still plagued right up to the turn of the century and beyond by 'so-called butter-farmers ... who present themselves as apparently honest countryfolk and peddle their mixtures of margarine, fat, etc. door to door as country butter which they have made themselves'.[27]

In South Germany, bread and potatoes gave way to some extent to noodles. These too were subject to widespread adulteration. Picric acid, for example, was mixed with urine and added to cheap dough to give 'egg noodles' a plausible yellow colour. Colouring agents were subject to few effective controls, and the use of lead chromate, copper oxide, nitrobenzene, and other noxious substances in cakes and confectionery had, said the 1878 report, 'made the confectionery workshops into complete factories for a virtually professional application of poisons'.[28] The wealthy could afford to buy expensive confectionery that was more or less guaranteed pure, but if the masses wanted to vary their diet or placate their children with a few chocolates, then it was only the very cheapest kinds of sweets that they could afford.[29] In order to reach this mass market, manufacturers and confectioners substituted the expensive genuine chocolate with mutton or veal fat, rice, and 'even starch-gum and rubber', while 'vanilla' chocolate was as often as not flavoured with benzoin or resin instead of genuine vanilla.[30] If the people of Hamburg wanted to indulge in the English habit of drinking tea with their bread and cakes, then they were quite likely to encounter used tea-leaves, dried, recycled, dyed with copper sulphate or chromate of lead, then dried and dusted with magnesium carbonate or soapstone and sold as new. Often the tea-leaves were mixed with other leaves such as 'ash, juniper, strawberry, whitethorn, dogrose, willow, elm', and coloured with Prussian blue and chrome yellow.[31]

Hamburg's most popular beverage was coffee. This offered rich oppor-

[26] BA Koblenz, R86/2114 Bd. 1: reports of the Chemisches Staatslaboratorium in Hamburg 1889–1892.
[27] StA Hbg, MK II A 1 Bd. 1, Bl. 87: *Hamburger Fremdenblatt*, 3 Oct. 1902.
[28] StA Hbg, MK II A 2 Bd. 1, Bl. 2: Bundesrats-Drucksache 25, 9 Feb. 1878, p. 30.
[29] Ibid, pp. 72–3.
[30] Ibid., pp. 34–5.
[31] Ibid., pp. 72–3.

tunities to the unscrupulous adulterator, who might mix it with burnt corn, chicory, or even sand. 'Raw green coffee-beans', continued the report,

are copied from clay or other pastes in factories that exist specifically for this purpose ... Unroasted beans are coloured in all sorts of ways. There are even special factories in Hamburg which deliver all shades of colouring for this purpose. The constituents are Prussian blue, chrome yellow (lead chromate), corn yellow, various kinds of ochre, indigo ... A highly reprehensible kind of coffee colouration consists further of rolling the beans in barrels with lead balls ... Roast coffee-beans are also artificially produced, partly from clay with burned sugar, partly from dough, partly from already ground roast coffee with a mixture of dough.[32]

Coffee, as we have seen, was consumed almost daily by Hamburg's working classes, and the cheap varieties they bought are more than likely to have been mixed with illicit substitutes. 11 out of 26 samples of coffee examined by a private medical investigator in 1878 were found to be adulterated.[33] By contrast, wine was not a popular drink in Hamburg, so the widespread falsifications to which it was subject—10 out of 28 cases in the same investigation in 1879[34]—had little impact on the city's diet. Beer, however, was widely consumed, and here a whole bagful of tricks was employed by brewers, wholesalers, landlords, and bartenders to reduce costs. As early as 1810, one observer complained that 'the brewers are using many kinds of substitutes because of the present high price of hops'.[35] Imperial Health Office investigations revealed that in the 1870s cheap added sugar often replaced the natural sugar which should have been produced from the malt, and old, used, or rotten hops were frequently substituted by benzoic acid or gingered up with a variety of substances including aloes, belladonna, 'Spanish pepper', buckbean, gentian root, picric acid, or an opium alkaloid.[36] If the beer became cloudy it was sometimes clarified with bisulphate of lime, tannin, or sulphuric acid and alum. Cautious landlords occasionally added borax to their beer so that it would keep longer, while coriander was sometimes put in to increase the lifespan of the foam once the beer was poured into the glass.[37] Repeated attempts to control the quality of beer by legislation ran into the problem that checks and controls were almost impossible to enforce with any thoroughness or consistency given the manpower and technology available. By the late nineteenth century, beer formed a major part of the working man's diet. Traditionally it was supposed to be brewed according to the 'purity

[32] Ibid., p. 71
[33] BA Koblenz R86/2114 Bd. 1: *Jahresbericht des Vereins gegen die Verfälschung der Lebensmittel in Hamburg* (Hamburg, 1879), report of Dr Niederstadt. In most cases, Niederstadt's figures were implausibly low, and the true rate of adulteration of these substances is likely to have been a good deal higher.
[34] Ibid.
[35] Scholz, *Freimüthige und bescheidene Rügen*, pp. 16–17.
[36] Ibid., pp. 50–9.
[37] StA Hbg. MK II A 3a Bd. 1, Bl. 2, 16, 87, 98.

principle' (*Reinheitsgebot*) which laid down that it was to contain nothing but malt, hops, yeast, and water.[38] In the nineteenth century however, this was very far indeed from the truth. A spot check of 33 beers carried out in Hamburg in 1894 revealed 23 to be adulterated, with serious consequences for their quality in terms of nourishment. Even Bismarck was moved in 1877 to complain of 'the complete lack of any connection between these fluids and what one normally calls beer and wine'.[39] Beer consumption, at least, began to decline from the turn of the century onwards. James Roberts has argued convincingly that nineteenth-century German workers drank beer for sustenance as much as for its alcoholic content. The fact that it was from about 1900 that a decline in beer drinking really became noticeable is more evidence that workers were at last finding it possible to afford more wholesome forms of nourishment, just as the rise in beer consumption from 1850 into the 1870s may be taken as an indication of an overall fall in working-class nutritional standards during those decades. Widespread adulteration seems to have made it an even less satisfactory substitute for other forms of sustenance than has hitherto been supposed.[40]

Food adulteration was undoubtedly extremely widespread in big cities like Hamburg and Berlin in the mid-nineteenth century. Its true extent is of course almost impossible to estimate. Most of the available data comes from the 1880s and 1890s. In 1890, for example, it was reported that out of 240 tests on foodstuffs and drinks carried out in Berlin, 63 (or 24%) found evidence of adulteration, ranging from pepper consisting partly of ash to cognac 'that did not have any cognac in its contents'.[41] The scale of adulteration practised two decades or so before may well have been even greater. The 1878 report led to a law of 1879 establishing quality controls over staple foods throughout the German Empire, but it was more or less a dead letter in Hamburg because there was no one competent to carry out the necessary investigations. There was, to be sure, a state chemical laboratory in the city, but this was responsible for investigating everything from forensic evidence in criminal cases to the cement used in building construction. It only undertook nutritional tests if it received complaints from the public. For most of the 1880s the policemen trained in the laboratory were mainly occupied with 'other official duties'. Serious random checks do not seem to have been instituted until 1889, and even then almost exclusively on butter, which had presumably been the

[38] Ibid., *Hamburgischer Correspondent*, 10 Mar. 1895. For the eventual institution of controls in Hamburg, see below, pp. 171, 529–30. Present-day German beer is usually advertised as having been brewed according to the *Reinheitsgebot* since the Middle Ages.

[39] StA Hbg, MK II A 3a Bd. 1, Bl. 98; Bismarck is quoted in Heischkel-Artelt, *Ernährung*, p. 169.

[40] J. S. Roberts, *Drink, Temperance and the Working Class in 19th-Century Germany* (London, 1984), pp. 43, 112–15.

[41] BA Koblenz R86/2068 Bd. 1: *Reichsanzeiger*, No 133, 4 July 1890.

subject of widespread complaints.[42] Characteristically for Hamburg, the public debate on the subject in 1878 led to the foundation of a voluntary association to tackle the problem (the *Verein gegen die Verfälschung der Lebensmittel in Hamburg*), established in 1878. Inspired by master artisans, innkeepers, bar owners and others who stood to lose financially by some aspects of adulteration, it tried to get the Senate to set up a separate investigation office to deal with the problem, but without success, and it does not seem to have been in existence very long.[43] Not until the founding of the Hygienic Institute in 1892 did the Senate employ trained chemists who could carry out spot-checks on food and drink and provide the police with the evidence necessary to secure a conviction under the terms of the law of 1879.[44] The adulteration revealed by the Hygienic Institute's investigations was very extensive. The Institute was initially seriously understaffed, and it was some years before it was able to record a reduction of fraudulent practices to a more or less acceptable level. It would seem reasonable to conclude that it was only from about 1900, at least, that Hamburg's poor could be confident that the cheap food on which they depended for their existence was basically free from harmful additives or illicit dilutants. However, adulteration continued to be practised well after the turn of the century; a report issued in 1902 took some 132 pages to list all the varieties of adulteration still in use,[45] and as late as 1909 the liberal daily *Frankfurter Zeitung* was complaining once more of an 'increasing falsification of foodstuffs' and asserting 'above all it is the consumer sector of the great cities and the industrial areas that is flooded with inferior products'.[46]

Adulteration was dangerous to people's health in a number of ways. Some of the additives used were poisonous if taken in large quantities or consumed over a lengthy period of time. Copper sulphate, lead chromate, and other minerals could cause death if consumed in sufficient quantities. They could leave trace elements of lead, copper, or arsenic which would accumulate in the body and gradually weaken the digestive system. Alum could also inhibit digestion and thus lower the nutritional value of food. Above all, however, the substitute of worthless substances for real food—gum instead of chocolate, water in beer, chalk in flour, and so on—lowered their protein or calorie content and further weakened what was for most of the poor an

---

[42] Ibid., 2114 Bd. 1: reports of Chemisches Staatslaboratorium in Hamburg, 1886–1891. This seems to have been true of most German towns in 1879 (ibid., 2104 Bd. 1–2).

[43] Ibid., 2114 Bd. 1: *Jahresbericht . . . gegen die Verfälschung* (n. 33 above).

[44] Other parts of Germany did not follow suit until 1894 (Spree, *Soziale Ungleichheit*, p. 110). For detailed evidence on the difficulties of detecting and prosecuting adulteration, see E. Schmauderer, 'Die Beziehungen zwischen Lebensmittelwissenschaft, Lebensmittelrecht und Lebensmittelversorgung im 19. Jahrhundert, problemgeschichtlich betrachtet', in Heischkel-Artelt, pp. 131–97.

[45] BA Koblenz R86/2107 Bd. 3: 'Ergänzungen zu der Übersicht über die Jahresberichte der öffentlichen Anstalten zur technischen Untersuchung von Nahrungs- und Genussmitteln im Deutschen Reich für das Jahr 1902'.

[46] Ibid., 2068 Bd. 2: *Frankfurter Zeitung*, 17 July 1909.

already inadequate diet.[47] If the poor were enjoying a more varied diet at the end of the nineteenth century than they were at the beginning, then it may not always have been in the sense intended by those historians who have advanced this claim. Finally, as John Burnett has remarked, there was also a moral dimension to food adulteration, for here we have an important section of the middle class accepting fraud and deception as a normal agency of commerce. 'Business morality', concludes Burnett, in words which might equally apply to Hamburg's merchant and manufacturing community as to London's, 'was never lower than at the time when Christian observance was at its most ostentatious'.[48]

II

Adulteration was perhaps the most dramatic aspect of the decline in the quality of food in industrializing Germany. The separation of producer and consumer led to comparable dangers to health, however, in the form of declining standards of hygiene. Not that food in the countryside was particularly clean, of course: but at least it was easier to get it fresh, and the potential sources of contamination were many fewer in number. Most foodstuffs in nineteenth-century Hamburg were not sold in shops, or even on the markets. 'With reference to the traffic in most foodstuffs', it was reported in 1900, 'there still exists in Hamburg the old custom of sale by itinerant traders who offer them with street-cries and bring them into the consumers' houses. Only hotels and restaurants, large institutions, and the people who live near the Hopfenmarkt and the Messberg are accustomed to buy their food from the markets held in these places; there are no covered markets at all.'[49] These picturesque tradespeople may have enlivened the street scene with traditional Low German cries and songs advertising their wares, but their business naturally exposed the food they sold to a host of sources of infection. In 1899, for instance, there were complaints about the low standards of hygiene observed by the owners of fruit-barrows: 'One often sees such tradespeople offering their wares', wrote an irate reader to a local newspaper: 'Their clothing is not very clean, and is in addition subject to all the street dust of the day. Their hands are extraordinarily filthy. And their goods are open to every kind of dust and impurity and are often enough of inferior quality to begin with.'[50] Milk, which was subject to a series of special investigations in the 1890s, was particularly unhygienic. Vast quantities of milk were consumed in the city—over 60 million litres in 1897, for example,

[47] Burnett, *Plenty and Want*, pp. 118–19.

[48] Ibid., p. 120

[49] *Die Gesundheitsverhältnisse*, p. 75. For further reminiscences, see StA Hbg, FA Merck II 9 Konv. 4a, Heft II, pp. 2–3, Erinnerungen und Aufzeichnungen von Heinrich Merck.

[50] StA Hbg, MK II A 9a: *Hamburger Fremdenblatt*, 30 July 1899.

which worked out at roughly 100 litres per person annually. By 1906 the inhabitants of Hamburg were drinking 282,000 litres of milk a day. Three-quarters of this was delivered directly to the consumers by some 1,000 to 1,500 milkmen, who were mostly independent salesmen working on their own.[51] They refused to allow the farmers to cool the milk before they bought it because it was easier to remove the cream when it was warm.[52] After removing the cream they often added a yellow dye to make what was left look like the full-cream milk that the customers preferred. In 1894, when checks were first instituted, 25% of all samples were found to have added water or too low a fat content, and before controls were even a threat, the proportion was certainly much higher: in 1878, for example, a private medical investigation carried out in Hamburg found 36 out of 47 samples of milk to be adulterated, or nearly 80%.[53] The water added was often dirty and full of harmful bacteria. 23% of the samples investigated in 1895—and nearly all of those examined in July—had borax and boracic acid added to prevent it going off; indeed, some dealers did not shirk at using formaldehyde for the same purpose.[54]

When the milkmen bought their supplies from the farmers they put the milk into wooden, red-painted pails which they then carried through the streets on carts pulled by dogs. These pails were seldom cleaned very thoroughly, and there were complaints in the 1880s about the 'unsatisfactory *covering* of the pails ... which hang from the cart without lids in the rain, wind, heat, or dust'. 'There is little to be said in respect of a *control* of the milk trade in our city', added the report.[55] Some attempts were made, above all in the Law Concerning the Milk Trade of April 1894, to improve the hygienic standards of the milkmen and force them to fit their pails with covers. The Law prescribed that the pails had to be regularly cleaned and fitted with covers. It did not, however, force the milkmen to keep the pails covered. And, as the Hygienic Institute in Hamburg reported in 1900:

When one goes for a walk in the morning and observes the various milk-carriers and milk-carts, and follows the manipulations which take place on the cart, one sees how on occasion not only the dog that pulls the cart quenches his thirst by lapping the dripping milk-pails, but also how other dogs also strike up relationships of various kinds with the milk-pails that are often set down on the pavement or on the stairs in front of the houses, and when one reflects on all the other dangers that are connected

[51] Ibid., 3a Bd. 1 Bl. 61: *Bericht des Hygienischen Instituts ... 1897*; ibid Bl. 120: *Hamburgischer Correspondent*, 13 Feb. 1903; ibid., 1 Bd. 1 Bl. 87: *Hamburger Fremdenblatt*, 13 Oct. 1906.

[52] Ibid., 3a Bd. 1, Bl. 80 (pp. 12–13); ibid., Bl. 3: *Correspondenz des Milchwirtschaftlichen Vereins*, 17 (1882), 5.

[53] BA Koblenz R86/2114 Bd. 1: *Jahresbericht ... gegen die Verfälschungen*, report of Dr Niederstadt (cf. n. 33, above).

[54] Ibid., Bl. 80 (pp. 12–13). Borax was introduced only in 1895; before this, the problem of preserving the milk was even more severe.

[55] Ibid., Bl. 3. *Correspondenz des Milchwirtschaftlichen Vereins*, 17 (1882), 5.

with this decentralized milk trade, one is constantly confronted with the question of where one can hope for the help that is absolutely necessary in improving such circumstances, which are completely unworthy of a great city of Hamburg's importance.[56]

If the addition of chalk, gypsum, flour, and other thickeners was a relative rarity by this time, the general hygienic conditions in which milk was produced were still very poor.[57] Only in the 1890s did sterilization devices seem to have become generally available, and even here they were beyond the pockets of most people.[58] Little was done before the turn of the century to reduce the possible risk of infection from tubercular cows; investigation was difficult, pasteurization expensive and the slaughter of tubercular cows came up against powerful vested interests. If the British experience is anything to go by, then up to 50% of cows may have been infected by the time they reached the slaughterhouse.[59]

Milk was only one of a whole range of foods whose hygienic quality left more than a little to be desired. The Foodstuffs Law passed in Hamburg in 1870 aimed to remove what were later described as 'serious nuisances in the food trade', but it had little practical effect because the courts proved unable to build up a firm tradition of dealing with these cases. Preserved foods, canned fish or fish paste especially, were the cause of frequent mass poisonings in the 1880s and 1890s, and these continued after the turn of the century. Fresh foods were just as dangerous. Rotten fish was sold cheaply to the poor and also led to outbreaks of food poisoning.[60] Hygienic conditions in bakeries were often extremely primitive; Wilhelm Wachendorf, for example, recalled the presence in the Niedernstrasse in the 1880s of 'an old bakery that was famous for its round loaves, although—or perhaps just because—one often had to cut out firebugs that had been baked into them.'[61] Butchers and meat-sellers continued to colour rotten mince with cochineal to give it a fresh appearance or to put carmine in sausages to disguise their high grain content.[62] Diseased animals were frequently slaughtered illegally, and the meat put cheaply onto the market. In the 1870s there were some celebrated cases in various parts of Germany where people were taken seriously ill, some fatally so, after eating contaminated meat. 206 people were affected in Wurzen and 197 in Zeitz, for example,[63] and further mass poisonings continued

[56] Ibid., Bl. 80 (*Bericht ... 1900*, pp. 12–13). For the 1894 law, see StA Hbg, MK II A 3g Bd. 1.
[57] See StA Hbg, MK II A 1 Bd. 1, Bl. 2: Bundesrats-Drucksache Nr. 25 (9 Feb. 1878), pp. 40–8.
[58] BA Koblenz R86/2215 Bd. 1, *passim*.
[59] Smith, *The People's Health*, pp. 212–13.
[60] BA Koblenz R86/2271 Bd. 1, *passim* (esp. *Norddeutsche Allgemeine Zeitung*, 2 Aug. 1898, *Berliner Tageblatt*, 29 Apr. 1906).
[61] Helmut Wachendorf, 'Im Gängeviertel', p. 20.
[62] StA Hbg, MK II A 13a Bd. 1 Bl. 158–9, 170 c/d.
[63] Ibid., I Bd. 1, Bl. 2: (*Bericht ...* pp. 35–40).

regularly up to 1914.[64] Not only diseases such as anthrax and tuberculosis, but also dangerous parasitic infections such as trichinosis were passed on to humans in this way. Measly or condemned meat often appeared in sausages, or minced with healthy meat to disguise its flavour and appearance. The situation may have been improved in Hamburg by the early introduction (in 1753) of a ban on slaughtering other than in approved slaughterhouses, the construction in 1839 of a central slaughterhouse in the Neustadt (replaced by a much larger one in St Pauli in 1892), the promulgation of a ban on the sale of measly meat in 1855, and the outlawing of the sale of meat from animals infected with trichinosis in 1866. But there was no proper inspection of meat until 1894, and even after that it remained difficult to control the presence of diseased meat in cheap mince and sausages.[65]

Food of all kinds was a common source of infection and disease in the great cities of nineteenth-century Germany. Conditions were probably almost as unhygienic in the countryside, where checks and controls were extraordinarily difficult to operate. But at least the countryfolk were not as exposed as the town-dwellers to the perils of adulteration, and their close proximity to the sources of supply made storage less of a problem. Fruit and vegetables, milk and butter, cheese, bread, and meat were all exposed to many dangers *en route* from the farm to the city streets. Even before they reached the retailer they were liable to widespread adulteration, reducing their nutritional value and in some cases making them positively dangerous to health. As they were carted by the salespeople from house to house, often after being adulterated once more, they were open to all the hazards of the environment, from soot and smog to dust and dirt and the unwanted attentions of grubby street-urchins and passing dogs and other animals. When they got into the home they were stored in unrefrigerated, often unhygienic conditions where they were liable to infection from all the multifarious elements of domestic squalor with which they were surrounded. The well-off, with their armies of domestic servants and acres of storage space, were able to some extent to overcome these problems. Those who could afford to buy good cuts of meat and to throw away stale bread and sour milk were spared the dangers that these foodstuffs posed to their health as well as their disagreeable effects on the palate. As the *Frankfurter Zeitung* pointed out in 1909, 'the cheaper the goods which the public is forced to buy, the greater the risk it runs of receiving adulterated products for its money';[66] and the same principle applied to poor-quality, rotten, or polluted foods as well.

It is not possible in the present state of knowledge to say with any certainty whether things were as bad elsewhere, but the sheer size of Hamburg and its

---

[64] See the collection of these cases in BA Koblenz R86/2273 Bd. 1.

[65] See the comments ibid., 2107 Bd. 3, 'Ergänzungen . . . (n. 45, above) on the legal problems involved in enforcing regulations on the grain content of sausages.

[66] BA Koblenz R86/2068 Bd. 2: *Frankfurter Zeitung*, 17 July 1889.

population make it quite likely that only in Berlin were conditions so very unfavourable for the purity and preservation of food; Hamburg's status as a centre of food-processing industries, and its tenacious hold on customs such as the sale of foodstuffs in the streets, may have made the quality of food even worse than in the capital city. As we saw in Chapter 1, the rise of rents for working-class housing from the middle of the century and above all in the 1880s must have compelled widespread cut-backs in food expenditure among proletarian families, and the situation became desperate with the sharp jump in food prices in 1888–90 and the widespread unemployment that characterized the economic downturn of 1890–2. It was unfortunate that these developments took place at a time when the monitoring of food hygiene and quality was unimproved and the pressures on retailers and middlemen to adulterate their wares particularly strong. The average manual labourer in Hamburg entered the last decade of the nineteenth century on a diet no better that that of his or her predecessor in the early part of the century, and in many respects quite possibly a good deal worse.

III

As the example of food suggests, the physical environment in which the inhabitants of Hamburg lived went through a number of important changes in the nineteenth century. Although it is obviously rather risky to generalize, we may hazard a guess that the financial crisis of the state, the poverty of the overcrowded population, and the confusion of the administration in the first fifteen years of the century led to a deterioration in the quality of the environment: to judge from the comments of contemporaries such as Rambach and Scholz, the administration of the city seems to have been in such a bad way that the streets were hardly cleaned, the food-sellers were allowed to offer even the most obviously rotten food for sale with impunity, and the habits of the population left a great deal to be desired as far as hygiene and cleanliness were concerned. The return of ordered and solvent government, the reorganization of the police, and the reform of the street-cleaning system after the end of the Napoleonic Wars may well have eliminated some of the worst abuses, although the banning of pigs from the city centre was possibly a retrograde step. However, the steady growth of the population, and the continuous rise in economic activity, which brought increasing numbers of horses onto the streets, soon seems to have led to a renewed deterioration, if the complaints that began to be voiced in the 1830s are to be believed.

The Great Fire of 1842 brought major improvements to the environment in the form of the centralized water-supply and sewage systems created by William Lindley, to which must be added the public bathhouse opened in 1855. However, although these innovations gave Hamburg a well-deserved reputation for its progressive stance in sanitary matters, they were all in fact direct consequences of the disaster of the fire, or linked to it by one means or another, and without it they would certainly not have occurred so quickly or so comprehensively. Once they had been introduced, they were not significantly improved, and by the beginning of the 1880s Hamburg was in reality no longer the centre of progressive attitudes to sanitary reform that it had been before Lindley was forced to leave the city in 1860. In other respects the environment began to deteriorate once more after the middle of the century. The transition from the lowest-tender to the highest-bidder form of contract for street cleaning and waste removal in 1850 was soon followed by a decline in profits from dung caused by the increased use of cheaper fertilizers by farmers and the decline in supplies consequent upon the extension of the sewage system. Contractors cut costs all round, and reduced efficiency was the result; and by the time the lowest-tender system was reintroduced in 1869 the population had begun to grow so quickly—above all in the suburbs—that contractors were no longer able to keep pace. Only in 1886 did matters begin to improve when the state finally took over, and even here the adjustment doubtless took time; an incineration plant for rubbish, for example, was not established for another decade.

The growth of population from the 1860s also began to overload the sewage system, and the volume of untreated effluvia discharged into the Elbe began to become a serious health hazard by the middle of the 1880s. Meanwhile over 5,000 lavatories were still not connected to the sewers and many of them continued to discharge their contents directly into the fleets. Hamburg's rivers and streams also began to suffer from sewage discharged into them from municipalities and factories upriver from the early 1880s. The water-supply remained unfiltered because of disputes about who was to bear the cost of constructing filter-beds, and the danger of serious infection became steadily greater as all these sources of pollution became more powerful. The expansion of ancillary industries and the growing use of coal for heating in the ever-increasing number of domestic dwellings in the city and suburbs led to worsening air pollution, once more in the 1880s. Health hazards posed by overcrowded and verminous living conditions continued and may also possibly have become more serious. Rats plagued the harbour in increasing numbers as more ships came and went. The expansion of the suburbs across formerly rural territory where pigs and other animals were still kept created more nuisances. Finally, the problem of food adulteration and hygiene seems to have grown worse as the city expanded, and no effective means were found to deal with it before the 1890s. It is possible, therefore, to speak of a general deterioration of the urban environment in Hamburg beginning in the late 1850s and continuing unabated until the end of the 1880s.

The history of the environment, however, is also the history of people's changing perceptions of it. In the observations of Rambach at the beginning of the nineteenth century it is possible to detect the beginnings of a crusade by the emerging medical profession for a general sanitization of society under their own guidance; while in the fulminations of Scholz against the filth that was choking the streets of Hamburg in 1810 one may see not only a reflection of the chaos caused by the Napoleonic occupation but also a metaphorical expression of the desire to be rid of the French. Later on, the chorus of complaints about the environment that began to be heard in the 1830s, was cut off by the reforms that followed the Great Fire, but raised its collective voice again with increasing shrillness from the late 1850s onwards, was overwhelmingly a bourgeois chorus, led by doctors, lawyers, Citizens' Clubs, Citizens' Assembly deputies, and other members or organs of the dominant classes.

The growth of concern about the environment was part of a general growth of middle-class consciousness in the period 1850–80. The bourgeoisie and petty-bourgeoisie began to set themselves apart from the working class. The values which moulded their lives included not only hard work and thrift but also orderliness and self-discipline. Dirt was disorder, and the bourgeois perception of dirt was in part a symbolic identification of an opposite against which they could measure the extent of their own social achievement. The distance which they sought to put between themselves and the working class was expressed in a growing bourgeois perception of the common people as dirty, smelly, and unhygienic; and this perception reinforced itself through the rapidly-spreading use of perfumes and deodorants to which it gave rise. The middle classes began to distance themselves from their own bodily functions; modesty, shame, and ultimately prudery, became the bourgeois equivalents of the aristocratic code of honour. The changed perceptions which these attitudes embodied could be directly affronted when, for example, the rapid growth of population in a district such as Barmbeck or the Billwärder Ausschlag brought about a clash between rural and working-class life-styles and the sensibilities of the bourgeois members of the local Citizens' Club.[67]

But these perceptions were not merely conditioning influences on the physical sense of smell. They embodied a more general fear of the mob, as William Lindley's enthusiasm for the social and political benefits of the public washhouse clearly suggested. It was not that lack of cleanliness would lead to revolution; rather, lack of cleanliness was merely the outward expression of an inner rejection of bourgeois norms and so of bourgeois society. This perception could act as a reinforcement of bourgeois fears and bourgeois feelings of moral superiority over the working class, but with occasional exceptions such as Lindley's washhouse it did not lead to a general cleansing and moralizing offensive against the proletariat until class antagonisms had

[67] M. Douglas, *Purity and Danger* (London, 1975); N. Elias, *Über den Prozess der Zivilisation* (2 vols.; Frankfurt, 1969); Corbin, *Pesthauch*.

reached a really dangerous pitch. By 1890, when this was indeed the case, the middle classes in Hamburg were confident enough of their own incorporation of the virtues of cleanliness and orderliness to be ready to force them upon the working class should the latter's dirt and disorder become a serious threat. Such a threat was not necessarily seen in direct, personal terms: the most general perception of environmental pollution, whether it was of evil-smelling rivers or dung-strewn streets, could be a metaphorical translation of the fear of social disorder as well as embodying a direct attempt to banish it from the public space inhabited by the bourgeoisie. The very language used to describe pollution—'*verpestet*', '*pestilenzartig*', '*gemeinschädlich*', '*Ausdünstungen*' ('contaminated', 'pestilential', 'a common danger', 'exhalations')—suggested a force that would spread to infect the whole of society unless it was brought under control. Environmental pollution was real enough in late nineteenth-century Hamburg; but for Hamburg's dominant classes, it appeared not so much a direct physical consequence of the capitalist expansion which they themselves had done so much to create, as a symbolic expression of the threat from below which was bringing that expansion into question.

3

Matters of Life and Death

a. Patterns of Mortality

I

HISTORIANS seem generally agreed that in the nineteenth century, as Robert Woods and John Woodward have recently remarked,

the urban environment ... was generally more unhealthy than the countryside. Infectious diseases were more likely to be endemic; epidemics developed more frequently and were easily maintained; poor sanitary conditions meant that food, milk and water supply were liable to be contaminated; whilst overcrowding provided both a source of psychological tension and an aid to the easy communication of disease.[1]

There is ample evidence to support Woods and Woodward's claim. Anthony Wohl has pointed out that 'it was not that rural conditions were good but that many elements necessary for good public health ... were much more difficult to provide in the congested and burgeoning cities'.[2] In 1876, the death rate per 1,000 inhabitants of the 22 biggest towns and cities in Prussia was 30.0; for Prussia as a whole it was only 27.5. And there was no really marked decline in death rates for most of the century. It was not until well into the last quarter of the century that mortality in Berlin and other great cities finally began the decline which eventually brought it down to modest levels.[3]

These persistently high levels of mortality were also present in nineteenth-century Hamburg. Almost until the end of the century Hamburg's death rate averaged around 25 per 1,000 population per year. Normal urban death rates in advanced industrial societies in the late twentieth century average

---

[1] R. Woods and J. Woodward (eds.), *Urban Disease and Mortality in Nineteenth-century England* (London, 1984), p. 20.

[2] A. S. Wohl, *Endangered Lives: Public Health in Victorian Britain* (London, 1983), p. 3. See also G. Rosen, 'Disease, Debility and Death', in H. J. Dyos and M. Wolff (eds.), *The Victorian City: Images and Realities* (London, 1973), pp. 625–67; B. Luckin, 'Death and Survival in the City: Approaches to the History of Disease', *Urban History Yearbook* (1980), pp. 53–62; D. J. Loschky, 'Urbanisation and England's Eighteenth-Century Crude Birth and Death Rates', *Journal of European Economic History*, 1 (1972), 697–712.

[3] R. Spree, *Soziale Ungleichheit vor Krankheit und Tod: Zur Sozialgeschichte des Gesundheitsbereichs im Deutschen Kaiserreich* (Göttingen, 1981), p. 169; A. E. Imhof, *Die gewonnenen Jahre. Von der Zunahme unserer Lebensspanne seit dreihundert Jahren, oder, von der Notwendigkeit einer neuen Einstellung zu Leben und Sterben. Ein historischer Essay* (Munich, 1981), p. 208.

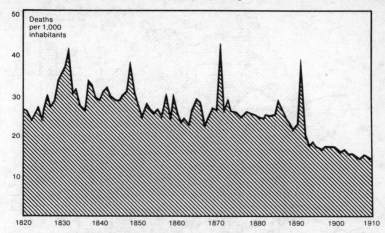

Sources: Die Gesundheitsverhältnisse Hamburgs im 19. Jahrhundert (Hamburg, 1901), 106–7; *SHS* 16, (1912), 59. Figures are for city and inner suburbs to 1871; state territory thereafter

FIG. 2. Mortality rate in Hamburg, 1820–1910

little more than 10 per 1,000 population. Right up until the last decade of the nineteenth century, as Figure 2 shows, the general mortality rate fluctuated within fairly narrowly-defined limits and failed altogether to undergo any permanent, long-term decline. In the 1880s it was considerably higher than that of Hamburg's smaller Hanseatic counterpart, Bremen, which stood at 20.4‰; higher too than that of the financial centre of Germany, Frankfurt, where the death rate was only 19.6‰. Leipzig, where it was 21.6‰, was another major German town that could claim to be a good deal healthier than Hamburg. Other cities, however, had a more readily comparable death rate in the 1880s. Dresden, for example, suffered 23.8 deaths per 1,000, and Düsseldorf, with 24.0‰, or Cologne, with 26.6‰, also experienced similar levels of mortality. There were appreciably higher mortality rates in Munich (30.8‰), Breslau, (30.5‰), and Chemnitz (32.1‰). By international standards, Hamburg's mortality rates were about average for a large city at this period. Liverpool's average annual death rate for the 1880s has been calculated at 25.8‰, for example, and Manchester's 26.6‰. So while Hamburg was by no means exceptionally unhealthy compared to other cities, it certainly had nothing to boast about in respect of its mortality rates either.[4]

[4] W. Matti, 'Bevölkerungsvorgänge in den Hansestädten Hamburg und Bremen vom Anfang des 19. Jahrhunderts bis zum Ersten Weltkrieg', *ZHG* 69, (1983), 103–56; *Hygiene und Soziale Hygiene in Hamburg* (Hamburg, 1928), p. 34; *SHS* 16 (1894), 59; *Die Gesundheitsverhältnisse Hamburgs im 19. Jahrhundert* (Hamburg, 1900), pp. 166–7 (these rates are for the city and

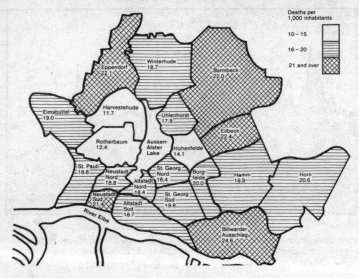

Source: calculated from *SHS* 15 (1894), 57, 67, 77, 87, 97

MAP 18. Average annual mortality rate, by district, Hamburg 1887–91

   These global mortality rates concealed wide variations between the various districts of which the city was composed. In the mid to late 1880s someone living in the inner city was over one and a half times as likely to die as someone living in Harvestehude, while an inhabitant of the Billwärder Ausschlag was about twice as likely to die as an inhabitant of Rotherbaum. These were the extremes, of course; but as Map 18 shows, death rates in the Neustadt Süd, Barmbeck, and other predominantly working-class districts were much higher than in the wealthier districts around the Alster. These differences between the districts of Hamburg present a powerful picture of social inequality in the face of death and disease. But the figures tell us nothing in themselves about the causes of the inequality they reveal. Nowadays heart failure and cancer are the most important causes of death in the advanced industrial nations. A century ago they were relatively unimportant in statistical terms. The major killers were the infectious diseases. In part the difference is caused by the decline of fatal infections among infants; in part it reflects the fact that many cases of cancer and circulatory failure were not recognized as such a century ago, but were classified under the symptoms

suburbs only), 311; J. J. Reincke, *Der Typhus in Hamburg, mit besonderer Berücksichtigung der Epidemieen von 1885 bis 1888* (Hamburg, 1890), p. 2; Woods and Woodward, *Urban Disease and Mortality*, p. 184.

which they occasioned. The category of 'death from old age' (*Altersschwäche*), which underwent a remarkable rise and fall in the medical statistics during the nineteenth century, is only one example of this difference in classification.[5] Nevertheless even when these considerations are taken into account, we are still left with the undeniable fact that infectious diseases caused far more deaths among adults in the nineteenth century than they do today.

Chief among these killer diseases was tuberculosis. Its main causative agent was the tubercle bacillus, discovered by Robert Koch in 1882. The bacillus could affect animals as well as humans and may have been transmitted in milk from infected cows. It was also carried in the droplets expelled by victims when coughing or spitting. These infected other people directly or through food or other objects in which the droplets landed. After entering the human body, the bacilli began to multiply and destroy the tissue around them. They could effect almost any part of the body, especially bones and joints, the lymph nodes (in the form known as scrofula), and the intestinal tract. These varieties of tuberculosis, which were not always recognized as manifestations of the same disease in the nineteenth century, mainly affected infants and children. Among adults, however, tuberculosis was primarily a disease of the lungs. In all its aspects it was relatively slow to act; among adults, indeed, often extremely so. The bacilli could be contained by calcification of the infected areas, and periods of remission could occur. In the great majority of cases, this is what indeed happened. But in some, the bacilli continued to multiply, and vital tissues, whether in the lungs or elsewhere, were progressively destroyed, until death eventually ensued.[6]

Tuberculosis was extremely common in the nineteenth century. A survey of European cities reported in 1930 that an average of 20% of children had been infected by the age of 2; half by the age of 5; and 90% by the time they were 15. Only three out of every hundred adults showed a negative reaction to the tuberculin test, which gave a positive result if they had at any time suffered tubercular infection. Given the fact that almost every town-dweller seems to have suffered from the disease at one time or another, it is hardly surprising that even a relatively low number of deaths per 100 cases (or case-specific mortality rate) still made tuberculosis the greatest of all the killer diseases. It had been estimated that nearly four million people in England and Wales died of it between 1851 and 1910. About three-quarters of these

[5] C. Conrad, 'Sterblichkeit im Alter, 1715–1975, —Am Beispiel Berlin: Quantifizierung und Wandel medizinischer Konzepte', in H. Konrad (ed.), *Der alte Mensch in der Geschichte* (Vienna, 1982).

[6] G. Cronjé, 'Tuberculosis and Mortality Decline in England and Wales, 1851–1910', in Woods and Woodward, *Urban Disease and Mortality*, pp. 79–101 (here pp. 80–3); F. B. Smith, *The People's Health, 1830–1910* (London, 1979), pp. 287–93. For another local study, see C. Pennington, 'Tuberculosis', in O. Checkland and M. Lamb (eds.), *Health Care as Social History: The Glasgow Case* (Aberdeen, 1982), pp. 86–99. Pennington's main concern is with medical policies of prevention and treatment, not with the incidence of the disease.

deaths were from tuberculosis of the lungs. Worst affected were young adults: in the age group 20–24, almost half of all recorded deaths were from tuberculosis in this period.[7]

Tuberculosis had a particularly severe effect in industrial cities. The worst-affected part of Germany in 1892–3 were the Ruhr, Upper Silesia, central Franconia, and the Palatinate with the adjacent area on the right bank of the Rhine. All these areas contained large centres of industrial activity and industrial pollution. Dust in factories and in the atmosphere was a predisposing factor in tuberculosis and other respiratory diseases, and by forcing people to keep their windows shut to keep the smoke and soot out, atmospheric pollution also reduced ventilation and so helped spread infection in the home. The death rate from tuberculosis exceeded 4.5 per 1,000 population aged 15–60 in the provinces of Münster and Osnabrück, while it was only slightly less (still over 4.0‰) in the provinces of Cologne, Düsseldorf, and Minden; all of these included major industrial centres on the lower Rhine. For Hamburg the rate in 1892–3 stood only a little lower, at just under 3.5‰. In the North German countryside as far east as Bromberg and Köslin it was just over 2.5‰, while further east still it was less than 2.0‰. Hamburg was thus roughly in the middle, about average for a major German city. When we compare its experience with that of other countries, we find that it was, once again, far from exceptional. Urban mortality rates from tuberculosis of the lungs in Britain stood at 3.6 per 1,000 inhabitants of all ages in the period 1881–90. Over the whole of England and Wales, the death rate was 2.8 per 1,000 in the 1850s, 2.3‰ in the 1870s and 1.99‰ in the 1880s. So Hamburg's death rate from tuberculosis was about the same as that of an average town in England at the same period.[8]

These figures suggest that the overcrowding, malnutrition, air pollution, and poverty which were so important in the spread of tuberculosis were common to almost all industrial towns in Europe in the late nineteenth century. Despite the peculiar obstacles which Hamburg's social and political structures placed in the way of effective reforms in the field of public health, they seem in this respect to have been no more intractable here than anywhere else in the urban-industrial world. As tuberculosis gradually declined in virulence in most European cities, so it declined in Hamburg too. As Figure 3 clearly shows, there was a clear downward trend in mortality from the disease from the early 1850s until the early 1860s. The Hamburg medical

[7] Cronjé, 'Tuberculosis', pp. 81–5.

[8] *Das Deutsche Reich in gesundheitlicher und demographischer Beziehung. Festschrift, den Teilnehmern am XIV. Internationalen Kongresse für Hygiene und Demographie Berlin 1907 gewidmet vom Kaiserlichen Gesundheitsamte und vom Kaiserlichen Statistichen Amte* (Berlin, 1907), Plate 18; Cronjé, 'Tuberculosis', pp. 95, 86; if we add on deaths from extra-pulmonary tuberculosis, we get another 0.7‰ for the 1850s, 0.6‰ for the 1870s, and 0.6‰ for the 1880s. *SHS* 20 (1902), 14. It was estimated that there were perhaps 9,000 people suffering from the disease in Hamburg in 1896 (StA Hbg, MK III G 1 Bd. I, Bl. 74: *Hamburger Fremdenblatt*, 27 Nov. 1896).

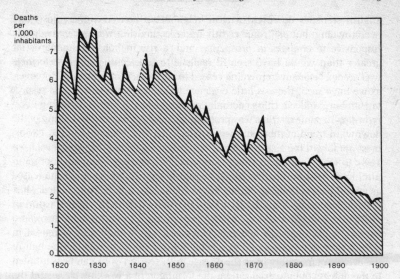

Source: *Die Gesundheitsverhältnisse Hamburgs im 19. Jahrhundert* (Hamburg, 1901), 284

FIG. 3. Tuberculosis mortality in Hamburg, 1820–1900

authorities considered this trend 'a phenomenon that can hardly be explained ... except by the reconstruction of the city which began after the Great Fire'. Apart from this, they also thought that a 'general increase in prosperity and the concomitant improvement in the whole way of life of the people, namely in respect of nutrition', played an important role in reducing tuberculosis mortality over the period in question.[9]

This opinion is difficult to verify. We have already seen how similar statements made in Hamburg by Senate Secretary Lappenberg bore little resemblance to the real facts. Some writers have pointed to improvements in diet in the search for the causes of tuberculosis mortality decline in the nineteenth century; but there is no firm evidence for an overall improvement, as we saw in Chapter 2, although it remains possible that increased potato consumption may have reduced the intake of harmful toxins from cereals and so contributed to the decline in a very specific way.[10] In her recent study of tuberculosis in England and Wales, Gillian Cronjé has played down the influence of a possible improvement in housing conditions in reducing tuberculosis mortality. The

[9] *Die Gesundheitsverhältnisse*, p. 284.
[10] Woods and Woodward, *Urban Disease and Mortality*, p. 68; D. J. Oddy, 'The Health of the People', in T. C. Barker and M. Drake (eds.), *Population and Society in Britain, 1850–1980* (London, 1982), pp. 121–39; M. K. Matessian, 'Death in London, 1750–1909', *Journal of Interdisciplinary History*, 16 (1985), pp. 183–98.

English statistics do reveal a clear relationship between tuberculosis and overcrowding, but as Cronjé rightly remarks, housing was not immediately responsive to changes in prosperity, and 'a rise in housing standards far greater than would have seemed realistic to nineteenth-century reformers was needed before overcrowding ceased to affect the death rates'.[11] Moreover, as we have seen, there is little evidence for an improvement in this respect in Hamburg: indeed, things actually got worse in the 1880s. Growing over-crowding in some districts was probably a major reason for the halting of the downward trend of tuberculosis mortality after the beginning of the 1860s, most notably in the Neustadt Nord, where it remained at the same level from 1885 to 1890, and the Altstadt Nord and Süd, where a decline did not set in until 1889. In some districts the death rate for consumption actually increased as working-class housing of the cheapest kind began to be constructed. Most striking here was Winterhude, where mortality rose from 1.4 per 1,000 in 1885 to 2.1 in 1889 and 3.5 in 1891. Death rates from this cause increased by 22% in Winterhude between 1885 and 1895; they also increased in Eilbeck over the same period by a total of just over 8%. Probably the halt in the decline of mortality from the disease in the early 1860s can be attributed to the process of industrialization, the formation of a working class, and the deterioration of the environment that began at that time. In general, as Map 19 indicates, the highest mortality rates from tuberculosis were all in the inner city areas (the Altstadt and Neustadt) or the inner suburbs (notably St Pauli, where they increased in the northern half of the district from 3.1 per 1,000 in 1885 to 3.3 in 1891). Outlying districts, such as Barmbeck and the Billwärder Ausschlag, where overcrowding was less severe, suffered markedly lower tuberculosis mortality, despite the fact that they were among the four poorest districts in terms of income. A contributory factor may have been the tendency of the disease to strike men more than women: nearly twice as many men as women over 20 died from the disease in Hamburg in 1892, for example; they were more liable to catch it at work, and the inner-city areas had a relatively high ratio of men to women (10% more at this time).[12]

Despite this qualification, a clear relationship can be established between income levels and tuberculosis mortality. The richest districts, Rotherbaum, Harvestehude, and Hohenfelde, had the lowest annual death rates from consumption in the period 1885–94, while the highest death rate of all was in the Neustadt Süd, one of the four poorest districts in the city. Poverty increased the likelihood of death from tuberculosis not only because it often meant living in cramped and overcrowded housing which favoured the spread of the disease, but also because it condemned those who suffered from it to an impoverished diet that weakened their resistance once the disease had struck. In Hamburg during the years 1896–1900—the only period for which

[11] Cronjé, 'Tuberculosis', p. 101.
[12] *Die Gesundheitsverhältnisse*, p. 291; see also pp. 57 and 68–71, above.

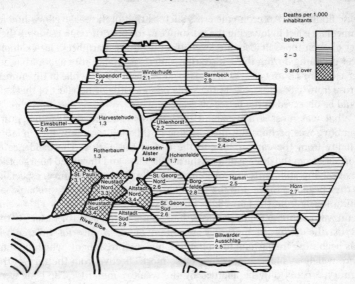

Source: MS 1894, Plate 3

MAP 19. Average annual deaths from tuberculosis, by district, Hamburg 1885–94

such figures are available—the likelihood of dying from tuberculosis declined steadily as income rose. Average annual mortality from tuberculosis of the lungs stood at 6.6 per 1,000 taxpayers earning between 900 and 1,200 Marks a year, and 5.6 per 1,000 earning between 1,200 and 2,000 Marks a year. These represented, very roughly, the bulk of the working class and the lower parts of the petty-bourgeoisie. For the very poor, who fell below the tax threshold altogether, the figures are likely to have been even higher. In the more prosperous classes, however, the disease was far less dangerous. Of every 1,000 taxpayers earning between 2,000 and 3,500 Marks a year, only 3.6 died annually from pulmonary tuberculosis in this period, while for those earning between 3,500 and 5,000 Marks the figure was 2.3‰ and for the well-off and the rich, earning over 10,000 Marks a year, it was only 1.9‰. The death rate from tuberculosis among the lowest class of taxpayers was thus nearly three and a half times as great as among the highest class. Comparable figures available for Brunswick in 1864–73, where the death rate from tuberculosis was 4.3‰ per year among the poorest class earning less than 100 Marks a year per head of population, 3.4‰ among those earning 100–200 Marks, 2.8‰ among those earning 200–250 Marks and only 1.9‰ among those earning over 250 Marks, confirm the typicality of these findings.[13] An economic crisis such as that of the early 1890s had an immediate effect in lowering the resistance of the poor through reducing their diet to even more inadequate levels than usual. In Barmbeck, for example, after declining during the 1880s, tuberculosis mortality rose again from 2.2 per 1,000 in 1890, to 2.3‰ in 1891, and 2.7‰ in 1892, while in Uhlenhorst it rose from 1.8‰ to 2.3‰ in the same period. Little or no effect of this kind could be observed in the better-off areas.[14]

What was most striking about tuberculosis rates in nineteenth-century Hamburg was perhaps not their decline in the long term, but their relative stability from the early 1860s to the end of the 1880s. The incidence of mortality from the disease among the middle class and the grand bourgeoisie, whose living standards improved dramatically from mid-century, especially as they began to move into the villa quarters round the Alster, probably fell continuously from the late 1840s onwards.[15] But from the early 1860s this trend was counteracted by the growth of an impoverished proletariat. By the 1870s, the notion of high, dry mountain air as a cure for tuberculosis was beginning the fashion for sanatoria, but such treatment, which became more widely available and perhaps also more effective from the turn of the century,[16] could only be afforded by the wealthy minority. The poor were merely treated with liberal doses of cod-liver oil.[17] Already by the 1880s, therefore, the better-off sufferers may have been able to lower their mortality rate to a significant extent by such treatment.[18] Before this, they could perhaps afford treatment by calomel, opium, or venesection, and after the middle of the century expectorants such as ipecacuanha and stimulants like brandy or ammonia. The poor could not.[19] In any case, however, none of the available treatments apart from sanatoria seems to have had a positive effect.[20] Hospital treatment for consumption was virtually unobtainable. The poor quarters of the city continued to house families where the father or, less frequently, the mother stayed at home, racked by uncontrollable coughing, unable to work, and gradually becoming weaker and less capable of looking after themselves,

[13] Ibid., p. 287; and Dr Reck, *Die Gesundheitsverhältnisse der Stadt Braunschweig in den Jahren 1864–1873 und die Verbreitung der Cholera daselbst in den Jahren 1850 und 1855. Von Dr. Med. Reck* (Brunswick, 1874), copy in Stadtarchiv Berlin, Rep. 01 GB 258. The per capita figures involve a division of income per taxpayer by the number of household members and do not, of course, represent average income per worker: see pp. 577–8 below.

[14] Ibid., p. 281; cf. Cronjé, 'Tuberculosis', p. 98.

[15] See, more generally, R. Kropf and H. Rauter, 'Erklärungsansätze zum Einfluss der Ernährung auf die Gesundheit und Lebenserwartung der Menschen im 19. Jahrhundert', in Konrad, *Der alte Mensch*, pp. 185–204.

[16] *Die Gesundheitsverhältnisse*, p. 291. See also D. Blasius, ' "Volksseuchen": Zur historischen Dimension von Berufskrankheiten', *Sozialwissenschaftliche Informationen für Unterricht und Studium*, 6 (1977), 55–60.

[17] Cronjé, 'Tuberculosis', pp. 99–100.

[18] SHS 20, 12–13.

[19] See also Smith, *The People's Health*, p. 288.

[20] Ibid., pp. 290–1.

until they eventually died: a process that was bound to impose a further burdening of economic hardship and emotional suffering on the families, often for years on end.[21]

II

If overcrowding and poor ventilation were major causes of high mortality rates from pulmonary tuberculosis, then malnutrition, inadequate sanitation, and unhygienic living conditions gave rise to a whole further range of often fatal illnesses. Perhaps the most important, regularly recurring fatal infections of this kind among adults were typhus and typhoid. These are now considered to be two quite separate diseases, but until the middle of the nineteenth century they were usually conflated, largely because of the similarity of their symptoms. Typhus manifested itself in red spots all over the body (apart from the face, the palms of the hand, and soles of the feet), sometimes coming together to form a general rash, and typhoid victims broke out in an angry red rash as well. In both diseases the sufferers developed a very high temperature, and nausea and delirium were common features too. Typhus was the more dangerous: it killed between a fifth and a half of those it affected, while mortality from typhoid seems to have fluctuated between a seventh and a fifth of those affected (about 15–20%). Death in typhus cases usually occurred from heart failure, while in typhoid it was more common from diarrhoea and abdominal haemorrhage. The most striking difference between the two diseases was in their mode of transmission. The typhus germ, *Rickettsia prowazeki* (first discovered in 1909), was transmitted from person to person by the human body louse; the micro-organism responsible for typhoid was transmitted by infected individuals, usually through contamination of water, milk, and foodstuffs by their faeces. Both diseases were thus associated with diet and overcrowded and unhygienic living conditions, though the ability of typhoid to be carried in an unfiltered water-supply made its incidence potentially more random.[22]

Although typhus traditionally reached epidemic proportions in times of warfare and famine, both diseases also took their toll of the European population year in, year out, for most of the sixteenth, seventeenth, and eighteenth centuries. The extent of their depredations in the nineteenth century is hard to judge. Hamburg's medical statisticians were forced to admit that it 'cannot be doubted that well into the most recent period, some cases of pneumonia, pleurisy, meningitis, tuberculosis, etc. with "typhoid" symptoms have been erroneously diagnosed as typhoid'. They thought that the diagnosis of typhoid

[21] On tuberculosis generally, see R. Dubois, *The White Plague. A History of Tuberculosis* (London, 1961).

[22] See B. Luckin, 'Evaluating the Sanitary Revolution: Typhus and Typhoid in London, 1851–1900', in Woods and Woodward, *Urban Disease and Mortality*, pp. 102–19.

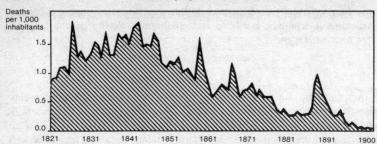

Source: Die Gesundheitsverhältnisse Hamburgs im 19. Jahrhundert (Hamburg, 1901), 222. Figures up to *c.* 1850 include typhus; the 1859 peak probably includes cholera cases

FIG. 4. Typhus/typhoid in Hamburg, 1820–1900

had improved since the 1840s, but still advised caution in interpreting the figures.[23] Certainly a decline in deaths from the two diseases seems to have occurred in Hamburg since the middle of the century, from an annual average of around 1.5 per 1,000 inhabitants in the period 1825–45, to an annual average of around 0.5‰ in the period 1880–90. This may have been partly due to a decline in typhus, and partly to the improvement in diagnosis, as we have seen. As Figure 4 shows, this decline was interrupted by serious epidemics in the mid-1850s, the mid-1860s, and the late 1880s. And it left Hamburg one of the worst-affected German cities, whose death rate from typhoid and typhus in the period 1878–87 was exceeded only in Königsberg, where it stood at 0.6‰, and Posen, where it stood at 1.0‰. Both these towns were in the far east of the German Empire, where Polish and Russian migrant labourers and generally backward social conditions, especially in the surrounding countryside, encouraged typhus to reach levels unknown further west, with major epidemics occurring in 1880 and again in 1890. In Frankfurt, Cologne, Dresden, Leipzig, Bremen, Nuremberg, and many other cities the death rate from these causes was a half or a quarter that of Hamburg, and even in Munich and Berlin it was a good third less in this period. Assuming that it was only in the east that typhus was a serious problem by this time, this leaves Hamburg with the highest typhoid mortality of all German cities in the 1880s.[24]

The major reason for this pre-eminence of Hamburg as a centre of typhoid was beyond doubt the pollution of the local water-supply. As we saw in Chapter 2, Hamburg's centralized but unfiltered water-supply was capable

---

[23] *Die Gesundheitsverhältnisse*, p. 222.

[24] Reincke, *Der Typhus*, p. 4; *Die Gesundheitsverhältnisse*, p. 315; BA Koblenz, R86/1048 Bd. 1, *passim*. The documents in BA Koblenz, R86/1041 Bd. 1 make it clear that by the beginning of the 1880s medical statisticians distinguished between typhus and typhoid but were not aware of the role of the louse in transmitting the former.

Table 2. Average annual sex-specific typhoid morbidity rates by district, Hamburg 1885–8, among adults.

District	Male cases per 1,000 male population aged 15 and above	Female cases per 1,000 female population aged 15 and above
Altstadt Nord	11.6	7.4
Altstadt Süd	11.0	7.7
Neustadt Nord	10.6	7.5
Neustadt Süd	10.2	6.1
St Georg	10.2	5.6
St Pauli	7.9	6.0
Rotherbaum	12.5	9.0
Harvestehude	16.1	12.7
Eimsbüttel	3.1	3.4
Eppendorf	5.3	5.7
Winterhude	3.8	3.7
Uhlenhorst	7.5	5.6
Barmbeck	6.6	4.4
Hohenfelde	6.0	6.1
Eilbeck	6.7	4.0
Borgfelde	8.3	5.6
Hamm	6.6	7.1
Horn	4.1	2.9
Billwärder Ausschlag	9.8	6.0
All districts	N = 1805 Mean = 8.3	N = 1307 Mean = 6.1

NB: The figures may also include typhus cases, though by this time it was usual to distinguish between *Flecktyphus* (typhus or spotted fever) and *Unterleibstyphus* (typhoid fever).
Source: calculated from J. J. Reincke, *Der Typhus in Hamburg. Mit besonderer Berücksichtigung der Epidemieen von 1885 bis 1889* (Hamburg, 1890), p. 19, and *SHS* 16 (1894), 24–5 (see also below, Statistical Appendix).

by the 1880s of spreading diseases to almost every house in the city, and the dangers of the contamination of the water-supply by untreated sewage were increasing all the time.[25] This was an almost classic recipe for a typhoid epidemic, and it is not surprising, therefore, that one duly occurred in 1886–7. In 1887, in particular, typhoid mortality in Hamburg reached levels unknown since the 1850s (save in the epidemic year of 1865). It was most probably because it was spread by the central water-supply that the disease showed relatively little observable variation in its impact from district to district.[26] As Bill Luckin has observed, 'in contrast to typhus, typhoid has traditionally affected a wide range of both poor and relatively affluent, particularly in societies in which water and foodstuffs have been exempt from effective public health regulations'.[27] Certainly, as Table 2 shows, the poor

[25] See above, pp. 138–51.
[26] Reincke (*Der Typhus*) opposed this view; but for reasons outlined at length below, pp. 276, 384, his opinion on the subject must be discounted.
[27] Luckin, 'Evaluating the Sanitary Revolution', p. 104.

districts in the Altstadt and Neustadt had high average annual typhoid morbidity rates (i.e. rate of cases per 1,000 population) in the years 1885–8, but the highest were in the wealthy district of Harvestehude.[28] This did not mean, however, that there were no social variations at all in the impact of typhoid. Dr Johann Julius Reincke, in his detailed study of the epidemic of the mid to late 1880s, argued that more men than women were affected in the inner city, St Pauli, and St Georg, while the reverse was true in Harvestehude, Eimsbüttel, Hohenfelde, and a few other districts. He put this down to the fact that there were large numbers of young, badly paid male immigrant workers in the inner city, and of young female domestic servants in the wealthier suburbs. Both groups he regarded as particularly susceptible to the disease. But his figures were suspect because they did not take account of the fact that over a third of all cases were among infants and children below the age of 15. Among adults, certainly, the female typhoid morbidity rate was markedly higher in Harvestehude, at 12.7‰, and Rotherbaum at 9.0‰, than it was in any other area: in the Altstadt, for instance, it averaged 7.6‰, and even in the Billwärder Ausschlag it only reached 6‰. Nine out of every 100 victims were female domestic servants, and it is quite probable that they suffered disproportionately because they were more likely than most to come into contact with contaminated food, infected water-closets, and the like. Adult women apart from domestic servants made up a further 17% of the sufferers, and were exposed to infection from broadly similar sources.[29]

At the same time, however, the wealthy districts of Harvestehude and Rotherbaum also had the highest proportion of adult male victims, at 16.1‰ and 12.5‰ of the local adult male population respectively. The difference between these and other districts was not so striking as in the case of female morbidity, but it was there all the same. One can only speculate as to the reasons. There were a number of wells in the district, and some of them may have been infected. But without knowing precisely who was affected it is impossible to reach any firm conclusion on the causes of the high male morbidity rate. These figures cast some doubt on the argument that cases among domestic servants were largely responsible for the high female morbidity rates in these districts. Easier to explain is the broad overall difference between the inner city, with its average morbidity rate of 10.9 per 1,000 inhabitants, and the outer suburbs in general, where morbidity was much lower (6.6‰ in Barmbeck, for instance, 5.3‰ in Eppendorf, 3.8‰ in Winterhude). In the inner city the high proportion of young male harbour workers among the population seems to be the most likely explanation; accustomed to drink directly from the river, they were highly exposed to infection when the river was contaminated with the typhoid germ. Female morbidity rates in the inner city were a good deal lower than the male, largely, it seems

[28] Reincke, *Der Typhus*, p. 14.
[29] Ibid., p. 13.

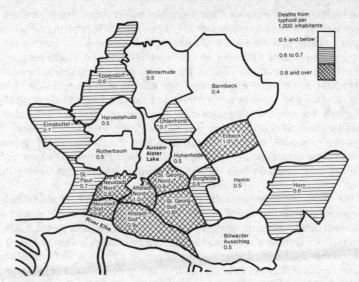

Deaths from
typhoid per
1,000 inhabitants

0.5 and below

0.6 to 0.7

0.8 and over

Eppendorf 0.6

Winterhude 0.5

Barmbeck 0.4

Harvestehude 0.5

Eimsbüttel 0.7

Uhlenhorst 0.7

Eilbeck 1.0

Rotherbaum 0.5

Aussen-Alster Lake

Hohenfelde 0.5

St. Pauli 0.7

Neustadt Nord 0.8

Altstadt Nord 1.0

St. Georg Nord 0.8

Borgfelde 0.6

Hamm 0.5

Horn 0.6

Neustadt Süd 0.9

Altstadt Süd 0.9

St. Georg Süd 0.8

Billwärder Ausschlag 0.5

River Elbe

Source: calculated from J. J. Reincke, *Der Typhus in Hamburg* (Hamburg, 1890), 18–19

MAP 20 Average annual typhoid mortality, by district, Hamburg 1885–8

reasonable to conclude, because of the higher risk run by male harbour workers.[30]

On the whole, therefore, while there was no indisputably clear relationship between social factors and typhoid morbidity, there is some evidence to suggest that occupation played a role in determining the distribution of the disease. This was perhaps more likely in a port such as Hamburg than Berlin. The social factors in the impact of typhoid emerge much more clearly when we turn to mortality rates. Map 20 shows how the highest mortality rates in the epidemic of 1885–8 were in the inner city, with St Georg and St Pauli not far behind. The typhoid mortality rates in the outer suburbs were only between a half and two-thirds as high as those of the Altstadt: the outlying district of Eilbeck was something of an anomaly in this respect, with its typhoid mortality of 1 per 1,000 inhabitants, but this may well have reflected a local source of infection. It is certainly possible that the high rates in the inner city also included typhus cases, encouraged by the overcrowded and often verminous conditions in which people in these districts lived. But given the fact that it was relatively common by this period to distinguish between typhus and typhoid, it seems more likely that the high mortality in the inner city was associated once more with its proximity to the pestilential waters of

[30] See also below, pp. 450–65.

the harbour and the canals. Poor sanitation and cramped living conditions may well have contributed to mortality here, since it was particularly high among infants in these districts. Resistance to disease was also lower among the local population, since case-specific mortality rates (i.e. deaths per 1,000 cases) here were relatively high: 8.4% of cases in the Altstadt and Neustadt were fatal, and 7.7% of those in the inner suburbs of St Georg and St Pauli, but only 5.9% of those in Rotherbaum and Harvestehude. These generally relatively low case-mortality rates make it incidentally clear that it is typhoid that we are dealing with: typhus was a great deal more fatal in its impact.[31] It seems reasonable to conclude, therefore, that the distribution of typhoid was to some extent socially uneven, and that the fall in mortality from mid-century may well have been greater among the better-off than among the poor.

The decisively important fact was the high overall typhoid mortality in Hamburg during the second half of the 1880s. In every single district it exceeded that of the worst-affected parts of London in the same period.[32] After tuberculosis, typhoid was the most frequent cause of death among Hamburg's inhabitants aged 15–25 over the whole period 1872–96, and one of the major causes of death in virtually all other age groups.[33] Many of the factors which had helped bring about a decline of typhoid in other European cities were still not present in Hamburg by the beginning of the 1890s. The water-supply had not been filtered, food and milk were not adequately protected, sewage was poured untreated into the river, sanitation was inadequate, and overcrowding in the inner city actually increased during the 1880s as refugees streamed in from the houses demolished to make way for the new harbour.[34] The failure to improve the urban environment in these respects led directly to the typhoid epidemic of the mid-to-late eighties. Increased overcrowding may even have led to a small growth in the incidence of typhus, though this seems on balance rather unlikely. Luckin has suggested, plausibly, that typhus was more associated with populations tolerant of body lice (in the case of England and Wales, this meant the Irish)[35] than with specific environmental conditions. The only people likely to have fallen into this category in Hamburg were Polish migrant labourers. These seldom stayed in the city very long, and the Polish population of Hamburg was never very large. It is mainly to the failure of the Hamburg Senate and Citizens' Assembly to introduce effective sanitation and water-supplies, therefore, that we must look for an explanation of the high typhoid mortality of the mid-to-late 1880s.

[31] See the Statistical Appendix for a further discussion of these points.

[32] Luckin, 'Evaluating the Sanitary Revolution', pp. 108–9.

[33] *Die Gesundheitsverhältnisse*, p. 315. However, the status of this statistic is rendered problematical by the incidence of typhoid in 1892. See the discussion of this point in the Statistical Appendix.

[34] See above, p. 69.

[35] Luckin, 'Evaluating the Sanitary Revolution', pp. 108–9.

III

Tuberculosis and typhoid acquired their pre-eminence as killer infections in the nineteenth century not least because they affected all age-groups more or less equally, with the exception of infants and the over-70s.[36] Other infectious diseases, however, had a less even age distribution, notably the childhood infections of measles, whooping cough, scarlet fever, and diphtheria. Over the whole period 1872–96 measles killed an annual average of 3 per 1,000 population aged 0–1 in Hamburg and 2.2‰ aged 1–5; whooping cough killed an average of 6 children per 1,000 aged 0–1 and 2‰ aged 1–5 every year; scarlet fever killed an average of 0.4 per 1,000 infants aged 1–5 and 0.6‰ children aged 5–15 annually; and diphtheria proved fatal for some 1.8 infants per 1,000, 4.4‰ children aged 1–5, and 1.3‰ children aged 5–15 on average every year. Taken altogether, these four infections killed 11.2‰ infants, 9.0‰ children aged 1–5, and 2.0‰ children aged 5–15 each year in this period. On occasions they reached more serious levels: diphtheria hit a particular high point in 1886, when morbidity reached the level of 7.1‰ of the whole population.[37]

Epidemics of all these diseases were often localized in character, and tied to specific sources of infection. Diphtheria and scarlet fever were frequently transmitted by contaminated milk, and so could easily reach the houses of the well-off as well as those of the poor.[38] The medical statistics reveal no clear social pattern to the incidence of these diseases in Hamburg. Nor were Hamburg's death rates from these infections particularly bad in comparison to those of other towns. Like diphtheria and scarlet fever, measles and whooping cough were also diseases that were often transmitted by droplet infection, so that overcrowding, poor ventilation, and cramped living conditions would seem to have been important factors in encouraging a higher incidence. Measles and whooping cough were widely supposed to be diseases of the poor, who were believed to be more exposed to infection and less able to resist it when it occurred.[39] Comparison of the incidence of these diseases by district yields no clear pattern of distribution. There was no visible decline in whooping cough or measles until the mid-1920s. Death rates from diphtheria and scarlet fever actually increased during the late 1870s and 1880s.[40] Here, too, environmental factors—contamination of food and milk, and overcrowded housing—seem to have played some role in the spread and impact of infection.

If they were all diseases of the young, then the elderly and the old were exposed to other threats to their health which were even more clearly linked

---

[36] *Die Gesundheitsverhältnisse*, p. 315.
[37] Ibid., pp. 169–206, 315.
[38] Smith, *The People's Health*, pp. 136–51.
[39] Ibid., also pp. 104–10.
[40] Hamburg figures in *Die Gesundheitsverhältnisse*, pp. 169–206, 315, and *Hygiene und Soziale Hygiene in Hamburg*, pp. 56–8.

to the environment. Leaving aside the still common catch-all category, 'death from old age' (*Altersschwäche*), by far the commonest cause of death among Hamburg's inhabitants aged 50 and over was acute respiratory disease—mainly bronchitis and pneumonia. The death rate in 1872–96 from acute respiratory diseases was 5.4 per 1,000 inhabitants of Hamburg aged 50–70 in an average year, while for those aged 70 and over it was as much as 22.4‰. In the same age-group of the over-70s, by contrast, deaths from heart failure were running at an annual average of 7.9‰ in this period, and deaths from cancer at 8.0‰. These figures have to be treated with due caution, since deaths from 'other causes' (mostly 'old age') were given as 68.4‰ per annum in these years; many if not most of these would now be classified as heart failure or cancer. Nevertheless, the high figures for deaths from acute respiratory infection were still very impressive. An inhabitant of Hamburg aged over 70 in this period was some 24 times more likely to die from this cause as someone aged between 25 and 50, and over a hundred times more likely to die from it as a person aged between 15 and 25.[41] Overall, from 1881–90 an average of 13.2‰ of the population died of acute respiratory infection in Hamburg every year; a further 12.5‰ died from 'catarrh and influenza', and another 6.7‰ from chronic respiratory infection. This added up to something like the same proportion of the population as died from pulmonary tuberculosis each year (32.5‰ as against 29.9‰). In other words, one in sixteen of the city's population died from respiratory diseases each year.[42] Cold, damp living conditions, and constant exposure to atmospheric pollution were all factors that contributed to this high death rate and made it likely—though in the absence of satisfactory statistical evidence it cannot be proven—that it was a good deal higher in the poorer classes and districts of the city than it was in the richer.

Not all of these various infections were declining in their incidence in Hamburg during the nineteenth century. Typhoid underwent a dramatic resurgence in the late 1880s, and its incidence before mid-century was too uncertain to permit the conclusion of a long-term decline. Respiratory diseases seem to have been as widespread in 1890 as they were a century before.[43] Neither scarlet fever nor diphtheria significantly decreased in incidence before the late 1880s. The greatest killer of them all—tuberculosis—did decrease in deadliness from the 1840s to the 1860s, at least for the middle-class sector of the population. Any effect that this might have had on overall mortality rates was, however, offset by a simultaneous increase in another area—that of infant mortality. We have already seen how some infectious diseases singled out the very young as their main victims. Infants and young children were exposed to many more perils than these, as we shall now see.

[41] Ibid., p. 315. These figures may also have included some lung cancer and tuberculosis cases.
[42] *SHS* 15 (1904), 104.
[43] *Die Gesundheitsverhältnisse*, pp. 169–77.

IV

By far the largest single element in the death rate in nineteenth-century Hamburg was the very high level of infant mortality. In the 1870s and 1880s, infant mortality was some ten times greater than the mean annual mortality of the city's population as a whole. Nearly one child in every four born in these decades died before reaching its first birthday. In the 1880s, Hamburg's average annual infant mortality rate stood at 24.2 per 100 live births. This was slightly lower than the comparable rate in Berlin (27.8) and discernibly lower than that of Munich (33.3) or Chemnitz (36.7), but it was very much higher than that of Frankfurt (17.9) and those of Hamburg's sister Hanseatic towns of Bremen (21.1) and Lübeck (18.2). In its infant death rates, Hamburg thus fell somewhere around the middle of the spectrum of the larger German cities. But it was a good deal worse off in this respect than, for example, England and Wales, where infant mortality was at an annual average of around 14 per 100 live births in the 1880s; by comparison, even the poorest districts of English industrial towns such as Bradford had lower infant mortality rates than the average for all districts of Hamburg in the last quarter of the nineteenth century.[44]

Moreover, infant mortality actually became a more serious problem in Hamburg as the century progressed. From 1840 it climbed for the first time above 20 deaths per 100 live births a year. It reached a height in the 1870s and 1880s. In the 1820s, roughly a fifth of all deaths in Hamburg were of infants under one year of age; by the 1880s this proportion had increased to a third. The medical authorities were forced to confess in 1900 that

Despite all the sources of error which vitiate the figures for the earlier decades, it can hardly be doubted that relatively fewer children died in the period before the Great Fire than after it. This is certainly not a reflection of the general sanitary circumstances of the city in this period, but rather it indicates that in those days, before the abolition of the guilds and the rise of industry, the majority of parents lived in much better social and economic circumstances than the swarms of our present workers who marry young and lack the experience and the means to care for their progeny as well as their predecessors did.[45]

Of course, this reasoning, with its social-conservative overtones, cannot be accepted entirely at face value. Many of its claims are difficult or impossible to verify or disprove. It was particularly striking that the authorities made

[44] See in general Smith, *The People's Health*, pp. 65-135; and Wohl, *Endangered Lives*, pp. 10–42. For a detailed local study, see B. Thompson, 'Infant Mortality in Nineteenth-century Bradford', in Woods and Woodward, *Urban Disease and Mortality*, pp. 120–47. For detailed figures, see *Die Gesundheitsverhältnisse*, pp. 313–15, and H. Meyer-Delius, 'Die Säuglingssterblichkeit in Hamburg seit dem Jahre 1820', *Hamburger Ärzteblatt*, 19 (1965), Nos. 3–4. For the general demographic background, see Matti, 'Bevölkerungsvorgänge', pp. 103–56.

[45] *Die Gesundheitsverhältnisse*, pp. 144–5.

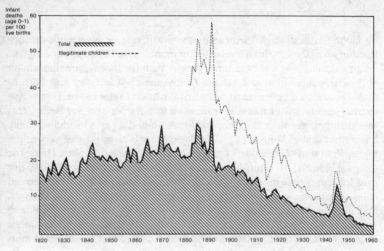

Source: Hugo Meyer-Delius, 'Die Säuglingssterblichkeit in Hamburg seit dem Jahre 1820', *Hamburger Ärtzeblatt*, 19 (1965), 3

FIG. 5. Infant mortality in Hamburg, 1820–1960

the city's reconstruction under the leadership of the Senate after the Great Fire of 1842 responsible for the decline in tuberculosis mortality but blamed the increase in infant mortality on the working classes. We have to bear in mind, too, that the birth rate in Hamburg was increasing up to the 1880s, when it briefly exceeded 40 live births per 1,000 population—doubtless a consequence of the very immigration of young workers of both sexes which the medical authorities so deplored. This in itself goes a long way towards explaining the fact that infant deaths increased from a fifth to a third of all deaths in the city between 1820 and 1880; infants simply made up a higher proportion of the city's population at the latter date. and so would have accounted for an increasing proportion of overall deaths in any case.[46]

Nevertheless, even when these factors are taken into account, it is still clear that a higher proportion of infants was dying in the 1870s than had been the case half a century before, as Figure 5 makes plain. A look at the specific varieties of infant death helps explain why this should have been so. The commonest occasion of infant deaths in nineteenth-century Hamburg was 'vomiting and diarrhoea', often known as 'summer diarrhoea'. The average annual death rate in Hamburg from this cause among infants aged 0–1 was 71‰ in the period 1872–96. Infant mortality from this cause

[46] Ibid., see also Matti, 'Bevölkerungsvorgänge'.

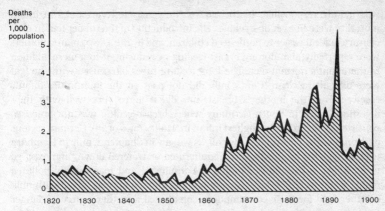

Source: *Die Gesundheitsverhältnisse Hamburgs im 19. Jahrhundert* (Hamburg, 1901), 207

FIG. 6. Deaths from 'vomiting and diarrhoea', Hamburg 1820–1900

increased perceptibly in the second half of the nineteenth century, as Figure 6 indicates. In 1879–83, vomiting and diarrhoea killed some 46.6‰ of infants born in Hamburg; in 1884–9, this figure rose dramatically to 74.1‰. There is no evidence that this rise was the result of changes in the practice of diagnosis or registration, and indeed the obviousness of the symptoms makes it unlikely that it could have been. Two further major causes of infant mortality, convulsions, which killed 30.0‰ of infants born in 1879–83 and 30.4‰ in 1884–9, and wasting or atrophy of the newborn, which killed 30.7‰ of infants born in the city in 1879–83 and 53.4‰ in 1884–9, were also mainly symptomatic of gastro-intestinal disorders caused above all by poor and unhygienic nutrition. Together these three digestive-related ailments accounted for 61% of all infant deaths in the years 1884–9.[47]

The official statistical handbook for Hamburg, in reporting these figures, concluded in 1891 that 'the causes of high infant mortality are to be found in inadequate child nutrition, and mainly in the fact that cow's milk or artificial substitutes are being used for natural feeding to an ever-increasing degree'.[48] Infant mortality was invariably highest in the summer months, reaching a peak in August, when the mean annual infant mortality rate stood at 34 per 1,000 inhabitants aged 0–1 in the years 1872–96, as against 21‰ or 22‰ for the months of February to May, October and November.[49] This suggests that food, and above all milk, going off in the summer heat,

[47] *Die Gesundheitsverhältnisse*, pp. 145, 315, 317; *Statistisches Handbuch für den Hamburgischen Staat* (2nd edn., 1891), p. 58.
[48] *Statistisches Handbuch*, loc. cit.
[49] *Die Gesundheitsverhältnisse*, p. 317.

was mainly responsible. In the 1820s these seasonal variations in infant
mortality were not yet observable. The introduction of the rubber teat in mid-
century made it easier to bottle-feed children, and by the 1880s many mothers
were reportedly abandoning breast-feeding or reducing it to a mere addition
to the infant's normal diet. The long feeding tubes often used with the teat
were difficult to clean. Cow's milk did not pass on the immunities infants
received from the mother's breast, nor did it agree very well with their
digestion. Areas in South Germany where breast-feeding was not practised
consistently recorded the highest infant mortality rates of any German regions
in the nineteenth century. Above all, as we saw in Chapter 2, milk in Hamburg
was unhygienic and dirty, often adulterated or watered down, and exposed
to all kinds of infections. Finally, the unfiltered and increasingly polluted
mains water in which infants were bathed, and which was mixed with milk
or other food for their consumption, constituted a further source of danger
for their poorly developed digestive systems. The fact that mains water reached
a steadily growing proportion of the city's population from the 1850s
onwards, was, in all probability, a significant contributory factor to the
increase in infant mortality rates in these decades.[50]

The other major causes of infant deaths were respiratory infections and
general debility. According to one estimate, respiratory infections accounted
for 31 deaths per 1,000 infants in Hamburg in the years 1872–96; a rather
different method of classification gave respiratory disease as the cause of
death of 26 per 1,000 infants born in the years 1884–9. 10% of all infant
deaths in these years were attributed to this cause. Finally, general debility,
associated above all with premature birth, accounted for 38.9 deaths per
1,000 infants born in 1879–83 and 45.8‰ for the period 1884–9. 17.8% of
all infant deaths in the period 1884–9 were attributed to 'general debility of
the new-born'. Between them, these three major factors—debility, respiratory
infections, and gastro-intestinal disorders—accounted for the overwhelming
majority of infant deaths in the mid-to-late nineteenth century. Almost 9 out
of every 10 infants in Hamburg who died before reaching the age of 1 in the
years 1884–9 died of one of these causes. The rest were largely accounted
for by the infectious diseases discussed in the previous section.[51]

Infected water and milk accounted for a high proportion of infant deaths
from gastro-intestinal disorders; damp, cold housing, poor ventilation, and
the notorious Hamburg smog of the autumn and winter months encouraged
pleurisy, pneumonia, and bronchitis among infants as well as the aged;

[50] A. E. Imhof, ''Unterschiedliche Säuglingssterblichkeit in Deutschland, 18. bis 20. Jahrhundert—Warum?'. *Zeitschrift für Bevölkerungswissenschaft*, 7 (1981), 343–82; Meyer-Delius, 'Die
Saüglingssterblichkeit'; W. R. Lee, 'Primary Sector Output and Mortality Changes in Early XIXth
Century Bavaria', *Journal of European Economic History*, 6 (1977), 133–62. M. W. Beaver, 'Population, Infant Mortality and Milk', *Population Studies*, 27 (1973), 243–54.
[51] *Die Gesundheitsverhältnisse*, p. 315; *Statistisches Handbuch*, p. 58. See also the discussion by
Thompson, 'Infant Mortality', pp. 120–47.

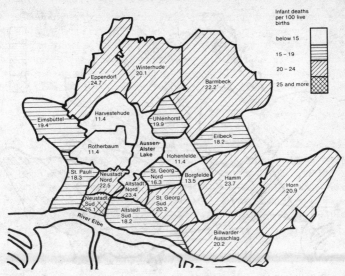

Source: calculated from *MS* 1894, 44 and *SHS* 20 (1902), 26–7

MAP 21. Infant mortality, by district, Hamburg 1894

unhygienic living conditions, poor sewage-disposal, dirt, and vermin all spread infections to which infants were particularly susceptible. Most of these factors affected the poor more than the rich. This was true, as we have seen, even of atmospheric pollution, which was worst in the poorest areas near the factories and the harbour. Poverty was thus the underlying cause of the greater part of infant mortality. The historian Reinhard Spree has shown that while infant mortality in Prussia was falling in the middle classes in the second half of the nineteenth century, it was actually increasing in the families of unskilled workers and to a lesser extent skilled workers and domestic servants, not least because of the higher illegitimacy rates in these groups.[52] Comparable figures are not available for Hamburg, but there were, as we might expect, differences in infant mortality rates between the richer and poorer city districts. Figures for infant mortality are only available for Hamburg by district from 1894 onwards, by which time they had begun to decline from their peak in the 1880s, but the differences are still clearly discernible. As Map 21 indicates, the highest rates were in the Billwärder Ausschlag, Horn, Neustadt Süd, and Uhlenhorst, while the least-affected districts were Harvestehude, Rotherbaum, and Hohenfelde. A child born in

[52] Spree, pp. 170–1.

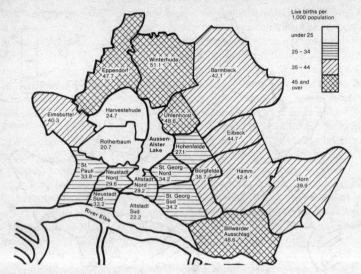

Live births per
1,000 population

under 25

25 – 34

35 – 44

45 and
over

Winterhude
51.1

Eppendorf
47.7

Barmbeck
42.1

Eimsbüttel
40.3

Harvestehude
24.7

Uhlenhorst
48.6

Eilbeck
44.7

Rotherbaum
20.7

Aussen-
Alster
Lake

Hohenfelde
27.1

St.
Pauli
33.8

Neustadt
Nord
29.6

St. Georg
Nord
34.2

Borgfelde
38.7

Hamm
42.4

Horn
39.9

Altstadt
Nord
29.2

Neustadt
Süd
33.2

Altstadt
Süd
22.2

St. Georg
Süd
34.2

River Elbe

Billwärder
Ausschlag
48.6

Source: MS 1892, Table 13g

MAP 22. Crude birth rate, by district, Hamburg 1892

the Billwärder Ausschlag was three times as likely to die before reaching the age of one as a child born in Harvestehude. The difference ultimately reflected the vast differences in income between the two districts, which can be observed from Map 4.

These differences would have been even more striking in reality than they appear in the cold light of statistics because, as we can observe from Map 22, the birth rate was higher in the poorer districts than in the richer ones. More children meant it was less easy to care for each one; in general a smaller number of births went together with lower infant mortality. The better-off not only had fewer children but had servants to look after them as well, and lived in far less overcrowded conditions. Poverty was a cause of infant mortality in many ways. Undernourished mothers often gave birth to premature or underweight babies, whose chance of survival were generally very poor. Women who had grown up in poor circumstances suffering from rickets and other vitamin deficiencies often had contracted pelvises, from which still-births were frequently the result. (These ran at between 3 and 4% of all births in Hamburg in the 1880s.) If an operation was necessary to assist birth, dangerous complications for mother and child often followed.[53] Lack of

---

[53] Imhof, 'Unterschiedliche Säuglingssterblichkeit', p. 360; *Statistisches Handbuch*, p. 47. More generally, see E. Shorter, *A History of Women's Bodies* (London, 1983), Chs. 2–5.

washing and cleaning facilities, dirty and verminous living conditions, and damp, airless, sunless rooms helped spread infection and weaken resistance.[54] Infant mortality was higher among the poor in many parts of Germany. In Berlin in the period 1883–8, for example, the infant mortality rate among the children of civil servants was 22.3%, while it reached 36.7% among the children of day-labourers.[55] Even more striking than these social differences, however, were the varying infant mortality rates among legitimate and illegitimate children. In Prussian towns in the period 1893–7, for example, 19.7% of legitimate children died in the first year of life, but 37.3% of illegitimate children.[56] In Hamburg, when records began in the early 1880s, the mortality rate among illegitimate infants was over 40%, where it remained for a whole decade, as we can see from Figure 5. This was almost twice the average infant mortality rate of the city. In the late 1880s, indeed, as we can see from Figure 5, nearly half, and in two years at least, well over half of all illegitimately born infants died before reaching the age of one.

Hamburg's illegitimacy rates were not particularly high for nineteenth-century Germany. In the 1870s, around 9.5% of all births in the city were illegitimate; in the 1880s the proportion rose to 10.6%, and in the 1890s to 11.8%.[57] In some parts of Catholic Bavaria it was more than twice this level.[58] Nevertheless, the very high death rates of illegitimate infants meant that illegitimacy must be accounted a major factor in infant mortality. Since the illegitimacy rate was around 10%, and illegitimate infant mortality roughly twice as high as legitimate, we can say that about one in every five infant deaths in Hamburg was the death of an illegitimate child. Illegitimacy rates were certainly very high in the poverty-stricken Alley Quarters of the Altstadt and Neustadt, contributing no doubt to the reputation of these areas as centres of immorality and disorder. They were only a quarter as high in the wealthy districts of Rotherbaum and Hohenfelde. But in general illegitimacy rates and infant mortality rates in Hamburg's districts were not very closely related. This was because, as Map 23 suggests, the illegitimacy rate was relatively low in the newer working-class districts such as Barmbeck or the Hammerbrook, and in St Georg Süd. Illegitimate births were concentrated in the inner city, the home of casual port labourers, prostitutes, and other single people. The type of housing in these central districts made it easy to rent single rooms, and the proportion of lodgers in households in these areas was

[54] For the influence of these factors on cholera, see below, Chapter 5.
[55] Imhof, 'Unterschiedliche Säuglingssterblichkeit', p. 358.
[56] Ibid., for a more general discussion, see Spree, *Soziale Ungleichheit*, pp. 49–92 ('Soziale Ungleichheit im Spiegel der Säuglingssterblichkeit').
[57] *SHS* 20 (1902), 1.
[58] W. R. Lee, 'Bastardy and the Socioeconomic Structure of South Germany', *Journal of Interdisciplinary History*, 7 (1977), 403–25.

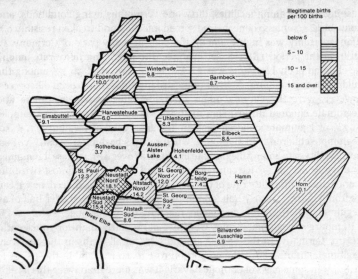

Source: SHS 20 (1902), 7

MAP 23 Illegitimate births per hundred births, by district, Hamburg 1892

also very high.[59] It seems reasonable to suppose that unmarried mothers were probably generally poor, perhaps young, lacking social support networks and often forced to work long hours for their living. All these factors had an adverse effect on the survival rates of their children.

Once more, lack of hygiene and sanitation, social deprivation, poverty, and malnutrition led to higher mortality rates among the poor than among the better-off. Recently, Reinhard Spree, in a pioneering study of social inequality in the face of death and disease, has emphasized the influence of the high birth rate of the working class in producing high infant mortality. While overcrowding was certainly an important factor, it is important none the less to stress that it was not a high birth rate as such that led to high infant mortality, but rather a high birth rate in the context of poverty and general social deprivation. Spree suggests that the better-off, in adopting family limitation in the late nineteenth century, were taking the lead in bringing about 'an increase in rationality in their way of life ... a growing awareness of the possibility of controlling their own fate and of their ability to break with traditional, fatalistic, and especially religious and mystical norms and

[59] For example, 18% of households in the Neustadt Nord were single-person households, as compared to 5.7% in Barmbeck (*SHS* 20 (1902), Uebersicht ID).

values'.[60] Yet Spree also emphasizes socially differentiated access to the health-related infrastructure (housing, sanitation, and clean water-supplies), as well as social variations in medical attendance; and it has to be said that there is little evidence of 'mystical and religious norms' dominating the attitudes of the notoriously secularized and hard-headed Hamburg working class in the late nineteenth century. Moreover, given the need of the working-class family for extra income and the high (though often concealed) level of child labour at the time, it may have been perfectly rational for working-class families to have lots of children. Similarly, civil servants may well have limited their family size in response to the arguably irrational demands of a status-conscious society for them to lead a life-style with a high degree of conspicuous consumption.

Nevertheless, as we saw in Chapter 2, Spree is correct to note that access to sanitation, and to a lesser extent to clean water, and the exercise of high standards of domestic hygiene, differed according to social class. While Spree emphasizes the importance of education in the adoption of high standards of cleanliness and hygiene, however, the employment of servants to keep the home clean, together with the possession of individual bathrooms and toilets and other necessary facilities, made hygiene relatively easy for the wealthy. Moreover, the influence of the medical profession in bringing about a lowering of infant mortality rates—a point which Spree's concept of a 'rational' attitude to the problem would seem to emphasize—is by no means easy to establish. Of course, this does not mean to say that the medical profession was unaware of the high levels of infant mortality that plagued Hamburg in the late nineteenth century: on the contrary, they registered these levels with a good deal of concern, as we shall now see.

b. *Doctors' Dilemmas*

I

In 1804 Senator Bartels of Hamburg was bold enough to complain publicly that 'public health care is more neglected here than it is in any small country town'.[1] This view was not his alone. In 1802 a visiting physician went out of his way to bemoan 'the lack of a good medical police' in Hamburg.[2] These complaints were not simply reflections of the lamentable state of public health in the city at the turn of the century. They were also the expression of a powerful new ideology. 'Medical police', the phrase used by the visiting doctor

---

[60] Spree, *Soziale Ungleichheit*, p. 92.

[1] Quoted in *Die Gesundheitsverhältnisse*, p. 64.

[2] Cited in M. Lindemann, 'Producing Policed Man: Poor Relief, Population Policies and Medical Care in Hamburg, 1750–1806', Ph.D. thesis (Cincinnati, 1980), p. 222.

in 1802, was one of the great slogans of the day. It did not mean a body of men: rather, a set of checks and controls, though these did of course mean employing people to operate them, such as poor law doctors. Its meaning was most extensively delineated in Professor Johann Peter Frank's *System of a Complete Medical Police*, published in no fewer than six substantial volumes in 1779.[3] Frank's work has been described by a recent historian as a 'totalitarian Utopia':[4] it foresaw a time when the state would intervene in almost every sphere of daily life, from conditions of work to marriage, pregnancy, and the upbringing of children, in order to ensure the health of present and future generations. The intention behind Frank's proposals was to demonstrate the value of the medical profession, who of course would be responsible for carrying out the main tasks of his 'medical police', in fulfilling the population policy of the Absolutist state. The Central European monarchs of the eighteenth century were constantly complaining about the underpopulation of their territories (in part a consequence of the Thirty Years' War of 1618–48), and continually seeking ways and means of overcoming the resulting shortage of peasants, workers, and soldiers and thus increasing the amount of their revenues and the size of their armies. Some Absolutist states, such as Prussia, went to considerable lengths to encourage immigration and passed far-reaching law reforms designed to increase the birth rate, for example by allowing easy divorce for childless couples.[5] In this context, therefore, Frank's proposals could be sure of a sympathetic hearing.

At the same time, however, there were clear limits to the state's willingness to adopt the idea of 'medical police' in the circumstances of the eighteenth and early nineteenth centuries. The medical historian George Rosen once suggested that the concept with its 'authoritarian and paternalistic character' was characteristic of the German political system, with its absence of 'individual freedom and initiative'.[6] But, as Ute Frevert has pointed out, the Absolutist state was well aware of the impossibility of putting the idea into effect with the rigour and comprehensiveness that Frank desired.[7] It lacked the manpower to carry out even a fraction of Frank's proposals, and communications in eighteenth-century Germany were so bad that large parts of the countryside were able to escape central government control for long periods of time. The creation of a 'complete system of medical police' would also cost far more money than the state was willing or able to afford. Moreover,

[3] J. P. Frank, *System einer vollständigen medicinischen Polizey* (6 vols.: Mannheim, 1779–88).

[4] U. Frevert, *Krankheit als politisches Problem 1770–1880. Soziale Unterschichten in Preussen zwischen medizinischer Polizei und staatlicher Sozialversicherung* (Kritische Studien zur Geschichtswissenschaft, 62: Göttingen, 1984), p. 66.

[5] Cf. Ibid., pp. 23–8.

[6] G. Rosen, *From Medical Police to Social Medicine. Essays on the History of Health Care* (New York, 1974), p. 143.

[7] Frevert, *Krankheit*, p. 354 n. 116.

the Prussian state regarded the pretensions of the medical profession as outlined by Frank and his colleagues with a justified degree of scepticism.

For the medical profession of the late eighteenth century was far from being the generally respected body that it was later to become. Physicians who obtained a university medical degree were often ill-equipped for the practical exigencies of dealing with the sick and the dying. Armed with only a theoretical knowledge, they still owed their allegiance in the main to the humoral doctrines of the ancient Greeks. Illness, they were taught, was the expression of an imbalance in the four 'humours' of the body: blood, phlegm, and yellow and black bile. Blood-letting through the application of leeches and vomiting induced by purgatives were the commonest treatments, designed to reduce a supposed excess of one humour or another, while the external or internal application of alcohol, herbal medicines, and chemical remedies was employed to top up whichever humour was supposed to be deficient. Not only were these treatments seldom effective, but they were also very similar to those employed by women of all classes in treating minor ailments and illnesses. The doctors had to contend with rivals in the form of surgeons (*Wundärzte*), whose practical anatomical training made them better equipped to deal with broken bones and similar disorders. Even if their social status was lower because they were trained through apprenticeship and not at a university, the surgeons were none the less popular because the results of their work were often obviously successful in a way that consulting doctors found very hard to emulate. Finally, given the uncertain effects of formal medical treatment, the doctors were also forced to tolerate the widespread activities of unqualified and often fashionable quacks and charlatans, whose treatments were frequently no more dangerous and no less effective than their own.[8]

The physicians of the day may thus have been a learned profession, but they by no means enjoyed a monopoly in the field of medical treatment. Moreover, since there was no state health insurance or state medical care, they were mainly dependent for their income on patients' fees. This meant in practice that they spent much of their time visiting the wealthy in their homes and attending to the whims of propertied hypochondriacs. The growth of an urban bourgeoisie in late eighteenth-century Germany created a growing market for the services of the medical profession, especially given the value which that class placed on an ordered, moderate, disciplined, and healthy life-style. Buoyed up by this increasing demand, academically trained physicians also tried to improve their position by taking advantage of the Absolutist state's known desire for a larger and more healthy population. The result was the increasing popularity in the late eighteenth century of the concept of 'medical police', which found gradual expression in the introduction of new medical regulations by a number of German states in this

[8] Ibid., pp. 36–44.

period. These regulations fell far short of the total medicalization of society advocated by Frank. But they none the less brought important gains to the medical profession. The new regulations laid down tougher sanctions against 'quacks' and 'charlatans', established basic rules of medical conduct, and set up a machinery for dealing with major epidemics and caring for the chronically ill. Many, if not most academically trained physicians were also engaged as state medical officers (*Physici*), charged with overseeing the operation of the medical regulations, examining apothecaries and midwives, and looking after the local hospitals, in return for a modest income that did something to reduce their dependence on the uncertainties of the private market. The growing influence of the concept of 'medical police' meant a substantial rise in the medical profession's income and prestige.[9]

Since 'medical police' and medical regulations owed their existence above all to the Absolutist state's population policies, it is scarely surprising that a liberal trading city such as Hamburg, which had no interest in increasing its population, and indeed maintained guild regulations partly to restrict it, was slow to follow the Prussian example. It was not until 1796 that the first draft of an official set of Medical Regulations (*Medizinal-Ordnung*) for the city was prepared. The chaos of the ensuing years, particularly during the lengthy French occupation, helped delay the implementation of these Regulations for over two decades. During this time the Senate was put under strong pressure from the surgeons and apothecaries for the preservation of their privileges and equal pressure from doctors who argued that the 'examination of surgeons is a laughable farce' and demanded the punishment of 'quacks'. The Senate seems eventually to have decided that although in principle free trade was better than monopoly, the organization of medical services came into the category of preventive policing rather than guild regulation or mercantile competition. So the regulations finally came into effect on 19 February 1818, creating a Health Committee (*Gesundheitsrat*) consisting of two members of the Senate, six other non-medical members, two medical officers (*Physici*), two other physicians, and one apothecary. The Health Committee was charged with advising the Senate on public health and medical care, and had the duty of preparing memoranda on all proposed legislation affecting sanitary and medical matters. It was characteristic of the administrative practice of the city that public health was put in the hands of a mixed body of Senators, laymen, and professionals, and that full-time medical officers were not employed. The medical officers were part-time officials with no more than an advisory function, and they retained their own private practice at the same time as their membership of the Health Committee. Their main duties were to examine corpses found in suspicious circumstances, and perform other

⁹ Ibid., Ch. 1; see also C. Huerkamp, 'Ärzte und Professionalisierung in Deutschland. Überlegungen zum Wandel des Arztberufs im 19. Jahrhundert', *Geschichte und Gesellschaft*, 6 (1980), 349–82.

functions of a police doctor (e.g. in rape cases), to report on the health of military recruits, to conduct examinations of doctors, surgeons, apothecaries, and midwives, to certify lunatics, to prosecute quacks, and to deal with epidemics. The Health Committee successfully pursued some of the major goals of 'medical police' in the first half of the nineteenth century, including the introduction of the mandatory notification of all cases of infectious disease, medical post-mortems, and of course regulations against 'quacks and charlatans'. But its lay-dominated composition and its purely advisory status were increasingly resented by the medical profession as time went on.[10]

By the end of the 1860s, demands for the reform of Hamburg's Medical Regulations from the local physicians had become too strong to ignore. Dr Hermann Gustav Gernet, one of the city's two medical officers, declared in 1870: 'a reform of our medical system ... is now unavoidable, because one cannot work these days with the old forms, which have in part become completely unusable.'[11] The amateur and part-time organization of medical services were, he argued, inappropriate for a large industrial city and seaport such as Hamburg had now become. Gernet pointed enviously to England, where the all-powerful Medical Officers of Health were taking the lead in sanitary reform. 'What we lack', he wrote, 'to start with is medical legislation which is in tune with the times and in accordance with today's high level of medical science and experience, and then we lack a unified, centralized medical administration.' The existing Medical Committee he regarded as 'a completely inappropriate organ', and he urged its replacement by a professional medical administration led by a full-time Medical Officer without a private practice.[12]

But the reform which he and his colleagues succeeded in persuading the Senate to introduce in a law of 26 October 1870 fell some way short of these ambitious hopes. True, the Health Committee was replaced by the Medical Board (*Medizinal-Kollegium*), on which the medical profession was in a clear majority. The two Senators remained on the new Board, but there were only two other lay members, the number of medical officers was increased to four and that of the other physicians to three, and the apothecary was joined by a chemist. From 1880 the medical director of the General Hospital also had a seat on the Board. It now consisted therefore of eight medical members and

[10] For the regulations, cf. H. Rodegra, *Das Gesundheitswesen der Stadt Hamburg im 19. Jahrhundert unter Berücksichtigung der Medizinalgesetzgebung (1586–1818–1900)* (Sudhoffs Archiv, supplement 21; Wiesbaden, 1979). There is a brief summary of the salient points in *Die Gesundheitsverhältnisse*, pp. 64–5. For influence by pressure groups and Senate reactions, see StA Hbg, Senat, Cl. VII, Lit. Lb, No. 23a, Vol. 1, Bd. 1, Bl. 3, 10, 12, 20, 22; ibid., Lit. Mb, No. 1, Vol. 1a2, Bd. 2, Bl. 39b, 62, and Rambach's letter of 29 Apr. 1804; ibid., Vol. 144, No. 1, No. 4. On the functions of the Medical Officer, see ibid., Lit. Lb, No. 23a, Vol. 75, Fasc. 3: 'Die amtliche Thätigkeit eines Hamburger Physicus. Zusammenstellung aus der Zeit von Mitte November 1833 bis Mitte November 1863 von Dr Buek, sen.'.

[11] H. G. Gernet, *Die öffentliche Gesundheitspflege in Hamburg* (Hamburg, 1870), pp. 3–5.

[12] Ibid., pp. 27–32.

six laymen. But if the medical profession had succeeded at last in establishing control over Hamburg's supreme medical authority, it had not succeeded in getting the authority itself any more power. Its functions remained advisory as before, and the presence of the two Senators on the new Board was evidence that the Senate still reserved to itself the final power of issuing public health regulations. One of the medical officers was made Medical Inspector (from 1878 Chief Medical Officer, or *Medizinalrat*) and charged with the general supervision of public health and the medical profession in the city. But his functions were still only advisory, and he still carried out his duties part-time. The real power was wielded by the President of the Medical Board, a Senator, who usually occupied the position of Chief of Police at the same time. The first doctor to be appointed Medical Inspector was said to have 'caused amazement when he demanded to be given an office'.[13] No paid officials or civil servants were appointed to work for the Medical Inspector or later the Chief Medical Officer, thus continuing the tradition of government by amateurs that the Hamburg Senate considered so important. Finally, the Medical Regulations of 1818 were not revised, and indeed they remained in force right up to the end of the century.

II

The Hamburg Medical Regulations of 1818 and the changes in composition of the Hamburg Medical Board which took place in 1870 have—along with subsequent changes in the 1890s—been described by their most assiduous chronicler, Heinrich Rodegra, as model achievements of a city administration that remained progressive and responsive to the interests of the inhabitants by succeeding 'in achieving a tight organization without too much encroachment on personal freedoms and privileges'. Rodegra regarded the regulations as the product of continual efforts by the Senate 'to provide the population once more with the security of being treated by really qualified physicians if they fell ill, and thus to put an unconditional end to the abuse of quackery'.[14] But there is no evidence for the existence of such an intention on the part of the Senate, and as Ute Frevert has remarked, 'the reference to the alleged wish of the authorities to provide every citizen with a "really qualified physician" seems at least naive, and in any case unhistorical given the very precarious situation of medicine and physicians at the time'.[15]

In reality, the medical policy of the Hamburg Senate in the nineteenth century evolved under the pressure of two contradictory influences. On the one hand, as we have seen, the great merchants whose views ultimately

[13] *Die Gesundheitsverhältnisse*, p. 65.

[14] Rodegra, *Das Gesundheitswesen*, pp. 191, 185, cited in the critical review by U. Frevert, in *Archiv für Sozialgeschichte*, 23 (1983), 772–4.

[15] Ibid., p. 773.

determined the Senate's actions wanted to reduce economic regulation to a minimum and preserve a maximum of free competition as the basis of the city's economy. From this point of view they were bound to be suspicious of the medical profession's claims to a monopoly in the health market, its efforts to dominate the state's medical board and its attempts to 'medicalize' society through the extension of the medical regulations. During the lengthy preparations of the Medical Regulations of 1818, for example, the Senate Commission charged with the task had initially proposed not to include any clauses penalizing 'quacks' at all, on the grounds that free competition was as desirable in medicine as elsewhere.[16] Similar doubts clearly lay behind the long delay in bringing in the Medical Regulations of 1818, the failure to replace them with a more interventionist set of regulations in 1870, and the reluctance to allow the medical profession anything more than an advisory role in the area of public health. 'Medical police', if carried out to anything like the extent which the doctors advocated, would not only go against the ideology of free competition and the night-watchman state, it would also involve the Senate in a great deal of public expense. On both counts, it was not surprising that it was rejected.

On the other hand, the influence of Hamburg's liberal ideology was to some extent countered by the fact that the doctors, as academically qualified professionals, themselves belonged to Hamburg's dominant classes. The demands of the medical profession could not simply be dismissed as the demands of lowly artisan guilds might be. Hamburg's doctors were men of education, breeding and substance. Some of them even came from the ranks of the great merchant families, increasingly so as the century went on, and the medical profession became more respectable. Dr Johann Julius Reincke, for example, who was born in 1842 and subsequently became one of the city's leading physicians, was related by marriage to the Sieveking family, one of whom, Hermann Sieveking (born in 1867) also entered the medical profession;[17] Senator Johann Otto Stammann (1835–1902) was the son of a doctor, as was Senator Gerhard Hachmann (1838–1904). Yet the social prestige of medicine was still not very high. One can easily cite comparable examples of Senators who were the sons of apothecaries—Senator Versmann, for example, or Senator Johann Heinrich Burchard (1852–1912)—and the social distance between these two professions for most of the nineteenth century seems to have been relatively narrow. For a member of one of

[16] Rodegra, *Das Gesundheitswesen*, p. 47.

[17] 'Stammbaum der Familie Reincke, zusammengestellt für den Familientag am 29. Dezember 1899' (copy in StA Hbg library); biographical notes in H.-G. Freitag, *Von Mönckeberg bis Hagenbeck. Ein Wegweiser zu denkwürdigen Grabstätten auf dem Ohlsdorfer Friedhof* (Hamburg, 1973); for the general background, see C. Huerkamp, 'Die preussisch-deutsche Ärzteschaft als Teil das Bildungsbürgertums: Wandel in Lage und Selbstverständnis vom ausgehenden 18. Jahrhundert bis zum Kaiserreich', in W. Conze and J. Kocka (eds.) *Bildungsbürgertum im 19. Jahrhundert* (Stuttgart, 1985), 358–88.

Hamburg's grand bourgeois families, becoming a doctor was always second-best to joining the family firm or entering the legal profession, and it may have been the choice of some who seemed for one reason or another unable to stand the strain of overseas service or daily attendance at the Exchange. It was surely not by chance, for instance, that one of the few members of the powerful and wealthy younger branch of the great Amsinck family to become a doctor, Johannes Amsinck (1823–99), was sickly as a child and grew up with a pronounced limp. Nevertheless, the decision to become a physician was one that could be respected: and even if they did not belong to one of the great families, Hamburg's doctors could find their place in the social world of the governing circles through a shared university or student corps experience, participation in the city's leading political and administrative institutions or geographical proximity to the great merchants in the better-off living quarters of the town: Dr Gernet, for example, was a neighbour of the Mercks, Woermanns, and other grand families in Harvestehude. Doctors played an important part in the city's formal and informal charitable institutions. Their income of course qualified them for the privileges of citizenship. They played an important role in the Citizens' Clubs; and they were also eager to secure election to the Citizens' Assembly, where they regularly constituted between 5 and 6% of the membership in the decades after the reform of the constitution in 1860.[18]

So Hamburg's medical profession constituted a group that had to be listened to in the inner councils of the dominant classes, even if it was, especially in the early part of the century, a strictly subordinate group. As Gernet wrote in 1863, there was

a certain unmistakable mistrust among the two professions which have hitherto ruled the roost here, the lawyers and the merchants, with regard to the efforts of the medical profession ... This mistrust may indeed have its origin partly in a somewhat jealous fear of an encroachment by the doctors on the more or less undisputed rule hitherto exercised by these two professions, but mainly it results from a scarely believable ignorance and indifference on the part of the majority with regard to what one might call public health care ... Most of them think that the task is basically done when occasional police ordinances have been issued and the business of the police and court doctors taken care of ... We are undoubtedly behind other states in this respect.[19]

[18] O. Hintze, *Die Niederländische und Hamburgische Familie Amsinck*, (Hamburg, 1932), iii. 72; A. Cord, 'Die Soziale Schichtung der Hamburger Bürgerschaft von 1859 bis zum Jahre 1921. Ein Beitrag zur parlamentarischen Geschichte des Kaiserreichs' StA Hbg, Handschriftensammlung 1023; Hamburg, 1961, Statistischer Anhang, 'Gesamtdarstellung 1859–1921', col. I; StA Hbg, FA Merck II 9 Konv. 4a Heft II, p. 11.

[19] H. G. Gernet, *Auch ein Votum über die Medizinal-Reform* (Hamburg, 1863), pp. 3–4. On the insecure social status of 19th-century medical men, see M. H. Kater, 'Professionalization and Socialization of Physicians in Wilhelmine and Weimar Germany', *Journal of Contemporary History*, 20 (1985), 677–701.

Like the lawyers, the doctors were caught between two opposing forces that shaped their consciousness. On the one hand, as subordinate members of Hamburg's dominant classes, if they wanted to retain their place at the dinner-table or the sick-bed of the merchant families upon whom they depended for their income, they could not afford to question the primacy of trade, the belief in free competition, or the abhorrence of the paternalist state that were the central dogmas of Hamburg's ruling class. On the other hand, they were exposed to the interventionist ideology of 'medical police' through their university training and their wider medical contacts. Unlike the English medical profession, who gained their qualifications in the private medical schools controlled by the profession itself, the German doctors received their medical education at state-run universities. Since Hamburg steadfastly refused to found its own university, aspiring doctors, like aspiring lawyers, were forced to go to a university in Prussia or South Germany to gain the qualifications necessary for the pursuit of their career. This brought them under the influence of professors of medicine who, like Johann Peter Frank, were staunch advocates of the interventionist ideology of the 'medical police'. Here, too, they made friendships with similarly minded medical men from other parts of Germany. These contacts were renewed at medical congresses and conventions held outside Hamburg, to which of course the Hamburg doctors regularly went.

These contradictory influences on the medical profession found a dramatic expression in a split which occurred in a commission set up to discuss the proposed reform of the Medical Regulations at the beginning of the 1860s. The four medical representatives on the Medical Committee wanted an advisory Medical Board led by a Senator and a general approach which recognized 'peculiar local circumstances' and so 'did not depart too far from the existing situation' (while of course 'not leaving out of account ... the demands of modern times'). The majority, however, representing the medical profession organized in the Doctors' Club, wanted an English-style system which separated medicine from policing and established sanitation as a whole separate system of government. They demanded that 'the tasks of the medical administration be infinitely extended in this direction'; 'the whole, great influence of a public health service under scientific leadership should be brought to bear'. The two sides were unable to agree and the minority resigned from the commission in protest. Even though the majority mobilized 111 doctors behind a petition in support of its proposals in May 1862, the official minority, led by the two Medical Officers, stood the best chance of getting their proposals through. Apart from anything else, they were clearly going to be a lot cheaper than those of the professionals.[20]

The Senate was prepared to compromise its principles of free competition

[20] Huerkamp, 'Ärzte und Professionalisierung', in general. For the debates of the 1860s in Hamburg, see StA Hbg, Senat, Cl. VII, Lit. Lb, No. 23a, Vol. 75, Fasc. 1a, pp. 1–4, 26 ff.

in the case of the medical profession, as it did by agreeing in the end to include sanctions against 'quacks' in the medical regulations of 1818. In return, the Hamburg doctors were expected to accept the primacy of trade and to restrict themselves to taking an advisory role in public health matters. Only when the pressure from the medical profession in the rest of Germany became overwhelming, as in the 1860s, did local doctors make a serious attempt to bring Hamburg into line with other parts of Germany. Where national medical opinion was less than clear, however, they found it difficult if not impossible to resist the pull of Hamburg's hegemonic ideology. In the uneasy relationship between the grand bourgeoisie and the medical profession, it was generally the grand bourgeoisie that retained the whip hand. Only in exceptional circumstances and at moments of extreme crisis could the constellation of forces change in the medical profession's favour.

III

A characteristic example of medical intervention in society in nineteenth-century Hamburg can be found in the attempts of the authorities to deal with the problem of infant mortality. The state in Hamburg repeatedly intervened to try and reduce the high numbers of infant deaths; but it saw the problem in characteristically voluntaristic terms, as lying not so much in the inadequacies of Hamburg's urban environment or the inequalities of the distribution of wealth, as in the actions of a single group of individuals, namely wet-nurses and foster-parents.

It had long been the custom to send infants and children out into the nearby countryside if they could not be adequately cared for in the city. 'Hamm and Horn', reported a local doctor in 1851, 'are literally flooded not only with foster-children from the Hamburg Poor Law Board but also with the children of (mostly unmarried) private individuals.' Some women were said to be looking after and attempting to breast-feed three babies from the city at the same time. There were no checks and controls on these women, he complained, and he noted that he had found 'one such foster-child of the Hamburg Poor Law Board staying in the most lamentable circumstances with the dirtiest, most drunken, and most dissolute people, the Wiske couple in Horn'. These foster-parents had already lost one of their own children through neglect. A number of children in the district had been infected with syphilis by their parents, who none the less were still taking in foster-children from the city.[21] Another doctor reported in December 1850 that the foster-parents frequently blamed the foster-children for bringing infections from the city, whereas the reverse was just as often true. Controls were non-existent, he said. He urged the Senate to demand references for the 'moral way of life' of

[21] StA Hbg, MK II C 2 Bd. 1, Bl. od–e (5. 1–3), letter dated Mar. 1851.

these women, as well as a medical examination in each case.[22] In fact there were extensive regulations in force, which demanded a previous examination of the wet-nurses, forbade them to take more than one suckling infant at a time, and laid down certain minimum standards of care. These had been in existence since 1822, and even before that there had been various schemes of registration, mostly of a voluntary kind not directly enforceable by the state.[23] These regulations, as Dr Hermann Gernet confirmed some three decades later, had not been very effective, and in 1852 the authorities were forced to confess 'that the way in which so-called foster-children have hitherto been farmed out for breast-feeding or care in country districts leaves much to be desired and in particular is lacking any supervision or control'.[24] The infants were kept in dark, dank, and dirty rooms, exposed to disease and the whims of drunken foster-mothers; many of them were lucky, wrote Gernet, not to fall into the hands of 'angel-makers' whose aim it was to bring them to an early grave.[25]

The wet-nursing business has been held responsible by many observers for a very large proportion of infant deaths in the eighteenth and nineteenth centuries. Hugo Meyer-Delius, in his study of infant mortality in Hamburg since 1820, published in 1965, singled out for special mention these so-called 'angel-makers' (*Engelmacherinnen*), wet-nurses and foster-mothers who deliberately neglected their charges, especially if they were illegitimate, often at the prompting of the natural mother, and usually with fatal results.[26] An official Senate document issued in 1893 declared 'that in the absence of a general control of fostering, innumerable children in their first years of life fall victim to carelessness and neglect or even to the disgraceful trade of so-called "angel-making"'. Repeated attempts to regulate the trade in 1852, 1873, and afterwards thus had little effect.[27] Indeed in 1894 the *Hamburgischer Correspondent* declared that 'the number of parents and mothers who, lacking all feelings of conscience, seek to get their children off their hands by farming them out at the cost of a small amount of money, has increased to the most alarming degree. And', the paper added, 'it is well enough known what fate frequently awaits these unhappy beings.'[28]

In eighteenth and early nineteenth-century Hamburg, it was overwhelmingly the poorest classes, and above all unmarried mothers, who sent

[22] Ibid., Bl. of.
[23] Ibid., Bl. oh: 'Verhaltungs-Massregeln für diejenigen, welche Kinder vom Waisenhause in Kost nehmen'. See also M. Lindemann, 'Love for Hire: The Regulation of the Wet-Nursing Business in 18th-century Hamburg', *Journal of Family History*, 6 (1981), 379–95.
[24] StA Hbg, MK II C 2 Bd. 1: 'Bekanntmachung der Landherrschaft der Geestlande', 10 Dec. 1852. Gernet's report is in ibid., Bl. ok ff.
[25] Ibid.
[26] Meyer-Delius, 'Die Säuglingssterblichkeit'.
[27] StA Hbg, MK II C 2 Bd. 1: 'Allgemeine Beaufsichtigung des Kostkinderwesens' (Drucksache für die Senats-Sitzung, Nr. 172, 7 July 1893).
[28] Ibid., Bl. 68: *Hamburgischer Correspondent*, 5 May 1894.

out their babies to wet-nurses in the country. The well-off employed wet-nurses in their own homes, and it was in fact for these wet-nurses that the regulations were mainly intended and enforced.[29] William L. Langer has suggested that the disposing of unwanted babies to wet-nurses in European society was part of a wider pattern of the control of family size through infanticide which prevailed right up to the second half of the nineteenth century. Thomas McKeown indeed considered that the decline of infanticide in the nineteenth century was, with the decline in starvation, the only major contributory cause to the growth in European population apart from the decline of infectious diseases.[30] No one would wish to underestimate the sufferings of those infants and young children who fell victim to the 'angel-makers' and dirty, negligent, or diseased foster-parents, but nor should anyone overestimate the extent of these practices or the contribution they made to infant mortality. It is characteristic, for example, that when Hugo Meyer-Delius mentioned the fact that an 'angel-maker' was condemned and executed in Hamburg as late as 1904, he neglected to add that the woman in question had been murdering the infants in her charge without any hint that she should do so from their mothers, and that it was in fact the enquiries of the distraught parents that eventually brought her to justice.[31] The innumerable and never-ending complaints of doctors and officials about the iniquities of wet-nursing and foster-parenthood were part of a more general discourse among the concerned educated classes which placed the blame for death, disease, and deprivation on the moral failings of the poor themselves. This discourse has been taken up more recently by those historians who argue that the great majority of people in the past were callous or indifferent towards the health and well-being of their children. Philippe Ariès, Lawrence Stone, and Edward Shorter have all suggested that lack of effective con-traception, material poverty, and already high infant death rates led to a brutal neglect of children; the role of mercenary wet-nurses in effectively killing off unwanted infants occupies quite a prominent place in their argu-ments.[32]

Unmarried mothers in nineteenth-century Hamburg, especially if they were alone or rejected by their families, often had little option but to send their infants to foster-parents in order to continue earning a living. Many women died in childbirth, and the poor law authorities were likewise compelled to send the surviving infants to a wet-nurse. Malnourished mothers were often unable to produce enough milk to feed their own infants. Poor married women often had to work long hours outside the home; official regulations

[29] Lindemann, 'Love for Hire'.

[30] T. McKeown, *The Modern Rise of Population* (London, 1976), pp. 66–7, 146–7.

[31] StA Hbg, MK II C 3 Bd. 1, 116, 116a: *Hamburger Neueste Nachrichten*, 19 Apr. 1903.

[32] E. Shorter, *The Making of the Modern Family* (London, 1976), pp. 169–90; L. Stone, *The Family, Sex and Marriage in England, 1500–1800* (London, 1977), pp. 470–7; P. Ariès, *Centuries of Childhood* (London, 1975), pp. 353–90.

providing for maternity leave and time off work for nursing mothers during the day were not introduced until the end of the 1870s and in any case were frequently ignored. Until the invention of the rubber teat in the middle of the nineteenth century, infants could not easily be fed cow's milk in sufficient quantities,[33] and wet-nursing was the only real alternative. None of these facts is evidence of a callous indifference towards infants on the part of poor mothers. On the contrary, there is abundant evidence of affection and emotional involvement between parents and children in past societies, and the contrary view has become prevalent not least because so many historians have taken their evidence from court cases and other documents dealing with those parents whose behaviour attracted the attention of the authorities.[34] Infanticide, abandonment, and the farming out of infants to wet-nurses were not very widespread in the nineteenth century; no figures were ever supplied by the Hamburg authorities, but the numbers involved do not seem to have been very large.

More crucially still, whatever the shortcomings of wet-nurses, the infants who were put in their care were almost certainly better off than those who were not breast-fed at all. There is abundant statistical evidence available to show that infants who were breast-fed stood a far better chance of survival than those who were not.[35] Given the unhygienic state of milk supplies in the nineteenth century, this was scarcely surprising. Numerous investigations failed to establish with any certainty that children who were put out to wet-nurses suffered higher mortality rates than those who were not. Certainly, as we have seen, illegitimate children were far more at risk, but although it was sometimes claimed that the great majority of illegitimate infants were sent to wet-nurses,[36] there is no firm statistical evidence to back up this assertion. The Association for the Protection of Foster-Children in Altona and Ottensen, active in the urban areas immediately bordering on Hamburg, reported in 1880, for example, that 67% of the illegitimate children who died in these areas in 1879 before reaching the age of one had not been breast-fed. Infant mortality in Altona in 1870 was 20.8%, but it stood at 37.3% for illegitimate infants.[37] Those who had not been breast-fed had, of course, by definition, not been sent to wet-nurses. Failure to breast-feed the infant, for whatever reason, thus seems to have been a much more important cause

---

[33] Bread or meal wrapped in cloth and soaked in cow's milk was usually given to the infant as a substitute for the breast; see Meyer-Delius, 'Die Säuglingssterblichkeit'.

[34] For some general points along these lines, see S. Wilson, 'The Myth of Motherhood a Myth: The Historical View of European Child-rearing', *Social History*, 9, (1984), 181–98; A. Wilson, 'The Infancy of the History of Childhood: An Appraisal of Philippe Ariès', *History and Theory*, 19 (1980), 132–53. A useful guide to the whole subject is M. Anderson, *Approaches to the History of the Western Family, 1500–1914* (London, 1980), esp. Part 3.

[35] See especially Imhof, 'Unterschiedliche Säuglingssterblichkeit'.

[36] StA Hbg, MK II C 2 Bd. 1, Bl. 12–13.

[37] Ibid., Bl. 33–4.

of high mortality rates among illegitimate children than farming out to unscrupulous wet-nurses.

Once again the Senate, the Citizens' Assembly, and the responsible officials, including members of the medical profession, found it easier to blame high infant mortality rates on the immorality of the working classes than to look for the infrastructural causes for which they themselves were responsible. Police action could be taken against erring wet-nurses, and regulations introduced to curb the worst excesses of the trade in orphaned infant paupers, but these were responsible for only a tiny fraction of the infant deaths that occurred in the city. When it came to tackling the major causes of infant mortality—poor housing and overcrowding, polluted water, unhygienic milk, public dirt, and disease—the Senate and the Citizens' Assembly were unable for decades to do anything decisive. A serious improvement of the situation would not have been possible without drastic state intervention in society, affecting the vital interests of all fractions of capital.

IV

Even in areas where medical intervention in society was relatively simple, Hamburg was reluctant to act. Perhaps the most striking example of this reluctance can be found in the case of smallpox. Smallpox is a contagious disease whose symptoms include high fever, headache, and vomiting and above all the characteristic massed eruptions of the skin, which produce scabs all over the body and leaves those victims who recover horribly disfigured by deep pockmarks.[38] In the eighteenth century it was one of the commonest of all diseases. Epidemics swept across Europe at irregular intervals, attacking mainly infants and young children but affecting all age-groups to some degree. One German doctor estimated in 1798 that four out of five children caught the disease, 5% of the whole population lost their 'health and beauty' because of it, and 10% died from its effects.[39] No cure for smallpox has ever been found, but in the eighteenth century there were some attempts at prevention by inoculating people with the infection in a diluted form. This practice probably did more in the end to spread the disease than to contain it, for while some may have acquired immunity in this way, a few actually fell victim to the disease in its full force as a result of inoculation and so became centres of further infection.[40] This did not stop the medical profession

---

[38] Smith, *The People's Health*, pp. 156–69.

[39] Frevert, *Krankheit*, p. 69.

[40] McKeown, *The Modern Rise of Population*, pp. 11–13. For possible examples of epidemics accidentally induced by this method, see A. Perrenoud, 'Contribution à l'histoire cyclique des maladies. Deux siècles de variole à Genève (1580–1810)', in A. E. Imhof (ed.), *Mensch und Gesundheit in der Geschichte* (Husum, 1980), pp. 175–98.

from recommending inoculation, not least because it brought them substantial fees from the well-off clients upon whom they mainly practised it.[41]

In 1798, however, the British doctor Edward Jenner publicized a new preventive technique that quickly proved its worth. This consisted of vaccinating the client with cowpox, a related disease that gave those injected with it immunity against the far more serious scourge of smallpox. The new technique was not without its problems. It was not always completely efffective, it was often incompetently administered, and it was frequently so unhygienic that other diseases, including syphilis, are known to have been transmitted by the unsterilized needles used in the procedure. Vaccination in the early nineteenth century was a strange and frightening treatment and it often had painful and unpleasant side-effects.[42] Moreover, as Thomas McKeown has pointed out, mass vaccination was not necessarily effective as a preventive measure because immunity did not last very long and the early nineteenth-century state was incapable of ensuring that vaccination was truly universally administered. Still, the advantages appeared to the medical profession to outweigh the disadvantages, and historians have recently been too sceptical about its achievements. The technique was undoubtedly effective in reducing the incidence of smallpox, above all where it was combined with rapid identification of the victims at the beginning of an outbreak, isolation, containment, and a determined effort to identify and vaccinate the victims' contacts.[43]

Within a very short space of time the doctors were able to persuade the King of Prussia to issue an edict urging local authorities to encourage their subjects to be vaccinated. At the same time, the continued use of the innoculation method, which had justifiably aroused a good deal of popular suspicion, was prohibited by law. While the doctors had mainly been innoculating the better-off people who constituted the vast majority of their clients, the Prussian state, which clearly saw the military and economic advantages of reducing the incidence of smallpox among the population at large, now removed the medical monopoly of preventive treatment and allowed surgeons, pastors, teachers, and midwives to perform vaccinations as well. A whole series of official regulations was passed on the subject, culminating in the introduction of compulsory vaccination in Prussia in 1818. Bavaria had required its citizens to be vaccinated since 1807; Baden, Hesse, and other German states effectively followed this example in the next few years. As the historian Ute Frevert has pointed out, the Prussian state preferred to achieve its end in this area by indirect means rather than the more costly methods of direct compulsion. But since it refused to allow children or young people to be enrolled in school, apprenticed, confirmed, taken into service, or

[41] Frevert, *Krankheit*, pp. 70–1.
[42] Ibid.; see also Smith, *The People's Health*, p. 160.
[43] McKeown, *The Modern Rise of Population*, pp. 106–9.

recruited into the army unless they produced a vaccination certificate, the result was in effect the same. Moreover, direct compulsion and forced vaccination were used during smallpox epidemics, and the police punished the parents of children who caught the disease if it turned out that they had not been vaccinated. Thus vaccination became very common. 66 vaccinations were performed in Berlin for every 100 births on average in 1844–63, for example, and 70 in Bavaria in the years 1862–71. In Prussia deaths from smallpox were said to have fallen from 40,000 a year before the introduction of compulsory vaccination in 1818 to a 'mere' 3,000 a year by 1826.[44] In 1816 smallpox mortality in Prussia stood at 0.5 deaths per 1,000 inhabitants; in subsequent decades up to 1860 it seldom rose above 0.1 or 0.2 per 1,000 in any year. In Brandenburg the smallpox death rate fell from 2.2‰ a year in 1776–80 to 0.2‰ a year in 1816–50, after the introduction of compulsory vaccination; while in Württemberg the total annual number of deaths from smallpox fell from 23,000 in 1780–89, 32,000 in 1790–9, and 22,000 in 1800–9 to less than 1,000 in 1811–30. Those cases that continued to occur were either in people who had not been vaccinated, or in those who had not had the necessary booster injection, whose importance was not yet fully recognized.

The reduction of smallpox through compulsory vaccination was perhaps the one indisputable achievement of nineteenth-century medicine in its narrower sense in directly bringing about a significant reduction in mortality. Yet it was achieved at the cost of massive state intervention in the free disposition of the individual over his or her own body. Compared with the even more drastic compulsion used in Bavaria, the Prussian system of vaccination may indeed have been relatively lax, but compared to the situation in Hamburg, Prussia's tightly drawn network of rules and regulations requiring the production of the all-important vaccination certificate amounted in reality to 'executive coercion'[45] of the most effective kind. And indeed it was widely perceived as such. Compulsory vaccination was an easy enough step in late-Absolutist Prussia, where the paternalistic direction of the population by the state was an everyday occurrence. But it was a different matter altogether in self-consciously liberal Hamburg, where state inter-

---

[44] Frevert, *Krankheit*, pp. 71–3; Smith, *The People's Health*, pp.160–1; C. Huerkamp, 'The History of Smallpox Vaccination in Germany: A First Step in the Medicalization of the General Public', *Journal of Contemporary History*, 20 (1985), 617–35, here pp. 624–5; BA Koblenz R86/1097 Bd. 1: Tabellen zur Veranschaulichung der Pockensterblichkeit in Deutschland und im Auslande, Table II; ibid., 1215 Bd. 1: Gutachten über den Einfluss der einmaligen und wiederholten Einimpfung der Schutzpocken auf die Verbreitung und Gefährlichkeit der Menschenblattern, sowie auf die Gesundheit der Geimpften innerhalb der Staaten des Norddeutschen Bundes und thunlichst auch die übrigen Staaten (Königliche Wissenschaftliche Deputation für das Medicinalwesen, Berlin 28 Feb. 1872, MS). See also H. A. Gins, *Krankheit wider den Tod. Schicksal der Pockenschutzimpfung* (Stuttgart, 1963).

[45] Frevert, *Krankheit*, p. 74.

vention of this kind in the liberties of the individual subject was viewed with the deepest suspicion.

For decades after the general introduction of compulsory vaccination in the rest of Germany, Hamburg continued to hold out in favour of voluntary methods. The medical profession, as we have seen, was not in a very strong position in the city in the first half of the century, and indeed until the introduction of the new medical regulations of 1870 its influence on the Senate remained very limited. As far as individual practitioners were concerned, patients could always be vaccinated privately, and many of the better-off citizens undoubtedly took this step, providing Hamburg's medical men with a substantial source of income in the process. But the erection of free vaccination stations, as in Berlin, was another matter altogether. No one could be found to pay for them: certainly not the Senate. The Doctors' Club set up a vaccination station but doctors could seldom be found to serve in it. In 1871 it was described as 'completely orphaned' by the profession. Only 12 people were vaccinated in 1856, though in epidemics more was done, and the annual average number of vaccinations through the 56 years of the station's existence was 720. Even this was not much, however, given the hundreds of thousands of people who lived in the city. Hamburg's medical men shared enough of the dominant ideology of the city to regard the enthusiasm of their Prussian colleagues for compulsory vaccination as somewhat misplaced in the Hanseatic context. True, as Dr Hermann Gernet pointed out in 1856, children were only taken into the city poor school if they had been properly vaccinated, and compulsory vaccination was also in force in the Hamburg-controlled district of Bergedorf beyond the city limits. But Bergedorf was jointly administered with Lübeck until 1868; and while such restrictions were permissible for the disfranchised poor and for rural subjects, they were intolerable for free citizens. Regulations introduced in the epidemic of 1823 were never enforced. In Hamburg, as Gernet reported, 'the great mass of the uneducated, especially the poor, does not recognize the need, or is too indolent and is afraid of the cost'.[46]

By this time, in fact, the Hamburg medical profession was beginning to exert increasing pressure for a greater say in the city's affairs—pressure which found at least a partially successful expression in the promulgation of the new medical regulations of 1870. Moreover, half a century of the successful reduction of smallpox deaths by compulsory vaccination in other German states (even, from 1835, in England),[47] had left Hamburg's physicians feeling distinctly uneasy about what could all too easily be presented as the city's backwardness in this respect. It must have been embarrassing for them to

[46] Gernet, report of 20 Oct. 1856, in StA Hbg, MK II D 1, Bd.1, Bl. 0a; S. Dworak, *Die Entwicklung des Impfwesens der Stadt Hamburg. Die Entwicklung der Pockenschutzimpfung von 1800 bis 1940*, MD thesis (Hamburg, 1984), pp. 31, 36, 45–6.
[47] Smith, *The People's Health*, pp. 160–1.

confess to their colleagues from other parts of Germany, when they met at conferences and congresses which were becoming an increasingly important feature of medical life at this time, that they had been unable to persuade their government even to take this simple, universally acknowledged step towards the improvement of health standards in the population at large. And, of course, the threat of a smallpox epidemic remained in these circumstances a very real one. As Gernet remarked in 1856, 'we have in part the compulsory vaccination that obtains in the surrounding states to thank for the fact that smallpox mostly only shows itself here sporadically'.[48]

Accordingly, the Hamburg medical profession made a determined attempt to secure the introduction of compulsory vaccination during the 1860s. Their proposals were consistently rejected by the Citizens' Assembly, with—among other things—the argument 'that compulsory vaccination is an outrageous interference in the rights of people to freedom and liberty!'[49] Dr Buek, the city's Chief Medical Officer, failed to get a vaccination law adopted in April 1860,[50] and Dr Caesar Gerson, one of the most vocal champions of an increased medical intervention in Hamburg society, was also unsuccessful when he tried to persuade the Citizens' Assembly to introduce compulsory vaccination later in the decade.[51] Such a measure, it was said in the Assembly in 1871, was a measure which 'encroaches upon personal freedom and liberty, and upon the most basic right of the individual, that of the freedom to dispose of his body as he wishes, more than any other measure promulgated in the common interest'.[52] No doubt behind these grand statements of principle there also lay the fear that compulsory vaccination would cost the state a good deal of money to enforce. And given the fact that there had been no major epidemic outbreak of smallpox in Hamburg in the nineteenth century at all, there must surely have been a great deal of complacency as well. In the end, such measures hardly seemed necessary. After all, as Hermann Gernet remarked in 1870, 'Hamburg, on the whole, is a healthy place; epidemics almost never occur here to such a devastating degree as they do in other places'.[53]

Scarcely a year later, however, Gernet's smugness was shattered as soldiers returned to Hamburg from service in the Franco-Prussian War carrying the smallpox virus with them. Soon hundreds of the city's inhabitants had been stricken with the disease. At first, the Hamburg medical authorities seemed

[48] Gernet, report of 20 Oct. 1856, loc. cit.

[49] StA Hbg, MK III B 1 Bd. 1: *Hamburger Nachrichten*, 14 June 1871.

[50] StA Hbg, MK II D 1, Bd. 1, Bl. 1.

[51] Ibid., 5 Bd. 1: 'Reform' (various clippings, 1860); ibid., III B 1 Bd. 1, Bl. 20: *Hamburger Fremdenblatt*, 19 July 1871.

[52] Ibid., II D 1, Bd. 1: Bericht des von der Bürgerschaft am 13. September 1871 niedergesetzten Ausschusses (Nr. 2), Oct. 1871.

[53] Gernet, *Die öffentliche Gesundheitspflege*, p. 32.

determined to take no notice at all of the outbreak. As a liberal newspaper, the *Hamburger Fremdenblatt*, complained on 19 July 1871,

Still our Medical Board is shrouding itself in deep silence. The smallpox epidemic is spreading more and more, and the death rate is growing and growing, yet we can observe not a single measure that has attempted to relieve the suffering or prevent the evil from spreading further. The public is right to put the question: 'What then indeed do we have a Medical Board for?' . . . Even in the preparation of the statistics on the spread of the disease and its mortality there is a negligence which should not occur in a civilized modern state.[54]

There had already been some 900 deaths from smallpox by the end of May. And this was only the beginning. Altogether some 4,053 inhabitants of Hamburg died from smallpox in 1871. This was equivalent to a death rate of 15.4 per 1,000, which made the smallpox outbreak of 1871 the greatest of all epidemics in nineteenth-century Hamburg, more severe in its incidence than any visitations of cholera or typhoid, including the cholera epidemic of 1892. 9,055 victims were hospitalized, of whom 908 died.[55] If this ratio of deaths to cases held good for those not treated in hospital, then there may have been as many as 40,000 cases altogether. 29% of all deaths in Hamburg in 1871 were caused by smallpox.[56] The disease was above all a scourge of infants and young children. The death rate among those aged 0–1 was as high as 89‰, though the high infant mortality from other causes meant that only 24% of infant deaths during the year could actually be ascribed to the disease. But smallpox caused 47% of all deaths among 1–5 year olds, with a mortality rate of 33‰, and exactly half of all deaths among those aged 5–15, generally the healthiest age-group in the population, where smallpox mortality only reached 8‰. Among older age-groups the epidemic did not cause more than 10 deaths per 1,000 population in 1871, but even so it was still responsible for 30% of deaths among those aged 15–50 and 21% of deaths among those aged 50–70.[57] These were truly terrifying figures. And they were not paralleled anywhere else in Germany. In Berlin there were some 5,216 deaths, a mortality rate of only 6.3 deaths per 1,000 inhabitants, less than half that experienced by Hamburg, although there was a smaller epidemic the following year as well, with another 1,198 deaths (a mortality rate of 1.4‰). In 1871 no other German city apart from Danzig even began to approach these rates. 'Hamburg', as the offical medical history of the city later admitted, 'distinguished itself in the whole of Germany through the severity of its smallpox epidemic'.[58]

[54] Clipping in StA Hbg, MK III B 1 Bd. 1, Bl. 20.
[55] *Die Gesundheitsverhältnisse*, pp. 163–4.
[56] StA Hbg, MK II D 1 Bd. 1, Bl. 58: 'Materialien zur Impffrage'.
[57] See *MS 1872* for these figures.
[58] *Die Gesundheitsverhältnisse*, pp. 163–4; BA Koblenz, R86/1097 Bd. 1: Tabellen zur Veranschaulichung der Pockensterblichkeit in Deutschland und im Auslande, Table II. In London

The smallpox epidemic of 1871 gave rise to a storm of protest which concentrated on the failure of Hamburg to introduce a compulsory vaccination law. As Hermann Gernet conceded on 13 July, significantly, despite his earlier criticisms, a defender of the Senate and the medical authorities on this occasion, 'it is unbelievable how large the number of people who have not been vaccinated was and is in this city'. The *Hamburger Nachrichten* concluded on 20 July: 'The number of deaths from smallpox appears greater in comparison to the number of inhabitants in Hamburg than in any other large European city, for example in London, because here not even the first vaccination is compulsory in law.'[59] Dr Fischer, who had practised for thirty years in a vaccination centre in Westphalia, agreed that the epidemic was worse in Hamburg than anywhere else, and he strongly criticized the past inaction of the city authorities in this area.[60] Already on 3 August the Senate set up 15 vaccination stations and put an extensive vaccination programme into action.[61] Beyond this, however, the epidemic presented the opponents of compulsory vaccination in the city with an unanswerable case for its introduction. Such was the scale of the disaster that the Senate was compelled to take immediate action to restore public confidence. A law on compulsory vaccination was passed in the same year and, as Chief Medical Officer Dr Johann Caspar Theodor Kraus reported two years later, 'it soon became clear that the public demand was greater than expected'.[62] After the shock of 1871, vaccination against smallpox was suddenly in vogue, and the disease never visited the city again in epidemic form. But Hamburg had only just forestalled the Reich by its action: three years later, in 1874, the Imperial Vaccination Law (*Reichsimpfgesetz*) made smallpox vaccination compulsory across the whole German Empire. After this, the death rate from smallpox fell dramatically everywhere in Germany; from 0.2 or 0.3‰ in a normal year in Prussia to less than 0.05‰ from 1876. In the epidemic years of 1871–2 some 125,000 people died in Prussia of smallpox; in 1877 the number was only 88. The incidence of the disease in Hamburg became negligible after 1872.[63]

The smallpox epidemic of 1871, like the medical regulations passed the

the same year smallpox mortality was 2.4‰; Vienna, Danzig, and Breslau also all suffered epidemics in 1872, Vienna with a mortality rate of 5.4‰. Mortality from smallpox in the German army in France in 1870–1, as further tables in the file indicate, was 0.4‰. Bismarck's wars had already caused a jump in smallpox mortality in the 1860s, from 0.3‰ in 1863 to 0.5‰ in 1864 and 0.6‰ in 1866, sinking back to 0.2‰ in 1868–70, its normal rate (deaths per 1,000 Prussian population, ibid., Table II; in absolute terms an increase from about 5,000 to nearly 12,000 in 1863–6).

[59] StA Hbg, MK III B 1, Bd. 1: *Hamburger Nachrichten*, 13 July 1871.
[60] Ibid., *Hamburger Nachrichten*, 14 July 1871.
[61] StA Hbg, Polizeibehörde I, 84, Gesundheitsrath 3 Aug. 1871.
[62] StA Hbg, MK II D 1 Bd. 1, Bl. 176, report of 22 Apr. 1873.
[63] BA Koblenz, R86/1097 Bd. 1: Tabellen zur Veranschaulichung der Pockensterblichkeit in Deutschland und im Auslande, Table II; ibid., Tafeln zur Veranschaulichung der Wirkung des Impfgesetzes in Deutschland.

year before, demonstrated that the influence of the medical profession in Hamburg had its limits. Despite over a decade of pressure, the doctors had been unable to persuade the Senate to spend money on compulsory vaccination at a time when it existed almost everywhere else in Germany. The drive for greater medical intervention in society had come up against the powerful Hamburg ideology of the night-watchman state. At the same time, the alacrity with which the local medical profession jumped to the Senate's defence once the epidemic had broken out was perhaps an even more significant pointer to its position in the city's power structure. Those who, like Caesar Gerson, launched a frontal attack on the Senate's failure to bring about medical reforms, were in a minority. To voice open criticism of the Senate was to align oneself with the reviled Hamburg 'democrats'. Gaining acceptance as part of Hamburg's ruling fraction depended on closing ranks when a crisis came. The medical men exacted a price for their loyalty, of course. It was as a direct result of the smallpox epidemic of 1871 that the changes in the Medical Board agreed in 1870 were actually put into effect.[64] The doctors knew that in the end they had more to gain from showing solidarity with the authorities than from going over into opposition.

Smallpox was a disease that, like so many others, was spread especially by overcrowding and ill-ventilated living and working conditions, and so it was, like that other great affliction of the nineteenth century, tuberculosis, above all a disease of the poor. Unfortunately there are no statistics for the Hamburg epidemic of 1871 that can demonstrate this point; but figures from Brunswick for 1864–73 show that average smallpox cases in the income group earning less than 75 Marks per capita per year were running at 5.1‰, while the rate among those earning 75–100 Marks was only 2.8‰, descending to 2.3‰ among those earning 100–150 Marks, 1.2‰ among those earning 150–200 Marks, 0.8‰ among those earning 200–250 Marks, and 0.3‰ among those earning more than 250 Marks. The distribution of deaths was similar, with a 0.6‰ smallpox death rate in the lowest income group, 0.3‰ in the next two up, 0.2‰ in the 150–200 Mark group, and no deaths at all in the higher income brackets.[65] As for Hamburg, the reaction of the Senate to the outbreak of the 1871 epidemic was simply to pretend it was not there. Concealment and inaction were the watch-words of the day. No doubt the Senate was concerned not to damage trade by prompting other ports to impose a quarantine on Hamburg ships. Perhaps too it was afraid of arousing popular panic through a dramatic public announcement. This pattern of behaviour was entirely characteristic of Hamburg's authorities in the face of epidemic disease, and it was repeated on numerous other occasions during the nineteenth century, as we shall see in the following chapters. Nevertheless, smallpox differed from all other epidemic diseases of the era in one crucial respect:

[64] StA Hbg, MK III B 1 Bd. 1, Bl. 47: *Hamburgischer Correspondent*, 21 June 1871.
[65] Reck, *Die Gesundheitsverhältnisse der Stadt Braunschweig*.

unlike typhoid, tuberculosis, or cholera, smallpox could easily be prevented by a simple medical prophylactic in the administration of a vaccine. If the Senate and the medical profession were incapable of pushing through even such an uncomplicated measure as this in time to prevent a disaster occurring, then what hope was there in the case of the other killer diseases, whose prevention required the most far-reaching reforms of the sanitary and social infrastructure?

c. *The Challenge of Cholera*

I

In the early 1830s European society was suddenly confronted by the appearance of an entirely new and very serious disease: Asiatic cholera. It came to Europe as a consequence of European mercantile and industrial enterprise, and once it had arrived, it fastened on to the industrial society that was then in the making and exploited and exaggerated many of its most prominent aspects, from urbanization and overcrowding to environmental pollution and social inequality. The disease had long been endemic on the Indian subcontinent. But the expansion of the British Empire, with its frequent and large-scale movements of goods and people, and the rapid growth in trade between India and Europe that accompanied the industrial revolution in the United Kingdom, combined in the early nineteenth century to export the disease to the rest of the world. By 1819 the major outbreak that had begun in Bengal two years before had reached Mauritius; by 1824 it covered the whole of South-East Asia. More ominously still, it had been carried by traders across Afghanistan before being halted by a military cordon sanitaire in Astrakhan in 1823. It was indeed by this route that it eventually reached the West. After a brief respite in the mid-1820s, it returned to Persia and crossed the Caspian once more, making its way north to Orenburg, at the south-western edge of the Urals, in August 1829. From this new centre it was spread by merchants travelling to and from the great annual fair in Nijhni-Novgorod, as well as making its way independently up the Volga past Astrakhan, where this time the military cordon sanitaire failed to work. In September 1830 it reached Moscow. And in 1831 a major Russian military campaign against a rebellion in Poland spread it rapidly further west. By July it had reached the port of Riga, on the Baltic.[1]

Reports of the horrifying and deadly effects of the new disease soon began

---

[1] M. Durey, *The Return of the Plague. British Society and the Cholera 1831–32* (Dublin, 1979), pp. 7–18; R. J. Morris, *Cholera 1832: The Social Response to an Epidemic* (London, 1976), pp. 21–4.

to reach Western Europe. It began to affect the victim through a vague feeling of not being well, including a slight deafness. This was followed fairly quickly by violent spasms of vomiting and diarrhoea, vast and prolonged in their extent, in which the evacuations were usually described as being like 'rice-water'. In this stage up to 25% of the victim's body fluids could be lost. This led, not surprisingly, to a state of collapse in which, in effect, the blood coagulated and ceased to circulate properly. The skin became blue and 'corrugated', the eyes sunken and dull, the hands and feet as cold as ice. Painful muscular cramps convulsed and contorted the body. The victims appeared indifferent to their surroundings, though consciousness was not necessarily lost altogether. At this stage death would ensue in about half the cases from cardiac or renal failure, brought on by acute dehydration and loss of vital chemicals and electrolytes, or the victim would recover more or less rapidly. The whole progess of the symptoms from start to finish could take as little as 5 to 12 hours, more usually about 3 or 4 days. Modern medical science would add that the incubation period appears to last for a minimum of 24 hours and up to a maximum of 5 days, and though the carrier state may last longer, it too is usually of similar duration (roughly 24 hours to 8 days).[2]

The most important causative agent in the disease is now agreed to be a microscopic bacillus known as *Vibrio cholerae*. It thrives in warm and humid conditions, above all in river water (up to 20 days). It multiplies very rapidly when the water is warm, though it can survive in colder temperatures. Although the bacillus is transmitted most easily in water, it can also survive on foodstuffs, especially on fruit and vegetables which have been washed in infected water. It can live in butter for up to a month. Milk also provides a hospitable environment. These facts are important because the disease can only strike if the bacillus enters the human digestive tract. In effect, it can only be caught by putting an infected foodstuff or other substance into the mouth. It is transmitted easily enough by touching the mouth with infected hands. This opens up a further range of possibilities. The bacillus survives for up to 15 days on faeces and a week in ordinary earth dust. Infected clothes and linen, especially the bed-linen of victims, are important sources of transmission, should they be touched by others who then later unsuspectingly put hand to mouth. Person-to-person transmission usually occurs indirectly through infection of food or clothing or bathroom and toilet facilities. The bacillus can also be transmitted by flies as far as their limited range takes them. The best way to combat the bacillus is through scrupulous personal hygiene. Frequent washing of the hands, especially after contact with infected persons and things (e.g. communal lavatories), is vital. During an epidemic, bacilli in the water-supply, in milk, or on foodstuffs can be killed by heat (boiling or baking). The bacillus cannot withstand acid. This includes some

---

[2] Durey, *The Return of the Plague*, p. 216.

gastric juices and most disinfectants. It only lasts for a few minutes in wine or spirits, a few hours in beer. It can be prevented from entering the water-supply by the process of sand filtration. This introduces hostile bacteria into the water and the cholera bacilli are quickly exterminated. It follows from all this that cholera epidemics tend to break out in warm and humid weather. They are often spread by infected water-supplies, especially if allied to inefficient sewage systems. Personal contacts also play a role. Dirty and overcrowded living conditions and shared toilet facilities are especially dangerous. On a wider geographical scale, the disease is spread by victims and carriers as they move about the country. River-water is sometimes infected and spreads the disease as it flows downstream. All these factors marked out an insanitary port city such as Hamburg as a major potential centre if the disease should continue to spread.[3]

For nineteenth-century sensibilities, cholera was a disease truly terrifying in its effects. Society had in many ways come to terms with infant deaths and with long-term, permanently present killers such as consumption. A whole set of attitudes had evolved to help people confront the reality of such everyday deaths. This was 'the Age of the Beautiful Death', as Philippe Ariès has described it, when literature was full of edifying death-bed scenes, in which death crept up on people slowly, transformed their physical suffering into an ethereal beauty, and lent them, in its slow but inexorable progress, a moral purity unattainable in everyday life.[4] Death's permanent presence in the family made its emotional costs easier to bear. In most cases where death was exceptionally sudden and violent, as on the battlefield, it was usually possible to come to terms with it through the ideology of heroism, chivalry, or self-sacrifice. Even an ignominious death, by suicide or on the gallows, had its appointed rituals—the suicide note, often with its claim to a noble motive, the last meal of the condemned, the speech from the scaffold.[5]

Death from cholera was, almost by definition, anything but beautiful. It was a new disease, which people found hard to fit into the patterns of coping with death evolved across the preceding centuries. Moreover, the occurrence of cholera epidemics was sufficiently rare for people to be able to suppress their consciousness of its visitations. The threat which it posed was not permanent, and therefore not psychologically manageable. Its impact was unpredictable, its causes unknown or disputed. It affected every group of the population.[6] Thus when a cholera epidemic did occur, it stamped itself on the

[3] Ibid., pp. 216–18.

[4] P. Ariès, *The Hour of our Death* (Harmondsworth, 1981), pp. 409–72.

[5] A. Alvarez, *The Savage God: A Study of Suicide* (Harmondsworth, 1971); J. McManners, *Death and the Enlightenment: Changing Attitudes to Death among Christians and Unbelievers in 18th-century France* (Oxford, 1981), pp. 368–408.

[6] A. E. Imhof, 'Mensch und Körper in der Geschichte der Neuzeit: Reflexionen über eine internationale Tagung in Berlin vom 1.–3. Dezember 1981', *Beiträge zur Wissenschaftsgeschichte*, 5 (1982), 195–207, here p. 203.

public consciousness with all the force of a natural disaster. Tuberculosis, though a great killer, was usually a slow disease. It spread through the city's population at a pace so leisurely that no one could notice whether it was increasing or decreasing in incidence. Cholera raged through the population with terrifying speed. People could be walking about normally, with no symptoms one day, and yet be dead the next morning. The mere onset of the symptoms could sometimes be enough to kill. People were appalled by the terrifying and unpredictable suddenness with which the disease struck. A businessman could leave his house in good order in the morning and return from work in the evening to find a note on the door saying his wife and family had been taken to hospital after being stricken down during the day. A woman could begin her supper in good health but not live to eat the pudding. Such stories, and the fact of their wide circulation during epidemics, attested to the fact that the suddenness with which cholera attacked people was one of its most frightening aspects.[7]

In addition, the symptoms of cholera were peculiarly horrifying to nine-teenth-century bourgeois sensibility. Consumptives exhibited few symptoms that caused embarrassment or discomfort in the onlooker, and then only from time to time. On the whole, they merely became pale and interesting. Even typhoid, despite some unpleasant symptoms, was considered socially acceptable and claimed a number of prominent victims. It presented symptoms of fever that took some weeks to progress and could be understood in terms of a drama of life and death, so that spectators were frequently present at the bedside to watch the whole performance and converse with the patient in his or her moments of lucidity.[8] Not so cholera. The blue, 'corrugated' appearance of the skin and the dull, sunken eyes of sufferers transformed their bodies from those of recognizable people, friends, family, relatives, into the living dead within a matter of hours. Worse still, the massive loss of body fluids, the constant vomiting and defecating of vast quantities of liquid excreta, were horrifying and deeply disgusting in an age which, more than any other, sought to conceal bodily functions from itself. Bourgeois society, as we have seen, took increasing pains, as the century wore on, to make private the grosser physical acts of daily living and to pretend that they did not exist.[9] Cholera broke through the precarious barriers erected against physicality in the name of civilization. The mere sight of its symptoms was distressing; the thought that one might oneself suddenly be seized with an uncontrollable, massive attack of diarrhoea in a tram, in a restaurant, or on the street, in the presence of scores or hundreds of respectable people, must have been almost as terrifying as the thought of death itself. It is telling that while

[7] C. A. Schröder, *Aus Hamburgs Blütezeit* (Hamburg, 1921), pp. 80–1. See also Plate 17.
[8] T. Mann, *Buddenbrooks* (Harmondsworth, 1968), for one example.
[9] N. Elias, *Über den Prozess der Zivilisation* (Frankfurt, 1978).

quiet diseases such as cancer and tuberculosis were widely used as literary metaphors, cholera's apperance in the literature of the nineteenth century is rare. The literary critic Susan Sontag has pointed out the contrast:

In *Death in Venice*, passion brings about the collapse of all that has made Gustav von Aschenbach singular—his reason, his inhibitions, his fastidiousness. And disease further reduces him. At the end of the story, Aschenbach is just another cholera victim, his last degradation being to succumb to the disease afflicting so many in Venice at that moment. When in *The Magic Mountain* Hans Castorp is discovered to have tuberculosis, it is a promotion. His illness will make Hans more singular, will make him more intelligent than he was before. In one fiction, disease (cholera) is the penalty for a secret love; in the other disease (TB) is its expression. Cholera is the kind of faculty that, in retrospect, has simplified a complex self, reducing it to a sick environment. The disease that individualizes, that sets a person in relief against the environment, is tuberculosis.[10]

Like syphilis, whose metaphorical power was also limited, cholera was felt to be a vulgar and demeaning disease. Its reputation as a disease of the poor only strengthened its repulsiveness. Cholera could only function as a term of abuse, as applied by Trotsky to Stalin, or Langbehn to the Jews.[11] It was a synonym for pestilential horror, nothing more. A cholera epidemic of serious dimensions was severe in terms of the sheer suddenness and rapidity of its onslaught: this was a disease which killed people within hours of the appearance of the first symptoms, and could kill thousands within weeks of the initial outbreak. And it was severe in psychological terms: this was a disease which had no mitigating features, there was no means of coming to terms with the degrading violence it inflicted on the human body, and no consolation in the event of it gaining the victory over life.

Such was the nature of the disease that broke out in Hamburg on 5 October 1831, when a sixty-seven year-old former sailor called Peter Petersen, who mainly lived from begging, fell ill with 'violent vomiting and diarrhoea'. Police surgeon Hauptfleisch found him on 6 October suffering from severe cramps, 'the extremities ice-cold, hands and feet blue, and eyes sunken'. At 6 p.m. on 6 October 1831, Petersen died.[12] At this point the authorities learned of another case that had occurred on 2 October on board a barge that had travelled down the Elbe from Wittenberge. It is most likely that the disease had entered the city by this route, through infection of the river-water upstream from Hamburg, where the barge lay in quarantine in the port of Geesthacht. Probably Petersen had for some reason come into contact with

---

[10] S. Sontag, *Illness as Metaphor* (Harmondsworth, 1983), p. 41.

[11] Ibid., pp. 84–5. For a study of the anti-Semitic German writer Julius Langbehn, see F. Stern, *The Politics of Cultural Despair* (New York, 1966).

[12] J. C. G. Fricke, *Geschichtliche Darstellung des Ausbruchs der asiatischen Cholera in Hamburg* (Hamburg, 1831); J. Michael, *Geschichte des ärztlichen Vereins und seiner Mitglieder* (Hamburg, 1896), p. 125.

the river water; or it had infected the sour milk which he often drank. Several of the 41 inhabitants of his cellar lodgings, who 'consisted in their entirety of vagabonds and beggars' as a history of the epidemic written later in the same year subsequently noted, also fell ill with the same symptoms. So too did some of Petersen's companions in the begging trade.[13] Soon cases were being reported all over the city. Already on 11 October 14 new cases were reported; on 16 October there were 44, and on the 18th day the epidemic reached its height, with 51 new cases. Thereafter it declined rapidly. Hamburg breathed again.[14] The epidemic had, all things considered, been a good deal less severe than many people had feared.[15]

In the meantime cholera swept on westwards, reaching Britain later in October 1831 and America and Canada in the following year.[16] But it had not yet disappeared from Hamburg. The epidemic was officially regarded as having ended in January, and the various precautionary measures ordered by the authorities were relaxed. No cases occurred in February or March. Already on 1 April, however, a new case was reported, and eight further cases, with five deaths in all, were confirmed before the Senate, on 27 April 1832, finally concluded that cholera had broken out once more. The disease spread throughout May and June, reaching a first peak on 16 June, when 92 cases were reported within the space of a few hours. In July it declined, so that towards the end of the month there were only half a dozen or so new cases reported each day. But in August it grew in intensity once more, with 30 new cases reported on the 26th. Throughout September and October it showed no signs of departing, with anything between 5 and 15 new cases occurring each day. In November it finally began to abate. The last case was reported on 17 December. All in all, 3,349 people in Hamburg fell victim to the disease in the epidemic of April–December 1832. 1,652 of them died.[17] In the end, therefore, Hamburg was quite seriously affected by the epidemic of 1831–2.

How the medical profession and the authorities dealt with the new disease depended on what they thought caused it. Here opinions were divided. The obvious model to which cholera seemed to conform was the plague. Certainly the Russians acted on this basis. The Medical Council of St Petersburg reported in 1830 that cholera was a contagious disease and that in some instances quarantine measures had proved undeniably effective. Some Indian doctors

[13] Fricke, *Geschichtliche Darstellung*, pp. 26–7.
[14] Ibid., p. 91.
[15] StA Hbg, Senat, Cl. VII, Lit. Ta, Pars 2, Vol. 11, Fasc. 17, Inv. 1a: *Hamburger Fremdenblatt*, 27 Oct. 1892; and Michael, *Geschichte des ärztlichen Vereins*, p. 127.
[16] Durey, *Return of the Plague*, Morris, *Cholera 1832*; C. E. Rosenberg, *The Cholera Years 1832–1959* (Chicago, 1962); G. Bilson, *A Darkened House: Cholera in Nineteenth-century Canada* (Social History of Canada, 31; Toronto 1980).
[17] StA Hbg, Senat Cl. VII, Lit. Ta, Pars 2, Vol. 11, Fasc. 17, Inv. 1a: *Hamburger Fremdenblatt*, 27 Oct. 1892.

thought the same.[18] Two Berlin medical men, writing in 1831, argued that it was 'solely and exclusively caused and transmitted by an infectious material' which was spread in people's breath, in their clothing, in their excretions, and in the things they touched. They drew optimistic conclusions from their theory. If cholera was caused by a miasma, they declared, there would be no means by which the individual citizen could protect himself.[19] A contagionist theory placed the means of prevention in everyone's hands. These views were echoed by Thomas Jensen, also writing in 1831, who claimed that it was 'very probable' that the disease 'spreads through contact with infected people and goods and through breathing in their poisonous exhalations'. Jensen, it should be noted, was a preacher, not a medical man.[20] Nevertheless, yet another pamphlet, issued in Berlin with official backing in 1831, agreed that cholera was transmitted by touch, through clothing, and in the breath of the victims.[21]

The doctrine of contagion was a very old one. It went back at least as far as the plague writings of the sixteenth century, which postulated transmission by touch, by infected clothing or goods, and (exceptionally) inhalation of an infected atmosphere.[22] By the 1830s, however, many medical scientists seriously doubted the adequacy of the contagionist model. A second type of theory stressed instead the importance of local miasmas, in which the air was polluted by factors peculiar to certain localities under specific conditions. This too was an old theory, with parallels in medieval plague medicine.[23] More recently it had gained credence through its application to the problem of yellow fever in the United States by Benjamin Rush and Daniel Webster. A substantial number of Indian doctors favoured this kind of explanation for cholera, though they were unable to persuade many people in Europe of the validity of their arguments in the 1820s.[24] Even before the disease arrived in Hamburg the local medical profession was split over the issue. On 21 June 1831 the Doctors' Club decided to meet once a week to study and discuss the reports of cholera coming in from further east and prepare for its possible arrival. Letters from doctors in Königsberg, St Petersburg, Warsaw, and other cities where the disease had broken out were read aloud and debated. Here

---

[18] Morris, *Cholera 1832*, pp. 28–9. Durey, *Return of the Plague*, p. 110.

[19] E. Horn and W. Wagner, *Wie hat man sich vor der Cholera zu schützen und was hat man bei ihrem Eintritt zu ihrer Heilung und zur Verhütung der weiteren Verbreitung zu thun? Zur Beruhigung des Publikums beantwortet von dem Geheimen Medizinal-Rath und Professor Dr. Ernst Horn und dem Professor und Stadt-Physikus Dr. Wilhelm Wagner in Berlin* (Berlin, 1831).

[20] T. H. Jensen, *Belehrungen, Ermunterungen und Tröstungen für den Bürger und Landmann wegen der Cholera. Von einem Landprediger* (Altona, 1831).

[21] *Anweisung zur Erhaltung der Gesundheit und Verhütung der Ansteckung bei etwa eintretender Choleraepidemie. Von der Königl. Preussischen obersten Medicinal-Behörde in Berlin zum Druck befördert* (Hamburg, 1831), p. 7.

[22] Durey, *Return of the Plague*, pp. 105–6.

[23] Cf. J. Nohl, *The Black Death: A Chronicle of the Plague. Compiled from Contemporary Sources* (London, 1961), 4.

[24] Durey, *Return of the Plague*, p. 106.

the first battles took place between the 'contagionists' and 'miasmatists'. As the author of the Club's official history noted in 1896, 'the opposing parties fought with roughly the same means as they do today, and just as they do today, everyone stuck at the end of the debate to his original point of view'. After the disease had broken out in Hamburg, the arguments between the two main spokesmen, Steinheim the contagionist and Buek the miasmatist, became so violent, 'that they could not be held to parliamentary forms even by the three adjudicators appointed by the Club. So the controversy was stopped and the adjudicators resigned.'[25]

What particularly impressed the anticontagionists was the universal failure of quarantine. Time and again this was the major reason given for concluding that the disease was not contagious. Typical was the view of Dr K. G. Zimmermann, one of the most assiduous chroniclers of the disease in Hamburg. He pointed out that quarantine measures had proved useless all over Europe. Yet despite this, not every locality into which cholera had entered had seen an epidemic outbreak. The existence only of isolated outbreaks in some areas proved that 'the conditions for the development of such an epidemic had not yet reached maturity in these places'. Zimmermann declared that contagionism was 'long since untenable'.[26] And indeed of the forty-odd pamphlets on cholera published in Hamburg in 1830–2, very few attempted to advance a contagionist view. So certain were some writers of the non-contagious character of the disease that they predicted in advance of its arrival that cholera would never reach Hamburg. Dr H. W. Buek, the City Medical Officer (*Stadtphysikus*), whom we have already encountered as an anticontagionist in the Doctors' Club, gave it as his firm opinion in December 1830 'that this oriental form of disease should appear in the heart of Germany ... seems to me ... to be very unlikely, indeed almost unthinkable'.[27] Yet appear it did; and soon the idea of contagion was in disrepute because quarantine had failed to work. Doctors began to be converted to the idea that cholera was produced by a miasma.[28] F. Siemerling, writing in 1831, called it *malaria animata* or 'animated swamp-air' released by rotting plants in marshy land. He ascribed vast numbers of diseases to this influence. Siemerling was a doctor in Stralsund; his pamphlet was printed in Hamburg,

[25] Michael, *Geschichte des ärztlichen Vereins*, pp. 123–6.

[26] K. G. Zimmermann, *Nachtrag zu der geschichtlich-medicinischen Darstellung der Cholera-Epidemie in Hamburg im Herbste und Winter 1831–1832* (Hamburg, 1832), vii. Cf. Rosenberg's conclusion that it was the failure of quarantine that brought victory for the anticontagionists in the USA (*The Cholera Years*, p. 80).

[27] H. W. Buek, *Die bisherige Verbreitung der jetzt besonders in Russland herrschenden Cholera, erläutert durch eine Karte und eine dieselbe erklärende kurze Geschichte dieser Epidemie* (Hamburg, 1831), p. 30.

[28] *Noth- und Hülfsbüchlein bey der Cholera-Epidemie für den Landmann und für diejenigen, denen nicht gleich ärztliche Hülfe zu Gebote steht* (Hamburg, Aug, 1831); *Zur Beruhigung für Jedermann bei Annäherung der Cholera, Schreiben eines Familienvaters in St Petersburg an seinen Freund in Deutschland* (Hamburg, 1831).

and his miasmatism was shared by many members of the city's medical profession.[29] Dr F. von Brandenburg agreed that a miasma was responsible but argued it was produced by melting icebergs, which sent up infected clouds then blown towards Europe. Cholera, he declared, was an advanced form of rheumatism, an idea that seemed to be connected with the view of cholera as a kind of extreme cooling down of the body. The ultimate origins of the disease thus lay in the 'chaotic-chronic con- and destructive system of eternally active Nature'.[30] A more conventional view was taken by Dr J. C. Buchheister and the apothecary C. Noodt, both of whom were employed in the special Cholera Hospital set up in Hamburg in 1832. They firmly declared that cholera was 'an epidemic disease ... occasioned by a miasma called forth from the sickly earth'. They suggested, moreover, that the miasma had had its first effect on fowl; where such sickness had raged in the weeks before the coming of the cholera 'some gooseherds reported that of sixty geese, only four remained alive after a fortnight'. Typhoid and other fevers they described as mild forms of cholera.[31]

If cholera was caused by a local miasma, then how was the disease transmitted from place to place? One writer, Karl Preu, noting that it appeared to travel along waterways, hypothesized that the miasma was carried along by 'the strong airstreams that prevail along such great rivers'. From there it sank into the ground on the river banks. He denied that the miasma was produced by any particular type of weather.[32] Dr C. F. Nagel, writing in Altona, went further in the direction of a 'contingent contagionism'. He argued that the disease was in part the consequence of conditions in the ground the nature of which was not yet properly understood; it also seemed to be carried by 'infection by people, perhaps also by goods and effects'. However, though he practised in Danish-ruled Altona rather than free-trade Hamburg, Nagel did not go so far as to argue for quarantine and isolation as preventive measures. He preferred instead to place his main emphasis on personal behaviour. 'Nothing encourages the outbreak of this disease more than excessive, persistent fear of the same.' If people kept calm and avoided a 'disorderly ... way of life', they would be safe. In particular

[29] F. Siemerling, *Entschleierung der Cholera nebst dem sprechendsten Beweise ihrer Nicht-Contagiosität, und Angabe der Heilmittel, so wie des einzig und allein auf Vernunft basirten Vorbeugungsverfahrens gegen das Einathmen der Malaria animata (belebten Sumpfluft). Auf den Altar der Menschheit niedergelegt von Dr. Fr. Siemerling zu Stralsund* (Hamburg, 1831).

[30] F. v. Brandenburg, *Der Sturz der Cholera morbus nebst den sie begleitenden Attributen des Irrthums und des Vorurtheils oder die gediegene Antwort auf die Frage: Woher entstand die Cholera?— Was war deren Character? (angesehen als Krankheitsstoff), und Welches waren die eigentlichen Mittel zu deren Beseitigung? Alles aus grossen Natur-Ereignissen hergeleitet,—in dieser Schrift erklärt und zur bessern Verständlichkeit in Gesprächsform abgefasst* (Hamburg, 1832).

[31] J. C. Buchheister Dr. and C. Noodt Apotheke, *Erfahrungen über die Cholera Asiatica in Hamburg im Herbste 1831* (Hamburg, 1832).

[32] K. Preu, *Was haben wir von der Cholera morbus zu fürchten? Ein Versuch, die aufgeschreckten Völker zu beruhigen* (Nuremberg, 1883), pp. 38–9, 61.

dirt, damp, and neglected living conditions, and above all, the 'abuse of alcoholic beverages' encouraged infection. 'Old drunkards' were particularly vulnerable. Thus Nagel inserted his theory within a powerful current of opinion which ascribed disease to the moral weakness of the victims.[33]

The tendency to ascribe infection to moral failings or psychological disturbance in the victim was very widespread. 'Just don't be afraid!' people were advised, 'be moderate and sober!'[34] Fear, wrote Wilhelm Cohnstein of Glogau, in a pamphlet circulating in Hamburg before the outbreak of cholera, had a 'paralysing influence on the nervous system'. Cohnstein too offered a combination of miasmatist and contagionist theories, but laid the main stress on psychological factors. 'Gaiety and a cheerful courage are well known to be the best prevention against all epidemics and infectious diseases.' Indeed, some medical writers thought that cholera could be explained almost entirely in terms of individual predisposing factors. The assiduous Dr K. G. Zimmermann, for instance, considered both contagionism and miasmatism equally erroneous. If the disease was caused by a miasma, he asked, why had it not broken out before? He preferred to ascribe it to unknown 'repeated cosmic-telluric influences' in the city which caused the ganglious system to be suddenly 'feverishly over-excited'. Thus fear caused by seeing a victim led to the observer going down with the disease as well. 'Contagion', concluded Zimmermann, 'is only *psychological*.'[35] The disease was in effect a development of various kinds of fever that had been present in Hamburg for many years. 'Sadness and fear', agreed another pamphlet published in 1831, easily caused people to succumb.[36] The conclusion seemed to be that cholera was caused by a sudden upset in the internal equilibrium of the body—an idea that perhaps owed something to the old doctrine of humours but which bears on the other hand a striking resemblance to modern notions of psychosomatic illness.

In general, therefore, three basic explanations of cholera seem to have been circulating in Hamburg in the early 1830s: the contagionist, the miasmatist,

[33] C. F. Nagel, *Nachricht an das Publikum über die zweckmässigsten Verhaltungsmaassregeln bei einer etwaigen Erscheinung der morgenländischen Brechruhr (Cholera morbus). Auf Befehl Sr. Exzellenz des Herrn Geheime-Conferenzraths Grafen von Blücher, Altona, entworfen von Dr. C. F. Nagel* (Altona, 1831); cf. *Der Hamburgische Beobachter*, 45 (22 Oct. 1831), p. 170; Frevert, *Krankheit*, pp. 125-35.

[34] *Stimme aus Danzig über die Cholera. Zur Beruhigung Aller, die sie fürchten* (Danzig, 1831), pp. 12-13. For general considerations on the ascription of illness to immorality, see A. Labisch, '"Hygiene ist Moral—Moral ist Hygiene". Soziale Disziplinierung durch Ärzte und Medizin', in C. Sachsse and F. Tennstedt (eds.), *Soziale Sicherheit und Soziale Disziplinierung. Beiträge zu einer historischen Theorie der Sozialpolitik* (Frankfurt-on-Main, 1986), pp. 265-85.

[35] W. Cohnstein, *Trost- und Beruhigungsgründe für die durch das Herannahen der Cholera aufgeschreckten Gemüther, nebst Angabe aller gegen diese Krankheit bisher empfohlenen Schutzmittel* (Glogau and Lissa, 1831); K. G. Zimmermann, *Die Cholera-Epidemie in Hamburg während des Herbstes 1831. Historisch nach ihrer Entwicklung und Verbreitung sowie in ihrem pathologischen und therapeutischen Verhalten dargestellt von K. G. Zimmermann, Dr. med. et chir* (Hamburg, 1831), pp. 27-8, 77-9, 84.

[36] Jensen, *Belehrungen*.

and the moral or psychological. These were of course not necessarily wholly incompatible with one another. Dr S. L. Steinheim, described as a 'zealous contagionist' and a leading opponent of miasmatism in the Doctors' Club debates of 1831, also advocated what he called a 'doctrine of polarity' according to which cholera affected people by changing the balance of 'sympathies' and 'antipathies' within the body. 'The claim that cholera only seizes those who are predisposed by a faulty diet or depressed emotions', he asserted, ' . . . is completely without foundation.'[37] Miasmatists were much more likely to emphasize the influence of a moderate life-style in keeping the miasma from affecting the body. Many writers were in fact 'contingent contagionists' who accepted the existence of a means of transmission of the disease from place to place along rivers or through the air, but also insisted that an outbreak in a given locality was dependent upon local conditions, whether in the atmosphere or the soil, that would determine whether a miasma was created or not. Yet again, many miasmatists, citing the evident ineffectiveness of quarantine, poured scorn on the idea of any kind of transmission from place to place, as we have seen. All in all, as the author of the *History of the Doctors' Club* ruefully noted, the epidemic of 1831–2 was quite unable to produce a consensus in the medical profession on the nature and causes of the disease.[38]

However, the experience of the first epidemic was enough to persuade most medical men in Hamburg—as in other parts of Europe—that whatever else cholera was, it was not a contagious disease in the accepted meaning of the word. As Zimmermann remarked in 1832, 'a conviction that cholera is not contagious has become so fixed here, as everywhere, among the medical and lay public, that it would be difficult to bring them over to any other point of view'.[39] It was particularly important that the Chief Medical Officer of the city, *Stadtphysikus* Dr Heinrich Wilhelm Buek (1796–1879), was from the outset a convinced anticontagionist; his influence was doubtless a contributing factor to the spread of anticontagionist views in the Hamburg medical profession after 1831. In his official report on the next major cholera epidemic to hit the city, in 1848, Buek repeated 'that an *import*, a transmission from one victim to another, an assumption that is still to be found here and there, has *not* happened here'. This was proved, he considered, by the fact that the first cases to occur broke out in different parts of the city and were thus not connected. Yet 'the manner in which cholera is *spread*', he was forced to confess, 'is still a riddle, nor has the present epidemic given us any clues to it'.[40] Indeed, so insoluble did the problem seem that the Doctors' Club

[37] S. L. Steinheim, *Bau- und Bruchstücke einer künftigen Lehre von den Epidemieen und ihrer Verbreitung, mit besonderer Rücksicht auf die asiatische Brechruhr* (Altona, 1831).

[38] Michael, *Geschichte des ärztlichen Vereins*, p. 125.

[39] Zimmermann, *Nachtrag*, vii; 'Privatschreiben aus Berlin', 22 Sept. 1831, quoted in *Der Hamburger Beobachter*, 42 (Vol. 15, No. 4, 15 Oct. 1831), p. 167.

[40] StA Hbg. MK III A 2 Bd. 1, Bl. 81, 91.

did not think it worth discussing at all in 1848-9.[41] The medical profession remained anticontagionist in its majority (as Buek remarked, contagionism could now only be found 'here and there'). But its unity was essentially negative: the doctors could agree on what cholera was not, but they were completely at a loss when it came to explaining what it actually was.

II

By 1860, however, all this had changed. A new theory of cholera had been developed which seemed to offer the answer to all these problems. Its author was the Bavarian scientist Max von Pettenkofer.[42] Pettenkofer was born in 1818 in Lichtenheim. He spent his childhood in the care of his uncle, an apothecary in Munich. He studied medicine and graduated in 1843 from Munich University. But his background probably helped determine that he should concentrate on pharmacology. He soon went to study at Giessen with Justus Liebig, the founder of organic chemistry. The experience seemed to liberate Pettenkofer's creative scientific energies; before long, he had made a variety of important inventions and discoveries in an astounding number of different fields. He was partly responsible for developing a method of preparing meat extract which ultimately led to the Oxo cube. He devised a copper amalgam for filling teeth. He created a new kind of 'good German cement'. He invented a way of producing gas from wood which was used to provide illumination for the theatre and the main railway station in Munich. He originated a new method of restoring cracked varnish on old pictures. He made significant improvements to Bavaria's official coinage. These were only a few of his achievements. They were all incidental to his main work, which was in the field of public hygiene. He poured his inexhaustible energy into a vast quantity of publications in this area. They included fifty-five articles and books on a wide variety of topics in environmental health, among them a paper on the detection of zinc in the atmosphere and a demonstration that air permeated the soil by proving that a canary could survive being sandwiched between two layers of earth.

---

[41] Michael, *Geschichte des ärztlichen Vereins*. For the contemporary debate on cholera elsewhere in Europe, see R. McGrew, *Russia and the Cholera 1823-32* (Wisconsin, 1965), Durey, *Return of the Plague*, and (for Spain) E. R. Ocaña, 'Hygiene y Terapeutica Anticolericas en la Primere Epidemia de Colera en España 1833-1835', *Asclepio*, 24 (1982), 71-100.

[42] Pettenkofer received the 'von' title quite late in life, but to avoid confusion I have used it throughout. The best account of his theory of cholera is probably that given in C. E. A. Winslow, *The Conquest of Epidemic Disease. A Chapter in the History of Ideas* (Princeton, 1944), pp. 311-36. See also the following contributions by Pettenkofer himself: *Untersuchung und Beobachtung über Verbreitung der Cholera, nebst Betrachtungen über Massregeln derselben Einhalt zu thun* (Munich, 1855); 'Cholera', *The Lancet*, 2 (1884), 769-71, 861-5, 904-5, 992-4, 1042-3, 1086-8; 'Causes of Cholera', *Medical Press* (London, 1869), p. 405; 'Zum gegenwärtigen Stand der Cholera-Frage', *Archiv für Hygiene*, 4 (1886), 249-354, 397-545; ibid. 5 (1886) 353-445, ibid. 6 (1887), 1-84, 129-233, 303-58, 373-441; ibid. 7 (1887), 1-81. See also Plate 16.

Pettenkofer was thus cast in the heroic mould of the great nineteenth-century inventors. Over the years, however, he became best known for his writings on cholera. There were seventy-one of these in all, running into thousands of pages. As early as 1869, he suggested that cholera was in part caused by a germ or fungus, and he conceded from the start that this agent could travel from place to place. But he did not believe that the agent could infect a victim without the intervention of other factors. Thus one can describe him, at best, as a 'contingent contagionist'. In reality, the extent to which he was influenced by the ideas of the contagionists should not be overstressed. In his own day, and indeed in his own mind, Pettenkofer was the best-known and most implacable of the contagionists' opponents. His ideas evolved and changed in various respects over the years, but the central elements in his mature theory remained constant, and it is important to look at them briefly since their consequences proved to be practical as well as theoretical.

Pettenkofer's theories of cholera took their starting-point in the ideas of his mentor Justus Liebig. These stressed, among other things, the importance of the fermentation of decomposing matter as an influence on the receptivity of a given area to epidemic diseases.[43] Pettenkofer began to apply these ideas in his account of the 1854 epidemic in Munich, published the following year. While accepting the existence of an infectious element which enabled cholera to be transported from one place to another, he denied that the disease was spread 'by contagion in the narrow sense of the word'. Nor, he asserted, could it possibly be carried by drinking-water. Indeed, he wrote that 'in my report in Munich, I have disposed, once and for all, of causation by drinking-water'. Nor, finally, was the disease carried in infected clothes or goods. It was most probably transmitted from place to place by human beings, even those who had not suffered the symptoms of cholera. But they could have no effect unless they infected the soil with their excreta. Influenced by Liebig's work on fermentation, Pettenkofer developed over the decade 1855–65 an elaborate theory of the conditions under which a cholera miasma could arise. It depended, he argued, on a series of changes in the level of the water-table or 'ground-water'. The water-table would suddenly rise, and the moisture content of the soil increase. These events were followed by a dry period in which the water-table dropped and the moisture content of the soil fell. Thus a layer of soil would be left above the water-table; cholera would 'germinate' in this soil, provided of course that the soil had been infected with the cholera germ. A miasma would then be created, in which the disease was transmitted through air polluted by the germination process. Thus people living on high ground, or even on the upper storeys of apartment blocks, could enjoy a relative immunity, while those living on low-lying or marshy land, in cellars,

---

[43] For an account of Liebig's ideas, see M. Pelling, *Cholera, Fever and English Medicine* (Oxford, 1978), Ch. 4.

or in cramped and confined conditions, where the circulation of air was restricted, were most at risk.

Pettenkofer thus became the self-appointed champion of the 'localist' school, which emphasized meteorological influences operating through changes in the water-table. Though he accepted a contagious element in cholera, he did not consider it very important, and the bulk of his writings on the subject was devoted either to proving that the disease could not be transmitted by drinking-water, or to elaborating and further refining his own 'ground-water' theory and providing a statistical basis for its major assertions. On these fundamental points he did not change his mind over the decades. Pettenkofer's theory achieved widespread currency, helped by his enormous influence in the field of hygiene, a discipline of which indeed he has some claim to be regarded as the founding father. He was appointed associate professor of medical chemistry at Munich University in 1847 and full professor (*Ordinarius*) in 1855. Meanwhile, in 1850, he had been made court apothecary by King Maximilian II of Bavaria, whose attention he had attracted by devising a method of manufacturing reproduction antique red stained glass. In 1864–5 he served as Rector of Munich University and used his influence with the court to get hygiene recognized as a full subject in all three Bavarian universities. Pettenkofer then took over the newly created chair in this subject at Munich. He built up a school of disciples. By the turn of the century there were over thirty directors of institutes of hygiene or professors in the subject in German and other universities who had been his pupils and owed some allegiance to his ideas. Pettenkofer eventually persuaded the Bavarian government to build an Institute of Hygiene in Munich, largely by threatening to leave for another, similar post in Vienna. It was opened in 1878 with Pettenkofer himself as director. By now, his ideas were also being disseminated in two specially created journals, which he and his pupils edited and largely wrote, the *Zeitschrift für Biologie* and the *Archiv für Hygiene*. Finally, in 1890 he was elected President of the Bavarian Academy of Sciences.[44]

Pettenkofer owed his prestige and influence not to his studies of cholera, but rather to his all-round abilities as a propagandist for public health. Nevertheless, his reputation here helped ensure that his ideas on cholera were officially adopted as well. In 1876 he was invited by the Imperial government in Berlin to become head of the newly created Imperial Health Office (*Reichsgesundheitsamt*) attached to the office of the Chancellor (at that time Bismarck). Pettenkofer, unwilling to abandon teaching, declined the offer but agreed to act as Scientific Adviser. In this capacity his influence on

[44] For these and other details of Pettenkofer's life and thought, see C. Childs, 'Obituary: Geheimrath Max von Pettenkofer, of Munich', *Transactions of the Epidemiological Society*, NS 20 (1901), 118–125; A. S. Evans, 'Pettenkofer Revisited', *Yale Journal of Biology and Medicine*, 46 (1973), 161–76; E. E. Hume, 'Max von Pettenkofer's Theory of the Etiology of Cholera, Typhoid Fever and Intestinal Diseases: A Review of his Arguments and Evidence', *Annals of Medical History*, 7 (1925) 319–53 (with full bibliography).

the Imperial Health Office's policy towards cholera in the late 1870s was decisive. Indeed, he had already been playing a determining role in Berlin's attitude towards the disease for some years, and his views were widely influential as early as the mid-1860s. He was the leading force in the Cholera Commission for the German Empire, which was also attached to the Imperial Chancellery and in some ways was a forerunner of the Imperial Health Office. Both these medical bodies were established to co-ordinate the approach of all the member states of the German Empire to epidemic and infectious diseases. They could use the authority of the Chancellery to impose their policies on all the federated states of the Empire. In 1873, for example, the Cholera Commission 'on behalf of the Imperial Chancellery' sent out a 'Plan for Investigation and Research into the Origins and Prevention of Cholera' to the federated states. The plan was printed as an official document for the *Bundesrat*, the Federal Council. It demanded elaborate information on the local climate and geology of affected areas. In the case of ships with cholera among the crew, these details were to be supplied for the port of embarkation. The document was drawn up jointly by Pettenkofer and August Hirsch, a professor in Berlin who shared most of his ideas on the subject of cholera.[45]

In the 1860s and 1870s, therefore, there can be little doubt that Pettenkofer's 'ground-water theory', and his dismissal of the notion that cholera was a water-borne disease, dominated official and medical approaches to the cholera problem in Germany. His ideas were never undisputed, and many doctors continued to emphasize moral and other factors in the aetiology of cholera. But Pettenkofer's influence is unmistakable not only in a large body of medical writings on cholera by many different commentators, but also in official policy as well. How can it be explained? Certainly it would not have been possible without his indefatigable energy and the ceaseless flow of publications on cholera that streamed from his pen. Equally certainly, it owed a lot to his enormous reputation in the field of social hygiene, with which the problem of cholera had long been recognized as having an intimate though hotly disputed connection. But there were more general reasons for Pettenkofer's influence. Pettenkofer was a pioneer of preventive medicine. He advocated a broad approach and believed strongly in public education as a means of improving public health. Against some opposition from his own university, he was a determined popularizer of his own views, both on paper and by word of mouth. He was an advocate of temperance, of cleanliness, of regular bathing, of a 'rational diet', of warm clothing, and above all of fresh

[45] Bundesrath 1873, Drucksache 151: *Untersuchungsplan zur Erforschung der Ursachen der Cholera und deren Verhütung. Denkschrift verfasst im Auftrage des Reichskanzler-Amts von der Cholera-Kommission für das Deutsche Reich* (copy in StA Hbg, MK II; another copy in StA Bremen 2-M.6.l.4.k.7). For the Imperial Health Office, see G. Göckenjan, *Kurieren und Staat machen. Gesundheit und Medizin in der bürgerlichen Welt* (Frankfurt, 1985), pp. 329–40; Göckenjan, however, underestimates the early influence of the Office and appears to regard it as bacteriologically oriented from the beginning.

air. Indeed, if anyone deserved to be called a 'fresh-air fanatic' it was Max von Pettenkofer. He opposed drinking not least because it took place in 'the horrible atmosphere' of smoke-filled, overcrowded taverns. He maintained that 'our children's health suffers when they are exposed for a number of hours to the atmosphere of ill-ventilated schoolrooms'. He poured well-deserved scorn on the Germans' traditional horror of draughts. He admired the English habit of maintaining an open fire in every parlour because, as he perceptively remarked, 'the English fireplace is a very poor heating device but good for ventilation'. All these improvements could be achieved, he thought, by means of public education and propaganda. Legislation was not only largely unnecessary, it was also impracticable.[46]

Pettenkofer was, to be sure, an advocate of state regulation and reform where he considered it absolutely necessary in order to reduce the possiblity of creating an unhealthy miasma through contamination of the soil. He insisted on the provision of adequate sewage and waste disposal. He believed that every dwelling, even a garret apartment, should be supplied with water from a central source, because this meant people were more likely to wash frequently than if they had to fetch the water from a distance.[47] The water, therefore, had to be clean, for if foul water was repeatedly used for washing it could turn the surfaces which it affected into breeding-places for disease.[48] It was largely due to Pettenkofer's insistence that a slaughterhouse was constructed in Munich in 1878, that the city acquired a new water-supply from the mountains, and that a new sewage system was installed, channelling the waste into the river downstream from the city and so preventing it from getting into the soil, where he thought it did so much harm. Pettenkofer warned against regarding sewage disposal and the provision of a fresh water-supply as all that were necessary to the improvement of public health, however. He asserted that a nutritious diet and fresh air were far more important. Moreover, he does not seem to have thought it necessary to provide a filtration system for the water-supply. It was enough for the water-supply to avoid direct contamination by contact with ground-water in the soil. Thus spring-water carried from the mountains was superior to water drawn from wells in the city. The water with which he arranged for Munich to be supplied certainly was not filtrated, and indeed, shortly after the water began flowing a massive typhoid epidemic hit the city, spread by the new supply system. Pettenkofer continued to believe none the less that epidemic diseases could not spread in water. He did advocate reducing overcrowding in houses 'partly by education and partly by regulations', but again he insisted that 'we do not solve the problem by providing the poor with the most

[46] H. Sigerist (ed. and trans.), 'The Value of Health to a City. Two Lectures, Delivered in 1873, by Max von Pettenkofer', *Bulletin of the History of Medicine*, 10 (1941), 473–503, 593–613.

[47] Ibid., p. 597.

[48] Hume, p. 343.

necessary food, housing and clothing unless we at the same time educate
them in painstaking cleanliness.'[49]

Pettenkofer was careful to present these limited measures of state intervention in a way acceptable to liberals. Hygiene, he wrote, was to health as
economics was to the economy.

Just as the effort to obtain greater profits, and not merely fear of losses, is the driving
force in economics, so too it must be in hygiene as a doctrine of health. Hygiene (as
a subject) must establish and investigate all the influences exerted on the organism
by its natural and artificial environment, in order to increase its well-being through
this knowledge. Health really is a form of property or capital, which is to be sure
usually inherited, but which must also be acquired by its owner and can be increased
as well as reduced.[50]

Pettenkofer sought to prove that prevention would result in a massive saving
in hospital costs by reducing disease. It thus offered municipal authorities a
substantial return on their initial investment. He called hygiene 'health
economics'. Such preventive measures as proper sewage disposal and the
provision of drinking-water were analogous to the minimal state intervention
necessary to guarantee the smooth running of the economy, rather like the
standardization of weights and measures or—in Hamburg—the construction
of the harbour. Once they had been provided, the real responsibility for health
and well-being lay with the individual.

In keeping with this voluntaristic approach to health, Pettenkofer was
opposed to the massive state intervention favoured by the contagionists.
Prevention, he believed, was all; once an epidemic had actually broken out,
the state could do nothing to check its progress. In a major series of articles
published in 1886–7, Pettenkofer declared that quarantine measures were
useless against cholera. They would always be ineffective, he said. They were
irrelevant to the decisive factor, which was the condition of the soil. The
isolation of cholera cases after the outbreak of an epidemic, he wrote, 'is
equally useless; and so is the special cholera hospital'. Moreover, he added,
'it is obvious that I consider the disinfection of the excreta of cholera patients
to be as ineffective as the isolation of cholera patients'. This was because
'cholera patients produced no effective infectious material'. Flight was a
reasonable precaution since it removed people from the miasmatic local
influences. The closing of markets, fairs, and other gatherings would achieve
nothing, unless they were held in a locality where the soil factor was powerful.
Finally, he continued to deny categorically that cholera was transmitted by

[49] Sigerist, 'The Value of Health', pp. 605–6.
[50] Quoted in H. Schipperges, 'Zur "Wirtschaftslehre von der Gesundheit" bei Max von Pettenkofer', *Die Heilkunst* 89 (1976), 321–3.

drinking-water, so all measures during an epidemic to provide people with alternative supplies of pure or boiled water were futile.[51]

The parallels between Pettenkofer's theory of cholera and liberal theories of the state are obvious. Pettenkofer attracted the adherence of medical opinion by offering a synthesis of many previous accounts and linking it to the established scientific principle of fermentation. But his ideas also had a broader appeal. His emphasis on sanitation, cleanliness, fresh air, and a rational diet were more than welcome to the German middle classes at a time when the urban environment was rapidly deteriorating, and when bourgeois consciousness of the presence of dirt and excrement, noxious vapours, and polluted or adulterated food was growing stronger. The stress he laid on termperance and regularity accorded strongly with bourgeois values, as did the belief he expressed that hygienic improvement depended above all on the individual. But the seductiveness of Pettenkofer's theories went even further than this. As we shall now see, they found a ready response not only because of the values which they expressed and the promise of environmental improvement which they held out, but also because of the direct appeal they directed to bourgeois self-interest.

III

When cholera first appeared on the European scene, governments everywhere went to great lengths to try and halt its progress. In Russia, military cordons were thrown around infected areas; in the Habsburg Empire, stringent quarantine measures were introduced. These activities were almost invariably ineffective. Not only did they fail to stop the cholera, they also provoked widespread popular unrest. The government and military presence in the stricken areas, the isolation of hospitalized victims, and the sudden appearance of large numbers of doctors, including many from other areas and countries who had come to observe the disease, convinced many Russian peasants that the government was trying to kill them off. Several physicians and officials were massacred amid widespread rioting. In the Habsburg Empire castles were sacked and quarantine aid officers and doctors were slaughtered. When the disease reached Prussia, official efforts to control it met with a similar response. Popular resentment against official interference in the

---

[51] Hume, 'Max von Pettenkofer's Theory', pp. 373, 327–8. Reinhard Spree (*Soziale Ungleichheit*, pp. 116–17) gives the impression that Pettenkofer's influence worked in favour of isolation and quarantine. The reverse was in fact the case (see pp. 251–3, 255–6, 261–3 below). For further details of Pettenkofer's views on medical policy see Winslow, *The Conquest of Epidemic Disease*, pp. 311–36. The account of Pettenkofer's ideas in Göckenjan, *Kurieren und Staat machen*, pp. 115–19, goes further in stressing the lack of implications for sanitary reform in Pettenkofer's work, but only deals with the earliest version of his ideas and so underplays the importance of climatic factors and overlooks the emphasis Pettenkofer placed on safe sewage and water-disposal systems to avoid contamination of the ground-water.

livelihood of journeymen, peasants, traders, and many others found symbolic expression in the belief that the disease was the product of poisoning by physicians engaged in a secret campaign to reduce the excess population. The doctors, it was said, were being paid 3 Talers for every cholera death reported to the king. In Stettin the authorities reported in September 1831 that

Since the outbreak of cholera in Stettin, the view has become widespread among the lower class of people in this place, who are those most exposed to this plague, that the disease is a means chosen or at least encouraged by the well-off, by which they can rid themselves of the poor. This delusion has become so deeply rooted that despite the most careful preparations in the cholera hospital which has been set up here, it has been possible to admit the victims to it only against great resistance on the part of their relatives and friends. On the first of this month mobs gathered and riots took place at several places in the city, and ... they have taken on the most dangerous character.

Crowds had tried to prevent cholera victims being removed from their homes, and then had stormed and looted the house of the responsible official. Order was only restored by the local militia, who wounded 5 of the rioters (some of whom subsequently died) and arrested a further 29. In Memel a crowd broke into the cholera hospital and took a patient back to his home, demanded that cholera corpses be buried in the churchyard, and claimed 'that the butcher Schadewaldt has been boiled alive in a steam bath by the doctors and this treatment has led to his death'.[52]

Most serious of all, a major public disturbance broke out in Königsberg, caused partly by a sharp increase in food prices following on the imposition of quarantine and a cordon sanitaire around the city. On 28 July, it was reported, a plasterer suffering from cholera died after taking vitriolic acid internally instead of having it rubbed on his body; 'the people who do not want to believe in the existence of cholera ... took the ... view that the doctors were poisoning the victims in co-operation with the apothecaries'. The police refused the man burial in the churchyard 'and by this ... measure aroused the fury of the people, whose religious feelings were outraged by it'. A crowd stormed the police station and 'all the police files, cupboards, chairs, and other furniture were thrown into the street and destroyed, with cries of "there is the cholera, in there, it must be destroyed!" ' Troops were called,

---

[52] Durey, *The Return of the Plague*, pp. 18–19, citing reports from Riga; GStA Berlin, Rep. 84a, 4179: Oberlandesgerichts-Präsidium Stettin to Justizministerum, 3 Sept. 1831 (Bl. 41). Since June an official commission had been active in Stettin in order 'to inspect all the dwellings of the poorer class of people ... and to effect the removal of those who live too close together to roomier and better-ventilated dwellings'. For events in Memel, see GStA Berlin, Rep. 84a, 4178, Bl. 185–8 (reports of 23–5 July 1831), and Stadtarchiv Berlin, Hauptstadt der DDR, Rep. 01, GB 217; *Berlinische Nachrichten*, 13 June 1831. For another example of popular resistance, see Frevert, *Krankheit*, p. 131. Riots in Paris in 1832 seem to have had only a very indirect connection with the epidemic: A. P. E. Leca, *Et le choléra s'abattit sur Paris 1832* (Paris, 1982), pp. 205–38.

and the cavalry arrived but was blocked by the heaps of police files lying around on the market-place. The crowd then streamed into the suburbs, breaking windows as they went, 'manhandled doctors, completely demolished two pharmacies', and broke into a gun-shop to arm themselves. Rescue for the helpless authorities came only from the *Rector Magnificus* of the university and 100 armed students, who with 50 junior civil servants, the militia, and the remnants of the troops opened fire on the crowd, killing 7 and wounding a substantial number of rioters and dispersing the rest. The damage caused was estimated at 14,660 Taler, and 177 people, mostly journeymen and labourers, were arrested and fined. The authorities concluded with relief 'that this riot neither originated with a political group nor expressed any more general dissatisfaction with the government of the state'. But it was highly alarming all the same.[53]

Public order was very much at the front of the mind of authority as the cholera epidemic spread across Eastern and Central Europe in 1831. Even Hamburg did not escape; in September 1830 popular unrest in the city expressed itself in prolonged though minor anti-Semitic disturbances.[54] Nevertheless, in common with the authorities elsewhere in Europe, the government of the city-state proceeded in the summer of 1831 to impose restrictions on the movement of people and goods in an attempt to stop the approach of the cholera epidemic. Incoming ships and river barges were subjected to medical quarantine from the summer of 1831 until the beginning of 1832.[55] From 8 October the Senate refused to issue clean bills of health to ships leaving the port.[56] For the duration of the 1831 epidemic, Hamburg was under medical quarantine with severe restrictions on trade.

The Hamburg Senate was no less energetic in the measures which it took to combat the disease once it actually arrived. In July 1831, indeed, well before the outbreak of the disease, it issued an elaborate set of ordinances, to come into force immediately the epidemic broke out, as it eventually did in October. A General Health Commission was established, with special local commissions for the various districts of the city. All cases were to be reported to these commissions as soon as they broke out. 'Houses in which there are

[53] GStA Berlin, Rep. 84a, 4178, Bl. 66 (Oberlandesgericht Königsberg (Präsidium) to Justiz-ministerium 17 June 1831); Bl. 177 (the same, 29 July 1831); ibid. 4180, Bl. 10, 18 (records of the trial), 23.

[54] H. G. Husung, 'Volksprotest in Hamburg zwischen Restauration und Revolution 1848', in A. Herzig, D. Langewiesche, and A. Sywottek (eds), *Arbeiter in Hamburg: Unterschichten, Arbeiter und Arbeiterbewegung seit dem ausgehenden 18. Jahrhundert* (Hamburg, 1983), pp. 79–88; M. Zimmermann, 'Antijüdischer Sozialprotest? Proteste von Unter- und Mittelschichten 1819–1835', ibid., pp. 89–94; H. G. Stühmke, ' "Wo nix ist, hett de Kaiser sien Recht verlor'n" oder "Der Stein auf dem Sofa der Frau Senatorin". Die Hamburger Unruhen vom 31. August bis 5. September 1830', in J. Berlin (ed.), *Das andere Hamburg. Freiheitliche und demokratische Bestrebungen in der Hansestadt seit dem Spätmittelalter* (Hamburg, 1981), pp. 49–68.

[55] Fricke, *Geschichtliche Darstellung*; StA Hbg, Senat, Cl. VII, Lit. Ta, Pars 2, Vol. II, Fasc. 17, Inv. 1a: *Hamburger Fremdenblatt*, 27 Oct. 1892.

[56] Michael, *Geschichte des ärztlichen Vereins*, p. 125.

people stricken with cholera will be signified with a poster, on which the word "cholera" is written, so that everyone knows that they are infected.' Such houses were to be isolated and disinfected. A special commission was established, to supervise disinfection work. This included chlorine fumigation in the streets, to clean the air. The cheap lodging-house where the disease had broken out was evacuated and fumigated some five days after the first case was reported, and other affected houses were similarly treated. Burgomaster Bartels ordered the publication of a regular cholera newspaper, produced in co-operation with the Doctors' Club and containing statistical and medical information on the epidemic. The authorities ordered the creation of two special cholera hospitals where victims would be treated in isolation. The General Hospital in St Georg was sealed off, no patients were discharged, and visitors were banned. All these measures, of course, were predicated on the assumption that cholera was an infectious disease.[57]

But they met with increasing criticism as time went on. In the first place, they were clearly unable to prevent the arrival of the disease or its spread through the city and beyond. Secondly, in Hamburg as elsewhere, they were seen as posing a threat to public order. Like other German cities, Hamburg was walled in the 1830s, but its expansion with the growth of trade had already led to the creation of a substantial built-up area of urban settlement outside the walls, in St Pauli and St Georg. The inhabitants of these areas resented their exclusion from the governing institutions of the city and had been petitioning for equal rights for some time, with little success. When the General Health Commission was founded in July, the Chief of the St Georg Battalion of the Citizens' Militia demanded a seat on it, and was dubbed a 'trouble-maker' for his pains. The incident led to a series of demonstrations in which the inhabitants of the suburb attempted forcibly to prevent the nightly closure of the city gate, the symbol of their exclusion from equal participation in the city's affairs. Eventually the problem was solved, but it was now felt in the Senate that any further organizational measures against the epidemic might easily offend popular sensibilities in a similar way. Finally, the measures taken in 1831 were very expensive. They involved, for example, the employment of some 700 workers to carry out the hospitalization, quarantine, and fumigation measures ordered by the Senate, as well as the construction of the special hospitals and isolation wards where the sick were housed.[58]

Medical and bourgeois opinion all over Europe was now mobilizing against quarantine and the other interventionist policies adopted in the face of

[57] Fricke, *Geschichtliche Darstellung*, pp. 26–7; *Verordnung, betreffrend die Organisation des Gesundheits-Polizeywesens für die Freie und Hanse-Stadt Hamburg, deren Vorstädte und Gebiet, für den Fall des Ausbruches der Asiatischen Cholera* (Hamburg, 1831, copy in StA Hbg); Michael, *Geschichte des ärztlichen Vereins*, p. 125; *Der Hamburgischer Beobachter*, 42 (Vol. 15, No. 4, 15 Oct. 1831), pp. 166–7.

[58] Husung, 'Volksprotest', p. 83.

the first cholera epidemic. Quarantine, maintained a pamphlet published in Danzig in 1831, was not only useless but dangerous. It exhausted state finances, disrupted trade, and so increased poverty. It caused terror and panic flight in the population and prevented the support of the afflicted and isolated families by welfare agencies. The question of the contagious or non-contagious character of the disease was thus a vital one:

The well-being of states and peoples depends on how this question is answered. Or shall the exhausted forces of poor divided Germany be entirely consumed in a vain struggle with the invisible demon at 39 state boundaries?—shall trade and industry completely collapse and everything become impoverished because of the continuation of the quarantine? Shall the labouring classes be deprived of a living and driven to desperation, shall the flames of rebellion now be fanned by a poisonous breath from the East while we still look anxiously to the West?[59]

There was thus ample support for the decision of the Hamburg authorities to drop early in 1832 all the precautions they had taken against cholera the previous year. These precautions had contributed, it was believed, to 'fear and terror' among 'the gentlemen who frequent our Exchange', and the sealing-off of the borders by the Prussian and Danish authorities had done untold damage to trade.

The Senate was fortified in its decision by the general swing of medical opinion against contagionism, and by the fact that the epidemic had in the end proved a good deal less severe than originally feared. The quarantine measures were thus not renewed; and the state sanitary stations (*Sanitätswachen*) set up to deal with the disease were disbanded. When cholera broke out with increased virulence later in the year, the burden of combating the disease was placed entirely on the medical profession. The Doctors' Club set up a sanitary station in its rooms, staffed by two physicians at a time, working shifts, during the day. There were no medical services available after 10 p.m. To the Doctors' Club also fell the task of compiling lists of the sick and the dead. It was the medical profession, not the state, that arranged for hospitalization of victims and supplied ambulancemen and nursing staff, though expenses could be claimed for these measures, in arrears, from the authorities. There were no quarantine measures and no isolation wards: cholera patients were simply put alongside the normal hospital inmates. No official announcements were made of new cases, or even of the presence of an epidemic. It was hardly surprising, therefore, that while the 1831 epidemic cost the authorities fully half a million Marks Courant, that of the following year cost them only twenty thousand, even though it was considerably more severe.[60]

[59] *Stimme aus Danzig über die Cholera*, pp. 5, 11.
[60] StA Hbg, Senat, Cl. VII, Lit. Ta, Pars 2, Vol. II, Fasc. 17, Inv. 1a: *Hamburger Fremdenblatt*, 27 Oct. 1892. Michael, *Geschichte des ärztlichen Vereins*, p. 127; *Der Hamburgischer Beobachter*, (Vol. 15, No. 4, 15 Oct. 1831), p. 167.

The widespread concern with cholera as a problem of individual morality found its way into the handbooks of medical advice on how to prevent the disease. Disease appeared here as the consequence not so much of immorality as of emotional disorder or excitement—the very factor which was also seen as at the root of the riot and rebellion with which cholera was so often associated. Virtually all the early literature, including the official leaflet issued in 1831,[61] prescribed personal cleanliness and much of it also offered dietary advice, including the avoidance of 'acidulous, watery foods and those which cool down the stomach and abdomen'.[62] Miasmatists stressed the need for fresh air, while the widespread belief that cholera was an extreme form of 'the common cold' led many to urge the importance of keeping warm.[63] Most widespread and insistent of all was the advice to avoid physical or emotional excess. Many doctors in 1831 considered that fear of the disease was a sure invitation for it to strike.[64] Correspondingly they urged people to lead a sober and moderate life and to avoid any kind of upset.[65] People were told to avoid 'passions', to trust in God, and to maintain an 'orderly way of life'.[66] The classic formula was provided by the Prussian physician Wilhelm Cohnstein, who declared that a calm and positive frame of mind was best maintained by 'unconditional trust I: in Divine Providence and II: in the orders of the authorities'.[67] The authorities in Berlin themselves encouraged citizens to lead a 'regular way of life', to avoid fear, sorrow, and 'excessive mental exertion'. 'Such states of mind, on the other hand, as are connected with a pleasant spiritual mood, like cheerfulness, gaiety, optimism, etc., increase the strength of the body and thereby make it less receptive to sickness.'[68]

The association of cholera with individual immorality was thus expressed in the very theories which medical men developed to account for it. It was felt that emotional excess could lead to increased receptivity to infection. But there was another reason for the widespread assocation of cholera with lack of self-restraint. Not only did it lead to public disorder in itself, but the threat

[61] Siemerling, *Entschleierung der Cholera; Beruhigung für Jedermann und Ermahnung an Viele. Zur Verminderung der Furcht vor der Cholera morbus, und Befestigung des Vertrauens auf die Güte Gottes, von einem Mitfühlenden und zur Beruhigung Anderer fern beitragender Mitbürger geschrieben,* (Hamburg, 1831); *Zubereitung auf die Cholera* (Bergedorf, 1831); *Anweisung,* p. 7.

[62] *Verständlichste und bewährteste Belehrungen über die mit Gefahr bedrohende pestartige Krankheit Cholera morbus. Mit einem Recepte versehen, welches das sicherste Schutzmittel wider die Cholera lehrt, und alle hierüber schon erschienene und vielleicht noch erscheinende Büchlein übertrifft und überflüssig macht. Nach den Hauptresultaten ärztlicher, in Indien, Persien, Russland und Polen gemachten Erfahrungen sorgfältig zusammengestellt. Nur nicht ängstlich!* (Hamburg, 1831); Jensen, *Belehrungen.*

[63] *Verständlichste und bewährteste Belehrungen; Zubereitung auf die Cholera;* Horn and Wagner, *Wie hat man sich vor der Cholera zu schützen . . .*

[64] See above, pp. 234–5.

[65] *Stimme aus Danzig über die Cholera;* Buchheister and Noodt, *Erfahrungen.*

[66] *Beruhigung für Jedermann und Ermahnung an Viele; Verständlichste und bewährteste Belehrungen.*

[67] Cohnstein, *Trost- und Beruhigungsgründe.*

[68] *Anweisung.* For a useful discussion of the roots of this emphasis on moderation in medical theory, see Göckenjan, *Kurieren und Staat machen,* pp. 76–8, 90–1.

which it posed was magnified by the fact that it generally appeared at moments of tension in European society, because social and international conflict both led to large-scale troop movements which tremendously accelerated the pace and scale of epidemic infection. In 1830 these troop movements were taking place everywhere in Europe, from Poland, where the Russian army was engaged in putting down a major nationalist uprising, through to the West where military engagements were taking place in many countries in connection with the successful or unsuccessful revolutions of that year. During the revolutionary upheavals of 1848–9 there were even more extensive troop movements, with the Russian army in Vienna and the Prussians marching as far west as Baden, in the deep south-west of Germany. Similarly, Bismarck's wars of 1866 against Austria, and of 1870–1 against France, both brought cholera to Hamburg and spread it to other areas as well.[69] Because the disease was notoriously liable to appear at moments of acute political tension, it is hardly surprising that the first reaction of the authorities was to appeal for calm.

Such an appeal, understandably enough, was issued with greater force than ever in the revolutionary year of 1848. On that occasion, Dr Friedrich Simon, a Hamburg medical practitioner, urged that inns and bars be closed early for the duration of the epidemic and urged his readers to lead 'a moderate, sober, and regular life-style' and 'to avoid any excesses'. Not only did this mean the avoidance of alcohol. It also meant, Simon explained, that

altogether a state of mind that is as evenly balanced as possible is an essential and important means of protection ... Tiring intellectual exertions, especially deep into the night, have a disadvantageous effect; but strong and long-lasting spiritual excitements of other kinds, powerful passions and changes of mood, even exaggerated joy and sprightliness, are just as much to be avoided.[70]

In 1848 there was no doubt that for the Hamburg Senate the preservation of public order was the first priority. In July, the medical representatives on the Health Committee held a meeting to discuss measures to be taken in view of the fact that after an interval of sixteen years, cholera was once more approaching the city from the east:

The first thing that we feel impelled to express, before anything else, is the wish that the public be alarmed and disturbed as little as possible. Therefore we would like to see the avoidance of all sensation during the preparations and right up to the actual outbreak of the epidemic. We do not want the release of public notices calling attention to this so widely feared disease, nor, later, when the epidemic has really broken out, do we want measures to be taken which allow the disease to appear as particularly dangerous or extraordinary.

[69] A. Aust, 'Vor 80 Jahren: Die Cholera in Hamburg. Soziale und hygienische Missstände und ihre Folgen', *Die Heimat. Monatsschrift zur Pflege der Natur- und Landeskunde in Schleswig-Holstein und Hamburg*, 79 (1972), 302–11.

[70] F. Simon, *Schutzmassregeln gegen die asiatische Cholera* (Hamburg, 1848), pp. 13–15.

Such measures, in their opinion, would only cause panic and make things worse. The previous epidemic had, they argued, showed beyond doubt that cholera was not a contagious disease. So it was decided on these grounds not to establish a quarantine, not to isolate the sick, nor to make any special arrangements for burying the victims. Such measures, the doctors warned, 'are no help at all, but rather cause endless damage by getting people excited'. The most that was necessary was the printing of a pamphlet advising people what to do in the event of an epidemic, together with arrangements to feed the poor, control the quality of food in the markets, ensure the cleanliness and airiness of doss-houses, and hospitalize the victims should there be any. These arrangements were to be supervised by a medical Cholera Commission, which was also charged with compiling daily lists of cases and deaths.[71]

The official advice issued to the citizens of Hamburg in 1848—after the outbreak of the epidemic—added considerably in detail to the familiar refrain of the need to lead an orderly life. Indeed, it hardly mentioned anything else. 'Those', it warned

who are accustomed to eat and drink more than the human being actually needs, those who lead a dissolute life, and find pleasure in drinking, gambling, and nightly carousals, should restrict these bad habits ... One should avoid strong passions, whether of an exciting or depressing kind. One should avoid any strong outburst of joy, irritation, or anger, and avoid excessive indulgence in carnal love.

Anything which could cause a chill or excessive acidity in the stomach was to be avoided, including all kinds of fruit, whether raw or cooked, milk, fat, watery vegetables, and above all spirits. On the other hand, a diet of meat washed down with 'a moderate amount of a good red wine' was declared to be 'advantageous'. Most people in Hamburg could not even afford a bad red wine, and lacked the means to buy even the poorest meat every day of the week. But the advice was likely to be reassuring to Hamburg's bourgeoisie, and the avoidance of milk and raw fruit would also be of some advantage. Moreover, the pamphlet also advised people not to drink water unless it came from a well or was boiled. Those who followed this advice would have stood a better chance of avoiding cholera than those who did not.[72]

The unusually strong concern with public order, reflecting the fact that the political conflicts and disturbances of the revolutionary year reached their height in the first week in September, just as the cholera broke out, led once more to a policy of inaction on the part of the Hamburg authorities. Clearly they were anxious not to give further cause for lower-class discontent, which

[71] StA Hbg, MK III A 2 Bd. I, Bl. 3ff.: meeting of 5 Aug. 1848.
[72] *Wie ist das Erkranken bei der herrschenden Cholera-Epidemie zu vermeiden, wie erkennt man die Krankheit, und was ist bei derselben bis zur Ankunft eines Arztes zu thun? Zur Beruhigung und Belehrung des Publicums hg. von dem Hamburgischen Gesundheits-Rath September 1848* (copy in StA Hbg, MK III A 2 Bd. I, Bl. 62).

had already led to barricades and demonstrations in August.[73] As in 1832, therefore, virtually nothing was done to cope with the epidemic. The official Senate file on the 1848 outbreak is entitled 'File concerning the epidemic of so-called Asiatic cholera which took place in Hamburg in 1848, against which no quarantines, hospitals, or otherwise important preventive measures were taken'. The Senate, indeed, decided on 23 October 'not to release any regular reports on the state of the cholera epidemic, but instead to issue a reassuring article on the progress of the disease and its decline'. To protect Hamburg ships from quarantine measures being imposed by foreign ports, the Commerce Deputation even argued on 1 November that the practice of noting on ships' health passes the fact that cholera had broken out in Hamburg should immediately be stopped.[74] As before, the Doctors' Club arranged an information and assistance centre in its rooms, manned by its members in two-hour shifts. The centre dealt with 640 cases between 12 September and 9 November. In the Jewish Hospital, cholera was treated as contagious, and patients were put in isolation wards. The other hospitals, however, did not follow this practice.[75]

IV

The epidemics of 1832 and 1848 thus established a firm tradition in Hamburg, according to which the state did virtually nothing to prevent or combat the disease, and took no steps to confirm or announce its presence in the city. The burden of coping with cholera fell instead on the medical profession and voluntary organizations such as the Doctors' Club. Here too, as we have seen, anticontagionism reigned supreme. The Chief Medical Officer, Dr Buek, had been an anticontagionist even before the arrival of cholera in 1831; he remained one in the epidemic of 1848. There were further minor epidemics in the 1850s, as Figure 7 indicates, and more serious ones in 1859 and 1866. The Doctors' Club did not discuss the epidemics of the 1850s in any great detail, but in 1867 a debate on the cholera outbreak of the previous year revealed the supporters of Pettenkofer to be in the ascendant. Two lectures, by Dr Benjamin and Dr Engel-Reimers, on the relationship between cholera and ground-water, met with no contradiction or objection of any kind from the assembled medical men. Correspondingly there was little change in the arrangements taken for coping with cholera through the minor outbreaks

---

[73] D. Bavendamm, '"Keine Freiheit ohne Mass". Hamburg in der Revolution von 1848/9', in Berlin, *Das andere Hamburg*, pp. 69–92; H.-W. Engels, '"Wo ein St. Paulianer hinhaut, wächst so leicht kein Gras wieder." St. Pauli und die Revolution von 1848/9', ibid., pp. 93–115.

[74] StA Hbg, Senat, Cl. VII, Lit. Ta, Pars 2, Vol. 1.

[75] StA Hbg, MK III A 2 Bd. 1, Bl. 93.

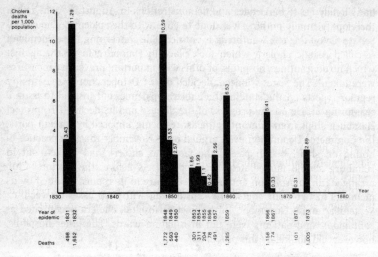

Year of epidemic	Deaths
1831	498
1832	1,652
1848	1,772
1849	593
1850	440
1853	301
1854	311
1855	204
1856	78
1857	491
1859	1,285
1866	1,158
1867	74
1871	101
1873	1,005

Source: L. v. Halle, F. Wolter, G. Koch, *Die Cholera in Hamburg in ihren Ursachen und Wirkungen* (Hamburg, 1895), Part II, Table 1

FIG. 7. Cholera in Hamburg before 1892

of the 1850s and the more serious ones of 1859 and 1866.[76] By the 1860s these were clearly showing the influence of Pettenkofer's ideas in the attention they paid to preventing excreta from contaminating the ground; this seems to have involved a slight increase in official activity during the epidemic of 1866. But the tradition of inactivity was only strengthened by the appointment of Buek's successor as Chief Medical Officer, Dr Johann Caspar Theodor Kraus, a 'convinced supporter of Pettenkofer's views', as his obituary subsequently noted. Born in Altona in 1826, he had studied in Kiel and was 47 at the time of his appointment as Chief Medical Officer in Hamburg in 1871.[77] His report on the cholera epidemic of 1873 revealed a pessimistic, even fatalistic attitude towards the possibility of prevention. The various measures urged on the authorities in the epidemic, declared Kraus, were of 'relatively

[76] The explosive nature of the outbreak in 1859 suggests that it was spread by the water-supply; all the epidemics of the 1850s probably derived from reservoirs of the disease that survived in Hamburg over the winter, or were imported from other parts of Germany. Cf. StA Hbg, MK III A 2 Bd. 1, Bl. 81–3, 91, 96, 163–5, 199–200; Bd. 2, Bl. 7.

[77] For the policies adopted in the 1860s, see StA Hbg, Polizeibehörde I 49 Bd. 1: Physicats-Gutachten von Dr. Buek, 13 Feb. 1864, and *Hamburgischer Correspondent*, 8 Aug. 1866. For the epidemic of 1859, see Dr. Buek's 'Physicats-Bericht' of 22 Aug. 1859, in StA Hbg, Senat, Cl. VII, Lit. Ta, Pars 2, Vol. 6. See also Michael, *Geschichte des ärztlichen Vereins*, pp. 149–50, and entry for Kraus. Buek resigned aged 74 in 1871 when the new Medical Regulations came into effect (StA Hbg, Senat, Cl. VII, Lit. Lb, No. 23a, Vol. 75, Fasc. 3).

little value'. Disinfection was useless because it was impossible to do it thoroughly enough to kill all the germs. Quarantine was futile because individuals would always manage to slip through the net. In the

worse affected areas the pollution of the ground and the ditches near to dwellings by refuse, and the unsatisfactory drinking-water, can be regarded as causes of the disease's spread. But the removal of these causes by thoroughly implemented waste-disposal laws, ordinances, and arrangements and through the provision of pure and healthy drinking-water cannot be quickly achieved in view of the fact that the population is so large.

So Kraus foresaw many obstacles in trying to apply Pettenkofer's principles of hygiene to Hamburg. Moreover, his interpretation of Pettenkofer's theories seemed to emphasize the great man's doubts about the possibility of preventing an epidemic. This was not the kind of attitude calculated to persuade the Senate to improve matters. In fact the energetic and irascible Chief Engineer Franz Andreas Meyer was far more effective in bringing pressure to bear for sanitary improvements than the pessimistic Dr Kraus, with his general belief in the ineffectiveness of state intervention. 'During the cholera epidemic', declared Kraus after the events of 1873,

some people feel themselves called upon to report individual sanitary nuisances, namely those which offend their sense of smell, and to press for improvement. But a thoroughgoing improvement encroaches upon a good few real or imagined rights and customs, and demands on the one hand such a mass of preparations and on the other the expenditure of so much money, that it must appear out of the question; while an improvement in isolated instances is no use at all.

Kraus's document of 1873 was almost entirely negative in tone. Right at the beginning of his term of office, he seems to have decided that nothing could be done to prevent the outbreak of cholera.[78]

Kraus's conduct in the 1873 epidemic brought him a good deal of criticism.[79] In early September questions began to be asked in the Citizens' Assembly about the epidemic. Dr Buek, now representing the Medical Board, reported that 'the epidemic has kept within moderate bounds and, it is hoped, will continue to keep within them'. This was not good enough for the 'democrats'. On 10 September the 'democrat' Dr Banks reminded the Citizens' Assembly that although Kraus published weekly morbidity and mortality statistics, 'the rumour was going round already in July that these publications were wrong because cases of cholera had already occurred within that time, they just had not been made public'. Cholera, he declared, has been in the city since late June, but full lists of cases and deaths had not been published until August.

[78] J. C. T. Kraus, *Die Cholera in Hamburg im Jahre 1873* (Hamburg, 1873).
[79] For the following see *Bürgerschaft*, Sept.–Oct. 1873; also StA Hbg, FA Petersen D30 Bd. 2, Kraus to Petersen 7 Mar. 1883.

Now it is very regrettable that Hamburg authorities apparently knowingly publish erroneous facts. Such a thing has never been known before and cannot be too strongly condemned; nothing can have a more demoralizing effect. Rumour has been wicked enough to claim that this has happened in order to protect certain mercantile enterprises which feared losses if the facts were made known ...

Worse was to follow. The official spokesman in the Citizens' Assembly, Dr Buek, felt unable to reply in detail to Banks's accusations, since he lacked both the necessary information and the permission to impart it from the Medical Board. This did not satisfy the 'democrats', and another deputy, Dr Caesar Gerson, broadened the scope of the attack to ask why there had been no disinfection, why there was insufficient manpower to transport the sick, and why special hospitals had not been erected. A week later, Buek returned with the necessary authorization. Kraus had told him, he informed the Assembly, that the June and July cases had originally been recorded as 'cholerine' or *cholera nostras*. The publication of these cases was according to an 'absolutely definite plan, which rests on the distinction between cholera that only occurs sporadically, and genuine Asiatic cholera'. However, by the end of July the sporadic pattern of deaths had been replaced by an epidemic pattern which left no doubt about the fact that the earlier cases had in reality been Asiatic cholera. The statistics were therefore revised. Buek added that 'there was no occasion ... for a system of such grandiose measures as Dr Gerson has demanded ... Apart from the high costs, they would certainly have had the disadvantage that they would have disquieted the population'; a thoroughly traditional reply, as we have seen. This reply was hardly calculated to reassure the Senate's critics. Moreover it pointed once more to Kraus's determination to delay as long as possible any confirmation of the presence of Asiatic cholera in the city. The 'absolutely definite plan' to which Buek referred seems to have involved medical officials automatically registering even fatal cases of cholera as *cholera nostras*, so long as they only occurred occasionally or 'sporadically'. In 1873 medicine still diagnosed according to the symptoms in this case. Diagnosis through isolation and culture of the bacillus was not introduced for cholera for another decade. The symptoms of *cholera nostras* could indeed be similar to those of the more severe and far more dangerous Asiatic variety, though in really serious cases of Asiatic cholera they were in fact unmistakable. Kraus was determined not to admit the presence of the disease until the pattern of cases became epidemic.

One of the most striking features of the history of medical administration in nineteenth-century Hamburg was the continuity of senior personnel. Dr Buek was closely involved in dealing with all the epidemics from 1831 to 1873; Dr Kraus, whose first experience of cholera came in 1873, was still in office in 1892. As we shall see, nothing happened between 1873 and 1892, not even Koch's discoveries, to make Kraus change his mind on the subject of cholera. In 1892, as in 1873, Kraus and the medical authorities were still operating to an 'absolutely definite plan' which obliged them to deny the existence of Asiatic cholera in Hamburg until after the disease had reached epidemic proportions. This policy could be justified to some extent by the anticontagionist views which Kraus espoused, but there could be little doubt that it had its origins in the fear of the quarantine measures that would immediately loom over the city if an official declaration of a cholera epidemic was made. Even in 1873 there were those who disapproved of such a policy. In the Citizens' Assembly, indeed, the 'democrat' Dr Banks had effectively accused Kraus of a cover-up; 'the saying has been proved once more that lying is an art'. Kraus reacted to this attack by submitting his resignation to the Senate—a demonstrative act designed to rally support, rather than a serious admission of error or guilt. The Senate, satisfied that Kraus had taken the right course in delaying the confirmation of the disease, refused to accept the resignation. No doubt prompted from above, 'Hamburg's physicians', declared Kraus on 29 October, 'have declared in an address submitted to me on 11 October that they would like me to stay'. Armed with these tokens of official support, Kraus now demanded that the Citizens' Assembly record its official dissent from Banks's attack. This was demanding too much even of a body that found the 'democrats' something of a nuisance. Kraus had to be satisfied with reassurances from Banks and from the President of the Citizens' Assembly that there had been no accusation of lying and no personal element in the affair. Nobody, he was informed, had intended to criticize any individual in the Medical Board or the Medical Inspectorate. The debate ended with a repetition of these assurances from the chair after Banks had repeated his view 'that in the publications which are under attack, cases and deaths caused by cholera have been deliberately wrongly classified as having been caused by *cholera nostras*'. After this, the Assembly clearly felt that enough had been said, and voted not to support a motion for an inquiry into the conduct of the authorities during the epidemic. Such a stormy controversy was highly unusual in the Citizens' Assembly, and it may be that Dr Banks's strong language already expressed the beginnings of the schizophrenia which was soon to take him into a mental hospital in Bonn, where Kraus found him ten years later 'definitely mentally ill' and suffering from 'persecution mania and delusions'. But however much he might have overstated his case, the Citizens' Assembly clearly felt that Banks had good reason for voicing his dissatisfaction with official conduct in the epidemic of 1873.

The influence of Pettenkofer since the 1850s had diverted the attention of the medical profession to the soil factor. In many cases, it was agreed in 1874 that 'one is inclined to regard possible harmful substances in the soil as a direct cause'.[80] But Pettenkofer and his supporters never thought it was possible to eliminate these 'harmful substances' altogether. Improved sewage

---

[80] StA Hbg, MK III A 2 Bd. 2 Bl. 83 (supplement to No. 91 of *Altonaer Mercur*—19 Apr. 1874).

disposal would certainly help, they thought; and indeed great improvements had taken place in this area since mid-century. The faith they placed in a centralized water-supply, uncontaminated, as drinking-wells often were, by infected 'ground-water', was not matched by any corresponding belief in the importance of filtration. In most respects, the influence of Pettenkofer in Hamburg simply confirmed the existing way of doing things. In 1873, as in all previous cholera epidemics since the defeat of contagionism in 1831, the medical profession and the Senate did their utmost to avoid official confirmation of the disease's presence in the city, and once they were forced to concede this point, made no attempt to impose quarantine, to isolate the victims, or to mount a campaign of disinfection. By 1871 at least the Senate was agreeable to undertaking a limited amount of state action, lending the police to collect the sick and the dead, and providing funds to stop the contamination of the ground-water. But the avoidance of financial costs and the maintenance of public order remained the highest priorities. Those who disapproved of this policy of state inaction remained a tiny minority.[81]

d. *Empire of Germs*

I

How far did Hamburg's practice diverge from that of other parts of Germany in the question of cholera? In the present inadequate state of research two examples must suffice. The first is the much smaller but equally bourgeois and trade-oriented Hanseatic city of Lübeck. Like Hamburg, Lübeck was an autonomous federated state within the Empire. Here the Senate established a special Sanitary Commission to deal with cholera if and when it arrived. The Commission was provided with considerable powers. The doctors who sat on it in 1831 thought that the disease was contagious, and the commission established extensive quarantine, disinfection, and isolation provisions, which were first applied to ships coming from Riga in June. In September the Senate also stationed a cordon sanitaire round the city. The cordon was applied rigorously to travellers from Hamburg once cholera had broken out there in October. The villages under the Senate's control were required to put up notices on the road if cholera broke out, informing travellers that the disease was present: they would then be sealed off and supplied with food from outside.

---

[81] The only example I have found is a local doctor who argued in 1873 that the cholera victims spread infection and should be isolated: 'Ueber den Verlauf der Cholera im Sommer 1873 in Eimsbüttel', in StA Hbg, MK III A 2 Bd. 2 Bl. 62–78. For evidence of a parallel policy of suppression of the facts and appeals for calm in the plague of 1712–14, see A. Wohlwill, *Hamburg während der Pestjahre 1712–14* (Hamburg, 1893), pp. 58–61. For the epidemic of 1871, see StA Hbg, Polizeibehörde I 49 Bd. 2, Vol. 1. The authorities still recommended private fumigation at this stage.

These and other measures, based on the eighteenth-century experience of the plague, went much further than the precautions taken in Hamburg, where medical opinion, as we have seen, was less unanimously contagionist. However, as soon as the disease broke out (which it did only in June 1832), the quarantine and cordon sanitaire were abandoned. Since this was the city's first experience of the disease, the Senate was evidently quite happy to stick to at least some of the elaborate and expensive measures devised in 1831 to deal with it. The Sanitary Commission organized the transport of the sick to an isolation hospital (or their isolation at home), and it paid for the burial of the dead and the support of those made paupers by the epidemic. Altogether Lübeck had to deal with 1,243 cases and 695 deaths from June to August 1832. 10% of the Senate's expenditure for the year, a total of 88,700 Marks in all, went on dealing with the epidemic.[1]

Well before the end of 1832, however, the Lübeck Senate had already begun to retreat from the strongly interventionist stand it had so far taken. It had officially decided on 27 June 1832 not to make any official announcement of the disease's presence or to issue daily lists of cholera deaths, because this would unsettle the general public and damage trade by calling forth quarantine measures from foreign ports. On the advice of Hamburg's Senator Dammert, who informed his colleagues in Lübeck 'that in general it is assumed here that cholera is not contagious', the ban placed in 1831 on burials inside the city walls was lifted. In September 1832 the Sanitary Commission closed its office. Meanwhile medical opinion in Lübeck came round to an anti-contagionist position, combined as elsewhere with a strong emphasis on personal disposition for the disease. As a consequence, the Senate undertook no quarantine or disinfection measures in the epidemic of 1848, nor did it attempt to isolate the victims in a special hospital. Only 125 cholera patients were hospitalized, during an epidemic in which no fewer than 500 people died from the disease, in sharp contrast to the epidemic of 1832, in which every effort had been made to get all the victims into hospital. The police did nothing beyond opening a health office to keep account of the progress of the disease. So inactive was the Senate that the Lübeck Doctors' Club was forced to enquire, the day before the epidemic broke out, whether there were any plans to engage ambulancemen and nurses, whether a hospital was to be made available to victims, and whether indeed any measures had been taken at all to deal with the disease. The same inactivity characterized the Lübeck Senate's behaviour during the epidemics of 1850 (in which 506 people died), 1853, and 1856–9.[2]

By this time, however, the views of Max von Pettenkofer were beginning to influence the medical profession in Lübeck. In 1856 they were taken up

[1] D. Helm, *Die Cholera in Lübeck. Epidemieprophylaxe und -bekämpfung im 19. Jahrhundert* (Kieler Beiträge zur Geschichte der Medizin und Pharmazie, 16; Neumünster, 1979), pp. 12–27.

[2] Ibid., pp. 25–32.

by Senator Theodor Curtius, who issued a public demand for a clean-up of the ground, where, according to Pettenkofer, the cholera germ bred. Curtius's plea for improved sewage disposal and sanitation, proper drainage, and a centralized water-supply was echoed by the Doctors' Club in 1862. At the same time a local doctor, Emil Cordes, launched an Association for Research-ing the Local Causes of Cholera in Lübeck (*Verein zur Erforschung der localen Ursachen der Cholera in Lübeck*), which attacked the Senate for doing nothing about the disease. These initiatives led to a series of sanitary reforms in the 1860s. A central water-supply, filtrated because of the high mineral content of the local water, began operating in 1867, new regulations were introduced to improve and extend the sewage system in 1869, and plans were laid for the construction of new suburbs outside the city walls. Pettenkofer's views seemed to be vindicated in Lübeck by the fact that there were no more cholera epidemics in the city after this, with the exception of a minor outbreak in 1866.[3]

At the other extreme from Lübeck in terms of size and power in nineteenth-century Germany was the Kingdom of Prussia. Significantly, the cholera files in the archive continue without a break a series of files opened in 1804 on quarantine regulations against bubonic plague. The same measures were initially deployed in 1831 as in 1804. A commission of doctors and civil servants set up to study cholera before its arrival concluded after examining the literature that it was caused by 'a contagion developed in an infected individual' rather than an 'infectious substance spread through the air'.[4] Quarantine, fumigation, controls on the movement of persons, cordons san-itaires, and public education about the disease were justified in terms unim-aginable in Hamburg: 'the disadvantages that follow from this for the individual will be far outweighed, as every unbiased person will feel, by the security that will be gained for the generality.'[5] The commission promised that 'considerable success' would come from these measures, and regarded an outbreak in Berlin as a 'scarcely to be apprehended eventuality'. Despite a penalty of 'several years' gaol or confinement in a fortress' for breaking quarantine, or even death if the breach resulted in a cholera outbreak,[6] cholera duly arrived and took its course. The Berlin authorities ordered the isolation of victims in their houses and the fumigation of dwellings; with true Prussian thoroughness they also ordained that all dogs and cats in infected houses should be put down and birds should have their wings clipped. Only in one respect did they make a concession to the miasmatist standpoint; from 23 September 1831 to 15 February 1832, exceptionally, 'the smoking of

[3] Ibid., pp. 33–51.
[4] GStA Berlin, Rep. 84a, 4178, Bl. 21: *Vossische Zeitung*, 19 May 1831.
[5] Ibid., Bl. 72–3 (Allerhöchstverordnetes Gesundheits-Comité für Berlin).
[6] Ibid., Bl. 78: Gesetz wegen Bestrafung derjenigen Vergehungen, welche die Uebertretung der—zur Abwendung der Cholera—erlassenen Verordnungen betreffen, 15 June 1831.

tobacco is permitted in public places and streets here, and in the Tiergarten, in order not to remove protection from those who believe this to be effective against cholera'. But soon the most severe of these measures was rescinded. In September the cordons sanitaires, it was concluded, 'have already had a damaging effect on the business traffic of the inhabitants and threaten to ruin the prosperity of many families and become more fatal for the country than the disease itself'. The cordons were thus relaxed, then lifted altogether; traffic was freed and by the end of October quarantines were also dropped. The government began to consider a pardon for those who had been caught breaking the quarantine regulations now that these had proved ineffective.[7]

Up to this point, official policy for dealing with cholera had developed in much the same way in Prussia as it had in Hamburg and Lübeck. From here onwards, however, paths began to diverge. The next general instruction issued by the government Cholera Commission was much concerned with the maintenance of public order: it admonished local police forces not to remove cholera victims from their homes against the wishes of the head of the family, told them to avoid 'unusual gatherings of people', and advised burial of cholera victims only after nightfall. But compulsory reporting of cases, isolation, disinfection, checks on river traffic, and the issuing of clean bills of health were continued. Its work done, the Cholera Commission was dissolved early in 1832 and from now on the measures it had drawn up were enforced by police action and by locally based sanitary commissions.[8] This interventionist policy was strengthened in a comprehensive set of regulations which was issued in 1835 and formed the basis for subsequent Prussian procedure in cholera epidemics. Asiatic cholera, declared the 'Lessons on Infectious Diseases' attached to the regulations, 'is infectious and is ... spread further by infection under the most varied kinds of climatic, seasonal, weather, wind, territorial, etc. conditions'. It conceded merely that receptivity to infection could vary from person to person. Otherwise the document was thoroughly contagionist. So too were the regulations, which for the most part repeated those already in existence providing for special commissions to be set up by local government, isolation of all victims, control of river traffic,

---

[7] Ibid., Bl. 233: Abändernde Bestimmungen der Instruction über das bei dem Ausbruche der Cholera zu beobachtende Verfahren, 5 Apr. (1 June 1831); ibid., 4179, Bl. 81: *Vossische Zeitung*, 13 Sept. 1831; ibid., Bl. 215: *Vossische Zeitung*, 31 Oct. 1831; ibid., Bl. 229: *Das Tribunal von Königsberg*, 22 Oct. 1831; Stadtarchiv Berlin, Rep. 01 GB 257: *Amts-Blatt* 24 (17 June 1831), p. 101; ibid., 218: *Berlinische Nachrichten*, 15 Feb. 1832. Further details in ibid., 217: *Berlinische Nachrichten von Staats- und gelehrten Sachen*, 6 May 1831, 11 May 1831, and subsequent issues. Similar developments in Vienna can be followed in ibid., 218: *Berlinische Nachrichten*, 20 Oct. 1831. The number of deaths from cholera in the Habsburg Empire to that date was said to total 233,000.

[8] GStA Berlin, Rep. 84a, 4180, Bl. 37–9: Instruction über das im Betreff der asiatischen Cholera in allen Provincen des Preussischen Staates zu beobachtende Verfahren, 5 Feb. 1832; Stadtarchiv Berlin, Rep. 01 GB 257: *Intelligenz Blatt*, 18 Feb. 1832.

Table 3. Cholera morbidity and mortality in Berlin, 1831–73

Year	Cases	Deaths	Population	Cases per 1,000 population	Deaths per 1,000 population
1831	2,274	1,423	229,843	9.9	6.2
1832	613	412	234,171	2.6	1.8
1837	3,557	2,338	265,394	13.4	8.8
1848	2,407	1,595	400,557	6.0	4.0
1849	5,361	3,552	401,802	13.1	8.8
1850	1,185	711	405,707	2.9	1.8
1852	247	165	413,517	0.6	0.4
1853	1,405	940	415,425	3.4	2.3
1855	2,172	1,385	419,241	5.2	3.3
1866	8,186	5,457	658,251	12.4	8.3
1871	68	55	826,341	0.1	0.8
1873	1,074	740	918,841	1.2	0.8

Source: E. H. Müller, *Die Cholera-Epidemie zu Berlin im Jahre 1873. Amtlicher Bericht* (Berlin, 1874); copy in Stadtarchiv Berlin Rep. 01 B 220

fumigation, and disinfection, and so on.[9] These regulations were legally binding and were still in force in 1850.[10]

Berlin escaped more lightly from cholera in 1832 than in 1831, but this in no way prompted a relaxation of the measures: indeed, they were probably held in some measure responsible for the decline.[11] However, as Table 3 shows, the disease returned to the capital in 1837, and in 1848, 1849, and 1850.[12] There were also minor outbreaks in 1852, 1853, and 1854, and a serious one in 1855, when over 1,300 people died from cholera in the capital city.[13] The outbreak in 1837, in the absence of any cases in Hamburg that year, suggests that seaports were not particularly vulnerable to cholera at this time; it was river-borne traffic that acted as the major route of transmission from the east, and so in principle almost any major town could be

[9] Ibid., Bl. 157–8: Sanitäts-polizeiliche Vorschriften bei den am häufigsten vorkommenden ansteckenden Krankheiten (nebst Anhang: Belehrung über ansteckende Krankheit) (1835); the quotation is from p. 15 (Bl. 189) of the 'Belehrung'.

[10] Ibid., 4181, Bl. 57 (Nr. 53): Erkenntniss des Königlichen Ober-Tribunals vom 26. Februar 1855.

[11] Stadtarchiv Berlin, Rep. 01 GB, 218: Beilage zum 7ten Stück des Amtsblatts der Königlichen Regierung zu Potsdam und der Stadt Berlin: A. Uebersicht des Ganges und Umfanges der Cholera in den einzelnen Ortschaften der Provinz Brandenburg seit dem am 9. August 1831 stattgefundenen Ausbruche der Krankheit bis ult. Januar 1832. Altogether it was estimated that over 30,000 people in Prussia died of cholera in 1831 (ibid., *Berlinische Nachrichten*, 20 Feb. 1832). For a local study, see A. Stollenwerk, 'Die Cholera im Regierungsbezirk Koblenz (1832)', *Jahrbuch für westdeutsche Landesgeschichte*, 5 (1979), 241–72.

[12] Stadtarchiv Berlin, Rep. 01 GB 219: *Berlinische Nachrichten*, 8 Feb. 1851.

[13] Ibid., *Vossische Zeitung*, 16 Nov. 1855; *Berlinische Nachrichten*, 6 June 1856.

infected. The most frequent and most serious visitations tended generally to be in the eastern provinces, nearest to Russia, where ordinary road traffic also acted as a transmitter.[14] Nevertheless, there was no change of policy. In 1852 for example another outbreak was announced in Berlin. Although, it was reported, the epidemic was in no way a large one, 'however, it has not been thought permissible to withhold an official announcement from the public, so that everyone will be in a position to adopt the advisable caution in his way of life'. The contrast with Hamburg could not be more striking. It was underlined by an official announcement issued by the Berlin authorities in 1866, during the epidemic of that year, stating that cholera was infectious, providing for strict measures of isolation and disinfection, demanding the immediate reporting of all cases, and setting up government commissions to deal with the disease.[15]

By this time, however, the influence of Pettenkofer had already begun to make itself felt. Already in the instructions issued in 1866 and quoted above, the authorities had been forced to concede that while cholera was 'positively only spread by means of human traffic', and therefore quarantine, isolation, and disinfection were still justified, nevertheless it was most likely to strike in places where the agent 'gets into the soil ... with human excreta'.[16] Pettenkofer's report on the Munich epidemic of 1866 was studied in Berlin,[17] and in 1867 an official report on the Berlin epidemic of the previous year treated Pettenkofer as the leading authority on the subject and paid close attention to the state of the ground in the affected areas.[18] From now on, discussion of cholera in Berlin concentrated mainly on the need for a thorough application of Pettenkofer's views.[19] New police regulations were issued in 1867 providing for the disinfection and cleaning of gutters, cesspools, and public lavatories; and these were widely applied in the epidemics of 1871 and 1873,[20] neither of which, however, approached that of 1866 in severity. Essentially, therefore, it was only in the epidemics of 1871 and 1873 that anticontagionism had any major influence on Prussian policy towards cholera. By and large the authorities—and above all the military authorities,

[14] Ibid., *Vossische Zeitung*, 9 Sept. 1852. In 1831–2, 1837, and 1848 a total of 33,000 people died of cholera in the districts of Königsberg, Gumbinnen, Marienwerder, and Danzig combined; the death rate was 8‰, 2‰, and 4‰ in each of the respective epidemics (ibid.).

[15] Ibid., *Amtsblatt der Königlichen Regierung zu Potstam und der Stadt Berlin*, 21 June 1866 and 26 June 1866. The 1866 epidemic, with a mortality rate of 5.9‰, was by far the largest in 19th–century Prussia; nearly 115,000 people died, and the epidemic affected other parts of Germany, such as Baden, for the first time (A. Fischer, *Geschichte des deutschen Gesundheitswesens* (Berlin, 1933), ii, p. 557). See also G. Fleischer, *Die Choleraepidemien in Düsseldorf* (Düsseldorf, 1977).

[16] Stadtarchiv Berlin, Rep. 01 GB 219: *Amtsblatt der Königlichen Regierung zu Potsdam und der Stadt Berlin*, 21 June 1866 and 26 June 1866.

[17] Ibid.

[18] Stadtarchiv Berlin, Rep. 01 GB 220: *Berlinische Nachrichten*, 4 Oct. 1867, discussing the official report on the 1866 epidemic by Dr Müller on behalf of the Royal Sanitary Commission.

[19] Cf. Ibid.: *Berlinische Nachrichten*, 3 Sept. 1871.

[20] Ibid. (E. H. Müller, 'Die Cholera-Erkrankungen zu Berlin im Jahre 1871', p. 121).

who were of course concerned about the danger of the disease spreading in the army (a matter of no small importance in 1866 and 1871)—continued to operate in the traditional mould of bureaucratic interventionism. Official policy during the epidemic of 1871 was still to disinfect the belongings of victims, to hospitalize those who fell ill with the disease, and to urge the avoidance of 'impure drinking-water'. Indeed, local officials in the countryside frequently imposed measures that went far beyond those allowed by the regulations in 1835. These remained officially in force well into the 1890s, unaffected by the spread of anticontagionism in the medical profession.[21]

This policy aroused considerable opposition from merchants and others who disliked the disruption to trade[22] and from municipal authorities who not only shared this view but objected to the expense caused by the measures ordered.[23] Isolation was particularly criticized from the very beginning. 'The quarantines are too costly', complained the citizens of Berlin as early as October 1831, 'they limit our earnings', and in any case 'the cordons sanitaires are only enforced against the poorer class of people', they were 'frightening', and 'the disease has also not shown itself to be infectious'.[24] Anticontagionism seems to have been widespread among the urban bourgeoisie in Prussia from the moment they felt the adverse effects of quarantine and isolation. It was shared in large measure by the medical profession. In 1868, for example, of 39 doctors in the Merseburg province who submitted opinions of Pettenkofer's views in response to an enquiry, 4 disagreed, 6 approved, and 29 agreed, with some criticisms, mostly on the grounds that Pettenkofer was too much of a contagionist![25] Public opinion in Berlin was soon declaring, however, 'that it is desirable for the city council to pay a bit more attention to Pettenkofer's cholera theory'. These feelings were above all directed towards the reform of Berlin's system of sewage and waste disposal, which at this time, as we have seen, still relied mainly on open gutters in the streets: and indeed the spread of Pettenkofer's views may well have played a role in the major reforms which the city undertook in the second half of the decade. There was clearly a feeling that the authorities were looking at the wrong thing. Given the tenacity with which the Prussian police held to the implementation of disinfection and isolation measures in 1871, it was hardly

---

[21] Ibid.: *Berlinische Nachrichten*, 24 Aug. 1871 (reporting Polizei-Präsidium 'Bekanntmachung' 21 Aug. 1871); and RT 21 Apr. 1893, 1960–1, speech of Freiherr von Unruhe-Bornst; cf. below, pp. 493–502 for the 1890s.

[22] GStA Berlin, Rep. 84a, 4178, Bl. 280: *Allgemeine Zeitung*, 14. Aug. 1831; Stadtarchiv Berlin, Rep. 01 GB 257: Stadtverordneten-Versammlung to Magistrat Berlin, 22 Sept. 1831.

[23] Ibid.: 'Verhandelt Berlin den 2ten September 1831 in der Plenar-Sitzung des Magistrats'.

[24] Ibid.: 'Auszug aus den Erklärungen der Schutz-Commissions-Vorsteher in Berlin für oder wider die Beibehaltung der vorgeschriebenen Maassregeln hinsichts der Wohnungssperre auf das Magistrats-Circular vom 25ten September: und auf die am 13ten Octobr. erlassene Rückfrage an einzelne, die sich zuerst noch nicht bestimmt ausgesprochen hatten pp', replies nos. 36, 31, 6, 5.

[25] Stadtarchiv Berlin, Rep. 01 GB 220: *Berlinische Nachrichten*, 12 July 1868.

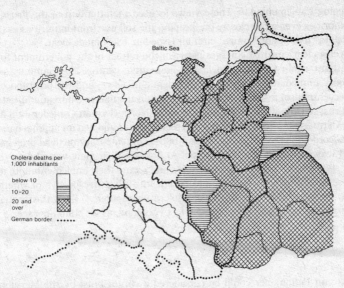

Baltic Sea

Cholera deaths per
1,000 inhabitants

below 10

10–20

20 and
over

German border ......

Source: StA Hbg, MK III W4, Bl. 136

MAP 24. Deaths from cholera on the Russo-German border, 1873

surprising that a protest meeting was held in Berlin at which demands were made to 'take account of the Cholera Regulations of Griesinger, Pettenkofer, and Wunderlich, issued in 1866'.[26]

As the influence of Pettenkofer grew, so the Prussian and Reich authorities gradually seem to have relaxed their traditional policing of epidemics. After 1831, indeed, cordons sanitaires no longer seem to have been employed; but even the tightening of controls on river traffic across the borders seems to have been abandoned by 1873, and there is no mention in the sources of any quarantine arrangements. As Map 24 shows, such traffic continued to be the vector that spread the disease unchecked across from Russia to the Eastern Prussian provinces in 1873. The foundation of the Imperial Health Office in 1876 gave Pettenkofer, as we have seen, further opportunity to impose his views. Already in 1877 it was urging more investigation of the meteorological and ground-water conditions in German towns and declaring that 'cleanliness and the renewal of air' were the key to defeating epidemics, because an efficient disinfection programme 'will certainly never be capable

---

[26] Ibid., Bl. 65b–66: Bericht über die am Montag dem 7. August 1871 durch den Redacteur Wegener im Concertsaal zu Berlin abgehaltene Versammlung.

of being implemented'.[27] These views focused the attention of the Prussian authorities ever more closely on 'keeping the soil free from impurities', as an official Prussian government circular issued in 1883 made clear.[28]

Yet a clear contrast emerges between the retreat of the government from the fight against cholera in liberal mercantile centres like Hamburg and Lübeck immediately after the first epidemic in 1831, and the persistence of interventionism for another 35 to 40 years in the military-bureaucratic state of Prussia. Only with the foundation of the North German Confederation and the German Empire do the Prussians seem to have adopted an approach more in accord with the anticontagionism of the contemporary medical profession and wide sectors of the bourgeoisie. At bottom, their view was always that the state had to 'take certain measures and secure their implementation, and these measures are necessarily to be put into effect irrespective of whether they correspond to one theory of cholera or another'.[29] Even this partially liberal era, moreover, did not really last very long, as we shall now see.

II

Max von Pettenkofer could be considered a contagionist by the Merseburg doctors because he postulated the existence of a cholera germ carried by human beings, even if he did maintain that this germ was harmless unless it fermented in the soil. He thus departed from his mentor Liebig in regarding fermentation as caused by a living organism rather than a chemical process. To this extent he can be counted among a number of scientists who helped pave the way for germ theory and bacteriology, and encouraged others to start the hunt for the germ which he, in common with many others, believed to be an essential part of cholera's causative mechanism. By the 1870s, this hunt was truly under way. Its leading figure at this time was the Frenchman Louis Pasteur. Like Pettenkofer, Pasteur too had started with an interest in fermentation. His researches led him to the theory that fermentation was caused by a living organism carried in the air. Following on this, he developed a more general germ theory. This was confirmed by his discovery of bacilli in diseased silkworms in 1868, accompanied by a successful formula for preventing contagion. This opened the way to more discoveries of this kind. In 1880 Pasteur turned his attention to 'chicken cholera', a kind of fowl pest. He not only demonstrated that it was caused by a germ, but by injecting chickens with a weak culture of the germ he also managed to produce

[27] BA Koblenz R86/9, Bd. 1: Denkschrift über die Thätigkeit des Kaiserlichen Gesundheitsamtes vom Jahr 1877, pp. 8–10.

[28] GStA Berlin, Rep. 84a, 4180, Bl. 84 (Ministerium der Geistlichen, Unterrichts-und Medicinalangelegenheiten, circular of 19 July 1883).

[29] RT 21 Apr. 1893, Col. 1954 (Secretary Boetticher).

immunity. Subsequently he was able to repeat this procedure with rabies. These discoveries made Pasteur famous all over Europe.[30]

Germ theory, of course, was far from being Pasteur's invention. It was already being developed in various ways by other scientists, including some in Germany. One such was the pathologist Jakob Henle, who taught at Göttingen University during this period. Henle was especially interested in the changes brought about in human tissues and internal organs by disease. He developed a set of rules for proving that a micro-organism was the cause of a disease. These rules were subsequently refined by Henle's most brilliant pupil, Robert Koch (1843–1910), the son of a Prussian mining official. They eventually became known as 'Koch's postulates'. They dictated that the agent or micro-organism had to be isolated from a diseased subject. It then had to be used experimentally to induce the same disease in an animal. Next, the micro-organism had to be isolated from the diseased animal. The experiment had to be repeatable. The micro-organism had to be present in all diseased subjects. Using this procedure, and taking advantage of improvements in microscopic technology made in the 1850s and 1860s, Koch began to investigate the cattle and sheep disease, anthrax, once he had settled down as a local physician in the rural district of Wollstein in 1872. As a country doctor, Koch was constantly confronted by anthrax as a serious disease which sometimes affected humans. By 1876 he had successfully isolated the anthrax bacillus and re-infected experimental animal subjects. He worked out the organism's life history and demonstrated the significance of the spore stage. A lecture on the subject at the University of Breslau, and a subsequent paper, brought him instant recognition. Between 1871 and 1881 he published a number of works on the principles of bacteriological investigation (including the staining of bacteria with aniline dyes and the use of microphotography). In 1880, as a mark of his achievements, he was given a laboratory at the Imperial Health Office in Berlin with assistants who included Georg Gaffky (1850–1918), later to play a role in the Hamburg epidemic along with Koch himself.

Koch's move to Berlin inaugurated the period of his most celebrated discoveries. In 1882 he discovered the cause of tuberculosis, the tubercle bacillus. Up to this point, tuberculosis, the greatest killer disease of the nineteenth century, had not even been recognized as a single entity by some schools of thought.[31] His discovery made Koch into Germany's leading bacteriologist. National prestige dictated that Koch should be dispatched to Egypt on the outbreak of a cholera epidemic there in 1883. The French, whose medical science had won international fame through the bacteriological discoveries of Pasteur, were known to be sending a team, and the race to discover and isolate the causative agent of cholera was now on. Koch arrived in Alexandria

[30] M. Pelling, *Cholera, Fever and English Medicine, 1825–1865* (Oxford, 1978) p. 1.

[31] Winslow, *The Conquest of Epidemic Disease*, pp. 307–10.

with his assistants, including Georg Gaffky, and fifty German mice, on 24 August 1883. As he wrote, they 'were able to track down a few cholera victims, and even one cholera corpse, on the day of our arrival, in order to be able to begin our investigations straight away'.[32] Unfortunately, all the attempts to infect the mice were fruitless, and further investigation proved impossible because the epidemic was virtually over. While the rival French expedition went home in disappointment, however, Koch refused to give up. He set off with his assistants for Calcutta, where the disease was endemic. By 7 January they had finally succeeded in identifying and producing a pure culture of the micro-organism which, because of its shape, Koch labelled the 'comma bacillus'. This, he announced on 2 February, after further experiments, was the cause of cholera.

On their return to Germany, Koch and his assistants were fêted as national heroes. They were greeted by the German Emperor, and showered with honours. Koch was made a member of the Order of the Crown, Second Class (with star), and Gaffky and Fischer were elevated into the Order of the Red Eagle, Third Class (medical discoveries were prestigious, but still by no means comparable with the achievements of military men). After the reception by the Emperor, the Imperial Health Office held another reception, in which it gave Koch a life-size bust of the aged Wilhelm I. His assistants received framed photographs of the old man. Such were the marks of esteem which counted in Berlin. They signified the close ties between the Imperial Health Office and the established system of government. Koch for his part was well aware of the political significance of his discovery. In one of the numerous banquets held in his honour that summer, he declared that 'the result of the expedition is especially welcome for Germany: it means a rise in the reputation which German science has achieved abroad because of its successes, and thus he can only be thankful to have been entrusted with such an honourable task'. The government recognized the political importance of Koch's discovery by introducing a special bill into the Reichstag to provide members of Koch's team with a reward of 135,000 Marks between them. The introduction of the bill, which rapidly passed into law amid general acclaim, emphasized once more that 'this valuable achievement is regarded beyond the borders of our fatherland as a brilliant testimony to the persistence and thoroughness of German science'.[33]

Koch could now be assured, therefore, of vigorous backing from the Imperial government in imposing his views on cholera prevention on medical authorities throughout the Empire. Already in June 1884 he was made a member of the Prussian Privy Council (*Staatsrat*) and co-opted onto the

---

[32] B. Möller, *Robert Koch, Persönlichkeit und Lebenswerk 1843–1910* (Hanover, 1950), p. 514: Koch to Emmy Koch, 25 Aug. 1883.

[33] Ibid., p. 151. Möller's account makes it clear that 1884 is the correct date for Koch's discovery, not 1883 as is sometimes given. See also Plate 15.

Cholera Commission for the German Empire. This had hitherto been controlled by Pettenkofer. Soon, however, Koch became the dominant force. In the same year he organized a course of the diagnosis and prevention of cholera, in which 146 doctors took part, including 97 civilian (i.e. non-military) doctors from all parts of Germany and 20 other countries. In 1885 he became full professor (*Ordinarius*) of Hygiene at the University of Berlin, and was appointed Director of a specially created Institute for Infectious Diseases in 1891. These positions enabled him to influence large numbers of pupils in favour of his ideas and methods. His influence was further spread by his senior pupils such as Georg Gaffky, who took up a Chair of Hygiene in Giessen in 1888. With another close collaborator, Carl Flügge (1847-1923), Professor of Hygiene at Göttingen 1883–7 and Breslau 1887–1906, Koch founded a journal for the propagation of his ideas, the *Zeitschrift für Hygiene und Infektionskrankheiten*. Thus Koch and his pupils were rapidly taking over the field of hygiene, which had been founded as an academic discipline, and hitherto dominated, by Max von Pettenkofer.[34]

Koch was a strong believer in the value of quarantine and disinfection. His observations in Calcutta and his own experiments confirmed his belief that the cholera bacillus survived best, indeed multiplied most rapidly, in water, including drinking-water. Infection, he argued, took place above all through the pollution of water by infected individuals and the drinking of this water, or the eating of foodstuffs (especially fruit) washed in it, by others. Koch therefore arranged for quarantine measures to be imposed on people coming from infected areas. He urged that especially sharp controls be placed on river traffic. Quarantine measures on most goods, he believed, were unnecessary, but an exception had to be made for dirty clothing. Koch argued that the bacillus could not survive immersion in boiling water, so the Imperial Health Office urged the boiling of all water during an epidemic. Carbolic was particularly effective against the bacillus in Koch's view, and he saw here a chance to impose on local authorities the principles of disinfection he had worked out in a series of experiments in the early 1880s. In an epidemic, from now on, all infected or possibly infected clothing and bedding, in which Koch found the bacillus multiplied very rapidly, would have to be treated with carbolic, by order of the Imperial Health Office. Strict quarantine and comprehensive disinfection were in Koch's view the two best methods of preventing cholera.[35] Thus, in a remarkably short space of time, anticontagionism had been ousted from the commanding heights of the Imperial Health Office and replaced with a new variant of the contagionist theory whose practical consequences were much the same as those of the old. Koch was now issuing a stream of advice from Berlin on how to prevent cholera

---

[34] StA Hbg, MK III A 2 Bd. 2, Bl. 152, for the 1884 course. More generally, cf. Möller, *Robert Koch*, esp. p. 161.
[35] Möller, op. cit.; see also pp. 313–14 below.

by the very methods which Pettenkofer had spent the previous thirty years denouncing as utterly useless. The change in official doctrine might not have been so easy without the existence of a central directing authority. But the educational courses with which Koch was now indoctrinating medical men from all over Germany threatened to reduce Pettenkofer to the role of an impotent spectator watching from the sidelines as his life's work in this field was destroyed.

What were the reasons for Koch's triumph? The standard medical histories present it as a simple story of the victory of true science over obscurantist error. In fact, however, the reasons for the ascendancy of contagionism from the mid-1880s were a good deal more complicated, as indeed were the reasons for the previous hegemony of miasmatism. Medical theories do not simply prevail because of their intrinsic merit. Social, economic, and political factors are also involved. In many ways Koch's discovery of the cholera bacillus in 1884 rested on extremely shaky foundations. Cholera is a disease that is virtually impossible to reproduce in animals, so it is not surprising that Koch encountered so many problems in establishing the agency of the bacillus in 1883–4. 'Koch's postulates' simply did not work in this case. By the very rules which he himself developed, Koch failed to discover the cause of cholera, as indeed anyone else attempting this task would fail. His announcement, on 2 February 1884, rested in effect on the assumption that normal procedures did not apply. Moreover, it had been shown more recently that Koch was in fact not the first person to discover the cholera bacillus at all. The Judicial Commission of the International Committee of Bacteriological Nomenclature now credits the Italian scientist Filippo Pacini (1812–83) with the discovery of *Vibrio cholerae* in 1854. At least four other scientists working along similar lines in the 1850s also have a claim to be regarded as the discoverers of the bacillus, though in every case their claim is a good deal less strong than Pacini's.[36]

So why did Koch get the credit? The conclusion seems inevitable that his success was determined above all by social and political factors. Three influences in particular played a crucial role. The first was nationalism. We have already seen how the French and German governments sent their rival teams to Egypt in the hope of being first in the race to discover the cause of cholera.

---

[36] Pelling, *Cholera, Fever and English Medicine*, p. 3. Pelling disputes the validity of the miasmatist/contagionist distinction; but while her objections may be justified in terms of scientific theory alone, the distinction was clear enough to contemporaries, not least because it was always understood in terms of its implications for quarantine. See R. Cooter, 'Anticontagionism and History's Medical Record', in A. Treacher and P. Wright (eds.), *The Problem of Medical Knowledge* (Edinburgh, 1982), pp. 87–108. The debate dates from the classic equation of contagionism with conservatism and miasmatism with liberalism in E. H. Ackerknecht, 'Anticontagionism between 1821 and 1867', *Bulletin of the History of Medicine*, 22 (1948), 562–93. For further details on Koch's discovery, see N. Howard-Jones, 'Choleranomalies', *Perspectives in Biology and Medicine*, 15 (1975), 422–33.

A great deal of national prestige was invested in the outcome. This, after all, was little more than a decade after Germany had defeated France in a major war. The very same year that saw Koch's discovery, 1884, also saw the beginning of that high point of the age of imperialism, the 'scramble for Africa'. At the same time as the Germans, the French, the British, and other nations were engaged in a desperate race to annex territory in the name of civilization, they were also involved in a furious competition to conquer disease in the name of science. No wonder, then, that Koch was acclaimed as a hero on his return. Such was the publicity given to his achievement by the German government that no one could remain ignorant of the fact that the vibrio had now been discovered.

Secondly, Koch's discovery was not simply a boost to the national prestige of the young German Empire. It also coincided with an increasing tendency of the German state to interfere in German society. In 1879 the era of free trade came to an end, when import tariffs and quotas were introduced, and the previous year had seen the passing of the Anti-Socialist Law. Koch's contagionist view of cholera implied comprehensive quarantine measures. In the new state-interventionist climate of the 1880s, the Imperial government in Berlin was not disinclined to impose these. The widely held thesis that anticontagionism was dominant when liberalism and free trade were dominant is exemplified in the German case with extraordinary neatness, for Pettenkofer's years of influence, the 1860s and 1870s, coincided with the era of free trade in Germany, while Koch's influence became paramount as protection was adopted. Moreover, Pettenkofer was a liberal, whose appointment in Munich had been blocked by conservative ministers until the very eve of the Revolution, in 1847; while Koch was very much the non-political, but basically conservative Prussian civil servant and so more congenial to the government in the conservative 1880s, when National Liberals such as Pettenkofer were looked on with less favour in Berlin.

Thirdly, Koch's advocacy of strong state intervention also accorded with the need for the German Empire to begin to impose itself on its various constituent federated kingdoms, principalities, and states. The Imperial Health Office, created in 1876, was one of a small number of such central governmental institutions in the German Empire. As we have already seen in the case of Hamburg, most functions of internal government (as opposed to foreign and military affairs) were decentralized and administered at the level of the federated states. Koch's activities in the Imperial Health Office, in contrast to those of his predecessor Pettenkofer, represented a marked increase in the interference of the central government in the internal affairs of the states. In the Imperial Health Office, Berlin possessed an important instrument for binding the Empire together and imposing its will on the provinces. Correspondingly, the Office was inevitably identified with Prussian domination, above all after the Prussian Koch replaced the Bavarian Pettenkofer as its most influential figure.[37]

These were the major determinants of the political triumph of Koch's theory. But it is possible to go further and argue that there were other reasons for its success, reasons connected not with its political implications but much more with its actual scientific content. Roger Cooter has recently suggested that miasmatism can be seen not simply as a reflection of specific social and economic interests, but also as a theory which embodied itself a 'mediation of the constitutive changes in social relations of production contingent upon the advance of urban industrial capitalism'. The notion of a *miasma*, of infection through the air, of poison from an unseen source was, Cooter argues, a scientific rendering of Adam Smith's 'unseen hand' that ruled the lives of individuals in the capitalist economy. The miasmatists' concentration on the atmosphere

minimalized the importance of immediate personal contact (the basis of mutual aid) and elevated the importance of an external depersonalised environment through which man's relation to man would have to be negotiated. Air can thus be seen in the thought of anticontagionists as a means of alternatively conceptualising the emergent realities of the industrial capitalist urban environment: harbouring unknown poisons, the air took on the distinguishing hostile qualities of life in new industrial towns. Like the town, the air required purification and, in this sense, air conveys the Utilitarian-inspired ambition to moralise individuals by moralising society's social framework.[38]

And because it so defied 'common sense' and traditional explanations of the transmission of epidemics, miasmatism arrogated to specialists of statistics and science the sole power of prevention. The mere avoidance of personal contact, in the miasmatists' view, was futile; only scientifically guided reforms to remove the source of the miasma would ever have any lasting results.

From this point of view it is easy to see why bacteriology was able to attract such widespread support within the medical profession. By postulating an unseen bacillus as the agent of the disease and providing the technique with which it could be identified and killed, Koch was able to reformulate contagionism in terms that made professional medical science even more indispensable to the disease's prevention. Indeed, the very simplicity of Koch's theory enabled medical scientists largely to dispense with the services of meteorologists, statisticians, and others whose contribution had been vital to

[37] Göckenjan, *Kurieren und Staat machen*, p. 113, attempts to apply Ackerknecht's formula to Germany but dates the resurgence of contagionism to the 1850s because the first part of the decade was the classic period of reaction; however, the eventual triumph of contagionism should be dated to the 1880s not the 1850s. For discussion of Ackerknecht's ideas in a different context, see E. R. Ocaña, 'La dependencia social de un comportamiento cientifico: Los médicos españoles y el coléra de 1833–35', *Dynamis*, 1 (1981), 101–30.

[38] Pelling, *Cholera, Fever and English Medicine*, p. 3; Cooter, 'Anticontagionism', p. 99.

the miasmatist model, as even the most cursory examination of the cholera monographs of Pettenkofer and his school quickly reveals. Miasmatism gave the central role in cholera prevention to the generalists in the broad, inter-disciplinary field of social hygiene—in fact, to men such as Pettenkofer himself. Bacteriology removed it from them and gave it to highly specialized laboratory scientists like Koch. The civil authorities once more took up quarantine, isolation, and disinfection as the chief weapons in the fight against cholera, but where this had formerly been a kind of traditional administrative reflex in the face of any major epidemic disease, it now assumed the guise of a systematic war against an identifiable enemy carried out under the clear direction and supervision of specialist medical scientists. Even the avoidance of personal contact was now given a scientifically validated form in the destruction of the bacillus through medically approved actions such as washing, disinfection, boiling water, and so on. Seen in this light, Koch's achievement was to reinterpret contagionism in terms compatible with medical professionalization.

It is perhaps rather more difficult to accept the suggestion that cholera theories may be regarded as symbolic representations of industrial capitalism. In some ways, as we have already seen, the notion of a miasma as the causative agent in epidemic disease was a very old one, going back at least as far as the Middle Ages. Moreover, while it may be plausible to link it with the rise of industrial capitalism in England, this still leaves us with the question of its dominance in the medical profession of Germany, where the industrial age had not yet begun in 1830, and Russia, where it was not to begin for another half-century. Capitalist relations of production certainly existed in Hamburg in the first half of the nineteenth century, but it is just as certain that they did not exist in the Tsarist Empire at that time. Yet miasmatism was equally influential in both. It is also very difficult to fit the bacteriological approach into this model. This was indeed the age of cartel formation in Germany, in the wake of the severe economic depression of 1873–8; the beginnings of the transition from competitive to monopoly (or, as West German historians like to say, 'organized') capitalism. It is very difficult, however, to imagine how Koch's theory of cholera could be regarded as a symbolic representation of this transition, or why the change in relations of production rendered the symbolic content of miasmatism unsatisfactory in this respect.

Despite these problems, it seems reasonable to suppose none the less that theories of cholera did carry with them a heavy load of political symbolism. Most obvious, of course, was the conservative notion of revolutionary ideology as a poison. The idea of a deadly bacillus transmitted by carriers and infected individuals throughout society had an obvious relevance to bourgeois and official fears of the peril of socialism, which were at their height during the 1880s, the period of the Anti-Socialist Law in Germany and of widespread

panic in official circles in other countries. It was not until later that bacteriological imagery became commonplace in politics—above all, with the
Nazis. But likely enough government officials in Berlin were aware of the
parallel in the 1800s, if only subconsciously. German theories of cholera in
the 1880s were political in another, more obvious respect as well. Pettenkofer
and his followers always described themselves as 'localists'. Their theory
emphasized the paramountcy of *local* conditions in the causation of disease.
As early as 1831 indeed, miasmatists were arguing 'that cholera assumes a
different character in every town and demands different treatment, which is
why no general means of dealing with it has yet been found'.[39] In this
sense, Pettenkofer was a kind of scientific particularist, and the persistence of
miasmatism in Hamburg reflected the strength of particularism there. Local
conditions required specific remedies based on a knowledge of local conditions.
Every part of Germany had its own individual characteristics, and had to be
treated accordingly, by those who were familiar with them. By contrast,
Koch's theory was centralist in character, emphasizing the spread of the
disease from a single, central source. The consequence of contagionism was
the central co-ordination of measures to combat the disease and its spread. The
same measures could be applied everywhere. And under Koch's supervision, if
necessary against the objections of local authorities, they were.

The relationships that existed between medical science, economic interest,
and political ideology in nineteenth-century Hamburg were thus far from
simple. Neither miasmatism nor contagionism was a monolithic or coherent
set of beliefs. Nor for that matter was liberalism or conservatism. To underline
the complexities of these relationships it is worth digressing for a moment to
look at the life and opinions of Rudolf Virchow, who was not only the leading
pathologist of the period but also a well-known figure in left-liberal politics.
Virchow was a Reichstag deputy for many years, and a well-known supporter
of many liberal causes. He was such a persistent and outspoken critic of the
government that Bismarck once actually challenged him to a duel. Among
Virchow's many claims to fame was his coinage of the term *Kulturkampf*, or
clash of civilizations, to denote the battle between the state and the Catholic
Church in the 1870s—a struggle in which, like the vast majority of liberals,
he strongly supported the Bismarckian state in its effort to defeat what they
regarded as the threat of obscurantist Ultramontanism. As a leading figure
in left-wing liberalism, Virchow was a convinced supporter of free trade
and actively opposed the introduction of the 1878 tariffs in the Reichstag.
Unfortunately, and perhaps rather surprisingly, the standard biography of
Virchow, by Erwin H. Ackerknecht, treats his medical and his political
activities quite separately and does not attempt to draw any connections
between them. But everything that we know about Virchow's politics would

[39] *Der Hamburgische Beobachter*, 45 (22 Oct. 1831), p. 171.

seem to suggest that he was likely to have been strongly anticontagionist in his approach to epidemic disease.[40]

In many respects this was indeed the case. In 1848 Virchow took an anticontagionist line on typhus and typhoid, and in his studies of cholera he was highly sceptical of its allegedly contagious qualities. However, he rejected Pettenkofer's theories as they were developed in the 1850s, and accused their author of an excessive dogmatism and determinism in relation to the influence of 'ground-water' in producing miasmas. As late as 1884 he was still sharply critical of Pettenkofer's emphasis on the soil. In 1868, Virchow modified his earlier views and argued for a 'fungus' as the agent of cholera. He welcomed Koch's discovery of the bacillus in 1884 and as time went on he became increasingly contagionist in his approach to the disease. By 1892 he was arguing in an exchange with Pettenkofer that cholera could be passed on from person to person, or through any one of a number of intermediaries, including the water-supply. Yet Virchow's views on cholera were something of an exception to his general approach to the aetiology of diseases. He refused to accept that diphtheria was caused by a bacillus and he rejected Semmelweis's account of puerperal fever. Most notably of all, he opposed the theory that the tubercle bacillus was the cause of tuberculosis, even though Koch's discovery of the bacillus had been so widely acclaimed. So Virchow was in no sense a simple 'contagionist' at any stage of his career.[41]

Virchow in fact thought any simple, mechanical explanation of disease was wrong, whether it was Pettenkofer's 'ground-water' theory or Koch's bacteriology. He regarded the claims of the bacteriologists to have discovered the fundamental principle of infectious disease as excessive in their nature and unfortuate in their effect. As a radical liberal, Virchow pursued what Ackerknecht has called 'a sociological epidemiology that appeared in the nineteenth century between the climatic and the bacteriological concepts of epidemics'.[42] The great epidemics, he thought, were primarily social in their causes. Because they mostly affected the poor, it followed that poverty was the major determinant of their incidence. Epidemics were

artificial ... attributes of society, products of a false civilization that is not distributed among all classes. They point towards deficiencies produced by the structure of state or society, and strike therefore primarily those classes which do not enjoy the advantages of civilization. Do not crowd diseases point everywhere to deficiencies in society? One may adduce atmospheric or cosmic conditions or similar factors. But never do they make epidemics by themselves. They produce them only where people

[40] E. K. Ackerknecht, *Rudolf Virchow, Doctor, Statesman, Anthropologist* (Madison, Wisconsin, 1953), esp. p. 188; see also F. Stern, *Gold and Iron. Bismarck, Bleichröder and the Building of the German Empire* (London, 1977), p. 55.

[41] Ackerknecht, *Rudolf Virchow*, pp. 107, 116, 124–5; see also M. von Pettenkofer, 'Rudolf Virchow's Choleratheorie', *Berliner Klinische Wochenschrift*, 21 (1884), 485–91 (including reply by Virchow).

[42] Ackerknecht, *Rudolf Virchow*, p. 126.

have lived for some time in abnormal situations because of bad social conditions ... Epidemics resemble great warning signs on which the true statesman is able to read that the evolution of this nation has been disturbed to a point which even a careless policy may no longer ignore.[43]

Virchow's remedies for epidemics were therefore primarily social. Neither quarantine and disinfection nor fresh air and effective sanitation were what was really needed, but prosperity and social reform. In his celebrated report on typhus in Upper Silesia in 1848, he maintained that the best way of preventing a recurrence was to provide the inhabitants with efficient industry, improved agriculture, new roads, communal self-government, education, prosperity, liberty, and democracy. Because epidemics were caused by social crises, the remedy lay in social reform. Virchow did argue for sanitary improvements along English lines, and was indeed influential in the creation of an effective sewage system in Berlin in the 1870s. But he never ceased to believe in democracy as the primary prophylactic. The physician in his view should not be an improving municipal administrator like Pettenkofer or a bacteriological scientist like Koch, but a political democrat and social reformer like himself.[44]

This stance was very unusual by the late 1880s. Left-liberals like Virchow were in a political minority; radical doctors were even more of a rarity. Nevertheless, despite his quarrels with Pettenkofer, Virchow sided with the Munich professor on most of the key issues: in his rejection of the most ambitious and far-reaching of the bacteriologists' claims; in his scepticism towards the theory that virtually all infectious diseases were caused by microorganisms; in his belief that prosperity improved health; and finally, in his concentration on environmental improvement rather than laboratory science as the best means of combating disease. Where he parted company with Pettenkofer was above all in his insistence on political change, democratic reform, and economic prosperity as the prerequisites of good health. Virchow did not believe in socialized medicine or a National Health Service, although he did want a national Ministry of Health (staffed by doctors). He was a libertarian, who was also closely wedded to the idea that the medical profession should be the guide to sanitary reform, and strongly opposed to the idea of state control. He argued that freedom from authoritarian government alone guaranteed freedom from infectious disease. Democracy was the best medicine for epidemics. Given Virchow's identification with the most extreme wing of the left-liberals, and considering the radical political implications of his epidemiology, it was small wonder that his ideas found little resonance in Hamburg. In the vast outpouring of literature that came from the pens of Hamburg's medical men on the subject of cholera before 1892, there were

[43] Ibid., pp. 16–19, quoting Virchow, *Gesammelte Abhandlungen: öffentliche Medizin*, i. 55. (Translation by Ackerknecht, slightly amended.)

[44] Ackerknecht, *Rudolf Virchow*, pp. 124–5, 129–32; see also P. Weindling, 'Was Social Medicine Revolutionary? Rudolf Virchow and the Revolutions of 1848', *Bulletin of the Society for the Social History of Medicine*, 34 (1984), 13–18.

few echoes of Virchow's theories, indeed scarcely any mention of them. Pettenkofer's views were more congenial from a number of points of view: they committed their adherents to limited sanitary reforms rather than sweeping political change; they emphasized voluntary action rather than state interference; they made fewer concessions to contagionism; they prescribed prophylatic measures that could be presented as largely having been put into practice in the 1840s by the schemes of William Lindley; they dictated inaction once an epidemic had broken out. Virchow's theories lacked the seductive symbolic charges carried by the views of Pettenkofer and Koch: their political character was obvious enough, and not at all to the liking of Hamburg's dominant classes. Finally, while Pettenkofer had established himself as an expert in the field of cholera, by the sheer volume of his publications if by nothing else, Virchow's real medical reputation was as a pathologist, and his writings on cholera were few in number and easily discountable as politically determined ventures into a field not really his own. It was not until the exceptional circumstances of 1892, as we shall see, that Virchow's 'sociological epidemiology' made any real impact on Hamburg.

What Virchow's theories made explicit was none the less what was common in a greater or lesser degree to all theories of cholera and other infectious diseases in this period: the indissoluble connection between medical science, economic interest, and political ideology. It has been necessary to establish the case for the importance of these connections at length not only because it has been disputed in recent literature, but even more because without this, it is really impossible to understand the attitude of the Hamburg authorities and the Hamburg medical profession to epidemic disease in the mid and late nineteenth century, and even more important, it is impossible to grasp the reasons why Hamburg, alone of all European cities, was to experience a major cholera epidemic in 1892. As we shall now see, the arguments between Pettenkofer, Koch, Virchow, and their various supporters were not merely abstruse academic disputations; however much they might have been influenced by social and political considerations, both conscious and unconscious, they also in their turn had a material effect on the policies that the state adopted to meet the challenge which cholera posed.

III

The triumph of Robert Koch in 1884 brought the immediate resurgence of contagionism in a new, infinitely more powerful form, and mobilized the resources of the state to a degree unknown since the era of the cordons sanitaires in 1831. Almost immediately, as we have seen, Koch's views were implemented to the full extent of their rigour in Prussia. How were they received in Hamburg? As the medical historian Norman Howard-Jones has complained, 'In all the books of medical history, the facts are grossly over-simplified. Koch, it is said, "discovered" the cholera vibrio in 1884 and one is left with the impression that that was the end of the matter. The truth is quite otherwise. For many years antagonists of Koch were almost as vocal as protagonists.'[45] There were a number of reasons why Koch's many critics, both lay and professional, were able to continue opposing his ideas for so many years. In the first place, as we have already seen, his identification of the cholera vibrio rested on somewhat shaky foundations, for the nature of the disease made it virtually impossible to satisfy 'Koch's postulates' by reproducing it in an experimental animal subject. Moreover, this was not the first time Koch had been skating on thin ice. His discovery of the cause of tuberculosis in 1882 bears some interesting similarities to his discovery of the cause of cholera two years later. Koch accompanied his announcement of the discovery of the 'tubercle' with a demonstration that the bacillus was transmitted in the sputum of infected sufferers. Tuberculosis was therefore infectious. This conclusion was widely resisted within the medical profession. Its members frequently regarded such practices as the ostracism of consumptives and the incineration of their belongings after their death as barbarous relics of a superstitious medieval past. They considered Koch's reassertion of the infectious character of tuberculosis as a resurrection of a discredited and outmoded theory. Koch also subsequently announced that the substance he had developed to help diagnose the disease—'tuberculin'—would cure it as well. Initial tests did, to be sure, come up with some impressive results. But it soon became apparent that tuberculin only acted on the tissues in which the bacillus grew, not on the bacillus itself. Indeed, it actually seemed to activate the bacilli in areas where they were dormant. Koch's claim that he had discovered a cure for consumption proved to be bogus. None was in fact developed until the development of streptomycin after 1945. So although Koch was fêted by the Imperial authorities, professional medical men were entitled to a degree of scepticism about his work.

The fact that Koch's views were so loudly supported by Berlin was not seen in Hamburg as any reason for giving them particular credence. Moreover, Pettenkofer's continued criticism of the contagionist approach greatly strengthened the Hamburg doctors in their adherence to the miasmatic views which they had espoused for so long.[46] A characteristic product of these views, for example, was the elaborate report issued by Dr Johann Julius Reincke on the typhoid epidemic of the late 1880s. It was written entirely according to Pettenkofer's ideas, with elaborate charts of temperature, rainfall, and all the other factors which Pettenkofer considered so important. Air, concluded

[45] N. Howard-Jones, 'Gelsenkirchen Typhoid Epidemic of 1901, Robert Koch and the Dead Hand of Max von Pettenkofer', *British Medical Journal*, 13 Jan. 1973.

[46] Pettenkofer also had many pupils in leading positions. See H.-H. Eulner, 'Hygiene als akademisches Fach', in W. Artelt *et al.* (eds.), *Städte-, Wohnungs- und Kleidungshygiene des 19. Jahrhunderts in Deutschland* (Stuttgart, 1969), pp. 17–33.

Reincke in 1890, was the principal means of infection.[47] An outside observer reporting on Hamburg's medical profession noted that the localist or miasmatic view was 'exclusively dominant' in 1886.[48] The priorities of protecting trade, avoiding government expenditure, and maintaining public order were even more urgent now that Koch's influence was making it difficult to avoid the imposition of quarantine and isolation and the mounting of elaborate disinfection measures once a cholera epidemic was officially confirmed. Thus the Hamburg medical profession, which, as we have seen, belonged to the city's dominant classes and had close if subordinate relations with the mercantile grand bourgeoisie, became more determined than ever to avoid such an official confirmation taking place.

In the long term, however, it was clearly going to be impossible to prevent supporters of Koch's views from obtaining medical posts in the city. One of the first breaches in the miasmatist front came early in 1892, with the appointment of a new Director of the New General Hospital in Eppendorf. The man who took up the job was Professor Theodor Rumpf. Born in 1851 near Kassel, in Hesse, Rumpf was an outsider, who had spent much of his previous career in Bonn, where he became a professor in 1887. He was to be one of the major figures in the drama that began to unfold in the city not long after his appointment. Rumpf came to the city as a convinced supporter of Koch; indeed, he lectured in Wiesbaden in 1893 in support of Koch's theories. Rumpf was clearly an able and energetic administrator, but he seems to have been somewhat lacking in tact, and as a newcomer he clearly aroused the suspicion of the local medical profession. Moreover, not only was he an outsider, but his position was also fatally weakened by the fact that his own field of specialization was neurology, which was so far removed from the question of cholera that he could easily be accused of ignorance. Rumpf was to have a difficult time during the epidemic, and to some extent his memoirs, published in 1925, provided the occasion for a belated revenge on those he considered had slighted him. Nevertheless, they do not appear to be mendacious, and they are at least worth taking into account. For Rumpf's views on cholera, a subject on which he was in fact no more ignorant than most of his colleagues, were clearly unwelcome to the Hamburg medical men, above all to Kraus, 'a splendid fellow, who urgently requested me during our earliest discussions just not to report any cases of *cholera nostras* as real cholera, nor to diagnose a cholera epidemic from isolated cases of cholera, because the publication of such reports would cause immeasurable damage to Hamburg's trade'.[49] This conversation, it should be noted, took place shortly after Rumpf's appointment early in 1892. Once an epidemic was

[47] Reincke, *Der Typhus*.

[48] F. Hueppe, 'Die Cholera–Epidemie in Hamburg 1892', *Berliner Klinische Wochenschrift*, Vol. 30, No. 4 (1893).

[49] T. Rumpf, *Lebenserinnerungen* (Gotha, 1925), p. 41.

officially declared, there would be little that the city could do to stop Koch and the Imperial Health Office from imposing on it the quarantine and other measures which it considered so futile and so damaging. Quarantine would undoubtedly be declared by Prussia on the Hanseatic port; and foreign trade was effectively an Imperial matter, in which Hamburg was now dependent on the overall policy of the Customs Union, which it had joined in 1888. So the decisive issue now became that of diagnosis.

Here too things had changed since 1873. In earlier epidemics, diagnosis had been not merely according to symptoms, but also, as we have seen, according to the pattern of cases over time: isolated cases were not an epidemic and so were not diagnosed as Asiatic cholera; only in a full-scale outbreak could the disease fairly be called 'real'. This practice even allowed Kraus to order the retrospective re-diagnosis of earlier cases once the presence of an epidemic had finally been confirmed. Though Rumpf's account of his meeting with Kraus shortly after his appointment suggests that this was still the 'absolutely definite plan' that the Chief Medical Officer had in mind in 1892, the triumph of bacteriology in Berlin undoubtedly introduced a new factor into the diagnostic process. Ever since the mid-1880s the Imperial Health Office had been insisting that the only proper way to diagnose Asiatic cholera—as distinct from other, less virulent intestinal infections—was to take a sample from the stool of a suspected victim, isolate it, then produce a pure culture which showed the characteristic rapid growth of the bacillus which—in Koch's view—caused the severe symptoms of the Asiatic cholera. In theory, therefore, the diagnosis of a single case in this way, or at most a 'non-epidemic' handful of individual cases, would be enough to oblige the Chief Medical Officer and the Senate to declare the presence of Asiatic cholera in the city, with all the fateful consequences that this implied.

In practice, however, circumstances were not quite so unfavourable to a renewed application of Kraus's plan in 1892 as they at first sight appeared. In the first place, it was clear that until a full bacteriological diagnosis actually was achieved, the Senate would be under no pressure to declare the presence of an epidemic. In other words, any number of cases could occur exhibiting the characteristic symptoms of Asiatic cholera, but without the achievement of a bacteriological diagnosis none of them would be recorded as such. Secondly, such a diagnosis was notoriously difficult to obtain. Even Koch had had problems in producing a pure culture of the bacillus in 1883–4. Clearly some progress had been made in the appropriate techniques since then. But few doctors in Hamburg were at all familiar with them. Nobody occupying a position of influence in the city's medical profession in 1892 had been on Koch's course on cholera diagnosis in 1884; no new courses had been held since that date. The production of a rapidly growing colony of the bacillus depended on placing the culture in a solution whose constituents had to be correctly mixed and placed in the most favourable conditions for quick growth. Things could easily go wrong if the experimenter was inexperienced. Moreover, the Doctors' Club, the key social and professional institution of the Hamburg medical men, which met regularly to discuss scientific problems, did not discuss cholera at all in the fifteen or more years leading up to 1892. This was largely because the usual procedure in the Club was for the speaker to bring a patient along and demonstrate whatever problem was exhibited, something clearly out of the question with cholera. It also probably reflected a general consensus in the local profession that Koch's procedures were wrong-headed anyway, and that the miasmatic view was so self-evident as to be no longer worthy of debate.[50] Thus there was hardly anyone in Hamburg in 1892 who was capable of achieving a swift diagnosis of Asiatic cholera according to the officially approved procedures. This meant, in effect, that Kraus's plan of delaying an official announcement of the disease's presence in the city until it had reached epidemic proportions was still reasonably viable.

Sixty years of dealing with cholera epidemics had created a tradition that remained undisturbed in all its essentials by the discoveries of the 1880s. The medical profession remained overwhelmingly anticontagionist. Local doctors were largely unfamiliar with the procedures for the bacteriological diagnosis of cholera. They remained convinced of the impossibility of the disease being conveyed in the water-supply. They shared the concern of the Senate, made more acute by the ascendancy of contagionism in Berlin, that a hasty or premature announcement of the discovery of Asiatic cholera in the city would invoke quarantine measures that would severely damage Hamburg's trade. The Senate for its part was content to continue its long tradition of non-intervention. It had no contingency plans for an epidemic. Disinfection and isolation, it thought, were as useless as quarantine, and almost as expensive, so no plans for disinfection or isolation were drawn up. Hospitalization and burial could be dealt with as before, by the medical profession or by private citizens, so no plans were drawn up for these measures either. In any case, the years of frequent severe epidemics now seemed to be over. By 1892 almost two decades had passed by since the last visitation of Asiatic cholera, and even that had been a minor one by the standards of 1832 or 1849. No one suspected that cholera was about to strike again, with a ferocity and a severity unparalleled in all its previous history in the city.

By the early 1890s the spread of a railway network across the Russian Empire, from the Caucasus to Congress Poland, had provided cholera, a disease of the industrial age to the last, with an unprecedentedly swift new means of transport from Central Asia to the German border.[51] In 1892 a

[50] *Verhandlungen des ärztlichen Vereins zu Hamburg 1881–1890* (Hamburg, 1890).

[51] J. N. Westwood, *A History of Russian Railways* (London, 1964), p. 61. For detailed evidence of the transmission of cholera by railways, see P. Bourdelais and J. Y. Raulot, 'Sur le rôle des contacts interhumains dans la transmission du choléra, épidémies de 1832 et 1854', *Bulletin de la Société de Pathologie Exotique*, 71 (1978), 119–30.

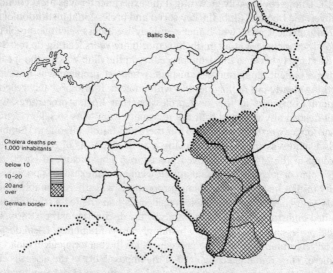

Source: StA Hbg, MK III W4, Bl. 136

MAP 25. Deaths from cholera on the Russo-German border, 1894

fresh outbreak spread from Afghanistan to Russia in this way, causing numerous deaths and widespread disturbances. It reached Moscow by July and Kiev
by the middle of August. Acting on the advice of Koch and the Imperial
Health Office, the Prussian authorities sealed the border, this time, as Map
25 suggests, with a good deal of success.[52] From 18 July migrants bound for
the United States via Hamburg and Bremen were transported across Germany
in special sealed trains. These were not allowed to stop except for technical
reasons, and the passengers were not allowed to alight at any intermediate
point on the journey. If by any chance they did so, the station was cleared
of people and disinfected after the train's departure. This device was to
be used again during the First World War, when the German authorities
transported the bacillus of Bolshevism across their territory in the form of
Lenin and his friends, returning from their Swiss exile to strife-torn Russia.
But in 1917 the German government had every hope that the ideological

[52] (G. Gaffky), *Amtliche Denkschrift über die Choleraepidemie, 1892* (Kaiserliches Gesundheitsamt,
Berlin, 1895), pp. 1–15; T. Deneke, 'Die Hamburger Choleraepidemie 1892', *ZHG* 49 (1949),
124–58, here pp. 128–9; N. M. Frieden, 'The Russian Cholera Epidemic, 1892–93, and Medical
Professionalisation', *Journal of Social History*, 10 (1977), 538–59. The effectiveness of border
controls is also shown (for 1892) by Map 27, below.

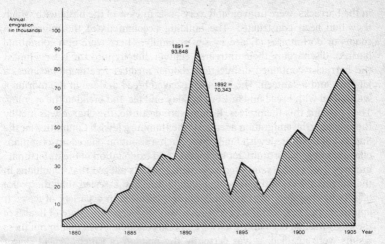

Source: Imre Ferenczi (ed.), *International Migrations*, Vol. I (New York, 1929), 808

FIG. 8. Russian citizens leaving Hamburg and Bremen for the USA, 1879–1905

infection would spread as fast as possible on reaching its destination. A quarter of a century earlier, in 1892, they did everything they could to extinguish the biological infection *en route*, by instituting regular medical checks and disinfection procedures on the trains.[53]

As Figure 8 indicates, unusually large numbers of migrants were travelling through Hamburg and Bremen at this time, driven by the famine of 1891–2 and the expulsion of Jews from Moscow early in 1892 to seek a new life across the Atlantic Ocean.[54] Special barracks, jointly financed by the Senate and the Hamburg–America Line, were built in the harbour to house these people before they embarked. The great majority of the migrants were transferred directly from the special trains into the barracks. Here they were immediately subjected to a medical examination and made to hand over their belongings for disinfection. 'A smaller number of emigrants who possessed sufficient means and wanted to stay in emigrants' lodging-houses in the city', as an official report noted, 'were released, after medical examination and disinfection, with the permission of the doctor.'[55] Provisions for the majority,

[53] (G. Gaffky), *Amtliche Denkschrift über die Choleraepidemie 1892*, p. 19.
[54] R. G. Robbins, *Famine in Russia 1891–1892* (New York, 1975), pp. 170–1. The total of overseas migrants leaving Hamburg in 1892 had reached 102,059 by the end of August (I. Ferenczi (ed.), *International Migrations* (New York, 1929), i. 808); StA Hbg, Auswanderungsamt II E IV, No. 9 Bd. 1; also StA Hbg, Auswanderungsamt E 1, No. 2 Bd. 1, Bl. 52 (Jahresbericht der Behörde für das Auswanderungswesen für das Jahr 1892).
[55] StA Hbg, Auswanderungsamt IE I, No. 2, Bd. II, Bl. 52 (Jahresbericht der Behörde für das Auswanderungswesen für das Jahr 1892).

in the barracks, were unavoidably very basic in view of the haste with which they had been constructed. The building accommodated the migrants in rooms or dormitories divided by sex or family. There were also communal latrines, discharging their untreated effluvia directly into the river. Finally, the barracks contained disinfection rooms, medical treatment facilities, a kitchen, and a canteen. The inmates received bread and tea in the morning, warm food with bread and meat at midday and tea and bread in the evening. They paid for this themselves. If they were destitute, the charge was met by the shippers, the emigration agents, or the Hamburg Jewish Committee for the Support of Destitute Jewish Emigrants. Such a situation offered unscrupulous officials ample opportunity for corruption and exploitation of the unfortunate inmates. Just over a year later, newspaper reports alleged that conditions in the barracks were filthy beyond description. They asserted that the police officers in charge of the emigrants had misbehaved in a variety of ways. It appeared that the doctor whose duty it was to oversee the state of health of the migrants had been dismissed for immoral conduct.[56] Whether or not these claims were justified, it was certainly the opinion of Chief Medical Officer Kraus that the medical examination to which the migrants were subjected on arrival at the barracks was less than thorough.[57]

In 1892 the authorities were confronted with the problem of preventing these migrants from bringing cholera with them from Russia to Hamburg. To make things more difficult, the medical authorities in the city were not convinced that there was any danger of the disease being brought in by this means. As we have seen, Kraus and the great majority of his subordinates were supporters of Pettenkofer's view that cholera could only strike as a result of local circumstances. The quarantine measures, the medical examinations, the disinfections, the sealed trains—these were all measures ordered by the Prussian authorities, or by the Imperial Health Office acting under the influence of Koch. As late as 20 August 1892, Kraus expressed his scepticism of the policy, proposed by Senator Hachmann the previous day, of isolating the migrants for observation in the barracks. He wrote that 'The benefits of isolation are illusory if the emigrants are released into the migrant lodging-houses in the city after what must always in the circumstances be a merely superficial observation in the sheds on the quay.'[58] Kraus was not so much concerned to stop these contacts as to prevent a policy of total isolation. Even when a policy of confining all new arrivals to the barracks was eventually adopted, on 22 August, the agents who were arranging their passage were still allowed to come and go as they pleased. Moreover, many of the migrants stayed in cheap lodging-houses in the inner-city Alley Quarters. A report

[56] StA Hbg, Auswanderungsamt II E II, No. 4, Bd. 1: *Hamburger Freie Presse*, 10 Oct. 1893 and 26 Jan. 1894.
[57] StA Hbg, Auswanderungsamt II E I, No. 1a 2, Bd. 1, Kraus to Hachmann.
[58] Ibid.

issued in May 1893 concluded that conditions in 10 out of the 39 emigrants' lodging-houses were bad, with dark rooms, narrow staircases, overcrowding, and unsatisfactory facilities. That is to say, over a quarter of the lodging-houses did not satisfy even the most basic hygiene requirements of the authorities. Twelve more, or just over 30%, were described as 'mediocre', including two located in the Niedernstrasse. Only a minority—fifteen, or just under 39%—were actually given the accolade of 'good'. It is more than likely that a number of these had made serious efforts to improve their facilities in the wake of the cholera epidemic. These lodging-houses operated on a very considerable scale, which is perhaps not surprising given the vast numbers of migrants with which the city had to deal. Altogether the 39 listed in the report of May 1893 could house 1,865 migrants, making an average of just under 48 each. There were still 142 migrants staying in such places in mid-September 1892.[59]

These migrants, as the authorities in Berlin noted in 1892, 'mostly came from areas where cholera has been widespread this year'.[60] From these areas, above all around Kiev, Podolie, Poltava, Chernigov, and Volhynia, some time in the second week of August, they brought the disease to Hamburg.[61] Soon

[59] StA Hbg, Auswanderungsamt II E V No. 1, Bd. 2, Bl. 55: report of 15 May 1893; ibid., Beiheft 2, Bl. 4. See also Plate 8.

[60] (G. Gaffky), *Amtliche Denkschrift über die Choleraepidemie 1892*, p. 18.

[61] The origin of the epidemic has long been a subject of controversy. Koch thought it came from Russian migrants (StA Hbg, FA Versmann VI A 6, entry for 26 Aug. 1892). He considered the sanitary arrangements in the barracks inadequate (reported in Deneke, 'Die Hamburger Choleraepidemie 1892', p. 139). Theodor Deneke, however, argued that it came via Le Havre from the Seine, which had been infected by waste from Pasteur's laboratories (op. cit., p. 131). He was in fact writing in 1941 under the impression of the Nazi conquest of France and probably still during the Nazi-Soviet pact, and his thesis, complete with a defence of Russian policy (p. 131) and references to New York as the 'capital city of world Jewry' (p. 129) bears clear marks of political bias. There was cholera in Paris and Le Havre in 1892, but there is no evidence that it was brought to Hamburg either by ship or by rail; and it had probably reached France by steamship from Syria, not from Pasteur's laboratory. Cholera only broke out in Le Havre on 15 Aug.. It could easily have been carried by train from Kiev in three days (Westwood, *Russian Railways*, pp. 90, 155, Appendix 11), reaching Hamburg within the incubation period. The first case was officially confirmed in Kiev on 16 Aug., so it was probably there on the 11th if not before, given the usual delays in official announcements. Deneke pointed out that there were no cases in the barracks until 25 Aug., but there were 22 cholera deaths on the *Moravia*, which set sail on 17 Aug. (none of them crew) (see below, pp. 316–17). There were also cases in the lodging-houses (StA Hbg, Auswanderungsamt II E I No. 2, Bd. 2, Bl. 52). The bacillus did not have to enter the harbour in vast quantities to infect the water upstream in the conditions of Aug. 1892, and it would have travelled upstream faster from the quays and the fleets than from French ships anchored downstream. Finally, in 1893 Deneke argued that the infection came from Russia, not France (StA Hbg, MK II F 5, Bl. 28, Deneke to Hachmann, 28 Feb. 1893). It is remarkable that his article, with its Nazi phraseology and thrust, could still be published, without amendment, in the journal of the Hamburg Historical Society in 1949 (*ZHG* 40 (1949), pp. 124–58); however, the leading figure in the local history establishment in Hamburg at this time, Professor Kurt Detlev Möller, Director of the Staatsarchiv, was dismissed for his openly expressed Nazi sympathies in 1948 (only to be reinstated in the early 1950s!). See Werner Skrenntny, ' "Hier war alles vernünftiger als anderswo". Hamburg und die Aufarbeitung der NS-Zeit', in GAL-Fraktion in der Hamburger Bürgerschaft (ed.), '*Es ist Zeit für die ganze Wahrheit' (K.v. Dohnanyi). Aufarbeitung der NS-Zeit in Hamburg: Die nichtveröffentlichte Senatsbroschüre* (Hamburg, 1985), pp. 17–47.

they had infected the harbour with the bacillus, from the primitive latrines in the barracks, from the chamber-pots and earth closets in use in the Alley Quarters where so many of them stayed, directly via the fleets, or by water-closets discharging through the sewage system into the river downstream. Probably the bacillus was in the harbour on 14 August and possibly as early as the 13th. In the harbour the bacillus found conditions that were ideal for it. The water was warm as a result of a long spell of very hot weather; a water temperature of 22°C was recorded in the river towards the end of the month. Now, therefore, once it had reached this hospitable environment, the bacillus began to multiply exponentially, with the astounding rapidity characteristic of micro-organisms in conditions ideally suited for their growth. It was already in the sewage system and its outlet above Altona by 15 August at the latest; at the same time it was in all likelihood swarming quickly upstream and downstream from the migrants' barracks and the mouths of the Alster and the fleets. It would only be a matter of time before the first cases were reported. The question was, would the danger be recognized quickly enough for action to be taken to stop the outbreak becoming a major epidemic?

4

The Great Epidemic

a. From Concealment to Catastrophe

I

THROUGHOUT July and August 1892 the civil and medical authorities in Hamburg were well aware that a new epidemic was threatening their city. Senator Johannes Versmann noted its approach anxiously in his diary as early as 3 August.[1] As we have seen, Koch's views on the causes of the disease, and the means by which it was spread, had been imposed upon the authorities everywhere. The responsible medical officers were obliged to investigate every suspicious case for signs of the presence of the cholera vibrio. But most doctors in Hamburg were without any experience in identifying the bacillus, and many 'could not bring themselves to the decision to take on the *very grave responsibility* of pronouncing the diagnosis "cholera Asiatica"'. Pressures on medical men in Hamburg to avoid such a diagnosis, with all the damage to trade implied by the quarantine measures that would inevitably follow, were, as we have seen, very strong. Indeed, in 1892 as in 1873, the policy of Chief Medical Officer Johann Caspar Kraus was to follow an 'absolutely definite plan' of not diagnosing isolated cases as cholera at all, and waiting until an epidemic had actually broken out before confirming the disease's presence.[2]

Cases of people suffering acute digestive disorders were common enough in the summer, and the local doctors probably groaned with irritation at having to go through the laborious process of investigating each one for the presence of the cholera vibrio. Nor were their investigations likely to have been characterized by any particular sense of urgency. And the question of diagnosis was bound up with all kinds of scientific and medical disputes which got in the way of a smooth application of Koch's methods. So it was when Dr Hugo Simon, a doctor in the neighbouring Prussian town of Altona, found a building worker, Sahling, whose job it was to inspect the sewage outlet and other constructions on the Kleiner Grasbrook, at three in the morning on the night of 14–15 August. Sahling had fallen ill suddenly on his way back from work, and was suffering violent spasms of vomiting and diarrhoea. Simon

---

[1] StA Hbg, FA Versmann, VI A 6, entries for 3 and 18 Aug. 1892.
[2] See above, p. 254.

immediately diagnosed Sahling as suffering from Asiatic cholera on 15 August. But Simon was at odds with his superior, Medical Officer Dr Wallichs, who he believed had blackballed him from the Hamburg Doctors' Club on the grounds of Simon's supposed anti-Prussian sympathies. Wallichs refused to accept his diagnosis without evidence of the presence of the bacillus. It was not found. Simon was obliged to note the cause of death, which occurred on 15 August, simply as 'vomiting with diarrhoea'.[3]

The next day, however, brought some indication that cases such as Sahling's were occurring with noticeable frequency even for the hot period of mid-August. In the night of 16–17 August, another building worker, the twenty-four-year-old mason Köhler, was brought into Eppendorf General Hospital in Hamburg exhibiting similar distressing symptoms. He died on the evening of the 17th. On the same day, a bacteriological investigation of his stool was set in motion under the direction of the hospital's director, Professor Theodor Rumpf, and his assistant Dr Rumpel. It revealed 'apart from many other micro-organisms, in particular the *bacterium coli*, some curved and remarkably large rod-shaped bacilli'. Puzzled by these unusual 'rod-shaped bacilli', which they had not seen before, Rumpf and his assistant decided to carry out an autopsy.[4] The doctor in charge of these operations, *Physikus* Dr Erman, was a decided opponent of Koch's views; indeed, he subsequently wrote an article ridiculing the idea that cholera was spread by means of the water-supply.[5] Erman noticed once more the presence of the 'rod-shaped bacilli'. He went on, therefore, to try and produce a culture of the bacillus. But he had still not managed to do this by 20 August.[6] Meanwhile, an increasing number of such cases were beginning to occur: two more on 16 August, four more on the 17th, and no fewer than twelve on the 18th.[7] Altogether 31 cases received medical attention on 19 August. And now, for the first time, doctors began to be seriously concerned. A private medical practitioner sent a warning that he suspected Asiatic cholera in one of his patients on Friday 19th, and several more such warnings reached the Chief Medical Officer for Hamburg, Dr Johann Caspar Kraus, on the 20th. As one doctor wrote a few days afterwards, 'I knew already on Saturday that there

[3] StA Hbg, Senat, Cl. VII, Lit. Ta, Pars 2, Vol. 11, Fasc 16, Inv 9, esp. Anlage 1 zu 8 (deposition of Simon, 10 Sept. 1892) Anlage 3 zu 8 (deposition of Reincke, 17 Sept. 1892), and Anlage zu 8a (deposition of Regierungspräsident Zimmermann, Schleswig, 26 Oct. 1892). J.J. Reincke, 'Die Cholera in Hamburg', *Deutsche Medizinische Wochenschrift*, 3–4 (1893), conceded the possibility that this might none the less have been the first case of cholera in Hamburg in 1892. See also the discussion in the official *Amtliche Denkschrift über die Choleraepidemie 1892*, by Georg Gaffky.

[4] See the report in StA Hbg, Senat, Cl. VII, Lit. Ta, Pars 2, Vol. 11, Fasc 16, Inv. 9, which attempts to clear up the circumstances of the epidemic's outbreak.

[5] *Hamburgischer Correspondent*, 9 Sept. 1892.

[6] StA Hbg, Senat, Cl. VII, Lit. Ta, Pars 2, Vol. II, Fasc 16, Inv 9, Anlage zu 7.

[7] The clearest account is that of Reincke, 'Die Cholera in Hamburg'. It provides the basis for the following paragraphs.

was no doubt about a diagnosis of cholera Asiatica.'[8] More generally, as we shall see, rumours of cholera were already rife in the city's population at large by this time.

On 19 August, the symptoms of cholera began to appear in the neighbouring city of Altona. Two people, a Swedish sailor and a Hamburg cigar worker, were taken ill on 19 August with every appearance of having been struck down by Asiatic cholera. The military physician Dr Weisser, who had considerable experience of bacteriological investigation, established a suspicion of the presence of the bacillus in the two men on 20 August. He immediately reported it to the Altona district physician. This was in strong contrast to the procedure adopted in Hamburg, where the responsible medical officers, including Rumpf, had been afraid to report even the 'suspicion' of Asiatic cholera, though the symptoms they had observed were more than merely suspicious. By this time further cases with the classic symptoms were appearing in the Altona Hospital. The District Medical Officer announced the probability of cholera to the police on 20 August. The Prussian governor of the province (Schleswig-Holstein) was formally telegraphed on the 21st, and he in turn notified the authorities in Berlin without delay.

While these moves were going on in Altona, events were occurring in Hamburg which would have been farcical had they not been taking place in a context of such tragic potential. At the Eppendorf General Hospital, as Dr Erman was continuing to pore over his bacteriological culture plates, cases displaying the unmistakable features of Asiatic cholera were coming in with increasing frequency. One of them was a twenty-year-old worker, Rubbert, from Wilhelmsburg, admitted on 21 August. On the morning of the 22nd the presence of the bacilli was established in Rubbert's stool. Professor Rumpf, now thoroughly alarmed, went to the Old Hospital at St Georg, where five cases of this sort had been admitted the previous night. By the time he got back, the decisive breakthrough had occurred. On his return from holiday on 22 August, Dr Eugen Fraenkel had descended upon the unfortunate Dr Erman and had taken over the plates on which he was still trying to cultivate bacilli obtained from investigations of the original case of the mason Köhler, who had been admitted six days before. Fraenkel, who was familiar with Koch's methods, succeeded in a few hours in carrying out the task that Erman had been unable to perform for almost a week. By midday on 22 August Fraenkel had produced pure cultures of the bacillus not only from the autopsy of Köhler but also from investigations carried out on other victims, including one brought in the same morning. No doubt inspired, or instructed by Fraenkel, Erman himself managed to produce a pure culture of the bacillus on the 22nd

[8] StA Hbg, Senat, Cl. VII, Lit. Ta, Pars 2, Vol. 11, Fasc. 17, Inv. 4: *Die Post*, 235 (28 Aug. 1892).

as well, from samples from a worker, Koch, who had been admitted on the 19th.

This sudden flurry of activity on 21 and 22 August meant that an official announcement of the presence of Asiatic cholera was now only a matter of hours away. Yet the chapter of fateful and absurd delays had not yet come to an end. On 20 August Erman had told Dr Kraus, Hamburg's Chief Medical Officer, that the bacillus had been found in the samples from which he subsequently succeeded in developing a culture on the 22nd. Kraus, however, was still operating to the 'absolutely definite plan', last used in 1873, of not taking cognizance of individual cases. So he did nothing. He did not even pass on the news to his superior, Senator Gerhard Hachmann, President of the Medical Board. He could feel strengthened in his resolve to do nothing by the fact that Rumpf had officially diagnosed Köhler's ailment as *cholera nostras*, not true Asiatic cholera, on the evening of the 20th. Now, on the morning of 22 August, however, Rumpf arrived at Kraus's office to inform him that Asiatic cholera was indeed present in the city. The symptoms, he said, were unmistakable, and the bacilli had already been found in a number of cases. Fraenkel and Erman were already working on the cultures and one of the plates was already showing suspicious, if not absolutely incontrovertible signs of growth. There was no doubt, therefore, as Rumpf told Kraus, that this was Asiatic cholera. But Kraus refused to give any official response to the news. Rumpf, in a rage, returned to the Eppendorf Hospital and sent Kraus an official state telegram announcing the presence of the disease. Though hardly necessary in terms of communicating the information, which Rumpf had imparted to Kraus in person less than an hour before, this action put the announcement in black and white and made it open, official, and impossible to ignore. So Kraus left his office in the early afternoon and made his way to Senator Hachmann, to whom he duly announced the 'suspicion' that the disease was present. He added, however, that unless a pure culture of the bacillus could be obtained, the suspicion could not be confirmed and no further action should be taken.[9]

Meanwhile, as Kraus was talking with the Senator, a second telegram arrived at his office. It was from Rumpf, announcing that Fraenkel had succeeded, where the others, including himself, had failed in producing a pure culture of the cholera bacillus from the stool of one of the victims. It is not certain whether Kraus returned to his office the same afternoon and read the telegram, or whether he simply went home. Whatever the case, it was not until the morning of 23 August that he got around to communicating Fraenkel's confirmation of the disease to Senator Hachmann and the auth-

[9] For these events, see Reincke, 'Die Cholera in Hamburg'; T. Rumpf, *Lebenserinnerungen* (Gotha, 1925), pp. 42–3; StA Hbg, FA Versmann, VI A 6, entry for 8 Sept. 1892; T. Rumpf, 'Die Cholera in den Hamburgischen Krankenanstalten', *Jahrbuch der Hamburgischen Staatskrankenanstalten*, 3 (1891–2), pp. 34–7.

orities in Berlin. Hamburg's collegial system of government meant that Hachmann could do nothing on his own initiative. All decisions had to be taken by the Senate in plenary session. So there would in any case have been no point in announcing the presence of the disease on the 22nd, since the Senate was not due to meet until two days later. It was sufficient for Hachmann to report it on the 23rd, in time to get the item onto the agenda for the regular Senate meeting on the 24th.[10]

While all this was going on, Dr Kraus and Senator Hachmann still refused to admit the presence of the disease in public. Indeed on 22 August Hachmann explicitly assured the American Vice-Consul Charles Burke that there was no cholera in Hamburg.[11] Around the same time—it is unfortunately not possible to ascertain the exact date—Friedrich Werner, Assistant Pastor in South Hamm, had a similar experience with one of Hachmann's colleagues.

One morning as I was saying goodbye to Senator Schemmann in the rural district administration office [*he wrote in his memoirs*), he took me aside and asked me to calm people in my circle of acquaintances if there should be any talk of an outbreak of Asiatic cholera in Hamburg, and to explain the real situation to them. He could assure me that there was no Asiatic cholera in Hamburg. But the Senator, as I was to learn by personal experience on the very same day, was absolutely wrong.

For immediately on returning to his parish, Werner was called to administer the last rites to a woman in the neighbourhood, and the doctor, passing him on the staircase, told him that it was beyond doubt Asiatic cholera that the woman was suffering from. She died the same night, and Werner was called to several other cases the next day. There is no corroboration for Werner's story, but the fact that Hachmann was doing exactly the same thing as Schemmann on 22 August makes it seem plausible enough.[12]

By this time the medical authorities and the Senate had been overtaken by the Prussian government and the Imperial Health Office. The Altona medical officials who had already established the presence of the disease on the 21st, two days previously, had set the wheels of the Prussian and Imperial governments in motion. On the same day the Prussian Minister of Health had been notified of the presence of cholera in Altona by the governor of Schleswig-Holstein. He had ordered cultures of the bacillus to be sent to Robert Koch in Berlin, adding that all measures necessary to deal with a full-scale epidemic should be taken without delay. On 22 August Dr Weisser went by train from Altona to Berlin with the culture of the cholera bacillus (fortunately, his fellow-passengers were presumably unaware of what he was carrying!). Koch examined it in his laboratory and on the same day assured the Minister that

[10] StA Hbg. FA Versmann, VI A 6, entry for 26 Aug. 1892.

[11] *Export*, 40 (6 Sept. 1892).

[12] Kirchenarchiv Hg, D166: Pastor Friedrich Werner, 'Erinnerungen aus meiner Amtstätigkeit in der Gemeinde Süd-Hamm' (MS 1937), pp. 22–3.

cholera had indeed broken out in Altona. Early on 23 August the Minister ordered Koch to travel to Hamburg to investigate the 'cholera-like' symptoms reported in recent cases there. All of this took place before the Hamburg authorities had managed to get round to announcing the presence of the disease on their side of the Hamburg–Altona boundary. It was not until later on the same day, 23 August, that the Imperial Health Office in Berlin was officially informed by Hachmann and Kraus that there was a cholera epidemic in Hamburg, and not until the 24th, at least eight days after the first case, that the Senate met to consider what to do.[13]

Had the first case of cholera been diagnosed on 18 August, as it should have been, the Senate might possibly have been able to issue warnings to the city's inhabitants to take precautionary measures such as boiling their drinking-water. By the 24th, it was too late. At this time North Germany was going through a prolonged heat wave, and the river level was so low that the tide was pushing even further upstream than usual. In this environment, with the water at 22°C, the cholera bacilli multiplied with extraordinary rapidity. Soon they were pouring into the river with the excreta of infected boatmen and bargees miles above the harbour. By 19 or 20 August at the latest, they were also pouring into the main intake of Hamburg's central water-supply.[14] As we saw in Chapter 2, numerous objections and delays had meant that the filtration system proposed for the central water-supply in the 1870s had only been approved in 1890. It was not due to come into operation until 1894. The water was taken directly from the river into reservoirs. From there, it was pumped straight into the city's houses at a rate of up to 160,000 cubic metres a day. A heat wave such as that of August 1892 probably meant that it was being consumed even more heavily than usual, while the low level of the Elbe meant that an unusually high proportion of the river-water was being extracted. So once the river-water was infected as far upstream as Rothenburgsort, where the intake for the central water-supply was situated, it would only have been a matter of hours before it reached people's houses. Most probably it was already coming through the taps of domestic users by 19 or 20 August. The results were not long in making themselves manifest. By 23 August every area in the city was affected. Thousands of people had unsuspectingly drunk the contaminated water, and soon they began to fall ill with the symptoms of cholera and to infect each other. Fruit and other

[13] (G. Gaffky), *Amtliche Denkschrift über die Choleraepidemie 1892*, pp. 3–4; also StA Hbg, Senat, Cl. VII, Lit. Ta, Pars 2, Vol 11, Fasc 16, Inv. 9, for these events.

[14] T. Deneke, 'Die Hamburger Choleraepidemie 1892', *ZHG* 49 (1949), pp. 124–58 (here p. 135), following *Amtliche Denkschrift über die Choleraepidemie 1892*, suggests that the bacillus entered the water-supply as early as 17 Aug., but neither author presents any evidence to back up this claim. Deneke's suggestion that it was only on the 19th that the bacillus infected the water-supply 'to its full extent' is more easy to accept. The really explosive increase of the disease began on 25 Aug., so counting back a maximum incubation period of 5 days, with the addition of a day or so for the water to reach the taps from the river, gives us the 19th. See Reincke, 'Die Cholera in Hamburg', pp. 10–12, 14.

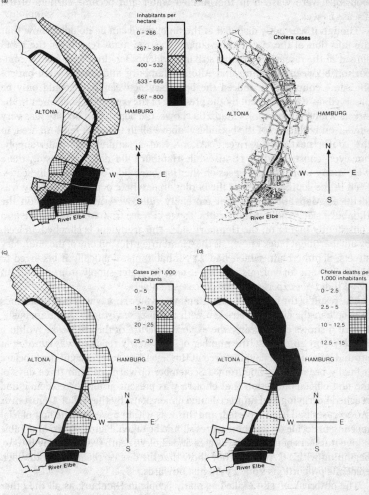

Boundary between Hamburg and Altona

(a) Population density on the Hamburg–Altona boundary, December 1891 (Hamburg), December 1890 (Altona)
(b) Cholera on the Hamburg–Altona boundary August–November 1892: individual cases
(c) Cholera on the Hamburg–Altona boundary August–November 1892: morbidity rates
(d) Cholera on the Hamburg–Altona boundary August–November 1892: mortality rates

Source: T. Deneke, 'Nachträgliches zur Hamburger Cholera-Epidemie', *Münchener Medizinische Wochenschrift*, 41 (1895), 6–7

MAP 26. Cholera on the Hamburg–Altona boundary, August–November 1892

foodstuffs were washed in the infected water and became carriers of the disease as well.

Though it was hotly disputed at the time, there can be no doubt now that the infection of the city's water-supply was the main reason for the rapid spread of the disease. The most striking evidence for this came from a comparison between Hamburg and Altona. Hamburg and Altona were part of the same conurbation, indeed the boundary between them could only be observed, as we have seen, by the presence of the patrolling policemen in the streets which it crossed. As Map 26a shows, the population density was very similar on both sides of the boundary, above all in the most built-up area, in the south, next to the river.[15] Altona had a sand-filtered water-supply, however, constructed in 1859, while Hamburg did not. As a result, there were many more cholera cases on the Hamburg side, as Map 26b indicates. Even in the southern parts of the border area, where population density was identical, Map 26c shows that morbidity rates were much higher on the Hamburg side. And mortality rates, as we can see from Map 26d, were also consistently higher on the Hamburg side. The argument is clinched, indeed, by an apartment block known as the 'Hamburger Hof' on one of the boundary streets, Schulterblatt, which had 345 inhabitants. Politically it belonged to Hamburg, but for various reasons it took its water-supply from Altona. In 1892 it did not experience a single case of cholera.[16]

The result of the infection of the Hamburg water-supply was that thousands of people in the city were stricken with the disease virtually simultaneously. Figure 9 shows quite clearly the explosive nature of the outbreak. Within a few days, on 26 August, the number of cases newly reported was running at around a thousand a day. It stayed at this level for a total of eight days, before it finally began to decline from 2 September onwards. Within three days of the first official admission that cholera was present at all, the epidemic had reached horrifying and unprecedented dimensions. By the end of August over 7,000 cases had been reported: and this was within a week of the first official meeting to decide on what measures should be taken. Figures 9–10 and Table 4 give numbers of new cholera cases and cholera deaths reported day by day, beginning with 16 August. They show that the disease really began to reach epidemic proportions from 25 August onwards.[17]

The outbreak of 1892 killed as many people in Hamburg as all the other

[15] The map was originally compiled by the Prussian army doctor Schumberg in Oct. 1892. The fact that investigations at this time failed to discover bacilli in the water-supply was used by miasmatists to support their case, but was in reality a consequence of inadequate investigation. When by error a small quantity of infected water entered the supply in the autumn of 1893, the presence of the bacillus was clearly demonstrated in the river, the water pipes, and in domestic water tanks. See J. Dunbar, 'Zum derzeitigen Stand der Wasserversorgungsverhältnisse im hamburgischen Staatsgebiete'. *Vierteljahresschrift für öffentliche Gesundheitspflege*, 37 (1905), 537–80.

[16] Deneke, 'Die Hamburger Choleraepidemie 1892', p. 142.

[17] For more detailed analysis of the reliability of the official figures, see the Statistical Appendix.

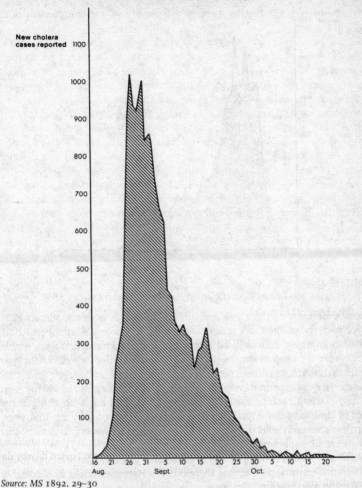

Source: MS 1892, 29–30

FIG. 9. Cholera cases in Hamburg, August–October 1892

cholera epidemics of the nineteenth century combined. The proportion of the population that died was 13.4‰, at least according to the official statistics; it may have been higher. This was much greater than in 1832 or 1848. In comparison with cholera outbreaks at other times and other places, however, the epidemic in Hamburg in 1892 appears somewhat less severe. True, cholera mortality rates in London never exceeded 6.6 deaths per 1,000 population even in the worst epidemic, that of 1849. But in Glasgow in 1832

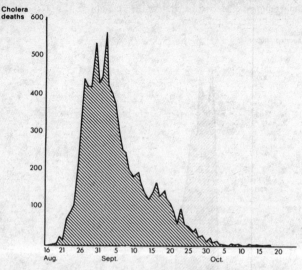

Source: MS 1892, 29–30

FIG. 10. Deaths from cholera in Hamburg, August–October 1892

cholera mortality ran at 15‰, and in Paris in the same year it was 21.8‰. More severely affected still was Dublin, with 30 cholera deaths per 1,000 population. These figures paled before those of Stockholm in 1834, where there were 43 cholera deaths per 1,000 population, or St Petersburg two years earlier, where cholera mortality also reached the 40‰ level. And even these high rates appeared insignificant compared to those suffered by Hungary in 1873, when cholera mortality reached 65‰. Half a million Hungarians died of cholera and the total population of the country fell by 2% that year. The most severely affected area so far uncovered by historians was not in Europe at all, but across the Atlantic, in Montreal, where one in every thirteen inhabitants died of cholera in 1832, a mortality rate of 74‰. Seen in a broad nineteenth-century perspective, therefore, the Hamburg cholera epidemic of 1892 was by no means startlingly severe.[18]

Yet in terms of its impact on the city itself the epidemic appears in an altogether different light. Figure 11 gives the crude monthly death rate in Hamburg, from all causes, between 1886 and 1893. In no month apart from August and September 1892 did it exceed a rate of 3 per 1,000 population,

[18] R. J. Morris, *Cholera 1832: The Social Response to an Epidemic* (London, 1968), pp. 80–3; M. Durey, *The Return of the Plague. British Society and the Cholera 1831–2* (Dublin, 1979), p. 52; L. Madai, 'Les Crises de mortalité en Europe dans la deuxième moitié du XIXe siècle', in H. Charbonneau and A. Larose (eds.), *The Great Mortalities: Methodological Studies of Demographic Crises in the Past* (Liège, 1979), pp. 157–70; J.-C. Robert, 'Le Choléra de 1832 dans le Bas-Canada: mesures des inégalités devant la mort', ibid., pp. 229–56.

Table 4. Daily reported cholera cases and deaths, Hamburg 1892

Date	Cases	Deaths	Date	Cases	Deaths
16 Aug.	2	—	15 Sept.	294	141
17	4	2	16	344	167
18	12	—	17	285	130
19	31	8	18	221	143
20	66	24	19	237	126
21	113	17	20	192	112
22	249	70	21	171	94
23	338	89	22	160	59
24	358	107	23	134	96
25	608	218	24	109	59
26	903	313	25	91	52
27	1,024	414	26	70	44
28	936	427	27	69	45
29	925	428	28	58	26
30	1,008	537	29	36	27
31	850	435	30	46	16
1 Sept.	863	444	1 Oct.	23	22
2	843	561	2	26	11
3	732	426	3	15	11
4	664	402	4	17	10
5	627	371	5	13	7
6	446	308	6	6	2
7	430	257	7	9	6
8	362	249	8	15	5
9	337	202	9	8	5
10	351	185	10	1	4
11	325	197	11	14	2
12	317	168	12	2	5
13	241	140	13	5	3
14	286	125	14	8	4

From 15 Oct. to 12 Nov.: 26 cases, 20 deaths
To 19 Sept.: 16,944 cases, 8,594 deaths
To 12 Nov.: 16,956 cases, 8,605 deaths
Source: MS 1892, pp. 29–30.

not even in the typhoid epidemic of 1887. By contrast, the gross mortality rate in August 1892, at nearly 8‰, was some four times as high as what we normally would have expected. In September, at almost 12‰, it was nearly six times the normal rate. 55% of all deaths in August were from cholera: in September it caused 70% of all deaths. Another way of assessing the impact of cholera on mortality rates is to calculate what is known as *excess mortality* for 1892. Taking the average annual death rate from all causes over the preceding period, how much greater was the death rate from all causes in 1892? If we construct an index of annual mortality with the mean for 1882–

[19] Calculated from *SHS* 20 (1902), Uebersicht 1E (pp. 12–13). See also *MS* 1892, Table 15 h/i. Excess mortality in 1831 was 122, in 1832 it was 136, and in 1849 it was 127 (calculated from *SHS* 20, loc. cit., and *Beiträge zur Statistik Hamburgs* (Verein für hamburgische Statistik, Hamburg 1854), Table 5). In all these years, the cholera mortality rate was lower (see above, Figure 7).

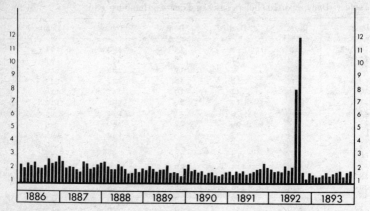

Source: MS 1892, 16

FIG. 11. Monthly death rates (per 1,000 inhabitants) for Hamburg, 1886–93

91 as 100, then the figure for 1892 is 160.[19] By this measure, the impact of cholera on mortality patterns in Hamburg in 1892 was quite considerable. Cholera in 1892 was not simply replacing other causes of mortality, it was adding to them. It represented a considerable, measurable extra burden of suffering and death.

Of course other serious diseases, like tuberculosis, took a heavy toll, month by month, year in, year out, rather than striking in spectacular but isolated outbreaks as cholera did. From 1872 to 1895, for example, tuberculosis killed over 46,000 people in Hamburg, and even diphtheria nearly 9,000, while cholera accounted for a total of only 9,631. But in 1892 cholera outdid all other causes of death, despite the fact that it was effectively confined to only one and a half months out of a total of twelve. Figure 12 gives the absolute numbers of deaths from the eight major causes of death in Hamburg in 1892. It represents in fact a transitional stage in the art, or science, of diagnosis, where some 'causes' of death, especially among infants, were merely descriptions of symptoms.[20] With this reservation, however, the figures give a roughly accurate impression of the major causes of death in Hamburg in 1892. Only the various infant ailments, taken together, came anywhere near causing the number of deaths brought about by cholera. Even some of these, especially in the category 'vomiting with diarrhoea', were probably cholera cases.[21] Among predominantly adult diseases, tuberculosis, that great scourge of the nineteenth century, caused less than a fifth as many deaths as cholera,

[20] See A. E. Imhof, *Die gewonnenen Jahre. Von der Zunahme unserer Lebensspanne seit dreihundert Jahren, oder, von der Notwendigkeit einer neuen Einstellung zu Leben und Sterben. Ein historischer Essay* (Munich, 1981), pp. 219–23.

[21] For a full discussion of problems of diagnosis, see the Statistical Appendix.

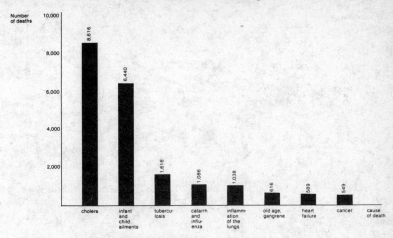

Note: 'Infant and child ailments' includes deaths from 'weakness of the newborn' (1,059), 'convulsions' (905), wasting (1,683), and 'vomiting with diarrhoea' (2,793), all in children aged 0–5. Many of the cases of 'vomiting with diarrhoea' in August and September were probably cholera (see the Statistical Appendix, below)

Source: SHS 19 (1902), 12–13

FIG. 12. The eight major causes of death in Hamburg, 1892

while the major killers of the twentieth century, heart failure and cancer, were still relatively insignificant in their impact. Even if we assume that the great majority of tuberculosis cases were lung infections, and put them together with the fourth and fifth major causes of death (catarrh and influenza, and inflammation of the lungs) to form a more general category of respiratory diseases, the total number of deaths in this category—3,740—is still less than half the number of deaths caused by cholera in 1892. The sharpness of cholera's impact compared to that of endemic diseases can be measured by the calculation that, had cholera struck Hamburg in 1892 with only the same, relatively mild impact with which it had hit the city two decades previously, in 1873, it would still have constituted the major cause of death in that year apart from infant and child ailments. But the impact of cholera in 1892 was more than four times greater than in 1873.[22] Its overall impact on mortality rates was correspondingly much more serious in 1892 than 1873.

The impact of cholera on Hamburg in 1892 was immeasurably heightened

---

[22] *Die Gesundheitsverhältnisse Hamburgs im 19. Jahrhundert* (Hamburg, 1901), pp. 128–9 and 151, and 'Ueber die Tuberkulose in Hamburg und ihre Bekämpfung', *Sonder-Abdruck aus dem Hamburgischen Correspondent* (Hamburg, 1896).

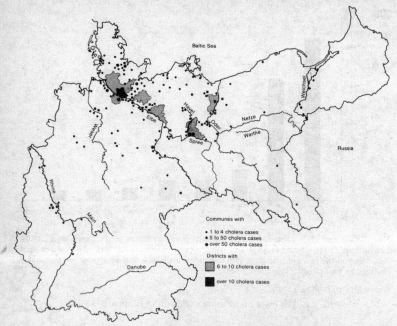

Source: (Georg Gaffky), *Amtliche Denkschrift über die Cholera-Epidemie 1892* (Berlin, 1895)

MAP 27. Cholera in the German Empire, 1892

by the fact that no other German or indeed West European city suffered a major epidemic in this year. As Map 27 shows, the disease was concentrated above all in Hamburg and the surrounding areas, and along the Elbe. Almost all cases in the rest of Germany were a result of infection from Hamburg, not from elsewhere. Even the endangered areas along the Russian border stayed immune. The overwhelming majority of cases and deaths, as a comparison of Figure 13 with Figures 9 and 10 reveals, were in Hamburg. There were many reasons why the rest of the Empire was able to avoid the disease. The quarantine imposed on the borders was initially the most important factor. Hamburg was particularly vulnerable because of the traffic in Russian migrants. But so too was Hamburg's sister-city of Bremen, of all towns in Germany the most nearly comparable. A comparison with the experience of Bremen in 1892 therefore will serve to point up more precisely the reasons for Hamburg's unique prominence in the cholera epidemic of that year.

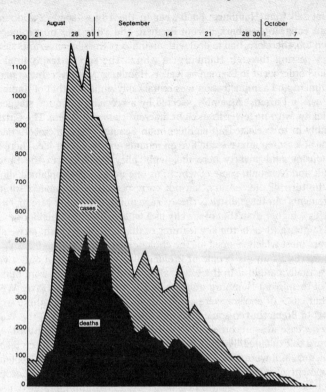

Source: (Georg Gaffky), *Amtliche Denkschrift über die Choleraepidemie 1892* (Berlin, 1895)

FIG. 13. Cholera in the German Empire, 1892

II

The Hanseatic town of Bremen was less than a third the size of Hamburg, with just under 180,000 inhabitants in 1890. But it made up for this by its activities as a trading centre, in which it more than held its own in competition with its sister port. Bremen's shipping company, the North German Lloyd, hated rival of the Hamburg–America line, was a major carrier of transatlantic migrants. From 1881 to 1885 a total of 127,000 non-German emigrants left Bremen, nearly all destined for the Americas. This number was not far short of the 190,000 who left Hamburg in the same five years. By the turn of the century, indeed, Bremen had overtaken its rival, dispatching 680,000 non-German emigrants to overseas ports in 1901–5 compared to only 480,000 who set sail from Hamburg. Each year in the 1890s, some 25,000 non-German emigrants embarked from Bremen, and 1892 was no exception.[23] Bremen too, therefore, had to deal with an influx of Russian emigrants similar to that passing through Hamburg in 1892. The special trains from the Russian border went to Bremen as well as Hamburg. Moreover, the system of government and administration was remarkably similar to that of Hamburg. There was a Citizens' Assembly, elected by a procedure of quite staggering complexity, with no fewer than eight different classes of voters. The Citizens' Assembly in turn elected an eighteen-man Senate, whose members had to include at least ten lawyers and five merchants and served for life. There was bad housing and poverty here too, with 'alley dwellings' in the Bremen Altstadt and Neustadt, some of which, as one authority complained shortly after the turn of the century, 'do not correspond even to modest sanitary requirements'. In these districts the average annual mortality rate in 1890–4 was 33% higher than that of the city as a whole.[24] Bremen therefore shared with Hamburg three of the key features of that city's life which, as we shall see, were most widely blamed for the cholera epidemic.

Yet in 1892 only six people in Bremen died of cholera, and only two of them actually caught it in the town: all the rest brought it in from outside, three of them from Hamburg and the fourth by barge up the River Weser. No other cases of cholera were confirmed in the town, except these six. In the port of Bremerhaven some miles downriver, at the mouth of the Weser, only one case was recorded.[25] How can this astonishing contrast with Hamburg be explained? A combination of factors seems to have been responsible, acting, as it were, like a series of safety nets at each stage in the potential development of an epidemic. In the first place, the medical profession in Bremen seems to have been much better organized and more alert to the dangers of an epidemic than its counterpart in Hamburg. As early as 1883, the Bremen Doctors' Club had debated the achievements of the new science of bacteriology.[26] In 1884 some of the local doctors had taken part in Robert Koch's course in Berlin on the cholera bacillus, its culture, and measures to be taken against it—though in 1892 the Bremen police obviously thought it advisable for such a course to be repeated.[27] As a result, elaborate preparations were made in the same year for protection against infectious diseases. A Quarantine Office was set up in Bremerhaven, yellow flags were stockpiled,

[23] H. Tjaden (ed.), *Bremen in hygienischer Beziehung* (Bremen, 1907). pp. 29, 381–2. The other Hanseatic city, Lübeck, was much smaller and had little to do with the emigration traffic.

[24] H. Schwarzwälder, *Geschichte der Freien Hansestadt Bremen* (Bremen, 1976), ii. 221; Tjaden, *Bremen in hygienischer Beziehung* pp. 172–3.

[25] StA Bremen, 3-M. 1. r. 18–5, notice of 8 Sept. 1892; (G. Gaffky) *Amtliche Denkschrift über die Choleraepidemie 1892*, pp. 9–10.

[26] H. Tjaden, *Bremen und die Bremische Ärzteschaft seit dem Beginne des 19. Jahrhunderts* (Bremen, 1932), pp. 132–3.

[27] StA Bremen, 3-M. 1. r. 18–1, 24 Aug. 1892 (Polizeidirektion Bremen to Senator Marcus).

a disinfection machine was purchased, and isolation barracks were established. At Bremerhaven it was easy to stop ships before they reached Bremen; traffic in general, indeed, was easier to control on the Weser than it was on the Elbe.[28] The medical profession in Bremen seems to have had full support from the Senate in these questions. They co-operated in responding quickly and positively to the flood of warnings of the approaching epidemic sent by Caprivi's office in the summer of 1892. Already on 15 July the Senate made contingency plans for the erection of a special cholera hospital. On 21 July it announced special administrative arrangements for the immediate reporting of any *suspected* cases of cholera.[29] This was important. It meant that the Bremen Senate and medical authorities would not wait for a full diagnosis to be achieved—though even that was likely to be reached more quickly than in Hamburg. Any cases even suspected of being cholera would immediately be placed in the isolation barracks, where the bacteriological diagnosis would then be carried out. In this procedure they were following long-established Prussian practice, and it is clear indeed that as a smaller, less wealthy town than Hamburg, Bremen was far less able to protect its own traditions and had been far less stubbornly particularist. Ever since the early 1870s it had been Hamburg that had taken the lead in preserving Hanseatic traditions, including those which Bremen had proved unable to defend for itself. By the early 1890s, Bremen was following the Prussian model in the fight against infectious disease. There was a general acceptance of cholera's infectious qualities. Accordingly, the civil and medical authorities had confidence in the effectiveness of quarantine and isolation. A major cholera epidemic, they thought, would be far more damaging to the city's interests than the temporary inconvenience of trade restrictions. Their belief that cholera was spread by its victims led the Bremen authorities to place a high priority on prompt and comprehensive preventive measures. This meant acting on the merest suspicion of cholera, rather than waiting for the results of a full diagnosis.[30]

The vigilance of the Bremen authorities continued through late July. On the 27th, tighter controls were imposed on the Russian migrants. From now on they could only stay in approved lodging-houses, at least until early August. The Quarantine Office in Bremerhaven was on special alert from 9 August.[31] On 11 August the Senate distributed to the local press an elaborate, officially approved set of instructions on how to avoid catching cholera. Readers were warned against eating fruit and advised to boil milk and water

---

[28] Ibid., 3-Q. 1. b. 1. *passim.*; H. Falliner, 'Zur historischen Entwicklung des Bremischen Quarantänedienstes', *Bremer Ärzteblatt*, 9 (1978), 36–52; and ibid., 3-Q. 1. b. 3, *passim.*

[29] Ibid., 3-M. 1. r. 18–1, reports and correspondence of 15, 21, and 27 July.

[30] Ibid., 18–2. For another example of the greater tenacity of Hamburg's particularism, see p. 35 above.

[31] Ibid., 18–1, reports and correspondence of 27 July and 9 Aug.

before drinking it. Cholera, the notice declared, was carried in the evacuations of the sick, and people should wash and disinfect their hands frequently. Public gatherings were to be avoided and no one should take in visitors from areas already infected.[32] This advice was repeated in a major publicity campaign on 26 and 27 August.[33] What is particularly impressive is that it had already been issued publicly and officially in Bremen long before the outbreak of the epidemic in Hamburg. Once the epidemic there had begun, the Bremen authorities were even more vigorous, banning markets and dances,[34] ordering an immediate medical quarantine on trains from Hamburg from 24 August, and carrying out carefully all the vast mass of instructions now flowing in from Berlin.[35] A Bremen Senator attended a special meeting called by Koch in Berlin on 27 August, and when Koch himself visited the city on 3 September he seemed to be satisfied that all the necessary steps had been taken.[36] Even this much, as we shall see, was beyond the Hamburg authorities, who proved initially unable to respond to the advice sent from Berlin. But this was less important than the fact that many precautions were already in force in Bremen well before the outbreak of the disease. The question, as we have seen, was not so much how Bremen avoided catching the disease from Hamburg, as how Bremen avoided catching it at the same time, and from the same causes. Here, in the greater vigilance of the medical authorities, we have at least part of the answer.

Thus people in Bremen were forewarned. They were already taking precautions by early August. Those few suspected cholera cases that did occur in the city were immediately isolated in the cholera barracks constructed earlier in the summer. Even had they escaped the attention of the authorities, however, and infected the Weser with the bacillus, the town had a second line of defence. Up to 1873 the people of Bremen had taken their water from public and private drinking wells. By that time the growth of the town's population had long outstripped the capacity of these wells to provide it with an adequate supply of water. As a result of a decision taken in 1857, a central water-supply system was constructed between 1871 and 1873. Part of the reason for the long delay between the decision and its execution was the fact that initial attempts to obtain naturally filtered water, on the lines of the Hamburg system in operation until 1893, proved unsuccessful. The water was taken from the Weser not far upstream from the town, but in experimental storage reservoirs it became mixed with water from the water-table and the resulting supply was undrinkable because of its high iron content.

[32] Ibid., 18–5, *Bremer Courier*, 221, 11 Aug. 1892.
[33] Ibid., *Weser Zeitung*, 27 Aug. and poster of 26 Aug.
[34] Ibid., 18–4 and 18–8. The same can be said of Lübeck. See D. Helm, *Die Cholera in Lübeck. Epidemieprophylaxe und -bekämpfung im 19. Jahrhundert* (Kieler Beiträge zur Geschichte der Medizin und Pharmazie, 16, Neumünster, 1979), pp. 52–62.
[35] StA Bremen, 3-M. 1. r. 18–1, notice of 24 Aug.
[36] Ibid., reports of 24 Aug. and 3 Sept.

No method existed at the time for removing iron from water, so it was decided instead to construct a sand-filtrated water-supply. As we have seen, this method of filtration was by far the most effective means of preventing bacilli entering the water. The new system provided immediate dividends as the typhoid morbidity rate declined rapidly from 6.7 cases per 1,000 population in 1872 to 3.9‰ in 1873 and 0.7‰ in 1877, after which the disease virtually disappeared. In 1875, 5,000 houses were connected to the mains, and by 1890 it was reaching the great majority of households in the city. Thus, quite unintentionally, Bremen had secured its drinking-water against Asiatic cholera.[37]

Even had this not been the case, it is likely that Bremen's population would have been significantly protected against secondary infection—the passing-on of the disease from one person to another—by another respect in which it differed from Hamburg, indeed a feature of the town that was unique in Germany. For Bremen, partly because of its relatively slow pace of growth, more because of peculiar local traditions, was a town of one-family houses. Even as late as 1900, no building in Bremen was inhabited by more than ten households, and over half of all the buildings used for living purposes consisted of only one household. The number of inhabitants per house in Berlin in 1900 averaged just over 50, in Hamburg it was in excess of 23, but in Bremen it totalled less than 8. These houses were not necessarily hygienic or well-built, and at least a third of the so-called one-family houses seem to have been used by more than one family. But when all these criticisms have been made, it remains the case that overcrowding on the scale on which it existed in many parts of Hamburg was virtually unknown in Bremen, even in the hygienically unsatisfactory houses of Bremen's Altstadt and Neustadt. Thus even had a cholera epidemic broken out in the town, it would have been slower to spread, and thus easier to contain, than the epidemic in Hamburg.[38]

The experience of Bremen and the rest of Germany outside Hamburg in 1892 underlines the effectiveness of the precautions advised by Koch. Certainly, as the historian Reinhard Spree has pointed out, quarantine, disinfection, and isolation, as practised earlier in the century, were far from satisfactory. But the evidence from 1892 and 1894 suggests that the state had managed to achieve an effective degree of application of these methods by the last decade of the century. After rejecting the influence of quarantine, disinfection, and isolation on the mortality rates of infectious diseases, Spree goes on to claim that a much clearer impact could be observed in the case of sewage disposal and water-supply. In particular, he regards the provision of

[37] Tjaden, *Bremen in hygienischer Beziehung*, pp. 62–4. Lübeck's water supply had been filtered since 1867 (Helm, *Die Cholera in Lübeck*, pp. 10–11).
[38] Helm. op. cit., pp. 165, 170–1; G. Albrecht, 'Das Bremer Haus. Ein Sonderfall in der deutschen Baugeschichte um 1900', in L. Niethammer (ed.), *Wohnen im Wandel* (Wuppertal, 1979). pp. 233–51 (esp. pp. 248–50).

a centralized water distribution network and a properly constructed waste-disposal system as decisive.[39] Yet the construction of a central water-supply could actually increase morbidity rates, as in the Hamburg cholera epidemics of 1892 and (possibly) 1859, and the Munich typhoid epidemic which occurred shortly after Pettenkofer's reforms, if it was unaccompanied by the provision of a sand-filtration system to remove bacteria. Similarly, the mere provision of a waste-disposal system had relatively little effect by itself; what mattered was the proportion of households it covered and the way in which the sewage was disposed of. Here again, global statistics are of little use; only local studies can tell the full story, as indeed Spree himself has pointed out.[40]

The local example of Bremen suggests that Hamburg experienced a major cholera epidemic in 1892 for three basic reasons. Last in order of importance, and coming into operation only when the other two factors had had their effect, was the chronic overcrowding, poverty, and malnutrition which, as we saw earlier, existed in virtually all the poorer areas of the city, above all after the new harbour construction of the 1880s.[41] This acted as a 'multiplier' of the disease by facilitating its rapid spread from person to person. It could only come into action because the disease was carried to virtually every household in the city by mains water. The failure of the Senate and the Citizens' Assembly to agree on a proper filtration system for the water-supply until it was too late, and the failure to implement a comprehensive system of sewage disposal and treatment, must be accounted the principal reasons for the epidemic proportions reached by the disease.[42] Other cities such as Bremen did not experience a major epidemic because they possessed a sand-filtrated water supply. Most important of all was the Hamburg authorities' policy of concealment and delay.[43] They failed to issue advance warnings and instructions along the lines of those distributed by their counterparts in Bremen. They failed to make proper contingency plans for an epidemic. They failed to act on suspicion of an outbreak. They failed to reach a clear diagnosis of the earliest cases. And they failed to take any steps to confirm the presence of the epidemic for over a week after the disease first manifested itself.

It was above all the initial delay that allowed what might have been a relatively minor outbreak, confined mainly to the harbour area and the inner city, to become a major epidemic affecting every part of the town. Had the first cases been competently diagnosed, the population could have been warned to avoid using unboiled water and to take all the necessary hygienic precautions as early as 19 or 20 August. Such warnings could have been

[39] R. Spree, *Soziale Ungleichheit vor Krankheit und Tod: Zur Sozialgeschichte des Gesundheitsbereichs im Deutschen Kaiserreich* (Göttingen, 1981), pp. 117–18.

[40] Ibid., p. 123. Spree notes the importance of filtration but seems to assume that all centralized water supplies were filtered.

[41] See Chapter 1c, above.

[42] See Chapter 2c, above.

[43] See above, pp. 285–90.

issued even earlier, on the 17th or 18th, had Hamburg followed the example of its Hanseatic sister-city and acted on the first appearance of the symptoms rather than waiting for a full diagnosis. Indeed, as we have seen, the Bremen authorities issued such instructions as early as 11 August, well before the appearance of any sign of the disease. If the Hamburg authorities had acted promptly, they might not have been able to stop the bacillus entering the water-supply, but they could have saved thousands of lives by warning people against drinking it. But it does not seem to have occurred to anyone in Hamburg that there was a danger of the water-supply being infected. The first person to point to this possibility was Koch himself, during his tour of the city on 24 August.[44]

It was scarcely surprising that the medical and state authorities in Hamburg were soon taken to task for their tardiness. Robert Koch himself opened the assault with a strongly worded attack on the doctors in charge of the initial diagnosis. Their ability to carry out bacteriological investigations, he declared, left a great deal to be desired. Though he did not mention them by name, he was clearly referring to Rumpf and Erman, as every medical man in Hamburg who read the article would know.[45] Rumpf's reputation never really recovered from this criticism from one of the most powerful names in German medicine.[46] The Senate had to face even more serious charges than mere incompetence. Imperial Chancellor Caprivi sent a personally signed letter to Burgomaster Johann Georg Mönckeberg complaining 'in a rather irritated tone' about the delay in the Senate's official announcement of the disease.[47] As if this were not serious enough, the press started bringing the matter out into the open in an even more explicit form. On 29 August the liberal daily newspaper, the Hamburg *General-Anzeiger*, attacked 'tactics of delay and concealment of the Hamburg authorities in the face of the epidemic'. It asked pointedly why the Senate had failed to apply successfully the quarantine measures with which the Prussians had managed to ward off the disease.[48] On 15 September the *Kölnische Volkszeitung* repeated this accusation, and declared: 'an accursed special-interest policy, a fatal regard for particular concerns, caused the concealment of the danger even though it was pregnant with potential disaster ... Conscientious physicians, who had been very prompt in drawing the attention of the authorities to the existence of cholera, were scolded as being timorous and over-zealous.'[49] Already on 25 August

[44] Rumpf, 'Die Cholera', p. 38. Rumpf added that he immediately telephoned Senator Lappenberg warning him of this possibility.

[45] R. Koch, 'Über den augenblicklichen Stand der Cholera-Diagnose', *Zeitschrift für Hygiene und Infektionskrankheiten*, Vol. 14 (1893), 319–23.

[46] For Rumpf's subsequent reputation, see M. Nonne, *Anfang und Ziel meines Lebens* (Hamburg, 1972), p. 96.

[47] StA Hbg, FA Versmann VI A 6, entry for 29. Aug 1892.

[48] StA Hbg, Senat, Cl. VII, Lit. Ta, Pars 2, Vol. 11, Fasc. 16, Inv. 24: *General-Anzeiger*, 29 Aug. 1892.

[49] Ibid., Fasc 16, Inv. 27: *Kölnische Volkszeitung*, 15 Sept. 1892.

the respectable *National-Zeitung* was voicing the suspicion that the authorities in Hamburg had 'concealed' the epidemic. It quoted the *Schlesische Zeitung*, which alleged that the disease had already been in the city for a fortnight. And on 28 August it referred pointedly to 'the motives ... out of which the presence of cholera in Hamburg was kept secret for eight whole days'.[50] The trade unionist *Eisenbahn-Zeitung* opined on 31 August that only pressure from Koch himself had forced the Hamburg authorities to confirm the presence of the disease. It talked of 'the negligence of the Hamburg Senate' and of 'the facts which the Hamburg authorities, for reasons which are easy to guess, had kept secret for some days'.[51] The London *Times* also criticized the reluctance of the authorities to give official recognition to the outbreak of the epidemic. On 29 August it criticized the 'lamentable apathy and secretiveness of the Hamburg authorities'.[52] On the whole, however, the British press thought this was no more than could be expected. As the *St James' Gazette* remarked on 25 August, 'It is always difficult to get at the exact truth about visitations of this kind, since the sanitary authorities of foreign cities are not fond of publishing true and particular accounts of the progress of epidemics'.[53] From 24 August onwards the eyes of the world were on Hamburg. The national and international press were clear from the outset that it was only in Hamburg that a really serious epidemic had broken out. As the London *Times* reported, while 160,000 people had died of cholera all over Europe up to the end of August 1892, no single town had suffered really badly, with the exception of Hamburg. In Moscow, for instance, there had been only 160 deaths, in St Petersburg 550 (although later there were to be more). Like other papers, *The Times* printed long and circumstantial accounts of the Hamburg epidemic, while other outbreaks, in Paris, Le Havre, or Rouen, were relegated to the sidelines. 'The worst news', it declared, 'comes from Hamburg'; and soon, like other newspapers, it sent a special correspondent to the scene of the disaster.[54]

III

The Senate in office in Hamburg on 1 September 1892 and in whose hands lay the responsibility for combating the cholera epidemic, consisted of nine lawyers and nine merchants; their average age was 61 years and 2 months. The two serving Burgomasters in 1892 were men of different generations.[55] First Burgomaster was Carl Petersen, who was eighty-three years of age and had been a Senator since 1855, after taking part in the 1848 Revolution on

[50] Ibid., Fasc 17, Inv. 4: *National–Zeitung*, 25 and 28 Aug. 1892.
[51] Ibid.: *Eisenbahn-Zeitung*, 31 Aug. 1892 (No. 204).
[52] Ibid., Inv. 7: *The Times*, 27 Aug. 1892.
[53] Ibid.: *St James' Gazette*, 25 Aug. 1892.
[54] Ibid.: *The Times*, 27 Aug and 10 Sept. 1892.
[55] *MdB* (biographies in StA Hbg, files in Lesesaal).

the side of the moderates. In his day, he had been well known for his own culture, his quick wit, and his passionate involvement in the issues of the time: 'his words', complained one of his colleagues disapprovingly, 'overshot the mark'.[56] In May 1892 he had caught a cold which soon turned into a serious illness. By the summer of 1892 he was no longer able to carry out his ceremonial functions or attend Senate meetings. Throughout the epidemic he was incapacitated; at the beginning of September at his own request he was taken from his summer home in Övelgönne to his house in the city, where his condition improved sufficiently for him to receive visitors. 'My poor Hamburg!' he is said to have exclaimed on his sick-bed, 'I lie here idle and can't help in anything!' On 14 November, after a brief relapse and fever, he died.[57] The formal powers of the Burgomaster therefore rested during the epidemic with his deputy, Second Burgomaster Johann Georg Mönckeberg, who was over thirty years younger than his colleague. Mönckeberg had belonged to the Senate for over sixteen years, and had already served his first double term as Second and First Burgomaster in 1889 and 1890. Mönckeberg was a Hamburg patrician in the classic mould. Rich, well connected, and not without a touch of arrogance,[58] he was undoubtedly an able and successful man. He was one of those rare individuals, essential for Hamburg's system of government, whose intellect and background had brought them to the Senate at an early age. His letters and private notebook reveal him to have been humane and tolerant, but with a very high opinion of himself and a sharp eye for the weaknesses and failings of others. He possessed in full measure the legendary coolness and reserve of the Hamburg grand bourgeois. Not only was he a competent administrator, he was also above all a skilful diplomat who knew how to present the policy of the Senate to its best advantage. Too young to have been a committed member of the Old Hamburg Particularists, he had nevertheless known many of them personally, and his time in the Senate indeed overlapped with some of the grand figures of nineteenth-century Hamburg particularism like Kirchenpauer. Mönckeberg was in a difficult position in 1892. With the First Burgomaster terminally ill, he had to chair the Senate and give it a lead in policy matters himself. Yet as Second Burgomaster he lacked at least some of the necessary authority. His position as sole active Burgomaster in 1892 was also weakened by the fact that he was, at fifty-three, the third youngest member of the Senate, despite his sixteen years' service.[59] Five of the merchant Senators had served for longer, and most of the junior legal Senators were older than he was. In a

---

[56] StA Hbg, FA Mönckeberg 21a, Bl. 276–8.

[57] Petersen D23: Carl Friedrich Petersen (1809–92), Letzte Krankheit und Tod; A. Wohlwill, *Die Hamburgischen Bürgermeister Kirchenpauer, Petersen, Versmann* (Hamburg, 1903) pp. 25–60, 193.

[58] Cf. his comments cited in Chapter 1a, above.

[59] *MdB* entry for Mönckeberg.

society where informal hierarchies were especially influential, this probably represented a considerable limitation on Mönckeberg's authority.

Moreover, Mönckeberg also had to contend with one legal Senator vastly senior to him in age, Johannes Versmann, whose turn it was to take a year out of the Burgomaster's chair and return to the status of an ordinary Senator. Not only had Versmann been First Burgomaster the year before Mönckeberg took office, he had also served as Burgomaster for most of the 1880s and had been in the Senate for over thirty years.[60] Versmann too was in a difficult position. There was no provision in Hamburg's constitution for anyone to step into a Burgomaster's place should he be seriously incapacitated by illness, and Versmann in theory at least had no more rights than any other Senator. He thus had to be careful about intervening in Mönckeberg's responsibilities. But Versmann had been the dominant figure in the Senate for nearly two decades, and he was not the man to stand idly by should things go badly wrong. His ability to recognize political realities and to persuade his colleagues to come to terms with them was undiminished; but his most important quality, perhaps, at this stage, was his sensitivity to national politics. In the 1880s he had been Hamburg's Plenipotentiary Representative on the Federal Council, the formal ruling body of the German Empire, made up of representatives of all the federated states, including Prussia. Coupled with his long experience of national politics, this gave Versmann an unrivalled knowledge of how Hamburg's affairs were regarded nationally and a sure feel for the national repercussions of local affairs. By 1892, at seventy-one years of age, he was far from well. For much of the summer, indeed, he was plagued with lumbago and other pains in his limbs to such an extent that he seriously thought of resigning from the Senate.[61] But by August he was beginning to recover and put such thoughts behind him. More of a handicap, perhaps, was the absence on holiday of Senate Syndic Roeloffs, Versmann's right-hand man, upon whom he relied very heavily to put his ideas into action. Events were to prove, however, that Versmann himself had lost none of his capability for decisive action in a crisis.

After Mönckeberg and Versmann, the most important member of the Hamburg Senate in 1892 was Senator Gerhard Hachmann. Aged fifty-four at the time of the epidemic, he had had a somewhat chequered career. By 1892 he had been in the Senate for seven and a half years, and had acted as Chief of Police and President of the Medical Board since 1886. The son of a Hamburg physician, Hachmann had studied in Leipzig and Heidelberg. He had a remarkable gift for music and languages, but he proved, to begin with, a failure as a lawyer; when he began his practice in the 1860s, he lacked the ability to plead in open court and had to take on a partner to deal with commercial cases. This was a disaster in two respects; first he had cut himself

---

[60] For Versmann's biography, see Chapter 1a, above.
[61] StA Hbg, FA Versmann VI A 6, entry for 6 Aug. 1892.

off from the quickest and safest route to success as a lawyer—and eventual entry into the Senate—and secondly, his partner, a cousin, soon quarrelled with him over family matters and resigned. Hachmann tried to win over the young Johann Georg Mönckeberg as a partner, but Mönckeberg later recorded that he 'did not believe that this partnership would be of advantage' to himself, and after a brief partnership with someone else, Hachmann gave up his practice.[62] His next venture in the 1860s was even more disastrous. He became Director of the Hanseatic Building Society. In this capacity he not only lost all his fortune but also saddled himself with the responsibility for much of the society's property, 'which caused him concern to the end of his life'. His luck finally began to turn when he went back to the law and took on a more reliable partner, Embden. Their practice was soon brilliantly successful and in 1868 Hachmann was elected to the Citizens' Assembly. Here he discovered for the first time his true abilities as an orator. In 1868 he was elected Secretary to the Assembly and in 1869 Deputy President. Finally in 1877 he became President, a post he used, in contrast to his predecessor, to represent the views of the Assembly and defend its rights in negotiations with the Senate with a skill and tact that won admiration on both sides of the table. Largely on the strength of this performance, he was elected to the Senate in 1885.

Hachmann seems to have had several qualities which were particularly useful in his career; first, his evident talent for conciliation, secondly his shrewdness in choosing competent subordinates to whom he could delegate a great deal of business, and thirdly his abilities as an administrator, where he had a marked taste for innovation. It was Hachmann, for example, who called in the noted expert Emil Münsterberg to reorganize the poor-relief system in Hamburg along the lines of the Elberfeld system. Above all, perhaps, Hachmann was one of those Senators, like Mönckeberg and Versmann, who liked hard work and took his duties seriously. Yet for all these laudable qualities, he lacked the ability to go out on a limb in defence of his own views. His tendency was to seek a consensus. Moreover, as a man who made a point of delegating authority, he surrendered his judgement rather too often to others, especially if they had some professional expertise which he basically lacked. As Police Chief he had proved far less able than his predecessor to resist the pressures in favour of a hard line exerted by Berlin. He was similarly inclined as President of the Medical Board to go along rather too easily with the opinion of the doctors. Mönckeberg's verdict on him was a harsh one, but in the light of the events of 1892 it does not seem unjust. 'I have known him since youth', he wrote, 'and am of the opinion that his rich gifts and talents were not matched by any corresponding sharpness of judgment or strength of will.'[63]

[62] StA Hbg. FA Mönckeberg 21a, Bl. 279–80; and for the following quotations.
[63] Ibid., and *MdB* (n.55 above). See also Plate 2.

The first meeting of the Senate after the official announcement of the presence of Asiatic cholera in Hamburg took place on Wednesday 24 August. Beyond receiving the report of Senator Hachmann, as Police Chief and President of the Medical Board, to the effect that cholera cases had been officially confirmed in the city, it did very little. Arrangements were made for cases to be reported, though as things turned out, these arrangements proved to be embarrassingly ineffective. Checks were instituted on ships for cholera cases. Those on which cases were found were isolated and prevented from leaving harbour.[64] Even this mild interference in the city's trade and merchant enterprise met with opposition from the shipowners who were directly affected. The main worry of senior members of the Senate such as Versmann was still the potential damage to Hamburg's trade from quarantine measures imposed in foreign ports against ships coming from Hamburg. It was only after 25 August, for instance, that the day-to-day problems of coping with the epidemic took over from the subject of quarantine as the main item of worry in the pages of Versmann's diary.[65] Perhaps the Senators' inaction can be explained by the fact that they were awaiting the advice of the discoverer of the cholera bacillus, Robert Koch, who, they had been officially told by Berlin on 23 August, was being sent to Hamburg as the Chancellor's official representative. But the likely truth was that they were still hoping that the epidemic was not serious and that quarantine measures could be avoided. Moreover, there were no contingency plans to deal with an epidemic, not least because Chief Medical Officer Kraus thought that little could be done. If they had taken energetic measures to deal with the epidemic before Koch arrived, they would have been able to present the Professor and the Chancellor with a *fait accompli*. They could thus have warded off further interference in Hamburg's affairs from Berlin.

The neighbouring Prussian city of Altona had taken the approved measures with such alacrity that all Koch could do when he went there on 25 August was to approve what the local authority had already done. But Koch's writ had run for years in Prussia. The Altona doctors were likely to follow Koch's principles even in the great man's absence. Things were very different in Hamburg. The Senate and its medical officers had steadfastly refused to accept Koch's theories and methods. Yet, by 1892, there was no real alternative to Koch's methods in terms of practical, politically feasible administrative action. It was, characteristically, Versmann who was the first to recognize this fundamental political reality. Carefully and methodically, he drew up a list of the various measures taken in Altona, noting that they had received the great Koch's seal of approval. As so often, Versmann proved more clear-sighted than his colleagues. But he did not have the authority, as a mere Senator, to put these measures into effect, although it soon became evident

[64] StA Hbg. Senat, Cl. VII, Lit. Ta, Pars 2, Vol. 11, Fasc. 17, Inv. 3, for the various ordinances.
[65] Ibid., FA Versmann, VI A 6, entry for 24 Aug. 1892.

that he had been the only member of the Senate to instruct himself in this manner.[66]

When Robert Koch arrived on 24 August to inspect the city before making his own recommendations to the Senate, he was thus confronted by a situation in which virtually no action had been taken. The responsible Senator, Gerhard Hachmann, had so far confined himself to following the advice of Chief Medical Officer Kraus.[67] Kraus had no intention whatever of following the example of his colleagues in Altona. As far as he was concerned, the situation in 1892 was no different from that of 1873, when he had thought the measures later advocated by Koch, such as quarantine, disinfection and isolation, were useless and impracticable.[68] As the author of Kraus's obituary subsequently commented,[69]

He was a convinced supporter of Pettenkofer's views, unimpressed by the pointless hyperactivity which was then the order of the day; and because he made no effort to display such hyperactive behaviour, he was considered indifferent and negligent ... He knew from his own experience that a city might indeed be protected from the visitation of an epidemic by sanitary reforms, but that once an epidemic had actually broken out, all measures taken would be in vain.

According to Professor Rumpf, the Director of Hamburg's New General Hospital in Eppendorf, Kraus was a constant source of delays and confusions. When Rumpf suggested to Kraus that they should go together to meet Robert Koch as he arrived at the station on 24 August, to give him the latest information on the epidemic, Kraus flatly refused.[70] Instead, when Koch arrived at the Medical Office with Rumpf at 9 a.m. on the 24th, he had to wait half an hour before Kraus turned up for work. A true Prussian in his punctuality, Koch was evidently unimpressed by this casual attitude on the part of the city's Chief Medical Officer.[71] This boded ill for Kraus. After a brief interview with Kraus, which evidently increased rather than diminished his dissatisfaction with the Chief Medical Officer's competence, Koch set off on a tour of the city's hospitals accompanied by a posse of officials. Just before half-past eleven, they arrived at the New General Hospital in Eppendorf, where Theodor Rumpf, the Director, was waiting to meet them. Koch, as Rumpf later proudly recalled, 'asked me straight away whether we had any cases of cholera. I gave him the number of cases we had, whereupon Koch turned round and said to his companions: "The first man in Hamburg who's

[66] StA Hbg, FA Versmann, VI A 6, entry for 25 Aug. 1892.

[67] For Kraus, see above, p. 253.

[68] See above, pp. 253–4.

[69] J. Michael, *Geschichte des ärztlichen Vereins und seiner Mitglieder* (Hamburg, 1896), entry for Kraus.

[70] Rumpf, *Lebenserinnerungen*, pp. 42–4.

[71] StA Hbg, Cl. VII, Lit. Ta. Pars 2, Vol. 11, Fasc. 16, Inv. 9, Nr. 13: report of 14 Sept. 1892. Kraus lived in Altona. The Citizens' Assembly had repeatedly complained about this (*Bürgerschaft*, 29 Oct. 1890).

telling us the truth!" ' Rumpf then showed Koch the patients, let him examine the cultures and secured his agreement to the various measures he had ordered to be taken. Koch was subsequently to submit Rumpf to some very harsh criticism. For the moment, however, they seemed to hit it off, and they agreed to meet for dinner in Weinschmidt's restaurant.[72] Koch and his retinue then went on to inspect the other city hospitals, the disinfection centres, and the barracks for the Russian emigrants,[73] before going for a brief walk through some of the worst-affected areas in the 'Alley Quarters' of the city centre.

Koch was evidently shocked by the seriousness of the epidemic. On 25 August he wrote to his mistress, the eighteen-year-old art student Hedwig Freiberg, giving his first impressions of the state of affairs:

When I came to Hamburg, I thought I would encounter a few patients, and that it would not really be certain whether they had cholera or not. But how different was the situation which I actually found! Within a few days the sickness had gained ground with giant strides, and already the dead were numbered in hundreds. Yesterday I was on the move for the whole day, from one hospital to another, to the emigrants in the harbour, and on the ships. I felt as if I was walking across a battlefield. Everywhere, people who had still been bursting with health a few hours before and had begun the day full of *joie de vivre*, were now lying stretched out in long rows, shot down by invisible bullets, some with the characteristic rigid stare of the cholera victim, others with broken eyes, others already dead: no lamentations were to be heard, only here and there a sign or death-rattle. It is a sight that always has something gruesome about it, even for the physician, and even when he has already often experienced something of this kind before. This is cholera, which has clearly made its entry here in its most frightful form. If the epidemic continues to spread in the same way as it has in the last few days, the situation may become really terrible.[74]

If he was alarmed by the extent which the epidemic had already reached within a few days of its outbreak, Koch was even more shocked by the miserable housing and living conditions he found in his walk through the Alley Quarters in the inner city. 'I have encountered nothing worse than the workers' accommodation in the Alley Quarters, neither in the Jewish district in Prague nor in Italy', he remarked. 'In no other city have I come across such unhealthy dwellings, such plague-spots, such breeding-places of infection.' It was at this point, indeed, surveying the narrow alley-ways, the tumbledown buildings, the insanitary courtyards, and the stinking waterways of the old city, that he evidently recalled his experiences in Alexandria and Calcutta and, turning to his companions, uttered the remark which was to do more than any other single statement to discredit the government of Hamburg, its

[72] Rumpf, *Lebenserinnerungen*, p. 43.
[73] StA Hbg, Cholerakommission 27: Erster Bericht.
[74] B. Möller, *Robert Koch. Persönlichkeit und Lebenswerk 1843–1910* (Hanover, 1950), p. 630. Koch subsequently divorced his first wife and married his mistress, a step which so shocked contemporaries that the citizens of his home town voted to remove a plaque earlier erected in his honour.

social policy, and the political system on which it rested. 'Gentlemen', he said, 'I forget that I am in Europe.'[75]

Coming from a conservative such as Koch, this was strong stuff. Spoken at the height of the age of imperialism, the remark was calculated, as no other could have been, to wound the sensibilities of Hamburg's dominant classes. Indeed, as it was repeated across the country, the press, the politicians, and the bourgeois public were compelled to admit a sense of shame that such a comment, whose truth they instinctively accepted, could have been made in Germany. It was to have a very considerable long-term effect. More immediately, however, Koch was faced with the problem of galvanizing the Hamburg authorities into some kind of action. After his tour of the Alley Quarters he went on to a second, more formal interview with Chief Medical Officer Kraus, this time with Senator Hachmann in attendance. The interview with Kraus and Hachmann did not go well, as he told Rumpf when they met in Weinschmidt's restaurant later the same evening. There had been 'unpleasant clashes'.[76] Koch's unequivocal declaration that the infection was being carried by the river-water, and his proposals for quarantine and disinfection measures, we may surmise, met with more or less open scepticism not only from Kraus but from Hachmann as well. Moreover, Koch would not have been impressed by the absence of any measures such as those already taken in Altona. He arranged, therefore, for a conference to be held the next day, in which he would give Hachmann and Kraus his official advice, backed with all his authority as the discoverer of the cholera bacillus and the representative of the Imperial Chancellor, and based on the observations he had made in his tour of inspection on the 24th.

Despite the fact that the Senate had officially taken cognizance of the epidemic on 24 August, therefore, it was not until Koch met Senator Hachmann and various responsible officials in formal conference on the 25th that any serious steps were taken to combat the disease. Most of the conference was taken up with a sharp lecture from Koch. The immediate problem, he announced, was to secure an uncontaminated water-supply. The police were to arrange for water wagons of a local brewery (the *Bill-Brauerei*) to be commandeered and to tour the working-class area of the Hammerbrook with supplies of fresh water. Boiling stations were to be set up on the streets, and public notices were to be issued to people warning them against drinking

---

[75] Koch's famous phrase is mentioned in the *Hamburger Freie Presse*, 26 Nov. 1892 (copy in StA Hbg, PP S3496 Bd. 1). The earlier quotation from his tour can be found, without a source reference, in A. Aust, 'Vor 80 Jahren: Die Cholera in Hamburg. Soziale und hygienische Missstände und ihre Folgen', *Die Heimat. Monatsschrift des Vereins zur Pflege der Natur und Landeskunde in Schleswig-Holstein und Hamburg*, 79 (1972), 302–11. These quotations suggest that Koch and the bacteriologists were not so indifferent to the social determinants of disease as is sometimes supposed (e.g. by G. Göckenjan, *Kurieren und Staat machen. Gesellschaft und Medizin in der bürgerlichen Welt* (Frankfurt, 1985), p. 56).

[76] Rumpf, *Lebenserinnerungen*, p. 43.

unboiled water or milk. Public baths were to be closed, and the sale of raw fruit from street barrows was to be banned.[77] Infected houses were to be disinfected. Every effort was to be made to prevent the further spread of the disease. All these, and other suggestions, came from Koch. They were ratified formally by the Senate, meeting on 26 August. Following Koch's further advice, the Senate closed all schools on 26 August, and public dances and public meetings were all banned. On the 27th dances held in bars, inns, and places of entertainment were also suppressed. At the same time visits to the prisons, the workhouse, the poorhouse, and other similar institutions were stopped. Meanwhile, it was decided to print and stick up posters warning people not to drink water without having boiled it first. A plainly worded leaflet on cholera, written by Dr Paul Sachse, a Berlin medical official, was also to be printed and distributed.[78] Finally, the police 'sanitary column' of six trained ambulancemen was placed on alert and received reinforcement, while measures were taken to increase the number of ambulances, which at the outbreak of the epidemic totalled four.[79]

Koch, in other words, had forced the Senate to take action. Many of the measures which he pressed it into taking were considered by Senators to be exaggerated. Versmann thought that the ban on dances was an excessive precaution,[80] while Kraus did not trouble to hide his belief that virtually all the measures taken were pointless. Part of the reason for this scepticism lay in the fact that the authorities were still not convinced that the epidemic was a really major one. It is revealing of the delays and uncertainties in the official reporting of cholera cases that the figures which Versmann recorded in his diary were constantly being revised upwards. On 23 August he noted that there had been 123 cases to date. Already when he sat down to record his next entry, the next day, he was forced to admit that this figure was a gross underestimate, and that the true figure was in fact 219. It was only on 26 August that he finally conceded that the cholera 'is apparently very severe'. He now thought there had been 295 cases up to and including 23 August.[81] In fact there had been no fewer than 815 (eight hundred and fifteen!).[82] But while they remained throughout this period in ignorance of the epidemic's true extent, ultimately the real reason why the authorities had been inactive was because they did not really believe that Koch's theory of the causes of the disease was correct. The measures taken on 25 August were taken largely against their will.

[77] StA Hbg, Cholerakommission 27: Erster Bericht.
[78] StA Hbg, Senat, Cl. VII, Lit. Ta, Pars 2, Vol. 11, Fasc 17, Inv. 3.
[79] StA Hbg, Cholerakommission 27: Erster Bericht, Zweiter Bericht (Bl. 56).
[80] StA Hbg, FA Versmann, VI A 6, entry for 26 Aug. 1892.
[81] StA Hbg, FA Versmann, VI A 6, entries for 23, 24 and 26 Aug.
[82] See above, Table 4.

IV

In agreeing to Koch's demand for a major publicity campaign to instruct people on how to avoid infection, Hachmann and his colleagues had not initially realized the magnitude of the task they were undertaking. It was not too difficult to draft and print a poster warning people to boil water before drinking it, and 20,000 copies were duly ordered from a local printer and posted up around the city. But Sachse's leaflet on 'Precautions against cholera' was an altogether different proposition. Koch was insistent that each household in the city should receive a copy immediately. At a rough calculation, that meant at least 250,000 copies would have to be printed and distributed virtually overnight. Hachmann and his colleagues knew only one organization that was capable of carrying out such a task. On 27 August he authorized his subordinates to contact the Social Democrats. Would they agree to print the leaflet on the party press and to use the party's well-oiled leafleting organization to distribute it throughout the city?[83]

It did not take the Social Democratic leaders long to agree, especially since the police promised to pay everyone who took part in the distribution a sum varying between 3 and 10 Marks according to the hours worked. The Social Democratic printing house Auer and Co. ran its presses throughout the night of 27–8 August and a quarter of a million copies were ready by the next morning. The costs of printing were covered—but no more than covered—by a grant of 2,000 Marks from the police.[84] Even here, however, there were delays. To begin with, Hachmann let nearly two days pass before the request was made to the Social Democrats to print and distribute the leaflet. He could in theory have asked them already on 25 August, after the decision to circulate the leaflet had been taken. Instead he waited until the 27th. This might have been because he was locked in debate with colleagues about the advisability of co-opting the Social Democrats in the performance of this task. But there is no record of any kind of debate or discussion on the subject. It is far more likely that Hachmann and his colleagues waited so that the distribution would take place on the next available Sunday (28 August) and so avoid any disruption of work, with its consequent loss of profit to the employers. Had the distribution taken place on the 26th or 27th, thousands of Social Democratic party workers—overwhelmingly manual labourers—would have had to take time off work, and since they would have done so at the request of

[83] An earlier version of the following account was published in R. J. Evans, 'Die Cholera und die Sozialdemokratie: Arbeiterbewegung, Bürgertum und Staat in Hamburg während der Krise von 1892', in A. Herzig, D. Langewiesche, and A. Sywottek (eds.), *Arbeiter in Hamburg. Unterschichten, Arbeiter und Arbeiterbewegung seit dem ausgehenden 18. Jahrhundert* (Hamburg, 1983), pp. 203–14.

[84] StA Hbg, PP S3469: Versammlungsbericht (Sozialdemokratischer Verein für den 3. Hamburger Wahlkreis, Mitgliederversammlung am 13. Oktober 1892).

the police, it would hardly have been possible for their employers to have imposed disciplinary or financial penalties for it.

But an operation on this scale proved in the end too much even for Hamburg's superbly organized Social Democratic Party to mount in such a short period of time. It was forced to confess that 'the requirement of carrying out this task between Saturday night and Monday morning could not be fulfilled as we had wished, because several branch chairmen were not present in Hamburg at the time'. It seems, therefore, that a good number of active Social Democrats had fled the city in the early days of the epidemic. Thus the party association for the third (and largest) Hamburg Reichstag electoral district ordered a new batch of leaflets—this time without a subvention from the police—and repeated the entire operation on Tuesday 30 August and the following day, 'because it was not satisfactory' the first time.[85] This meant that the operation was now taking place during working hours, which entailed still further delays.[86] It was not until Wednesday 31 August, there-fore—a whole week after Koch had persuaded the Hamburg authorities to distribute the leaflet—that instructions on how to avoid infection finally reached every household in the city.

Meanwhile, Hachmann had also begun to busy himself with another problem, one which he evidently regarded as considerably more pressing than that of the leaflets. This was the question of what to do with the hundreds of Russian migrants who were still in the city, staying in the emigrants' barracks and the lodging-houses. All of them had limited funds; some of them were destitute. None of them had expected to be in the city for more than a few days; neither they nor the various agencies which supported many of them could be expected to maintain them for the weeks or even months for which they would have to stay in the city once quarantine measures were imposed by outside ports, including New York, as they surely would be. The burden of supporting them would thus in all probability fall upon the Hamburg Senate. Faced with this prospect, Hachmann and his colleagues determined to be rid of them as quickly as possible, and in retrospect it is clear that they were none too scrupulous about how they did so.[87]

The best that could happen from the authorities' point of view was that the emigration should take its normal course. Already one steamship of the Hamburg–America Line, the *Moravia*, had left Hamburg on 17 August, carrying the bacillus with it; 22 passengers had died of cholera by the time the ship arrived in New York. The ship had been supplied with a clean bill of health by the American Vice-Consul in Hamburg, Charles Burke, acting on the advice of the Hamburg medical authorities. Burke was naturally worried by the possibility that cholera might reach his own country by courtesy of the

[85] Ibid.

[86] Ibid.: *Vorwärts*, 8 Dec. 1895.

[87] For background on the emigration business see Chapter 1b, above.

Hamburg–America Line. However, he claimed later to have been reassured by Hachmann as late as 22 August that there was no cholera in the city. On 21 August another ship, the *Rugia*, left Hamburg with a clean bill of health and a cargo of cholera germs; here too several cases occurred on the crossing.[88] The next sailing was due to take place on 26 August, when the Hamburg–America Line's *Normannia* was to sail for New York. The American Vice-Consul was persuaded, once more, on 25 August to give the ship a clean bill of health. No one can be certain now whether Hachmann and his colleagues were aware that cholera had broken out on the *Moravia*, which had sailed some eight days previously; there is no record of any ship having been in contact with the *Moravia* and having docked in Hamburg before the 25th, and Marconi's system of wireless telegraphy was not patented until 1896 and did not receive its first maritime use until the following year. But even if, as seems likely, the Senate was unaware that cholera had broken out on the *Moravia*, it was still acting irresponsibly when it persuaded Burke to give a clean bill of health to the *Normannia* on the 25th, particularly in view of the fact that many of its passengers had been staying in lodging-houses, and even more in view of Koch's stated opinion that it had been the migrants who had brought cholera to the city in the first place.[89]

On 26 August, none the less, the *Normannia* duly began steaming down the Elbe. It had hardly reached the sea when the first passengers began to fall ill with all the unmistakable symptoms of Asiatic cholera. On 26 August the ship's 'Sickness Log' recorded that two people, a man of thirty-three and a baby girl of eleven months, had been admitted to the sick bay from the 'tween decks suffering from cholera. A third passenger, a man of forty-five, travelling cabin class, was in fact the first to fall ill; but perhaps out of consideration for his social status, perhaps out of disbelief that his case could be cholera, his symptoms were put down to 'vomiting and diarrhoea' and he was said to have died, on 31 August, 'in a diabetic coma'. But the other cases left no doubt that cholera was on board. After the ship had called in briefly at Southampton on the 27th, the journey quickly became a nightmare. Two more cases were reported on 27 August, both cholera; another, labelled 'acute intestinal catarrh' on the 28th and three more on 29th. One passenger wrote back to Hamburg that 'the poor children on the ship were dying ... like flies'. Soon a total of ten people had died. This implies that at least twenty people were affected by the disease, although the 'Sickness Log' recorded a total of

[88] S. Winkle, 'Chronologie und Konsequenzen der Hamburger Choleraepidemie von 1892', *Hamburger Ärzteblatt*, 37 (1983), 421–30, here p. 423.

[89] *Export*, 40 (6 Sept. 1892), gives a full account of these events. The Senate claimed that the clean bill of health was issued on the 24th; but this leaves the question of why it was issued two whole days before the ship sailed (StA Hbg, Senat, Cl. VII, Lit. Ta, Pars 2, Vol. 11, Fasc 14: 'Zu den in der amerikanischen Presse erhobenen, von deutschen Zeitungen wiederholten Beschwerden über die Ausstellung reiner Gesundheitspässe nach Ausbruch der Cholera hierselbst'.)

only twelve cases. Some of those affected, to judge by their names, were probably migrants from Russia, but it is impossible to be sure. The attitude of the captain and crew during the terrible journey evidently left a great deal to be desired. One passenger claimed that the German crew 'have no hearts'.[90]

On 3 September the *Normannia* reached New York. She was immediately placed under strict quarantine by the immigration authorities. Armed patrols sealed her off completely. The passengers must by now have been desperate with fear of the disease that was still raging through the ship. The epidemic reached its height on 7 September, when no fewer than 14 new cases were recorded, though by now the ship's medical officer, in an attempt to deceive the New York authorities as to the true nature of the sickness, had stopped calling it cholera and was recording all cases as 'vomiting and diarrhoea' or 'acute intestinal catarrh'. Altogether 53 passengers and crew fell ill with symptoms of cholera. Attempts by passengers to swim ashore were dealt with ruthlessly by the American immigration officers, and conditions on board were deteriorating ('everything is in chaos', as one passenger complained).[91] On 4 September, however, the 'tween-deck passengers were taken off the ship and put into isolation. Some of those who had been taken ill were kept under observation for several weeks. Eight stokers from the crew of the *Normannia* were kept in quarantine in New York until 8 October. All their effects were burned, for which they received 80 to 120 Marks compensation each. Meanwhile, after being held on board for another week, the cabin passengers were eventually allowed off on 10 and 11 September. On 12 September, however, as these passengers were about to land on Fire Island, they were greeted by a crowd of 300 oyster-fishers, armed with oars, revolvers, and other weapons. The crowd shouted to the immigrants to go back to New York and threatened to use force to prevent them from landing. The Governor of New York's official agent, charged with accommodating the immigrants in the Surf Hotel, read out the documents empowering him to take over the hotel, but a local official declared that he did not recognize the Governor of New York's authority. The crowd meanwhile threatened to throw the Governor's agent into the water, and he retreated in confusion. A second attempt was rebuffed by a lawyer brandishing a court order, which already at that time was as potent a weapon in the United States as a revolver, and just as popular. Eventually, indeed, a large number of passengers were unable to obtain entry into America at all and had to return to Europe. The affair quickly led to a drastic tightening-up of the American immigration laws.[92]

While these events were going on across the Atlantic, the Hamburg auth-

[90] StA Hbg, Hafenarzt I 77: Auszug aus dem Kranken-Journal des Dampfschiffes "Normannia". The passenger's letter is printed in StA Hbg, PP S3490 Bd. 1: *Vorwärts*, 17 Oct. 1892.

[91] StA Hbg, Hafenarzt I 77, loc. cit.; ibid., PP S3490 Bd. 1: *Vorwärts*, 17 Oct. 1892.

[92] StA Hbg, Auswanderungsamt II E I No. 3, Bd. 10, Doc. J, No. 202; StA Hbg, PP S3490 Bd. 1: *Vorwärts*, 17 Oct. 1892, *General-Anzeiger für Essen und Umgegend*, 19 Oct. 1892, and *General-Anzeiger*, (Hamburg) 12 Nov. 1892.

orities were preparing a last, desperate effort to rid themselves of the remaining migrants before it was too late and quarantine measures were finally imposed. Above all they were determined to ship off those whose passages had already been paid for by relatives or prospective employers in America. Some were sent out during the next few days on another vessel of the Hamburg–America Line, the *Scandia*, which lost 32 passengers from cholera by the time it docked in New York on 9 September. Other migrants already on their way through Prussia were diverted to Stettin and shipped on the *Polaria*. The last ship to leave Hamburg for America was the Hamburg–America Line's *Bohemia*. The Senate proposed to ship all the remaining prepaid passengers on this vessel on 1 September. Already, non-German companies were refusing to take any more passengers from Hamburg because of the cholera epidemic. The police ordered all emigration agents dealing with prepaid passengers to embark them on the *Bohemia* without delay. However, the Hamburg–America Line lodged a formal objection with the authorities on 30 August. It protested that it had enough problems in trying to embark its own passengers without being forced to transport 'tween-deck prepaid passengers booked with other lines. If the company was forced to take other prepaid passengers, it would have to pay back considerable sums of money for the tickets of those of its own passengers whom it was obliged to turn away. The Senate responded by threatening the Line with a claim for all the costs involved in keeping the emigrants in Hamburg for the duration of the epidemic. So the company, under protest, gave in, and the *Bohemia* set sail with 682 passengers on 1 September. It was not until 3 September that Hachmann at last conceded that there could be no further shippings, since foreign quarantine measures meant that the passengers would no longer be allowed to land.[93]

The Hamburg authorities could thus congratulate themselves on having disposed of virtually all the emigrants who had arrived in the city since the middle of August and who initially had threatened to become a burden on the city's exchequer for as long as the epidemic lasted. The only exceptions were some 260 migrants who declared that they would prefer to go to England rather than be shipped off immediately to America. The British, however, refused to have them. The Prussians said they would not allow them to return by rail through their territory to Russia. So they were stuck in Hamburg. They were shortly joined by another 240 who had been refused entry into the United States on arrival, or who had been turned back from British ports *en route*. For the duration of the epidemic, therefore, these migrants remained imprisoned ('totally cut off') in the barracks, prevented by police sentries from going out or receiving visitors.[94] So the Senate's tactics

[93] StA Hbg, Auswanderungsamt II E IV No. 1, Bd. 1; and Auswanderungsamt II E I No. 1a3; see also M. Just, 'Hamburg als Transithafen für die osteuropäische Auswanderung in die Vereinigten Staaten' (Museum für Hamburgische Geschichte, Schausammlungen Heft 5, Hamburg, 1976), p. 9; Winkle, 'Chronologie', p. 19.

[94] StA Hbg, Cholerakommission 27: Zweiter Bericht, Bl. 63.

had been less than a complete success. Moreover, news of the deception soon became public. Charles Burke, the American Vice-Consul, indignant at having been made to look a fool, lodged a public protest with the Senate, and so the whole affair came to light. It did not do Hamburg's reputation any good.

The most controversial measure that resulted from Koch's advice in the conference held on 25 August was a massive and comprehensive programme of disinfection. All affected houses were to be thoroughly disinfected, and people were to bring infected bedding and other material to disinfection centres for treatment or destruction by burning. A special disinfection centre was to be established to treat ships on the river and in the harbour. Food shops in infected areas were shut down by the police until they were disinfected.[95] The resources available in Hamburg for such a programme would have been inadequate even had the epidemic not taken on such vast dimensions during the succeeding week. But in a situation where the number of new cases announced each day soon totalled over a thousand, they were virtually non-existent. A doctor from Vienna, arriving on 28 August, complained that the disinfection arrangements were thoroughly ineffective: 'two sprinklers filled with carbolic were standing in the hospital grounds and were used to spray the ambulances and the ambulancemen as they left the hospital: such was the procedure of "disinfection"'. All the disinfection arrangements were 'improvised', he noted, and he complained: 'The authorities are not undertaking a disinfection of the dwellings where cholera cases have occurred, but are leaving this to the people themselves. Only movable property is being disinfected, with improvised disinfection devices.'[96] In general, indeed, the attitude of the authorities three days after Koch's meeting with the Senate seemed to have changed little. The same doctor went on:

As soon as I arrived I went to see the Police Chief, Senator Hachmann, in the City Hall. There I was told that Senator Hachmann was engaged in a very important conference with the veterans' associations about the festivities for the anniversary of the Battle of Sedan. I was let in after half an hour. All my questions received evasive answers. Although Hamburg had been surprised by the epidemic, opined the Police Chief, everything was none the less in apple-pie order.[97]

Moreover, this was not all that was amiss. In his first report to the Senate on the measures ordered by Koch, on 28 August, Hachmann gave no hint that he recognized the urgency of the situation.[98] A special Cholera Commission was to be established to take charge of the fight against the disease, but

[95] StA Hbg, Cholerakommission 27: 1. und 2. Bericht des Polizei-Chefs und Präses des Medizinalkollegiums Hachmann.
[96] StA Hbg, Senat, Cl. VII, Lit. Ta, Pars 2, Vol. 11, Fasc. 17, Inv. 4: *Die Post*, 2 Sept. 1892.
[97] Ibid.: *Die Post*, 3 Sept. 1892.
[98] StA Hbg, Cholerakommission 27: 1. Bericht des Polizei-Chefs und Präses des Medizinalkollegiums Hachmann.

Hachmann was in no hurry to set it up, and it had not yet come into being five days after Koch's visit.

It was not long before Senator Johannes Versmann began to conclude that nothing very effective would be done unless he took a hand in the matter himself. He was appalled at Hachmann's inactivity. There were, he noted in his diary, delays in establishing the Cholera Commission, which was only 'finally set up on 31.8'. The Imperial Chancellor's numerous letters and telegrams, mostly giving detailed instructions and advice from the Imperial Health Office, had been properly forwarded to the relevant Senators, but none of the Senators actually seemed to have read them. Senator Hachmann, who was nominally responsible for fighting the epidemic, as Versmann noted, 'apparently thought that everything was in perfect order'. Versmann could see, however, that it was not. He clearly considered Hachmann to be incompetent, and referred scathingly to 'his unbelievable first report of 28 Aug.'. So he took action himself to put things right. On 28 August, Senate Syndic Roeloffs, Versmann's right-hand man, returned early from a holiday in the Black Forest and went straight to see his chief. The Senator immediately arranged for him to 'place himself at Hachmann's disposal' the next day. This was in fact a thinly disguised take-over of Hachmann's duties by Versmann, acting through Roeloffs, and it was scarcely surprising that Hachmann objected to this and other arrangements made at the same time, such as the immediate establishment of the Cholera Commission.[99] But with Versmann now taking a firmer grip on the administration, determined to ward off criticism—or worse, direct intervention—from the Chancellor in Berlin, by adopting an energetic approach, there was little that Hachmann could do. At the first meeting of the Cholera Commission, on 1 September, Versmann now put forward all the proposals and measures he had noted down over the previous days. A number of them were measures already taken in Altona, approved by Koch on 25 August, and carefully listed by Versmann in his diary. 'At last things are moving', noted Versmann with satisfaction on 2 September.[100] Soon 68 water wagons were touring the streets, 43 boiling-stations were in operation, fresh orders were being issued to close markets and other public gatherings, and medical and sanitary checks on the stations and in the harbour were being tightened up. Most important of all was the disinfection programme, which the Cholera Commission decided was not proceeding with sufficient rapidity.[101]

The dimensions which the epidemic had taken on now made a comprehensive disinfection of houses impossible without engaging a large number

[99] StA Hbg, FA Versmann VI A 6: Tagebuch von Johannes Versmann, entries for 24, 25, 26, 29 and 31 Aug.

[100] Ibid., entry for 2 Sept. See the Protokolle of the Cholerakommission (in Vol. 27 of the Commission's files) for the various measures taken. See also Plate 25.

[101] StA Hbg PP S3469: Meldungen für die Sanitätskolonne 24 July 1893, and for the following details.

of extra people to do the job. The idea was that mobile 'disinfection columns'
or 'sanitary columns' would be set up, each equipped with a disinfection unit
on a cart, and sent out into the city to do the work. At 6 p.m. on 1 September
the police once more turned to the Social Democrats and asked if the
party could provide 400 'trustworthy workers' to man the columns. Once
more, the Social Democrats appeared to the authorities as the body best able
to mobilize a large number of reliable and efficient people in a short space of
time. It was agreed that each worker would be paid 6 Marks a day for his
pains—'much too tiny a sum, if one takes into consideration the dangers
which these brave men were exposed to', as a Social Democratic newspaper
remarked on 1 October.[102] Once more, the party responded with alacrity. The
very next morning, on 2 September, at 8 a.m., the 400 workers selected by
the party reported for duty and the newly organized disinfection columns
immediately set to work.

Very quickly, however, it began to emerge that the Social Democrats had
not been too careful in their selection of the 400. On 3 September the
Chairman of the Cholera Commission reported

that the activities of the sanitary columns attached to the 21 disinfection centres as
they were carried out yesterday have given rise to many complaints, because many
shady elements have found their way into the 400 workers accepted by us and placed
at our disposal by the Social Democratic Party. These shady elements have been
responsible for robberies and excesses of all kinds. Since a reduction of their numbers
seems admissable, a muster of the same has been ordered, and every column is to be
placed under the leadership of a reliable police officer.[103]

The police, understandably enough, had no time during the epidemic to check
the credentials of those employed in the disinfection columns, but when
things were quieter they set to work, and by 24 July 1893 they were able to
produce a full report. Altogether during the epidemic some 671 men had
worked in the disinfection columns. Their names were known, since they had
to be registered in order to receive payment for the work, and they were then
checked against available police and court records. A total of 82 had been
previously convicted, of a wide variety of offences. Most of these were minor
contraventions, illustrating the extent to which the poor of Wilhelmine
Germany habitually broke the law in order to survive, the dimensions of the
constant petty war they waged with officialdom, and to some degree also the
more violent and disorderly side of the culture of poverty in lower-class
Hamburg. Convictions included offences such as forging official documents,

---

[102] Ibid.: *Vorwärts*, 6 Sept. 1892, *Glückauf*, 1 Oct. 1892. See also Plates 26 and 27.

[103] StA Hbg, Cholerakommission 1 Protokolle: 3. Sitzung. Theft and extortion by corpse-
bearers, ambulancemen, and quarantine officers is one of the classic themes of plague literature.
See J. Delumeau, *Angst im Abendland. Die Geschichte kollektiver Ängste im Europa des 14. bis 18.
Jahrhunderts* (Reinbek bei Hamburg, 1985), i. 179.

Table 5. Previous convictions of workers employed in the disinfection columns in Hamburg, 1892

Offence	Number of Convictions	Offence	Number of Convictions
Theft	55	Receiving stolen goods	3
Embezzlement	28	Using a false name	3
Begging	44	Causing a nuisance	22
Causing a domestic dis-turbance	15	Causing excessive noise	3
Slander	16	Deserting the colours	3
Resisting an official	14	Vagrancy	5
Fraud	12	Contravening food regulations	3
Causing actual bodily harm	12	Assault	3
Morality offences	4	Street offences	11
Causing damage to property	6	Others	27
Threatening behaviour	3		

Source: StA Hbg, PP S 3469: Meldungen für die Sanitätskolonne, 24 July 1893.

false accusations and numerous others listed in Table 5. The presence in the list of eleven convictions for contravening the police traffic and street regulations is accounted for by the fact that a substantial minority of the members of the disinfection columns were street traders thrown out of work by the epidemic. Altogether, of the 82 disinfection column workers with previous convictions, 15 were street traders; the majority were either listed as 'worker' (45), that is, unskilled labourers, or by trade. Most of the latter were trained, skilled workers, often belonging to a guild (22). They included 3 lightermen, 3 mechanics, a smith, a locksmith, a tailor, a basketmaker, a journeyman stonemason, a turner, a stevedore, a carter, a sailor, a boiler-cleaner, an upholsterer, a fisherman, a lithographer, a waiter, and a mes-senger-boy. Most of these involved, apart from the street traders, probably worked in the harbour.

Few of those involved could be called professional criminals or habitual offenders. Typical were individuals such as the worker Friedrich Georg Baack, born in 1856, sentenced in 1877 to ten days' imprisonment for theft, in 1878 to four weeks for the same offence, and in 1881 to four weeks for embezzlement; or the worker Johann Hagdstein, born in 1834, who had nine convictions for begging and vagrancy, one for theft, one for embezzlement, one for fraud, and one for wounding; or the trader Franz Kämpfer, born 1846, with one conviction under the traffic laws (1891), or the the worker Karl Krieger, born 1849, one conviction, also 1891, for theft. Such examples of petty offenders made up the majority of those in the list. There were, however, some more serious offenders, such as the trader Bernhard Feindt, born in 1855, who had three convictions for theft, earning him 5 years' penitentiary, four convictions for fraud, with three years and five months' imprisonment, and one conviction for causing a nuisance, which had earned him two days in gaol; or the worker Carl August Hochheim, born in 1844, who had been convicted of theft and fraud in 1879, 1880, and 1882 and of theft, wounding, and threatening behaviour in 1889; or the journeyman tailor Carl Hokendorf, born in 1853, evidently a pimp, sentenced in 1880 to two years' penitentiary for repeated offences against the morality laws; or the worker Justus Völcker, born in 1858, with 3 convictions for causing a nuisance, 5 for theft, one for begging, one for using a false name, one for causing a domestic disturbance, one for resisting arrest, and one for a morality offence.[104]

It is likely to have been the behaviour of characters such as Völcker that gave most cause for complaint against the activities of the disinfection columns; but given the temptation, and given the wretched economic situation of August–October 1892, it is probable that a good number of those employed in the columns, and not only those with previous convictions, took the opportunity to steal goods and valuables from some of the disinfected houses. Some scattered evidence of their activities emerged subsequently. A machine worker whose wife and four children had died in the epidemic, and who had himself spent several weeks in hospital, suffering from cholera, eventually returned to his home to find many of his belongings stolen and all the rest seriously damaged by disinfection.[105] A worker was caught stealing a golden cross and chain from the house he was disinfecting and was subsequently tried and imprisoned.[106] Two disinfection workers were gaoled for a week each in January 1893 for demanding payment on delivery of disinfected possessions back to their owners.[107] An ambulanceman with several previous convictions was convicted not only of removing clothes from the homes of those he carried off to hospital but actually of stealing several beds as well.[108] There were also general accusations that workers in the sanitary columns 'had behaved in a rough and frivolous manner'.[109] The yawning gulf between the patriotic intentions of the Social Democrats and the bald realities of crime and insult were a graphic reminder of the gap that existed between Social Democratic respectability and working-class norms.[110]

Even more serious than the theft and rudeness was the carelessness with which the disinfection columns went about their task. As the disinfection columns set enthusiastically to work, spraying carbolic over everything in sight, complaints soon began to come in. One inspector of disinfected houses

[104] StA Hbg, PP S3469: Meldungen für die Sanitätskolonne 24 July 1893.

[105] Ibid., S3490 Bd. 1: *Hamburger Tageblatt*, 10 Nov. 1892.

[106] Ibid., S3649: *Hamburgischer Correspondent*, 18 Apr. 1893.

[107] Ibid., S3490 Bd. 1: *Hamburger Echo*, 31 Jan. 1893.

[108] Ibid., Bd. 2: *Hamburgischer Correspondent*, 2 Feb. 1893.

[109] StA Hbg, Senat, Cl. VII, Lit. Ta, Pars 2, Vol. 11, Fasc. 17, Inv. 5: *Hamburger Fremdenblatt*, 1 Oct. 1892.

[110] See R. J. Evans (ed.), *The German Working Class 1888–1933: The Politics of Everyday Life* (London, 1982). The work of the disinfection columns also led to subsequent disputes about compensation from the authorities (StA Hbg, PP V327–30, V494, V495, V327–61).

in St Georg Nord criticized the lack of an efficient disinfection apparatus and noted:

As has already been mentioned, the unsatisfactory construction of the disinfection machines caused damage to the items disinfected, mainly through damp. This led to people being afraid of having their beds, clothing, etc. disinfected. Thus it has been the direct occasion for the concealment of cases of illness, not only of cholera but of infectious diseases in general. We must therefore call particular attention to this problem, and add that, according to our doctors, new diseases can be caused by lying on beds that are wet through after disinfection.[111]

Another, in Barmbeck, referred to 'items burned and ruined during disinfection by the police' and provided straw sacks for those whose beds were no longer usable.[112] Friedrich Werner, Assistant Pastor in South Hamm, reported too that he was obliged to arrange for much of the disinfected bedding to be replaced.

Where beds had been badly affected by disinfection, which at the beginning of the epidemic had not been carried out very carefully, the necessary steps were taken and thankfully accepted. The situation often indeed appeared unutterably wretched. The beds smelt bad and were wet when they were brought back from the disinfection centre, and there was a penetrating smell of chlorine and other substances in the rooms.[113]

The depredations of the disinfection squads occupied the courts for months afterwards, as they tried to sort out who was responsible for the destruction. Characteristic was the case of a domestic servant who died of cholera at the height of the epidemic. Her employers, showing a proper sense of civic responsibility, promptly took her clothes and personal effects to a disinfection centre, where they just as promptly disappeared—whether from the dissolvent effects of carbolic, or, as seems more likely, into the hands of the centre's employees, the court did not say. The dead servant girl's father, as her heir, then brought a lawsuit against her employers, for compensation, and was awarded the full sum, on the grounds that the employers had taken the effects to the disinfection centre at their own risk, that they could have got the girl's father to do this himself, and that the legal rights of heirs to property must be protected even at a time which demanded that individuals make sacrifices for the good of the majority. The judgment attracted hostile comment in the bourgeois press; but it was not overturned.[114]

Disinfection soon transformed the atmosphere of the city in a way that some found reassuring—'chlorine is now the best perfume', as one inhabitant

[111] StA Hbg, MK III A 13: Bericht der Gesundheitskommission St Georg-Nordertheil, p. 3.
[112] Ibid.: Bericht der Gesundheitskommission Barmbeck, p. 8. Cf. StA Hbg, Allgemeine Armenanstalt II, 211, Bl. 51: *Hamburger Fremdenblatt*, 21 Sept. 1892.
[113] Kirchenarchiv Hbg, D166, p. 26.
[114] StA Hbg, Meldewesen B43: *Hamburgischer Correspondent*, 21 July 1893.

of the city wrote in her diary[115]—but others found unpleasant. Already on 30 August Burgomaster Mönckeberg noted that 'we have the pleasure of encountering carbolic, Lysol, creolin, and other evil substances everywhere', his wife complained that 'everything smells of Lysol' and his daughter wrote that the smell of disinfectants 'was polluting the air'.[116] The smell of carbolic and Lysol was reported to be everywhere on 3 September.[117] The aroma lingered on in the city long after life had otherwise returned to normal, thus providing a constant reminder of the possibility of infection, should people be inclined to relax and forget that it could still be there. A visiting reporter noted at the end of September that 'the general street scene betrays nothing of the present epidemic, but was none the less reminded by the various official posters on the houses and advertising columns, or every now and then by a noseful of the odour of creolin or chlorine, that one is in a city which is suffering a visitation of cholera'.[118] Indeed, over forty years later, Leo Lippmann, who lived through the epidemic in his youth, wrote that 'when I go past our old house on the Schwanenwiek, I sometimes think even today that I can smell the sharp tang of Lysol, which was poured over the floors, into the washing-up water, and into the drains as a disinfectant at that time'.[119] A curious by-product of the campaign was the appearance on the streets of swarms of mice, driven out of disinfected houses by the repellent effects of carbolic.[120] The disinfection campaign may have done something to reduce the number of fresh infections in the end, although certainly not before the beginning of September, when it was at last organized on a comprehensive basis. It certainly promised to be more effective than the traditional method of fumigating the streets with flammable chlorine solution, abandoned on Koch's instructions some years before.[121] But its effect on the olfactory structure of public space was very similar. Suddenly the putrescent aromas of the great city, observable in hot summer weather such as the inhabitants of Hamburg were experiencing in August 1892, and exaggerated to an unbearable degree by the massive choleraic excretions of those who were taken ill on the streets, on trams, and in other public places, disappeared

[115] StA Hbg, FA Birt, 6, Tagebuch von Friederike Birt, 23 Sept. 1892.

[116] Carl Mönckeberg (ed.), *Bürgermeister Mönckeberg. Eine Auswahl seiner Briefe und Aufzeichnungen* (Stuttgart and Berlin, 1918), p. 20; Tagebuch Elise Mönckeberg 12 Sept. 1892; Tagebuch Tilli Mönckeberg 30 Aug. 1892 (both in private possession).

[117] StA Hbg, FA Neubauer 1, p. 28.

[118] StA Hbg, PP S3490 Bd. 1: *Karlsbader Volkszeitung*, 28 Sept. 1892.

[119] StA Hbg, FA Lippmann A 4, Bd. 1, p. 32.

[120] StA Hbg, PP S3490 Bd. 1: *Hamburger Fremdenblatt*, 22 Apr. 1893.

[121] Chlorine was traditionally the basis for cholera disinfection and fumigation. See F. F. Runge, *Vom Chlor, seinem Nutzen, seiner Anwendung und ausserordentlichen Wirksamkeit zum Reinigen der Luft und zur Abhaltung ansteckender Stoffe; besonders auch in Bezug auf die uns bedrohende Cholera. Nach den 'Grundlehren der Chemie für Jedermann' des Herrn Professors F. F. Runge in Breslau* (Hamburg, 1831).

1. Burgomaster Johann Georg Mönckeberg (Staatsarchiv Hamburg. Bildsammlung) 2. Senator Gerhard Hachmann (Staatsarchiv Hamburg. Bildsammlung)

3. Senator Johnannes Versmann (Staatsarchiv Hamburg. Bildsammlung)

4. Dr Heinrich Gieschen, President of the Property-Owners' Association 1878–96 (from Renate Hauschild-Thiessen, *Hundertfünfzig Jahre Hamburger Grundeigentümer-Verein.* Grundeigentümerverein zu Hamburg, 1982)

5. The Hamburg fleets (Herrengrabenfleet at low tide; Staatliche Landesbildstelle, Hamburg)

6. Flood in the Neustadt (drawing by C. Förster, in J. C. W. Wendt and C. E. L. Kappelhoff, *Hamburgs Vergangenheit und Gegenwart. Eine Sammlung von Ansichten*, Hamburg, 1896, p. 259)

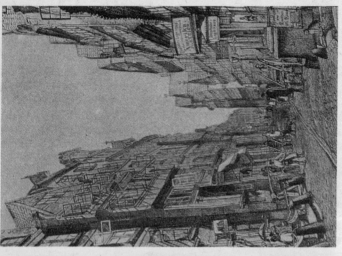

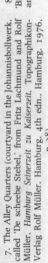

7. The Alley Quarters (courtyard in the Johannisbollwerk, called 'De scheebe Stebel', from Fritz Lachmund and Rolf Müller, *Hamburg Seinerzeit zu Kaiserzeit*, Topographikon-Verlag Rolf Müller, Hamburg, 4th edn., Hamburg, 1976. p. 38)

8. Emigrants' lodging-house and rag-dealer's shop (in the 'Binnen-kajen', after a drawing by Ebba Tesdorpf, in Wendt and Kappelhoff, *Hamburgs Vergangenheit und Gegenwart*, p. 209)

9. A one-room apartment in the Alley Quarters (Rademachergang, 1896, Staatliche Landesbildstelle Hamburg)

10. Toilets in the Alley Quarters (communal closets in the 'Langer Jammer' about 1890, Staatliche Landesbildstelle Hamburg). Not every toilet was connected to the sewage system by 1890

11. William Lindley, sanitary engineer (Staatsarchiv Hamburg, Bildsammlung)

12. The German Crown Prince on a tour of the Hamburg sewers (print by H. Kaesebers, 1895, Museum für Hamburgische Geschichte)

13. Clearance of dwellings to make way for the new harbour, 1880s (demolition of the Brook- and Kehrwieder peninsula, 1885, from Lachmund and Müller, *Hamburg Seinerzeit*, p. 10)

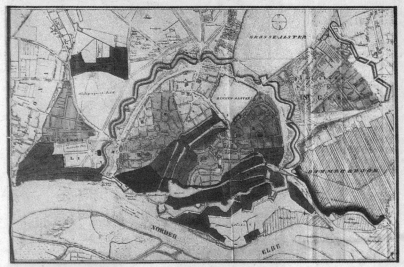

14. Cholera in Hamburg 1832. Mortality was highest along the rivers and fleets. (Map from J. N. C. Rothenburg, *Die Cholera-Epidemie des Jahres 1832 in Hamburg*, Hamburg, 1836, copy in library of Staatsarchiv Hamburg)

15. Robert Koch (Staatliche Landesbildstelle, Hamburg)

16. Max von Pettenkofer (BBC Hulton Picture Library)

17. (*right*). A cholera case in the tram (from *Über Land und Meer, Deutsche Illustrierte Zeitung*, 4 (1892), p. 80, Staatliche Landesbildstelle Hamburg)

18. (*below*). Hospitalization of the sick ('Enlèvement de cholériques dans la Niedernstrasse,' *L'Illustration* 2586, 17 Sept. 1892, p. 233, Staatsarchiv Hamburg, Plankammer 272, Medizinalwesen Mappe I)

19. The city ambulance (Staatsarchiv Hamburg, Medizinalkollegium II N3, Vol. 1, Bl.82)

20. A cholera death in the home ('Verwaist', *Die Gartenlaube*, 43 (1892), p. 717, Staatsarchiv Hamburg, Plankammer 272, Medizinalwesen Mappe I)

21. Cholera barracks and field hospital in Hamburg, 1892 ('Armee-Feldlazareth, errichtet für Cholerakranke,' No. 4 from *Hamburger Bilder aus der Cholera-Zeit*. Lichtdruck und Verlag von Knackstedt und Näther, Hamburg-Eppendorf 1892, in Staatsarchiv Hamburg, Plankammer 272, Medizinalwesen Mappe I)

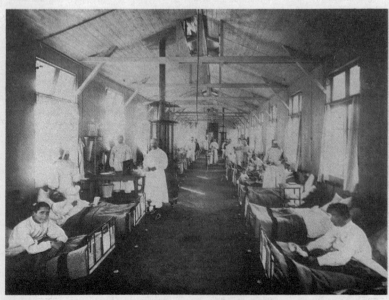

22. Inside the cholera barracks, October 1892 ('Inneres einer Cholerabaracke vor dem Marienkrankenhaus,' Staatliche Landesbildstelle Hamburg)

23. The municipal cemetery during the 1892 epidemic ('Begräbnisstätte der Choleraleichen,' *Illustrierte Zeitung* 2569, 24 Sept. 1892, p. 375, in Staatsarchiv Hamburg, Plankammer 272, Medizinalwesen Mappe I)

24. Burial in a mass grave ('The Cholera-Stricken City: An Open Grave in the Cholera Cemetery at Hamburg', *The Graphic*, 46, No. 1, 193, 8 Oct. 1892, p. 424)

25. Distribution of boiled water during the epidemic ('Verteilung gekochten Wassers am Messberg, No. 3 from *Hamburger Bilder aus der Cholera-Zeit*. Lichtdruck und Verlag von Knackstedt und Näther, Hamburg-Eppendorf, 1892, in Staatsarchiv Hamburg, Plankammer 272, Medizinalwesen Mappe I)

26. A disinfection squad poses for the camera in front of the disinfecting machine. Note the two policemen. ('Angestellten des provisorischen Desinfektionsanstalts', photographed by an amateur (Herr Feuerbach), 1892, G35d1 in Staatsarchiv Hamburg, Plankammer 272, Medizinalwesen Mappe I)

27. The disinfection squad at work ('Eine Desinfektionskolonne vertheilt Anweisungen', *Illustrierte Zeitung* 2569, 24 Sept. 1892, p. 344, in Staatsarchiv Hamburg, Plankammer 272, Medizinalwesen Mappe I)

28. Fear in Hamburg: the chemist does a roaring trade. Note the advertisement for alternative medicine on the side of the building; also the many domestic servants doing errands for their employers. ('Vor einer Apotheke,' *Illustrierte Zeitung* 2569, 24 Sept. 1892, p. 344, in Staatsarchiv Hamburg, Plankammer 272, Medizinalwesen Mappe I)

29. *The Hunters Hunted:* cartoon from the magazine *Kladderadatsch,* 25 Sept. 1892. 'The newspaper *The Bavarian Fatherland* reports that the local authorities in Augsburg have postponed the beginning of the hare-hunting season because of the danger of cholera.' (Staatsarchiv Hamburg)

30. *The Cholera-free Town Council:* cartoon from the magazine *Kladderadatsch,* 25 Sept. 1892. 'The firm Scaremonger & Co. has patented a cholera-proof aldermanic bench, which is being purchased forthwith by the city fathers in Augsburg, Peine, Ballenstedt, Altruppin, and other places.' (Staatsarchiv Hamburg)

31. *Bismarck Disinfected:* cartoon from the magazine *Kladderadatsch,* 25 Sept. 1892. Former Imperial Chancellor Otto von Bismarck (with pipe), his dog, and his son Herbert, on their way from the Bismarck home at Friedrichsruh, just outside Hamburg, to Vienna for Herbert's wedding, are stopped at the Austrian border by officials who prepare to spray them with carbolic. In fact they had already left Vienna on 26 June. The caption reads: 'A certain honorary citizen of Hamburg is glad it is not now that he has to tread on Austrian soil; otherwise he would be thoroughly disinfected by higher authority' (Bismarck was made an honorary citizen of Hamburg in 1871). (Staatsarchiv Hamburg)

FEAR OUTSIDE HAMBURG

32. The charitable effort: a temporary soup-kitchen erected during the epidemic ('Speisehalle, Hansaplatz', photographed by an amateur (Herr Feuerbach), P51–918a Staatsarchiv Hamburg, Plankammer 272, Medizinalwesen Mappe I)

33. Clearance of the Alley Quarters, 1913 (demolition of the district south of the Steinstrasse, from Lachmund and Müller, *Hamburg Seinerzeit*, p. 89)

34. (*right*) *The Cholera says Farewell*: cartoon from the magazine *Deutsche Wespen*, 30/42 ('Der Abschied der Cholera'). As Cholera leaves Hamburg with his haul of corpses, the citizens, dressed in characteristically archaic style, hasten to prevent his return by closing the gate, over which stands the legend 'Administrative Reform'. The caption reads: 'Hopefully the gates of Hamburg will be closed behind the departing Cholera in such a way as to prevent the terrible guest's return.' (Staatsarchiv Hamburg)

35. (*below*). Remember the dead: a memorial placard (Staatsarchiv Hamburg)

under purifying clouds of disinfectant, and all seemed to be healthy and clean again.

Up to the end of August, however, there was little concrete evidence of this sort to reassure the public that anything was being done. The Senate had been forced to take action by Koch on the 25th, but public life only began to be affected by the closure of schools, dances, and entertainments on the 26th and 27th, leaflets providing advice on hygiene were only distributed on a comprehensive scale on the 31st, a separate administrative body to organize the fight against the disease only began to work on 1 September, a disinfection campaign of adequate dimensions was only launched on the 2nd, and even this soon proved to have damaging side-effects. Moreover, these delays and confusions had not gone unnoticed by the public. Hamburg's administration was already coming under attack from without for its tardiness in publishing an official confirmation of the epidemic and for the deception it practised on the Americans over the state of health of the migrants it was still dispatching to New York at this time. Worse was to follow; for it soon became clear that the arrangements made by the city for the hospitalization and treatment of the victims were equally rudimentary and inadequate.

b. *Healing the Sick*

I

There were few contingency plans in Hamburg even for a relatively mild outbreak of cholera, let alone for one as disastrous as that of 1892. As we saw in Chapter 3, in every epidemic after 1831 the Senate had sought to avoid what it regarded as unnecessary expenditure by placing the burden of coping with the disease on to the shoulders of the Doctors' Club. But in 1892 the Doctors' Club played almost no role in combating the epidemic. The official history of the club explained this by saying 'that the Doctors' Club as such had become too cumbersome for such tasks because of its large membership, and that therefore such purposes had to be achieved by other means'. The state had taken no measures in any previous epidemic since 1831 to provide extra ambulancemen or additional facilities for treating the sick. Advised by men, such as Chief Medical Officer Kraus, who believed that isolation was a waste of time and money, the Senate had never erected any special cholera hospitals or wards after the initial outbreak. By 1892 some limited contingency plans did exist, but in general the Senate probably considered that the facilities of the new General Hospital in Eppendorf were adequate for any emergency that could arise. The explosive spread of the cholera epidemic in 1892 thus caught it unprepared.[1]

Senator Gerhard Hachmann, as Chief of Police and President of the Medical Board, was the man responsible for co-ordinating measures to deal with the epidemic. A colleague later reported that he 'did not ... let his equanimity be disturbed' despite the 'alarming news' which was continually reaching him in the last week of August 1892. He maintained 'the greatest calm and collectedness and thereby had a calming effect on all the city officials'.[2] Whether this was competence or merely complacency was doubtful, as we have already seen, Versmann for one clearly thought it was the latter. Yet if Hachmann failed to tackle the epidemic with any sense of urgency, this was not least because he persistently underestimated its true extent. The epidemic reached a first peak on 27 August, with over 1,080 new cases reported, and a second peak, also with over 1,000 new cases, on the 30th. The highest number of deaths on a single day—561—was recorded on 2 September. Only then did a real, though gradual, decline set in.[3] Yet most people already thought the worst was already over by the 29th. Koch's deputy Dr Rahts declared on that day 'the epidemic has come to a standstill, or is perhaps still advancing a little, but in view of the present measures it is probable that within a pretty short space of time it will retreat and come to an end'.[4] On the 30th, just as the epidemic was reaching its second dreadful peak, Senator Versmann noted that the 'cholera transportations have declined somewhat',[5] while his colleague Burgomaster Mönckeberg remarked in similar vein that 'the epidemic seems, to be sure, to have fallen off a little in recent days', though he was cautious enough to add that 'the situation can change again from day to day'; and Senator Gustav Hertz thought on 2 September that the worst was over because he noticed fewer hearses on the streets than the day before.[6] During the whole of the first week of the epidemic, therefore, the authorities were unaware of its true extent. This was not the least of the reasons for Hachmann's complacency up to the point of Versmann's intervention on 28 August. Added to the lack of any contingency plans for an epidemic, this led to a situation of rapidly increasing chaos.

Hamburg did not even possess any proper facilities for taking the sick into hospital. At the outbreak of the epidemic there were only four ambulances and a total of six ambulancemen in the city. This number was increased as

[1] Michael, *Geschichte des ärztlichen Vereins*, p. 207.

[2] Carl August Schröder, *Aus Hamburgs Blütezeit*, (Hamburg, 1921), p. 79.

[3] See Table 4, above.

[4] StA Hbg, Senat, Cl. VII, Lit. Ta, Pars 2, Vol. 11, Fasc. 17, Inv. 4: *Freisinnige Zeitung*, No. 202, 30 Aug. 1892.

[5] StA Hbg, FA Versmann VI A 6, entry for 30 Aug. 1892.

[6] Mönckeberg, *Bürgermeister Mönckeberg*: Johann Mönckeberg to Carl Mönckeberg, 30 Aug. 1892, p. 20; StA Hbg, FA Gustav Hertz B17, letter from Frau Hertz to Else, 2 Sept. 1892.

part of the initial response to cholera on 25 August.[7] But the ambulances were very slow and it took up to three hours to get from the city centre to Eppendorf, including the time needed to harness the horses. The two main ambulances could only take one patient at a time; the 'Smallpox Cab' and another coach seated four each, but were unsuited for cholera patients. A 'Hamburg doctor' wrote to the *Vossische Zeitung*, a well-known liberal newspaper in Berlin, on 26 August, complaining that there were still only eleven ambulances in the whole of Hamburg. 'The sick and the dead lay for 5–6 hours before being taken away.'[8] In these first days of the epidemic, the sick often had to lie for up to 15 hours in police cells, 'on cold stones or floors' until they 'implored to be finally taken away'.[9] Even as late as 7 September there were still complaints that those unfortunate enough to fall victim to the disease were waiting for up to 12 hours before being taken to hospital. 'Is there no Moltke here then?' asked one newspaper, appalled at the chaos and desperate for suggestions as to how to impose some organization on it all.[10] By 28 August the number of ambulances had been increased to 30, and a total of 150 ambulancemen were in action, many of them volunteers, though many of them were paid by the state.[11]

Even this, however, was not enough in a city where over a thousand people were falling victim to the disease every day. Karl Wagner, a journalist from Vienna who served as an ambulanceman for two days at the height of the epidemic, left one of the most vivid accounts of conditions at the time.

The vehicles which were to be used were horse-drawn coaches from which the upholstery had been removed, so that the patients, whom we had to wrap in blankets, were carried on the bare wooden seat-frames. Almost inconceivably, five to seven large holes had been cut in the floor of the coach, through which the patients' excretions flowed onto the street!!! To begin with I fetched a 14-year-old girl, an old woman, and a boy; the woman died on the way ... The dwellings I entered were begrimed with dirt, so that I was more nauseated by them than by the cholera itself. During my service I transported 132 patients, of whom almost half died on the way.[12]

So chaotic was the organization of the hospitalization service that husbands were often transported to different places from their wives, and parents were

---

[7] StA Hbg, Cholerakommission 27, Erster Bericht; MK II N 3 Bd. 1, Bl. 59, 62, 82, 88 ('Das Kranken-Transportwesen in Hamburg, Seine Entwicklung und Organisation', 1892).

[8] StA Hbg, Senat, Cl. VII, Lit. Ta, Pars 2, Vol 11, Fasc. 17, Inv. 4: *Die Post*, 28 Aug. 1892.

[9] StA Hbg, PP S3490 Bd.1 *Hamburger Fremdenblatt*, 28 Oct. 1892.

[10] StA Hbg, Senat, Cl. VII, Lit. Ta, Pars 2, Vol. 11, Fasc. 17, Inv. 2: *Hamburger Nachrichten*, 7 Sept. 1892. See also J. Jungclausen, *Acht Tage Cholerakrankenpflege* (Hamburg, 1892). Moltke was the victorious Prussian general of 1866 and 1870–1.

[11] StA Hbg, Cholerakommission 27, Erster Bericht.

[12] Wagner's account was frequently reprinted. See for example *Die Misserfolge der Staatsmedicin und Ihre Opfer in Hamburg* (Hamburg, 1892), pp. 30–1; or StA Hbg, PP S3490 Bd. 1: *General-Anzeiger für Essen und Umgegend*, 19 Sept. 1892. In the article, Wagner claimed to have arrived as early as 18 Aug. in order to report the epidemic. Presumably this was a misprint for 28 Aug.

separated from their children, when several members of a family were taken ill.[13] Friedrich Werner, Assistant Pastor in Hamm noted that 'in the early days, when great confusion reigned, many people did not even know where the victim removed from their house had been taken to'.[14] Karl Wagner claimed that cases of heart failures or strokes, where the patient had collapsed in the street, were brought straight into hospital with the cholera victims.[15] Max Nonne, a doctor in the Eppendorf General Hospital, even reported that many healthy people had been transported 'by mistake' in the ambulances.[16]

Once they got to hospital, the cholera victims had to suffer further horrors. The two main hospitals in Hamburg had 3,820 beds between them, the majority of them already occupied by medical or surgical patients. Yet from 26 August over 400 new cholera cases were arriving every day. By the end of August over 3,000 cholera cases had been admitted.[17] They required isolation as well as treatment. The two hospitals both had new directors in 1892, neither of whom had had any previous experience of hospital administration. Professor Theodor Rumpf, the director of the New General Hospital in Eppendorf, had taken up his duties in the spring and was evidently finding it difficult to fit into the Hamburg scene. The director of the Old General Hospital in St Georg, Captain Weibezahn, was even less experienced. A former army officer, he had taken up his duties on 1 August and had therefore had less than three weeks to accustom himself to the institution of which he was now in charge before it was confronted with the gravest crisis in its history. His inexperience became dramatically apparent right at the beginning. Evidently ignorant of the standard precautions against infection, Weibezahn went down with cholera himself almost immediately, and although he eventually recovered, the Old General Hospital had to function without its director for the duration of the epidemic.[18] Like other people in Hamburg, however, he was unaware to begin with of the true extent of the disaster.

On 22 August Rumpf advised Senator Lappenberg, who was responsible for the overall running of the hospitals, that preparations would have to be made for dealing with the expected increase in admissions now that it was clear that cholera had broken out, and on the 23rd it was agreed to construct eight cholera barracks in the grounds of the Old General Hospital and the small Sailors' Hospital. Plans already existed and it was hoped the buildings could be opened by the end of the month. But it soon became clear that this

[13] StA Hbg, Senat, Cl. VII, Lit. Ta, Pars 2, Vol. 11, Fasc. 16, Inv. 27: *National-Zeitung*, 28 Aug. 1892, quoting private correspondence.
[14] Kirchenarchiv Hbg, D166: Pastor Friedrich Werner, 'Erinnerungen aus meiner Amtstätigkeit in der Gemeinde Süd-Hamm' (MS 1937).
[15] See above, n. 12.
[16] Nonne, *Anfang und Ziel*, p. 95. See also Plates 18, 19 and 20.
[17] Rumpf, 'Die Cholera', pp. 38–40.
[18] Ibid., p. 48.

would be too little, too late. Many patients already in the hospitals were discharged or moved to small private institutions, but on 27th August Rumpf took more drastic action and moved many of the remaining 2,400 surgical convalescents and less seriously ill patients from the hospitals to emergency infirmaries set up in empty school buildings. The construction of the barracks was completed ahead of schedule on 29 August, and more were ordered to be built. Even this was not enough. Driven to despair by his inability to accommodate cholera patients by conventional methods, Rumpf telegraphed the Prussian Army General Staff on 28 August and requested a field hospital with 500 beds and the necessary staff. This was a dramatic confession of Hamburg's failure to deal with the crisis unaided. The field hospital was set up on 7 September, and the second set of barracks was opened on the next day. A final, additional set of barracks, known as 'Station Erica', built under the supervision of Chief Engineer Franz Andreas Meyer, was opened on the 20th. Altogether 1,784 emergency hospital beds were eventually made available. But all these arrangements came too late to save the situation.[19]

Even Rumpf was forced to admit 'that a shortage of space in the hospitals was observable on the 26th and 27th', and he added that it was also very difficult 'to obtain the necessary staff at the beginning'. Behind these bland phrases lay a world of misery and horror in the hospitals. At first, most cases were admitted to the Old General Hospital because it was nearer the city centre. From 26 August an attempt was made to get the situation under control by closing each hospital for admissions for 12 hours on alternate days, then for the whole 24 hours, 'so that the break could be used to put the admission lists in order, remove the numberless dead and put their beds in order again, and set up new wards'. But as Rumpf admitted, this arrangement 'could not ... be carried out with full rigour'.[20] And in so far as it was, it only seemed to cause further problems; an ambulanceman later complained 'that we were not told when the hospitals in St Georg and Eppendorf were closed, so that we often had to drive the sick and the dead around for hours'.[21] On the cholera wards, conditions in the last week of August were described as 'frightful'.[22] In St Georg, it was reported, 'the rooms are really terribly overcrowded; often there were sixty patients lying in one ward, where there is scarcely place for thirty'. 'Wailing and screaming, groaning and moaning, echo gruesomely through the room.' The number of doctors in the two hospitals—35—was quite inadequate, and although Rumpf appealed for volunteers from other towns, most of the 90 or so who eventually came did not arrive until after the beginning of September: local religious and charitable organizations provided a few extra nurses, but here too most

[19] Ibid,, pp. 37–42, 48.
[20] Ibid., pp. 35, 39–40, 47, 157. See also Plates 21 and 22.
[21] Wagner, *Die Misserfolge*.
[22] StA Hbg, Senat Cl. VII, Lit. Ta, Pars 2, Vol. 11, Fasc. 17, Inv. 4: *Die Post*, 3 Sept. 1892.

of the volunteers—eventually no fewer than 600 in all—also started work well after the epidemic was into its second officially registered week.[23]

The scenes in the hospital wards before the end of August were widely reported in the press. They did not make comfortable reading. 'In the large, airy rooms', wrote one volunteer nurse,

there lay, in bed after bed in a row, the poor patients, here contorted in powerful muscular convulsions, there begging the nurse for a bedpan or a drink; some had violent attacks of vomiting and befouled the bed and the floor in a nauseating manner; others lay in their last moments, a loud death-rattle in their throats, and many passed on in my very presence ... A powerfully built man belonging to the seafaring profession had died, and his corpse had to be taken into the corridor. His skin tinged with blue, his face distorted by pain, his eyes opened wide, he lay on his bed, which in his last moments he had massively befouled. To touch the corpse seemed impossible to me, the penetrating stench that rose from the last evacuation of his bowels into the bed almost robbed me of my senses ...[24]

Outside the ward, he reported, the dead lay 'in long rows' along the corridors waiting to be collected and taken away. Dr Gustav Hülsemann, from Soest, who began work in the Hamburg epidemic in 26 August, noted that it took up to ten hours for corpses to be removed from the wards on which he was working. Often bodies lay in their beds or in the corridors for several hours more until they could be removed; they were laid out on the grass in the hospital grounds in long rows, and specially hired cabinet makers

had the dreadful task of nailing down the coffins or wooden crates, of which there were often 100 standing in the garden at the same time. These could by no means be closed as quickly as appeared necessary. In addition there were flies and bluebottles swarming around the half-open coffins, and carrying the germ of the disease away with them.[25]

So small were the softwood boxes used for coffins, indeed, that they were popularly known as 'nose-squashers (*Nasenquetscher*)'.[26]

Furniture vans and other closed vehicles were commandeered as makeshift hearses, and the public mortuaries were asked to take in as many bodies as they could, but as late as 7 September complaints were still being received that corpses were lying in houses for up to 12 hours before being collected.[27]

[23] Ibid., 2 Sept. 1892; Rumpf, 'Die Cholera', pp. 43–8; cf. also 'Erinnerungen aus der Cholerazeit 1892', *Neue Hamburger Zeitung*, 23 Feb. 1898, in StA Hbg, PP S3490 Bd. 3.

[24] 'Meine Erlebnisse als freiwilliger Krankenpfleger in den Cholerastationen des Alten Allgemeinen Krankenhauses zu Hamburg', *Magdeburgische Zeitung*, 14 Nov. 1892, in: StA Hbg, Senat, Cl. VII, Lit. Ta, Pars 2, Vol. 11, Fasc. 17, Inv. 5. Another, slightly different version also appeared in the *Hamburg-Altona Generalanzeiger* on 5 Nov. 1892 (copy ibid., Inv. 1a).

[25] *Export*, 6 Oct. 1892, quoting *Soester Kreisblatt*, 15 Sept. 1892; StA Hbg, PP S3490 Bd. 3: *General-Anzeiger*, 11 July 1912:

[26] Aust, 'Vor 80 Jahren'; *Die Heimat*, 79 (1972), 302–11.

[27] StA Hbg, Senat, Cl. VII, Lit. Ta, Pars 2, Vol. 11, Fasc. 17, Inv. 2: *Hamburger Nachrichten*, 7 Sept. 1892.

and Carl August Schröder later reported that 'large open spaces in various parts of the city were boarded off. Numerous corpses were stored there in the open, before they were driven off by day and night to Ohlsdorf' (where the main city cemetery lay).[28] Hearses and furniture vans could be seen rumbling though the streets on their way to the city cemetery at Ohlsdorf in a virtually unbroken procession from the hospital.[29] Here the bodies were buried, in numbers running as high as 500 a day, in mass graves 60 feet long by 12 feet wide by 3 feet 6 inches deep, by 250 grave-diggers working by day and night in shifts.[30] These scenes not only aroused horrified comment from outsiders like Karl Wagner, the journalist from Vienna, or Gustav Hülsemann, the doctor from Soest, who complained that 'Hamburg had nothing prepared for such an epidemic',[31] but also widespread fears of hospitalization among the local population. As Wagner observed, many of the sick 'resisted being taken away and had to be removed with the help of a constable'.[32] Theodor Rumpf is said to have confessed that 'there exists in Hamburg a certain antipathy towards the hospital because the doctors there are suspected in the city of performing too many experiments on the patients'.[33] There was a good deal of resistance to the removal of the children of victims from infected houses too.[34] Clearly the nineteenth-century hospital had an unsavory reputation in the community at large. Cholera rioters in previous epidemics, and in Russia during 1892 itself, almost invariably took doctors and hospitals as their main object of attack.[35] Given the chaotic and horrifying circumstances that obtained in Hamburg's hospitals in the last week of August 1892, such suspicion would seem on the face of it to have been justified. But it is also important to ask whether there is any hard evidence to support this view, to examine the experiences to which the victims were subjected by the doctors, and to ask whether they made any difference to their chances of survival.

Long after 1800, hospitals in Germany cared overwhelmingly for socially disadvantaged people such as the chronically ill single labourer, the prostitute and the pauper, the old without a family to look after them. Most patients were supported by poor relief. The middle classes and as far as possible the petty bourgeoisie paid for home care. They avoided hospital treatment because there was no separate accommodation for them apart from the mass of poor patients. As time went on, the hospitals served increasingly as places where physicians and surgeons could receive practical medical training and experiment with new treatments. Hospital fevers and infections gave these insti-

[28] Schröder, *Blütezeit*, p. 79.

[29] StA Hbg, FA Lippmann A4 Bd. 1, pp. 32–3.

[30] Aust, 'Vor 80 Jahren'. See also Plates 23 and 24.

[31] *Export*, 8 Oct. 1892 (n. 25, above).

[32] Wagner, *Die Misserfolge*.

[33] StA Hbg, Senat, Cl. VII, Lit. Ta, Pars 2, Vol. 11, Fasc. 1b: *Hamburgischer Correspondent*, 21 Oct. 1892, article by Ferdinand Hueppe.

[34] Jakob Loewenberg, *Aus Zwei Quellen* (Berlin, 1914), pp. 286–8.

[35] See Chapter 3c, above.

tutions a widespread reputation as being more a 'source of mortality than of the healing that was sought'; the determination of the sick to stay away from them was strengthened by the military discipline imposed on patients. Patients who died could also be anatomized, a fate which caused widespread fear and resentment on religious grounds.[36] In the second half of the nineteenth century, the development of anaesthetics and antisepsis, and the increasing construction of hospitals with segregated facilities for different classes of patients, began to alter this situation. But they still retained their popular reputation as centres of experimentation, and public hostility remained widespread right up to the turn of the century and beyond. The experience of the 1892 cholera epidemic in Hamburg gives us a chance to see whether or not popular fears were justified.[37]

Relatively few cholera victims were hospitalized in the earlier Hamburg cholera epidemics. In 1831 and to the end of January 1832, a total of 326 victims were treated in hospital, including 247 males and 79 females, out of an estimated total of 940 victims;[38] in 1832, 430 cases were admitted; in 1848, 517 cases out of 3,687 were treated in hospital, or only 14%; there was a high proportion of old people among them. Most of the patients were considered by the doctors to be living in circumstances too poor for them to be cared for properly at home.[39] Even fewer cases were hospitalized in 1849— 163 out of 1,191.[40] By 1892 the situation had changed with the construction of the New General Hospital in Eppendorf and the introduction, in the previous decade and a half, of state-sponsored health insurance. The wealthy were still treated at home, but the hospital was no longer a place for paupers: it had become a centre for the medical treatment of the masses. Nevertheless, it remained the case that the doctors were generally prepared to use the mainly working-class patients they treated as subjects for theraputic experiments. Angry exchanges in the press resulted, for example, from the activities in Eppendorf of Professor Ferdinand Hueppe, a Rhinelander born in 1852 who had qualified in Berlin, served in the Imperial Health Office, and since 1889 held a chair at the Charles University in Prague. He had been an early admirer and collaborator of Koch's but now disagreed with many of his views.[41]

Hueppe was on holiday, taking the waters at Bad Reichenhall, when the news broke that Hamburg had been hit by cholera. He immediately wrote to

[36] U. Frevert, *Krankheit als politisches Problem 1770–1880* (Göttingen, 1984), pp. 74–83; Göckenjan, *Kurieren und Staat machen*, pp. 214–41.

[37] For a critical examination of the negative reputation of 19th-century hospitals, see J. Woodward, *To Do the Sick No Harm: A Study of the British Voluntary Hospital System to 1875* (London, 1974).

[38] K. G. Zimmermann, *Nachtrag zu der geschichtlich-medicinischen Darstellung der Cholera-Epidemie in Hamburg im Herbste und Winter 1831–1832* (Hamburg, 1832), p. 49.

[39] StA Hbg, MK II A 2 Bd. 1, Bl. 95.   [40] Ibid., Bl. 163.

[41] H. A. L. Degener (ed.), *Wer Ist's?* (Berlin, 1909); additional biographical information from Paul Weindling (Oxford).

Theodor Rumpf announcing that he had recently, after several years' research, discovered a medicine 'which has a specific effect on cholera bacteria—roughly in the same way as quinine on malaria'. He requested permission to test this new medicine, 'which it has not been possible to procure in large quantities up to now, and ... [which] ... I ... cannot let out of my own hands', on cholera victims in Hamburg. On receipt of Hueppe's letter, on 25 August, Rumpf replied accepting the offer, and Hueppe arrived on 2 September and was put in charge of women's ward number 26 and men's ward number 41 at the New General Hospital, where he remained until 21 September. He refused to reveal to Rumpf the secret of his remedy; but Rumpf gathered from discussing its alleged effects with the professor 'that it has to do with a disinfection of the intestine and that the substance in question has already been taken by healthy people in large quantities without ill effect'.

Rumpf was perhaps a little unwise to accept this offer; but as he later explained, Hueppe was well known and well respected, and his scientific credentials were impressive. Nevertheless, the results were disastrous. In the first place, Hueppe seems to have sought to boost his own reputation by putting it about that he had been specifically invited to Hamburg to deal with the epidemic, whereas in reality he had invited himself. This annoyed Rumpf sufficiently to cause him to initiate a controversy in the press over the invitation once Hueppe had departed. Much more serious than this rather trivial dispute, however, was the fact that Hueppe's method seemed only to be killing off the patients at an alarming rate. Of the 31 cases who entered the women's ward number 26 between 3 September and Hueppe's departure, 15 died by 1 October; while of the 22 cases entering the men's ward number 41 after Hueppe took it over on 4 September, 5 turned out not to have the disease at all and 11 of the remaining 17 died. In all, the average case-specific mortality rate in Hueppe's wards was 57%, which was considerably higher than the average case-specific mortality for all wards in the same period. Hueppe attempted to deny or explain away this allegation. He argued that the statistics should have been based on cases already in the wards when he arrived as well as those who came in after he began his work. He alleged that some of the deaths were in fact not from cholera but from other causes such as 'inflammation of the lungs'. He suggested that those who died had been treated not by his method but by Rumpf's, carried out by junior doctors working in Hueppe's two pavilions. All this was highly unpersuasive. Those who worked with Hueppe on the wards thought that he was a 'great optimist' if he thought his treatment stood any chance of success. More damaging to Rumpf, perhaps, was the fact that Hueppe declared that conditions were so chaotic as to be quite unsuitable for the proper conduct of a scientific experiment; and it was probably his attack on the management of the hospital that was the real cause of Rumpf's ire. Hueppe's own attitudes and motives in approaching the epidemic were amply revealed, however, by his statement that he had been amazed on his arrival in Hamburg to be given administrative responsibilities in running two pavilions, instead of simply having been provided with facilities to conduct his experiments, and by his conclusion that while 'Herr Rumpf is a specialist in nervous disorders, he has never hitherto concerned himself with any aspect of cholera research. On the other hand my researches have extended knowledge of cholera in many directions.'[42]

Hueppe's treatment was in fact a kind of purgative procedure. This was nothing new. In some ways, it is true, medical views of cholera therapy had changed since 1831. It had become conventional to distinguish between different stages of the symptoms, of which there were agreed to be two. The first displayed the well-known loss of body fluids and violent muscular cramps, while in the second stage, delirium occurred and the disease somewhat resembled typhoid. It had also become usual to distinguish between 'mild', 'moderate', and 'serious' cases, usually on admission to hospital. Treatment could thus be varied according to the severity of the symptoms and the stage they had reached. Yet for all these changes, commentators were forced to conclude that the treatments used in 1831–2 were 'still used today, for cholera therapy has made only marginal progress since then'.[43]

With reference to the treatment of cholera [concluded Dr G. Häger] the last great epidemic in Hamburg in 1892 did not bring to light any innovation of lasting value. On the contrary almost all therapies which have been applied before, as well as many new ones which according to our observations up to this point can achieve nothing in practice, have been extensively tried out.[44]

The influence of Koch's discovery of the bacillus simply served to provide a new justification for existing practice. The continuity of treatment methods over sixty years of cholera in Hamburg was truly remarkable.

Even before they began work in 1892, the doctors were less than sanguine about the prospects of success. It was clear, they noted

that there is at the moment no specific cure for this infection in its acute form, and that all treatments recommended as such have not stood up to tests. The epidemic had convinced us once more that we must restrict ourselves to treatments of the symptoms in the first place ... As far as the *mild* and in particular the *moderately severe* forms, the concern in the first place was to remove the poisonous agent of the disease from the body, to render it harmless by introducing medication, to return to the body the warmth it has lost, to regulate the altered circulation, and in more exceptional cases even to stop an excessive loss of body fluids.[45]

[42] StA Hbg, Senat, Cl. VII, Lit. Ta, Pars 2, Vol. 11, Fasc. 1b: *Hamburgischer Correspondent*, 8 and 21 Oct. 1892; StA Hbg, FA Versmann XI 313: Max Versmann to Arnold Versmann, 7 Sept. 1892 (for the 'great optimist' quotation).

[43] StA Hbg. Senat, Cl. VII, Lit. Ta, Pars 2, Vol. 11, Fasc. 17, Inv. 1a: *Hamburger Fremdenblatt*, 27 Oct. 1892.

[44] *Jahrbücher der hamburgischen Staatskrankenanstalten*, 3 (1891–2), p. 111.

[45] Ibid., pp. 140, 143.

The most widely used treatment for cholera cases was thus purging. A warm 2% solution of tannin was administered repeatedly in quantities of one or two litres at a time. The doctors maintained that this treatment brought about a visible improvement in the patient's condition. On occasion creolin or soap was substituted for the tannin, with what results we are not told. The large quantities in which the solution was administered may have had the effect in some cases of countering the dehydration which is the most serious of the cholera problems. The doctors thought that such solutions would 'wash out' the alimentary canal and perhaps kill the bacilli.[46]

More drastic purgatives were also employed. The doctors administered to a large number of patients 'the treatments familiar from earlier epidemics; the idea that these might develop disinfectant antibacillary effects in the digestive tract led to their being chosen'. These disinfections were not administered in large quantities, which is perhaps just as well, since they included not only ammonium chloride, chlorhydric acid, lactic acid, bismuth, calomel, iodine, and quinine, but also creosote, hydrochloric acid, strychnine, and arsenic! Given the nature of the substances which the desperate medical staff were pouring down the unfortunate patients' throats, it is hardly surprising that their most frequent effect was to induce further vomiting (or, as the official report primly recorded, 'the unwelcome side-effects caused by their bad taste'). The most frequently administered substances were ammonium chloride and calomel, the latter a favourite since the earliest epidemic of 1830, in pure doses of up to half a gram. In the early stages of the milder cases, purgatives were administered with the idea of emptying the bowels before the bacillus had the chance to multiply. In serious cases, the repeated and severe vomiting made it pointless to administer disinfectants, and only calomel was used. An alternative strategy was to warm the body up—most patients felt extremely cold to the touch—and improve the circulation in hot baths, in water up to 36°C in temperature. These provided relief from the painful muscular cramps that usually accompanied the disease, and were popular with the patients. Attempts were also made to stimulate the heart by subcutaneous 10% infusions of camphor oil and ether. Other, more agreeable methods of stimulating the circulation included plying the patients with hot tea and coffee, or even with wine and champagne. This latter method proved rather expensive, however, and was discouraged by the hospital authorities.[47]

Calomel, which had been the most popular purgative employed in earlier epidemics, was a compound of mercury. This had the effect of turning the victims' excreta green, which in the 1830s was evidently regarded as a favourable sign. Chlorine and camphor were also used in 1831, sometimes mixed with other substances in potions or dissolved in wine.[48] More dra-

[46] Ibid., p. 143. [47] Ibid., pp. 143–5.
[48] Fricke, *Geschichtliche Darstellung des Ausbruchs der Asiatischen Cholera in Hamburg* (Hamburg, 1831), p. 29.

matically, arsenic was much favoured by a number of physicians, as were bismuth and ipecacuanha. These were all emetics, given to the patients to swallow with the aim of causing the poison to leave the body as soon as possible.[49] In 1848, a brief discussion of cholera therapies in the Hamburg Doctors' Club revealed that 'calomel and bismuth' were the most popular internal treatments.[50] Often they were administered in conjunction with opium, which provided some relief from the painful symptoms (notably muscular cramps) which usually accompanied the disease. Opium was also a favoured cholera medicine of Dr Buchheister at the Hornwerk Hospital in 1831.[51] Quinine, magnesium, and other substances were employed as well. Sometimes, in an alternative version of this strategy of driving the choleraic poison from the body, aromatics were used, and patients were treated with 'aromatic plaster in the area of the belly', or given quantities of aromatic tea.[52] Camomile flowers were the remedy adopted by 'an experienced practising physician' in Hamburg in 1831, who claimed, somewhat melodramatically, to have concocted the recipe 'according to the very extensive and definite pronouncements of a particularly clear-sighted somnambulist'.[53]

The strategy of improving the circulation and pulse rate by warming the body up had also been frequently employed in earlier epidemics. In 1831 the Hamburg Doctors' Club devoted a good deal of attention to 'the use of massage and warm baths, especially steam baths', and listened to an enthusiastic lecture 'on the favourable effects of rubbing oil into the body'.[54] Ammonium rubs were another method used to try and restore circulation to the surface and extremities of the body.[55] Victims were to be kept warm at all times[56]

---

[49] S. Hahnemann, *Sicherste Heilung und Ausrottung der asiatischen Cholera* (Leipzig, 1831); W. Cohnstein, *Trost- und Beruhigungsgründe für die durch das Herannahen der Cholera aufgeschreckten Gemüther, nebst Angabe aller gegen diese Krankheit bisher empfohlenen Schutzmittel* (Glogau and Lissa, 1831); *Unfehlbares Mittel gegen die Cholera* (Hamburg, 1831); K. Preu, *Was haben wir von der Cholera morbus zu fürchten? Ein Versuch, die aufgeschreckten Völker zu beruhigen* (Nuremberg, 1831), p.136; F. Simon, *Abfertigung und Warnung vor einem gewissen Krüger-Hansen und seinem, im Hamburger Correspondenten vom 7. September d. J. empfohlenen Mittel gegen die Cholera, von Scheue-Niemand* (Hamburg, 1831); *Glückliche Heilung der Cholera asiatica auf homöopatischem Wege, nach einem Schreiben des Dr. Schröter in Lemberg an die Versammlung homöopatischer Aerzte zu Naumburg* (Leipzig, 1831).

[50] Michael, *Geschichte des ärztlichen Vereins*, p. 148.

[51] Fricke, *Geschichtliche Darstellung*, pp. 29–30.

[52] StA Hbg, Senat, Cl. VII, Lit. Ta, Pars 2, Vol. 11, Fasc. 17, Inv. 1a: *Hamburger Fremdenblatt*, 27 Oct. 1892.

[53] *Entdeckung und Beleuchtung des bisher unbekannt gebliebenen Wesens und eigentlichen Sitzes der Cholera morbus nebst der Darstellung der Behandlungsart und der Schutzmittel gegen dieselbe für Gesunde. Für Jedermann fasslich dargestellt von einem erfahrnen praktischen Arzt nach den sehr ausführlichen und bestimmten Aussagen einer besonders hellsehenden Somnambule* (Schlafwachenden) (Hamburg, 1831).

[54] Michael, *Geschichte des ärztlichen Vereins*, p. 124.

[55] *Protocoll-Extracte der ersten bis sechsten Sitzung sämmtlicher Aertze Riga's in Betreff der daselbst herrschenden Cholera-Epidemie vom 30. May bis 4. July 1831.*

[56] T. H. Jensen, *Belehrungen, Ermunterungen und Tröstungen für den Bürger und Landmann wegen der Cholera. Von einem Landprediger* (Altona, 1831); A. B. Siedenburg, *Dr. A. B. Siedenburg's Heilverfahren bei der Cholera morbus nebst krankengeschichtlichen Belegen* (Hamburg, 1831).

and were to be given frequent hot baths.[57] Presumably only the better-off among the victims could afford to follow the advice given in 1831 by two Berlin doctors, Professor Horn and Professor Wagner, whose patients were told to lie for three-quarters of an hour in a bath filled with wine heated to a temperature of 30°R (i.e. 24° C).[58] Even more exotic were the 'frictions' employed by Dr Buchheister in Hamburg in the same year as a treatment for one cholera patient—'I had him', reported the doctor, 'roughly brushed with brushes steeped in rum'.[59] Success in this treatment was measured by the appearance of sweat, an indication that the body fluids were beginning to flow again. One pamphlet issued in 1831 even told its readers not to let the victims sleep until they had been made to sweat.[60] The advice to induce sweating by hot compresses, warm rubs, warm drinks, and so on, was repeated with official backing in Hamburg in 1848.[61] It was also widely used in 1892, when hot baths were an almost standard treatment for cholera victims once the initial chaotic period of the epidemic was over.

A third type of therapy very widely used in 1831 was blood-letting. Police surgeon Hauptfleish reported in 1831, for example, that he and his colleagues had treated cholera victims with 'blood-letting, Spanish flies, leeches' among other methods,[62] and Dr Buchheister, at the Hornwerk Hospital, had also used bleeding.[63] At a meeting of the Doctors' Club held in 1832 to discuss the treatment of cholera, bleeding was revealed as the most widely used of all treatments.[64] Blood-letting was used because it was thought to revive circulation near the surface of the body, where it was clearly impaired by the onset of cholera symptoms. In his study of the 1832 epidemic in Great Britain, Michael Durey has claimed that blood-letting was 'a reflex action on the part of the physician as soon as he entered a sick room, in much the same way as a modern general practitioner automatically reaches for his thermometer. 'It was', he has argued, 'the essential preliminary action, clearing the way for

[57] *Zur Beruhigung für Jedermann bei Annäherung der Cholera. Schreiben eines Familienvaters in St. Petersburg an seinen Freund in Deutschland* (Hamburg, 1831).

[58] E. Horn and W. Wagner, *Wie hat man sich vor der Cholera zu schützen und was hat man bei ihrem Eintritt zu ihrer Heilung und zur Verhütung der weiteren Verbreitung zu thun? Zur Beruhigung des Publikums beantwortet von dem Geheimen Medicinal-Rath und Professor Dr. Ernst Horn und dem Professor und Stadt-Physikus Dr. Wilhelm Wagner in Berlin* (Berlin, 1831).

[59] Fricke, *Geschichtliche Darstellung*, pp. 29–30.

[60] *Zubereitung auf die Cholera* (Bergedorf, 1831).

[61] *Wie ist das Erkranken bei der herrschenden Cholera-Epidemie zu vermeiden, wie erkennt man die Krankheit, und was ist bei derselben bis zur Ankunft eines Arztes zu thun? Zur Beruhigung und Belehrung des Publikums hg. von dem Hamburgischen Gesundheits-Rathe September 1848* (copy in StA Hbg, MK III A 2, Bd. I, Bl. 62).

[62] C. Münchmeyer (Hofmedicus und Stadtphysicus in Lüneberg), *Kurzgefasste Rathschläge für Familienväter zu Vorbereitungsmassregeln und die diätische und ärztliche Behandlung von Cholera-Kranken in Privathäusern zu erleichtern und zu beschleunigen* (Lüneburg, 1831); A. B. Siedenburg, *Dr. A. B. Siedenburg's Heilverfahren bei der Cholera morbus nebst krankengeschichtlichen Belegen* (Hamburg, 1831).

[63] Fricke, *Geschichtliche Darstellung*, pp. 28–9.

[64] Michael, *Geschichte des ärztlichen Vereins*, p. 128.

a reasoned diagnosis to be made.'[65] In Hamburg, however, it was used as a treatment for cholera *after* diagnosis, as long as blood could be obtained. Moreover, the widespread assumption by medical historians[66] that it was no longer widely used in 1848 also seems to be erroneous. A debate in the Hamburg Doctors' Club revealed on the contrary that 'above all it was blood-letting that had the most adherents'.[67] After 1848, however, venesection fell out of favour. Nevertheless, there were, surprisingly, still circumstances in which it was used in 1892, as we shall shortly see.

A fourth strategy was to counteract the dehydration of the victim by applying intravenous infusions of saline solution. The originators of this method appear to have been Hermann and Jaenichen in Moscow, who proposed that 'the immediate cause of death is the thickening of the blood, which prevents its circulation'and suggested the injection of fluids to thin it out again. It was used by O'Shaughnessy and Latta in Great Britain in 1832, and it is from this source that it came to Hamburg and was discussed at a meeting of the Doctors' Club. 'On 3 July 1832', it was recorded, 'Gumprecht reported the successes which Latta had achieved in Edinburgh with intra-venous saline infusions. On 4 September Zimmermann reported that he had cured a serious case with this method.' However, other members reported failures with the method. The trouble was that the clumsy needles of the time introduced air into the bloodstream, causing an embolism or stroke, or poisoning of the bloodstream because they were not properly sterilized (septicaemia). The method does not seem to have been used in 1848, nor was it discussed again in the Doctors' Club.[68] In 1892 the treatment was certainly in use in the hospitals. It was thought to be of only limited benefit. There was general agreement 'that saline solutions cannot be seen as a cure for cholera, they are only an aid which in some cases can help the patient through the severity of the first phase, but are unable to prevent the disastrous conclusion of a "typhoid" stage should it occur'. The method was believed to strengthen the heart 'as a powerful stimulant, which encourages the heart to become active again', and also to help dilute 'the poisons which the agent of cholera excretes into the body'. That it helped counter the dehydration which was so decisive a symptom of the disease was considered rather less important. In 1892, some 1,659 hospital patients in Hamburg were given intravenous or subcutaneous infusions of between 1,500 and 2,000 cubic centimetres of saline solution, sometimes repeatedly. The results were dramatic:

The pulse recovers rapidly and becomes strong and full, the cyanosis and the grey colouring of the skin vanishes, the deeply sunken eyes come to life again, breathing

[65] Durey, *The Return of the Plague*, p. 124.

[66] N. Howard-Jones, 'Cholera Therapy in the Nineteenth Century', *Journal of the History of Medicine*, 27 (1972), 373–95.

[67] Michael, *Geschichte des ärztlichen Vereins*, p. 148.

[68] Ibid., p. 146; Howard-Jones, 'Cholera Therapy'; Durey, *Return of the Plague*, pp. 128–30.

grows deeper and more regular, and a blush returns to the face, sometimes with an outbreak of sweating. The patient feels an inner warmth and a significant improvement in his condition. Those who were previously lying in their beds in an apathetic, comatose state, not responding when they were addressed, not even reacting to the cut through the skin made when their veins were opened, often awaken as from a deep sleep as the saline infusion streams in, and the rough, hoarse cholera voice becomes clear and comprehensible. Under the influence of the warm saline infusion flowing into the body, the muscular convulsions decline and cease altogether. The picture is changed as if a magic wand had been waved, and the seriously ill patient is changed with the infusion into a patient on the way to recovery.

Although some of the patients so treated did indeed go on to recover from the disease, many eventually succumbed even after four or five subsequent infusions. The quantities of fluid administered, whether orally, intravenously, or subcutaneously, were in no way enough to compensate for the massive dehydration which the patients suffered, a fact which was instinctively felt by the patients themselves, for, as one volunteer nurse was obliged to explain, the doctors' policy 'of limiting the consumption of drinks in order to avoid further vomiting' met with widespread protests: 'the patients often saw evil intentions behind this restriction, and it was difficult to make them realize that drink was only denied them in their own interests'.[69]

Medical reports issued in 1892 went out of their way to stress that there was no question of air-bubbles being introduced into the bloodstream or of infections being causes by unsterilized needles, They were confident that the dangers that had led to the abandonment of this therapy in the mid-nineteenth century had now been overcome. Yet while the treatment was no longer positively dangerous, it was still thought to be disappointingly ineffective. In retrospect, it seems likely that this was because the infusions were not substantial enough in quantity, nor followed by the drinking of large amounts of fluids; it may also have been the case that the physiological balance of the solution was not the best possible for the patients. However, intravenous injections of saline solutions sometimes had unpleasant side-effects. Ida Neubauer, who dealt with discharged hospital patients in Winterhude, noted for example that one woman 'still had great boils from her salt injections'.[70]

II

How much difference did these therapies make to hospital mortality rates? The most promising treatment seemed to be the saline infusion. It seems that only serious cases were given intravenous infusions, usually on the first day. Out of 193 cases treated in this way by Dr Rieder in the Old General Hospital,

[69] *Jahrbücher der Hamburgischen Staatskrankenanstalten*, 3 (1891–2), p. 99; 'Meine Erlebnisse' (n. 24, above).
[70] StA Hbg, FA Neubauer 1, p. 30.

191 were classified as 'serious cholera, mainly *stadium algidum*'. 125 died, a case-specific mortality rate of 65%. Among the 80 remaining, untreated cases in Dr Rieder's cholera wards, the death rate was no less that 90%. 24 of these untreated patients died within 12 hours of admission and were 'in part admitted when they were already moribund'. Although there were similar cases among those treated with infusions, they were likely to have been fewer in number; treatment was not normally given to patients who were clearly dying on arrival. If we remove the 24 'moribund' cases from the untreated, we still get a mortality rate of 86%. Moreover, some of the 8 who recovered received subcutaneous infusions. 301 serious cases were treated with Cantani's tannic acid solution, 231 in the form of an infusion. The case-specific mortality here ran at 67%. Case-specific mortality among all 2,283 cholera patients combined ran at 79%, so here too the treatment may have made a small difference. However, some 80% of those serious cases who recovered had not received treatment with saline infusion at all, so in numerical terms the effect of the treatment really was marginal. And it may have been counteracted by other therapies.[71]

Individual patients were often subjected to a number of different treatments over a period of several days. For example the patient W., a woman aged 31, was admitted to hospital in Hamburg on 4 September 1892. The medical notes on her case described her as suffering 'numerous episodes of diarrhoea; this evening vomiting twice, many muscular convulsions, back and stomach pains, feet cold, totally collapsed, body cold, aphonic. About 8 o'clock face grey, eyes fallen in'. She claimed to have drunk only boiled water, but some of the people in her house had already died of cholera and she had most probably been infected, directly or indirectly, by them. She was given a subcutaneous infusion of 2,000 cc saline solution not long after being admitted, but this made little difference and she continued to complain of extreme thirst, so she was given another 2,000 cc of saline solution intravenously. This had the effect of restoring her pulse—previously the doctors had been unable to feel it at all—and arousing her consciousness. 'Patient spontaneously opens her eyes, asks how she is etc.' The next day her pulse remained strong. She suffered 'a great deal of diarrhoea, less vomiting'. This continued on 6 September, and her pulse began to fade again, so she was given 40 drops of creolin and 0.01 ml. morphine. On 7 September 100 g. of urine were removed with a catheter; on the 8th another 300 g. were taken out. The patient was still throwing up and complaining of stomach cramps, so she was given some 'bismuth powder'. A further infusion of saline solution on 9 September brought about another improvement in the pulse. The patient, it was reported, 'feels fresher'. She had stopped vomiting by 10 September,

[71] *Jahrbücher der Hamburgischen Staatskrankenanstalten*, 3 (1891–2), pp. 102–6, 150. For the eventual success of rehydration therapy see W. E. van Heyningen and J. R. Seal, *Cholera. The American Scientific Experience 1947–80* (Boulder, 1985), pp. 22–5, 65–9.

and diarrhoea had almost ceased, but she was now complaining of severe pains in her left side, 'stabbing pains in her right side', and 'palpitations'. On the 11th she suffered 'the onset of absolutely critical delirious episodes. *Casus gravissimus*'. She was given morphine to calm her down. At 9 o'clock on the morning of 13 September she died: 'completely acute *Exitus*', as the medical notes put it.[72]

In another case, however, large infusions of saline solution had a more beneficial effect, perhaps because they were administered in rapid succession. Patient G., admitted on 31 August, was 'almost unconscious on admission, collapse, could not be questioned, has enormous muscular convulsions, diarrhoea, and continual vomiting of blackish liquid masses'. His pulse could not be felt. Camphor injections were administered and the patient was given a number of hot baths. More important, in his first two days in hospital he received eight and a half litres of saline solution intravenously, in a total of five separate infusions. The medical report noted 'colossal vomiting, retching motions, and innumerable cholera stools'. The patient continued to throw up until 6 September, then began to recover. He was discharged on the 25th.[73] Other patients, however, were given large infusions of saline solution over a much longer period and still failed to recover.[74] There seemed to be no clear pattern to these cases; and although infusions were generally recognized as giving temporary relief, the general view was that they did not offer the promise of a satisfactory cure.

Cholera therapy in our own day is based on the recognition that, as Norman Howard-Jones pointed out in 1972,

The cause of death in cholera is a depletion of fluids from the body, due to the enormous losses of water and electrolytes resulting from persistent diarrhoea and vomiting. It is this loss of fluid that accounts for the tarry consistency of the blood and its virtual disappearance from the peripheral vessels. Cholera patients are in desperate need of rehydration therapy to restore the volume and fluidity of the blood, initially by the intravenous infusion of physiologically balanced saline solution, and later by the drinking of large quantities of fluids.

Thus in principle any treatment which further dehydrated the patient was likely to be positively harmful. All the various emetics and purgatives used in cholera cases had this effect, of course, because they induced yet more vomiting and diarrhoea. The conclusions drawn by Howard-Jones from this fact were drastic indeed. In the nineteenth century, he wrote, 'tens of thousands of cholera patients must have been despatched by their physicians to their graves' through the application of these therapies.[75] More recently,

[72] *Jahrbücher der Hamburgischen Staatskrankenanstalten*, 3 (1891–2), p. 107.
[73] Ibid., p. 108.
[74] Ibid., pp. 107–9, for further case-histories.
[75] Howard-Jones, 'Cholera Therapy'.

Michael Durey has sought to defend the medical profession of the time by claiming that such therapies in reality made very little difference. He argued that very little blood was let because it was only done as a preliminary precautionary method. In Hamburg, however, blood was let as a treatment, not as a precaution in 1831–2 and 1848, and so the quantities are likely to have been larger. In 1892, patients were sometimes relieved of up to 800 cc of blood in order to make room, as it were, for the saline solution. This was a large enough quantity to have a serious effect. Durey estimated that if more than 20 or 30 ml. were removed, the patient's situation would begin to deteriorate. He has also suggested that medical men would not have continued to let blood in cholera cases if it had had the devastating effects alleged by Howard-Jones.[76] But this, of course, is highly speculative. Similarly, in the case of purgatives and emetics, Durey has taken a remarkably positive view of calomel and its allies. He is too cautious to make any bold claims for their success. But the language in which he writes about them is far from neutral. 'Most medical men chose wisely ... relative effectiveness ... to suggest that calomel saved lives *on any significant scale* [*my italics*] would be altogether too sanguine ...' and so on. This adds up to a strong suggestion that these methods were indeed effective. On the whole, Durey concludes, the nineteenth-century medical profession did the best it could with the concepts and materials available to it, and he strongly hints that it was more likely to have saved the lives of cholera victims than to have hastened their demise, as Howard-Jones claims it did.

There are serious problems involved in trying to arrive at a convincing assessment of these rival arguments. Durey, for instance, has suggested that treatment in 1853–4 was effective because the mortality among cholera victims undergoing calomel and sulphuric acid therapy was 45–47%, whereas the normal case-specific mortality rate was 50–75%. But these figures are unsatisfactory because the other variables in the sample are unaccounted for: it might be, for example, that only the less severe cases were selected for treatment, or that treatment was administered mainly to victims in the age-group where case-specific mortality was lowest and the chances of recovery seemed best—and as we shall see in Chapter 5, case-specific mortality did indeed vary according to age. If those who were given calomel and sulphuric acid therapy were mainly in an age-group where case-specific mortality averaged 25–30%, and it was generally the milder cases that were selected for treatment, then a case-specific mortality rate of 45–47% would suggest the opposite of what Durey takes it to suggest, namely that calomel and sulphuric acid made things worse than they already were.

The general hospital statistics give some idea of how effective hospital treatment and care was in cholera cases in 1892. In all, 8,296 cholera victims

[76] Durey, *The Return of the Plague*, p. 123; *Jahrbücher der Hamburgischen Staatskrankenanstalten*, 3 (1891–2), p. 149.

were hospitalized in Hamburg in 1892. 3,994 of them died and 4,302 were eventually discharged. The case-specific cholera mortality rate for Hamburg hospital patients in 1892 was thus 48%. The mean case-specific cholera mortality rate for all cases was 51%, so—taking the innumerable possibilities of statistical error into account—hospitalization seems in general to have made little difference.[77] This represented something of an improvement on earlier epidemics. In 1848, for instance, the mortality rate among cholera hospital patients was higher than average, at 56%.[78] But in earlier epidemics, as we have seen, a much smaller proportion of cases was hospitalized. During the first two weeks of the 1892 epidemic, it seems clear that priority in admission was given to serious cases. Between 22 and 28 August, 79% of the cases admitted to hospital were classified as 'serious'; in the second week, from 29 August to 4 September, the proportion fell to 69%, and in the third week to 64%, remaining at this level for the rest of the epidemic. Given this pattern of admission, it is not surprising that hospital mortality rates were high in the first week of the epidemic. 67% of those admitted suffering from cholera between 22 and 28 August died. Already in the second week, to 4 September, the case-specific mortality rate among hospitalized patients had fallen to 56%. Thereafter, until 25 September, it hovered around the 50% mark, roughly the same as the case-specific mortality rate in the city as a whole.[79] In general, therefore, hospital mortality rates reflected changes in admissions policy rather than the effects of treatment.

So there is no conclusive evidence that hospitalization, taken overall, either helped or hindered a cholera victim's chance of recovery. A treatment such as saline or tannin infusions may have had a marginal effect in improving the patient survival rate; other treatments, such as the emetics and purgatives administered by Professor Hueppe and others, may have had a marginal effect in worsening it. Morphine and opium probably did much to ease the terrible sufferings of the victims. For those who were unfortunate enough to be hospitalized during the first two weeks of the epidemic, the experience must have been an alarming and frightening one, moderated only by the apathy and indifference which the middle stages of the illness seemed to bring, before delirium set in. Surrounded by patients exhibiting the most serious and extreme symptoms of the disease, attended only intermittently, if at all, by an overworked and undermanned staff of physicians and nurses, they can have had little hope of recovery. All around them two out of every three patients on the cholera wards were dying the frightful death that cholera brought. In the corridors and grounds, the bodies and coffins of victims were visible in their hundreds to those able to look. Often these early victims were taken to hospital without the knowledge of their family and relatives; isolated

[77] Ibid., Plate VII.

[78] StA Hbg, MK III A 2 Bd. 1, Bl. 95.

[79] *Jahrbücher der Hamburgischen Staatskrankenanstalten*, 3 (1891–2), Table, 1, p. 147.

and unable to contact those they knew and loved, they suffered and died alone, the most miserable of the epidemic's many victims.

c. *Fear and Panic*

I

The terror which patients must have experienced on the cholera wards was only the most extreme expression of a general fear that gripped the city's population in 1892. 'Wide circles of the population', as one observer noted, 'were gripped by a panic.'[1] The sight of the cholera victims and the hidden nature of the deadly menace made people 'nervous';[2] 'the population', it was reported, 'was seized by great fear and nervousness'.[3] 'The fear', wrote the domestic servant Doris Viersbeck, 'that a loved one could be affected by this terrible plague, and also the worry that one might oneself fall ill and then be pitilessly carried off under suspicion of having cholera to lie in bed among the victims (for one could read of such cases daily) put one into a feverish state of anxiety.' Even Senators' wives were said by friends to be 'sick with fear' and everywhere people came across 'anxious faces'.[4] Rumours of all kinds quickly became rife. Fear of cholera grew into a general fear: soon it was widely believed that typhus had broken out as well, and in one report it was even claimed that there was an epidemic of 'the black pox' in Hammerbrook.[5] Rumours were coursing through the city even before the outbreak of the disease was officially announced. As soon as they began to occur, cholera cases were reported in the local press, first of all in small, isolated notices in columns devoted to miscellaneous trivial news items, then in increasing numbers, until the coincidence of so many cases with 'cholera-like symptoms' became too alarming to overlook.[6] On 20 August, well before the presence of the disease in the city was officially announced, the *Hamburger Fremdenblatt* noted that rumours of an epidemic had been circulating in the city, although it was at pains to deny them. On 22 August, however, it reported that these

[1] StA Hbg, FA Buehl 2c, p. 37. See generally, on this subject, R. Baehrel, 'Épidémie et terreur. Histoire et sociologie', *Archives Historiques de la Revolution Française*, 23 (1951), 113–46.

[2] StA Hbg, FA Gustav Hertz B17, Rudolf Hertz to Gustav Hertz and Frau Hertz, 27 Aug. 1892.

[3] Ibid., FA Lippmann A20, p. 36.

[4] Doris Viersbeck. *Erlebnisse eines Hamburger Dienstmädchens* (Munich, 1907), p. 88; Tagebuch Elise Mönckeberg, 27 Sept., 28 Aug. 1892 (in private possession).

[5] StA Hbg, Senat, Cl. VII, Lit. Ta. Pars 2, Vol. 11, Fasc. 17, Inv. 4: *Kölnische Zeitung*, 30 Aug. 1892; StA Hbg, PP S3490 Bd. 1: *Vorwärts*, 4 Oct. 1892.

[6] *Hamburger Echo* (microfilm, StA Hbg), 20–4 August. 1892; *Hamburger Fremdenblatt*, 17–18 Aug. 1892 (microfilm, StA Hbg). The rumours circulating in the city before 24 Aug. are dramatized in Paul Schurek's fictional account of the epidemic, *Das Leben geht weiter* (Stuttgart, 1940), p. 74.

rumours had become 'alarming' and 'exaggerated' and demanded an official response.[7] Probably few people were aware of any danger before 18 or 19 August; but the 66 new cases that occurred on the 20th must have set a wave of speculation going, and the fact that 113 more people fell ill—often in public—with the symptoms of the disease on the 21st can have left little room for doubt in most people's minds that something was seriously amiss.[8]

These rumours and fears found their expression in a mass flight from the city on 22 August. Figure 14 shows that, taking account of the annual 10.5% increase in railway travel in this period, and the normal weekly increase in traffic on a Sunday, over 8,000 more railway tickets were purchased on 22 August, and nearly 4,000 more on 23 August, than would normally have been expected. From 24 August, immediately after the official announcement of the disease's presence, however, traffic began to fall off.[9] As a reporter for the *Kölnische Zeitung* remarked on 28 August, 'the spell which has lain more or less heavily on every soul is beginning to dissipate; the fear of cholera, which has indeed driven thousands from the city in the last few days, no longer has that uncanny character which trembled unspoken on everyone's lips'.[10] As this quotation suggests, the mass flight of at least 12,000 people (or 2% of the population) on 22–3 August did not go unnoticed.[11] 'That many weak spirits are running away', wrote Burgomaster Johann Georg Mönckeberg to his son on 30 August 1892, 'or commit the most unbelievable stupidities, in order as far as possible to preserve their petty lives, goes without saying.' His daughter was more forthright. 'Half humanity is leaving', she wrote in her diary the same day.[12] One inhabitant of Hamburg, in the city at the time, estimated on 25 September that 40,000 people had fled the city since the beginning of the epidemic.[13] The official report of the Imperial Health Office also noted 'that a large number of Hamburg's inhabitants sought to remove themselves from the danger of infection by going away'.[14] In similar vein, Georg Koch, head of Hamburg's Statistical Bureau, and in the city throughout the epidemic, reported on 2 September that 'many people of Hamburg have fled'.[15] 'Eutin, Gremsmühlen, Malente, the hotel *Zur Hol-*

[7] *Hamburger Fremdenblatt*, 20 and 22 Aug. 1892.

[8] For these figures, see Table 4, above.

[9] StA Hbg, Cholerakommission 13: Flüchtlinge. For the detailed calculations, see the Statistical Appendix, below.

[10] StA Hbg, Senat, Cl. VII, Lit. Ta, Pars. 2, Vol. II, Fasc. 17, Inv. 4: *Kölnische Zeitung*, 30 Aug. 1892.

[11] Cf. the reference to crowds who 'stormed the railway stations', in Aust. 'Vor 80 Jahren', pp. 302–11.

[12] Mönckeberg, *Bürgermeister Mönckeberg*, p. 20; Tagebuch Tilli Mönckeberg, 30 Aug. 1892 (in private possession).

[13] StA Hbg, FA Birt 6, Tagebuch von Friederike Birt, entry for 25 Sept. 1892.

[14] (G. Gaffky), *Amtliche Denkschrift über die Choleraepidemie 1892*, p. 6.

[15] Friederike Koch (ed.), 'Die Tagebuchaufzeichnungen Georg Kochs über die Hamburger Cholera-Epidemie des Jahres 1892', *Die Heimat. Monatsschrift zur Pflege der Natur- und Landeskunde in Schleswig-Holstein und Hamburg* 79 (1972), 353–4; 80 (1973), 23–4.

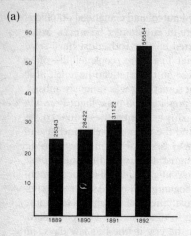

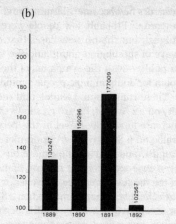

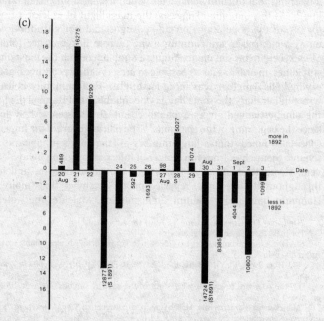

(*a*) Railway tickets bought in Hamburg and Altona on 20, 21, and 22 August 1889–92 (in thousands)

(*b*) Railway tickets bought in Hamburg and Altona from 23 August to 3 September 1889–92 (in thousands)

(*c*) Railway tickets bought in Hamburg and Altona in 1892 as compared with same day in 1891 (in thousands; S = Sunday)

Source: StA Hbg, Cholerakommission 13: Flüchtlinge

FIG. 14. The flight from the city, August 1892

steinschen Schweiz on the Kellersee', observed another reporter, 'were literally stormed by the inhabitants of Hamburg.'[16] The *Norddeutsche Allgemeine Zeitung*, a newspaper widely read in Hamburg's hinterland, complained that the inhabitants of the city had 'left the city in such large numbers' that they posed a serious threat to the surrounding area.[17] It was only in early October that, as the press reported, 'the refugees were gradually returning'.[18]

The overwhelming majority of these refugees were middle class. The *Norddeutsche Allgemeine Zeitung*, a newspaper of impeccably respectable views, alleged that it was the better-off citizens who fled in the early days of the epidemic.[19] The right-wing *National-Zeitung* agreed: 'the better-situated middle class is leaving the city'.[20] This accusation was subsequently repeated on many occasions by the Social Democrats,[21] and the Hamburg police countered such allegations by referring to 'the large number of workers who have fled the disease ... a factor which was particularly noticeable in the departure of the Polish workers'.[22] The official medical report by the Imperial Health Office also noted that 'numerous workers in factories which have reduced or ceased production because of the stoppage of trade, have turned to areas outside the city in their search for work'.[23] Polish migrant workers, in fact, generally left at this time to help with the potato harvest, so it is impossible to say with any certainty that they left to escape the cholera. Workers usually travelled on a Sunday, to avoid losing a day's pay, and going away on holiday was still an almost exclusively middle-class habit. Bourgeois business men could better afford to take time off than wage labourers could. It was not likely to have been the working classes who stormed the Schleswig-Holstein hotels. Of course, most of the middle classes did stay in the city during the epidemic. The *Hamburgische Börsen-Halle*, the in-house newspaper of the Exchange, in defending the bourgeoisie against the charge that it had fled the city, brought forward the following evidence, which was perhaps revealing of the city's priorities in more ways than it intended:

While mass meetings have long been voluntarily abandoned or forbidden as absolutely dangerous, the greatest daily mass meeting of our city, the Exchange, continues unaltered. Habit and sense of duty have—now as before, and even in the very worst days—led thousands thither for an hour or two; although they knew exactly the risks

---

[16] StA Hbg, PP S3490 Bd. 1: *Hamburger Echo*, 4 Oct. 1892.

[17] Ibid.: *Hamburgischer Correspondent*, 29 Sept. 1892.

[18] Ibid.: *Vorwärts*, 15 Oct. 1892 (reporting from Hamburg).

[19] Quoted in *Export*, 40, 6 Oct. 1892.

[20] StA Hbg, Senat, Cl. VII, Lit. Ta. Pars 2, Vol. 11, Fasc. 17, Inv. 4: *National-Zeitung*, 30 Aug. 1892. See the same file for a similar account in *Kölnische Zeitung*, 30 Aug. 1892 (report of 28 Aug.).

[21] See below, pp. 371–2.

[22] StA Hbg, Senat, Cl. XI, Gen. No. 2, Vol. 61, Fasc. 1: Denkschrift vom 4. Nov. 1892, p. 9.

[23] (G. Gaffky), *Amtliche Denkschrift*, p. 6.

they were running, they still attended. That is the 'pusillanimity of the coffee- and pepper-sacks'![24]

Here then was one rule for the rich and another for the poor; and it was perhaps surprising that while the Social Democrats agreed so readily to abandon their own meetings, they made no comment about the continued meetings of the Exchange. For here, whatever the *Börsen-Halle* might say, it was not simply the call of duty but also the lure of profits, or—more likely in the circumstances—the fear of bankruptcy that led the dealers to brave the dangers of contamination and frequent the crowded Exchange. Yet, while one reporter noted the usual scene in the Exchange on 6 September, with up to 2,000 people present, he added that perhaps 1,500 regular participants had been absent at the beginning of the month.[25] A week earlier, on 28 August, another reporter noted: 'the Exchange has hardly half the usual number of regular participants'.[26] And on 10 September a local newspaper complained that bills were being left unpaid because 'unfortunately a large part of the citizens in Hamburg who owe money and can pay it are away'.[27] So many stayed away after all.

Many middle-class Hamburgers were already away from the city on holiday when the epidemic broke out. Burgomaster Mönckeberg reported on 30 August that 'I am glad to say however that all those whose office and duty demand it are faithfully in their places and in part have broken off their holidays to return here'.[28] Caesar Amsinck, a member of one of the city's largest and most powerful families, also returned from holiday on 27 August to deal with the problems faced by his business.[29] Many officials, such as Senate Syndic Roeloffs, came back early from their holidays and most of the city's medical men who were away returned as soon as they heard the news.[30] Others came back for personal reasons. Ida Neubauer, governess to the children of the shipowner Carl Laeisz, returned from a holiday in Norderney against the advice of her doctor because she wanted to be with her brothers and sisters, who also lived in Hamburg.[31] Some were more hesitant. The Goverts family, also on holiday in the second half of August, and due to come back on the 1 September, spent the evening before their return trip arguing over whether or not to postpone their journey. They were especially worried because the head of the family, Dr Ernst Goverts, had a stomach

---

[24] StA Hbg, Senat, Cl. VII, Lit. Ta, Pars 2, Vol. 11, Fasc. 1b: *Hamburgische Börsen-Halle*, 12 Sept. 1892.

[25] Ibid.: Fasc. 17, Inv. 4, 6 Sept. 1892.

[26] Ibid.: *Kölnische Zeitung*, 30 Aug. 1892.

[27] Ibid., Inv. 2: *Hamburger Fremdenblatt*, 10 Sept. 1892.

[28] Mönckeberg, *Bürgermeister Mönckeberg*, p. 21.

[29] StA Hbg, FA Beneke, M94: Caesar Amsinck to Hugo Beneke 15 Sept. 1892.

[30] See above, p. 321.

[31] StA Hbg, FA Neubauer 1, p. 28.

upset. In the end, however, they kept to their plans.[32] But among the holiday-making classes there were many who delayed their return to the city. Pastor Gustav Ritter, for example, wrote to his wife Henny, who was in Travemünde when the epidemic broke out, advising her not to travel. Evidently she felt under some moral pressure to come back, for he added that she had no need to feel guilty about staying: after all, she had not fled the epidemic, she merely happened to be out of town when it struck. Henny Ritter stayed in Travemünde until 26 September, when the epidemic was virtually over.[33] Senior Pastor Behrmann actually sent his wife and children to Travemünde when the epidemic broke out, although they had only recently returned from a holiday there; and the small shipowning family of the Reuss-Löwensteins, who lived with a single domestic servant in St Pauli, left for Gremsmühlen on 27 or 28 August. They stayed with a well-off uncle until the epidemic was over.[34] More prominent families also took precautions of this kind. Rudolf Hertz, son of Senator Gustav Hertz, took his wife and child 'and the maid-servant (who beamed at the idea)' to Hanover on 28 August.[35] Gustav Petersen, son of Burgomaster Carl Petersen, wrote from his holiday—where the family remained throughout September—that he was reluctant to return, 'because of the cholera'.[36] Senator Refardt's daughter Edith wanted to go back to Hamburg, believing 'that my place is at home', but ran into strong objections from her family.[37] Senator Johannes Versmann, cautious as ever, sent his family to Kassel on 30 August. They returned a week later.[38] The Senators and responsible officials may have stayed at their posts, therefore, but a good many of them made sure that their families found their way to safety.

The fear which drove many of the bourgeoisie to flee the city was also expressed in dramatic changes in the conduct of those who remained. 'In the better classes', as one reporter noted, 'an exaggerated terror has frequently ... taken hold, so that many families are changing their whole way of life.'[39] The middle classes removed themselves from possible sources of infection as far as they could. 'One cut oneself off completely, lived like a prisoner', wrote Friederike Birt in her diary on 25 September.[40] 'Those who did not need to', remembered Max von Schinkel later, 'did not go on to the street at all', and Burgomaster Mönckeberg's wife noted on 28 August that 'all social

[32] Ibid., Goverts 76, Bd. 17: Tagebuch E. F. Goverts 31 Aug–2 Sept.1892.

[33] Ibid., Ritter D2, pp. 182–5.

[34] C. K. G. Behrmann, *Erinnerungen* (Berlin, 1904), p. 271; H. Reuss-Löwenstein, *Kreuzfahrt meines Lebens. Erinnerungen* (Hamburg, 1962), p. 36.

[35] StA Hbg, FA Gustav Hertz B17: Rudolf Hertz to his parents, 27 Aug. 1892.

[36] Ibid., FA Petersen G5: Gustav Petersen to Anna Petersen, 20 Sept. 1892.

[37] Ibid., FA Refardt G1: Edith Refardt, letter of 30 Aug. 1892.

[38] Ibid., FA Versmann, VI A6; Tagebuch Johannes Versmann, entries for 30 Aug. and 5 Sept. 1892.

[39] Ibid., FA Westenholz B XV 2, p. 16.

[40] Ibid, FA Birt 6, entry for 25 Sept. 1892.

invitations are being declined'.[41] Social life in these circles almost ceased. Jakob Loewenberg, young and on his own, found life very tedious during the epidemic. 'If only the evenings weren't so long! Where can one go? The cafés and restaurants are empty. One is looked at with astonishment if one enters them, and one becomes anxious if one is sitting completely alone in an enormous room.'[42] Those who usually frequented such establishments were staying at home. 'In the dismal cholera days', wrote Dr Ernst Goverts in his diary, ' ... we lived, like all our friends and relations, completely quietly, no one thought of being sociable.'[43] Doctors especially were almost obliged to live this kind of life. The director of the New General Hospital in Eppendorf, Professor Theodor Rumpf, reported in his memoirs that

My wife and I would have been completely alone in the difficult cholera period in 1892 if we had not met frequently with the Kümmel family. In those days Dr Kümmel was surgeon in charge of St Mary's Hospital. But because he also treated cholera cases, he and his family were avoided as posing a threat of infection. Absolutely without justification. If one takes care the danger of passing cholera on from person to person is very small.[44]

The well-off citizens of Hamburg were able to live this kind of isolated existence because they had servants to whom they could delegate the necessary contacts with the outside world. At the same time, this meant—as R. J. Morris noted of the 1832 epidemic in Britain—that servants now appeared to pose a threat of infection in middle-class houses.[45] Already on 28 August letters to the local press in Hamburg were urging domestic servants to stay at home. Attempts to keep them there led to conflicts when the servants wished to visit sick or dying relatives. Such visits struck terror into the hearts of their employers, who feared that they would bring the disease back with them. The Hamburg domestic servant Doris Viersbeck, for instance, recalled later of the household in which she worked:

Tradespeople were dealt with at the window, so that we did not come into close contact with them. Of course we were not allowed to go out, and we had no stomach for it either. Only on one occasion did my sister and I arrange to meet and pay a single visit to our brother, but what a shock was in store for us when we got to his door! There we were told that he had a mild attack of cholera and it would be better if we did not come into closer contact with him. No, we could not do that, because we had promised our employers to keep away even from the mildest cases. With a heavy heart we made our way home.[46]

[41] Max von Schinkel, *Lebenserinnerungen* (Hamburg, 1929), p. 127; Tagebuch Elise Mönckeberg, 28 Aug. 1892 (in private possession).

[42] Loewenberg, *Aus zwei Quellen*, p. 281.

[43] StA Hbg, FA Goverts 76, Bd. 17, entry for 14 Sept. 1892. For similar comments, see also ibid., FA Gustav Hertz B17: Else Hertz to Johanna Pfefferkorn, 25 Sept. 1892.

[44] Rumpf, *Lebenserinnerungen*, p. 44.

[45] Morris, *Cholera 1832*, pp. 92–3.

[46] Viersbeck, *Erlebnisse*, pp. 88–9.

Not all servants were as obedient as Doris Viersbeck. One, for example, continued to visit and be visited by her sister in the Hammerbrook, even though this was forbidden. Discovered by her employers, she was dismissed on 22 September. Outraged at such treatment, she sued them for unfair dismissal and claimed the wages and maintenance she was owed. But the court ruled that a domestic servant's contract of employment had to a certain degree the character of a 'family contract' which obliged her in general terms to avoid causing any danger in life and limb to other members of the household. Cholera, in the court's opinion, constituted just such a danger, especially since 'the relatives or acquaintances of domestic servants mostly live in such areas or quarters which have formed more or less strong centres of infection'. The court found in consequence that the dismissal was lawful.[47]

While the middle classes carried their already existing fear of contact with the proletariat to these extreme and previously unheard-of lengths, locking themselves away in their houses and instituting there a domestic regime of surpassing order and cleanliness for the duration of the epidemic,[48] the working classes expressed their fear in a very different manner. As Pastor Christian Stubbe lamented, 'it is a very disturbing but undeniable fact, not only in our city, but, as various temperance periodicals have reported, in other places as well, that during cholera epidemics the consumption of spirits increases enormously'.[49] Another commentator confirmed on 16 September 'that we have never seen so many drunks on our streets as in the period of this epidemic'.[50] Demand for alcohol was particularly strong among ambulancemen, corpse-bearers, grave-diggers, disinfection workers, and volunteer nurses, whose lot it was to come into close physical contact with the victims. Ambulancemen were given 'half a bottle of wine and cognac' with their lunch every day,[51] and even the police, charged with collecting the sick in the early days of the epidemic, bought themselves bottles of schnapps 'to wash down the nausea which overcomes one when one is rummaging around all day and night among the sick and the dead'.[52] So great was the demand that the authorities were forced to announce on 26 August that illegal sales of alcohol in the free port area would not be prosecuted;[53] and on 16

[47] StA Hbg, Meldewesen B43, Bl. 94: *Hamburgischer Correspondent*, 2 Dec. 1892. Katharina Schlegel kindly supplied the references in notes 4 and 46–7. See more generally K. Schlegel, 'Mistress and Servant in Nineteenth-century Hamburg: Employer/Employee Relationships in Domestic Service 1880–1914', *History Workshop Journal*, 15 (1983), 60–77.

[48] For further evidence along these lines, see Chapter 5a, below.

[49] C. Stubbe, *Hamburg und der Branntwein: Die ältere Mässigkeits- und Enthaltsamkeitsbewegung in Hamburg* (Berlin, 1911), p. 10.

[50] F. Wolter, 'Die Cholera in Hamburg', *Berliner klinische Wochenschrift*, 29 (17 Oct. 1892), pp. 1062–3.

[51] StA Hbg, PP S3490, Bd. 3: *General-Anzeiger*, 11 July 1912.

[52] Ibid., Bd. 1: *Hamburger Fremdenblatt*, 28 Oct. 1892.

[53] StA Hbg, Senat, Cl. VII, Lit. Ta, Pars 2, Vol. 11, Fasc. 16, Inv. 9: *Hamburgischer Correspondent*, 9 Sept. 1892.

September the disinfection workers were warned that they would only be reimbursed for the purchase of cognac in so far 'as the need for it became apparent on the occasion of sudden cases of illness among the men employed at the disinfection centres'. Under these circumstances it was hardly surprising that the poet Detlev von Liliencron, in Hamburg at the time, found 'the sanitary officials all drunk'.[54]

Drunkenness created some tension where the middle and working classes came into contact with one another. As one middle-class volunteer doctor complained early in September, 'to maintain discipline in the barracks during these night hours, when the nurses are all drunk from 2 o'clock onwards (probably in the belief that it is a protection) is difficult'.[55] Max Nonne, another doctor, remembered later that the wagoners who drove the hearses and 'also the nurses in the dissecting-room' were 'mostly very inebriated'. Under these circumstances, he complained, it was difficult for them to observe the proper hygienic procedures, and he often saw how, after off-loading the corpses at the mortuary, the wagoners, 'almost always drunk, were hosed down by the also mostly drunken disinfection workers with carbolic—in other words, a small trickle fell on to a part of their rubber coats'; a proper disinfection, in his view, it was not.[56] The belief that, as the refrain of the popular song had it, 'schnapps is good for cholera', was widespread among the proletariat. 'Cognac is the surest remedy', one of the characters in Jakob Loewenberg's autobiographical novel about the epidemic was made to remark;[57] ' "cognac", and a hundred times "cognac"', as another observer noted, 'can be found offered in shop windows, next to "cholera-bitters", "cholera wine", port wine, and other "preventive drinks"'.[58]

By drinking alcohol, people sought not only to fortify themselves against infection but also to dull their sense of fear. Cognac and beer were certainly safer to drink than water, but they could also make people careless. It was not for this reason, however, that the Medical Board warned the public on 9 September 'that the excessive consumption of spirits encourages rather than prevents the outbreak of the disease'.[59] There was a long tradition of medical writing which held that alcoholism was a major, indeed the major cause of receptivity to cholera. Writers in 1831–2 were virtually unanimous in ascrib-

[54] StA Hbg, MK III A 16, Bd. 1: Maes to Desinfektionsanstalten, 16 Sept. 1892, Bl. 89: pp. 16–23, here p. 16.

[55] StA Hbg, Senat, Cl. VII, Lit. Ta, Pars 2, Vol. 11, Fasc. 17, Inv. 4: *Marburger Volkszeitung*, 7 Sept. 1892.

[56] Nonne, *Anfang und Ziel*, p. 96. See also Aust, 'Vor 80 Jahren'.

[57] Loewenberg, *Aus Zwei Quellen*, p. 275.

[58] StA Hbg, Senat, Cl. VII, Lit. Ta, Pars 2, Vol. 11, Fasc. 17, Inv. 4: *Kölnische Zeitung*, 30 Aug. 1892. See also Schurek, *Das Leben geht weiter*, pp. 70–1. For similar observations in the American case, see Charles Rosenberg, *The Cholera Years 1832–1859* (Chicago, 1962), p. 122.

[59] StA Hbg, Senat, Cl. VII, Lit. Ta, Pars 2, Vol. 11, Fasc. 16, Inv. 9: *Hamburgischer Correspondent*, 9 Sept. 1892.

ing infection in large measure to 'excessive indulgence in alcoholic spirits',[60] and in warning that 'nothing makes the body more receptive to cholera than alcoholism'.[61] The victims, it was claimed, were 'without exception great drunkards, and some of them could empty 3–4 bottles of spirits a day'.[62] Dr Buek concurred in 1848 in the belief that it was 'the vice of drunkenness, which as is well enough known, brings cholera a particularly rich booty'.[63] It was above all schnapps, a working-class drink, that was held to cause the disease; wine, a middle-class beverage, was recommended on the contrary as a prophylactic and even used in medical treatment.[64] There was very little real evidence that alcoholism led to cholera. In 1832 it appeared that out of over 3,000 cases in Hamburg only 85 were 'notorious drunkards', and their survival rate, at 60%, was in fact rather better than average;[65] while even Dr Buek in 1848 was forced to concede that a mere 21 out of the more than 3,000 cholera cases recorded in Hamburg that year were known 'drunkards', hardly an impressive figure.[66] The discourse to which this seemingly ineradicable belief in the connection between alcohol and cholera ultimately belonged was the familiar one that ascribed illness and disease above all to moral weakness and lack of self-control, and linked them both to poverty as evidence that the unequal distribution of wealth and health was fundamentally the responsibility of the individual rather than of society as a whole.

Fear and panic were recognized as having a powerful influence on receptivity to cholera especially when they led the individual to take refuge in drink. They were portrayed as natural elements in the psychology of poverty, the last and most fatal products of a downward spiral of moral and physical integrity and self-respect that could only end in death. The victim, as one commentator wrote in 1831, was usually a 'person ruined by debauchery, but also ... the victim of poverty and ill-fortune, and put out of sorts by fear'.[67] Another claimed in the same vein 'that cholera draws its victims from the numbers of the drunk, of those who have abandoned themselves to dissipation, and of those who have been unnerved by heightened fear'.[68] Yet

[60] Jensen, *Belehrungen, Ermunterungen und Tröstungen*; Horn and Wagner, *Wie hat man sich vor der Cholera zu schützen?*

[61] *Anweisung zur Erhaltung der Gesundheit und Verhütung der Ansteckung bei etwa eintretender Choleraepidemie. Von der Königl. Preussischen obersten Medicinal-Behörde in Berlin zum Druck befördert* (Hamburg, 1831), p. 6.

[62] Fricke, *Geschichtliche Darstellung*, p. 26.

[63] StA Hbg, MK III A 2. Bd. 1, Bl. 84.

[64] *Anweisung*, p. 6.

[65] StA Hbg, Senat, Cl. VII, Lit. Ta, Pars 2, Vol. 11, Fasc. 17, Inv. 1a: *Hamburger Fremdenblatt*, 27 Oct. 1892.

[66] StA Hbg, MK III A 2 Bd. 1, Bl. 84.

[67] Jensen, *Belehrungen*. Per capita consumption of spirits in Hamburg was lower in 1831–2 and 1847–8 than in any other years from 1800–50, probably for economic reasons.

[68] J. A. P. Müller, *Verhaltungsregeln gegen Cholera morbus* (Hamburg, 1831).

there could be a rational fear of cholera as well, a fear which led the middle classes to bring a whole range of bourgeois virtues into play, from moderation and self-control to cleanliness and order. Even flight from the scene of the outbreak could be presented as a rational act, for had not Max von Pettenkofer proclaimed that cholera was the product of local circumstances, and that removing oneself from the locus of the miasma was the surest mode of self-protection? By 1892 the triumphs of Koch, and the fact that the precautions he ordained were endorsed by the authorities and legitimized by his status as discoverer of the bacillus, convinced the middle classes that 'in our social milieu, if one is only careful, there is nothing to worry about',[69] while proletarians were suffering heavily because they 'are unfortunately still very foolish, in part are not *able* to be on their guard as our sort are ... '.[70] Yet even though the middle classes could feel relatively secure if they took the recommended precautions, their fear of infection was so great that they could never be absolutely sure that they would remain immune, and so they hid themselves away or fled for more salubrious parts.

II

Fear not only drove people to drink, it also sent them to church. All over the city, as soon as the epidemic was officially announced, pastors began holding special services to pray for deliverance. As Senior Pastor Christian Behrmann said,

A sad fact now became apparent, namely that for the great mass of the people, we pastors are no longer that which we ought to be: friends in need, helpers towards faith and hope. We deceived ourselves in this matter, because we were still always called to surround certain turning-points in life with the aura of consecration; but what does that signify, if we are not called upon in the hour of need![71]

Assistant Preacher Werner, of Hamm, reported that his immediate superior, Pastor Palmer, returned from his holidays in Berchtesgaden on hearing of the outbreak of the epidemic: 'He immediately set up prayer-meetings every evening in the Trinity Church'.[72] Meanwhile his colleagues in the city parishes were attempting to organize pastoral care in the hospitals and cholera barracks. [73] On 2 September the Church Council (*Kirchenrat*) regularized these procedures, dividing the parishes into districts, arranging a supply of Bibles to the hospitals, and establishing systematic procedures for visiting the sick both in the hospitals and at home.[74] Not all pastors, however, followed these

[69] StA Hbg, FA Bertheau E 4a IV: Carl III Bertheau to Carl II Bertheau, 26 Aug. 1892.

[70] Ibid., FA Beneke M94: Caesar Amsinck to Hugo Beneke, 20 Sept. 1892.

[71] Behrmann, *Erinnerungen*, p. 281.

[72] Kirchenarchiv Hbg, D166: Pastor Friedrich Werner: 'Erinnerungen aus meiner Amtstätigkeit in der Gemeinde Süd Hamm' (MS 1937), p. 27.

[73] Ibid., Kirchenrat B. XVI. a. 2, p. 6; Behrmann, *Erinnerungen*, p. 281.

[74] Kirchenarchiv Hbg, Kirchenrat B. X. d. 11.

plans, and it may be doubted whether the church's ministrations were either regular or comprehensive. Pastor Gustav Ritter, for example, felt obliged on 10 September to offer to minister to the patients in the cholera barracks but was advised not to: 'Cholera', he was told, 'works like a very powerful poisoning process when it sets in strongly, and just as pastoral consolation has little point in cases of poisoning, so it has little purpose in cases of cholera, above all when 20 patients are crowded together on the ward.'[75] In most areas, daily services and evening prayer-meetings were arranged; even when these did not take place every day, they were held at least several times a week. The church authorities were cautious in their assessment of whether these services were a success:

The question whether a heightened need for religion has shown itself in the parishes as a result of this severe Divine Visitation could initially only be answered in the affirmative with considerable hesitation; but—praise God!—as these hard times have gone on, there has been no lack of concurring witnesses from the whole clergy, that after the first impact of the sickness, which laid claim on all our efforts to ward off its external threat, the spirit of religion and the need for religion did indeed begin seriously to come forth from broad circles of our population.[76]

Special services, such as that held on Sedan Day (13 September), were 'extraordinarily well-attended'. And the prayer-meetings in particular, it was reported, 'have enjoyed a very numerous attendance and have also been attended by classes of the population which otherwise stand aloof from the church'.[77] The Church Council hoped that 'many a broken link with the church has now been re-forged' through these prayer-meetings.[78] Certainly the enthusiasm of those who flocked to the churches at this time seems to have been genuine enough. Assistant Preacher Werner reported not only that the prayer-meetings in his parish were 'exceedingly well-attended in the first weeks' but also that the Ninety-first Psalm and the hymn 'Soar up to thy God, thou troubled soul' were especially popular: 'hardly ever has this hymn been sung so powerfully and so sincerely'.[79]

In many cases, preachers sought only to use the cholera as an image, without drawing any specific lessons from it.[80] On 21 September, for example, Senior Pastor Behrmann was said to have delivered a brilliant sermon likening the water-wagons to Christ's message, in a particularly topical and elegant comparison.[81] The lessons that the church sought to bring home to the

[75] StA Hbg, FA Ritter D2, pp. 183–4.

[76] Kirchenarchiv Hbg, Kirchenrat B. XVI. a. 2, p. 1.

[77] Ibid., Koch, 'Die Tagebuchaufzeichnungen Georg Kochs', entry for 25 Aug.; Kirchenarchiv Hbg, D166: Werner, 'Erinnerungen', p. 28.

[78] Kirchenarchiv Hbg, Kirchenrat B. XVI a. 2, p. 6.

[79] Ibid., D166: Werner, 'Erinnerungen', p. 27. See also n. 93, below.

[80] Behrmann, *Erinnerungen*, p. 280.

[81] StA Hbg, 622–1: FA Ritter D2, p. 186; Koch, 'Die Tagebuchaufzeichnungen Georg Kochs', entry for 28 Aug.

crowds of strangers who now filled the pews at its daily services and prayer-meetings were familiar ones. Both in the special address composed by Senior Pastor Behrmann, approved by the Church Council for reading in all the Hamburg churches and distributed to the public in 30,000 copies, and in a popular sermon of the time, 'I am the Lord Thy physician', which the Church Council ordered to be printed in an edition of 70,000 copies provided with specially inserted references to the cholera epidemic, the people were warned that the epidemic was God's punishment for their sins:

With deep emotion we must confess that unbelief and worldly pleasures of the most varied kinds have turned many away from God's Word and God's House. But now all should open their eyes to the uncertainty of earthly life, the evanescence of all worldly goods, the solemnity of the contemplation of Death and of the Last Judgement; so that nothing more remains but to cry out (Ps. 39.8): 'And now, Lord, what wait I for? My hope is in Thee'.[82]

Indeed cholera was used as an image in these sermons for a 'world sick unto death' from which God rescued the believer.[83] Such sentiments could help lessen the fear that gripped the sick or those in danger of infection; and mindful of such psychological functions of its ministrations, the church supplied special prayers and texts to cater for various states of mind induced by the epidemic, most notably, perhaps, 'Against the Fear of Death'.[84]

But there were also practical, secular messages conveyed in these texts. When the clergy led the congregation at a special service of thanksgiving for the end of the epidemic, on *Buss-und Bettag* (25 November), in confessing to God that 'we know Thy Visitation and feel that Thy Judgements are righteous!'[85] it was not simply the empty churches of the pre-cholera period that in their view had caused God to visit his wrath on the people of Hamburg. Carl Manchot, pastor in the parish of St Gertrud, for example, told his congregation on 18 September:

Every day we must all learn anew to suffer according to God's Will, by continuing to practise the self-control which has been demanded of everyone during this epidemic. Woe to the imprudent, who at this time do not righteously provide for themselves the protection which is entrusted to them; for whom the trouble is too great, the office too unwelcome. Woe to the wicked who at this time not only bring danger upon themselves, but also upon others.

'Duty, obedience, and faithfulness', were the virtues that Manchot preached to his parishioners. It was clear that he was doing more than simply adding a religious legitimation to all the warnings of the authorities about the

---

[82] Kirchenarchiv Hbg, Kirchenrat B. XVI. a. 2: Ansprache 'An unseren Gemeinden'; Behrmann, loc. cit. (n. 80). Verse 8 in the Luther Bible is verse 7 in the Authorized Version.

[83] J. Bernhard, *Ich bin der Herr, dein Arzt! Eine Zeitpredigt über das Evangelium des 14. Sonntages* (Lübeck, 1892).

[84] *Der Herr, dein Arzt, auch in der Cholerazeit, von H. G.* (Hamburg, 1892).

[85] Kirchenarchiv Hbg, Kirchenrat B. X. d. 12.

precautions to be taken against cholera. There was a general message here, too; that the citizens of Hamburg had failed to carry out the God-given tasks which they had been assigned; that forgetfulness of their duties to their superiors, failure to obey their masters, faithlessness in serving their betters, had brought on them the wrath of the Almighty. Nowhere is the German Protestant church's function as a legitimator of the existing structure of state and society more clearly revealed than in this sermon.[86]

It was all the more interesting, therefore, that another pastor, Albrecht Krause, speaking in St Catherine's on 2 October, chose the occasion to exercise some sharp social criticism. Krause (1838–1902) was a controversial figure whose early sermons in Hamburg in the 1860s had been officially reprimanded and whose promotion had been blocked for thirty years as a consequence. Hamburg, he declared, had indeed deserved the plague because of its worldliness: religion had virtually disappeared fom the city, young people were full of 'self-indulgence' and 'indulgence in worldly pleasures'. As a result, people had lost their sense of responsibility. Employers paid wages so low that no family man could be maintained from them; and therefore women went out to work and no longer kept house properly. The Alley Quarters had been allowed to remain as centres of poverty and degradation. 'The rich have lived in their palaces and let the homes of the poor become the objects of speculation.'[87] This message cannot have been welcome to the better-off members of his congregation. It was evidence that in some quarters of the Protestant church at least, a new spirit of social criticism was beginning to make itself felt; eventually, in the shape of figures like Adolf Harnack and Friedrich Naumann, it would feed an important strand into the resurgence of left-wing liberalism after the turn of the century.[88] Sixty years earlier, such radical sentiments would not have been heard from the pulpit.[89] Indeed, it was only the latitudinarianism of the Hamburg Senate that allowed them to be heard in 1892.

The church did not confine itself in 1892 to holding special services and delivering fulminatory admonitions. From the beginning of the epidemic local pastors were also active in visiting the sick and the dying. For many of them this was clearly a difficult experience. 'It is indeed not easy', wrote Pastor Gustav Ritter on 11 September, 'to witness pain and distress and death so suddenly and in such quantity.' Ritter, indeed, went into the houses of the

[86] C. Manchot, *Wie wir in unserer Noth nach Gottes Willen leiden* (Hamburg, 1892).

[87] A. Krause, *Hamburgs Anfechtung, Bewährung, Errettung: Predigt über Jacobus I. 12 aus der Zeit des Kampfes mit der Cholera am 2. Oktober 1892* (2nd edn., Hamburg, 1892). Krause was also a distinguished Kant scholar. For his career see StA Hbg, Zeitungsausschnitt-Sammlung A760.

[88] See J. J. Sheehan, *German Liberalism in the Nineteenth Century* (Chicago, 1978), and W. Struve, *Elites Against Democracy* (Princeton, 1973), ch. 3.

[89] But cf. Jensen, *Belehrungen*: 'It cannot be proven ... that this epidemic is a Divine Judgement, indeed it seems unbelievable, since it takes hold of the good and bad without distinction.' This is however the only example of such a sentiment to be found in the Hamburg cholera sermons.

afflicted only if summoned, and only when assured by a doctor that he 'considered that there was no danger if care was taken'.[90] Others were less timid, however; and the experience gave many of them, discouraged as they must have been by the general irreligiosity of the city's inhabitants, fresh enthusiasm for their work. For Friedrich Werner, Assistant Preacher in South Hamm, the most comforting and elevating aspect of his experiences during the epidemic was to be found at a victim's death-bed. With true Pietist fervour, he wrote:

To witness the home-coming to God of a soul which one has been able to serve as pastor, often in weakness and long without fruit, is a wonderful strengthening and a sweet reward for a pastor and a disciple of Jesus ... In death there is no unbelief, no philosophy can give peace of mind, but only the certainty that one is going to meet the Saviour. Christ has robbed death of its sting.[91]

Werner's account of the epidemic indeed consists mainly of a series of elevating death-bed scenes. It it clear that Werner—'I had no fear. I knew what the duties of my office were'—was a man of exceptional courage and devotion to his parishioners. In his memoirs he claimed that the 'ordinary people' were most important to him: 'I am a man of the people', he wrote, and he made it plain that he had little time for the world of fashionable or official religion in the great churches of the city centre.[92] Only twenty-seven at the time of the epidemic, and unmarried, he still had the recklessness and enthusiasm of youth. Arriving at the working-class apartment blocks of the Borstel-mannsweg, where the disease was already present, he found the courtyards full of weeping women, whom he gathered around him to read the Ninety-first Psalm. The rest of the day he spent in similar activities.[93] As Werner's account shows, the men who lived in such streets as the Borstelmannsweg were still out at work, so that it was mainly their womenfolk with whom the pastor had to deal. Secularization indeed was in particular a male phenomenon; in towns as well as in the countryside the great majority of Protestant communicants were women—in Hamburg in the late nineteenth century the proportion was about 64%.[94] For women, the Church offered an alternative set of social institutions to the male-dominated pubs and clubs of the working-class world of leisure; as the historian Hugh McLeod has pointed out, women may have welcomed the clergy's attacks on male drunkenness and violence and responded positively to a rare chance to meet each other outside the home, in a society where—at least according to contemporaries—companionate marriages were unusual among the working class. Thus women adhered to

---

[90] StA Hbg, FA Ritter D2, p. 184.

[91] Kirchenarchiv Hbg, D166: Werner, 'Erinnerungen', p. 26.

[92] Ibid., p. 16.

[93] Ibid., p. 23. Psalm 91 promised deliverance from 'the noisome pestilence' and assured the believer 'neither shall any plague come nigh thy dwelling'.

[94] P. Pieper, *Kirchliche Statistik Deutschlands* (Freiburg, 1899), p. 217.

religion while, increasingly, their menfolk abandoned it.[95] This was particularly true in the families of committed Social Democrats. At this time, in the early 1890s, there were only a handful of women in the party; the emergence of a mass Social Democratic women's movement only came after the turn of the century. It was not uncommon, therefore, for the wives of active Social Democrats to keep faith with the church even at the cost of serious conflict with their husbands.[96] The Social Democratic Party was actively anti-religious, seeing in the Catholic church a dangerous and powerful institution (many workers voted for the Catholic Centre Party) and a divisive influence in the labour movement, and regarding the Protestant church as the spiritual arm of the state.[97]

The conflicts which female piety and Social Democratic secularism could bring—or express—in the family are graphically illustrated in Pastor Werner's account of his ministrations in the Borstelmannsweg, a street so notorious as a hotbed of Social Democracy that the pastor took 'a good walking-stick' with him the first time he ventured down it. On one of many such occasions, he arrived in an apartment in the street to find that

A young woman was still struggling against the disease. I saw the fear in her eyes as they moved hither and thither. I bowed over her and said the Twenty-third Psalm and a few Biblical quotations and hymnal verses. Upon this she became quite peaceful, and the fear departed from her eyes. I asked her: 'Do you believe this?' She nodded: yes. 'Then', said I, 'you can die in peace, you are going to Jesus.' Suddenly a hand was laid on my shoulder and an angry voice said: 'Herr Pastor, leave off that nonsense, my wife doesn't believe it!' I did not concern myself with the man, but asked the woman once more: 'Do you believe this?' To the soft, scarcely audible 'yes' of the dying woman I replied once more, 'You can die in peace, you are going to Jesus in Heaven.' The husband took me into the next room. On the wall a large picture of 'Red Liberty' , on the table Godless publications with the title 'Make life here good and beautiful, there's no beyond, no Resurrection!' Word for word he added: 'That's my belief, my wife kicks the bucket today, perhaps I'll kick the bucket tomorrow!' I looked him very earnestly in the eye and spoke: 'Make no mistake, God is not mocked!' I left the room in a state of shock.

With macabre self-satisfaction, Werner added as a footnote: 'About a year later I heard that the man had died of an ignominious ailment.'[98] But Werner's ghoulish *Schadenfreude* at the reported fate of his adversary could not conceal the fact that the vast majority of Hamburg's inhabitants, above all in the working class, remained ordinarily indifferent to religion. There were other reactions equally hostile to the pastors' role in the epidemic. 'Now

[95] H. McLeod, 'Protestantism and the Working Class in Imperial Germany', *European Studies Review*, 12 (1982), 323–44, here pp. 337–9.
[96] Ibid., p. 337.
[97] H. Grote, *Sozialdemokratie und Religion* (Tübingen, 1968).
[98] Kirchenarchiv Hbg, D166: Werner, 'Erinnerungen', pp. 24, 27. Psalm 23 is 'The Lord is my Shepherd'. The 'Red Liberty' was probably a Social Democratic poster.

you want to convert us by force!' one man was heard to say on the street as copies of Behrmann's address on the cholera epidemic were distributed to the public.[99] One Social Democratic newspaper—though not a local one—complained during the epidemic that 'the oppressive feeling which burdened the people had to be increased still further by the threat of Hell and Divine Judgement'.[100]

How long did the religious enthusiasm brought on by the epidemic last? The Church Council, as we have seen, was bold enough to express the view that at least some lapsed Christians had been brought back into the church's fold for good by the experience, and there can be little doubt that this was so. More generally, too, the courage and devotion of a man like Pastor Werner probably did much to soften the hostility of suspicious or politically alienated parishioners: Werner himself remarked that as a result of his activities in the epidemic he was from then on generally trusted in the area 'even by people who were otherwise completely estranged from the church'.[101] Doubtless the charitable work in which the church engaged during the epidemic also helped win people over.[102] A slight increase in the proportion of the Protestant population attending communion was registered—from 8.98% in 1880–4 to 10.02% in 1891–5, and still at 9.58% in 1896–but this proportion was still the lowest in Germany even after the epidemic.[103] All the available evidence suggests that even if anti-religious feeling was marginally lessened, the religious enthusiasm exhibited by many people during the epidemic was only a temporary phenomenon. Pastor Werner, for example, reported that 'bit by bit, as the plague receded, the number of worshippers decreased'.[104] Eventually the daily prayer-meetings and special services were discontinued, leaving only the regular services to provide an opportunity for those few people who wished to continue to express their new-found religious fervour. It was also notable that religion played a minor role in legitimating state policy in Hamburg in 1892. Apart from anything else, the Senate itself had little faith in the efficacy of the measures which Koch had obliged it to take—the disinfection campaign, the water distribution, and so on. The policy it would have wanted to legitimize—a policy of inaction—was no longer possible. The advanced state of secularization among the populace, the active irreligiosity of the Social Democrats, the relative lack of public hostility to the medical profession, the strong and unified efforts of the authorities to educate the populace in simple ways of preventing infection, and the general acceptance of water-borne and person-to-person contagion as the major, and therefore in principle controllable cause of the disease, also reduced the value of religion

---

99 Behrmann, *Erinnerungen*, p. 281.
100 StA Hbg, PP S3490 Bd. 1: *Glück auf!* 22 Oct. 1892.
101 Kirchenarchiv Hbg, D166: Werner, 'Erinnerungen', p. 27.
102 See Chapter 6a, below.
103 Pieper, *Kirchliche Statistik*, p. 217.
104 Kirchenarchiv Hbg, D166: Werner, 'Erinnerungen', p. 27.

in backing up state policy. Since the 1830s, in Germany as elsewhere, a radical divorce had taken place between scientific theory and religious belief. Early nineteenth-century rationalism—epitomized in Strauss's *Life of Jesus* (1835)—had undermined some of the intellectual foundations of Christianity through the application of the techniques of secular scholarship. Natural science had not seemed irreconcilable with Christianity until much later. In 1892, however, religious discourse had become divorced not only from scientific discourse but from moral discourse as well: in earlier epidemics, the advice had been to trust in God and obey the authorities; the explanation for cholera had been a moral decline of which irreligion was undoubtedly a part. But by the epidemic of 1892 the discourse on the moral origins of the disease had largely secularized itself. The working class was blamed because it was careless, and drunken, and irresponsible, but not—except by the church—because it was irreligious. The church could provide a temporary refuge in a time of fear, and hence contribute to the important task of calming the population; but it could not do much that was directly supportive of the Senate's policy in the epidemic.

III

As much as they stormed the railway stations, crowded into the churches, or reached for the bottle, the frightened inhabitants of Hamburg also sought to help themselves by recourse to popular patent medicines. Apothecaries were besieged for preventive preparations; they were said on 28 August to be open virtually 24 hours a day. 'Drugstore owners and wine merchants competed with one another to recommend the "best" and "only effective" cholera prophylactics.'[105] So high was the demand for disinfectants that prices rocketed and unscrupulous pedlars began selling bogus imitations on the streets.[106] Nor surprisingly the chemical firm Schering recorded an increase in its annual profits of 250,000 Marks in 1892 over the previous year.[107] The Hamburg newspapers were also full of advertisements offering to disclose—at a price—some 'infallible remedies, which will nip the sickness in the bud within 48 hours'.[108] Most popular of all were 'cholera drops', which contained a small quantity of camphor and were sold (and drunk) in large quantities in 1892, as they had been in previous epidemics.[109] One innkeeper from Bromberg offered an unspecified remedy 'which also cures the cholera victim' for a payment of '50,000 Marks, fifty thousand Marks no more and no less'.[110]

[105] StA Hbg, Senat, Cl. VII, Lit. Ta, Pars 2, Vol. 11, Fasc. 17, Inv. 4: *Kölnische Zeitung*, 30 Aug. 1892.

[106] Ibid., Inv. 2: *Hamburger Nachrichten*, 3 Sept. 1892.

[107] StA Hbg, PP S3490 Bd. 1: *Hamburger Freie Presse*, 17 Dec. 1892.

[108] G. H. Sieveking, 'Nachklänge aus der Cholerazeit 1892', *Deutsche Medizinische Wochenschrift* 51 (1899), 1–5.

[109] StA Hbg, Senat, Cl. VII, Lit. Ta, Pars 2, Vol. 6, p.2.

[110] StA Hbg, MK III A 16 Bd. 1, Bl. 106–7.

Hospitals and administrators were deluged with letters and petitions offering remedies and prophylactics. Sometimes these were of a similiar vagueness and expense. The Medical Board, for example, received a magnificent letter from the 'Duca di Bustelli Foscolo, Generale di divisione; Inviato Straordinario e Ministrio Plenipotenziario della Republica di Honduras in situo 12 Lawence Road, Noting Hill [sic], W. London', offering 'un rémède *infallible*' and declaring its author's readiness to deliver 'le secret de la composition du dit rémède moyennant un compensation'.[111] More often, however, the petitioners were only too explicit in their proposals.

Thus from various sides came advice to the sick to drink tea or schnapps, or burned and ground rye flour, or mustard spirit, turpentine, chlorine, or other fluids. Often such remedies were drawn from older sources. 'Half a tablespoon of fine sea sand is much better than opium', wrote one petitioner. Traces of medieval medical theories could be found in the belief that 'freshly-prepared, warm cow-dung broth pushes the cholera out below, because it is slimy and already digested'. This latter cure was not easy to carry out in the city, as its author admitted; 'because this medicine must not be more than a day old, a sufficient number of cows has to kept in the vicinity'. Other writers favoured infusions of gunpowder; more palatable perhaps were proposals to consume quantities of raw onions or salted herrings, Berlin 'white beer', or even three tablespoons a day of Worcestershire sauce. Other writers favoured modern methods over old ones: running an electric current through the patient's bath or even electrifying his whole house, or pumping carbon monoxide or ether into the body, it was argued on various sides, would effectively kill off the bacilli. The problem was that it might also effectively kill off the patient. Preventive measures included camphor or menthol cigarettes, gargling with camphor, putting Lysol in one's morning coffee, rubbing the body down with petroleum—or covering it in chalk—or washing it down in chlorine. One Hugo Schüssler, a member of the Town Council in the Berlin suburb of Köpenick, offered an elaborate machine for boiling the main water-supply at its distribution point. As well as these forms of preventive disinfection, there were other suggestions designed to stop the bacillus entering the body by placing a muzzle round the mouth, or by drinking through the nose. Straight out of the Middle Ages came the suggestion that the City Fathers fire off cannon to set the air in motion and so kill the bacilli which the writer imagined were floating in it; or that the entire city should be covered in salt.[112]

Fortunately, perhaps, none of these suggestions was ever taken up by the Hamburg authorities. But free enterprise continued to offer a wide variety of preventive and curative suggestions. Most of these were individually inspired

---

[111] Ibid., Bl. 86–7.

[112] Sieveking, 'Nachklänge'; H. Schüssler, *Ein praktisches Mittel zur Verhütung der Cholera-Epidemie* (Köpenick, 1894).

and commerically motivated. Alternative medicine had little to offer to cholera patients and avoided treating them. The local newspapers were already sceptical in 1831. Reporting the treatment of cholera victims in Vienna, they noted that 'the allopathic physicians have certainly restored many cholera victims to health, but soon after, nervous disorders set in, perhaps caused by the violence of the treatment, and they ended in nervous fever and nervous breakdown'. It was admitted that 'the homeopaths ... have achieved admirable cures with veratrum, camphor, and phosphorus',[113] but this seems to have had little impact in Hamburg. In 1848 Chief Medical Officer Dr Buek remarked that 'homeopathy, which *boasted* that it had achieved such an exceedingly propitious effect in the earlier epidemic in some places, is only represented here in Hamburg as far as I know by one single well-known older physician'. Even he was reported to be treating his cholera patients allopathically. A total of 24 victims had put themselves in his care, of whom 16 had been cured. 'Instead of homeopathy a new goddess of fashion, hydropathy, has entered upon the scene, and it has worthily filled its place as far as the *boast* of its success is concerned.'[114]

Even here, however, cholera victims and their relatives do not seem to have sought alternative treatments with any great enthusiasm. The symptoms of the disease were too violent, its progress too swift, and its mortality rate too extreme, for people to put much faith in the mild prophylactics and cures which these movements offered. As in previous epidemics, so in 1892, popular opinion remained overwhelmingly contagionist. Those who had been employed in the disinfection squads or as grave-diggers and hearse-drivers frequently found difficulty in obtaining subsequent employment. As one of them explained, somewhat ruefully, 'I've been told in one place after another "we can't take on people who've worked on the cholera".' Indeed, many of these workers seem to have shared this view; 'of course, we're sitting here chock-a-block with bacilli', as one of them remarked, 'it's obvious people don't take us on'.[115] In these circumstances the remedies offered by homeopathists, hydropathists, and allopathists seemed hardly capable of driving the bacilli out. People rushed to purchase patent preventive medicines because these were not available from the doctors, just as they took to drink in part as a preventive measure, but when it came to cures, scepticism and disbelief were the order of the day. Experience seemed to indicate that once cholera struck, there was little hope of rescue. Proffered means of self-protection were grasped

[113] *Der Hamburgische Beobachter*, Vol. 42, no. 15, 15 Oct. 1831, p. 167.

[114] StA Hbg, MK III A 2 Bd. 1, Bl. 94. For further discussion of alternative medicine in 19th-century Germany, see W. Krabbe, *Gesellschaftsveränderung durch Lebensreform* (Göttingen, 1974), and Frevert, *Krankheit als politisches Problem*, p. 291. See also Plate 28.

[115] StA Hbg, PP V 327–30, Versammlungsbericht, 28 Oct. 1892. Charles Rosenberg also noted that popular opinion remained firmly contagionist in the USA throughout the century (*The Cholera Years*, p. 81).

eagerly by individuals, but few sought to enrol in collective movements of resistance such as it was the ambition of alternative medicine to provide.

Individual self-help of various kinds only served in many ways to increase the chaos and disorder into which the city seemed to be plunging. It was reported that

> the owners of earth closets were so afraid of the plague that they suddenly handed them over to the garbage disposal service. In some areas, e.g. on the Veddel, the quantities of this liquid stuff were so great that they could no longer be absorbed by the rest of the household rubbish but sprang forth from all the joints in the dustcart.[116]

The garbage contractors were suddenly obliged to cart away much more than usual, particularly when houses were cleared out by the disinfection columns, while their usual workers vanished equally precipitously from the scene. Similarly the labourers whose job it usually was to empty cesspools in areas like the Borstelmannsweg also disappeared, 'so that the cesspools filled up and overflowed, giving rise to a really dreadful situation in the surrounding areas'.[117] In the haste with which many houses and apartments were evacuated, pet animals were left unattended and cats and dogs began to befoul the rooms or run wild on the streets. Crowds began to gather outside the Eppendorf Hospital, and surrounded each ambulance as it came to fetch away the sick.[118] In the press, reporters started to fantasize about the possibilities the epidemic offered for dastardly acts of crime: 'How terrible', one wrote, 'must be the temptation which is offered to criminal minds at such a time, when they know that a few sips of this water taken by someone they hate, or want to get rid of, will in all probability cause death without it being traced back to a criminal act.'[119] In the Senate, knowledge of the public disturbances to which earlier epidemics had led—and which were taking place at that very moment in Russia—must have been a major cause for apprehension. Resistance to hospitalization was frequently encountered, as we have seen, and the belief that the hospitals were more centres of experimentation than treatment, also seems to have been as widespread in 1892 as it had been in 1831.[120] Public drunkenness and mass flight were further evidence of the panic and fear that gripped the city.

Despite all this, however, as Leo Lippmann remarked, looking back on the events of 1892, 'not *one* commotion, not *one* outrage has taken place'.[121]

---

[116] StA Hbg, Senat, Cl. VII, Lit. Cc, No. 3b, Vol. 58a, Fasc. 2: Baudeputation-Bericht betr. Abfuhr-Ordnung 30 Dec. 1892.

[117] Ibid.

[118] Ibid., Lit. Ta, Pars 2, Vol. 11, Fasc. 17, Inv. 2: *Hamburger Fremdenblatt*, 3 Sept. 1892; ibid., Inv. 4: *Die Post*, 2 Sept. 1892; Loewenberg, *Aus Zwei Quellen*, pp. 286–7.

[119] StA Hbg, PP S3460 Bd. 1: *Hamburger Fremdenblatt*, 28 Oct. 1892.

[120] See above, pp. 333–4; and, for 1831, when it was reported that people thought 'people are being sacrificed' in the hospitals, and there was a 'climate of opinion in the lower classes against the doctors' in which there was no evidence of 'the necessary trust', see *Der Hamburgische Beobachter*, Vol. 42, No. 15, 22 Oct. 1831, p. 170.

[121] StA Hbg, FA Lippmann A20, p. 36.

'Moreover', wrote Senator Gustav Hertz, with perceptible relief on 8 September, 'I must commend our Hamburg people: they have kept exemplary order and avoided every fearful or disturbing impulse ...' [122] The absence of any rioting or public disturbances in Hamburg in 1892 contrasted sharply with the experience of cholera at other places and other times. We have already seen how popular suspicion of doctors and popular resentment against hasty mass burials in secular ground led to rioting in Memel and Königsberg in 1831. The French historian René Baehrel has pointed to a close connection between 'épidémies et terreurs', and Jean Delumeau, in his study of fear in Western Europe, has noted the recurrence of popular conspiracy theories about the origins of epidemics from the fourteenth century at least up to the outbreak of cholera that occurred in France in 1884. Delumeau draws from this the conclusion that 'in the history of mentalities, of collective consciousness, we have to liberate ourselves from the chronology and the divisions of time that we know from the history of politics and the economy'. [123] Yet this pattern of behaviour—from terror released by the arrival of an epidemic, through the popular search for a scapegoat (usually the doctors or the authorities), to collective violence and revolt—was conspicuously lacking in Hamburg in 1892. This was not because the habit of collective violence had disappeared, or been channelled into purposeful political activity through the labour movement; there had been serious rioting in the Alley Quarters in 1890 and it was to occur again in 1897 and 1906, while food riots in the city were to break out once more during and shortly after the First World War. [124] The Alley Quarters were severely affected by cholera in 1892; indeed it was widely believed that they bore the main brunt of the epidemic. Yet there was no unrest, not even any small incident of collective hostility to the authorities in these areas during the epidemic.

Several reasons were responsible for this. The religious indifference of the Hamburg working class by the early 1890s removed a major cause of unrest detailed in official reports on earlier cholera riots, namely, popular religious outrage against secular mass burials of the dead. It also has to be remembered that earlier cholera riots often originated in the hunger and panic caused by sealing off towns and localities with military cordons sanitaires. In addition, the fact that cholera generally broke out, for reasons already discussed, at times when political unrest, social antagonisms, and even revolutions were already creating numerous impulses for popular violence, meant that cholera was as often as not a pretext for rather than a cause of violence; the accusation

[122] StA Hbg, FA Gustav Hertz B17.

[123] Baehrel, 'Épidémie et terreur'; Delumeau, *Angst im Abendland*, i. 189.

[124] See M Grüttner, 'Soziale Hygiene und Soziale Kontrolle. Die Sanierung der Hamburger Gängeviertel 1892–1936', in Herzig *et al.*, *Arbeiter in Hamburg*, pp. 359–72, esp. p. 361; and V. Ullrich, 'Massenbewegungen in der Hamburger Arbeiterschaft im Ersten Weltkrieg', ibid., pp. 407–18.

that the authorities, acting through the medical profession, were trying to kill off the poor was a symbolic expression of deep-seated, ultimately more realistic popular resentments of official repression and indifference to the plight of the masses. It is important to bear in mind the fact that—for all these reasons, but particularly because of the weakness of social antagonisms in Hamburg in 1831–2 and 1848—not only were there no serious public disturbances in Hamburg during the epidemic of 1892, there were none in any previous epidemic either, with the possible partial exception of 1831. Finally, the prestige of Koch's discovery and the rise in the status of doctors since the 1830s helped ensure that the medical profession aroused less hostility in 1892 than it had done sixty years before.

There can be little doubt, however, that the Social Democrats also played a role in calming popular fears in 1892. As Police Commissioner Rosalowsky wrote after the epidemic was over,

One characteristic of all Social Democratic demonstrations here incidentally is the exemplary order with which they are customarily carried out, so that the police authorities are almost never obliged to intervene. The leaders are most careful to avoid coming into open conflict with the authorities. In this connection the experiences which we had in last year's cholera epidemic are interesting. Already on 23 August, the day after the outbreak of the epidemic, leaders of the Social Democratic Party and trade unions, when approached by the police authorities, declared themselves ready to work towards obtaining a moratorium on political and trade union meetings during the epidemic. On 25 August the main organ of the local Social Democrats, the *Hamburger Echo*, printed a call to postpone 'all meetings that are not strictly necessary' until the plague was over. The promise of the paper's editors to avoid inflammatory articles was kept to the letter, and while a part of the bourgeois press unleashed unbridled attacks on the authorities, the *Hamburger Echo* forwarded critical articles and complaints which it received to the police authority.[125]

The official approach to the Social Democrats, indeed, seems to have been made on 23 August, even before the outbreak of the epidemic was officially announced. This was striking testimony to the paramountcy of the public order issue in Senator Gerhard Hachmann's mind. His role as Chief of Police clearly took precedence over his role as President of the Medical Board, and in retrospect it was rather unfortunate that both were combined. His action in contacting the Social Democrats on the 23rd showed that he could act quickly and decisively enough when he considered the situation warranted it, and when he was not dependent on the advice of professional experts.

Hachmann was not unaware of the fact that on the eve of the epidemic the Social Democrats were embroiled in a furious row with the Hamburg State Prosecutor Romen, who had attempted to discredit Social Democratic witnesses in the trial of a strike-breaker who had become involved in illegal activities. Romen—a Prussian by origin—had accused the witnesses of per-

[125] StA Hbg, Senat, Cl. XI, Gen. No. 2, Vol. 61, Fasc. 1: 'Denkschrift'.

juring themselves for political reasons: oaths, even the most sacred, he said, meant nothing to the Godless Party. The local party paper, the *Hamburger Echo*, responded with fierce attacks on the prosecutor, and several issues were seized by the police, who then brought a series of libel suits. On 9 August 1892, the Social Democrats held six mass meetings to demand Romen's dismissal, and individual protest meetings were still passing resolutions to this effect up to 20 August. Eventually, in 1893, the paper's editors were condemned, but Romen also resigned to take up a post elsewhere: things had become too hot for him in Hamburg. In August 1892, however, the party's agreement to suspend all meetings brought a welcome relief to the authorities, who had undoubtedly been forced onto the defensive by the campaign.[126]

Just as striking as the promptness of the police's appeal was the alacrity with which the Social Democratic leadership responded. Well before any official ban on popular assemblies and gatherings had been imposed, the Social Democratic Party had decided not to hold any of its own. More striking still was the self-censorship exercised by the party's daily newspaper, the *Hamburger Echo*. The decision to send in readers' complaints to the police can only be described as astonishing. Even if the editors considered that they were doing the authors of such letters a service by making their views known to the authorities despite the paper's self-imposed embargo on publication, they must surely have known that such action would mark these people down as trouble-makers in the eyes of the police. At a moment's notice, the Social Democratic press in Hamburg had become even more subservient to the Senate than its bourgeois rivals were. Indeed, the *Hamburger Echo* even went so far as to defend the Senate against criticism from the Social Democrats' main daily newspaper in Berlin, *Vorwärts*. 'We had the drama', as the police later reported, 'of the two Social Democratic papers, the Berlin *Vorwärts* and the *Hamburger Echo*, engaging in the most violent dispute with one another during the epidemic.' On 30 August the *Echo* denounced the *Vorwärts* for the 'untrue, exaggerated, sensation-seeking news' it was printing about Hamburg. On the 31st it explained that 'no patients will be cured or people protected from death by attacks on the authorities'. Even as late as 18 September the *Echo* was still pleading: 'it is an urgent necessity for the party press to comply with our repeated requests to describe things in Hamburg as they really are'. No wonder that Police Commissioner Rosàlowsky could report that the authorities had succeeded in 'making the Social Democrats serve the purposes of the police'.[127]

The services they performed lay first of all in legitimizing the actions of the medical profession. Elsewhere, in previous epidemics, it had almost always

[126] StA Hbg, PP S1365 Bd. 1, *passim*; see also A. Hall, *Scandal, Sensation and Social Democracy. The SPD Press and Wilhelmine Germany* (Cambridge, 1977), pp. 76–8.

[127] Ibid., p. 3; StA Hbg, PP S3420 Bd. 3: *Hamburger Echo*, 18 Sept. 1892; *Hamburger Echo*, 30–31 Aug. 1892 (microfilm in StA Hbg).

been the hospitalization of victims, the isolation of affected houses, or the mass burial of the dead, that had sparked off attacks on the doctors and then on the authorities. By distributing medical advice in the form of Sachse's leaflet, the Social Democrats endorsed the explanations of cholera purveyed by the medical profession under Koch's leadership. They reinforced the authority of the doctors, and although they devised a plan to set up their own 'sanitary columns' in the case of another epidemic, these were designed simply to be put at the disposal of the authorities, not to act as self-help organizations as were their equivalents in Berlin.[128] Moreover, by this time riots in Hamburg generally occurred only when the Social Democrats had already taken the lead in launching a public attack on the authorities, or when an already existing political or trade-union action provided the stimulus for violent action, as in the riots of 1890 during the gasworkers' strike, the disturbances of 1897 after the harbour strike, or the general suffrage demonstrations of 1906, which occurred during the first political general strike to be held in the city, indeed in Germany. By immediately refusing to criticize the authorities or call any public meetings of any kind, the Social Democrats in 1892 destroyed the possibility of a political stimulus for popular disturbances.

There were several reasons why the party co-operated with the police in 1892. It saw the distribution of pamphlets and the provision of workers for the disinfection columns in part as job-creation schemes at a time of high unemployment, and tried to ensure that the workers it provided were paid for their pains. The disinfection workers, indeed, were, as we have seen, all unemployed before they took up their posts. Subsequently the Social Democrats tried to get the credit for providing not only the disinfection workers but also the corpse-bearers and male nurses, although these had in fact been recruited by public advertisement. They also claimed later on that 'the distribution of leaflets ... was undertaken by the Social Democrats free of charge', although they were paid between 3 and 10 Marks for the job. Nevertheless, the second printing and distribution of the leaflets on 29–31 August had been done without payment, as a matter of honour, because the first attempt had been unsuccessful. The Social Democratic printers Auer and Company had only just been able to cover the costs of the first printing with the grant of 2,000 Marks paid by the police, and the subsequent claim of a Senator that they had done 'good business' with their co-operation certainly went too far. And it was not entirely true to assert, as the liberal *Hamburger Fremdenblatt* later did, 'that at that moment the Senate wanted to keep the Social Democrats in a good mood' and had only asked them to co-operate for this reason, 'otherwise the bourgeoisie would have been able to print and

---

[128] A. Labisch, 'Selbsthilfe zwischen Auflehnung und Anpassung: Arbeiter-Sanitätskommission und Arbeiter-Samariterbund', in *Alternative Medizin* (Argument-Sonderband 77, Berlin, 1983), pp. 11–26; StA Hbg, PP V494, *passim*.

distribute the leaflets themselves'.[129] Although the first part of this statement was certainly true, the rest equally certainly was not.

These claims and counter-claims continued to be advanced for years after the epidemic, as the Social Democrats attempted to show that they had stayed behind to fight the epidemic while the bourgeoisie had fled.[130] At the time, however, it was not so much a patriotic desire to do their duty that dominated their emotions, as a sense of pride and relief 'that', as Wilhelm Liebknecht, the leading figure in the national party alongside August Bebel, put it at the beginning of October 1892, 'the Senate no longer regards the Socialists as a gang of conspirators and revolutionaries with whom no dealings are possible, but rather as people who can be drawn into co-operation with it'.[131] Humble party workers in the city also expressed the same feeling. Reporting a Social Democratic meeting on 13 October, the police noted among other things the following speech from a party activist referring to his activities on a local health commission:

Comrade R. Müller, Eimsbüttlerstr. 14, auxiliary party worker in Eimsbüttel, says . . . that he is also a member of the Health Commission. Through this position the claim of Herr Dr Borghardt [*sic*], which he made in the Reichstag—that they hadn't gone so far as to use the Social Democrats to maintain law and order, the police could still do that on their own—is refuted, for in my own person there stands before you today a police officer; and I do believe that it was with some difficulty that Senator Dr Hachmann brought himself to sign my card.[132]

There were parallels here to the feelings of the Social Democrats in August 1914, when they responded with alacrity to the call of the state to rally round in a crisis. There were also the beginnings of a long-term co-operation with the state in the area of public health—although working for the police was, in the end, quite a different matter from taking part in democratic elections to the health insurance boards, and neither the local party's defence of the Senate against the attack by the Social Democrats in Berlin, nor its policy of passing on letters of complaint to the police, can ultimately be understood outside the immediate context of the shattering events of 1892.[133]

As in 1914, so in 1892, the Social Democrats expected a price to be paid

[129] StA Hbg, Senat Cl, VII, Lit. Ta, Pars 2, Vol. 11, Fasc. 24: *Hamburger Echo*, 2 Mar. 1906, *Hamburger Nachrichten*, 15 Feb. 1906.

[130] Cf. StA Hbg, PP S3425 Bd. 3: *Hamburger Echo*, 6 June 1893.

[131] StA Hbg, PP S3469: *Hamburger Echo*, 9 Oct. 1892.

[132] Ibid., Versammlungsbericht 13 Oct. 1892. The claim to be a 'police officer' was of course meant figuratively, and referred to Müller's role as an officer of the local Health Commission on which he sat. For the Health Commissions see below, Chapter 6c; for Burchard's speech in the Reichstag, see below, pp. 400–1.

[133] A. Labisch, 'Die gesundheitspolitischen Vorstellungen der deutschen Sozialdemokratie von ihrer Gründung bis zur Parteispaltung (1863–1917)', *Archiv für Sozialgeschichte*, 16 (1976), 325–70; and R. J. Evans, 'Die Cholera und die Sozialdemokratie: Arbeiterbewegung, Bürgertum und Staat in Hamburg während der Krise von 1892', in Herzig *et al.*, *Arbeiter in Hamburg*, pp. 203–14.

by the state for their loyalty. From this point onwards, their service during the cholera epidemic formed a constant refrain in the propaganda they directed at the Senate and the public at large. Eventually conservatives in the city came to regret that the Social Democrats had ever been approached. 'At that time', declared a writer in the *Hamburger Nachrichten* in 1906,

The Police Chief Herr Dr Hachmann could not know what a terrible mistake he was making as he turned to the Social Democratic Party organization with his request for co-operation. How the unscrupulous and loud-mouthed Social Democratic press has played up this fact and used it to further its own narrow party purposes![134]

During the crisis itself, however, there was every reason for the Senator to be grateful. The Social Democrats not only did nothing to criticize the Senate, they actually stepped in positively to defend it. The same could not be said of the bourgeois press. In the next act of the drama, indeed, the role it played was to be decisive.

d. *Guilty Men*

I

The official announcement on 24 August 1892 that an epidemic of cholera had broken out in Hamburg immediately prompted the city's trading partners to impose quarantine and health checks on ships coming from the Elbe. Many European governments restricted or banned the import of goods from Hamburg, especially used clothes, fruit and vegetables, hides and skins, rags, meat, dairy products, and the like; some enforced medical inspections on all incoming German ships.[1] The Danish border was sealed off and there were soon complaints about the 'inhuman' behaviour of Danish customs officials.[2] Some overseas governments banned not only all imports from Hamburg but refused to admit parcels sent through the post as well.[3] Foreign ships refused to sail to Hamburg, fearing infection once they arrived. Already on 17 September the *Kölnische Zeitung* reported that the damage to trade was 'incalculable':

The top German trading city has been anathematized and excommunicated; weekly gross turnover was 50 million Marks earlier; now it is only a few thousand, because

---

[134] StA Hbg, Senat, Cl. VII, Lit. Ta, Pars 2, Vol. 11, Fasc. 24: *Hamburger Nachrichten*, 15 Feb. 1903. The arguments about the Social Democrats' role in the epidemic are contained in the reports and paper clippings in StA Hbg, PP S3490 Bd. 3, *passim*.

[1] For a full list of quarantine and inspection measures see (Georg Gaffky), *Amtliche Denkschrift über die Choleraepidemie 1892*.

[2] StA Hbg, Senat, Cl. VII, Lit. Ta, Pars 2, Vol. 11, Fasc. 17, Inv. 1a: *Hamburger Tageblatt*, 22 Oct. 1892.

[3] StA Hbg, PP S3490 Bd. 1: *Hamburgischer Correspondent*, 30 Dec. 1892.

shipping is coming more and more to a standstill. The proud vessels which once ploughed their speedy furrows through the ocean to bring the treasures of the four corners of the earth to the 'northern Venice' now lie in many cases in foreign ports, held fast by the quarantine imposed on them.'[4]

This situation lasted not merely for several weeks, but for several months; extensive quarantine regulations were still in force at the end of the year.[5]

Just as serious were the restrictions imposed on Hamburg's contacts with the rest of Germany. While the Prussians quickly moved to seal off the border to any further Russian migrants, a special conference of the federated states held on 27 August drew up a range of quarantine measures which were implemented on the 29th. These concentrated on the disinfection and isolation of goods and obviously ill people coming from Hamburg, and on the composition and distribution of a number of leaflets for railway officials, river boat crews, and indeed the population in general. On 12 September strict controls were established on the Elbe, and Baron von Richthofen was appointed as a special Reich Commissioner for Public Health in the Elbe Basin, with the authority of Chancellor Caprivi behind him to ensure that his 'advice' was taken. Between 13 September and 29 November 1892 over 57,000 boats, barges and ships on the river were inspected and nearly 33,000 subjected to a thorough disinfection. Measures on a similar scale were taken on the Oder and the Rhine. The whole programme was co-ordinated by an Imperial Cholera Commission established on 11 September, chaired by the head of the Imperial Health Office, and consisting of representatives of a number of the federated states including Hamburg. The proceedings of its first meeting, on 12 September, were dominated by Robert Koch, who thought that the Spree and Havel might be infected with cholera, and persuaded the Commission to focus its attention on sanitary controls on the rivers; riverborne infection, he declared, was 'a factor ... to which no attention has been paid up to now'.[6]

These checks and controls, by land and by river, were not intended to be comprehensive. As Koch explained to the Commission on 1 November:

Intercourse with Hamburg spread the disease to nearly 300 places and at the beginning it looked as if the whole of Germany would shortly be infected with cholera. In order to prevent the country being flooded by infectious substances in this way, we observed a different procedure from earlier ones. Human traffic was not restricted as it had been on earlier occasions because experience has taught us that little will be achieved by this means. The definite and purposeful measures in force today (which are also valid for other epidemics) aim especially to submit the earliest cases in any

---

[4] StA Hbg, Senat, Cl. VII, Lit. Ta, Pars 2, Vol. 11, Fasc. 16, Inv. 22: *Kölnische Zeitung*, 17 Sept. 1892.

[5] StA Hbg, PP S3490 Bd. 1: *Hamburgischer Correspondent*, 30 Dec. 1892.

[6] *Amtliche Denkschrift*, pp. 16–21; BA Koblenz R86/2657: Sitzungsberichte der Cholera-Commission, 12 Sept., 19 Sept., 22 Sept., 26 Sept. 1892.

given place to a thorough treatment so that a local epidemic does not break out. In almost all the cases that were spread from Hamburg we succeeded in this way in becoming masters of the cholera.[7]

As Figure 15 shows, this policy met with a fair degree of success, and already by early September the spread of the disease across the German Empire had been effectively checked. But local authorities frequently went far beyond Koch's intentions. Many threatened dire penalties if anyone from Hamburg even dared set foot in their territory. Some poured disinfectant over all mail coming from the stricken city, thus ruining it entirely, and over postal and railway officials as well, irrespective of whether they had been to Hamburg or not. Communes and municipalities along Hamburg's borders often barred all imports from the city and forcibly disinfected refugees, or refused them lodgings, or simply deported them. Even Altona imposed a quarantine. In one village, it was reported, the local inhabitants attempted to wash down a refugee from Hamburg with arsenic, on the grounds that it killed vermin on cattle.[8] 'In some cases', recalled one inhabitant of the city, 'not only was all correspondence with Hamburg forbidden, but even telephone conversations from Hamburg to Berlin or Magdeburg were broken off at the other end in the lunatic, stupid fear that people might be infected in this way.'[9]

Citizens of Hamburg who found themselves outside the city's borders during the epidemic often had a difficult time. Olga O'Swald, the twenty-three-year-old daughter of one of Hamburg's richest merchants, was in nearby Travemünde, getting ready for her wedding, when the epidemic broke out. 'Every morning I received a telegram telling me if everyone was still in good health. It was nerve-wracking!' she later wrote. The wedding party arriving from the city on 3 September had to be disinfected, though the pastor, curiously, was exempted from this procedure. On their honeymoon, the young couple, 'armed with numerous health certificates' were twice examined by doctors in the train, and everywhere people avoided them. 'On the journey in the narrow-gauge railway to Heiligendamm', she wrote, 'I heard a lady say "They are surely from Hamburg, shall we go into the next compartment?" ... In Heiligendamm, where the rumour had got around, we were quite horribly stared at, very unpleasant ...' Later they were involved in a heated argument on their way to Berlin, where a gentleman on the train 'began to heap terrible curses on Hamburg'.[10] Travellers from the city had to contend with hostility and suspicion as well as with the physical indignities of medical examination and disinfection. Many who were already out of the city at the

---

[7] BA Koblenz R86/2657: Sitzungsberichte der Cholera-Commission, 12 Sept., 11 Nov. 1892.

[8] *Hamburger Cholera-Tropfen: Blüthen-Lese von Curiositäten aus ernster Zeit* (Hamburg, 1892); *Amtliche Denkschrift*, p. 22; StA Hbg, Senat, Cl. VII, Lit. Ta, Pars 2, Vol. 11, Fasc. 17, Inv. 1a: *Hamburgischer Correspondent*, 29 Oct. 1892.

[9] StA Hbg, FA Lippmann A20, Vol. 1, p. 36. See also Plates 29, 30 and 31.

[10] Ibid., FA Schramm K10/1, pp. 28–31.

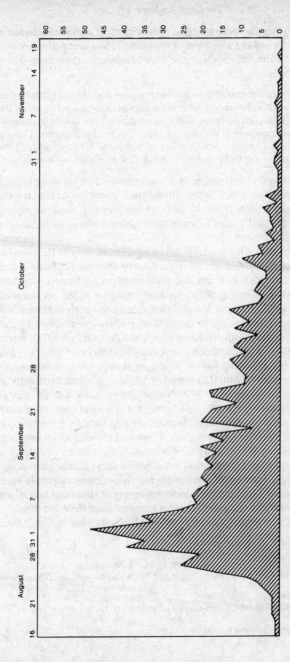

Source: (Georg Gaffky), *Amtliche Denkschrift über die Choleraepidemie 1892* (Berlin, 1895)

FIG. 15. Number of communes and districts in the German Empire reporting cholera cases in 1892, by day

outbreak of the epidemic were forced to obtain medical certificates declaring that they were 'free of the suspicion of cholera'.[11] Similar experiences were reported by Ida Neubauer, who returned from Norderney to Hamburg during the epidemic. She noted that

When a train from Hamburg arrived in Bremen everyone who got out had to put out their tongue to men in white coats (who in those days were an unfamiliar sight). This procedure did not lack a certain comic aspect. In Norddeich I was talking to a Senator from Bremen when a gentleman joined us and said 'You're from Hamburg. I have to tell you how outraged I am by circumstances in Hamburg.' My reply was: 'I think you should address yourself to the Hamburg authorities, it's nothing to do with me.'[12]

Travellers from Hamburg were forced in many places to have their luggage disinfected, a process which often ruined the contents.[13] 'The railway stations', reported Rudolf Hertz as early as 27 August, 'stink of carbolic and are sealed off, and I was virtually the only passenger on the way to Hamburg.'[14]

Railway traffic, as we have seen,[15] fell off sharply as soon as the presence of cholera was officially announced. By 17 September the *Kölnische Zeitung* was reporting that 'railway traffic has long since ceased to cover its costs; more and more trains are cancelled, because passenger traffic via Hamburg will not pick up again until the dreadful plague has completely vanished from Hamburg'.[16] The takings of the Prussian State Railways were down by 24% in September compared with the same month the previous year. The Altona District of the State Railways, indeed, took a million Marks, or 50%, less than in September 1891 from the sale of passenger tickets. On 6 September the 8.45 express from Berlin to Hamburg left without a single passenger on board. The three daily expresses to Berlin stopped running, leaving only six slow trains in operation on the line, including the overnight train. Quarantine measures on various international borders created further disruption, and even the celebrated Orient Express, which crossed through Germany on its way to the Habsburg Empire, had to stop running for a time.[17] As Figure 16 indicates, perhaps as many as 2,000 fewer people came to take up residence in the city in September 1892 than might have been expected; while Figure 17 shows a similar sharp drop in guests registering at Hamburg hotels, with a full recovery of traffic still not occurring even in November.

The effects of these measures on trade and business were severe. Already

---

[11] Ibid., FA Beneke M2: Urkunde vom 10. Sept.

[12] Ibid., FA Neubauer 1, p. 28.

[13] Ibid., FA Gustav Hertz D9 Bd. 2: Elisabeth Hertz to her mother, 28 Sept. 1892.

[14] Ibid., Rudolf Hertz to his parents, 27 Aug. 1892. For a similar report, see Nonne, *Anfang und Ziel*, p. 95.

[15] See above, Figure 14.

[16] StA Hbg, Senat, Cl. VII, Lit. Ta, Pars 2, Vol. 11, Fasc. 16, Inv. 22: *Kölnische Zeitung*, 17 Sept. 1892.

[17] Ibid., Fasc. 17, Inv. 1a: *Börsen-Halle*, 29 Oct. 1892.

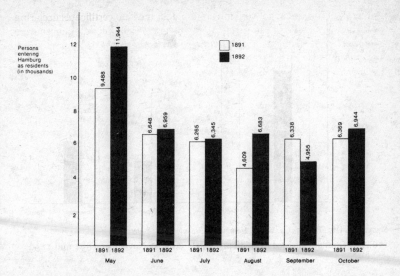

Source: StA Hbg, Senat Cl. XI, Generalia No. 2, Vol. 61, Fasc. 1: Denkschrift vom 4. Nov. 1892 (Einwohner-Melde-Bureau)

FIG. 16. Residential migration into Hamburg, May–October 1891 and 1892

on 2 September the head of the city's Statistical Bureau, Georg Koch, noted in his diary that 'upriver and overseas water-borne traffic has almost completely stopped'.[18] A reporter visiting the city on 6 September informed his readers that there were 'hardly a dozen coke or coaling ships' loading or unloading in the harbour; usually there were anything up to 200 at this time of year. 'Sad, deeply sad ... is the sight of the real traffic artery of Hamburg's trade, the harbour and the warehouse city.'[19] The bargees complained of the 'for the most part pointless and unfounded prohibition' of 'every possible commodity that customarily passes through Hamburg', and the numerous delays caused by the disinfection of river barges and the banning of night sailing: 'river shipping has thus lost money through this epidemic, and time, and that means once more money'.[20] Larger shipping companies suffered even more. The Hamburg–America Line recorded 'very heavy losses' because of the epidemic: profits, complained the company's annual report, were 'down by

[18] Koch, 'Die Tagebuchaufzeichnungen Georg Kochs über die Hamburger Cholera-Epidemie des Jahres 1892', *Die Heimat. Monatsschrift zur Pflege der Natur- und Landeskunde in Schleswig-Holstein und Hamburg*, 79 (1972), 353–4; 80 (1973), 23–4, entry for 2 Sept.

[19] StA Hbg, Senat, Cl. VII, Lit. Ta, Pars 2, Vol. 11, Fasc. 17, Inv. 4: *Marburger Volkszeitung*, 7 Sept. 1892.

[20] BA Koblenz, R86/864 Bd. 1, Bl. 17: Bericht des Hamburger Vereins Oberländischer Schiffer (1892).

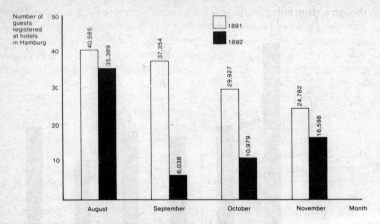

Source: StA Hbg, PP, S3490, Vol. 1: *Hamburger Fremdenblatt*, 7 Dec. 1892

FIG. 17. Guests registered in Hamburg hotels, August–November 1891 and 1892

millions'. Half a million Marks had to be paid back for unused 'prepaid' tickets alone.[21] 'Almost every merchant', indeed, as the Chamber of Commerce was forced to report in December, 'has to a greater or lesser degree suffered effective losses, which in many cases still cannot be calculated.'[22] Dividends were slashed, sometimes by as much as half, to reflect the steep fall in profits occasioned by the epidemic.[23] It was, as the Chamber of Commerce reported, 'a terrible year'.[24]

Very soon after the initial effects of quarantine made themselves felt, the Senate began to mount a counter-offensive. Already on 26 September, it succeeded in persuading the Imperial Cholera Commission to relax checks on goods sent by post.[25] On 5 November, indeed, it made a formal request to the Commission to have all the restrictions lifted and an official statement issued that Hamburg was 'free of infection'. This was rejected on Koch's advice because of what he saw as the continuing danger of the disease being spread from Hamburg to other parts; a second request, discussed by the Commission on 14 November, succeeded in getting most of the restrictions lifted even

[21] StA Hbg, PP S3490 Bd. 1: *Hamburgische Börsen-Halle*, 7 Nov. 1892; ibid., *Hamburgischer Correspondent*, 15 Mar. 1893.
[22] StA Hbg, Senat, Cl. VII, Lit. Ta, Pars 2, Vol. 11, Fasc. 16, Inv. 25: Handelskammer to Präses, Deputation für Handel und Schiffahrt, 19 Dec. 1892.
[23] StA Hbg, PP S3490 Bd. 1: *Hamburgischer Correspondent*, 30 Dec. 1892.
[24] 'Rückblick auf das Wirtschaftsjahr 1892', *Hamburgischer Börsen-Halle*, 2 Jan. 1893 (in StA Hbg, PP S3490 Bd. 1).
[25] BA Koblenz, R86/2657: Sitzungsberichte der Cholera-Commission, 26 Sept. 1892 (4. Sitzung).

though a clean bill of health was still refused.[26] A stream of complaints flowed from the Chamber of Commerce to various official bodies complaining that quarantine measures were being too strictly enforced.[27] This pressure was backed up by a publicity campaign in the local press, which carried lengthy denunciations of the quarantine measures and suggested that they amounted to a 'contravention of Imperial laws'.[28] 'In the time of greatest need', complained the *Hamburger Tageblatt* in an obvious appeal to national sentiment, 'our German brothers have with a few exceptions abused, abandoned, and attacked us.'[29] The interest of the Senate and the merchant community alike lay in removing the quarantine regulations as quickly as possible and securing a mitigation of their severity while they lasted. Their campaign to restore the freedom of trade and movement which the epidemic had so quickly destroyed was a striking demonstration both of the continuity of local opinion and its continuing divergence from the point of view taken in Berlin.

Yet underneath the surface, serious clashes of interest between the Hamburg state and local capital were also taking place. After the epidemic was over, the Senate refused to relax the restrictions which it had imposed on the migrant traffic; the Hamburg–America Line, afraid of losing the traffic to other ports, announced in its 1893 report that it had arranged to move its headquarters to Bremen and to operate exclusively from the Weser. Such a move would have been a devastating blow to the Hamburg economy, to which the Line's presence in the city was estimated to contribute some sixty million Marks a year. Faced with such a threat, the Senate knuckled under and rescinded the restrictions.[30] It was the first of a series of striking demonstrations of the power of capital to negate the state's intentions of reform in the wake of the epidemic. More immediately, it indicated that the united face which the Senate was encouraging Hamburg's citizens to present to the hostile world around them concealed serious differences of opinion within the city itself about the causes, course, and consequences of the epidemic.

II

Even before it was faced with the threats and intrigues of the Hamburg–America Line, the Senate had already begun to be confronted by growing opposition from within the city's dominant classes. The joint sovereignty of Senate and Citizens' Assembly meant that an emergency session of the

[26] Ibid., 12. Sitzung (5 Nov. 1892), 13. Sitzung (14 Nov. 1892).
[27] Ibid., 13. Sitzung; and StA Hbg, Senat, Cl. VII, Lit. Ta, Pars 2, Vol. 11, Fasc. 16, Inv. 25. Handelskammer to Präses, Deputation für Handel und Schiffahrt, 19 Dec. 1892.
[28] StA Hbg, PP S3490 Bd. 1: *Hamburgischer Correspondent*, 29 Sept. 1892.
[29] StA Hbg, Senat, Cl. VII, Lit. Ta, Pars 2, Vol. 11, Fasc. 17, Inv. 2: *Hamburger Tageblatt*, 20 Sept. 1892.
[30] L. Cecil, *Albert Ballin: Business and Politics in Imperial Germany 1888–1918* (Princeton, 1967), pp. 40–1.

latter had to be called as quickly as possible to approve the extraordinary expenditure needed to finance the disinfection and other measures decided upon. It met on 29 August. The Senate did not escape from it unscathed. It began well enough with a brief, factual speech by Hachmann describing the measures taken ('in part under the influence of *Geheimrat* Koch', as he was careful to point out) and a determined attempt by the Senatorial party to argue that preventive measures had been taken on time and that there had been no delays in the announcement of the disease's presence. But it soon became apparent that these bland statements were not going to be accepted without criticism—and not only by the reviled minority of 'democrats'. The first voice to be raised was that of a medical deputy, Dr Hagedorn, who told the Citizens' Assembly that it should not have taken more than 24 hours to produce a culture of the bacillus:

However, the Hamburg Medical Office, under the command of Medical Inspector Dr Kraus, needed three days to do it; thus the presence of Asiatic cholera in Hamburg was only confirmed on 22 August instead of on the 19th. Whereas the authorities in Altona had already reported the occurrence of Asiatic cholera to Berlin on 21 August, Dr Kraus only allowed a similar report to be sent 24 hours later. In this way there arose an inexcusable delay in the announcement of the disease, which has taken a terrible revenge on Hamburg. For this reason the earliest preventive measures adopted by the authorities were adopted too late.

In fact Kraus and his subordinates had been even more dilatory, as we know, and the delay had been not four, but seven or eight days. When Hagedorn had finished, Amandus Gérard, a deputy belonging to the Left-Centre Caucus, got up and immediately demanded Kraus's resignation. 'This affair,' he said, 'must surely sound the last post for this man as far as his career as a state official is concerned.' As Gerard made his demand, 'the crowded benches of the public gallery echoed with a peal of applause so loud and so long-lasting that the President threatened to clear the gallery if the audience applauded in this way again'.[31] Clearly Kraus was now in the firing line. 'If Dr Kraus is dismissed from office', commented *Vorwärts*, the organ of the Berlin Social Democrats, on 31 August, 'this would be quite justified.'[32]

Kraus was not only under attack because of his alleged concealment of the epidemic's outbreak. There was also a widespread feeling that he was conspiring to conceal the epidemic's true extent as it went on. On 27 August Rudolf Hertz reported to his father, Senator Gustav Hertz, that 'all the doctors ... are making horrified faces, talk of the unusual violence of the disease or say it is unprecedented in their own experience, and declare that the official figures are being falsified'. What confirmed this suspicion for Hertz was 'the lowness of the official figures in comparison with the large numbers of hearses'

[31] *Bürgerschaft*, 29 Aug. 1892; StA Hbg, Senat, Cl. VII, Lit. Ta, Pars 2, Vol. 11, Fasc. 17, Inv. 4: *Kölnische Zeitung*, 30 Aug. 1892.
[32] StA Hbg, PP S3490 Bd. 1: *Vorwärts*, 31 Aug. 1892.

that he saw in the streets.[33] The figures given by the newspapers were supplied by Kraus himself and were equally suspect. 'A Hamburg doctor' complained on 26 August that 'the newspapers, unfortunately, are suppressing a great deal'; 'one should just not rely on the reports of the local papers and the press releases of the authorities', he wrote; '... the number of victims is certainly greater than claimed by officials'.[34] Ignorance of the true dimensions of the epidemic may have been a reason for Hachmann's initial dilatoriness in dealing with it, as we have already seen.[35] But the suspicion that the official figures were incorrect continued even after the events of the 28th.[36] The press was particularly alert for evidence of suppression of the truth once that it seemed the authorities had tried to conceal the epidemic at its outbreak. 'Now that the truth is finally out', warned one newspaper on 28 August, 'one hopes that it will continue to be given its due respect even in Hamburg.'[37]

A particularly bad impression was made by an interview which Kraus gave to the press on the morning of 6 September. His attempts to deny that there had been any delays in the announcement of the outbreak of the epidemic were not convincing. 'You ask,' said Kraus,

whether cholera was already present before 20 August—I must deny that. The first case of Asiatic cholera was reported to me on 20 August, and two gentlemen from the New Hospital in Eppendorf, including the Senior Anatomist, were immediately entrusted with a bacteriological investigation. The result was that Asiatic cholera was confirmed at 1 o'clock in the afternoon on 22 August.

This was not only unconvincing, it was also untrue. Whatever Kraus himself had been told, the first case had been admitted to the hospital on 16 August and bacteriological investigations had begun long before the 20th. 'What', asked the reporter, 'do you think of the speech of deputy Dr Hagedorn in the Citizens' Assembly claiming that a culture of the comma bacillus can be achieved in 24 hours according to the present state of medical science? ...' 'If Dr Hagedorn can do it, let him—I can't.' Worse than this, it seemed to the reporter that the medical authorities in Hamburg were, at best, confused about, and at worst, deliberately concealing, the true extent of the epidemic. 'The newspapers', he said to Kraus, 'talk of 2,000 deaths which have not been reported by the Medical Office.' 'My officials will give you the necessary explanation,' Kraus replied, 'I can't read all the newspapers.' On turning to the officials, the reporter discovered that their recording of deaths and cases was several days in arrears. 'Today's list will be completed perhaps in a

[33] StA Hbg, FA Gustav Hertz B17: Rudolf Hertz to his parents, 27 Aug. 1892.

[34] StA Hbg, Senat, Cl. VII, Lit. Ta, Pars 2, Vol. 11, Fasc. 17, Inv. 4: *Die Post*, 28 Aug. 1892; *National-Zeitung*, 28 Aug. 1892.

[35] See above, pp. 314, 328.

[36] StA Hbg, Senat, Cl. VII, Lit. Ta, Pars 2, Vol. 11, Fasc. 17, Inv. 4: *Freisinnige Zeitung*, 30 Aug. 1892.

[37] Ibid.; *Die Post*, 28 Aug. 1892.

fortnight', he was told. One of the reporter's colleagues visited the place where the bodies were collected. 'The doctor who accompanied my informant complained about the earlier chaos in the mortuary.' It had long been impossible to conduct a proper count because the relevant papers were missing. It had probably only been after Versmann and Roeloffs had taken a grip on things that circumstances had at last improved. 'Now', boasted the doctor, 'the morgue is exemplary in its orderliness.' 'And the dead number?' '—over 5,000.' 'A terrible revelation', commented the reporter, '—but it was the truth which I was hearing.' His readers were left in no doubt that had it been left to Dr Kraus, the truth would not have been heard.[38]

And indeed it was undeniable that Kraus and his officials were publishing grossly underestimated statistics. At noon on 6 September, for example, the Senate announced that there had so far been 6,798 cases and 2,940 deaths up to that point. A week later, these figures had been revised to show that a total of 11,424 people had caught the disease by 6 September and 4,900 had died of it. This was more than a minor adjustment. 4,626 cases, or over 40% of the total, had been omitted from the official statistics, and so too had 1,960 deaths, likewise 40% of the total.[39] As Senator Johannes Versmann complained next day in his diary, Kraus should have corrected his figures. 'The figures were only put in order after Roeloffs had placed competent officials in the Medical Office!' Various officials were interviewed and it was discovered that Kraus had only reported cases communicated to him by the doctors; he had discounted cases reported by the hospitals on the grounds that these had already appeared in the returns sent in by the doctors. But of course it was inevitable in the circumstances of the epidemic that thousands of sufferers should be taken straight to hospital without receiving any prior medical attention. A further source of error, shocking in the extreme to German officialdom, was uncovered when it was revealed that an official had been applying his rubber stamp to the wrong documents. Thus partial figures were endorsed as final counts. Kraus had blundered again. 'This is bad!' commented Versmann in his diary. In his view the matter was a serious one.[40]

On 6 September, Hamburg's Cholera Commission met to discuss these discrepancies. Senator Gerhard Hachmann attempted to defend his Chief Medical Officer and declared that the figures published by Kraus were in reality more likely to be exaggerations than underestimates—graphic evidence of

[38] Ibid., report of 7 Sept. 1892 (the paper is unfortunately not named).

[39] StA Hbg: Cholerakommission 1: 6. Sitzung ibid., 9: Hamburger Echo, 15 Sept. 1892. Relying on the same figures for his private notes on the progress of the disease Georg Koch, head of the Statistical Bureau, underestimated the number of cases by 35% up to 27 Aug. and 40% up to 4 Sept. (Koch, 'Die Tagebuchaufzeichnungen Georg Kochs'). Exactly the same problems occurred in the previous 'explosive' outbreak of cholera in 1859: see StA Hbg, Senat, Cl. VII, Lit. Ta, Pars 2, Vol. 6: Physicats-Bericht 22 Aug. 1859.

[40] StA Hbg, FA Versmann VI A6, Bl. 124–6.

his continuing complacency on the subject. But Versmann and Mönckeberg rejected Hachmann's claim out of hand. The Commission decided formally to recognize that there were serious discrepancies between the various statistics issued, and admitted that their origin had to be explained to the press. The same evening Versmann and Mönckeberg agreed that Kraus should be suspended from office. Versmann convinced Mönckeberg that he should get Hachmann to call a meeting of the Medical Board the next morning before the regular session of the Senate, in order to make a formal recommendation to this effect and to suggest the provisional appointment of a successor. Versmann had some difficulty in getting Mönckeberg to issue the relevant instructions to the waiting messenger; there was, he reported, 'a very substantial difference of opinion between us about the significance and importance of this lamentable occurrence'; but in the end, as so often, he succeeded in persuading his colleagues to fall in with his suggestion. On 7 September the atmosphere in the Senate was so hostile to Kraus that long and serious consideration was given to a proposal that he be dismissed without a pension. Eventually a formula was agreed on whereby Kraus formally requested to be relieved of his duties on health grounds.[41] In his formal letter of resignation, Kraus gave his poor health as the reason. He had not felt able to resign while the epidemic was at its height, he wrote, but he could now the worst was over.[42] Kraus had in fact for some time been suffering from lung cancer; his obituary in the *History of the Hamburg Doctors' Club* later noted that he had been ill since 1891. 'Broken in body', and perhaps broken in spirit too by his disgrace, he left office the same day and did indeed die before the year was out. In the meantime his resignation provided the city's ruling fraction with a convenient scapegoat. Caesar Amsinck, a member of Hamburg's richest and most patrician merchant families and related to several of the Senators by marriage, wrote on 8 September that Kraus had been dismissed for suppressing the news of the epidemic in its first week, an assertion that was, to say the least, something of an oversimplification.[43] In the meantime, however, there was no doubt that the reputation of Hamburg's government had suffered another blow, and Hachmann himself was forced to admit publicly in the second formal report of the Cholera Commission, drafted by Roeloffs and issued on 13 September 1892, that the official figures had been 'very deficient' because of delays and omissions in doctors' reports and because of the lack of attention paid to reports from the hospitals.[44]

With the departure of Kraus, his duties passed into other, more energetic hands. Kraus's successor as Chief Medical Officer was the successful Hamburg

---

41 Ibid. (entry for 7 Sept.).
42 StA Hbg, Senat, Cl. VII, Lb, No. 23a, Vol. 88, Fasc. 7.
43 Michael, *Geschichte des ärztlichen Vereins*, biography of Kraus; StA Hbg, FA Beneke M94: Caesar Amsinck to Hugo Beneke, 8 Sept. 1892. Cf. Winkle, 'Chronologie', pp. 16–23, here p. 17.
44 StA Hbg, Cholerakommission 27: 2. Bericht, Bl. 50; and StA Hbg, FA Versmann VI A6, entry for 12 Sept.

doctor Johann Julius Reincke. Born in 1842, son of an Altona merchant, Reincke was an established figure in Hamburg society. A deputy in the Citizens' Assembly from 1879 to 1891, he belonged to the Senatorial party, the Caucus of Rightists, and was related by marriage to the Senatorial dynasty of the Sievekings.[45] Through his connections Reincke had built up a practice so successful that he was able to demand 15,000 Marks in compensation for lost income on taking over as director of the Medical Office: it was considered 'impracticable' to raise the salary attached to the post immediately, but Reincke was given an assurance that a raise would be considered once the epidemic was over.[46] Reincke had been a disciple of Pettenkofer as late as 1890, but the events of 1892 brought about in him a well-timed conversion to the contagionist doctrines of Robert Koch.[47] The Senate could rely on him to strike a suitable compromise between the dominant medical theory of the day and the needs and requirements of the state which he had now been called upon to serve. Pastor Ritter noted on 7 September that 'the reports of the medical authorities are admittedly so confused and unreliable that the Senate has taken the responsibility for compiling statistics of the epidemic away from it and given it to Georg Koch (Statistical Office), so that they can be rendered useful again'.[48] Koch found that 'the statistics of cholera cases and deaths kept up to now by the Medical Office were very incomplete and quite obviously yielded figures that were far too low'. As a result, as he complained in his diary, he had to go into the office on Sundays for the rest of September and most of October as well. However, within a week or so reliable figures had at last been produced: too late, to be sure, to rescue the Hamburg authorities from almost universal outrage at their persistent underestimation of the epidemic's true extent.[49]

The day after Kraus's enforced resignation, Senator Versmann sat down in his study to compose his customary diary entry. 'With the resignation of Dr Kraus as Medical Inspector', he wrote,

the first act of this tragedy has come to an end. As a result we are witnessing the raging of a cholera epidemic, of a hitherto unknown severity, which has already probably claimed 5–6,000 victims in the city and suburbs and threatens the danger of further loss of human life;

the moral discrediting of the Hamburg government and the Hamburg authorities in the whole civilised world;

poverty and destitution in wide areas of the poorer population and wholly incalculable damage to our national prosperity that will scarcely prove to be any less severe than that caused by the Fire of 1842;

[45] 'Stammbaum der Familie Reincke, zusammengestellt für den Familientag am 29. Dezember 1899' (copy in StA Hbg).
[46] StA Hbg, FA Versmann VI A6, Bl. 126: entry for 7 Sept.
[47] See above, pp. 191, 276.
[48] StA Hbg, 622–1: FA Ritter D2, p. 183.
[49] Koch, 'Die Tagebuchaufzeichnungen Georg Kochs'.

a discrediting, achieved at a single stroke, of our sanitary arrangements and their infrastructure, the sewage system and water-supply, which will swallow up many millions in the effort to make it good.[50]

Events were to prove Versmann correct. The first act was indeed over. After two weeks of chaos, the Senate had at last taken decisive steps to reassert its control over the course of events. But this was in reality only the beginning.

III

The 'moral discrediting of the Hamburg government' which Versmann recorded in his diary on 8 September had already started within a few days of the epidemic, with the discovery of the delays and confusions that attended the announcement of the disease's presence in the city. On 14 September the Citizens' Assembly met again to hear Burgomaster Mönckeberg ask for a vote of a million Marks to cover the cost of fighting the epidemic. Mönckeberg's comparison of the disaster with that of the Great Fire fifty years before, and his appeal to the patriotic sentiments of the deputies, were well received; but 'later', as Versmann noted in his diary that evening, 'the Senate speakers, unfortunately, did not intervene authoritatively, so that the speeches of the Citizens' Assembly deputies were allowed to compete with one another without hindrance in committing the most unbelievable indiscretions'.[51] By the time the Citizens' Assembly next met, on 1 October, far more than 'indiscretions' were on the agenda: Dr Heinrich Gieschen, President of the Property-Owners' Association, used the opportunity to launch one of the Caucus of Leftists' frequent attacks on the role of the notables in the electoral system. Picking up the complaints of the American Vice-Consul Burke, which by this time were arousing widespread public comment, Gieschen described the dispatch of the *Normannia* and other migrant ships with bills of good health[52] as 'nothing short of a crime'. No one, he said, could now doubt the disease was carried in the water-supply ('except Herr *Physicus* Erman', he added); a shameless enough statement given Gieschen's earlier attacks on Koch's theories when it was in the interests of the property-owners to delay the filtration of the water.[53]

'When the cholera has gone', he went on, 'we'll go back to muddling through in the same old way. It's not the fault of the Citizens' Assembly that there have been delays ... If we could rid today's Assembly of the notables, we could have more of an effect on the Senate.' How that greater influence might have been exerted during the debates on the water-supply since 1873

[50] StA Hbg, FA Versmann VI A6, Bl. 126: entry for 8 Sept. Characteristically Versmann used the word *Nationalwohlstand* to refer to the local Hamburg economy.
[51] Ibid., entry for 14 Sept.
[52] See above, pp. 316–19.
[53] Cf. Chapter 2c, above.

was a very different matter. Yet by 12 October, Gieschen was attacking the Senate in even harsher terms. 'If the Senate had not mixed up the filtration question with the problem of the water rate in 1887, it could already have been in existence by 1890.' Given the blame that the press was now casting on the property-owners for their role in the delay, Gieschen evidently thought that attack was the best means of defence. The tenseness of the atmosphere exploded into a rare moment of uproar as Carl Möring, the most senior of the merchant Senators, got up to complain that 'in recent weeks there has been a systematic campaign of maligning and casting aspersions upon the administration and its officials'. Gieschen interrupted with a shout of 'that's impossible!' which Möring promptly called 'an irresponsible expression', causing 'uproar' in the Assembly. 'Our system', concluded Gieschen, 'is hopeless. This fact is worse than the epidemic itself. Either reform it root and branch or the next disaster will be the end of us.'[54]

Gieschen's hypocritical diatribes were mild compared to the assault which was soon being launched on the city's political and social system by the local Social Democrats. For much of September, as we have seen, the Social Democratic *Hamburger Echo* refrained from criticizing the Senate in any way, and managed to deny a public outlet to possible protests by the small group of radicals in the local party's ranks. But as the police, referring to the attacks which had led to the resignation of Dr Kraus, noted, soon 'the attitude of the Hamburg press, the *General-Anzeiger*, the *Fremdenblatt*, etc. forced the Hamburg paper (i.e. the *Echo*) to adopt a far more radical posture than all the efforts of the more radical group in Hamburg had succeeded in doing'.[55] Events, thought the police, were now playing into the hands of the radical minority. The Social Democrats, under the influence both of the radicals and of the group of petty-bourgeois democrats who had joined the party at the end of the 1880s, now launched a two-pronged attack, aiming to gain the support both of the working class and of the petty bourgeoisie. As Police Commissar Rosalowsky reported,

The point of attack was supplied by Hamburg's constitution. By pursuing this point it was sought at the same time to put part of the Social Democratic programme into effect. Reform of the constitution would win the support of the non-Social Democratic petty bourgeoisie, while the point on which it was hoped to win the support of the mass of the labouring population was the alleged 'fight against unemployment'. Without doubt the moment chosen by the Social Democrats for the attack was the right one. The consequences of the epidemic weighed heavily on the people. Borders were closed everywhere, the harbour lay full of ships but none was being loaded or unloaded. The railways had stopped running. Nobody in the population thought of buying things or repairing them and nobody wanted to buy luxury goods, so that

[54] *Bürgerschaft*, 1 Oct., 12 Oct. 1892.
[55] StA Hbg, Senat, Cl. XI, Gen. No. 2, Vol. 61, Fasc. 1: Denkschrift vom 4. Nov. 1892, pp. 6–7; and for the following.

workers were without occupation and stared poverty ever closer in the face, while the small trader in his shop confronted ruin.

It was in this situation, therefore, towards the end of October, as the epidemic finally seemed to be over, that the Social Democrats, pushed on by the left opposition, and almost shamed into the act by the radicalism of the bourgeois press, began their campaign for full employment and constitutional reform.[56]

On 4 November the Hamburg Social Democratic party organization staged nine simultaneous mass public meetings on the theme of 'Cholera, the Hamburg Constitution, and the Social Democratic Party'. The meetings attracted huge audiences: according even to the bourgeois press, a total of 30,000 people attended the nine meetings.[57] At one meeting, held in Sagebiel's establishment, the attendance exceeded 6,000, and in Barmbeck, the party's leading local figure, Otto Stolten, according to police estimates, attracted an audience of 3,500.[58] All the meetings had a common theme: it was that the epidemic had been caused by the incompetence and greed of the Hamburg Senate. Such a catastrophe would not have occurred had the government of the city been in the hands of a democratically elected body. What was needed, therefore, to prevent a recurrence, was the immediate introduction of universal suffrage.[59]

With mostly only minor variations, all the nine speakers at the mass meetings echoed this theme in their addresses. Wilhelm Koenen, speaking to an audience of 2,000 at Hamm (500 according to the police), was perhaps the most radical. He began by declaring 'when the epidemic came, its arrival was concealed by the authorities and only described as "cholerine"'. This accusation does not seem to have been repeated by other speakers, although Ehlers, in Eilbeck, complained that it took 8 days to declare its presence.[60] But most followed Koenen in concentrating their attack on the fact that the Hamburg Senate had seen fit to delay the introduction of a filtrated water-supply in favour of other, more lucrative or—in the case of the grandiose new Town Hall—more prestigious projects. He declared that

The work on the sand-filtration beds is progressing ... at a snail's pace, just like all the projects that are undertaken for the common good. The propertied class is not very interested in speeding them up, because it's in a position to procure palatable drinking-water for itself. The construction of the free port was finished in the shortest time because it was in the interest of the propertied class. In the same way the construction work on the Council Palace has been speeded up.[61]

In echoing this complaint, other speakers added the charge that the Senate

[56] Ibid.
[57] StA Hbg, PP S3496: *General-Anzeiger*, 6 Nov. 1892, *Berliner Volkszeitung*, 6 Nov. 1892.
[58] Ibid.: *Versammlungsbericht*, 5 Nov. 1892.
[59] Ibid.: *Berliner Volkszeitung*, 6 Nov. 1892.
[60] Ibid.: *Hamburger Echo*, 6 Nov. 1892, 12 Nov. 1892, *Versammlungsbericht*, 5 Nov. 1892.
[61] Ibid.: *Hamburger Echo*, 12 Nov. 1892.

had also failed to take adequate steps to improve the housing in which Hamburg's poor lived. Emil Fischer, for example, declaring 'the bourgeoisie is to blame for the terrible catastrophe', added: 'bad drinking-water, bad housing, and bad nutrition for the great mass of the people are to blame for the cholera epidemic having been so great'. For, as another orator, speaking to an audience of over 1,500 in Eimsbüttel, asserted, it was not only the water-supply that brought cholera. 'Every child knows these days that unhealthy dwellings and hungry bellies are the preconditions of every disease.' It followed from this that 'it would have been necessary to have cleared out certain tenement blocks and torn them down'. A similar emphasis was placed on housing as well as on the water-supply by the speakers at Sagebiel's in Eilbeck, and at the Marienhof in Grünerdeich. It was summed up by Otto Stolten, speaking in Barmbeck. He said, beginning with a graphic image of wealth,

All that the people who travel on rubber tyres know of Hamburg are the villa quarters and the façades of the main streets. They know the Jungfernstieg but not the Niedernstrasse, the Springeltwiete, and similar areas (stormy applause) ... The 120 million that it cost to join the Customs Union were much easier to get than the $7\frac{1}{2}$ million that it is supposed to have cost to supply better drinking-water (lively applause) ... It needed a terrible catastrophe before the Senate would cast a glance at the poverty in the city.[62]

These, then, were the three major points of the speakers' attack on the Hamburg Senate: its neglect of the water-supply, its failure to improve working-class housing, and its undemocratic, plutocratic composition.

Most speakers did not go into the epidemic itself in any great detail: Karl Frohme, for example, said virtually nothing on it, and contented himself with the observation that 'since the epidemic ceased, everything has gone back into its old groove and every innovation is anxiously avoided'.[63] In this respect, the accusations brought by Wilhelm Koenen were far more circumstantial:

The transport of the sick and the dead has been carried out in a very inadequate manner ... When the epidemic broke out in Hamburg and many victims and corpses had to be transported, we thought that it would be all provided free of charge by the state. But far from it! Now that the epidemic has pretty well left us, the victims of cholera are being sent bills and if they are not in a position to pay, they even get the bailiffs round their neck. If the bourgeoisie had intervened earlier to fight the epidemic, Hamburg's trade would not have lost all those many millions ...

Indeed, during the discussion of this speech, one participant at the meeting went even further in his allegations, claiming that 'because trade would be damaged by the presence of cholera becoming known, and half the Senators

[62] Ibid.: *Versammlungsbericht*, 5 Nov. 1892.
[63] Ibid.: *Hamburger Echo*, 6 Nov. 1892.

are merchants, the disease was kept secret'. At this point, however, the officiating policeman called the speaker to order.[64]

All the meetings ended with a demand for universal suffrage, but they also appended specific points calling for slum clearance, the construction of new housing estates in the suburbs, linked by railway to the city centre, and the provision of work for the unemployed by the state.[65] The police saw in the constitutional demands a tactic of the Social Democrats to win over the petty bourgeoisie 'in order to bring about the entry of their members into the legislature'.[66] In addition, Rosalowsky thought that in the coming Reichstag elections of 1893, the Social Democrats, because of the losses they had sustained during the epidemic, were seeking 'a strong increase in members from the circles of the petty bourgeoisie which have up to now been hostile to it'.[67] But this tactic was only incidental to their main purpose, which was directed in the view of the police to changing the balance of political power in Hamburg itself. Hamburg was to form a precedent for the spread of socialism to other parts of Germany above all in the use of state funds for job creation and unemployment relief. Moreover, the campaign for the democratization of Hamburg's constitution clearly posed a serious threat to the dominant classes. This was almost the first time that the Social Democrats had really focused their attention on local political structures in the city-state. When the simultaneous calls for constitutional reform urged by the Caucus of Leftists and the property-owners are taken into consideration as well, this did not bode well for the continued hegemony of the mercantile interest.

IV

Yet more serious, in many ways, were the attacks that were launched on Hamburg from outside, beginning even before the end of August. The Social Democratic press in other parts of Germany shared none of the inhibitions that made the columns of the *Hamburger Echo* so reticent at this period. The organ of the Berlin Social Democrats, *Vorwärts*, was of the opinion as early as 31 August that not only should Dr Kraus be relieved of his office, but

the whole patrician clique that rules the Free and Hanseatic City of Hamburg, because of the rights its money-bags give it, must be cleared out straight away as well. Kraus is only an official of that clique of families that rules in Hamburg, while the great mass of taxpayers have 'nothing to say'. The driving-force of Hamburg's bourgeois policies is the shabbiest shopkeeper-interest; fear of damaging 'large-scale trade' was the main cause of those tactics of deadly silence whose calculations were reckoned

[64] Ibid.: *Hamburger Echo*, 12 Nov. 1892.
[65] Ibid.: *Der Grundstein*, 12 Oct. 1892: *Versammlungsbericht St. Georg*, 5 Nov. 1892.
[66] StA Hbg, Senat, Cl. XI, Gen. No. 2. Vol. 16, Fasc. 1; Denkschrift 4 Nov. 1892, p. 13.
[67] Ibid.: p. 17.

not in people's lives but in coffee sacks, not in citizens with rights but in petroleum tankers, and which threaten not just Hamburg but the whole of Germany.[68]

Other Social Democratic newspapers played further variations on these themes, declaring that Hamburg was ruled by 'special interests'[69] and describing the Alley Quarters in the city as containing 'circumstances which in parts are unworthy of a Russian village'.[70]

A Social Democratic paper in Munich even claimed there was an outbreak of typhus in Hamburg: 'here hunger-typhus, there warehouses brimming with bread and corn'. All concurred in blaming the epidemic on the rule of the merchants and the absence of democratic controls over the city government. *Vorwärts* attacked the Hamburg Senate in the most unbridled terms for its concealment of the epidemic in the first weeks. 'To have admitted openly, and straight away, that Asiatic cholera had come to Hamburg, would have meant reducing the booty of the shipowners, the coffee kings, the traders, the brokers, the speculators, the insurance agents by a few per cent; but property is holy, thrice holy.' The main organ of the Social Democrats was not impressed with the Senate's attempts to combat the epidemic either. 'The Hamburg money-bags coterie stands helpless and lost for ideas in the face of the epidemic, which is only reaping where the boundless dilatoriness of the administration, the most narrow-minded capitalist self-interest, the most unbelievable stupidity of an obsolescent, decayed, and inefficient clan regime have sown.' The paper called for a ruthless critique of Hamburg's ruling class and its 'rotten regiment of snobs'.[71]

A very different kind of attack on Hamburg's political system was launched from the quarter of the small but vociferous anti-Semitic movement that had emerged in Germany during the 1880s. The anti-Semitic *Deutsch-Soziale Blätter*, published in Leipzig, ran a series of articles in the second half of October on 'Hamburg on the Elbe: a Jewish-patrician Limited Company', offering a characteristic mixture of populist criticisms and demogogic solutions: 'Those who do not live in Hamburg', it began,

regularly fail to recognize the fact that Hamburg forms a territory that is strictly cut off from the rest of Germany. Its inhabitants are ruled by a most peculiar, stiff, and immovable mammonistic spirit of cliquishness. This spirit is fostered and cared for within a powerful ring of purse-proud merchant families and mainly produces internationalist and anti-patriotic inclinations. Indeed one has to say that within this ring there dominate moral views which reveal a decided antagonism against natural territorial notions of morality.

[68] StA Hbg, PP S3490 Bd. 1: *Vorwärts*, 31 Aug. 1892.
[69] StA Hbg, Senat, Cl. VII, Lit. Ta, Pars 2, Vol. 11, Fasc. 16, Inv. 22: *Kölnische Volkszeitung*, 14 Sept. 1892.
[70] Ibid., Inv. 27: *Kölnische Volkszeitung*, 5 Sept. 1892.
[71] StA Hbg, Senat, Cl. XI, Gen. No. 2, Vol. 16, Fasc. 1: Denkschrift vom 4. Nov. 1892, p. 16; StA Hbg, PP S3490 Bd. 1; *Vorwärts*, 31 Aug. 1892.

Hamburg was ruled, it went on, by a tiny group of 'Exchange-Senators' whose only interest was money and profit. This mercenary spirit had penetrated the majority of the population. 'One asks in Hamburg not "what kind of man is he?" but "how much is he worth?"' Status in Hamburg derived solely from income: cultural life consisted in a slavish following of the latest fashions, in tasteless luxury and display.

These circumstances, argued the anti-Semites, showed that the city was infected by 'the corrupting bacillus of Judaism'—a biological metaphor which lay close at hand, given the occasion of the articles, but which was none the less characteristic of the new, racialist anti-Semitism which had recently taken on an organized form in the German Empire. 'The whole state in Hamburg', the paper continued,

is these days in reality nothing more than a demesne for the cultivation of Jewish-patrician interests. The Senate owes allegiance to the Exchange, and several of its members are of Jewish origin. The decisive role in the Citizens' Assembly is played by pettifogging Jewish lawyers. They jabber down anything that dares to oppose the all-powerful Jewish influence. All the leading papers, the *Hamburgische Korrespondent*, the *Hamburger Fremdenblatt*, the *Hamburger Tageblatt* (the last-named the continuation of the defunct *Reform*) do nothing but carry out the Jews' business and up to a few years ago were still able to conceal the existence of a powerful anti-Jewish movement in the Reich from the average common man in Hamburg.

The paper complained of Hamburg's Jews that 'they make themselves unpleasantly apparent on the street, in the tram, in the omnibus, in the theatre, in the pubs, briefly, everywhere, in a manner that puts even the situation in Berlin in the shade'.

It was characteristic of the anti-Semites that they saw Jews everywhere; as Hitler remarked in *Mein Kampf*, when he became converted to anti-Semitism the scales dropped from his eyes and he suddenly saw Jews wherever he looked. Characteristic too were their association of Jews with dirt, a symbolic means by which they sought to separate the Jews from humanity, and suggest they were something lower. Thus 'unspeakable filth' was 'permanently piled up' in Hamburg's streets, while sexual circumstances in Hamburg 'defied all description' and 'the shamelessness of the Hamburg prostitutes on the streets borders on the unbelievable'. Finally, the epidemic itself had been caused not least by 'the mass arrival of Jewish emigrants and the impurity of the Hamburg water mains'. 'There is every justification', it concluded, 'for calling Hamburg a Godless city, a modern Sodom and Gomorrah'. The anti-Semites' diatribe culminated in the accusation that Hamburg was still a foreign body in the German Empire. It had never taken a leading role in German unification and its interests lay outside the Empire altogether. 'The patricians and their followers are a kind of half-breed Englishmen in their lack of any understanding for the national German cause.' Thus it was necessary for 'outside government to be forced upon them, a government which ruthlessly shows the money-bags the way back into the cupboard, when their interests come into conflict with those of the common good.' A Reich Commissioner should be installed to put Hamburg's house in order, and the constitution should be changed in order to destroy the power of the patriciate. Such proposals combined populism and authoritarianism in a manner entirely characteristic of the anti-Semites; and it was not the least of their concerns that they believed the existing conditions in the city to be almost ideally favourable to the growth of the 'Godless' Social Democratic Party, to combat which, indeed, the Berlin anti-Semites had originally come into being.[72]

The anti-Semites' accusations were fantastic nonsense, of course: Hamburg was not ruled by Jews, nor were there any men of Jewish descent in the Senate. It was true that the grand bourgeoisie in Hamburg was far less prejudiced against Jews than was, for example, court society in Berlin. This was not least because by the late nineteenth century the Jews of Hamburg belonged in the main to the better-off classes. As Map 28, giving the earliest available figures, indicates, half the city's practising Jews lived in the two richest districts, Rotherbaum and Harvestehude, and these districts undoubtedly contained many more baptized Jews. There was a small Jewish petty bourgeoisie, concentrated around the street-market known as the Jewish Exchange (*Judenbörse*) in the Neustadt; but there was no doubting the general assimilation of the city's Jewish community to the mercantile and professional bourgeoisie. Until 1860, Jews in Hamburg had not been fully emancipated; until 1849 they had not been permitted to join the guilds, and before 1851 they had been forbidden to marry Gentiles. But Jewish banking families such as the Warburgs and the Heines were accepted without difficulty as business and political allies of the leading merchants. Salomon Heine was elected an honorary member of the Patriotic Society as early as 1843, and prominent Jewish politicians such as Isaac and Albert Wolffson were able to make a successful career for themselves in the Citizens' Assembly, to which nine Jews were elected when the Assembly was established in 1859.[73] Albert Wolffson indeed became leader of the Caucus of Rightists and exercised such an influence on the election of Senators that he was generally known as 'King-maker Wolffson'.[74] At the turn of the century the Senate appointed as its Secretary and leading official in the Finance Deputation the Jew Leo Lippmann; in his memoirs, written after his abrupt dismissal by the Nazis in

---

[72] StA Hbg, Senat Cl. VII, Lit. Ta, Pars 2, Vol. 11, Fasc. 16, Inv. 22: *Deutsch-Soziale Blätter*, 16 Oct. 1892 *et seq.*

[73] E. Klessmann, *Geschichte der Stadt Hamburg* (Hamburg, 1981), pp. 465–7; H. Krohn, *Die Juden in Hamburg, 1800–1850* (Frankfurt-on-Main, 1967) and H. Krohn, *Die Juden in Hamburg 1850–1914* (Hamburg, 1974).

[74] StA Hbg, FA Buehl 2c, p. 47.

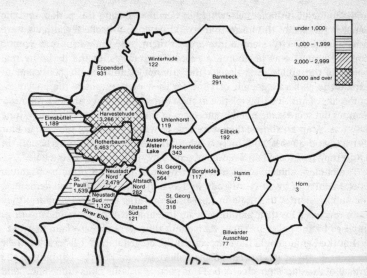

Source: SHS 24 (1909), 27

MAP 28. Jews in Hamburg (1905), by district: absolute numbers

1933, Lippmann recalled that he never encountered even a hint of anti-Semitism in his work for the Senate before the First World War.[75] Julius von Eckardt noted that there was little anti-Semitic sentiment in the Hamburg upper class 'and that even at a time when the plague of anti-Semitism was raging through the rest of Germany, one Jew was appointed as Director of the City Library and another as State Factory Inspector'. Moreover, he thought 'that great and important services have been rendered by the Jews of Hamburg in the assimilation of the city to the dominant conditions and arrangements of the new Germany'.[76]

However, he went on, 'despite their decided friendliness towards the Jews, the old Hamburg families ostracized the Jewish element as far as social life was concerned'. The Jews, 'whether baptized or not', lived in 'a world of their own'.[77] Jews could never be elected to the Senate; otherwise a man such as Albert Wolffson would long since have embarked upon a Senatorial career. Moreover, there had been anti-Semitic disturbances in 1819, 1830, and 1835, in which Jews had been attacked on the streets and forcibly ejected from coffee-houses. Yet these were in no way as serious as comparable

---

[75] StA Hbg, FA Lippmann A4, i. 2.
[76] J. von Eckardt, *Lebenserinnerungen* (Leipzig, 1920), i, 203.
[77] Ibid., p. 204.

anti-Semitic disturbances elsewhere in Germany during this period, and the Senate, mindful of the harm that would be done to trade if the Jews were driven from the city, stepped into protect them.[78] By the 1840s anti-Semitic popular protest was no more—a reflection, perhaps, of the declining real power of the guilds. And despite the attempt of anti-Semitic politicians to exploit the cholera epidemic of 1892 for their own purposes, there were no outbreaks of anti-Jewish violence in the 1890s either. Nevertheless, the Anti-Semites did score some notable successes in the Reichstag election of 15 June 1893. As Map 29 shows, they were able to win over 10% of the vote in four districts and almost 10% in two others (Hohenfelde and Rotherbaum). In 1890 they had scored an average of only 0.5% in Hamburg as a whole.[79]

The cholera epidemic certainly played a role in anti-Semitic propaganda in the winter of 1892–3. Already in 1891 the Anti-Semites had demanded the suppression of the trade in Jewish immigrants through Hamburg; they were rewarded for their agitation by an indefinite ban on all public meetings imposed by the police in 1891. As a result they were able to claim in 1892–3 that the Senate could have prevented the epidemic had it listened to their warnings, and at least some people believed them. But the banning of the transit of Russian migrants robbed this particular issue of its immediacy, and in June 1893 the Anti-Semites were able to hold public meetings once more as part of the election campaign. Attacks on the Senate over the suppression of Anti-Semitic meetings and the origin of the cholera outbreak played only a very subordinate role in the Anti-Semites' electoral propaganda in 1893. Like all Reichstag elections it was fought mainly on national issues—in this case, the Caprivi Army Bill, although the National Liberal campaign, in contrast to all the others, concentrated on the issue of Hamburg's representation in the Reichstag, as we saw in Chapter 1. The relative success of the Anti-Semites was due largely to the fact that they had regrouped under a new, more radical leadership after the fiasco of the 1890 election, and quarrels between the old Christian-Social Anti-Semites and the new racial Anti-Semites had been forgotten in the common campaign to get the local ban on meetings lifted. Differences did break out once more during the 1893 election campaign, but they did little real damage to the Anti-Semites' fortunes. ∗

What really won them support was the explicit appeal they were now directing to the petty bourgeoisie, particularly at a time when—partly as a result of the epidemic—small trading, retailing, and crafts were not doing well. The Anti-Semites were supported by numerous petty state employees, and were thought to have many sympathizers among lower customs officers and ordinary policemen, but their main support came from shopkeepers,

[78] M. Zimmermann, 'Antijüdischer Sozialprotest? Proteste von Unter- und Mittelschichten 1819–1835', in Herzig et al., Arbeiter in Hamburg, pp. 89–94.

[79] SHS 20 (1902), 92–3.

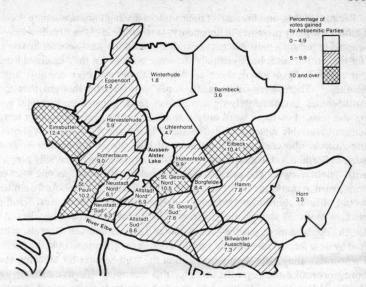

Source: SHS 20 (1902), 93

MAP 29. Anti-Semitic vote, by district, Reichstag election, Hamburg 1893

white-collar workers, and artisans, many of whom had apparently voted Social Democrat in 1890. Some artisans and some branches of the retailing trade (e.g. greengrocery) suffered badly in 1892–3 because of the epidemic, and white-collar workers may also have lost income during the commercial depression. It was precisely for these reasons that the Anti-Semitic Party gained so much support in a district like St Georg Nord where there was a relatively high proportion of petty-bourgeois votes. Indeed this district eventually elected the first Anti-Semite deputy to the Citizens' Assembly in 1898. Interestingly, the next district to elect an Anti-Semite was the Billwärder Ausschlag, near the harbour, where social antagonism between the petty bourgeoisie and the working class seems to have been considerable. It was also the favoured place for customs officers to live, and had the highest proportion of lower civil servants of any district apart from Eimsbüttel (which also scored the highest Anti-Semitic vote in the Reichstag election of 1893).[80]

---

[80] K.-G. Riquarts, *Der Antisemitismus als politische Partei in Schleswig-Holstein und Hamburg, 1871–1914,* Ph.D. thesis (Kiel, 1975), pp. 69–76, 183, 208: StA Hbg, PP S4296 Bd. 1, *passim*; ibid, S2424 Bd. 1–2, *passim*; S576 I Bd. 1, Bl. IIb, IIIc, IV, *passim*; Sta Hbg, PP S3625 Bd. 4: Vigilanzbericht 7995/II/1 (12 June 1893); ibid., 8645/II/1 (24 June 1893); *SHS* 20 (1902), p. 102 (F. Raab). For the damage caused to small shopkeepers by the epidemic, see StA Hbg, Senat Cl. VII, Lit. Ta, Pars 2, Vol. 11, Fasc. 16, Inv. 22: *Münchener Neueste Nachrichten,* 30 Oct. 1892, *Berliner Börsen-Courier,* 22 Sept. 1892: ibid. Fasc. 17, Inv. 2, Bl. 99, 106, 117, 125, 157, 173, 205; StA Hbg, PP S3490 Bd. 1: *Hamburger Fremdenblatt,* 12 Nov. 1892; C. Wischermann, *Wohnen in Hamburg vor dem Ersten Weltkrieg* (Münster, 1983), p. 262.

Because of this, and because of their attacks on 'high finance', some Social Democratic party members in Eppendorf—a stronghold of the Anti-Semites—wanted to put up a joint Reichstag candidate with the Anti-Semites in 1893, 'for the Anti-Semites have virtually the same aims as us; they emerged from our party, because where there are Social Democrats there are also Anti-Semites'.[81] There were undoubtedly some workers who thought that the Anti-Semites 'are absolutely right ... We've really got to keep a careful eye on the Jews'; but these were only a small minority, and such views were almost invariably rejected by active Social Democrats.[82] As Map 29 shows, the Anti-Semitic vote was low in areas of high Social Democratic support such as Barmbeck. Most workers thought the Anti-Semites were 'silly people' with 'idiotic views'. 'The rascals want a punch on the nose', as one worker was heard remarking, and they generally believed that the Anti-Semites would all join the Social Democrats in the long run.[83] Most Anti-Semitic election meetings were actively disrupted by Social Democratic hecklers. As for the establishment parties—the National Liberals and Left-Liberals, who had by now formed an electoral pact in a desperate attempt to oust the Social Democrats—they were deeply resentful of the Anti-Semites for breaking the bourgeois ranks and regarded them for this reason as 'effective succour for the Social Democrats'.[84] Ultimately, the Anti-Semites were marginal enough in 1892–3 for no one to have to worry particularly about their attacks on the Senate over the epidemic or their candidature in the Reichstag elections. Their fantasies, in which Hamburg appeared as 'Jewish' largely because of the ruling spirit of capitalist finance and mercantile free enterprise, could be dismissed for the moment as the irrelevant ravings of a disgruntled minority.

Far more serious than the antics of the Anti-Semites were the criticisms aimed at Hamburg's system of government by the respectable liberal and conservative press. The respected liberal *Vossische Zeitung*, published in Berlin, blamed the failure to provide a hygienic water-supply, the lack of preparedness for the epidemic, the bogus statistics, and the attempt to suppress the news of the outbreak, on Hamburg's 'patrician regime'. A copy of the article was sent to the Senate marked 'Shame! Shame! In the name of a hundred Berlin women'.[85] *Die Post*, a right-wing paper, argued that Hamburg's patriarchal system of government might have been good in its time, but it was now 'obsolescent and not capable of meeting the new demands of the age' so that

[81] StA Hbg, PP S3625 Bd. 5: Vigilanzbericht 20 Apr. 1893 (Wirtschaft von Schnönhobel, Eppendorf).

[82] Ibid.: 9 June 1893, Vigilanzbericht 7906 II/1.

[83] Ibid., Vigilanzberichte 7397 II/1 (31 May 1893); 7527 II/1 (3 June 1893); 7480 II/1 (3 June 1896); and other reports in the same file. See more generally R. Leuschen-Seppel, *Sozialdemokratie und Antisemitismus im Kaiserreich* (Bonn, 1978).

[84] StA Hbg, PP S3625 Bd. 5: *Hamburger Fremdenblatt*, 3 June 1893.

[85] StA Hbg, Senat, Cl. VII, Lit. Ta, Pars 2, Vol. 11, Fasc. 17, Inv. 6: *Vossische Zeitung*, 9 Sept. 1892.

'dilatoriness and occasionally corruption are there of their own accord'.[86] The favoured solution in most of the liberal and conservative press, ominously enough for Hamburg, was a take-over of the city's medical administration by the Reich. 'Here', as the *National-Zeitung*, mouthpiece of the National Liberals in Berlin, wrote on 28 August,

we have demonstrated by a highly sensational example that can give no pleasure even to the most hard-boiled of 'federalists', the damaging nature of the tactic, which has been in operation for the last decade, of treating not only the rights but also the wishes and prejudices of the governments of the individual states with kid gloves— as if it was not a matter of the interests of the German people, but merely a question of ensuring that a number of petty state authorities held on to all those functions which they possessed in 1866 or 1870.[87]

So widespread were such views that the Berlin correspondent of the London *Times*, writing on 29 August, thought it likely that public health in Hamburg would now be placed in the care of the Imperial Health Office in Berlin. Indeed, the liberal *Berliner Tageblatt* went so far as to exclaim 'the simplest thing is for us to place Hamburg under Reich authority and so put an end to this nuisance once and for all'.[88]

Particular excitement was caused in Hamburg by a series of articles in the organ of the Central Association for the Geography of Trade and for the Furthering of German Interests Abroad (*Centralverein für Handelsgeographie und Förderung deutscher Interessen im Auslande*), the magazine *Export*. Mercantile interests in Germany as a whole were suffering from the trade restrictions imposed at home and abroad as a result of the Hamburg epidemic, and they were not slow to lay the blame where they thought it belonged. The Senate, declared *Export*, had shown egoism and cynicism in its attitude to the water-supply, and caused unwarrantable delays in combating the epidemic once it had broken out. It urged its readers to consider switching their business to Bremen, and proposed that the sanitary administration of Hamburg be taken over by the Reich. Hamburg's defenders replied in the next issue and the controversy continued in subsequent numbers, quadrupling the sales of the magazine in Hamburg in the space of a few weeks. Not only in the pages of *Export*, but also more generally, the governing fraction of the Hamburg bourgeoisie reacted strongly to criticisms and suggestions of this kind.[89] On 12 September the *Hamburgische Börsen-Halle* launched a vigorous counter-attack against critics of the city's constitution. Complaining that the hostility of the rest of a now unified Germany was displaying to

[86] Ibid., Fasc. 16, Inv. 22: *Die Post*, 3 Nov. 1892.

[87] Ibid., Fasc. 17, Inv. 4: *National-Zeitung*, 28 Aug. 1892.

[88] Ibid., Inv. 7: *The Times*, 29 Aug. 1892; StA Hbg, PP S3496 Bd. 1: *Hamburger Neueste Nachrichten*, 21 Dec. 1897.

[89] *Export* Vol. 15, No. 37 (15 Sept. 1892) and Vol. 15, No. 40 (5 Oct. 1892); cf. *Die Nation*, 49 (3 Sept. 1892) and 50 (10 Oct. 1892).

Hamburg in the disastrous epidemic of 1892 made a depressing contrast to the sympathy displayed by the rest of a then disunited Germany in the disastrous Great Fire of 1842, the paper went on:

In the terrible stroke of fate that has suddenly fallen upon us, not only have we been denied any sympathy, but we have seen such harshness towards Hamburg, such coldness, that we have inevitably been deeply hurt and upset here. Indeed the experiences we have had since the outbreak of the epidemic have been deeply disturbing. A tendency to blame and malign has obtruded itself in the most hateful way, and no words have appeared to be too harsh, no calumny too violent for the unhappy city. The accusations levelled against our governing authorities have been monstrous, unmeasured.

Of course, the paper admitted, mistakes had been made. The filtration of the water-supply had been neglected for too long, not for lack of money, but for lack of energy. The epidemic, too, had caught the city by surprise. But, continued the paper, 'such an unprecedented, unexampled dissemination of the disease *could* not be prepared for'. And once it had broken out in its full fury, the epidemic had been confronted by an active and determined resistance. No one had lost their head; the authorities had done their duty; private citizens had spent vast sums of money on helping those worst affected. Yet all this had been ignored by the outside world, which had simply heaped abuse upon the city. Worst of all, in the eyes of the *Börsen-Halle*, were the unlimited and exaggerated quarantine measures taken by the rest of Germany. It was time, concluded the paper, for reason, moderation and human sympathy to prevail.[90]

The *Norddeutsche Allgemeine Zeitung* was having none of this. In a leading article published on 28 September the newspaper declared that it ill became the Hamburg press to attack the rest of Germany at a time 'in which the severe misfortune under which Hamburg is compelled to labour has found the active sympathy of the entire nation from throne to hovel'. Hamburg's campaign against the alleged maltreatment of its citizens in other parts of Germany, was, thought the paper, 'a move ... which is aimed at diverting attention from the causes and portraying as the greater evil not its own mistakes but the behaviour of third parties, although these none the less have to suffer under the danger of a further spread of this calamity'. The citizens of Hamburg were the ones responsible for the severity of the quarantine measures: they should not have left the city in such large numbers to escape the epidemic: 'The flight of the people of Hamburg has, quite naturally in the present circumstances, been followed by fear of the sickness in disease-free parts of the country, and if the consequences of this fear have been unpleasant for the refugees, they mostly have themselves to blame'.[91] This

[90] StA Hbg, Senat, Cl. VII, Lit. Ta, Pars 2, Vol. 11, Fasc. 1b: *Börsen-Halle*, 12 Sept. 1892.
[91] StA Hbg, PP S3490 Bd. 1: *Hamburgischer Correspondent*, 29 Sept. 1892.

was particularly serious coming from a paper generally regarded as standing close to government circles in Berlin.

Since the government was so critical of the Hamburg Senate, it is not surprising that the cholera epidemic was also drawn into the long-standing quarrel between the Emperor and his former chancellor Bismarck. At the end of November, Wilhelm II was reported as having delivered a speech in which he regretted that Hamburg had 'concealed' the first cholera cases and criticized the city 'in a very sharp tone of voice'. Bismarck immediately delivered a counter-attack in defence of the city of which he was an honorary citizen. Interviewed in Maximilian Harden's journal *Die Zukunft*, in October, Bismarck used the occasion of the epidemic to launch into a diatribe against the government in Berlin. The former Chancellor noted that he had expressed his sympathy to 'the Mayor, a personal friend of mine'—he meant Burgomaster Petersen—'and other acquaintances', 'Good God!' he exclaimed, 'I've looked after a good few cholera victims in my life and I have no fear.' Lending the Senate the dubious honour of his patronage, the former 'Iron Chancellor', now an angry old man in the political wilderness, was reported as expressing the wish to reverse government policy in the epidemic:

I'd like to talk again to my people of Hamburg. They have been done serious wrong by all this pharisaic invective; the boycott of Hamburg was unlawful, and it's the government's duty to restore freedom of movement with full effect immediately. It was also their duty once their consuls in Russia had told them of the cholera there, to have given a public warning of the epidemic threat; this applied particularly to Prussia, as the neighbouring state. If the government press is right, however, they did exactly what Hamburg is now being accused of—keeping quiet because they wanted to protect trading interests.[92]

This was utter nonsense, of course, and showed not only how Bismarck was prepared to seize on almost any pretext to attack his successors, but also how out of touch he was with the real course of events. As late as June 1893 his mouthpiece the *Hamburger Nachrichten* renewed the attack, this time with a furious denunciation of Robert Koch and his theory that cholera was waterborne. This brought a swift reply from the *Kölnische Zeitung*, which frequently carried material supplied by the government. In an article sent in from Berlin and clearly emanating from official circles, the newspaper accused the *Nachrichten* of attaching itself, unprecedentedly, to the cause of Hanseatic particularism simply in order to be able to criticize the government in Berlin. The liberal Hamburg *General-Anzeiger* rubbed salt into the wound by asking sarcastically how it was that the *Hamburger Nachrichten* knew more about cholera than the world-famous Professor Koch did.[93]

[92] Ibid.: *Hamburger Tageblatt*, 30 Nov. 1892; *Hamburgischer Correspondent*, 6 Dec. 1892; StA Hbg, Senat, Cl. VII, Lit. Ta, Pars 2, Vol. 11, Fasc. 17, Inv. 1a: *Hamburger Fremdenblatt*, 29 Oct. 1892; see also StA Hbg, FA Petersen D23; Bismarck to Carl Petersen, 11 Sept. 1892.

[93] StA Hbg, PP S3490 Bd. 1: *General-Anzeiger*, 1 June 1893.

Meanwhile the dispute had got as far as the Reichstag. On 22 February 1893 the cholera epidemic was the subject of a brief debate characterized, however, by a renewed willingness of Hamburg's Social Democratic deputies to adopt an uncritical stance. Senator Johann Heinrich Burchard indeed subsequently praised the speech of the Social Democratic deputy for Altona, Karl Frohme, as 'moderate' and 'apparently not demagogic' and remarked: 'Deputy Frohme has in my opinion put forward practical policies'. He had similar good things to say about the contribution of Wilhelm Metzger, one of the Hamburg Social Democratic Reichstag deputies, whom he described as 'calm'. But Hamburg did not come off so lightly in the Reichstag debate of 21–2 April 1893 on the Epidemics Bill. The Social Democratic deputy Emil Wurm launched a powerful attack on the 'terrible abuses' he believed that cholera had revealed in Hamburg. 'Has not the water question in Hamburg been delayed for decades in a manner that is, to the credit of all the other cities in Germany, without parallel?' The capitalist economic order forced workers into 'miserable living conditions', 'the worker has been robbed of air, light, and food' and 'then along comes the epidemic and the plague and kills off above all workers'. And, he charged, nothing had been done since the epidemic to remedy the situation. On the second day of the debate, this was followed up by another Social Democratic speech, this time from Hermann Molkenbuhr, who remarked that while comparably bad housing existed in many parts of Germany, it was unlikely to be reformed in Hamburg because of the influence of the property-owners in the Citizens' Assembly. A democratization of the Hamburg suffrage was required, together with an Imperial Housing Law, to force Hamburg and other states to put their housing in order.

Senator Burchard—Hamburg's representative in Berlin at this time—responded with a speech that combined a defence of the city's record with a promise of speedy reform and an emotional appeal to national unity and solidarity with the stricken city. At every stage of his speech, he was careful to emphasize that conditions in Hamburg were no worse than in other cities, constantly employing phrases such as 'in Hamburg as elsewhere'. He sought to turn the Social Democrats' attack by alleging that the insanitary and overcrowded conditions of much of Hamburg's housing were caused by 'workers from outside, in part foreigners' and won cheers of 'hear! hear!' from the Social Democrats by ascribing to these foreign workers a bad influence on the normally clean-living native German proletarians. Similarly, he fended off criticism of Hamburg's electoral system by defending the mass of small house-owners and putting the blame on speculative builders whose 'ruthless exploitation of building plots and sites' would, he promised, be severely dealt with. Burchard's speech was notable not only for the subtlety of its political appeal but also for the boldness of its factual mendacity. The water-supply, he argued, was used mainly for fire-fighting and toilet-flushing; drinking-water was mainly supplied by wells and filtration was only discussed as it began to be argued that the population had grown too fast for the wells to keep pace with it. There was widespread disagreement over the sanitary necessity of filtration, many people favoured obtaining water from Holstein instead of the Elbe, and in any case 'our authorities and technical officers were occupied to a most unusual degree by the preparatory work for joining the Customs Union'. This series of claims about Hamburg's water supply was very far from the truth, and it was hardly surprising that others stepped in the next day to contradict them.[94]

Burchard's defence of Hamburg's ability to run its own affairs was a masterly performance. But it was not carried off without important concessions having to be made on the way. The massive pressure for change exerted on the Hamburg Senate from within and without continued unabated through the winter of 1892–3 and seemed as powerful as ever during the Reichstag debates in April. Virtually all shades of political opinion, from the Social Democrats to the Anti-Semites, were agreed that Hamburg had to act quickly to improve its housing and sanitation, complete the filtration of its water-supply, and reform its amateurish and inefficient administrative system. Hardly a dissenting voice could be found from the general view that the epidemic had occurred not least because too much in the Hanseatic city was subordinated to the interests of trade; and scarcely anyone seems to have doubted that an extension of the franchise was necessary to ensure a more equitable representation of non-mercantile interests in the city's legislature. Behind all this lay the explicit threat of Reich intervention in the city's affairs, either partial, through legislation such as an Epidemics Law or a Housing Law, or total, through the installation of a Reich Commissioner or the city's absorption into Prussia. This massive pressure for change continued not least because of fears—characteristic for disasters such as that of 1892—of a repetition of the epidemic in 1893. 'The German Reich had to suffer', as one deputy put it in the Reichstag debate, 'because conditions obtaining in Hamburg were a danger to health, and because certain necessary steps had not been taken!'[95] Fear drove people both in Hamburg and outside to seek almost desperately for reforms that would prevent the disaster from recurring: reforms that, were they to be carried out in their full extent, would seriously undermine the hegemony of the city's dominant classes.

But what shape would these reforms take? Where would they be directed? It seemed generally agreed that the suffrage needed extending: but how far? No one doubted that the housing situation urgently needed improving, but was it that the Alley Quarters needed clearing, as some thought, or were there, as Burchard for example maintained, equally serious sanitary nuisances in the speculatively constructed tenement blocks in the outer suburbs? Few

[94] *RT* 20–1 Apr. 1893, Cols. 1952–71, 1978–84.
[95] Ibid., Cols. 1983–4.

were inclined to deny that dirty and unhygienic conditions existed, but whose fault were they—the Senate's, the proletariat's, or the immigrant population's? Upon the answers contemporaries gave to these questions depended the measures they considered it necessary to take; and upon the answers that the historian gives to them depends the assessment to be reached of the policies which eventually emerged to be implemented. It is now necessary to turn, therefore, to the question that lay at the heart of the whole debate on the Hamburg cholera epidemic of 1892: who suffered the most from the ravages of the disease, and why? In answering these questions, it is necessary to subject the available statistics to a close scrutiny; but we shall also be looking once more at qualitative evidence that reveals a great deal about class relations and the structures and values informing everyday life in the city.

5

Dimensions of Inequality

a. Income and Class

I

As we saw in Chapter 3, some of the most devastating infectious diseases in nineteenth-century Hamburg, including smallpox and tuberculosis and to a lesser extent typhoid, were above all working-class diseases. Was this true of cholera? Certainly many leading figures in Hamburg's bourgeoisie in 1892 believed this. On 26 August, for example, Carl Bertheau, the fourteen-year old son of the pastor of St Michael's church, noted that the victims of the epidemic were principally 'the people who live in the narrow streets and courtyards';[1] and the son of Senator Gustav Hertz noted similarly the next day that 'our district, by the way, seems to have been pretty well spared up to now'.[2] This belief was shared by the doctors. The medical officer for Wandsbeck, a Prussian community bordering on Hamburg, noted on surveying the impact of the disease in his area, 'once more we can confirm the conclusion that cholera mainly affects the lower classes of people'.[3] 'A Hamburg doctor' noted on 26 August: 'cases are mostly present in proletarian circles, the upper strata of society are less strongly affected'.[4] Four days later, on 30 August, Burgomaster Johann Georg Mönckeberg echoed this view. 'Up till now', he noted, 'cases are occurring only or almost only in the lower classes of people'.[5] On 20 September, Caesar Amsinck, a judge, son of Senate Syndic Wilhelm Amsinck and a member of one of Hamburg's largest and richest merchant families, wrote on the matter to his friend Hugo Beneke:

As terrible as this year's epidemic is, and as much as one has cause to be careful and on one's guard, still, mortality is virtually exclusively confined to the labouring population and so-called humble people ... Only *very few* cases have occurred in the

[1] StA Hbg, FA Bertheau E 4a IV: Carl III Bertheau to Carl II Bertheau, 26 Aug. 1892.
[2] Ibid., FA Gustav Hertz B 17: Rudolf Hertz to his parents, 27 Aug. 1892.
[3] StA Hbg, PP S3490 Bd. 1: *General-Anzeiger*, 21 Dec. 1892.
[4] StA Hbg, Senat, Cl. VII, Lit. Ta, Pars 2, Vol. 11, Fasc. 17, Inv. 4: *Die Post*, 235, 28 Aug. 1892 (report dated 26 Aug.).
[5] C. Mönckeberg (ed.), *Bürgermeister Mönckeberg. Eine Auswahl seiner Briefe und Aufzeichnungen* (Stuttgart and Berlin, 1918), p. 20.

circles of our acquaintances and our social standing; in these circles no more people have died than at other times.[6]

The propertied citizens whose opinions on the matter have survived were thus virtually unanimous in agreeing that a close connection existed between cholera and poverty. No one in 1892, as far as we know, ventured to contradict them at any stage of the epidemic; least of all the Social Democrats, who shared this view from the very beginning.[7]

Nevertheless, the historian cannot simply accept this view at face value, however impressive the unanimity with which it was held. The great majority of those who fell victim to the disease may have been poor; yet so too were the great majority of the city's inhabitants. It may be the case that the middle classes suffered in the same proportion as the proletariat, but their suffering was simply less visible because there were fewer of them, or because they tended to be treated privately, or at home, and were not carried off to hospital, or to a mass burial, in the glare of publicity which this necessarily involved. Once we start to look for hard evidence with which to test the validity of the contemporary view, the matter begins to seem rather less obvious. True, the first serious studies of cholera by modern historians did tend to confirm the contemporary view of the unequal social distribution of the disease. The French historian Louis Chevalier and his collaborators argued in their study of cholera in France in the 1830s and 1840s that the inhabitants of poor districts in Lille and Paris were harder hit than those who lived in the better-off areas (though one contributor, writing on Marseilles, suggested, without going into the subject any further, that professionals were badly affected as well). Poor diet, long working hours, unhygienic living conditions, and pre-existing economic crises were the chief factors responsible, in the view of these historians, for the higher cholera morbidity and mortality among the poor.[8] Similarly, Daniel Panzac noted in his article on the 1835 epidemic in Aix-en-Provence that workers, day-labourers, beggars, paupers, artisans, small traders, and small peasant farmers caught cholera in higher numbers than their proportion in the working population. In Panzac's view the better-off citizens were spared mainly because their chances of fleeing the town were better.[9] R. J. Morris, in his book on the 1832 cholera epidemic in Britain, concluded that the middle class, 'merchants, manufacturers and solicitors escaped', though medical men were an exception to this general rule. Wage-earners and the labouring poor, he suggested, bore the brunt of the epidemic, though rent-collectors, schoolteachers, and small shopkeepers were also

---

[6] StA Hbg, FA Beneke M 94: Caesar Amsinck to Hugo Beneke 20 Sept., 1892. One exception was the unfortunate Frau Hudtwalcker; cf. Tagebuch Elise Mönckeberg, 10 Sept. 1892 and Tagebuch Tilli Mönckeberg 3 and 9 Sept. 1892 (both in private possession).

[7] See Chapter 4d, above.

[8] L. Chevalier (ed.), *Le choléra. La première épidémie du XIXe siècle* (Paris, 1958).

[9] D. Panzac, 'Aix-en-Provence et le choléra en 1835', *Annales du Midi*, 86 (1974), 419–44.

affected, because they all came into close contact with the poor.[10] For all these authors, cholera provided a classic example of social inequality in the face of sickness and death.[11]

Already in 1961, however, Asa Briggs was beginning to cast doubt on this view. In his seminal article on cholera and society in the nineteenth century, Briggs pointed out that some highly industralized regions such as Lancashire, or Lyons, escaped the epidemic of 1832 altogether. Because of its 'eccentric' regional distribution, cholera was of little use as a barometer of social inequality. 'Many places with bad sanitary conditions escaped it, and in many places the rich (partly because of the mode of communication of the disease by water supplies) were not immune.'[12] More recently, Michael Durey has underscored this argument by suggesting that for 1832 in Britain, at least, there is no statistical evidence of social differences in morbidity and mortality rates from cholera. On the contrary, such evidence as there is points to the fact that the middle and upper classes were affected as well, especially if the epidemic was severe, or if it returned for a second time. In Durey's view, the decisive factor was the nature of the water-supply. A centralized water-supply increased the severity of the epidemic; a decentralized, locally based distribution system slowed down or stopped the spread of the disease. The nature of the water-supply had no connection with social class; so cholera, Durey concluded, was useless as an indicator of social inequality: 'cholera could not compare with the fevers, which relied predominantly on filthy conditions and overcrowding for their diffusion.'[13]

Briggs, Morris, and Durey all thought cholera was important mainly as a stimulator of social tension and a test of society's response to a crisis. By the late 1970s this approach had largely replaced the older emphasis on the disease as an expression of social inequality.[14] Nevertheless, the question of the social distribution of the disease has been raised again more recently by F. B. Smith, in his comprehensive survey of the people's health in nineteenth-century Britain. While both Morris and Durey were unable to provide a convincing statistical basis for their claims, Smith sought to construct one by working out cholera mortality rates per 1,000 inhabitants of rich and poor districts of various English towns, notably Hull, Liverpool, and London. In London, for example, he showed that cholera mortality rates in the poor districts of Bermondsey or Rotherhithe were between six and twelve times as

[10] R. J. Morris, *Cholera 1832. The Social Response to an Epidemic* (London, 1976), p. 93.

[11] See also M. Dineur and C. Engrand, 'Épidémie et pauperisme: le choléra à Lille en 1832', in M. Gillet (ed.), *L'homme, la vie et la mort dans le Nord au XIXe siècle* (Lille, 1972), pp. 41–78.

[12] A. Briggs, 'Cholera and Society in the 19th Century', *Past and Present*, 19 (1961), 76–96 (here p. 78).

[13] M. Durey, *The Return of the Plague. British Society and the Cholera 1831–32* (Dublin, 1979), pp. 47–9.

[14] M. Pelling, *Cholera, Fever and English Medicine 1825–1865* (Oxford, 1978); F. F. Cartwright, *A Social History of Medicine* (London, 1977), ch. 6.

high as they were in better-off areas such as Kensington or St James and Westminster in 1849 and 1853–4. By 1866, when a cholera epidemic struck London for the last time, no difference was discernible.[15] Briggs, for his part, argued that the moment when cholera lost its social unevenness occurred much earlier, in Britain at least: he placed it in 1848, when cholera 'affected all sections of the population'. By this time, he suggested, 'the barriers of class and character had been battered down' by the cholera epidemic, and were no longer revealed by it.[16]

Hartmut Kaelble has concluded in his recent survey of the literature that

The prosperous ... certainly did not stay completely immune from the disease. Nevertheless, such hard statistical material as is available does not show that the social impact of cholera was even. Even if the degree of inequality varied from place to place, poorer districts seem to have been more seriously affected than well-off districts, the lower and middle classes on the whole more strongly than the upper. After cholera epidemics had passed their high point in the 1850s or 1860s, these special social differences in mortality vanished, and with them an important, though sometimes rather eccentric seismograph of social inequality in the age of industrialisation.[17]

Yet there are unresolved problems in the studies which Kaelble cites in support of this conclusion. Panzac's analysis of cholera morbidity in Aix-en-Provence simply gave cases by occupation, which was only one determinant of social inequality among many. Smith compared districts, but was unable to control for other variables such as proximity to the river, the nature of the water-supply, and so on; his figures, in other words, were prone to what the statisticians call the 'ecological fallacy'. So these analyses, while suggestive, were not really conclusive. The same could be said for other studies of this kind not cited by Kaelble. For example, Arthur Imhof, who has pioneered German work in the field, uncovered social inequalities in the incidence of cholera in Halle in the period 1855 to 1874, which included three fairly serious epidemics. Cholera accounted for only 3.8% of all deaths in Class I (higher officials, doctors, lawyers, clergymen, large-scale merchants) but 10.0% of all deaths in Class IV (servants, manual labourers, untrained clerks). These figures have to be treated with caution, however, in the absence of cholera death rates in the two social groups in question.[18] The limitations of Imhof's sources do not allow him to delineate the social distribution of the disease in any real detail.

---

[15] F. B. Smith, *The People's Health 1830–1910* (London, 1979), pp. 230–4.

[16] Briggs, 'Cholera and Society', p. 85.

[17] H. Kaelble, *Industrialisierung und soziale Ungleichheit. Europa im 19. Jahrhundert. Eine Bilanz* (Göttingen, 1983), pp. 188–9.

[18] J. Conrad, *Beitrag zur Untersuchung des Einflusses von Lebenshaltung und Beruf auf die Mortalitätsverhältnisse, auf Grund des statistischen Materials zu Halle a. S. von 1855–74* (Jena, 1874), pp. 59–60, 152, expressed as pie-charts on p. 142 of A. E. Imhof, 'Mortalität in Berlin vom 18. bis 20. Jahrhundert', *Berliner Statistik*, 31 (1977), 138–45.

Because the 1892 epidemic in Hamburg was so isolated and so severe, it attracted not only the hostile attention of journalists and politicians but also the scientific curiosity of the statistical fraternity. Unlike most earlier epidemics, it occurred at a time when techniques of data collection and analysis were quite advanced: it took place, in fact, at the height of the first statistical age. As a result, more is known about the victims of the 1892 epidemic in Hamburg than about those of any other outbreak of the disease in nineteenth-century Europe. The great mass of available statistics is far from completely satisfactory. The influence of miasmatism can still be seen in the tables of ground-water levels and atmospheric pressure that adorned some of the major surveys. But on the whole the data were collected with Koch's bacillus theory in mind, unlike those of virtually all previous epidemics. This too increased their general usefulness. Finally, we also possess quantities of accurate and detailed statistical information about other aspects of Hamburg's population in the 1890s—far more so than is the case even for the period of the previous cholera epidemic two decades before. This means that we can go much further in correlating the incidence of cholera with other social indices than students of earlier epidemics have been able to do.

The rich and complex statistical material available for the 1892 cholera epidemic in Hamburg forms the basis for the present chapter, with the addition, where possible, of rather more scattered data compiled for earlier epidemics, both in Hamburg and elsewhere. Five main questions need to be answered: did cholera affect all income groups and social classes equally; did it hit the city's districts evenly or unevenly; did it have a greater effect on some occupations than on others; was its impact the same on young and old; and did it hit men harder than women? In addition, we also have to ask whether the patterns revealed by the statistics for Hamburg in 1892 were true for other times and other places as well, and we must explore the complex interconnections between the different dimensions of inequality which cholera revealed. Above all, the purpose of this chapter is to ask why: why were some kinds of people affected more than others, and how did this relate to the structures of society, politics, and mentalities in the city as a whole?[19]

II

We can begin simply enough by asking whether the poor were more likely to catch cholera and die of it in Hamburg in 1892 than the rich. Figure 18 shows the incidence of cholera by income group. There were only 85 cases and 49 deaths among those earning 10,000 Marks a year or more, and only 175 cases and 88 deaths among those earning 5,000 to 10,000 Marks a

[19] The presentation and evaluation of these statistics inevitably involves a number of rather technical questions, and as many of these as possible have been relegated to the Statistical Appendix, where they can be followed up by those who are interested.

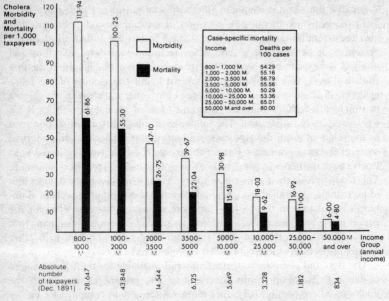

Cholera
Morbidity
and
Mortality
per 1,000
taxpayers

Income	Deaths per 100 cases
Case-specific mortality	
800 – 1,000 M.	54.29
1,000 – 2,000 M.	55.16
2,000 – 3,500 M.	56.79
3,500 – 5,000 M.	55.56
5,000 – 10,000 M.	50.29
10,000 – 25,000 M.	53.36
25,000 – 50,000 M.	65.01
50,000 M. and over	80.00

Morbidity

Mortality

Source: MS 1892, p. 38

FIG. 18   Incidence of cholera by income group, Hamburg 1892

year. Among those with a modest but sufficient income of 2,000 to 5,000
Marks a year, a much larger group, there were 928 cases and 524 deaths.
All the other victims whose income was known were earning less than 2,000
Marks a year. It is thus hardly surprising that cholera appeared to everyone
as a working-class disease, since the vast majority of those who caught it
were in the worst-off sections of the population. Yet once they had caught
the disease, there was little variation between the income groups in the death
rate. The number of deaths per 100 cases (or the *case-specific mortality rate*)
was about the same—between 50 and 57—for all the income groups save
the two highest. Since only five people in the top income group, those earning
50,000 Marks or more, actually caught the disease, the case-specific mortality
rate for this group is more or less without significance. The number of those
in the next income group, earning 25,000 to 50,000 Marks a year, is also
too small for the case-specific mortality rate to mean very much. In these
grand bourgeois circles, death from cholera was extremely rare even in 1892.
On the whole, it is clear that the difference between the income-groups was
a difference in morbidity: the poor were more likely to catch cholera than the
rich were, but once they caught it, they were no more likely to die of

it. Figure 18 may slightly exaggerate the differential impact of cholera by income group in 1892, for technical reasons explained in the Statistical Appendix, but on the whole it seems reasonable to conclude that the middle classes and above all the grand bourgeoisie, were correct in considering themselves relatively immune. Reliable material on other epidemics is hard to come by, but it would seem likely that this pattern was fairly typical for cholera epidemics in general. In Brunswick in 1850, for example—the only useful set of comparable figures that has so far come to light—the cholera death rate in streets with an average per capita annual income of under 75 Marks was 5.3‰, while the corresponding rate for the higher income group of 75–100 Marks was 3.0‰, for 100–200 Marks 1.4‰, and over 200 Marks 0.3‰.[20] But if the bourgeoisie were right to think of themselves as relatively immune, were they also correct in ascribing this immunity to the fact that they took all the necessary precautions, while the mass of the population did not? Any answer to this question must inevitably be impressionistic, but the available evidence certainly suggests that Hamburg's better-off inhabitants went to quite considerable lengths in following the advice of the authorities. Many bourgeois households initiated a regime of surpassing cleanliness and self-discipline during the epidemic. When he wrote later about his childhood experience of the epidemic, Albert Westenholz remembered above all 'eternally washing oneself and boiling and heating everything through'.[21] The lawyer Dr Buehl similarly recalled that in his house not only drinking-water and milk, 'not only washing-up water but even the water used to clean the floor was boiled'; while the bed-linen was sterilized in the oven. 'These precautionary measures lasted for weeks, even months'.[22] In the well-to-do Jewish family of Leo Lippmann, 'even the water drawn from an artesian well ten minutes away was boiled'.[23] On her return to Hamburg from holiday on 26 September, the pastor's wife Henny Ritter was surprised to find the house full of vessels containing boiled water.[24] In the household of Carl Laeisz, the shipowner, all the water was boiled and 'everything that was brought into the house, like bread, linen and so on, had to be heated to a fixed temperature in the oven'. Most hotels and guest-houses boiled their water too.[25]

The well-off were able to take such elaborate precautions largely because they possessed the inestimable advantage of having servants in the household.

[20] (Dr. Reck), *Die Gesundheitsverhältnisse der Stadt Braunschweig in den Jahren 1864–1873 und die Verbreitung der Cholera daselbst in den Jahren 1850 und 1855. Von Dr. med. Reck* (Brunswick, 1874), copy in Stadtarchiv Berlin Rep. 01 GB 258.
[21] StA Hbg, FA Westenholz B XV 2, p. 16.
[22] Ibid., FA Buehl 2c, p. 38.
[23] Ibid., FA Lippmann A4 Bd. 1, p. 32.
[24] Ibid., FA Ritter D2, p. 186.
[25] Ibid., FA Neubauer 1, p. 29; StA Hbg, PP S 3490 Bd. 1: *Karlsbader Volkszeitung*, 28 Sept. 1892.

'Our housemaids', wrote Senator Gustav Hertz complacently on 2 September, 'have made use of the instructions which have finally been issued and only use boiled water.'[26] We may assume that for those earning more than 5,000 Marks a year it was normal to have at least one servant; in the grand bourgeoisie, households with several servants were not uncommon. The epidemic meant a great deal of extra work for servants. Doris Viersbeck, who was employed as a domestic servant in a bourgeois Hamburg family at the time, recalled that 'in our house not a drop of water was used before being boiled; I had saucepans on the boil all day so as to boil as much as possible in advance. This was no small task, for not only washing and drinking-water, but also water for cleaning had to be boiled.'[27] It was easy enough for the well-off to impose high standards of cleanliness in their households when they had servants to boil their milk and water for them, and to clean and disinfect their homes and the things they used.[28]

In the working classes, where there were no servants to do all the boiling and carrying of heavy tubs of water, things were very different. On 30 August the police issued a public notice complaining that many people were still not heeding their advice to boil water.[29] Even after the epidemic was over, it was reported by a commission in St Georg Nord that 'in the circles of our population that were mainly affected by the disease, the observation of the indispensable sanitary instructions often left something, if not everything, to be desired'.[30] Dr Petri, a pupil of Koch's active in Hamburg during the epidemic, later wrote that 'posters were pasted onto the walls of houses near the outlet points of the water-mains forbidding people to use the water. None the less, women came from the nearby houses to continue without hesitation to get their water-supply from these mains taps, or in other words from the Elbe. When they were asked why they were doing so in spite of the ban, they replied that "nobody ever reads such posters—and in any case they could not read at all".'

In many working-class households the information sheet distributed by the Social Democrats probably met with the same fate.[31] As Else Hueppe, a doctor's wife who worked in the Eppendorf General Hospital during the epidemic, concluded, 'mostly ordinances and advisory notices are only framed for educated people or those who are already to some extent well situated, and as far as such people are concerned they are superfluous ... For the poor, the ordinances are ... mostly just simply incomprehensible and altogether

[26] StA Hbg, FA Gustav Hertz B17: Gustav to Else, 2 Sept. 1892.

[27] D. Viersbeck, *Erlebnisse eines Hamburger Dienstmädchens* (Munich, 1907), p. 88.

[28] See pp. 425–6, below, for further evidence on this point.

[29] Copy in StA Hbg, Senat, Cl. VII, Lit. Ta, Pars 2, Vol. 11, Fasc. 17, Inv. 3.

[30] StA Hbg, MK III A 3: St Georg Nord, p. 6.

[31] *Der Cholerakurs im Kaiserlichen Gesundheitsamte* (Berlin, 1893), p. 118, cited in S. Winkle, 'Chronologie und Konzequenzen der Hamburger Cholera von 1892', *Hamburger Ärzteblatt*, 37 (1983), 426.

impracticable.'[32] The Social Democrats were clearly aware of the practical difficulties of following the instructions they distributed; but their emphasis on the importance of education perhaps led them to underestimate the degree of incomprehension which the instructions met with in the class they claimed to represent. Many working-class households had no running water and had to fetch supplies, often from quite a distance. Some did not bother to take the even longer and more tiring route to the water wagons stationed in public places and offering pure water. Ida Neubauer commented on the distribution of pure water by the breweries but noted that 'some did not bother about it: "We might just die anyway!"' Such behaviour caused observers to comment on the 'fatalism' of the poorer classes in the face of cholera.[33] It often aroused the indignant attention of the better-off. 'I caught Frau Ewald today', wrote Pastor Ritter on 9 September, 'trying to take unboiled and undisinfected water for washing. People', he added in high dudgeon, 'really are too indolent and too easy-going.'[34] But they were in reality no more indolent than their superiors, who merely ordered their servants to take all the necessary precautions for them. For the working classes, such precautions were often expensive or even impossible to carry out. In Paul Schurek's novel about the cholera epidemic, *Das Leben geht weiter* ('Life goes on'), the wife of one of the characters exclaims as he explains the precautions to her, 'Boiling water for washing up, my God! You're normally so thrifty!'[35] As the Social Democrats' local daily newspaper, the *Hamburger Echo*, pointed out, 'in Hamburg, as in every other big city, one can count hundreds of proletarian dwellings without any heating. Many of them lack the fuel, the equipment and the labour to prepare the necessary supplies of boiled water.'[36]

Moreover, better-off families, as we have seen, predominated among the 12,000 to 15,000 people or more who fled the city at the outbreak of the epidemic or stayed away until it was over.[37] They could afford the travel costs and the time off, while most of the poorer inhabitants of the city could not. Those who stayed frequently cut themselves off from the world during the epidemic to a degree that was out of the question for the proletariat. It was easy enough to avoid contact with others when you lived in a detached villa and had servants to do the fetching and carrying. Not so for the *Mittelstand*, who still had the family shop or business to carry on. And it was even more difficult for those who lived in overcrowded apartment blocks, who had to

---

[32] F. und E. Hueppe, *Die Cholera-Epidemie in Hamburg 1892. Beobachtungen und Versuche über Ursache, Bekämpfung und Behandlung der asiatischen Cholera* (Berlin, 1893), p. 103.

[33] StA Hbg, FA Neubauer 1, p. 29; StA Hbg, PP S3490 Bd. 1: *Hamburger Nachrichten*, 3 Nov. 1892 (quoting *Die Post*).

[34] StA Hbg, FA Ritter D2, p. 183.

[35] P. Schurek, *Des Leben geht weiter* (Stuttgart, 1940).

[36] StA Hbg, PP S3490 Bd. 1: *Hamburger Echo*, 22 Sept. 1892. See also p. 426 and Table 15, p. 593, below.

[37] See Chapter 4c, above.

buy the necessities of life in the market or from street sellers or shops, and
who still had to go out every day to work. Conventions of neighbourliness
and mutual support in working-class communities, and the traditions of life
on the street or in the common courtyard, ensured that crowds gathered
whenever a victim was taken away, and that every ambulance, as one
observer reported, 'was surrounded by inquisitive people'.[38] It was especially
difficult for the working classes to keep an eye on their children. As the
Hamburger Echo noted, 'proletarian children are often left to their own devices
during the day because their father and mother have to go out to earn their
daily bread'.[39] This was inevitable during the epidemic, as the schools were
closed from 24 August to 13 October. On 13 September Senator Stammann
complained that as a result of the schools being closed children were running
about and playing in the streets everywhere, thus adding considerably to the
risk of infection.[40] Senior Pastor Christian Behrmann remarked too that
'children ... were playing in larger numbers than usual ... in the open air';
often, he wrote, their games were peculiarly 'appropriate to the moment: the
children had built themselves barracks and pegged out graveyards and were
carrying each other around as the sick and the dead'.[41] For middle-class
children, life was very different. 'We children', remembered Leo Lippmann,
'were almost never allowed to leave the house and the garden.'[42] While they
were at home, as Ernst Goverts recalled, the servants were required to keep
them constantly under observation, to make sure they followed the necessary
hygienic precautions and to prevent them from escaping.[43] If there was only
one servant, still it was likely that the middle-class mother would be at home
to watch over the children. Even in small family shops, business was slack
during the epidemic and wives who helped out behind the counter had more
time to attend to the family, though it was less usual for the *Mittelstand* to
have servants, and so more difficult to take the measures demanded.

III

It was not only in those aspects of hygiene that were aided by servants that
the middle classes found it easy to take preventive steps. One reason why
some of Hamburg's poorer families failed to follow the advice given by the
authorities was later supplied by Robert Neddermeyer, who was five years
old at the time of the epidemic and was the eldest of five children of a harbour

[38] StA Hbg. PP S3490 Bd. 3: *General-Anzeiger*, 11 July 1912.
[39] Ibid., Bd. 1: *Hamburger Echo*, 22 Sept. 1892.
[40] StA Hbg, Cholerakommission: Protokoll der 13. Sitzung (para. 173).
[41] C. K. G. Behrmann, *Erinnerungen* (Berlin, 1904), p. 278. For a dramatization of this point,
see Paul Schurek's novel about the epidemic, *Das Leben geht weiter*, in which one of the children
becomes bored at home, escapes supervision, is infected, and dies.
[42] StA Hbg, FA Lippmann A4 Bd. 1, p. 32
[43] Ibid., Goverts 76 Bd. 17, entries for 5 and 13 Oct.

worker and his wife. They lived, as we saw in Chapter 1, in grinding poverty: all five children slept in one bed, and the family subsisted on the father's weekly earnings of 18 Marks, together with the rent (2 Marks 50) paid by a lodger. The family was undernourished and the four younger children all suffered from rickets. It is against this background, then, that Neddermeyer's report of his experiences as a child during the epidemic has to be read. He wrote:

That which people normally regard as a terrible danger for once brought us poor devils unexpected pleasure. That perilous disease, cholera, broke out in 1892 in Hamburg and Altona ... scarcely anyone dared eat fruit at this time. But it was late summer, and the tradespeople were offering the most wonderful plums for sale. Because nobody wanted to buy them, they steadily went down in price. Instead of costing ten to fifteen Pfennigs a pound, they cost in the end only one and a half to two. So mother bought some. In my opinion, as a child, she was quite right to do so. In normal circumstances and at normal prices she could not buy us plums at all. At any rate we children now filled our stomachs with the magnificent fruit and—stayed healthy.[44]

A member of the bourgeoisie such as the hero of Jakob Loewenberg's auto-biographical novel on the epidemic, walking in the streets, reported that as a worker on the disinfection columns he was overcome by 'a kind of police consciousness'. He drove the children away from the drinking-fountains and snatched a basket of fresh plums from a boy and threw it into the gutter.[45] The officially appointed authorities, in the form of the Cholera Commission, also complained on 13 September that people were continuing to eat raw fruit, and predicted that this would lead to a rise in the incidence of cholera unless it ceased.[46] Sure enough, there were 23 more cases reported on 14 September than there had been the previous day.[47] The middle classes, however, enjoyed a varied and nutritious enough diet for them to be able to get by without fruit for a while.

The better diet that was enjoyed by the better-off may have secured them a further advantage in the face of the epidemic. Cholera, it may be recalled, caused extreme and dangerous symptoms only in a minority of cases. Often mild diarrhoea was the only result of ingesting the bacillus, and in a good number of cases there were no symptoms at all. The differential social dis-tribution of severe cases may therefore have been to some extent a reflection of differential resistance. The better-off may have had a better chance of ingesting the vibrio without any ill effects. Showing no serious symptoms, they would not have been recorded as cholera cases. The crucial factor here

[44] R. Neddermeyer, *Es begann in Hamburg ... Ein deutscher Kommunist erzählt aus seinem Leben* (East Berlin, 1980), p. 14.

[45] Loewenberg, *Aus Zwei Quellen* (Berlin, 1914), pp. 283–4.

[46] StA Hbg, Senat, Cl. VII, Lit. Ta, Pars 2, Vol. 11, Fasc. 17, Inv. 3.

[47] See Table 4, p. 295, above.

was the level of acidity of the stomach. The vibrio cannot survive in an acid environment, so the stomach acids must be neutralized if cholera is to survive in the host. The level of acid in the stomach is lowered by malnutrition or even by a poor diet, and it is also decreased by the presence of worms and other parasites. As the popular song had it,

> Yes, for cholera
> There's no cure
> In the world.
> If you're fat
> Thank God for that!
> If you're thin
> Then just give in!
> Yes, for cholera
> There's no cure
> In the world.[48]

Malnutrition was especially prevalent in the Hamburg working class at the time of the 1892 epidemic, particularly because food prices had risen sharply as a result of Hamburg's entry into the Customs Union in 1888, and the amount available to working-class families, particularly in the inner city, to spend on food had fallen at the same time because of the simultaneous rise in rents. Indeed, it is noticeable that the periods when prices for basic foodstuffs rose against a background of steadily increasing rents—the mid-1840s to the mid-1850s, 1873–80, and 1887 to the early 1890s—were all periods when epidemics hit the city. Cholera occurred in all three periods, with the addition of typhoid in the last one. Malnutrition, therefore, may well have been a significant conditioning factor in the high mortality rates of these years.[49]

Material factors such as these—diet, housing, ability to employ servants, money to support flight from the city, resources to keep the world of infection at bay—circumscribed the different responses that the epidemic elicited from different social classes. For the grand bourgeoisie, the strict domestic regime that had to be observed during the epidemic provided the opportunity of realizing the bourgeois virtues of order, cleanliness, thrift, and moderation to a degree hardly possible in normal times. As Senator Gustav Hertz noted complacently on 2 September, 'care, reason, the cessation of many a pleasure, bring of themselves a temperance which is in the end beneficial, as indeed the observation has long since been made that such an epidemic preserves

---

[48] Aufzeichnungen der Mathilde Bünz, Oldenburg (Holstein), ii. 44, in Deutsches Volkslied-Archiv: Schleswig-Holsteinsches Archiv A 95/463 (reference kindly supplied by Helga Stachow).

[49] See above, Chapter 2d, and more generally, J. M. May, *The Ecology of Human Disease* (New York, 1958), p., 38.

more life than it kills'.[50] The women who had to implement this regime of moderation and self-discipline were not so certain: 'How troublesome it now is to keep house!' exclaimed Burgomaster Mönckeberg's wife on 12 September.[51] While the middle classes, or at least their male half, rejoiced in the opportunity to implement a regime of painstaking order and self-discipline, the bulk of the proletariat greeted the admonitions of Koch and his associates with indifference. Workers were still imperfectly 'medicalized'; they were suspicious of official medicine, with its moralizing and disciplining drive powered by middle-class values and directed by middle-class doctors. To the inhabitants of the Alley Quarters, it represented yet another set of rules and regulations imposed by the state, and so was resented and evaded at will. In districts where even policemen had to patrol the streets two by two, there was little hope for the sanitary inspector; indeed, even health and welfare workers required police protection when they set about their business in these areas.[52]

In 1892 it was reckoned that there were some 20,000 casual workers in Hamburg, out of 90,000 manual labourers all told. As Michael Grüttner has noted in his fine study of the Hamburg port workers in this period, these casual labourers were alienated from the Protestant work ethic so dear to the Hamburg bourgeoisie; they often preferred the independence which the casual labour market afforded them to the regimentation that a regular job imposed. Their values emphasized living in the present: port workers, as a contemporary remarked, 'are men of the moment'; and this led not only to a contempt for authority, at home in the Alley Quarters as well as at work in the harbour, but also to an indifference to order and regularity, a disinclination to make plans or take precautions, and a tendency to let the future take care of itself.[53] More widely, in other parts of the Hamburg working class as well, the uncertainties of daily life, particularly at a time of depression such as the early 1890s, meant that men and women, unless they were particularly favoured with a steady and remunerative job, could scarcely afford to think beyond the next day's work or the next day's meal. Poverty condemned them to live in the present: the burdens of existence were great enough without all the extra work and worry involved in taking precautions against a danger both unseen and unknown. The social distribution of cholera was not simply a question of income, it was also a question of values; but the values that helped people to avoid infection also cost money to put into practice. They were beyond the pockets of most of Hamburg's working class in 1892.

---

[50] StA Hbg, FA Gustav Hertz B17: Gustav to Else Hertz, 2 Sept. 1892.

[51] Tagebuch Elise Mönckeberg, 12 Sept. 1892 (in private possession).

[52] See below, pp. 517–18, and U. Frevert, *Krankheit als politisches Problem, 1770–1880* (Göttingen, 1984), pp. 290–1.

[53] M. Grüttner, *Arbeitswelt an der Wasserkante. Sozialgeschichte der Hamburger Hafenarbeiter 1886–1914* (Göttingen, 1984), pp. 92–101.

b. *Social Geography*

I

No aspect of the social distribution of cholera has been so intensively studied as that of the disease's geography. This is mainly because the method of recording cases and deaths, by districts, made it easy in many places to compile figures along these lines. The geographical distribution of the disease became one of the central empirical aspects of the miasmatist–contagionist controversy, as one school of thought tried to match it with physical geography, the varying condition of the soil and the water-table by district, and the other tried to show that it was determined by the water-supply. Unfortunately, since this was what contemporaries were most interested in, this meant that attempts to correlate the geographical distribution of the disease with the social geography of the cities and towns which it struck were few and far between. August Hirsch, for example, in his very detailed study of the 1866 epidemic in Berlin, provided mortality figures not simply by district but by street and block as well; but he made no attempt to describe the social character of these localities, because his concern was to establish 'a positive, distinct dependence on the condition of the soil'.[1] Roderick McGrew's later investigation of cholera in Russia was able to provide absolute figures of cases and deaths in Moscow by district for 1830, but could not supply the overall population figure for each district.[2] Brita Zacke did provide cholera death rates for the various districts of Stockholm in 1834, but could not produce any other indices.[3] Dineur and Engrand could supply morbidity and mortality rates for the various districts of Lille for 1831–2, but that was all. However, for the five parishes of the town they were at least able to work out the percentage of registered poor in each parish. The parish in Lille with the lowest proportion of poor (24%) had the lowest cholera morbidity (12.5‰), but for all the other parishes the morbidity rate was roughly similar (19–23‰). This was despite variations in the proportion of poor in the population, so the figures were in the end rather inconclusive.[4] Michael Durey, in his study of the 1832 epidemic in Britain, presented a great deal of information on the geography of the disease but was concerned mainly with the distribution of the water-supply as a possible source of infection.[5] Only F. B. Smith has made

[1] A. Hirsch, 'Die Cholera-Epidemie des Jahres 1866 in Berlin. Vom statistischen Standpunkte geschildert', *Berliner Stadt- und Gemeindekalender und Städtisches Jahrbuch*, 1 (1867), p. 327.

[2] R. McGrew, *Russia and the Cholera 1823–32* (Wisconsin, 1965), pp. 91–3, 162.

[3] B. Zacke, *Koleraepidemien i Stockholm 1834. En Socialhistorisk Studie* (Monografien utgivne av Stockholms Kommunalforvaltning, 32; Stockholm, 1971).

[4] Chevalier, *Le choléra*, pp. 56–8.

[5] Durey, *The Return of the Plague*, pp. 27–76.

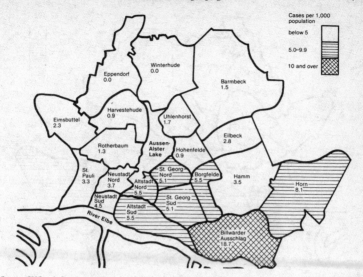

Source SHS 7 (1875) 49–50

MAP 30. Cholera morbidity rate, by district, Hamburg 1873

a determined attempt to use the social geography of cholera as a means of working out the disease's social distribution.[6]

There is plenty of information available on the varying impact of cholera on different parts of Hamburg in every major epidemic of the nineteenth century; we even possess morbidity and mortality rates for each individual street in 1832, 1848, 1859, and 1866.[7] But these figures tell us very little in themselves, and there are no readily available means of comparing them with the social composition of the streets concerned.[8] All that can be said with any certainty is that the disease was initially most virulent in the harbour area and around the fleets. This phenomenon did not escape the attention of contemporaries. In 1832 for example, it was noted that cholera raged 'initially more in the harbour, the river bank of the Elbe, its tributaries and canals, but gradually, from 11 October on, it penetrated more to the interior of the city and the inner suburbs ... but mainly stayed near the

---

[6] Smith, *The People's Health*, pp. 230–4; see pp. 405–6 above.

[7] For 1832, see J. N. C. Rothenburg, *Die Cholera-Epidemie des Jahres 1832 in Hamburg* (Hamburg, 1836), Table 4. For 1848, 1859 and 1866, see StA Hbg, BD B1749; for 1873, see *SHS* 7 (1873); for 1892, see StA Hbg, Cholerakommission 11: *Hamburgischer Correspondent*, 17 Dec. 1892.

[8] For general remarks on the inadequacy of earlier Hamburg statistics, see the Statistical Appendix, Section I, below.

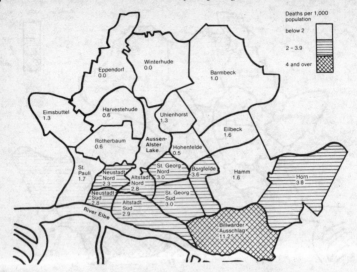

Source: SHS 7 (1875), 49–50

MAP 31. Cholera mortality rate, by district, Hamburg 1873

water'.[9] In 1873, what strikes the eye immediately when we look at the
distribution of cases (Map 30) and deaths (Map 31) is the greater concentration of high rates in the dockland area. The water-supply was probably
not affected in 1873, and in any case many people still took their water direct
from the harbour or the fleets at this date.[10] Substantial numbers also still
lived in the various districts south of the river. Steinwärder, for example, had
a population of 2,168 in 1873. Here the cholera morbidity rate, at 21.2‰,
was high by the standards of 1873, though mortality, at 6.7‰, was still low.
Outlying districts such as Eppendorf and Eimsbüttel were still largely rural in
1873, while the Neustadt had not yet suffered the overcrowding brought on
it by the influx of people expelled from the housing across the river pulled
down to make way for the new docks in the 1880s. The Altstadt Süd was
still a residential area in 1873, with small business and merchant premises;
the large office blocks and modern businesses which began to take over
towards the end of the century had not yet appeared. In short, the social
geography of the Hamburg cholera epidemic of 1873 suggests that proximity

---

[9] K. G. Zimmermann, *Die Cholera-Epidemie in Hamburg während des Herbstes 1831. Historisch
nach ihrer Entwicklung und Verbreitung so wie in ihrem pathologischen und therapeutischen Verhalten
dargestellt* (Hamburg, 1831), p. 40; see also Plate 14.
[10] See above, p. 144.

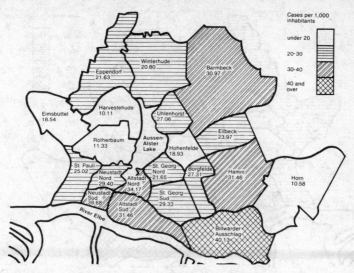

Cases per 1,000 inhabitants

under 20

20-30

30-40

40 and over

Winterhude 20.80

Eppendorf 21.63

Barmbeck 30.97

Eimsbuttel 18.54

Harvestehude 10.11

Uhlenhorst 27.06

Rotherbaum 11.33

Aussen-Alster Lake

Eilbeck 23.97

Hohenfelde 18.93

St. Pauli 25.02

Neustadt Nord 29.40

St. Georg Nord 21.65

Borgfelde 27.31

Hamm 31.46

Horn 10.58

Altstadt Nord 34.17

Neustadt Sud 39.68

St. Georg Sud 29.33

Altstadt Sud 31.46

River Elbe

Billwarder Ausschlag 40.13

Source: MS 1892, Table 33g

MAP 32. Cholera morbidity rate, by district, Hamburg 1892

to waterways was a more important determinant of morbidity and mortality than in 1892; it also indicates some of the changes that took place in the city's social geography over the intervening two decades.

Without a centralized water-supply to all parts of a city, the differential impact of cholera on a city's various districts cannot be considered a reliable index of social inequality in the face of the disease, since different districts depended on different water-supplies. This was particularly true of the earliest epidemics in Hamburg. It was only in 1892, when the overwhelming majority of the city's inhabitants took their water from the same mains system, that the differential impact of the disease on the city's various districts clearly reflected social and economic factors. And it is only for 1892 that we possess sufficient information about the social composition of the city's districts to enable us to test this hypothesis. Map 4 showed that there were wide variations in average per capita income between the various districts.[11] The patterns revealed there fit in quite well with those observable in Map 32, which indicates that an inhabitant of the Neustadt Süd was twice as likely to catch cholera in 1892 as someone who lived in Winterhude, Eppendorf, or St Georg Nord, and four times as likely to catch it as someone who lived in Rotherbaum or Harvestehude. Another way of saying this is that there

[11] See above, p. 57.

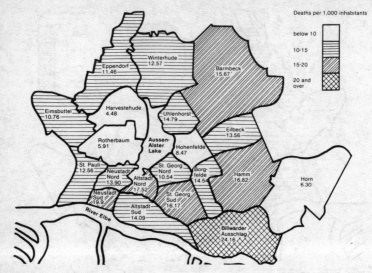

Source: MS 1892, Table 33c

MAP 33. Cholera mortality rate, by district, Hamburg 1892

was a clear negative correlation (-0.57) between the average per capita income and the rate of cholera morbidity in each of the twenty districts—that is, the higher the income the lower the morbidity rate.[12]

A very similar picture is presented by Map 33, which shows the cholera mortality rate by district in 1892. Here again the worst rates were recorded by the poorest areas (Billwärder Ausschlag, Neustadt Süd, Altstadt Nord, St Georg Süd, Hamm), though the differences were not quite so marked. The lowest mortality occurred, again predictably enough, in the wealthy 'villa quarter' of Harvestehude and Rotherbaum, while the other areas were somewhere in between. Thus an inhabitant of the Neustadt Süd, which had a cholera mortality rate of almost 20‰, was roughly twice as likely to die of cholera in 1892 as an inhabitant of St Georg Nord or Hohenfelde, or of Eimsbüttel or Eppendorf on the north-western outskirts of the city; and four times as likely to die of it as an inhabitant of Harvestehude or Rotherbaum, the opulent districts on the Alster. Those who lived in a newer working-class district such as Barmbeck were slightly better off than the poor of the two inner city districts, but were still roughly three times as likely to die of cholera as the inhabitants of the 'villa quarter'. The worst area, once more, was

[12] See the Statistical Appendix for an outline of the problems of the data and the methods used.

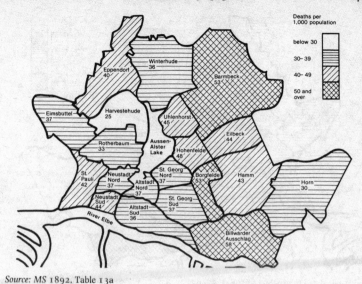

Source: MS 1892, Table 13a

MAP 34. General mortality rate, by district, Hamburg 1892

the wretched riverside district of the Billwärder Ausschlag. The correlation between cholera mortality and income level by district in Hamburg, 1892, works out at −0.61, which again is quite significant.

It is important to go beyond these basic statistics of cholera morbidity and mortality and ask how much difference the epidemic made to the normal level of mortality in the various districts. Cholera, as we saw in Chapter 4, did not simply replace other causes of death in 1892; it represented an additional burden of suffering. But if it did cause extra deaths, then how far did the proportion of extra deaths vary from district to district? A simple way of answering these questions is to work out the average annual death rate in each district over the previous five years (1887–91), as shown in Map 34. The number of deaths from all causes over the whole of 1892, per 1,000 inhabitants of each district, can then be expressed as a percentage of this 'normal' annual death rate. The resulting *excess mortality rates* are shown in Map 35. The first thing to notice is how the richest districts, Harvestehude and Rotherbaum, which usually had the lowest mortality rates in a normal year, also had excess mortality rates in 1892 that were among the lowest of any district. The same goes, to a lesser extent, for the third richest district, Hohenfelde, and the fourth richest, St Georg Nord, both of which also had a fairly low excess mortality in 1892. On the other hand, the poorest district

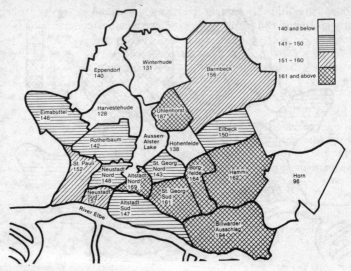

Sources: calculated from SHS 15 (1984), 57, 67, 77, 87, 97, and SHS 20 (1902), 7

MAP 35. Excess mortality, by district, Hamburg 1892 (1887–91 = 100)

of all, the Billwärder Ausschlag, also had the highest excess mortality of any district in 1892, almost double the normal rate, despite the fact that the normal rate was also the highest of any district. Similarly, Barmbeck, another of the four poorest districts in 1892, with a high normal mortality rate, also had high excess mortality in 1892. Another such district, the Neustadt Süd, site of some of the notorious Alley Quarters, also had high excess mortality in 1892. In these cases, therefore, it seems that cholera made most difference to the districts which already had high death rates, and least difference to those where death rates were normally low. Cholera did not simply reveal existing inequalities between Hamburg's districts, it actually made them worse.

The maps also reveal some interesting exceptions to this general pattern. Another of the four poorest districts in 1892, Horn, actually experienced a decline in mortality in 1892 despite the cholera epidemic. This was still largely a rural area, with the highest percentage of one-family houses and houses with gardens of any district in the city. Here the impact of cholera was so weak that it failed to make any impression at all on the decline in mortality rates that had been under way since the middle of the 1880s. Many of the farms and houses here were still not connected to the central water-supply, and so escaped. And by a curious coincidence, a major outbreak of foot-and-mouth disease among the bovine population of the district began early in August 1892. This led to extensive measures to prevent its spread, including the isolation of affected areas, in accordance with a law of 1873. This may well have cut off large areas of Horn from the rest of the city and so reduced the possibility of the district's human population being infected with cholera.[13] At the other extreme, Uhlenhorst experienced an exceptionally high level of excess mortality in 1892, despite being one of the richer districts. However, as we saw in Chapter 1, Uhlenhorst was sharply divided into a middle-class quarter near the Alster and a working-class quarter, running across into Barmbeck, and the high excess mortality was doubtless concentrated in the working-class quarters.[14] Cholera made relatively little difference to mortality rates in Winterhude, while in St Pauli, where the normal death rate was almost exactly the same, excess mortality in 1892 was 21% higher (152 as against 131 in Winterhude), reflecting the district's proximity to the deadly waters of the harbour. But these apparent exceptions do not shake the general conclusion, which was demonstrated, once again, in Eilbeck, where average per capita income was among the lowest, normal mortality rates exceeeded only by those of the Billwärder Ausschlag, and yet mortality in 1892 still ran at 150% of the norm: that is, cholera made more difference to the mortality of districts with a normally high mortality rate than it did to those with a normally low one.

II

How can the social geography of cholera as it emerged in 1892 be explained? To begin with, does the assumption made by Durey, that the nature of the water-supply was unconnected with social class, hold good for Hamburg in 1892, despite the existence of a central distribution system? In Winterhude, Eppendorf, Horn, and parts of Eimsbüttel there were a number of houses provided with water from private wells. Private water-supplies such as these generally remained uninfected. In Eppendorf, Winterhude, Barmbeck, Hamm, and Horn the cholera mortality rate among those supplied with mains water averaged out at 16.5‰.[15] Those supplied from wells here did indeed include many working-class houses, but a disproportionate number of wells belonged to the bourgeoisie. Apart from this, some institutions, such as the Alsterdorf Institute (575 people), the Pestalozzi Foundation in Barmbeck (94 people), the Central Prison in Fuhlsbüttel (1,100 inmates), and the House of Correction

---

[13] BA Koblenz, R86/1337 Bd. 1: Senate to Caprivi, 31 Aug. 1892 (No. 4356); *SHS* 19 (1900), 110.

[14] See p. 58.

[15] *MS 1892*, p. 42; T. Deneke, 'Nachträgliches zur Hamburger Cholera-Epidemie von 1892', *Münchener Medizinische Wochenschrift*, 41 (1895). For Durey's argument, see p. 406 above, and Durey, *The Return of the Plague*, pp. 47–9.

in Fuhlsbüttel (600 prisoners) also had their own water-supplies and experienced no cases of cholera at all. On the other hand, the Lunatic Asylum in Friedrichsberg, with 1,363 patients, drew its water from the mains and suffered 123 cases and 64 deaths.[16] But there were really very few private wells left in Hamburg by 1892, and in all the letters, diaries, and memoirs of the city's middle-class inhabitants there is not a single concrete reference to one having been in use.

Since the typhoid epidemic of the late 1880s, it had become customary to boil all drinking-water before use 'in many households, namely among propertied people', as the medical statistics for 1892 pointed out.[17] By this means, at least some bourgeois families remained immune. By the time the poorer people received instructions to boil their water, on 26 or 27 August, it was in many cases already too late. Apart from this, too, it is just possible that those people who lived on higher ground—notably in bourgeois areas such as Rotherbaum and Harvestehude—had a little more time to prepare themselves, even if they had not already been boiling drinking-water since the 1880s. The water pressure was weak in these areas, supplies were pumped in only intermittently, and a good deal of water was stored in tanks. In the low-lying, often poorer parts of the city, such as the Altstadt and the Neustadt, water was pumped in continuously and so infected supplies would have reached the consumer much more rapidly. This difference was accentuated by the fact that overall demand was higher in the more densely populated areas of the city centre than in the 'villa quarters' in the suburbs. Robert Koch also thought that intermittent pumping of water allowed the bacillus to settle in the pipes, or become stuck, so to speak, and perish.[18] In general the epidemic did reach its high point in the suburbs somewhat later than in the city centre. But the influence of the harbour was mainly responsible for this, and in any case per capita use of water was much higher in well-off houses with baths to fill, gardens to water, horses to feed, and stables to wash down. So of all these considerations, only the habit of boiling water was likely to have made a real difference, and this was not an aspect of water-supply, but of the treatment of water once supplied.

Far more important than this relatively minor factor was overcrowding. This meant that there was much more likelihood of infection spreading quickly, from person to person, in droplets in the air, or through foodstuffs and other household things being infected by carriers of the disease and then being touched or eaten by others. Lack of ventilation added to the danger of infection, and even more possibilities for the spread of cholera were offered by the existence of communal toilets. The reports of the local Health Com-

[16] J. J. Reincke, 'Die Cholera in Hamburg 1892', *Deutsche Medizinische Wochenschrift*, 3 1893). 9.

[17] *MS 1892*, p. 42.

[18] Durey, *The Return of the Plague*, p. 60.

Table 6. Morbidity and mortality rates for Heine's Platz, Hinter dem Strohhause 22, apartments with and without water-closets

Apartments	Inhabitants	Morbidity		Mortality	
		Absolute	‰	Absolute	‰
With WC	242	11	45.5	6	24.8
Without WC	368	28	76.1	16	43.5

Source: Mk III A 13, VI: St. Georg-Norderteil, p. 15.

missions on the infected houses indicate the kind of conditions which favoured the epidemic once it had entered a building.[19] The Health Commission for the Altstadt Süd found at Catharinenstrasse 4/5 the 'closet in the courtyard so full of dirt that it could not be entered', while in Lembkentwiete 4, where there were four cases of cholera, 'there is a closet which is used by 24 persons'. In the Neustadt Nord, the Health Commission found a single closet in the courtyard for the use of fifty people living in Marienstrasse 2, not to mention the fact that it was used by numerous passers-by. In St Georg Nord, the Health Commission compiled a special set of mortality and morbidity figures for a large block of apartments at Hinter dem Strohhause 22 and the adjoining buildings at Nos. 18–32, a block in which some of the apartments were provided with water-closets, and others had to make do with communal latrines. As Table 6 shows, rates were higher where toilets were shared. The reason why shared water-closets helped spread the epidemic was given by the Health Commission for Harvestehude, which remarked in its second report on the epidemic:

If a direct transmission of cholera from person to person is a possibility, then this means offers it the best opportunity. But far greater is the indirect damage which is caused by what in our experience is the customary gross neglect of the cleaning of closets of this kind, each family being inclined to leave this task to the others.[20]

Here again working-class families were reproached with laziness and failure to take hygienic precautions. In a class where all members of the family had to work long hours to make ends meet, where people were constantly worried and tired, where fetching and boiling water required repeated long trips up and down stairs, where even simply keeping an eye on the children demanded a major effort, such precautions were not easily carried out. The importance of servants in maintaining hygenic standards is underlined by the correlations between households with servants and cholera morbidity (-0.65) and mortality (-0.72) by district, which were higher than the correlations obtained

[19] These reports can be found in StA Hbg, MK III A 13. For the Health Commissions, see below, p. 517.
[20] Ibid.: Harvestehude, p. 19.

for income levels. Few working-class families had their own bathrooms, as we saw in Map 17. There was a strong negative correlation between the percentage of households with their own bathroom and cholera morbidity and mortality rates by district (Maps 32 and 33), the coefficients being respectively −0.66 and −0.69. These negative correlations between households with bathrooms and cholera rates were higher than those between income level and cholera rates. Less impressive, but still worthy of note, are the positive correlations between households without heating facilities (to boil water) and cholera morbidity (0.51) and mortality (0.37) rates by district, although by 1892 such households were so few in number that their presence in a given district did not correlate well with most other social indicators.[21]

A report from Johann Julius Reincke, who succeeded Johann Caspar Kraus as Chief Medical Officer of the city, described in graphic detail some of the sources of infection in a run-down working-class area:

In Kastanienallee number 37 we found that the leaky closets of the upper storeys were leaking into the water-tanks of the flats beneath; in another house, where a child had just died and the sick-room was still befouled with its excreta, the dirty nappies of another child suffering from diarrhoea were hanging over the stove above open saucepans filled with food. The kitchen was swarming with flies. In other places we found children without supervision since their parents were lying ill in bed.[22]

Particularly important in this context was the exactness of Reincke's descriptions. Every sentence implied a specific source of infection. By contrast, most writers contented themselves with vague but emotional descriptions of 'dark, damp, badly ventilated, small dwellings' in a very general way as centres of infection (*Seuchenherde* or *Choleraherde* were the most commonly used expressions). Reincke was one of the few doctors in Hamburg who supported Koch's theories, having been converted during the 1892 epidemic. He pointed out that it was very difficult to say exactly how much general factors such as lack of light and ventilation, or even dampness, came into play. Even if the dampness was so excessive that it could support the spread of the cholera bacillus across the area affected, the damp area would have had to have been very large for it to have constituted a really significant extra source of infection. Far more important as a source of infection were communal toilets and a faulty sewage system. Reincke noted that good housing could be inhabited by people with dirty habits, bad housing could be lived in by the cleanest of the clean. He did concede that poorer people were on average less clean than the well-off, a supposition that, as we have seen, was almost certainly correct. Like Senator Burchard, he thought that natives of Hamburg were cleaner and more hygienic than 'workers from the East with dirty

---

[21] See the Statistical Appendix, Section VII (and Table 15, below) for full details of the correlations and the sources on which they are based.

[22] Reincke, 'Die Cholera', p. 11. For the following, see *MS 1892*, pp. 14, 39–40.

Table 7. Cholera morbidity and mortality by average living space per person, Hamburg 1892

Square metres per person	Cases per 1,000 inhabitants	Deaths per 1,000 inhabitants	Deaths per 100 cases
less than 10	33.6	17.2	51.1
10–50	24.3	12.5	51.5
50–100	20.2	10.2	50.7
100–200	20.3	9.6	47.1
over 200	20.0	9.2	45.9

Source: (Georg Gaffky,) *Amtliche Denkschrift über die Choleraepidemie* (Kaiserliches Gesundheitsamt. Berlin, 1895), Appendix, p. 32.

habits', who lived in the poorest districts and added to their already high morbidity and mortality rates. But this argument was largely a product of local patriotism. By the early 1890s immigrants tended to be fairly evenly spread through the city's various districts. There is no evidence that they were more affected than native Hamburgers. Outsiders coming to the city during the epidemic tended in their turn to regard the native Hamburg working class as unusually dirty.[23]

By far the most important source of infection in working-class houses was the fact that a great many people lived in them. There was a fairly positive correlation between the number of inhabitants per square kilometre of built-up land, as shown on Map 3, and cholera morbidity and mortality, by district (Maps 32–33), in 1892 (the coefficients being 0.54 and 0.59 respectively). This again was a function of their poverty; and it should not be a surprise to learn that there is a reasonably suggestive correlation between rent levels and cholera morbidity and mortality. The correlation between the proportion of dwellings with an annual rent of less than 300 Marks and cholera morbidity by district was 0.42; the same for cholera mortality was 0.51. Many poor people, as we saw in Chapter 1, took in lodgers to help pay the rent, but this does not seem to have been a particularly important factor in the epidemic, though it attracted a lot of public comment. There was a mild though not very significant positive correlation between the proportion of households with lodgers and cholera morbidity and mortality by district, the coefficients being 0.41 for cholera morbidity and 0.32 for cholera mortality in 1892. Nevertheless, as Table 7 shows, the relationship between housing density and the incidence of the disease was unmistakable.

In sum, therefore, the social geography of cholera in 1892 underlined the fact that this was mainly a working-class disease. The impact of cholera on a district rose as per capita income fell, and it went together with overcrowd-

[23] C. Wischermann, *Wohnen in Hamburg vor dem Ersten Weltkrieg* (Münster, 1983), pp. 342–6; F. and E. Hueppe, *Die Cholera-Epidemie in Hamburg 1892*, op. cit., pp. 33–4.

ing, poor sanitation, and cheap accommodation. Yet this was not the whole picture. Contemporaries noted the association of cholera with poverty, but they also pointed to its concentration in the inner-city districts. As we have seen, while these districts were indeed hard hit, they were exceeded as centres of cholera by the Billwärder Ausschlag and rivalled by Barmbeck and Hamm. Hardly any commentators, however, described these latter districts as centres of contagion, though Senator Burchard did point to them as part of his attack on property speculators. In order to find out why this was so, we now have to turn to an investigation of the social geography of cholera on a more detailed level.

III

The Alley Quarters undoubtedly had exceptionally high cholera morbidity rates,[24] and some blocks within them had cholera morbidity and mortality rates in 1892 that were double the average for Hamburg as a whole, and higher than those of any other district in the city apart from the Billwärder Ausschlag.[25] But to get a real comparison we have to look at individual streets or blocks in the other districts as well. Such figures are not easy to come by, but the few that are available are suggestive. In St Georg Nord, for example, in a group of apartment blocks with courtyard at Hinter dem Strohhause 22, inhabited by 610 people, 39 inhabitants caught cholera in 1892, a rate of 60.8‰, and 22 of them died, a mortality rate of 34.2‰.[26] These buildings were relatively new. So too were the apartment blocks in the Abendrothstrasse (Uhlenhorst), where local investigations suggested a morbidity rate of 105‰ and a mortality as high as 40.2‰—exceptionally high by any standards.[27] Moreover, the worst-affected streets in the newly built-up areas on the outskirts of the city could certainly compare with the parts of the Alley Quarters and the criminal quarter which attracted so much attention.[28] Sometimes, indeed, the newspapers pointed out that recently constructed terraces were particularly liable to suffer high cholera morbidity and mortality rates. 'Uhlenhorst', it commented, 'is completely covered with terraces and small dwellings in its north-eastern part and the streets leading across into Barmbeck'.[29]

Other streets of terraced apartment blocks outside the old city centre also recorded high cholera morbidity and mortality rates in 1892. Eimsbüttel,

[24] StA Hbg, Kommission für die Verbesserung der Wohnverhältnisse, 25: Anlage 2.
[25] Ibid., 25: Auszug aus dem Protokoll, 14. Mai 1897; ibid., 25; J. J. Reincke, 'Betrifft ungesunde Wohnquartiere Hamburgs, Bericht an den Präses des Medicinal-Collegiums Senator Hachmann vom 13. Juli 1897', Anlage 3, 4, 5.
[26] Ibid; see also Table 6, p. 425, above.
[27] *Bericht der Gesundheits-Commission für den Bezirk Uhlenhorst über ihre Tätigkeit während der Cholera-Epidemie 1892* (Hamburg, 1892), Tables A, B, C.
[28] Street-by-street statistics are collected in StA Hbg, Cholerakommission 11.
[29] Ibid.: *Hamburgischer Correspondent*, 17 Dec. 1892.

commented the *Hamburgischer Correspondent*, 'had very many serious cases in some of the streets built-up with modern terraces'.[30] The statistics for Winterhude 'clearly reveal the deleterious influence of the numerous multi-storey houses which have been constructed since the opening of the new cemetery in Ohlsdorf'. Borgfelde had 'a few very bad streets, which are thickly occupied by terraces and workers' dwellings'. One Social Democratic investigator wrote after the epidemic:

If one wants to see dwellings that are tiny and cramped one needs to go not just to the Specksgang and visit the tenement situated there in the courtyard of house no. 7; one can also find such dwellings in other areas apart from the Alley Quarters. On the *sixth* floor of Bauermeisterstrasse no. 5 in St Georg there are families up to six strong living in *one* room (to which a small kitchen can also be added).

Yet this building had only been constructed seven years before.[31] It was not simply a case of such new buildings being overcrowded either. Often they were cheaply built by speculators out to make quick profits. They were just not solidly enough constructed to stand the strain of being lived in by large numbers of people; and the builders had not taken the trouble to provide them with proper sanitation.

One such street was the Borstelmannsweg, in Hamm, one of only a handful of built-up streets in this still fundamentally rural area. 3,486 people lived in the terraced apartment blocks of the Borstelmannsweg in 1892. The builders had not troubled to provide even the most basic communal facilities. As Pastor Friedrich Werner, at that time Assistant Preacher in the district, noted, the street lighting was so poor that people regularly risked falling into ditches if they went out at night. 'In persistent rainfall', moreover, 'or during a thaw, the Borstelmannsweg was so difficult of access that children who lived at the bottom end of the street were unable to get to their school on the Hammerlandstrasse despite the fact that boards had been laid across a few particularly bad places'. Worst of all, however, were the sanitary arrangements, Werner reported:

During the cholera epidemic I met Dr Taubmann the police doctor in the Borstelmannsweg, with Herr Jauch and a few other gentlemen. They told me that the health authorities had learned that the situation of the toilets in numerous dwellings in the Borstelmannsweg was not without fault, and that they wanted to have a closer look at the problem. I joined up with the gentlemen, and since I knew my Borstelmannsweg, I could even point them to many a nuisance there. The situation was indeed enough to make the flesh creep. The contents of the toilets went in many cases directly into the ditches behind the house.[32]

[30] Ibid.
[31] StA Hbg, PP S3490 Bd. 1: *Der Grundstein*, 5 Nov. 1892.
[32] Kirchenarchiv Hbg. D166, pp. 2–3.

Much of Werner's account of his activities during the epidemic, as we have seen, centred on the Borstelmannsweg. This is hardly surprising, since no fewer than 224 of its inhabitants fell ill with cholera, and 96 of them died. These figures represented a cholera morbidity rate for the street of 64.3‰ and a cholera mortality rate of 27.5‰. These rates were comparable with anything in the Alley Quarters or the 'criminal quarter' around the Niedernstrasse in the Altstadt Nord.[33] Nor could this be surprising, when the buildings in the street were so shoddily constructed. A Social Democratic investigator reported in 1892, for example, that the pipes carrying excrement down from the toilets on the upper storeys of Borstelmannsweg No. 137/139 were broken where they went through a cupboard under the stairs, 'so that the disgusting fluid mostly stands $1\frac{1}{2}$ feet high in the space there'.[34] Two men and seven children died of cholera in this part of the building, and conditions elsewhere in the terrace, as Werner's account suggests, were often almost as bad.

A police report of a general sanitary inspection of Hamm and Horn in 1892 summed up the problem and pointed once more to the serious conditions in the Borstelmannsweg:

The inspection has brought such disgraceful circumstances to light that it is incomprehensible how the planning authorities have allowed them to arise in the first place. Every spare inch of space has been exploited and the builders have gone and built on it at the cost of all hygienic considerations. Because of the high rents, the inhabitants are compelled to keep lodgers in the cramped, often half-lit rooms, which it is impossible to ventilate,—or to share the flat with another family. On top of this comes the fact that all the inhabitants of each house have to rely in common on a single closet situated in the courtyard. In the Borstelmannsweg in Hamm the old privies still exist in the thickly populated courtyards.[35]

As these examples suggest, some contemporaries were aware of the fact that the Alley Quarters were not the only 'centres of infection' in Hamburg. Thus the indefatigable Health Commission for St Georg Nord noted of a tenement block built in 1877/78 at Baumerstrasse No. 5, that the closets were dark, damp, and unventilated, that drainage in the kitchens was inadequate, and that the inner rooms were airless and without proper lighting. 'Similar abuses and faults exist in a large number of our modern multi-storey blocks and are to be seen as a major cause of the high incidence of cholera in these houses situated on main streets such as the Rostockerstrasse and Steindamm.'[36] These sentiments had more than a touch of miasmatism about

[33] See below, pp. 431–2.

[34] StA Hbg, PP S3490 Bd. 1: *Der Grundstein*, 5 Nov. 1892.

[35] Quoted in A. Aust, 'Vor 80 Jahren: Die Cholera in Hamburg. Soziale und hygienische Missstände und ihre Folgen', *Die Heimat. Monatsschrift zur Pflege der Natur- und Landeskunde in Schleswig-Holstein und Hamburg*, 79 (1972), 302–11.

[36] StA Hbg, MK III A13, p. 12.

them but, notably in their references to the inadequacies of the drainage, they were at least of some relevance to the epidemic. More to the point, they were uttered about a house that was less than 15 years old. Similarly, the Health Commission for Winterhude noted that by 7 September there had been 1ɔ4 cases in the district, 31 of these in Geibelstrasse alone, far more than in any other street. Here there were new houses, not old ones. The Health Commission explained the high incidence of cholera by alleging, quite without foundation, that they were mainly inhabited by foreigners, either from outside Hamburg or from outside Germany altogether. The Commission was thus able to put the blame on these people's supposed dirty habits rather than on the faults of the buildings they lived in.[37]

IV

Why did commentators concentrate so heavily on the older quarters of the city as centres of cholera? First, although there were streets and houses in the newer working-class suburbs as badly hit by cholera as any in the Altstadt or Neustadt, there were relatively fewer of them and they were less geographically concentrated. Nine out of the 20 streets listed by the *Hamburgischer Correspondent* in December 1892 as having a cholera morbidity rate in excess of 50 cases per 1,000 inhabitants were situated in the Neustadt. The two worst-hit streets were both in the Altstadt Nord. Similarly 15 of the 32 streets with the highest cholera mortality rate were in the Neustadt or the Altstadt Nord. Of the eight worst-hit streets in the city, where there were 60 or more cholera cases and 25 or more cholera deaths per 1,000 population in 1892, only three—the Borstelmannsweg in Hamm, the Stückenstrasse in Barmbeck, and Hinter dem Strohhause in St Georg Nord—were outside the inner city. So it seems reasonable to conclude that the city-centre districts had a greater concentration of streets and blocks with high cholera morbidity and mortality rates than the other, more outlying districts had.[38]

These inner-city districts were also more visible to the middle class than the outlying areas such as Barmbeck, Hamm, or the Billwärder Ausschlag were. It is notable that of all the adverse comments on these outlying areas quoted—and only a handful have come to light so far—two were made by Social Democratic investigators, one by a socially aware pastor who declared in his memoirs that he had always counted himself one of the 'humble people' and whose duties in any case took him to the area in question, and three appeared in the reports of local Health Commissions whose work involved a close inspection of the new housing blocks in their areas. General comments in the bourgeois press or by city politicians or other commentators were

[37] Ibid., p. 57. For another rare example of the perception that the Alley Quarters were no worse affected than new tenements, see StA Hbg. FA Roscher I a 1, p. 123.

[38] StA Hbg. Cholerakommission 11: *Hamburgischer Correspondent*, 17 Dec. 1892.

almost entirely concentrated on the Alley Quarters. The Borstelmannsweg
was never the subject of sensational reports in the newspapers, though
conditions there were every bit as bad as in the Neustadt, because the
Borstelmannsweg was out of town in a predominantly rural area and had to
be reached by carriage or on horseback along bad roads. Barmbeck was even
more remote from the centre of things. The Altstadt Nord and the Neustadt,
by contrast, were within walking distance of the Town Hall, the Exchange,
and the major business and trading quarters of the city. Business men and
government officials would have to pass through them to get to the harbour.
It was easy for officials to organize quick tours of these districts for visiting
investigators. Reporters could walk into them from their hotels. It was no
accident that it was these districts that Robert Koch and his team looked at;
there simply would not have been time to go further out and study conditions
in the tenements of Barmbeck and Hamm, given the very tight schedule to
which Koch was working during his stay in Hamburg.

   Koch's denunciation of hygienic conditions in the Alley Quarters soon
became the most famous of all comments on Hamburg's housing.[39] It did
much to focus the public's attention on the area. What horrified Koch were
mainly three aspects of living conditions in the area: the inadequate
sanitation, the dampness (especially the frequent flooding from the filthy fleets
at high tide), and the overcrowding. Adherents of Koch's views such as
Reincke pointed to the way in which these three factors interacted to increase
the likelihood of cholera being passed on through contact with infected faeces.
Where scores of people shared a single toilet, where there were no proper
washing facilities, where excrement was regularly thrown into the canals
and washed into the inhabited cellars and ground-floor apartments at high
tide, where people slept three or four to a bed, it was in Koch's view hardly
surprising that infection rates were high. Yet the general identification of the
older areas of the city as the centres of infection was not just the result of
Koch's celebrated remarks. It almost certainly reflected folk memory of earlier
visitations of the disease as well. For a good number of the houses and streets
which were particularly hard hit in 1892 had also suffered badly during
previous epidemics. A street such as the Grosser Bäckergang, for example,
was not only a notable centre of cholera in 1892, with 46.8‰ morbidity and
22.5‰ mortality, but also in 1873 (7.6‰ morbidity, 4.4‰ mortality), 1866
(5.0‰ mortality), 1859 (7.3‰ mortality), 1848 (10.9‰ mortality), and
1832 (35.0‰ morbidity and 23.1‰ mortality). In all these epidemics save
that of 1832, it was affected by cholera to a far greater extent than the city
in general. Of course, some of the worst-hit streets in earlier epidemics had
fallen victim to clearance schemes and were no longer there in 1892. This
applied particularly to the Brook Insel, in the Altstadt Süd, knocked down to

---

[39] See above, p. 313.

make way for the new harbour facilities created for the Customs Union in the 1880s. It had consistently been the worst-affected area of all during earlier cholera epidemics. 23 streets in the city suffered above-average cholera mortality rates in all the mid-century epidemics (1848, 1859, and 1866), and eight of these—more than a third—were on the Brook Insel. A long, narrow peninsula, it jutted out into the middle of the old harbour, and the possibilities of infection from the water, which served a variety of domestic uses, were clearly manifold. In the three mid-century epidemics it consistently suffered cholera mortality rates more than twice the city average. Despite the disappearance of this area, 22 streets in the rest of the city suffered cholera morbidity and mortality rates above the mean for the district in which they were situated both in 1873 and 1892. Four of these were in the Altstadt Nord, including the Springeltwiete and Steinstrasse, eight were in the Neustadt, and nearly all of them had recorded a significant number of cases and deaths in earlier epidemics as well.[40]

There were, therefore, several reasons why the attention of contemporaries was drawn to the Alley Quarters and the older parts of the city as centres of infection in 1892: there was a greater concentration of badly affected streets here than anywhere else, they were more visible to bourgeois commentators than the outlying districts were, they were the subject of a celebrated inspection and condemnation by Robert Koch, and there was most probably a folk memory of consistently severe visitations of cholera in earlier epidemics in streets such as the Grosser Bäckergang. Nevertheless, the fact remains that these districts by no means had a monopoly on suffering in 1892. Many newly built streets and blocks in outlying districts were also badly affected. Overcrowding, inefficient communal sanitation, lack of boiling facilities for water, and poorly ventilated rooms all helped spread infection, wherever they were situated. Insanitary houses were not always old.

c. *Occupation and Age*

I

Reliable statistics of the occupational distribution of cholera are notoriously difficult to come by. Even in the case of Hamburg in 1892, contemporaries despaired of any attempt to compile them, and only the massive occupational census of 1895 enables a retrospective calculation to be made. Most previous historians of cholera have been able to provide a breakdown of victims by occupation, but have not followed this up by linking it to the whole population by occupation. Dineur and Engrand's study of Lille in 1832 showed a virtual absence of cases among the free professions, *rentiers*, industrialists, and pro-

[40] See n. 7, above, and *SHS* 7 (1875), pp. 49–52.

prietors, a fair number among *commerçants* (a category which included many petty traders), and a large number of cases among labourers, especially textile workers. Similarly, R. J. Morris demonstrated that most victims in Britain in 1832 were artisans and labourers, but he was unable to convert absolute figures into rates per 100 occupied.[1] Roderick McGrew, in his study of the 1830 epidemic in Moscow, was rather more fortunate in being able to draw upon a contemporary study which did attempt such a conversion, but the categories used were legal rather than occupational, and so were not entirely satisfactory as socio-economic indicators. Similar problems beset Brita Zacke's study of the 1834 epidemic in Stockholm. The occupational classifications were partly legal, and there were no overall figures from which to calculate rates. However, they did suggest that nurses, cleaning women, and the female poor were particularly at risk, as were soldiers, sailors, and artisans.[2] Rollet and Souriac's study of the 1832 epidemic in the department of the Seine-et-Oise managed to produce cholera death rates, though it used an occupational census of 1851 to do so, but it only provided figures for three very broad groupings—farmers, *rentiers*, and 'artisan-workers'. In the majority of *arrondissements*, the last-named group accounted for about 70% of cholera deaths in 1832 but only just over 30% of occupied persons in 1851.[3] Most of these studies use the occupational distribution of the disease simply as a way of illustrating its greater impact on the poor. It is possible, however, to go beyond this and show that some occupations posed a specific risk on their own. If it turns out that people in some occupations were more likely to catch cholera and to die of it than people in others, and if these occupations were poorly paid, then we have discovered another important determinant of the proportionately greater impact of the disease on the poor—that is, provided that we can also show that those who did these jobs ran an extra risk of catching cholera in the course of their work, and did not simply catch it because they lived in overcrowded or insanitary housing, or because they could not afford servants.[4]

Figure 19 gives cholera morbidity and mortality rates for the twelve major occupations which supported the overwhelming majority of the city's population. They fall into five broad categories, which we shall look at in turn, beginning with those least affected, at the right-hand side of Figure 19, and proceeding to the left, as it were, finishing up with the occupations most seriously affected by cholera. In each case, the three main questions to consider are, first, how far the occupation carried with it a direct risk of infection from cholera, for example, through contact with infected excreta,

[1] Dineur and Engrand, 'Épidémie et pauperisme'; Chevalier, *Le choléra*, p. 90; Morris, *Cholera 1832*, pp. 88–97.

[2] McGrew, *Russia and the Cholera*, pp. 94–6; Zacke, *Koleraepidemien*, p. 165.

[3] C. Rollet and A. Souriac, 'Le choléra de 1832 en Seine-et-Oise', *Annales ESC*, 29 (1974), 935–65.

[4] See the Statistical Appendix for further discussion of these statistics.

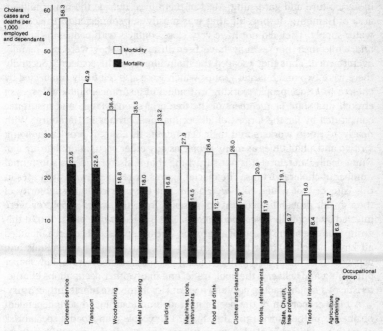

Total employed in these groups (with dependants) 1895: 456,122

Source: calculated from *MS 1892*, p. 32; *SHS* 18 (1898), pp. 102–18; *SHS* 21 (1903), pp. 114–16.

FIG. 19. Occupation-specific cholera morbidity and mortality rates for major occupations, Hamburg 1892

bedding, clothes, foodstuffs, or water; second, how far it carried a risk because most of the people employed in it worked in the harbour; and third, whether it was well or badly paid. Unfortunately there are no occupational statistics telling us about the location of people's jobs in Hamburg until 1900; so the 1900 figures will have to serve as an approximate guide to which occupations were concentrated in the harbour area (the free port, Altstadt Süd, Steinwärder, and Kleiner Grasbrook) in 1892, bearing in mind the changes that took place in the years between.[5] The figures that result are to some extent predictable, but a few at least are really quite surprising.

With these qualifications in mind, we can now turn to the occupational group least affected by cholera in 1892, which consisted of people working

[5] *SHS* 21 (1903), 90.

in agriculture and gardening. Most of them lived outside the main built-up area of Hamburg, in housing that was mostly not connected to the central water-supply. They did not have very close contacts with people in the city, and while their houses may have been insanitary, they were not usually overcrowded. Thus they escaped the main impact of the epidemic. Secondly there were two much larger groups which were also relatively unaffected by cholera in 1892: people working in trade and insurance, and employees of church and state or members of the free professions. Trade and insurance constituted by far the largest of all occupational groups in Hamburg. With nearly 154,000 workers and their dependants in 1895, it provided a living for two and a half times as many people as any other occupational group did. Numerically, therefore, it is not surprising that it also provided a substantial number of cholera victims. The official figures in 1892 show 1,537 cases in this category, of which 857 were fatal. But the overwhelming majority of these in all probability caught the disease from the water-supply or were infected by people in other occupations. The morbidity rate per 1,000 in this group was one of the lowest of all groups. The occupations it covered included all kinds of retail and wholesale trades (88,162 occupied individuals and dependants), banking, shipping, trading agencies, auctioneering, newspaper publishing and delivery, the book trade, and many other occupations characteristic of a major trading port and a great city in the late nineteenth century.

A high proportion of the people in trade and insurance had independent businesses of their own (36% in 1895). The people who stood a special risk of catching cholera at work were not these, but mainly the manual labourers employed by various branches of trade, such as stevedores, longshoremen, checkweighmen, porters, and so on—29,204 all told. Among retailers, milk, butter, cheese, and fruit traders also clearly ran a special risk. But these were not counted separately in the cholera statistics, and they only formed a relatively small proportion of the 'trade' category as a whole. Roughly speaking, the 'trade' category, with insurance, accounted for most of the *Mittelstand* in Hamburg in 1895—white-collar workers as well as shopkeepers and small traders. In 1900, some 20% of people in trade and insurance worked in the harbour area. This, no doubt, was the major risk that these people ran in 1892. Yet it is fairly safe to assume that most of them would not usually have thought of refreshing themselves from the waters of the Elbe, and that they were reasonably careful to avoid infection. Here, then, Hamburg's character as a centre of trade, shipping, and commerce served to reduce the impact of cholera rather than increase it. In 1886 only 32% of those employed in this group had a taxable income of less than 1,000 Marks a year; another 29% earned between 1,000 and 2,000 Marks a year; 22% earned between 2,000 and 5,000 Marks a year, and 17% earned over 5,000 Marks a year.[6]

[6] *SHS* 17 (1895). 67.

This was another influence that contributed towards reducing the impact of cholera on the middling and upper income groups in the city.

For much the same reasons, relatively few people working for the state, the church,[7] and the free professions were affected by cholera in 1892; in this occupational group indeed 744 cases and 386 deaths were officially recorded, but this was a very substantial occupational group, with nearly 50,000 people depending on it in 1895. The morbidity rate in this group was clearly below the average for all groups. Most people employed in this category (23,486) worked in the police force, as prison warders, as officials of one kind and another in local government at various levels, or in official welfare institutions (orphanages and the like). Those who worked in the harbour (a mere 8% in 1900) were probably more at risk than average. A newspaper report on 30 August noted that 'individual customs officials' had been stricken with the disease 'in the free port area'.[8] Also at risk were the police, whose duty it often was to deal with the sick and the dying on the streets. Especially in the early days of the epidemic, when ambulance services had not yet been organized, the main burden of dealing with the sick and getting them to hospital fell on the police.[9] In a letter to a local newspaper, one of these officers, or one of their sympathizers, painted a graphic picture of the risks they ran:

Ambulancemen were not available, so consequently the officers had to take a hand themselves if the sick and the dead were to be moved at all. In doing this, it frequently happened that the officers' clothing was befouled by the patients, who often had to be carried for long stretches on the way; the river-launches were polluted by the patients almost every time and had to be cleaned up by the officers. Then to the police stations! Because these are almost all very limited in space, the patients often had to be accommodated in the very rooms where the officers were staying, if they were not to be left lying on the streets, and here too the rooms were usually defiled by the patients. And this was the sight that had to be endured by the officers as they ate! Enjoy the meal, gentlemen![10]

Moreover, the officers then took their uniforms home for their wives to clean. All this greatly increased the risk of infection. Apart from the police, nurses, doctors, and hospital employees—5,365 of them in all—were also more at risk than average, but in 1892 all the evidence we have suggests that the great majority of them were very careful in observing the necessary hygienic precautions, unlike, perhaps, their predecessors in 1832. This category also included a substantial proportion of the professional middle classes. In 1886, 22% of those employed by church and state and 33% of those engaged in the

---

[7] For the Church's role in the epidemic, see Chapter 4c, above.

[8] StA Hbg, Senat, Cl. VII, Lit. Ta, Pars 2, Vol. 11, Fasc. 17, Inv. 4: *Freisinnige Zeitung*, 202, 30 Aug. 1892.

[9] See Chapter 4b, above.

[10] StA Hbg, PP S3490 Bd. 1: *Hamburger Fremdenblatt*, 28 Oct. 1892.

professions had an income in excess of 2,000 Marks a year. They probably ran a fairly minimal risk of infection at work. The numerical predominance of lower state officials such as policemen in this category helped redress the balance and produce a morbidity rate that was clearly below average, but not dramatically so.

Here, then, we have two occupational categories where the impact of cholera was well below the norm, as indeed might be expected. We now move on to a third category, where the impact of cholera might have been thought to have been relatively high, but where in fact it turned out to be no more than usual, or in one case indeed clearly below the mean. These are the three occupational groups that come under the headings of workers in hotels and refreshments, clothes manufacture and cleaning, and the food and drink industries. In all these groups, the risk of catching cholera came through the job itself, rather than through the work being done in the harbour area; less than 10% of workers in those categories, in fact, were employed in Hamburg's dockland in 1900. All these were rather mixed groups containing some workers who ran only a small risk of infection in the course of their work, and others who worked in jobs where the risk was a good deal higher. For example, many of those employed in the food and drinks industries worked in enterprises which used spring- or well-water rather than the centralized city water-supply. In 1895, 2,728 workers and their dependants relied on the brewery industry for a living, another 1,985 on distilling, and a further 435 on the bottling of wine and champagne. Pure water was also sometimes used in the mineral water and ice industries, which accounted for another 2,211 workers and dependants. These and other employees could also be expected to take more hygienic precautions (such as washing their hands) than most workers in other industries. Some of them, such as tobacco workers, millers, bakers and confectioners, and employees in the manufacture of noodles, macaroni, coffee, chocolate, ersatz coffee, and the like, were thus probably relatively safe even if their trade did involve using a lot of mains water. In 1900, moreover, only 8% of people in this occupational group were employed in the harbour area. The workers in this category who seem to have been most at risk were those who prepared cheese, butter, condensed milk, and other dairy products, who totalled 2,219 in 1895, though this figure also includes those engaged in the processing of all kinds of animal foods including for example salt fish. So all in all a morbidity rate of no more than average is roughly what we might expect anyway for those employed in the food and drinks industry.

Those engaged in the hotel and refreshments trade (a total of 23,876 including dependants) would seem on the face of it to have run a relatively high risk of infection, from cleaning up after guests, handling food, or catering for sailors and other people in the harbour area. Against this, however, must be set the fact that very few of them worked in the harbour area—only 9.8%

in the census of 1900—so that they would have been exposed to infection relatively late. Perhaps they too were more careful than most people to avoid infection and follow the rules for preventing cholera. A very high proportion were self-employed, and they were concentrated heavily in the income brackets generally associated with the *Mittelstand* and the upper reaches of the working class. In 1886, 49% earned less than 1,000 Marks a year, 40% between 1,000 and 2,000 Marks, and 10% between 2,000 and 5,000 Marks a year. They were further protected by the fact that trade in the hotels, restaurants, and bars slackened off considerably after 25 or 26 August. We might also have expected the morbidity rate for those in the clothes and cleaning trade to have been somewhat higher than average, since many of them had to deal with dirty and possibly infected clothes. Those employed in the laundry business and their dependants totalled 8,166 people, who most probably ran a very high risk of infection. Barbers and hairdressers, who with their dependants numbered 2,970 in 1895, were also exposed to cholera, since their jobs involved using a good deal of water from the mains and brought them into close contact with the public. The rest of the category, however, consisted mainly of shoemakers, tailors, needleworkers, and the like, whose trade—the manufacture of clothing—brought no particular risk. Moreover, only a tiny fraction of people in these groups—fewer than 3%, in fact—worked in the harbour in 1900. This was, one may assume, a major contributory factor in reducing the morbidity rate. And of course in so far as these jobs involved using water, it was often water that was hot enough to kill the cholera bacilli. Finally, the official advice distributed to all the inhabitants of Hamburg on the last weekend in August laid great stress on dirty clothing as a source of infection, and the disinfection campaign was aimed at the clothing and laundry of the victims even more than it was directed towards their housing or their sanitation and water-supply. All these influences, therefore, appear to have come together to reduce the impact of cholera on what would appear on the face of it to have been a fairly high-risk set of occupations.

There was a fourth category where cholera morbidity rates were at or rather below the average. This consisted of a number of industries which carried relatively little risk of catching cholera from the nature of the work itself, where the only real danger lay in the extent to which these industries were located in the harbour area. Only one of these industries—the machine tool and instrument industry—employed a large number of people and therefore appears on Figure 19. In 1900, no fewer than 44% of the workers in this group were employed in the harbour area, mainly in shipbuilding and ancillary trades. This no doubt accounts for the fact that the cholera morbidity rate was a good deal higher than we might have expected from the nature of the job. Similarly, the paper and leather industries, where the morbidity rate worked out at 28.6‰, were also located to a greater than average extent in the harbour area; in 1900 24% of workers in the paper industry and 13% of those in the leather industry worked in that area. Printers and those in associated trades suffered a cholera morbidity rate at roughly the average level in 1892—26.9‰—while in 1900 some 22% of them were employed in the harbour area. A similar discrepancy in the occupational group consisting of those who worked in the preparation and manufacture of matches and other lighting materials, oils, varnishes, and fats—a group employing some 5,525 people in 1895—is rather harder to explain. 37% of workers in this category were employed in the harbour in 1900, but the cholera morbidity rate was only 18.5‰ in 1892. Perhaps the rate was below average because of the hot and dry conditions in which they worked, or because their job demanded high standards of cleanliness, or because they wore protective clothing, or simply because they worked somewhat apart from the other employees in the harbour area. Even so, the morbidity rate here was only slightly below average, rather than dramatically so. By contrast, only 2% of those employed in the mining, saltworks, and stone industries worked in the harbour in 1900; but in 1895 these industries employed a mere handful of people—695 all told—so the morbidity rate of 19‰ may not be very accurate: all we can say is that it was around the average in this occupational group, or just below. In the textile industry, where only 10% were employed in the harbour in 1900 and the chemicals industry, where, again, 10% worked in the harbour in 1900, they ran at 19.3 and 18.0 per 1,000 respectively. Over half the employees in the textile industry were women, but this had no discernible effect on susceptibility to cholera.

II

The evidence for a close connection between cholera morbidity rates and employment in the harbour is strengthened still further when we turn to the next category of occupational groups, consisting of workers in building, metal processing, woodworking, and transport. Together these occupations provided a living for nearly 175,000 people in Hamburg in 1895. In two of these groups—building and woodworking—relatively few people were employed in the harbour area in 1900 (8% and 14% respectively). But in each case there were substantial numbers of workers who ran a high risk of infection because they worked actually on the waterfront itself, in timber yards or on the construction of quays, warehouses, and similar projects (including, for example, the filter-beds for the new water-supply). Moreover, the continuing construction of the harbour in the early 1890s and the high proportion of wooden sailing ships still being built, serviced and repaired in comparison to 1900 probably meant that there were proportionately more building and woodworkers employed in the port area in 1892 than there were eight years later. Other workers in these categories were also employed on and around Hamburg's numerous fleets, another source of infection. In the third occupational group in this category, metal processing, 20% of the workers were employed in the harbour in 1900. Here too there was a large number of shipbuilding workers. These categories included some of the worst-paid jobs in the city, which exposed those engaged in them to additional risks from poor housing, bad diet, and other factors influencing the spread of cholera. Although there was an élite of higher-paid and permanently employed workers in this category, 78% of Hamburg's building workers earned less than 1,000 Marks a year in 1886, a higher proportion than in any other trade except domestic service.

All these three groups had a cholera morbidity rate that was clearly above average, though not substantially so. The fourth occupational group in this category was that of the transport workers, where the impact of cholera was much higher than average. Just over 58,000 workers and their dependants fell into this occupational group in 1895. Some of them, such as railwaymen, tram drivers, postmen, and hansom cab operators, probably ran not much more than an average risk of catching cholera, though their jobs brought them into constant contact with the general public. The category of transport workers also, logically enough, included grave-diggers, who ran quite a considerable risk in 1892. A very large proportion of transport workers, however, depended on the harbour or on the river for a living, either as crew on inland or coastal shipping, or carrying people and goods around the harbour in boats and barges, or loading and unloading ships of all kinds on the waterfront. Some 45% of transport workers were employed in the harbour area in 1900. These people, for whom the harbour itself provided a living, ran a very high risk of catching cholera in 1892, as Figure 19 bears out. They included workers such as dredging operatives: it was noted for example that 'some 30 out of 300 workers employed in private dredging operations have died of cholera '. They lived in 'dredging barges', six to a cabin.[11] Like most workers in this category, they were also very poorly paid. 70% of Hamburg's transport workers earned less than 1,000 Marks a year in 1886. One very minor occupational group, with only 1,293 workers and dependants in 1895, was also especially hard hit by cholera. These were painters, sculptors, and artists, among whom 44 cases of cholera and 23 deaths were recorded by the medical authorities in Hamburg in 1892. Only 5% of the workers in this category were employed in the harbour in 1900. So the risk probably came from the constant use of mains water which their work demanded. Artists, too, may simply have been too undisciplined and disorganized to take the necessary precautions.

The most severely affected occupational group of all was that of domestic servants. There were nearly 22,000 workers and their dependants in this

[11] StA Hbg. Senat. Cl. VII. Lit. Ta, Pars 2, Vol. 11, Fasc. 17, Inv. 1a: *Hamburger Echo*, 22 Oct. 1892.

category in 1895. 855 domestic servants and their dependants were recorded in the official statistics as catching cholera in 1892, and 321 of them as dying from it. With a morbidity rate of over 58‰, they were twice as likely to catch cholera as people in the average occupational group. The Health Commission for Harvestehude provided five basic reasons for the high mortality and morbidity rates of female domestic servants:

1) handling water and dirt
2) if anybody comes into contact with unboiled water, it is domestic servants
3) maidservants come into contact in particular with uncooked foods whose consumption in the raw state is considered dangerous (raw fruit and vegetables, fresh milk, uncooked Elbe fish)
4) it cannot be doubted that maidservants, upon whom a major burden falls in the prevention of cholera (boiling water) are especially inclined to make life easy for themselves by neglecting their duties
5) in virtually every house the maidservant is assigned one of the worst, often most unfavourably situated rooms to sleep in. Many maids' rooms have insufficient light and air, especially in multi-storey houses, or are situated in the cellar.[12]

Of these points, the last one in the list, number 5, like so many explanations for the differential impact of cholera advanced in 1892, reflected the widespread belief that poor ventilation increased the chances of infection. This was only the case, however, when the room was inhabited by a carrier of the disease who could pass it on by droplet infection. More relevant by far are the first four points, though the fourth one undoubtedly reflected a common tendency on the part of the employers—and most of the members of the Health Commission for Harvestehude were probably employers of domestic servants—to accuse their employees of slackness. Domestic servants were also at risk because of their low pay. Though food and lodging were provided free of charge, the fact that over 10% of domestic servants earned too little to pay any tax, and of those who did pay tax, 93% earned less than 1,000 Marks a year, left them with few possibilities of improving their diet, which as we have seen was in all probability an important factor in weakening their resistance to the disease.

It seems clear, therefore, that people in some occupations did run a particular risk of contracting cholera. As we might expect, these occupations fell into two groups. First there were those jobs which involved working in the harbour and on the river as boatmen, fishermen, and quayside labourers as well as construction workers and those engaged in the myriad industrial occupations connected with the harbour, who all ran a high risk of infection from the contaminated water of the Elbe. They could either become infected by drinking the water in large quantities, as many of them did to quench their thirst in the hot weather of mid- to late August 1892, or simply by wiping

---

[12] StA Hbg. MK III A 13 (Harvestehude).

their mouths repeatedly with wet, unwashed hands, as was presumably a common enough habit. Similarly at risk were those in a second group of occupations which were not necessarily connected with the harbour in any direct way, but which involved handling contaminated food, clothing, and bedding, cleaning infected lavatories or living-quarters, or using contaminated water for washing, doing the dishes, cleaning, or other tasks. Domestic servants were most at risk in this group: workers in hotels, restaurants, and bars, in the second-hand clothes trade, and in the laundry business turned out in the end to be rather less vulnerable. Still, those who contracted the disease through their work were then quite likely to infect their families and those who shared accommodation or lavatory facilities with them. Work, then, was a major source of infection in the cholera epidemic of 1892.

It is likely that this was also the case in earlier epidemics—indeed, occupation probably played an even more important role in determining the distribution of cholera in 1831–2, 1848, 1859, 1866, and 1873 than in 1892. The influence of the centralized water-supply in spreading the infection to all parts of the city was much less important in most of these earlier outbreaks, with the possible, partial exception of 1859. As Hamburg became industrialized, so its economy diversified with the growth of manufacturing, reprocessing and service industries. The further back we go into its history, the more exclusive its dependence on trade and shipping, and the higher the proportion of its workers who were employed in the harbour. It is unfortunately not possible to compile occupation-specific morbidity and mortality rates for earlier epidemics,[13] but the scattered information that we do possess goes some way at least towards illustrating these trends. In 1832, for example, the highest absolute number of cases by occupation were among 'workmen (239), sailors (152), maidservants (137), boatmen and coxwains (83), innkeepers (64), washerwomen (60), cobblers (59), and joiners (54)'. No other occupation recorded more than 31 cases, and most suffered only a handful. The high number of cases among domestic servants, washerwomen, and innkeepers reinforces the conclusion that these were generally high-risk occupations: while the waterfront occupations were even more prominent in 1832 than sixty years later.[14]

A roughly similar pattern is observable in 1848. Here no fewer than 555 'labourers' caught the disease. The next highest numbers of cases were among servants and sailors (155 each), followed closely by boatmen (82) and joiners (73). If we add on ships' captains and ships' carpenters we get another 47 victims who worked on ships or in shipyards. Washerwomen, with 33 cases, seem to have been less hard hit in 1848, but innkeepers, with 50 victims,

---

[13] The insurmountable obstacles to such calculations are discussed briefly in the Statistical Appendix.

[14] Rothenburg, *Die Cholera-Epidemie*, Table. 5. See also Plate 14.

were again one of the worst-affected groups, along with tailors (58) and wagoners (37).[15] In general, the occupations that appeared at the top of the lists of cholera victims in 1832 and 1848 were therefore the same. In his official report on the 1848 epidemic, Medical Officer Dr Buek noted that many of the victims were in occupations 'which are carried out especially on and near the water', and this certainly seems to have been the case in 1831–2 as well.[16] Whether it was true of the 1859 epidemic is impossible to say, because less than a quarter of the cases had their occupations recorded.[17] For 1873, however, a broadly similar pattern is observable: 174 of the 693 who caught the disease were sailors, boatmen, or fishermen, a further 245 were 'workers' and another 810 were artisans of one kind or another.[18] Many of these were also most probably employed in the harbour.

While some of these vulnerable occupations were to be found in almost any nineteenth-century city—domestic service being perhaps the most notable among them—there is no doubt that Hamburg's status as a major sea and river port exposed its inhabitants to increased chances of infection in a number of ways. Not only did most cholera epidemics spread by sea-routes and waterways, thus putting ports at risk more than inland cities, but the disease was also particularly liable to infect sailors, boatmen, harbour workers, and others who made up such a high proportion of the workforce in the ports. Sailors and boatmen made up 14.4% of the victims of known occupation in 1831–2, 9.9% in 1848, 25% in 1873, and perhaps 4% in 1892.[19] Of all these epidemics, 1873 was by far the least serious, and the exceptionally high proportion of sailors and boatmen among its victims suggests that in the other, minor epidemics too, the disease's impact was greatest on those who worked on the river or on the waterfront. The three most severe of the Hamburg cholera epidemics—those of 1832, 1848, and 1892—were severe precisely because they managed to escape the harbour to a greater extent than the others.[20] But the declining proportion of sailors and boatmen among the victims from 1831–2 to 1848 and then 1892 also reflected the declining proportion of these occupations in the employment structure of the city as a whole. The impact of cholera on a city, in short, may well have reflected, among many other things, the presence in the city's workforce of particular vulnerable occupations. These in turn were overwhelmingly concentrated at the lower end of the social scale. There was a positive correlation between the proportion of wage-earning manual

[15] StA Hbg. Mk III A 2 Bd. 1: Bericht über die Cholera-Epidemie des Jahres 1848 von Physicus Dr. Buek.

[16] Ibid., Bl. 84.

[17] StA Hbg, MK III A 2 Bd. 2, Bl; 15 ff.

[18] *SHS* 7 (1875), pp. 49–52.

[19] Rothenburg, *Die Cholera-Epidemie*, Table 5; StA Hbg, MK III A 2 BD. 1: Bericht über die Cholera-Epidemie des Jahres 1848 von Physicus Dr Buek; *SHS* 7 (1875), pp. 48–52.

[20] See Figure 7, above.

labourers in 1895 and the 1892 cholera morbidity (0.62) and mortality (0.70) rates, and weaker but still suggestive negative correlations between cholera rates and white-collar workers (-0.56 morbidity, -0.56 mortality) and economically independent persons (-0.53 morbidity, -0.66 mortality) in the occupied population of each district.

III

The occupational incidence of cholera was also connected with its incidence by age, because different occupations had different age-structures, some being mainly for the young and others having a rather broader age-span. Those who worked for a living in nineteenth-century Germany were mainly adults in the prime of life. Child labour was common, but it was mostly part-time. At the other end of life, weakness and infirmity forced the retirement of the elderly from jobs which demanded physical strength and fitness. Most of the vulnerable occupations thus created an additional risk for young adults and the middle-aged in the cholera epidemic of 1892. Table 8 confirms the initial impression, shared by many contemporaries, that these were precisely the age-groups most at risk. The largest group of victims were mature adults; the second largest group were infants and young children. 697 cases, of whom 626 died, were infants below the age of one year, and a further 624 (with 490 deaths) were aged between 1 and 2. After this, the numbers of victims began to fall off quite rapidly, with 432 cases and 289 deaths among the 2–3 year-olds, 348 cases and 219 deaths among the 3–4 year-olds and 297 cases and 175 deaths among the 4–5 year-olds. So the very youngest seem to have been particularly hard hit. The fact remains, of course, that the bulk of the victims came from the middle years of life.[21]

Yet first impressions, as so often, were deceptive. When we turn to Figure

Table 8. Cholera deaths and cases by age group, Hamburg 1892

Age	Cholera Cases	% Cases	Cholera Deaths	% Deaths
0–5	2,398	14.1	1,799	20.9
5–25	1,731	10.2	776	9.0
15–25	1,959	11.6	744	8.6
25–50	7,127	42.0	3,520	40.9
50–70	2,002	11.8	1,369	15.9
70 and over	486	2.9	376	4.4
Unknown	1,253	7.4	21	0.2
TOTAL	16,956	100.0	8,605	100.0

Source: MS 1892, p. 31.

[21] *MS 1892*, p. 31, also for the following discussion.

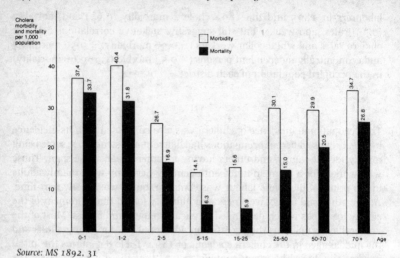

Source: MS 1892, 31

FIG. 20. Cholera morbidity and mortality rates by age-group, Hamburg 1892.

20, which shows cholera morbidity and mortality per 1,000 population in each age-group, we get a very different picture. There is a clear 'U-shaped curve', with the highest morbidity and mortality rates occurring in the under-fives and the over-twenty-fives. Infants aged 0–1 were over two and a half times as likely to catch cholera in Hamburg in 1892 than were children, adolescents, and young adults aged 5–25. The age-group 25–50 is rather a large one, but within it, it seems safe to say, the older people were, the more they were likely to catch the disease. Even more striking than the differences in morbidity between the various age-groups were the differences in mortality. Cholera mortality in Hamburg in 1892 was very high for children in the first two years of life; it fell to about half this rate for those aged 2–5 and 25–50; while children, adolescents, and young adults aged 5–25 fared even better, with a mortality rate less than a fifth of that of the infants. For the elderly and the old, death rates from cholera began to climb again; the over-50s were roughly 3 to 4 times as likely to die of cholera as the 5–25 year-olds; but they were still less likely to die of it than infants. This can be seen even more clearly if we look at deaths per 1,000 cases (the *case-specific mortality rate*) from cholera in Hamburg in 1892, by age-group. Rounded up, the rates on Figure 21 reveal that a staggering 90% of infants who caught the disease died of it. Cholera among infants was thus almost invariably fatal. For those aged 1–2, nearly 80% of whom died, it was scarcely less dangerous. After that, the rate fell quite rapidly, so that of those aged 15–25 who caught the

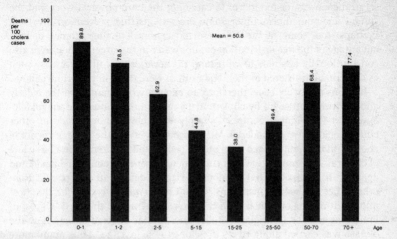

Source: MS 1892, 31. Mean case-specific mortality: 50.8%

FIG. 21.   Case-specific cholera mortality by age-group, Hamburg 1892.

disease, only 38% died of it. The rate was about average (nearly 50%) for the 25–50 year-olds, then climbed again with age until over three-quarters of people aged 70 and over who caught cholera in Hamburg in 1892 died of it.

Cholera thus had a strikingly different impact on different age-groups. Infants below 1 year of age were two and a half times more likely to catch cholera than adolescents and young adults aged 15–25; and if they caught it, they were more than twice as likely to die of it than were those in the 15–25 age group who caught it. The over-50s were similarly at risk, though not quite such a dramatic extent, with morbidity and mortality rates roughly twice those of adolescents and young adults. It would seem reasonable to conclude that the general capacity of the very young and the elderly or old to resist a severe disease such as cholera was relatively weak. This general lack of resistance was probably compounded by additional weaknesses in the digestive system and the vital organs, such as the kidneys, which were most seriously damaged by the disease. Infants were obviously more severely affected by digestive disorders than older children, and it is hardly surprising that cholera, with its brutal assault on the digestive organs, was so lethal in the newly born and under-ones. It was also difficult for these age-groups to maintain the strict standards of hygiene and cleanliness that were so important in keeping cholera at bay. The very young could not easily be taught to avoid infection.[22] The elderly and the old may have been too forgetful, or too

[22] Cf. pp. 412–13 above.

set in their ways, or too infirm to carry out the hard physical work and the careful and sometimes cumbersome precautions that prevention involved. Perhaps, too, some of the old were too confined to their homes to take advantage of the free distribution of pure water in the streets. They were also constitutionally less able to withstand the severe shock that a disease such as cholera administered to their bodies than were those in the prime of life.

It seems relatively easy, therefore, to explain why infants and the elderly and old were harder hit by cholera in 1892 than the young and the middle-aged. Yet this finding contrasts sharply with observations made in other cholera epidemics. As Roderick McGrew has observed, the greater impact of cholera on the middle-aged than on old people and children 'was a basic fact of cholera's epidemiology which subsequent experience confirmed again and again'.[23] It is possible that Hamburg in 1892 differed in this respect from other cities studied by historians. Inland waterways were by far the most important means of transport in the pre-railway age of the early 1830s, in France as well as in England. Rollet and Souriac showed clearly how the disease was carried along rivers in Seine-et-Oise in 1832. Thus many more industrial workers, indeed workers of all kinds, came into direct contact with polluted water in the course of their work in 1832 than was the case in 1892. Glasgow in 1832 was a major port. Cholera seems to have arrived there by canal from the east coast and got into the Clyde. Stockholm was also a major seaport, and even land-locked Lille was cross-crossed by canals which served as the major thoroughfares for industrial goods.[24] All these factors placed adult workers, who came into contact with infected water, more at risk than infants and the old. Yet even with the additional risk for adults in 1832, as compared with the situation sixty years later, it seems likely that the statistics provided by Morris and other students of the epidemics of the early 1830s still underestimate the incidence of cholera among infants and also, to some extent, among the old. The reason is not hard to see. The statistics provided by most of these authors are not age-specific cholera mortality rates. They either lack the figure of deaths from cholera (as in Morris's work) or they are unable to provide total population figures by age-group (as in the studies by Zacke, Rollet and Souriac, and Dechêne and Robert). Furthermore, in the pre-bacteriological era of the 1830s cases were all diagnosed purely on the basis of the symptoms found in the victims. In all the towns in question, normal mortality among infants was very high, as one would expect of the 1830s. Infant and child mortality in Lille (age 0–5) was as high as 21% in the early 1840s even in the well-off quarters of the

[23] McGrew, *Russia and the Cholera*, p. 44; see also Morris, *Cholera 1832*, p. 83; Chevalier, *Le choléra*, p. 166; Rollet and Souriac, 'Le choléra', p. 952; L. Dechêne and J.-C. Robert, 'Le choléra de 1832 dans le Bas-Canada: Mesure des Inegalités devant la mort', in H. Charbonneau and A. Larose (eds.), *The Great Mortalities: Methodological Studies of Demographic Crises in the Past* (Liège, 1979), pp. 229–56.

[24] Rollet and Souriac, op. cit., p. 952; Morris, op. cit., p. 83.

town; in the working-class districts it was as high as 59% in the same period.[25] In Glasgow the burial rate for the under-fives in 1830 was more than fifteen times higher than the cholera burial rate given by Morris for 1832.[26] Deaths in the youngest age-groups involving symptoms of vomiting and diarrhoea were extremely common in the summer months. Even in the bacteriological era of the 1890s many hundreds of cholera deaths were in all probability wrongly ascribed to 'vomiting and diarrhoea' among infants, and the same is true for deaths from 'old age' among the elderly.[27] This was a result of the fact that doctors were still describing the cause of death by symptom in some cases in 1892. In the 1830s, when virtually all deaths were classified according to symptom, the underestimation of cholera deaths in these age-groups must have been vastly greater.[28] The general belief at this time that cholera was mainly a disease affecting young adults and the middle-aged would have strengthened the tendency to record deaths among the very young as resulting not from cholera but from 'vomiting and diarrhoea', 'convulsions', 'debility', 'stomach catarrh', or some other similar cause instead. Drastic though such a conclusion may seem, therefore, it seems that all statistics on the age structure of victims in the cholera epidemics of the 1830s must be dismissed as worthless.

Such reliable contemporary studies as provide true age-specific mortality rates for cholera epidemics in the nineteenth century all show the same age structure of victims as revealed in the Hamburg epidemic of 1892. August Hirsch's study of the 1866 epidemic in Berlin, for instance, revealed a cholera mortality rate of 30‰ among infants, declining to 5‰ in the age-group 10–15 and 4‰ in the age-group 15–20. Among 20–30 year-olds, the death rate from cholera stood at 6‰, but after this, as we would expect from the experience of Hamburg in 1892, death rates began to rise again, reaching 9‰ in the age-group 30–40, and 11‰ in the age-group 40–50. Among 50–60 year-olds the mortality rate from cholera was 16‰, and among the 60–70 year-olds it was 18‰. The rate for the over-70s, at 19‰, was probably something of an underestimate. This pattern reflected the fact that cases of 'summer cholera' among infants during the epidemic had been counted as Asiatic cholera, a procedure evidently not followed in 1832. Hirsch's figures for Berlin in 1866, therefore, confirm the argument that cholera hit infants harder than any other group.[29] The same conclusion can also be drawn from the official statistics provided by the Hamburg authorities for the cholera

[25] Chevalier, *Le choléra*, p. 67.

[26] Morris, *Cholera 1832*, pp. 82–3.

[27] See the Statistical Appendix for further evidence.

[28] See in general A. E. Imhof, *Die gewonnenen Jahre. Von der Zunahme unserer Lebensspanne seit dreihundert Jahren, oder, von der Notwendigkeit einer neuen Einstellung zu Leben und Sterben. Ein historischer Essay* (Munich, 1981). Rollet and Souriac, 'Le choléra', pp. 936, 947–8, lay great stress on the problems and uncertainties of cholera diagnosis in 1831–2.

[29] Hirsch, 'Die Cholera-Epidemien', pp. 297–331, here p. 307.

epidemic of 1873. The highest morbidity and mortality rates occurred in the age-groups 0–1 and 1–2. The case-specific cholera mortality rate for infants under the age of 1 was 74%; it was the same for the 1–2 year-olds. In other words, roughly three out of every four infants who caught cholera in Hamburg in 1873 died of the disease. Among older children and adolescents, morbidity and mortality rates were much lower, declining to a low point in the age-group 10–15. Fewer than 40% of the children in this age-group who caught cholera failed to recover. From the age of 20 upwards, case-specific cholera mortality increased, reaching 50% in the age-group 25–30, 62% in the age-group 40–45, 66% in the age-group 55–60, and 80% in the age-group 65–70. This steady rise in case-specific mortality rates from late adolescence upwards conforms to the pattern which Figure 21 (above, p. 447) reveals for the 1892 epidemic.[30] When contemporaries noted of nineteenth-century cholera epidemics 'that', as one commentator on the Hamburg epidemic of 1832 put it, 'as has also been remarked at other times and in other places, middle-aged people from 31 to 40 are the most affected by the disease', this was 'perhaps because the number of individuals in this age-group is preponderant in the population'.[31] If we measure the cases and deaths by age against the actual composition of the population by age, what we find is something very different: as we have seen, the most vulnerable, the hardest hit, were not young adults and the middle-aged at all, but infants and old people. As far as there is evidence available, this seems to have held good for other nineteenth-century cholera epidemics as well. Nevertheless, of course, this is by no means the whole story. In order to proceed further, we now have to introduce a new dimension to the discussion: the differential effect of cholera on men and women, or the *sex-specific* impact of the disease.

d. *Male and Female*

I

Most students of cholera have paid little attention to its varying incidence between men and women.[1] R. J. Morris, for example, in his study of the epidemic of 1832 in Britain, not only ignored the question altogether, but even seemed to assume that all the victims were men ('when they died, the widows and orphans were left as an extra charge on the Poor Law').[2] Roderick McGrew mentioned the common belief in Russia at this time that women were more susceptible to cholera than men, but his figures showed that in

[30] *SHS* 7 (1875), pp. 44–52.

[31] Rothenburg, *Die Cholera-Epidemie*, p. 22.

[1] An exception is A. E. Imhof, *Die gewonnenen Jahre*; but the book's main concern is not with cholera but with mortality decline in general.

[2] Morris, *Cholera 1832*, p. 83.

absolute terms more men died than women, at least in Moscow in 1830–1, a fact which, in the absence of overall population figures for Moscow by sex, he was unable to discuss any further.[3] Dineur and Engrand provided absolute figures of cholera deaths by age and sex for Lille, which showed that many more women than men both caught the disease and died from it, in all age-groups from 15 upwards, but they added that 'this fact may perhaps simply be explained by a greater proportion of women in the population of Lille'. This supposition may be correct in view of the importance of textiles in the local economy, but no firm conclusions can be drawn in the absence of figures for the overall number of men and women in the town.[4] Brita Zacke showed that male victims outnumbered female in all age-groups below 50 in the Stockholm epidemic of 1834; the contrast was strongest in the age-group 30–39. She provided no overall population figures, however, so no definite conclusions could be drawn from these statistics.[5] Rollet and Souriac showed that excess mortality in the department of Seine-et-Oise in 1832 was greater among women aged 50–70 than among men in the same age-group, and roughly the same for both sexes in all other age-groups; but they were also unable to provide sex-specific cholera mortality rates.[6] The study of Dechêne and Robert on the 1832 epidemic in Quebec suffers from the same problem, so its claim that there were no differences in the impact of cholera on men and women must be treated with caution.[7]

Their problems not only reflect the general inadequacies of nineteenth-century statistics; they also illustrate the fact that contemporaries paid less attention to this aspect of inequality in the face of cholera than to any other. As a result, and in the absence of the original material, it is no longer possible to discover, either in absolute or in relative terms, how many men and women respectively caught cholera in Hamburg in 1892. However, we do have the material to enable us to work out how many men and women respectively died of the disease. In order to provide a proper basis for discussion, it is necessary to present these figures once more according to age-group.[8] Figure 22 shows the familiar 'U-shaped curve' with the highest death rates occurring among the very young and the elderly. It is slightly more detailed than Figure 20, so that we can see that death rates were indeed somewhat lower among the 25–30 year-olds than among those aged 30–60, a fact which Figure 20 does not reveal. Whereas Figure 20 on page 447 treated those aged 25–50 as one group, Figure 22, therefore, shows that mortality rates increased steadily from the 20–25 age-group upwards. The variations which Figure 22

[3] McGrew, *Russia and the Cholera*, pp. 44, 161.
[4] Chevalier *Le choléra*, p. 82.
[5] Zacke, *Koleraepidemien*, p. 166.
[6] Rollet and Souriac, 'Le choléra', p. 955.
[7] Dechêne and Robert, 'Le choléra', p. 229–56.
[8] For a discussion of the slight discrepancies between Figures 20 and 22, see the Statistical Appendix.

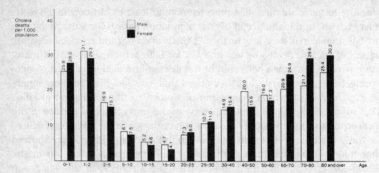

Source: calculated from *SHS* 20 (1902), 12–13. Age unknown: 12 male 9 female. Total of known age: 4,277 male; 4,339 female. Mean cholera mortality in 1892: 13.4 per 1,000 inhabitants

FIG. 22. Sex-specific cholera mortality by age-group, Hamburg 1892

shows between male and female death rates are on the whole not particularly significant, certainly not among the younger population. However, two interesting divergences are apparent among the over-forties. If (for the moment) we assume that the heavy involvement of men aged 15–60 in harbour employment, with its attendant danger of repeated contact with infected water, was counterbalanced by the extra risk of infection run (as we shall see) by women in childbearing age, roughly 15–40, then as this extra risk for women fell away among the over-forties, the continued employment in the harbour of men above this age-limit would have been the major factor accounting for the higher cholera mortality among males aged 40–60. Among the over-sixties, however, relatively fewer men worked in the harbour, and so the additional risk run by women in the course of carrying out their domestic duties—a risk to which we shall return in more detail a little later on—was enough to ensure that cholera mortality was higher among females aged 60 and above. All in all, however, given the inevitable margin of error involved in the compilation and calculation of the statistics, what emerges most clearly is the relative insignificance of male–female differentials in the overall impact of cholera.

When we turn to Figures 23 and 24, which provide, respectively, morbidity and mortality figures by age and sex for the cholera epidemic of 1873, a similar pattern emerges to that observable in 1892, with morbidity and mortality rates higher among men in their prime. Here men also seem to have suffered more than women in virtually all age groups below 60–70. Too much attention should probably not be paid to male–female differentials in the youngest age groups, where, as we have seen, problems of diagnosis

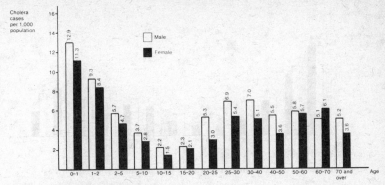

Source: calculated from *SHS* 7 (1875), 52

FIG. 23. Sex-specific cholera morbidity by age-group, Hamburg 1873

were particularly acute. In the highest age groups, however, a striking difference between the 1892 and 1873 figures immediately leaps to the eye: while mortality rates from cholera continued to rise quite clearly with increasing age from 25 upwards in 1892, they did not do so in 1873.[9] How can this discrepancy be explained? An important clue is provided by the fact that the course taken by the epidemic of 1873 was fairly undramatic. The first cases probably occurred in June, giving a total of 6 deaths. In July there was a steady trickle of cases, just a few each day, amounting to 116 in all, of which 76 were fatal. In August the epidemic climbed gradually to its peak, with an average of 20 deaths a day from 11 to 25 August, over 30 deaths a day over the next five days, then a gradual decline thereafter. This gradual spread of the epidemic strongly suggests that the bacillus did not get into the central water-supply in 1873. Most probably it lurked in the harbour area and in the fleets and was transmitted from person to person. This favoured its predominance among port workers, who were heavily concentrated in the age-group 20–50. The many other groups affected in 1892 did not run nearly so great a risk of infection in 1873. Mortality levels in the older population were lower because they were less exposed to infection. Only if the bacillus had entered the water-supply would the various influences favouring higher mortality rates with increasing age have come into play as they did in 1892.[10]

The same considerations may also hold good for the epidemic of 1848. In 1848 case-specific mortality stood at 62.0% for infants and children aged 0–5, then sank steadily to a low point of 29.9% for the 15–20 year-olds, before rising to a level of around 40% in the age-groups from 25 to 45. The pattern

[9] *SHS* 7 (1875), pp. 44–53.
[10] Ibid. Maps 30–31 (pp. 417–418 above) also suggest a concentration in the harbour area.

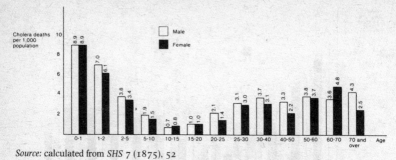

Source: calculated from *SHS* 7 (1875), 52

FIG. 24. Sex-specific cholera mortality by age-group, Hamburg 1873

is not dissimilar to that observable in the epidemic of 1873. The largest absolute number of cases was among men in the prime of life, between the ages of 20 and 40. Males still outnumbered females among the victims up to the age of 55, but thereafter the pattern was reversed. The cause was most probably the predominance of men in harbour jobs. Their multiple and repeated exposure to heavy doses of the bacillus was enough to explain their higher case-specific mortality rates in the age-groups 15–25 and 25–40.[11] Unfortunately case-specific mortality figures are all we have for the various age-groups in 1848; but it seems reasonable to conclude that the same patterns of morbidity and mortality by age occurred as in 1873, and for much the same reasons. Other possible explanations of the lack of a clear upward trend in morbidity and mortality rates with age in the Hamburg epidemic of 1873 do not really seem to fit the facts. There were no very significant differences in the age structure of the population between 1873 and 1892. The sharp rise in morbidity and mortality rates between the age-group 15–20 and the next age-group up the scale (20–25) in 1873 also suggests strongly that the prevalence of the disease among port workers is the most likely explanation. But for this factor, it is probable that morbidity and mortality rates would have risen in a gradual curve, remaining well below the levels actually attained until the age-group 40–50. Such a gradual rise is indeed what occurred in 1892. Here, then, we have an important link between the impact of cholera by age, by sex, and by occupation.

Yet these figures, of course, present the effects of cholera in isolation. They illustrate the impact of the disease in 1892 on the different age-groups in the population, and on men and women, without taking anything else into account. If we set these figures in the context of the *normal* pattern of mortality, we get quite a different picture. So far, we have just asked how

[11] StA Hbg, MK III A 2 Bd 1, Table IV.

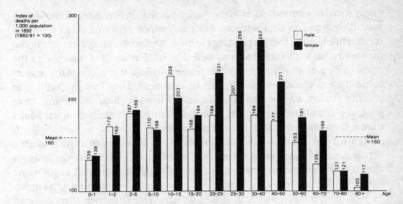

Source: calculated from *SHS* 20 (1902), 12–13

FIG. 25. Sex-specific excess mortality in Hamburg, 1892, by age-group (1882–91 = 100)

likely people of differing age and sex were to die of cholera. Figure 25 provides the answers to a further question, namely: how much *more* likely were people of differing age and sex likely to die in the cholera year (1892) than in a normal year? The statistics resulting from this approach provide rates of *excess mortality*, based on making the mean general mortality rate per annum in the previous decade equal to 100 and compiling an index, by sex and age-group, of the general mortality rate for 1892. Here the 'U-shaped curve', familiar from Figures 20 to 24, is reversed. Figure 25 reflects the fact that death rates among infants, small children, the elderly, and the old were so high anyway that even a massive cholera epidemic such as occurred in Hamburg in 1892 did not make a great deal of difference. It was the usually healthy sectors of the population, adolescents, young adults, and the middle-aged, who were hardest hit in comparison to a normal year. Seen in absolute terms, these age-groups were far less likely to die of cholera than either the very young or the elderly and the old. But they were even less likely to die of other causes, so that, seen in relative terms, cholera posed a greater threat to them than it did to the age-groups above and below.

This indeed was one source of the the extraordinary power it had to terrorize the contemporary imagination. The death of infants and old people was an accepted part of everyday life in the nineteenth century, and people had developed many ways of coming to terms with the emotional pain which it caused. The death of men and women in the prime of life was a far less normal or acceptable occurrence. The majority of these people were bread-winners, husband or wives, mothers or fathers, with central roles to play in major social institutions such as the family. Society, in Hamburg as elsewhere, was ill-equipped to deal with an epidemic which removed them from the scene while leaving their dependants behind. And people lacked the emotional means to cope with such losses as well. The sudden death of someone in the prime of life was an affront to human understanding. It was one of the aspects of the cholera epidemics most frequently commented on. This, no doubt, was another reason why contemporaries and, following them, historians, have generally considered cholera as a disease that hit normally healthy adults harder than any other sector of the population.

Figure 25 also reveals that excess mortality in Hamburg in 1892 was 47% higher among women aged 20–25 than among men of the same age; women aged 25–30 suffered an excess mortality 59% higher than men in the same age group did; and the excess mortality of women aged 30–40 was as much as 83% above that of men of the same age. The difference then declined slightly in the older age groups, but at 44% for the 40–50 year-olds, 28% for the 50–60 year-olds, and 37% for the 60–70 year-olds it was still far from negligible. There can be no doubt either that the cholera epidemic was the major, indeed virtually the only reason for the difference, since its occurrence was the only aspect in which mortality patterns in 1892 differed from those of a normal year. This is a very striking fact. It has been widely assumed as a result of Arthur Imhof's pioneering work on sex-specific mortality that women in nineteenth-century Germany generally had a higher death rate than men. In support of this thesis it has been argued that working-class women in particular were overburdened with work, undernourished compared to their menfolk, reluctant to seek medical advice, and excluded from coverage by sickness insurance. All this was to some extent true, although failure to seek medical advice probably did them little harm. But these factors were more than counterbalanced by the very high incidence of work-related accidents and illnesses to which men were exposed in the industrial environment. Imhof's data relate only to villages and very small towns, and he only intended them to illustrate the unequal burdens to which women were exposed in rural society. In large cities and industrial centres, all the evidence points to the fact that male mortality rates were higher than female throughout the nineteenth century.[12] This was the main reason why the impact of cholera showed up in such high female *excess* mortality rates. The very great

[12] Imhof, *Die gewonnenen Jahre*, pp. 144–6; for an example of the assumption that Imhof's findings apply to the urban-industrial working class, cf. Frevert, *Krankheit als politisches Problem*, p. 289. The proportion of women workers in the population by district seems to have had little connection with cholera rates. There were more than twice as many occupied women among the total female population in the Altstadt Nord and the Neustadt Nord as in the Billwärder Ausschlag or Barmbeck, though cholera rates were similar (R. Dasey, 'Women Workers. Their Employment and Participation in the Labour Movement. Hamburg 1880–1914', Ph.D. thesis, School of Slavonic and East European Studies, University of London, 1985, p. 85, and above, Chapter 5b).

difference it made to normal female mortality requires, therefore, careful consideration.

II

In so far as contemporaries noticed these differences in the sex-specific incidence of cholera, they were inclined to use them to support the ingrained prejudices of the middle-class male against the working-class female. The gentlemen of the Health Commission for the Neustadt Nord laid much of the blame for the epidemic as a whole at the door of 'the female sex, who take no pleasure in their home any more and do everything rather than dusting and cleaning their houses; how very different', they lamented in conclusion, 'things appeared in this respect twenty years ago'.[13] A local newspaper, the *Hamburger Tageblatt*, agreed that working-class women no longer knew how to keep house. The reason, it thought, was that young women now preferred to go into the factory instead of entering service. In domestic service, working-class girls had had no option but to learn the rudiments of keeping house and to acquire habits of cleanliness and hygiene:

There was compulsion: there the young girl, hardly out of school, was compelled to sit at home every evening and on her few free evenings to come home in good time according to the good old respectable custom. How seductive, by contrast, are the stories of her girlfriends who work in a factory or another industrial establishment. No housework, lunch in a café, and evenings free. So it's off to the dance. It's a jolly life for a young thing. On the dance floor she makes the acquaintance of smart young men, and in the end she marries one of them. The young woman has no conception of the duties which now confront her. She has no notion of how to make do with her husband's wages, in so far as these are handed over to her. Domestic discord and neglect of the household is the consequence—and dirt the result.

There was an urgent need, concluded the paper, to provide working-class girls with lessons in housekeeping,[14] a view that was shared by almost every shade of opinion in the bourgeois press. A reader of the left-liberal *Hamburger Fremdenblatt* declared on 24 August, as the epidemic was finally confirmed, 'women must be *competent*', and added: 'often housewives who used to work in factories and never learned to keep house are *not* competent, certainly not if they have also devoted every free hour to the pursuit of pleasure.'[15] It was also the opinion of a visiting German doctor that 'the worker's wife lacks any basis of domesticity, for she has been kept away from the home by modern factory life, and alienated still further from family and domestic life by Social

[13] StA Hbg, MK III A 13: Neustadt Nord.
[14] StA Hbg, Senat, Cl. VII, Lit. Ta, Pars 2, Vol. 11, Fasc. 17, Inv. 1a: *Hamburger Tageblatt*, 22 Oct. 1892.
[15] StA Hbg, Senat, Cl. VII, Lit. Ta, Pars 2, Vol. 11, Fasc. 17, Inv. 2: *Hamburger Fremdenblatt*, 24 Aug. 1892.

Democratic ideas about women's emancipation. These things', he added, 'occur with their consequences in all modern cities, but I have never encountered them in a drearier, crasser form than in Hamburg.'[16]

In reality, it was not women's failure to carry out the tasks which society ordained, but their very success in doing so, that proved fatal, and not for society, but for women themselves. There were few areas of life in the later nineteenth century where the sexual division of labour was so rigid and clear-cut as in the home. In all classes of society, it was women's role to buy, prepare, and cook food, to clean the house, including the toilets, to change babies' nappies, and to wash the bedclothes, indeed to wash everything, not only clothing but also the pots and pans, the dishes, and the knives and forks. All these activities, of course, constituted major hazards during the cholera epidemic. Women could catch the disease directly through coming into contact with contaminated food or water while cooking or even in the course of shopping. Their situation was particularly dangerous when there was already someone ill with cholera in the same household. Figure 26 contains a breakdown of households in which two or more cholera cases or deaths occurred, comprising about a quarter of all victims in Hamburg in 1892. The largest number of households in which two cases occurred were households where mother and child were affected; similarly with cholera deaths (about 30% of these households). It seems reasonable to conclude, therefore, that high female excess mortality in 1892 was in part caused by mothers catching cholera from their children.[17]

Pregnant women were also at risk. As an official medical report remarked,

Since the first appearance of cholera in Europe it has been observed that pregnancy beyond doubt constitutes a dangerous complication in cholera cases. Relatively more pregnant women than other women died in that first epidemic. Often the foetus dies at the onset of cholera symptoms, and in more than half the cases pregnancy is terminated, not to mention the fact that a high percentage of pregnant women die without giving birth.

Of the 115 pregnant women with cholera observed by this doctor, 28 stayed pregnant and recovered, 22 delivered their child and recovered, 40 delivered their child, usually dead, and died, and 25 died still carrying the child. This represented a mortality rate of 56% among the women. This was not spectacularly high, and perhaps it would be safest to conclude that pregnancy did not increase the female mortality rate to any very significant degree. In terms of human suffering, however, it presented a substantial extra burden on the women concerned.[18]

---

[16] F. and E. Hueppe, *Die Cholera in Hamburg 1892*, p. 33. Hueppe's wife Else, who was also in Hamburg during the epidemic, said much the same (p. 101).

[17] For further discussion, see the Statistical Appendix.

[18] A. Schütz, 'Über den Einfluss der Cholera auf Menstruation, Schwangerschaft, Geburt und Wochenbett', *Jahrbuch der Hamburgischen Staatskrankenanstalten*, 3 (1891–2), 63–95.

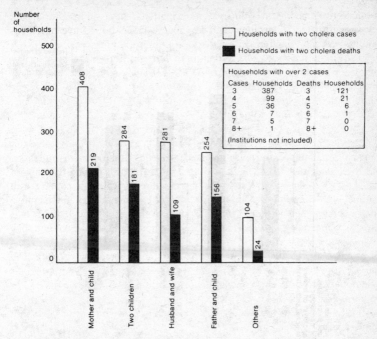

Source: MS 1892, 35

FIG. 26. Breakdown of cholera cases and deaths in households with two cholera cases or deaths, Hamburg 1892

A further source of danger for women lay in the hospital itself. There is some evidence that women who were taken into hospital fared less well there than men did. Figure 27 provides mortality rates for men, women, and children aged 14 years and under, in families where more than one member caught cholera, in the district of St Georg Nord. It shows that while men who were treated in hospital were no more likely to die than those who were treated at home, women and children were roughly twice as likely to die if they were taken to hospital than if they were allowed to stay at home. Put another way, it made little difference to a man's chance of survival if he was taken to hospital, but transportation to hospital made the situation very much more difficult for women and children. These figures, of course, only refer to one district in the city. But the differences in mortality rates are nevertheless very striking. How can they be explained? One might suggest that doctors, and perhaps families too, tended to be more reluctant to admit women, above all housewives and mothers, into hospital, than men. Women

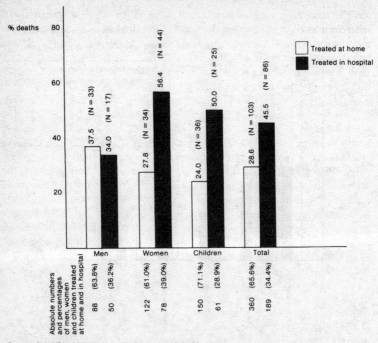

% deaths

Men   Women   Children   Total

Absolute numbers and percentages of men, women and children treated at home and in hospital

Men: 88 (63.8%) 50 (36.2%)
Women: 122 (61.0%) 78 (39.0%)
Children: 150 (71.1%) 61 (28.9%)
Total: 360 (65.6%) 189 (34.4%)

Treated at home
Treated in hospital

Source: StA Hbg, MK III A 13 St Georg Nord: Table A1

FIG. 27. Mortality rates among men, women, and children treated for cholera at home and in hospital, for St Georg Nord (families with more than one member suffering from cholera), 1892

were in general not covered by sickness insurance schemes. Unless they were serious cases, women were often treated at home so that they could continue to look after the children and the household as far as they were able; 66% of female patients in hospital were classified as serious, but only 59% of male.[19] However, the death rate among serious cases in hospital was lower (in every age-group above 5 years old) for women than for men, so in fact the overall death rate among hospital patients was only 47% for women and 45% for men in the age-group 21–40. Figure 27 does not support the theory that women were less likely to be hospitalized than men overall, so higher female death rates among hospital patients of all categories can only be partially explained by this factor.

While the numbers of male and female cholera patients admitted to hospital

[19] *Jahrbuch der Hamburgischen Staatskrankenanstalten,* 3 (1891–92), 146–7.

seem to have been roughly equal, men were on the whole admitted alone, whereas women were often admitted with their children (especially since this was the commonest combination of cases in a family). There may well have been difficulties in isolating mothers from children in hospital, and this may have increased the risk of infection from other children; but by itself it does not do much to explain the differences in mortality rates. The best clue, perhaps, is provided by the *weekly* statistics of cholera hospital cases. Among the hospital patients already mentioned, the death rate among male patients ran at 73% in the first week (22–8 August), while the death rate among female patients was only 60%. But the numbers of patients were relatively small, many of them were port workers, and the medical authorities, unprepared for so many patients arriving in the hospitals, were only admitting the seriously ill (83% of the male patients and 75% of the female). The second week of the epidemic, when over a third of all the patients in the sample were admitted, reversed the proportions, with a death rate of 59% among female patients and 52% among male. The discrepancies were particularly marked, once more, in the age-group 21–40. Twice as many people in this age-group as in any other were admitted in the second week of the epidemic. 49% of the women died, but only 44% of the men.

In all subsequent weeks, the case-specific mortality rate in this sample was under 50%. It was only in the first two weeks of the epidemic that large numbers of less serious cases continued to be treated at home, while the provision of hospital beds remained inadequate.[20] After this, virtually every cholera victim was hospitalized. The second week of the epidemic, when female death rates in hospital were much higher than male, saw the most chaotic and disorganized conditions in the hospitals, as the number of cases admitted reached its height before the cholera barracks and the field hospital had got under way. In these circumstances, perhaps, women and children may have found the strange institutional setting of the hospital more upsetting and more disorienting than men did. Men, after all, were used to institutional life, in the army, or in the all-male pubs and clubs that provided the basis for working-class social life outside the family in this period. Women and children, by contrast, may well have been shocked by their sudden removal from the home, and their resistance may well, in that case, have been lowered. But whatever the reason, hospitalization does seem, if the evidence from St Georg is to be trusted, to have been more dangerous for women than for men.

More important than this factor was the involvement of women in occupations seriously affected by cholera. Employment in the harbour was an overwhelmingly male affair, and in the initial stage of the epidemic there is little doubt that men were more seriously at risk from cholera than women

---

[20] See Chapter 4b.

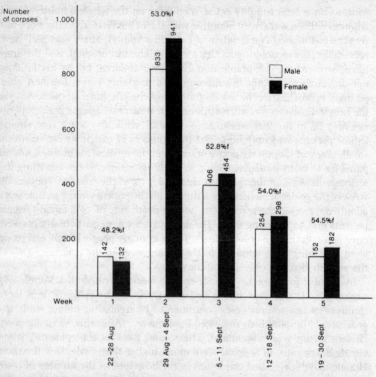

Note: The last week in September has been extended to the end of the month (in effect, the end of the epidemic)

Source: StA Hbg, Cholerakommission 6

FIG. 28. Cholera corpses delivered to the public mortuaries in Hamburg, by sex, 22 August to 30 September 1892

were. Figure 28 shows that in the first week of the epidemic more male corpses were delivered to the public morgues than female; and we have also seen that in the first week of the epidemic the mortality rate among male hospital patients was substantially higher than among female. For the rest of the epidemic, however, the relationship was reversed. Once the cholera had entered the water-supply, and once a large number of people had been affected, women started to catch cholera as a result of their domestic activities. Women's work in the 1890s represented, to a greater degree than either before or since, an extension of their domestic roles into the labour market. Thus women made up 53% of those employed in textiles in Hamburg in

1895, 59% of workers in the clothes manufacture and cleaning trade, and 39% of those involved in the hotel and refreshment business. Only about 2,000 people worked in textiles, but the other two trades were major employers. Moreover, 56% of those active in clothes and cleaning and 39% of those in the hotel and refreshment trade were (at least nominally) self-employed, according to the 1895 figures, and many of these people, again, were women. Both these trades had an average or slightly below average cholera morbidity rate, though the figures may be slightly underestimated because of the high proportion of the self-employed.[21]

It was in domestic service that working women ran the highest risk of infection. As we have seen, the morbidity rate among domestic servants and dependants was very high, over 58 per 1,000 in fact. Nearly three-quarters of workers in this category (73%, to be exact) were female, according to the occupational census of 1895. Their roles in middle-class households, as we saw earlier in this chapter, were likely to bring them into constant danger of infection. The low case-specific mortality rate for domestic servants in Figure 19 is deceptive. The rates, it must be remembered, were calculated for workers and dependants, including infants and small children, whose case-specific mortality rates were extremely high. Domestic servants were predominantly unmarried and so hardly any of them had children. Moreover, servants were concentrated in the age-group 15–35, where case-specific mortality rates were lowest anyway. These two features were unique to domestic servants and greatly lowered the case-specific mortality rate which they and their dependants suffered. Even so, cholera mortality in this group, at an estimated 23.6 per 1,000, was almost twice the average cholera mortality rate for the city as a whole in 1892, and more than that of any other occupational group. In the middle-class areas, indeed, cholera among women was predominantly a disease of servants. The Health Commission for Harvestehude, for example, reported that 26 out of the 47 women who caught cholera in 1892, some 65%, were domestic servants. Only 20 men caught the disease, and only 14 children. These figures suggest, once more, how domestic servants acted as a barrier between cholera and the bourgeoisie.[22] That this barrier was mainly female added further to the high excess mortality of women, above all in the age-group 20–30, but also to a lesser extent in the age-groups 15–20 and 30–40 as well.

The conclusion seems to be, therefore, that it was above all women's domestic roles, in preparing and cooking food, in washing, cleaning the house, and doing the dishes, and in looking after infants and small children

[21] See the Statistical Appendix for source references to this and the following paragraph.

[22] StA Hbg, MK III A 13 (Harvestehude). These figures are probably underestimates since they do not include cases of *cholera nostras* or 'diarrhoea with vomiting' which were subsequently added to the official statistics. See the Statistical Appendix for further discussion. The rigid hygienic regime existing in bourgeois households during the epidemic, and the segregation of servants' living-quarters, reduced the danger of servants infecting their employers.

that exposed them directly to infection by cholera and boosted their mortality rate far beyond what it normally was in the adult age-groups where it fell to their lot to fill these roles. A secondary, contributory factor to the increase in female excess mortality was the employment of women in dangerous trades, above all domestic service. Finally, there is some evidence that women succumbed more easily to the onslaught of cholera when removed from the home and placed in the alienating environment of the hospital, particularly in the second week of the epidemic, when conditions were at their most chaotic. Against this, of course, we have to set the fact that men were particularly vulnerable because of their concentration in port and river work.

Table 9. Sex-specific cholera morbidity and mortality rates for St Georg Nord, 1892

	Population	Cases	Deaths	Morbidity (‰)	Mortality (‰)	Case-specific mortality (%)
Women	16,222	526	220	32.4	13.6	41.8
Men	14,234	455	126	17.9	8.9	27.6
Children (14 and under)	9,938	342	148	34.4	14.9	43.5
TOTAL	40,394	1,323	494	32.8	12.2	37.3

Source: StA Hbg MK III A 13: St. Georg-Norderteil, Bl. 4

Suggestive figures in this context are provided by the district of St Georg Nord, whose social composition was mixed, with fewer than 5% of its inhabitants employed in the harbour in 1900. Table 9 shows that morbidity and mortality rates, in the absence of a substantial port labour force, were much higher for women than for men. In cities where there was no major harbour on the Hamburg scale, a similar pattern emerged. In the 1866 epidemic in Berlin, for example, in the 20–30 age-group, the cholera mortality rate among women, at 8‰, was more than twice that among men, which stood at a mere 3‰. It was greater for women in all higher age-groups as well, with the smallest difference being in the 50–60 year-olds and the highest among the over-70s, where 25‰ of the women died of cholera but only 12‰ of the men. Hirsch thought that pregnancy and childbirth made things more difficult for women who caught cholera,

but mainly the prevalence of women among the victims, which is indeed tremendous, is likely to be a consequence of the fact that the mature part of the female sex is more exposed to infection than the corresponding part of the male, because they are engaged in the handling and cleaning of the underwear and bed-linen that has been polluted by choleraic excretions.

Unlike Hamburg, Berlin was not first and foremost a port, but an administrative centre, so far fewer male workers were directly exposed to cholera in the course of doing their job than was the case in Hamburg in 1892. This accounts no doubt for the higher female cholera mortality rate (relative to the male cholera mortality rate) in the Prussian capital.[23]

In earlier epidemics in Hamburg, male cholera morbidity and mortality was far higher than female: in 1848, for example, cholera morbidity in the city, St Georg, and St Pauli stood at 26.6‰ for men, compared to 19.6‰ for women, while the mortality figures showed a similar difference (12.6‰ compared to 9.5‰). Dr Buek ascribed this not only to the predominance of men in the worst-affected occupations (sailors, boatmen, harbour workers) but also to the fact that drunkenness, which he held to be a major cause of infection, was a male vice. In some areas of the city the difference between the sexes was even more pronounced than on average: in St Pauli, for instance, a strong centre of port employment, male cholera mortality was almost double the female rate, at 14.5‰ compared with 7.9‰.[24] As port employment became relatively less dominant with the diversification of the local economy during the course of industrialization, so the predominance of men among the victims of cholera epidemics underwent a corresponding decline. Hamburg's status as a port ensured that male harbour workers were heavily represented among the victims even in 1892. Yet while this contrasted sharply with the situation in an inland administrative and industrial centre such as Berlin, Hamburg's experience cannot simply be dismissed as 'untypical'. Especially earlier in the century, inland waterways played a much more important role than in the railway age of the 1860s and after, and the rivers which flowed through all major inland towns also served as direct sources of domestic water in the days before municipal waterworks had become the norm. The typical sex structure of cholera victims in 1832 and 1848 may have been closer to that of Hamburg in 1892 than that of Berlin in 1866.[25] Rather than search for typicality, however, it is in the end more sensible to accept that the experience of individual towns varied according to the presence of vulnerable occupations, the nature of the water-supply, the extent and severity of the epidemic, housing and living conditions, and all the other variables discussed in this chapter. All of these factors depended in the last resort on the social and political structure of the city and the political and social beliefs of those who lived in it.

III

Social inequality in the face of cholera had many dimensions. Rich and poor, young and old, male and female were all affected by the disease to varying,

[23] Hirsch, 'Die Cholera-Epidemie', p. 309.
[24] StA Hbg. MK III A 2 Bd. 1, Bl. 84, Bl. 121, Table IX.
[25] E. R. Ocaña, *El coléra de 1834 en Granada. Enfermedad catastrófica y crisis social* (Granada, 1983), shows that the normal pattern of sex-specific mortality, with male death rates higher than female, was reversed in the cholera year of 1834 (p. 95).

measurable degrees, as were those who lived in different parts of the city and those who did different jobs. Yet these dimensions of inequality were also connected with one another in various ways. Fundamental to them all was the structurally determined poverty which was such a striking feature of Hamburg society in the late nineteenth century. Those who were denied the opportunity to acquire a skill, an education, or the training for a career—and these were the overwhelming majority of the population—were forced to sell their labour power cheaply. For men this meant above all unskilled work in the harbour; for women, domestic service, followed by marriage and housekeeping. All these kinds of work already increased the risk of infection from cholera in themselves, but the fact that they were poorly paid, or even, in the case of housework, not paid at all, made things even worse by condemning those engaged in them to live in overcrowded and insanitary housing, often without a bathroom or proper facilities for cooking and boiling water and milk. Malnutrition lowered their resistance; poverty prevented them from escaping the city altogether; the need to carry on working made it impossible for them to isolate themselves from possible sources of infection outside the home.

The better-off sections of Hamburg's population were protected from cholera by a number of influences. Their work seldom brought them into contact with the deadly waters of the harbour and the fleets; they could afford to live in spacious, well-ventilated accommodation, with their own kitchens, they were notoriously well-nourished, and they had the time and the money to flee the city if they wanted. Most importantly, they had servants. This was not a sign of extreme wealth, as it is today; on the contrary, it was almost a necessary part of being middle-class. Most people earning over 5,000 Marks a year probably had at least one servant. Over half of all the households in Hamburg's two most bourgeois districts, Harvestehude and Rotherbaum, had servants, and over 40% in the almost equally middle-class district of Hohenfelde. This enabled the bourgeois householders to arrange for all their water to be boiled, their children to be checked and controlled, their houses to be kept clean and disinfected, and their own dealings with the outside world to be reduced to a minimum. And besides this, they also had their own bathrooms, where they could be insulated from the danger of infection from other families. Of all the factors that enabled the middle classes to escape infection, the employment of servants, along with the possession of a dwelling with a separate bathroom, was by far the most significant.[26]

Yet the social distribution of cholera was also conditioned by other, less tangible factors. The uncertainties of proletarian existence encouraged values which paid scant attention to planning, saving, and taking precautions for the days ahead. Illness and death were already so familiar to the poor that

---

[26] In multiple regression analysis these turned out to be the only two significant independent variables. For more detailed discussion, see Section VIII of the Statistical Appendix.

fatalism seemed the only way of coping with their ever-present threat. Denied an adequate education, especially if they were women, for whom there was little effective schooling before the introduction of state primary education in 1871, they found it hard to read and understand the complex bureaucratic language of the instructions on avoiding cholera distributed to them by the Social Democrats. Even had they wished to take heed of these warnings, the sheer physical problems of putting them into practice in the absence of adequate heating facilities and water-supplies were overwhelming. All this was made a great deal worse by the large families that the poor continued to have. A high birth rate among the proletariat was not so much a product of ignorance, though ignorance there certainly was, as the outcome of a continued need for additional sources of income and support for the family. Once out of infancy the working-class child was put to work as soon as possible in part-time jobs, not only to help the family in general, but also to provide some degree of security against the possibility that illness or incapacity would rob the family of one of its major bread-winners. Infants and small children in large numbers were difficult to control in the absence of servants; they quickly became major sources of infection, because they were generally more susceptible to cholera than other age-groups were. Malnutrition and unhygienic living conditions combined to ensure that it was the children of the working classes who suffered most.

By contrast, the middle classes had already started limiting their families in the search for increased wealth and status. There was, indeed, a noticeable negative correlation between the birth rate and the presence of economically independent persons in the occupied population of each district (-0.69), matched by a corresponding positive correlation between the birth rate and the proportion of manual labourers (0.67). Children were a burden on the bourgeois family because of the expensive education they required; nor was it thought proper to send them out to work at an early age. Moreover, the bourgeois values of cleanliness and caution also came into play during the cholera epidemic; for some, indeed, it had been normal to boil the tap-water before using it since the typhoid epidemic of the late 1880s. The bourgeois respect for authority, especially when authority was incorporated in the figure of Germany's best-known medical scientist, Robert Koch, further encouraged the observation of the recommended precautions. This was made possible, of course, by the armies of servants that peopled the villa quarters around the Alster, but the regime of meticulous cleanliness and order instituted in many middle-class households during the epidemic and for some time afterwards was in many ways ideally suited to the bourgeois temperament. So much was this the case, in fact, that some middle-class inhabitants of the city, as we have seen, began to try and enforce these norms on complete strangers in the street, and waxed indignant when the working class failed to obey them.[27]

[27] See above, pp. 411-13.

Particularly strong was the indignation voiced by the dominant classes about what they regarded as the slovenliness of the working-class housewife during the epidemic. This was an age when the bourgeois ideal of 'separate spheres'—the home for women, the world for men—was at its height, and bourgeois anxieties about the influence of Social Democracy on the family were becoming steadily more acute. Social Democratic theory and propaganda were certainly more critical of the family as an institution than they were subsequently to become, but at this time the party had virtually no support among women, and the Social Democratic man was not yet interested in encouraging his wife to join the party, in contrast to the situation after the turn of the century.[28] There were 'separate spheres' in the working class too, as men led their own social life in pubs and clubs, trade unions, and party meetings, and left the home to their womenfolk to look after. Working-class women also had less contact with and trust in medical services than men. If they were unable to institute the new hygienic order demanded of them during the 1892 epidemic, this was because they lacked the facilities and often, too, the time to do so, especially if they were working long hours outside the home, as most of them did. Since mid-century a middle-class offensive directed at introducing bourgeois notions of cleanliness and order into the working-class family had been slowly gathering pace; charitable organizations (often run by middle-class women) had been attempting to establish domestic economy classes for proletarian housewives, books offering advice on how to keep house had been appearing in ever-increasing numbers, and even the law took a hand, with the introduction of obligatory lunch-breaks and maximum hours for working mothers.[29] Yet by the early 1890s this hygienic offensive had little to show for itself. Only after the turn of the century did it begin to register any tangible success. Just how far it had to go was amply demonstrated by women's experience in the cholera epidemic of 1892. In the absence of strict hygienic precautions, cooking, cleaning, and looking after infants in the circumstances of a cholera epidemic exposed women to a massively increased threat of infection and death compared to that of a normal year, when their domestic role brought them few such striking dangers and ensured that female mortality rates were usually lower than male. When women were carried out of their separate sphere and into the frightening, alien chaos of the cholera hospital, the resulting experience took a further toll, much greater than that exacted from men.

The epidemic of 1892 therefore not only affected different groups in the population in different ways and to different degrees, it also brought existing social antagonisms out into the open. The fundamental social reality was the

[28] See R. J. Evans, *Sozialdemokratie und Frauenemanzipation im deutschen Kaiserreich* (Bonn and Berlin, 1979).

[29] U. Frevert, ' "Fürsorgliche Belagerung": Hygienebewegung und Arbeiterfrauen im 19. und 20. Jahrhundert', *Geschichte und Gesellschaft*, 11 (1980), 420–46.

disproportionate impact of the disease on the working class. But perceptions of that reality, and even more, as we have seen, ascriptions of its origin, differed widely according to the social and political standpoint of the observer. The reaction to the epidemic was thus not a unified one, nor was it a simple response to an objective fact: rather, it was mediated through a whole existing range of economic interests, social antagonisms, and political ideologies. The pressures that built up during the epidemic were in many ways irresistible: pressures for sanitary reform and housing improvement, pressures for a drastic extension of state interference in society, pressures for the subordination of mercantile interests to the wider public good, pressures for democratic constitutional change. But while these pressures could not entirely be resisted, they could nevertheless be deflected, accommodated, or incorporated into the restructuring of bourgeois rule that was already under way. In the resulting process the parallelogram of forces which assailed the dominant classes in Hamburg in 1892 was realigned: the world the merchants made was now remade, but in ways that were often surprising and with effects that few in the autumn of 1892 would have been able to predict.

6

Remaking a World

a. *The Limits of Compassion*

I

THE impact of cholera on nineteenth-century culture has been a source of increasing fascination for historians over the last quarter of a century, as the growth of social history has turned their attention away from high politics, wars, and diplomacy to the everyday experience of ordinary people in the past. In 1961, Asa Briggs noted that 'a study of the history of cholera in the nineteenth century . . . is an important and neglected chapter in social history'; and in calling for further research on the subject, he enumerated a number of areas in which he considered its importance to lie. Cholera, he wrote,

hit the poor particularly ruthlessly, thriving on the kind of conditions in which they lived. Whenever it threatened European countries, it quickened social apprehensions. Wherever it appeared, it tested the efficiency and resilience of local administrative structures. It exposed relentlessly political, social and moral shortcomings. It prompted rumours, suspicions and at times violent social conflict. It inspired not only sermons but novels and works of art.[1]

Four years later, Roderick McGrew declared that 'cholera scored the European social consciousness, exacerbated contemporary tensions, intensified the impact of current social problems, and as it did so, revealed fundamental characteristics of European life and outlook'. He called for its study in terms of social psychology, as a 'massive social trauma which affected European culture, and which, if properly understood, could deepen historical perception'.[2] Similarly, Charles Rosenberg, writing in 1965, the same year as McGrew, noted that

an epidemic, if sufficiently severe, necessarily evokes responses in every sector of society . . . Values and attitudes, especially in the areas of religion, of traditionalism and innovation are, for example, inevitably displayed during an epidemic . . . An epidemic . . . provides a convenient and effective sampling device for studying in their structural relationship some of the fundamental components of social change.[3]

---

[1] A. Briggs, 'Cholera and Society in the 19th Century', *Past and Present*, 19 (1961), p. 76.
[2] R. McGrew, *Russia and the Cholera 1823–32* (Wisconsin, 1965), p. 3.
[3] C. Rosenberg, *The Cholera Years 1832–1859* (Chicago, 1962), p. 452.

And, writing more recently, Michael Durey has remarked that 'epidemics ... can ... be used as a medium whereby the whole of past societies can be studied, for their arrival always unsettled the normal functioning of society, and brought to the surface latent social antagonisms'. Society's response to cholera, he argued, could reveal 'much about its character which is not easily observable during periods of peace and relative harmony, or at least when underlying social tensions are hidden by the crust of formal social relationships'.[4]

As these quotations suggest, historians have not been slow to take up Asa Briggs's appeal for more research. Since the original appearance of his article a quarter of a century ago, a number of important monographs have appeared, and the subject can no longer be said to be a neglected one. First, a major point of his article was a call for international comparative research. 'Comparison of different national responses to cholera', he wrote, 'is revealing in illuminating general problems in comparative national history':

A systematic comparison of the role of cholera in modern social history at different times and in different places ... would have to take account of at least five sets of facts—first, the facts of demography, including antecedent and later mortality rates and the incidence of cholera in terms of area, occupation, age and so on; second, the facts of economic and social structure, and economic and social relations, including facts relating to the type and size of community and relations not only between rich and poor but between 'authorities' and 'subjects'; third, political circumstances, the immediate context of the cholera outbreaks; fourth, the structure of government, administration and finance, and the relationship of government effort to voluntary effort, including charity, and help from outside; and fifth, the extent of medical knowledge and popular attitudes towards that knowledge.[5]

Since Briggs wrote these words, there have been monographic studies of cholera in Britain, France, Russia, Canada, the United States, Spain, and Sweden, but none of them really attempts international comparison in a serious way; all operate very much within the confines of their respective national historiographies.[6]

Secondly, Briggs made a particular point of stressing comparisons between the initial epidemic of 1830–2 and subsequent outbreaks later in the century. Yet the monographic literature has concentrated overwhelmingly on the former. Norman Longmate devoted over half his general account of cholera

[4] M. Durey, *The Return of the Plague. British Society and the Cholera 1831–32* (Dublin, 1979). p. 1.

[5] Briggs, op. cit., p. 89.

[6] Durey, op. cit.; R. J Morris, *Cholera 1832: The Social Response to an Epidemic* (London, 1976); McGrew, op. cit.; Rosenberg, op. cit.; G. Bilson, *A Darkened House: Cholera in Nineteenth-century Canada* (Toronto, 1980); B. Zacke, *Koleraepidemien i Stockholm 1834. En socialhistorisk Studie* (Monografien utgivne av Stockholms Kommunalforvaltning, 32, Stockholm, 1971); F. Delaporte, *Disease and Civilization: The Cholera in Paris, 1832* (London, 1986); E. Rodriguez Ocaña, *El cólera de 1834 en Granada. Enfermedad catastrófica y crisis social* (Granada, 1983).

in Great Britain, *King Cholera* (1966), to 1830–2, the studies of Morris (1976) and Durey (1980) on Britain and McGrew (1965) on Russia deal exclusively with these years, Chevalier's earlier (1958) study of France again concentrates heavily on the outbreaks of the 1830s and 1840s, as does Delaporte's recent work (1986). The scholarly literature on cholera in Sweden is confined to the initial, devastating outbreak of 1834, and that on Spain almost exclusively to the same period (1833–5). This concentration is understandable, perhaps, because of the dramatic nature of the disease's first arrival in Europe. As McGrew has remarked,

The first epidemic ... came when the disease was generally unknown, and it wrote its effects on an unmarked slate. Ignorance sharpened social reactions; the administration, working without experience's guide, hastily devised expedients which clearly showed the weaknesses in its own organization, while the medical profession exhibited its resources and resourcefulness under the most difficult circumstances. Unprepared as Russia was for the cholera, her reaction had the special truthfulness of unconscious reflex.[7]

Yet the cholera epidemic of 1830–2 was only the first in a long series which haunted Western Europe almost until the end of the century and Russia even longer. There were subsequent severe outbreaks across Europe in 1847–9, 1853–4, 1865–6, 1873, 1884, and 1892–3.[8] These later epidemics have been of little interest to historians.[9] Partly this is because the shock of cholera wore off after the early 1830s, and so its power to challenge society was correspondingly diminished; partly it is a matter of source material, which—in the German case at least—is far more abundant for the epidemic of 1831–2 than for the outbreaks of the next half-century. But neither of these considerations holds good for 1892. Its very exceptionality, its uniquely late occurrence in the history of cholera, generated a vast outpouring of source material, enhanced by the fact that—unlike the earlier outbreaks—it fell squarely within the age of statistics, photography, and the mass newspaper press. Moreover, concentrated as it was in a single city, it brought to bear on the people and institutions who were held responsible pressures and challenges greater than any experienced since the original outbreak sixty years before.

For cholera, it has been argued, posed a general challenge to society and elicited an appropriately broad response. As Morris has remarked, cholera was 'a test of social cohesion. To follow the cholera track was not just, as some observers claimed, to follow the track of filth and poverty, it was to

---

[7] McGrew, op. cit., p. 5.

[8] See Chapter 3c, above.

[9] The epidemic of 1847–9, studied by Chevalier (ed.), *Le choléra. La première épidémie du XIXe siècle* (Paris, 1958), is a partial exception. See also N. M. Frieden, 'The Russian Cholera Epidemic 1892–93, and Medical Professionalization', *Journal of Social History*, 10 (1977), 538–59. Rosenberg, op. cit., also devotes some attention to the epidemics of 1849 and 1866.

watch the trust and co-operation between different parts of society strained to the utmost.' In his study of the British cholera epidemic of 1832, Morris asked, therefore, whether British society had the 'cohesion and stability to face the cholera'. He concluded that it did; the middle classes did not panic, and despite the fact that the epidemic was raging at the height of a deep and often violent political crisis over the Great Reform Bill of 1832, society none the less in a short while 'returned to stable equilibrium'.[10] Michael Durey, in his more recent and more thorough study, has devoted greater attention to the outbreaks of popular violence and rioting which accompanied the epidemic, but he concludes by referring to 'the essential stability of British society in 1832'. It was a stability which, as some historians have argued, was expressed in the way in which cholera acted as a stimulus to a whole range of sanitary reforms, to a series of transformations in the administration of public health, to the initiation of major schemes of slum clearance, and to long-term improvements in housing and living conditions. Finally, if the initial outbreak of this frightening and previously unknown disease did cause a certain amount of understandable panic in some quarters, public responses soon became calmer and more rational, thus providing further evidence of social stability.[11]

Cholera as a test of the social and political system has occupied a central place in most of the non-medical literature on the subject, and it provides a guiding thread that runs through the present study as well. But we need to be very careful and circumspect in handling this way of approaching cholera. Neither Morris nor Durey offers any guidance as to how social stability can be measured, nor how its breakdown can be defined. The only acceptable evidence of a collapse of social stability in the eyes of most historians who have dealt with the subject of British cholera in 1832 would probably be the occurrence of a social revolution on the lines of France in 1789 or Russia in 1905 or 1917, or the outbreak of civil war; a breakdown in the mechanisms by which different kinds of people in a given society tolerate each other's existence. But it takes a lot more than an epidemic to cause the destruction of a political and social system. The Aztecs and Incas of sixteenth-century America, while suffering appalling losses from new diseases imported by the invading Europeans, might have survived had they not been simultaneously confronted by a ruthless and unscrupulous enemy, equipped with infinitely superior weaponry, and determined to enslave and destroy them.[12] Even in John Wyndham's celebrated science-fiction novel *The Day of the Triffids*, which portrays a world in which the human race begins to return to a state of nature after having been struck blind by a passing comet, the final breakdown

---

[10] Morris, *Cholera 1832*, p. 17.

[11] Durey, *The Return of the Plague*, p. 215.

[12] Contrast W. H. McNeill, *Plagues and Peoples* (Oxford, 1977) with J. Hemmings, *The Conquest of the Incas* (London, 1970).

of society is only achieved by means of an invasion of man-eating plants. As Paul Slack has suggested, it seems that epidemics only led to a breakdown of social order where their impact was really extreme. Any society would be paralysed by the sudden death of the larger part of its members; where, as was always the case with cholera, in contrast to bubonic plague, only a small minority of people succumbed, the epidemic was more likely to lead to social reform than social collapse.[13] So while the idea of cholera as a challenge to society and as a test of its capacity to function effectively under stress is an important one, the metaphor of 'social stability' is too vague to get us very far. Just as important, it lacks any kind of concept of how societies change. It seems to imply that all societies are functionally self-regulating mechanisms which can only be disturbed by intrusions from without. Here too, there is a problem, for as we have seen throughout this book, cholera was a man-made disease, a product of industry and empire and the conflicts they generated, not merely a stimulus to change, but a consequence of it as well.[14]

It is scarcely surprising, therefore, that exaggerated expectations of the possible effects of cholera have been regarded by some historians with a high degree of scepticism. Margaret Pelling, for example, has pointed out that cholera was relatively unimportant as a cause of death and debility in the mid-nineteenth century; it was outweighed by other epidemic diseases such as typhoid, smallpox, and measles, and 'accounted for only a very small proportion of the area of highest mortality, which occurred among infants and young children'.[15] Moreover, as she noted, 'all the known epidemic diseases were exceeded in incidence and effect by the many forms of tuberculosis'. Pelling conceded only that it was 'assumed' by historians that cholera, because of its novelty and its sudden and devastating visitations, acted as a stimulus to reform. In reality, however, she argued,

probably on all levels, cholera was a distraction rather than an impetus to reform, and ... strenuous efforts had to be made at the time by reformers hoping to modify the reaction to it for their own ends. This is most clearly exemplified ... by the relation between interest in cholera, and concern over fever, of the greater importance of which as a perennial cause of death and debility, nineteenth-century public-health reformers were definitively aware ... Some effort was expended during the first epidemic, and a great deal more invested just before the second, some twenty years later, not to base the sanitary cause on the threat of cholera, but to force cholera, with respect to both theory and practice, into the same category as what was called 'the ordinary fever of the country'. It is partly as a result of these efforts that we are encouraged to assume that sanitary reform began with the first cholera epidemic.[16]

[13] P. Slack, *The Impact of Plague in Tudor and Stuart England* (London, 1985).
[14] See Chapter 3c, above.
[15] M. Pelling, *Cholera, Fever and English Medicine 1825–1865* (Oxford, 1978).
[16] Ibid., pp. 5–6.

Thus the independent effects of cholera on sanitary reform were slight, and its usefulness to the historian as a source of insights into the theories and experiences behind the sanitary movement of the nineteenth century limited.

There can be no doubting the devastating psychological effect of cholera, however, and its impact on infant mortality was far greater than historians such as Pelling have assumed. Cholera was not a distraction to reformers, not least because it was not as difficult as Pelling supposes to fit it into already existing theories of the causes of disease; they used it to reinforce their arguments, rather than discounting it as an aberration. In fact, a number of students of cholera previous to Pelling pointed out that the impact of cholera on sanitary reform was very limited. R. J. Morris stressed in his study of 1976 the lack of any real influence of the epidemic on sanitary improvement in Britain, and Charles Rosenberg noted in the case of the United States of America that all administrative reforms resulting from the epidemics were short-lived and left no permanent traces behind. The fundamental point of this argument commands respect, as a consideration of the German evidence readily indicates. It has been as widely argued in the German as in the British case that cholera was the "'great teacher" of practical hygiene and public health reform in the 19th century', as the sociologist Florian Tennstedt has called it. Tennstedt has argued that 'the danger of epidemics effected a series of measures of urban sanitation' right through the century up to and including the aftermath of the epidemic of 1892. But he presents no direct evidence to support this claim, relying instead on a single contemporary source which makes cholera responsible not only for improvements in the water-supply but also for stricter controls on foodstuffs, the construction of sewage systems, and the reform of medical regulations.[17]

As we have seen, the cholera epidemic of 1831–2 and 1848–9 did not lead to any major sanitary reforms. Sanitary movements, such as that led by Max von Pettenkofer in the 1850s and 1860s, or the German Association for Public Health (*Deutscher Verein für öffentliche Gesundheitspflege*), founded in 1875 but originating in a periodical first published in 1869, were not called into being solely by cholera, cast their net widely to catch typhoid and other fevers, and attempted to assimilate epidemics to their existing focus on improvements of the health-related infrastructure rather than the other way round. There is some evidence that public debate on sanitary reform reached new heights after 1866–7, but this was arguably not only because of the impact of the cholera epidemics of those years but also because of a stronger tendency towards the foundation of nationwide conferences and organizations in the wake of the establishment of the North German Confederation and (in 1871) the German Empire. In any case, as Ute Frevert has pointed

[17] F. Tennstedt, *Sozialgeschichte der Sozialpolitik in Deutschland. Vom 18. Jahrhundert bis zum Ersten Weltkrieg* (Göttingen, 1982), pp. 207–10; Morris, *Cholera 1832*, p. 197; Rosenberg, *The Cholera Years*, p. 98.

out, the sanitary reform movement which began in the late 1860s had little immediate impact on national or local administration. It was not until the late 1870s, when the danger of cholera was thought to have receded, that sanitary reforms began to take place in Berlin and elsewhere, and here, as we have seen, the impact of epidemic diseases was mainly indirect, and only one among a number of different influences.[18]

The standard reaction of Central European governments to the arrival of cholera in 1831–2 was to dust off their old files on the plague, dating from well over a century before, and reactivate the resources that had traditionally been mobilized against the great epidemics of the early modern period. Their reaction to the failure of these measures was either to continue them in a diluted form, where bureaucratic inertia continued to favour the application of policing techiques in the face of social threats, or to abandon them altogether where the interests of trade were strong enough to force through a policy of *laissez-faire*. It was only when the medical profession had gained sufficient social standing to make its influence felt, in the 1860s and 1870s, that medical ideas such as Pettenkofer's began to elbow policing techniques aside, and even then only against the background of broader changes in state–society relations in the era of incipient liberalism.[19] Cholera prevention was only one among many considerations here; in Hamburg, indeed, the major catalyst of sanitary reform was not the cholera epidemic of 1832 but the Great Fire, ten years later. The epidemic of 1873 did lead directly to an attempt to introduce measures such as the filtration of the water-supply and the extension of the sewage system, but, as we saw in Chapter 2, these attempts quickly ran in to opposition and met with little immediate success.[20] The German evidence, then, supports the view that the historian should be properly sceptical of William McNeill's thesis that micro-organisms have commonly transformed or destroyed state structures in world history.[21] As Bill Luckin has remarked, 'the "autonomous" impact of disease can be exaggerated at the expense of an analysis of the socio-political and economic nexus which largely determined mass epidemic mortality'.[22]

Yet there are good reasons for arguing that Hamburg in 1892 constituted something of an exception to this rule. This was to a large extent because of the fact that cholera failed to strike elsewhere. The outbreak in Hamburg

---

[18] U. Frevert, *Krankheit als politisches Problem. Soziale Unterschichten in Preussen zwischen medizinischer Polizei und staatlicher Sozialversicherung* (Göttingen, 1984), pp. 232–41; see also Chapter 3c, above, and G. Göckenjahn, *Kurieren und Staat machen. Gesundheit und Medizin in der Bürgerlichen Welt* (Frankfurt, 1985), p. 109.

[19] For this argument, see Chapter 3c, above.

[20] C. Wischermann, *Wohnen in Hamburg vor dem Ersten Weltkrieg* (Münster, 1983), pp. 333–5, points out the connection between the 1873 epidemic and the Sewage Law of 1875, but overestimates the importance of the latter considerably.

[21] McNeill, *Plagues and Peoples*.

[22] B. Luckin, 'States and Epidemic Threats', *Bulletin of the Society for the Social History of Medicine*, 34 (1984), 25–7.

thus caused everyone—quite correctly—to regard the peculiarities of the city's social and political structure as a major cause. But there was another reason too. Collective aggression in the wake of epidemics in medieval and early modern Europe was directed against Jews, witches, and other scapegoats, often outsiders to the community, but equally often hated groups within it; it was virtually never directed against the state,[23] until the state became sufficiently strong to be able to impose cordons sanitaires and special policing arrangements for the sick and the dead, which is to say, only in the age of absolutism which reached its height towards the end of the eighteenth century.[24] The stronger the state, the more likely it was to be blamed. Thus the objects of aggression in the cholera riots that flared across Europe at the beginning of the 1830s varied from the Tsarist bureaucracy at one extreme to British anatomists at the other: in Prussia, for example during the Königsberg riots of 1831, both seem to have been roughly equal targets of crowd anger, reflecting the intermediate status of Prussia between Russian absolutism and British *laissez-faire*. All over Europe, however, including the Tsarist empire, the medical profession paid for its claim to understand the causes of epidemics by becoming the object of widespread popular opprobrium. The authorities never took the blame alone.

As Luckin has argued, it was only much later, predominantly in the twentieth century, that the era of mass medicalization backed by national and local governments led to popular recriminations over mass mortality being directed solely at the state.

Anger and despair following mass mortality were most unlikely to make themselves felt at high levels of the state apparatus when society as a whole had become more fully medicalised: when, that is, reformers had become involved in the medical problems of new urban societies in north and north-west Europe and when mass consciousness had itself been imprinted by medical ideologies and (useful or useless) forms of medical explanation.

Since mass medicalization post-dated the epidemiological revolution, 'battle', he concludes, 'was therefore joined not over epidemics of typhus and typhoid but differentials in infant and maternal mortality and the relationship between unemployment and ill-health'.[25] When the cholera epidemic hit Hamburg in 1892, however, Germany was a society on the threshold of this transition to mass medicalization. A last rotten bloom of the age of epidemics, it fell in a period when the educative influence of Koch and the bacteriologists—purveyed in Hamburg through mass leafletting, comprehensive disinfection, popular newspaper reports, and the like—was already having a substantial

[23] J. Delumeau, *Angst im Abendland. Die Geschichte kollektiver Ängste im Europa des 14. bis 18. Jahrhunderts* (Reinbek bei Hamburg, 1985), i. 182–99.
[24] Luckin, op. cit.
[25] Ibid.

effect on public opinion.[26] Thus political activists of all shades quickly accepted Koch's theory that cholera was caused by unfiltered water, poor housing, and inadequate sanitation; they linked this to social inequality and the absence of constitutional democracy, and blamed the state.[27] The shock of cholera in 1892, far more than in earlier epidemics, generated massive pressures for social and political reform. It is now time to see how the dominant classes of Hamburg responded.

II

When a disaster such as that of the Hamburg cholera epidemic of 1892 occurs, two immediate responses are generally produced amidst all the recriminations. The first is the activation of charitable activities to help the survivors. These were not slow in coming. Along with the criticisms, massive sums of money also flowed into Hamburg from the rest of Germany and indeed the world. Emperor Wilhelm II alone donated 50,000 Marks for the care of orphans, a gesture which even won him recognition from the *Hamburger Nachrichten*, the organ of his arch-enemy Bismarck.[28] Far more important in every way, however, were the charitable activities which unfolded in Hamburg itself. Philanthropy, as we have seen, had always played an important role in legitimizing social inequality in the city;[29] in the crisis of 1892, which dramatized the differences of wealth and poverty in the city as never before, it quickly became central to the self-defence of the dominant classes. In subsequent years it became an essential element in their efforts to deflect the hostile accusations of their critics. As soon as the full dimensions of the epidemic became clear, as Carl August Schröder, a conservative lawyer and Senator from 1899 to 1918, later wrote, 'a common philanthropy developed, knowing no class differences or party antagonisms, but only seeking to help the afflicted and unite to fight against the plague'.[30] Senator Gustav Hertz pointed with pride to 'the vigorous and judicious practical activity which everyone is undertaking in the interests of all'. Community solidarity in the face of external threat and experienced disaster was what these and countless other similar statements never tired of emphasizing.[31]

The mobilization of Hamburg's philanthropic resources began as the collapse of trade and business in the wake of the quarantine imposed on the city from outside left merchants, traders, and industrialists with time on their

[26] See Chapter 4a, above.
[27] See Chapter 4d, above.
[28] StA Hbg. Senat, Cl. VII, Lit. Ta, Pars 2, Vol. 11, Fasc. 17, Inv. 1a: *Hamburger Nachrichten*, 22 Oct. 1892.
[29] See Chapter 1c, above.
[30] C. A. Schröder, *Aus Hamburgs Blütezeit* (Hamburg, 1921), p. 83.
[31] StA Hbg, FA Gustav Hertz B17: Gustav Hertz, letter of 8 Sept. 1892.

hands and little to do with it in the office.[32] On 31 August 1892, when the Chamber of Commerce issued a public appeal for the creation of an Aid Committee (*Hülfs-Comité*), 331 businesses and individuals responded. On 2 September a meeting at the Chamber resulted in the creation of an Executive Committee of 26 people, which called the following day for the founding of local Emergency Committees (*Notstandskomités*), one to be set up by each Citizens' Club. In those areas where political differences had led to the existence of more than one Citizens' Club, these were asked to join together. Meanwhile the Executive Committee ensured that at least four of its members were always present in the Chamber of Commerce during business hours (9 to 5) to co-ordinate the campaign. Two or three plenary meetings were also held every week; and the Executive Committee appointed commissioners from its own ranks to conduct business with each of the separate local Committees. There were 26 local Committees altogether, each of which was more or less free to organize itself as it wished. Normally they set up specialist and local sub-committees, so that before long an elaborate organization had come into existence, involving the participation of a total of some 1,500 people. After the epidemic was over, many of these local Committees expressed their pride in the work they had done by producing sumptuously bound, elaborately printed reports in which their charitable activities were outlined in minute and exhaustive detail. Not surprisingly, given the fact that they were organized by the Citizens' Clubs, and given the source of their original inspiration, these Committees were overwhelmingly male and middle class in composition. Schoolteachers were especially prominent; in Eimsbüttel they made up 77 out of the total of 131 members. In the poorest parts of the town a noticeable role was also played by the better-off sections of the petty bourgeoisie: thus in Neustadt Nord, for example, the Committee members consisted of 15 master craftsmen, 11 shopkeepers, 11 merchants, salesmen, or brokers, 2 owners of private schools, 4 teachers (2 male, 2 female), 2 hotel owners, 2 propertied *rentiers*, 2 dentists, 1 physician, and 1 'artist'. This was very similar to the social composition of the local Poor Law authorities. In some areas, such as Altstadt Nord, the Committee contained virtually all the local Poor Law overseers; in many other areas co-operation with the Poor Law authorities was very close.[33]

The activities which the Emergency Committees undertook were formidable in their range. They included the provision of boiled water, disinfectants, fresh clothing and bedding, food and rent, the initial care of convalescents, widows and widowers and orphans, the support of people whose furniture

---

[32] This point is made by Paul Schurek's novel about the epidemic, *Das Leben geht weiter* (Stuttgart, 1940), p. 215.

[33] L. von Halle, F. Wolter, and G. Koch, *Die Cholera in Hamburg in ihren Ursachen und Wirkungen. Eine ökonomisch-medicinische Untersuchung* (Hamburg, 1895), passim; *Bericht des Executiv-Ausschusses des Nothstands-Comités über seine Tätigkeit zur Bekämpfung des durch die Cholera vom Herbst 1892 hervorgerufenen Nothstandes* (Hamburg, 1893) (copy in StA Hbg, MK III A 13).

and belongings had been destroyed by disinfectant, or who had had to move house, and more generally the provision of money to those temporarily without income because of the epidemic (not only many workers, but also many shopkeepers, especially dairymen and greengrocers, as well). The official Poor Law had its hands full in maintaining the support of those who were already under its auspices before the outbreak of the epidemic, though some now required and received additional help from the Emergency Committees. The photographic records of the epidemic provide plenty of evidence of the variety of philanthropic initiatives, from soup-kitchens in hastily erected wooden huts in the city's main public places, to orphanages and crèches for the infant children of the unfortunate victims. While the men of the Citizens' Clubs took the lead in organizing this enormous charitable effort, it was often their womenfolk who did the actual work.[34] Professional cooks were engaged to prepare the food, which was purchased in shops whose owners were thought to have suffered during the epidemic, and potato-peeling was also carried out by paid labour, but the thick soups or stews which were prepared by these people were ladled out by women volunteers, including some 'charming young ladies'. One such, noted a reporter, 'said to me on one occasion, she would never again in her life feel such spiritual fulfilment, because her activity in the field kitchen allowed her to gain a deep insight into the endlessly wretched poverty of the lower classes of the population'. But, he went on to admit, 'this young lady belonged to the few who used their position in the field kitchen to track down deserving poverty'; most, he implied, thought little more of it.[35]

The district Committees operated on a very considerable scale. The Barmbeck Emergency Committee, for example, collected nearly 14,000 Marks by 17 September and eventually gathered in well over 20,000 from the district's inhabitants. Many donations, it was claimed, came from labourers and artisans who lived in this heavily working-class district. The bulk of the Committee's funds, however—114,000 Marks in all—came from the central fund. With this the Committee supported between about 1,500 and 2,500 individuals every month until March.[36] The Uhlenhorst Emergency Committee, to take another example, gave out nearly 5,000 daily grants to over 20,000 people between 3 September and 1 December. Most of these were members of families who received repeated donations, two or three times a week for several weeks.[37] Time and again these activities were used by the defenders of the Senate to demonstrate the solidarity of Hamburg's inhabitants

---

[34] Von Halle, Wolter, and Koch, *Die Cholera*, 3.1.

[35] StA Hbg, PP S3490 Bd. 2: *Hamburger Freie Presse*, 21. Jan. 1894, 'Bilder aus der Zeit der Choleraepidemie in Hamburg', by G. C. H. von Salz, IV: 'Die Feldküchen'. See also Plate 32.

[36] *Bericht des Vorstandes des Barmbecker Hülfs-Comites über dessen Tätigkeit während der Cholera-Epidemie im Jahre 1892* (copy in StA Hbg, MK III A 13).

[37] StA Hbg, PP S3490 Bd. 2: *Hamburgischer Correspondent*, 14 Dec. 1892: 'Vereins-Angelegenheiten'.

during the epidemic, the sense of duty and humanity of the bourgeoisie, and the overcoming of class barriers and divisions in the face of the common threat. But the realites of the charitable effort were far more complex and far less reassuring than this rosy picture of community spirit would seem to suggest.

In the first place, considerable friction was caused by the problem of what to do with the Social Democrats, who would clearly have to be consulted if the charitable effort were to penetrate to the quarters where it was most needed. A general report on the Emergency Committees' activities in 1892 noted of the Social Democrats

that the members of this party brought a particular expertise to bear on behalf of the aims of emergency welfare because they stood in absolutely immediate contact with the circumstances that created the emergency situation (in individual families). Thus the problem was less one of whether expert welfare workers could be found among the members of the party in question, as one of whether there was a danger that they might perhaps abuse such a position for party-political ends.[38]

Nevertheless, several of the district Committees approached individual Social Democrats for help and found a ready response. Here was another example of the long-awaited acceptance of the party into the civic community. In some cases indeed it was the Social Democrats who made the first approach. As the *Börsen-Halle* declared, reporting on the results,

Thus courage, energy, and philanthropy have been active here; social and political differences have been wiped out in this period of grievous trouble. The Social Democratic Party has joined the ranks, and its co-operation has been welcomed gladly because of its exact knowledge of the circumstances of ordinary people.[39]

This too was part of the legend, as the experience of individual district Committees soon began to show.

The Emergency Committee in Barmbeck, which was one of the strongholds of Social Democracy in the city, was made up of propertied gentlemen, the pillars of the local Citizens' Club. The Committee subsequently reported that the debate over whether or not to include the Social Democrats had come to a head on 4 September, and wrote:

Although it was the purpose of the same (i.e. the Committee) to spur on all sections of the population in our suburb, as its appeal emphasized, to lend a helping hand in the fight against cholera, nevertheless we could under no circumstances accede to the demand made to us by the Social Democrats to co-opt six of their members into the Committee and pay them 6 Marks a day from the funds at our disposal.

The idea that the six Social Democrats should receive a daily allowance for their work broke all the rules of amateurism by which such charitable

[38] Von Halle *et al.*, *Die Cholera*, p. 4.
[39] StA Hbg, Senat, Cl. VII, Lit. Ta, Pars 2, Vol. 11, Fasc. 1b: *Börsen-Halle*, 12 Sept. 1892.

activities distinguished themselves. This passage in the report was followed by two more sentences which were pasted over with a blank piece of paper. Time, however, has reduced the effectiveness of this form of censorship, and by diligent peering one can make out the following passage underneath:

There developed an excited exchange of views on the subject. Nevertheless the above-mentioned party undertook the distribution of the appeal and three of its members voluntarily joined our flock of welfare workers, to co-operate in our task as far as they were able.[40]

The Social Democrats themselves, too, reported that 'as we declared that we would claim compensation for this, because our people only lived hand to mouth, the tune suddenly changed and our assistance was dispensed with, since it was thought that we should volunteer for this work in an honorary capacity'.[41] None the less, the party then decided to pay its representatives on the Emergency Committees from its own funds, spending a total of 2,400 Marks over the four weeks in the process. It could afford to do this all the more easily since it received a total of nearly 18,000 Marks in donations to help fight the epidemic from supporters in Hamburg, in the rest of Germany, and in other countries, including many socialists in the United States.[42] It spent some 18,100 Marks on supporting those hit by the epidemic, but did not donate any of this money to the official Emergency Committees because it saw in them the representatives of the capitalists who had caused the epidemic and who should therefore be left to fund the major part of the rescue operation from their own pockets.[43]

On 13 October the Social Democratic Association for the third Hamburg Reichstag electoral district—the largest in the city—held a meeting to take stock of the situation. 352 of the Association's 3,000 members were present, and a number of them reported on their experiences in the various Emergency Committees. A. Backer reported that the Barmbeck Committee had accepted his co-operation and advice, and that he had also been able to work independently under its auspices. Similarly, H. Schneider declared himself fully satisfied with the way the Eilbeck Committee had accepted him, elected him onto the Committee itself, and approved his actions. But others had had a less happy experience. K. Scholz, for example, who with some of his comrades had approached the Uhlenhorst Committee, reported 'that the Committee had rejected their help and he had been told that he had done his duty; he had protested, and says he was then shown the door'. He was supported by C. Offen, who complained 'that he was not allowed to speak at the Committee meeting'. Eventually, however, when he did manage to speak, it was to

[40] *Bericht . . . Barmbeck* (n. 36 above), p. 6.
[41] StA Hbg, PP S3469: Versammlungsbericht, 3. Reichstagswahlkreis, 13 Oct. 1892.
[42] Ibid.: *Hamburger Echo*, 3 Nov. 1893.
[43] Ibid.: Versammlungsbericht, 3. Reichstagswahlkreis, 13 Oct. 1892.

suggest that all those with an income of 3,000 Marks a year should donate 3 per cent of it within four weeks, so it was not surprising that he did not get a friendly reception. Other representatives reported that various Committees had rejected their suggestions, accused the Social Democrats of wanting to take out of their hands the work they had begun, or even refused to discuss their proposals at all. In Eimsbüttel most of the sub-committees refused to accept Social Democrats as members at all. Altogether only one Social Democrat—Schneider in Eilbeck—was actually co-opted onto a district Emergency Committee. All the others were permitted to function only as 'assistants' in the sub-districts.[44]

Even here, however, there were evident clashes. One district was moved to complain 'that the reports of Social Democratic welfare workers were not always reliable, that namely not only had some people been admitted who were not in need, but others had been dismissed who were'.[45] This complaint pointed in fact to an even more fundamental problem than that of co-operating with the Social Democrats. Over the previous years, as we saw in Chapter 1, Hamburg had been preparing to go over to the so-called 'Elberfeld system', of poor-relief, which indeed was due to come into effect at the very time of the epidemic.[46] Given the close contacts of the Emergency Committees with the Poor Law authorities, and the fact that many Poor Law overseers took an active role in the Committees,[47] it was scarcely surprising that the charitable effort launched to relieve the misery caused by the epidemic was in large measure steered by the principles which the Elberfeld system had prescribed for the poor. The fundamental principle here was that work rather than alms should be provided; and rigorous checks should be instituted to ensure that only the deserving poor received support. The early, rather hurried creation of the Emergency Committees soon revealed that these principles were being widely flouted. Application to the Committees, it was reported,

was recognized, and indeed more or less at the same time in all districts, as relatively the easiest way to obtain benefits, so that some who could be proved to have work, or were able to get some, were seduced into letting themselves be supported at the cost of the Emergency Welfare because there were no civil disadvantages connected with the receipt of such benefits, rather than earning their own living, by doing a job of work.[48]

For, as this report suggested, the advantage of charitable donations from the point of view of the poor was that they did not entail loss of civil rights, as receipt of state poor-relief did.

[44] Ibid.
[45] Von Halle *et al.*, *Die Cholera*, p. 4.
[46] See Chapter 1d, above.
[47] See above, pp. 100 and 479.
[48] *Bericht des Executiv-Ausschusses* (n. 33 above), p. 11.

The committees tried therefore to steer the recipients of their charity towards self-sufficiency. As the central Emergency Committee noted,

> Bread, greengrocery, dairy, or stoneware shops were established or already existing businesses of this sort purchased, for a large number of women, some have set up a lunch-time restaurant, others have begun a laundry, three have learnt cookery, three have taken lessons in hairdressing, some were provided with funds to undertake a midwifery course, some have set up a business dealing in Dutch goods. Very many were just assisted, however, through being provided with a sewing machine.[49]

In the true spirit of the Elberfeld system, the Emergency Committees thus forced their charges into some of the more menial, exploited, and insecure of female occupations.[50] But they were of course continually concerned that such people should not get ideas beyond their station. Thus they rejected out of hand the suggestion that they should set up a lottery, profitable though this would be, because 'with the sudden flood of such a large sum of money into its coffers, the claims of the needy would naturally grow to such an extent that the Committee and the district Committees would find the task of working in a rational manner made extraordinarily more difficult'.[51] The propertied public also clearly thought the poor should remain poor, for many of the donations in kind received by the Committees, above all from well-wishers outside the city, were virtually useless: 'I myself have seen', wrote one Committee worker, 'what kind of rags people sent us'.[52]

The Committees were almost obsessively concerned to ensure that they were not cheated by claimants. On 13–14 October the Poor Law Board met to devise measures to ensure that 'the misuse and exploitation of charity can be prevented'. It quickly devised a firm division of labour between the Poor Law and the emergency relief agencies. The Committees also took careful steps to make certain that claimants did not receive benefits from other, private charities at the same time. All claimants were issued with identity cards on which the sums of their grants were noted as they received them. They were asked to appear regularly at the Committees' offices, which were initially manned 12 hours a day.[53] As one observer commented later, 'impudence, cheek, laziness, greed, immorality very often forced themselves into the ranks of genuine need and blameless poverty'.[54] So the Emergency Com-

[49] Ibid., p. 21.

[50] R. Dasey, 'Women Workers. Their Employment and Participation in the Labour Movement. Hamburg 1880–1914', Ph. D. thesis (Institute of Slavonic and East European Studies, University of London, 1985); and the same author's article, 'Women's Work and the Family: Women Garment Workers in Berlin and Hamburg before the First World War', in R. J. Evans and W. R. Lee (eds.), *The German Family* (London, 1981), pp. 221–55.

[51] *Bericht des Executiv-Ausschusses* (n. 33 above), p. 29.

[52] StA Hbg, FA Neubauer 1, p. 30.

[53] *Bericht des Executiv-Ausschusses*, p. 8; StA Hbg, Allgemeine Armenanstalt II 211, Bl. 36 (Bericht), and Bl. 43, No. 1a.

[54] StA Hbg, PP S3490 Bd. 2: *Hamburger Freie Presse*, 7 Jan. 1894 ('Bilder aus der Zeit der Choleraepidemie in Hamburg', by G. C. H. von Salz, II: 'Vertrauensmänner').

mittees did not hestitate to initiate prosecutions against those recipients who they felt were deceiving them. One person was convicted in December 1892 for obtaining support from two different Committees without informing either of them that the other Committee was involved. Similarly, one man employed as a messenger by the Eimsbüttel Emergency Committee during the epidemic was subsequently convicted of obtaining the princely sum of 14 Marks 50 Pfennigs from members of the Committee under false pretences. Another was convicted of obtaining a rather more significant amount, 270 Marks, from the Winterhude Emergency Committee in similar circumstances.[55] But bourgeois resentment was directed at more than mere cheating. The Emergency Committee for Winterhude, after listing the extensive resources which it had devoted to providing support for a total of 408 families, or 1,575 individuals, in distress over the late autumn and winter of 1892-3, felt constrained to add:

Not only 'cholera' but 'other' claimants sometimes developed most extraordinary views about their *right* to the monies sent in for *them*, and these naive opinions did not always come from a harmless limitation of the intellect ... It was in no way easy—and often simply impossible—to establish whether those who sought assistance had really honestly but unsuccessfully sought work.[56]

Here, then, were the poor in all their ambiguity in the minds of the propertied: naive and limited, or cunning and dishonest; not grovelling in gratitude for the help offered by their betters, but daring to assert their right to a share in the money administered by those who had exploited them.

This concern to ensure that only the grateful and deserving poor received support frequently led to considerable harshness. In his autobiographical novel about the epidemic, Jakob Loewenberg gave a biting portrayal of the activities of the Emergency Committees. On his disinfection rounds Loewenberg noted a family which clearly needed help, so he put their case to the Emergency Committee for his district:

The Chairman, a portly, robust individual, listened to me benevolently. The Secretary, apparently a Jewish gentleman, leafed through his minute book, rubbed his eyes, looked over the top of his glasses and put the quill into his full, dark hair. 'Might be right,' he said 'the case has already been noted, but not yet investigated. Herr Petersen has taken it up.'

Herr Petersen was not back yet. They discussed whether or not to grant support. 'Not so hasty! First check, then check again. No one goes hungry in Hamburg,' declared a corpulent, quite satiated-looking gentleman.

'But Herr Behnke,' countered another, 'if their situation is as the man there says it is—'

[55] Ibid.; *Hamburger Fremdenblatt*, 9 Aug. 1893, *Hamburgischer Correspondent*, 18 Apr. 1893, *Hamburgischer Correspondent*, 14 Feb. 1893.
[56] StA Hbg, MK III A 13, IX: *Bericht ... Winterhude*, p. 17.

'One mustn't immediately believe everything people say. You know of course that the old Michel couple also asked for support, and afterwards it turned out they had come into a lot of money.'

'Herr Petersen' is portrayed in the novel as something of a figure of fun—a benevolent gentleman who doles out money at every opportunity ('if there are children there', remarks the Chairman, 'you grant every request straight away'). But his benevolence is ill-rewarded, for he too falls victim to the epidemic in the end, while it is the hard-hearted who eventually survive.[57]

The ultimate failure of these charitable activities to bridge the class gap, whatever official reports might say, was lucidly explained by an inhabitant of Barmbeck, who wrote in to the local paper in terms which give an insight into the reasons why the vast philanthropic efforts of Hamburg's bourgeoisie failed to overcome the alienation of Hamburg's working class:

On the one hand healthy workers who really want to work cannot be receiving any particular benefit from these grants, because it is embarassing for them to have to live off charity; on the other hand, again, undeserving cases were taken into consideration, while the really needy preferred to go hungry rather than allowing themselves to be signed on by the Poor Law. In some places the distribution of benefits was carried out with a harshness that deterred even the boldest claimants, and on the other side the support was calculated at such a low level that even the most economical use of it could not protect recipients against slow starvation. And yet there were sufficient resources to help everyone generously. Thus at the rent-payment deadlines really large sums of money were handed over to landlords by the respective Aid Committees. I do not think that it occurred to the noble benefactors who provided the money that they were caring for Hamburg's property-owners; the money should in every case only be used for the really needy.[58]

The *Hamburger Echo* for its part suggested that the main concern of the Emergency Committees was to prevent the landlords from going bankrupt. Indeed the Committees did not stint when it came to paying rent support or reclaiming pawned goods: 25,000 Marks was spent by the Barmbeck Committee in this way,[59] and all the Committees of course purchased their food and goods from the small retailers whose representatives were frequently able to put the case for their status as the deserving poor to the other members of the Committees in person. Thus the Committees followed a pattern in Hamburg philanthropy that went far back into the nineteenth century.[60]

Frequently the agents of the Committees pried into the personal cir-

[57] J. Loewenberg, *Aus zwei Quellen* (Berlin, 1914), pp. 278–81.

[58] StA Hbg, PP S3490 Bd. 1: *Barmbecker Lokal-Anzeiger*, 4 Feb. 1893, 'Eingesandt'.

[59] Ibid., StA Hbg, PP S3490 Bd. 1: *Hamburger Echo*, 4 Oct. 1892; see also ibid., *Vorwärts*, 15 Oct. 1892; *Bericht . . . Barmbeck* (n. 36 above). For a furious attack on Social Democratic criticisms of this see *Hamburger Fremdenblatt*, 12 Oct. 1892 (copy in StA Hbg, PP S3420 Bd. 3).

[60] *Bericht des Executiv-Ausschusses* (n. 33 above), p. 21. See also p. 480 above; and StA Hbg, PP S1430 Bd. 1: *Versammlungsbericht* 4 Nov. 1892, for pressure from greengrocers on the Committees.

cumstances of claimants and withdrew support if a cholera widow, for example, was held to be cohabiting with and receiving support from a lodger.[61] Some claimants were even refused benefits because previous employers certified they were Social Democrats. It was reported that one particularly important assistance fund, the Altona Loan Fund of 1892, refused to help anyone suspected of belonging to the party.[62] Thus philanthropy was turned into an instrument of social discipline. No wonder that it aroused resentment. There were frequent complaints from claimants about the complicated bureaucratic procedures through which they had to go: above all, registered paupers affected by the epidemic or by disinfection measures found the Poor Law authorities unhelpful and continued to approach the Emergency Committees, who constantly complained about them as a result. The Rent Assistance Society, in its turn, reported that it had many 'unpleasant experiences' in the course of its work and complained 'it cannot count on being thanked for its trouble'.[63] Actual complaints from claimants are naturally difficult to come by. But one rejected claimant did write complaining that

They all seem to be really good chaps on the Emergency Committee, but they don't know much about poverty. Everyone gets a blue form for the rent, but where's the money?—does it go to the bank and earn interest, so that the gentlemen can buy wine to strengthen themselves with? They don't feel any poverty, they don't understand it.[64]

Given such differences of approach, it is hardly surprising that the Social Democrats found it difficult to work with the Emergency Committees. The blossoming of private charity during the epidemic provided Hamburg's dominant classes with political propaganda for future occasions; but it did little to reduce, let alone abolish, social antagonisms in the present.

III

A second reaction to disaster is generally to remove the perceived immediate cause so that it will not happen again, at least not in the same way or to the same degree. In the case of Hamburg, suspicion was concentrated on the water-supply. The Senate's response was to order work on the new filtration plant, due for completion in 1894, to be speeded up so that it would be ready before the summer of 1893 brought warm weather once more and with it the renewed threat of infection. Chief Engineer Franz Andreas Meyer worked day and night to get the new water-supply ready. Indeed, at one point in the spring of 1893, even the energetic Meyer complained to his friends that the

[61] StA Hbg, PP S3490 Bd. 2: *Hamburger Freie Presse*, 7 Jan. 1894.

[62] StA Hbg, PP S3490 Bd. 1: *Hamburger Echo*, 20 Dec. 1892; for another example see ibid., *Hamburger Echo* 10 Nov. 1892.

[63] StA Hbg, Allgemeine Armenanstalt II 211, Bl. 51–7: *Hamburger Fremdenblatt*, 21 and 27 Sept. 1892.

[64] Quoted in ibid.

task was wearing him out and threatened to retire. Nevertheless, about half the new filter-beds were brought into service on 1 May 1893 and the rest on 27 May. On 28 May the old water-supply inlet was closed, and from now on the city was supplied exclusively with sand-filtered water.[65] Yet anxiety about a possible recurrence of the epidemic did not diminish. The problem lay initially in the fact that isolated cases of cholera were regularly reported long after the main epidemic was over, as individuals were infected through contact with residual pools of the bacillus.[66] Just before Christmas 1892, for example, the *Frankfurter Zeitung* reported:

Anxiety about the renewed outbreak of cholera is growing among the populace. In fact the number of cases of cholera-like illness is by no means negligible. One often comes across the sick being carried away and the disinfection of coaches and streets. The only cases publicly reported to the Commission are those in which cholera has actually been confirmed.[67]

In fact, while occasional cases still occurred and some disinfection was still taking place, the transport of the sick had little to do with cholera; in a city of 600,000 inhabitants reporters were bound to come across ambulances every now and then. Nevertheless, in January 1893, as the *Hamburger Fremdenblatt* noted, people thought 'that as far as publication is concerned, the zealous identification of cholera which we are seeing today is almost more damaging than the sins of omission of August last year'.[68] The continual reporting of new cases caused repeated panics on the Exchange, and middle-class inhabitants of the city began to make preparations to leave in the spring; indeed it was reported that over a hundred people from Hamburg were staying in Wiesbaden by mid-January, while 'in many spas', as a Hamburg paper reported, 'namely in the Harz and in Thuringia, whole hotels have already been booked out by the inhabitants of this city for the whole summer'.[69]

Thus Hamburg's bourgeois press was faced with the task not only of defending the city's record during the real cholera epidemic in 1892 but also of continually rebutting accusations that a new one had broken out. Such rumours, as the *Hamburger Fremdenblatt* noted on 24 December 1892, were dangerous, because 'by this means the trading relations of Hamburg will be imperilled and nothing but damage done to the city and its inhabitants'.[70] A new case reported in May the following year should not have been reported,

[65] StA Hbg, FA Meyer B7b: E. Vermehren, 'Zum Gedächtnis für Franz Andreas Meyer'; ibid., B7a: 'Nachruf', in *Hamburgischer Correspondent* (undated); StA Hbg, Senat, Cl. VII, Lit. Ta, Pars 2, Vol. 11, Fasc. 16, Inv. 26, for the water supply in 1893.

[66] (G. Gaffky), *Amtliche Denkschrift über die Choleraepidemie 1892* (Kaiserliches Gesundheitsamt, Berlin, 1895).

[67] StA Hbg, PP S3490 Bd. 1: report in *Hamburger Fremdenblatt*, 24 Dec. 1892.

[68] StA Hbg, Senat, Cl. VII, Lit. Ta, Pars 2, Vol. 11, Fasc. 16, Inv. 27: *Hamburger Fremdenblatt*, 10 Jan. 1893.

[69] StA Hbg, PP S3490, Bd. 1: *Hamburger Tageblatt*, 20 Jan. 1893.

[70] Ibid., *Hamburger Fremdenblatt*, 24 Dec. 1892.

the newspaper remarked again in June 1893, for it had caused the press in New York to declare 'that the Asiatic enemy is again standing before the gates of Hamburg'. 'This incident', complained the *Fremdenblatt*, 'has again cost Hamburg millions!'[71] The *Hamburger Nachrichten* proposed in June 1893 that fresh cholera cases should no longer be publicly announced, in order to prevent these recurrent and economically damaging panics. This proposal drew a lengthy reply from the *Hamburgischer Correspondent*, a newspaper that closely reflected the views of the Senate:

It is precisely the prompt announcement of the most recent cases that has proved once more that the authorities keep their promise even where an isolated incident, which gives no cause for alarm, is concerned. As a result of this, foreign governments no longer allow themselves to be irritated by other reports, and their consuls have frequently been in a position to deny untrue reports about Hamburg written by unscrupulous correspondents in their domestic press, on the basis of the unimpeachable announcements with which they are provided. Hardly anyone could approve the forfeiture of this trust by the brief concealment of individual cases.[72]

If the announcement of new cases could not be suppressed, complained the *Hamburger Fremdenblatt* in June 1893, then at least the red notices still posted up in the city's streets advising people to take precautions against drinking impure water should now be removed. 'Certainly there is nothing to object to in the contents of the announcements', the paper declared, 'but the signature, which places in particular prominence the name "Cholera Commission of the Senate", must surely make an unpleasant impact on every stranger. No one can avoid gaining the impression that circumstances here are still extremely insecure, if one comes across the name "Cholera Commission" everywhere.'[73]

The newspaper was supported by others. The *General-Anzeiger* went so far as to accuse the *Hamburgischer Correspondent* and the *Börsen-Halle* of causing a panic on the Exchange by the premature publication of cases before they had been officially confirmed.[74] The left-liberal *Berliner Tageblatt*, declaring that cholera was not infectious, asked why it was necessary to publish every new case: this could only lead to 'damage to trade and transport' and therefore had to be avoided.[75] Anxiety, as Burgomaster Mönckeberg reported, reached a height on the first anniversary of the great epidemic.[76] Rumours were rife. On 14 August a hotel guest was heard to declare that cholera was in the city: 'We've got it already,' another said, 'it's just being kept secret; the

[71] Ibid., *Hamburger Fremdenblatt*, 1 June 1893.
[72] Ibid.: *General-Anzeiger*, 1 June 1893.
[73] Ibid.: *Hamburger Fremdenblatt*, 1 June 1893.
[74] Ibid.: *Hamburger Echo*, 19 May 1893.
[75] Ibid.: *Hamburger Nachrichten*, 3 June 1893.
[76] C. Mönckeberg (ed.), *Bürgermeister Mönckeberg. Eine Auswahl seiner Briefe und Aufzeichnungen* (Stuttgart and Berlin, 1918), p. 27: Mönckeberg to Carl Mönckeberg, 1 Sept. 1893.

disinfection carts aren't always going around for nothing. They don't want to damage the interests of Hamburg's merchants, but it can't be kept secret for long.'[77] Workers fully expected new quarantine measures to be imposed,[78] and the *Berliner Tageblatt* reported a 'panic fear' in Hamburg's population that doubtless caused a renewed mass exodus.[79] In fact there *was* a minor outbreak in September, as a small quantity of unfiltered Elbe water was accidentally let into the drinking-water supply. Five cholera deaths were announced on 18 September, but they had occurred on the 15th, a delay which, in the opinion of another paper, marked a recurrence of 'the fateful hushing-up system with which the Hamburg authorities operated last year'.[80] These renewed disruptions to business and trade caused a group of influential merchants and shipowners to send a deputation to the Senate requesting an embargo on the announcement of new cases.[81] The Senate gave in; representations were made in Berlin, and the Imperial Health Office agreed in October that no official figures would be published or announcements made should cases of cholera recur. Professor Theodor Rumpf, Director of the New General Hospital in Eppendorf, who had succeeded, a year too late perhaps, in achieving a prompt identification of the disease and sending the required bacteriological cultures to Berlin, was sufficiently upset by this decision to recall it with some bitterness over thirty years later.[82] Thus all the accusations of suppression and delay in 1892 had merely resulted in an even greater determination to repeat the same process in 1893. This did not bode very well for the fate of the other reforms which the great epidemic had begun to set in motion.

b. *Pettenkofer's Last Stand*

I

Although the epidemic of 1892 was fought in Hamburg as elsewhere by the classic contagionist methods of quarantine, isolation, and disinfection, this did not mean that medical and lay opinion in Hamburg was instantly converted from its previously anticontagionist standpoint, any more than the rapid completion of the water-filtration project in 1892–3 meant that the Senate accepted wholeheartedly that the disease had been carried in the water-supply. The truth was that Hamburg had little choice but to carry out the policies of the contagonists, however unpopular they might remain.

[77] StA Hbg, PP S3490 Bd. 2: Wirtschaftsvigilanzbericht 10657, 16 Aug. 1893.
[78] Ibid., Wirtschaftsvigilanzberichte 12294, 12345, etc., on 20–21 Sept. 1893.
[79] Ibid.: *Hamburger Echo*, 19 Sept. 1893.
[80] Ibid.: *Das kleine Journal*, 19 Sept. 1893.
[81] Ibid.: *Hamburger Nachrichten*, 19 Oct. 1893.
[82] T. Rumpf, *Lebenserinnerungen* (Gotha, 1925), p. 44.

'During last year's cholera epidemic,' noted Burgomaster Johannes Versmann in 1893, 'it was the Imperial Health Office and Prof. Koch who ran things here.'[1] His view was echoed almost word for word by the *Hamburger Fremdenblatt*, which complained early in 1893 'that it is really Herr Koch who is ruling Hamburg today. That is what is so serious and so dangerous about the present situation.' The paper poured scorn on the idea that the bacillus was the cause of the disease, but added: 'Herr Koch is the intellectual father of the cholera bacillus, and as long as he is in charge of the Imperial Health Office, the procedures in operation at the moment are scarcely likely to be changed.'[2] Burgomaster Johann Georg Mönckeberg was among the many members of Hamburg's ruling families who remained sceptical of Koch's views throughout the epidemic. On 30 August 1892 he wrote a revealing letter to his son Carl, who was studying at university. It was clear from this letter that the views of Max von Pettenkofer, Koch's arch-miasmatist rival, may well have found favour among the better-off because, among other things, they associated cholera directly with poverty and so offered them the promise of immunity: 'Up to now', he wrote,

the disease has exclusively, or almost exclusively, affected the lower classes of people, mainly in the areas near the Elbe and the harbour. But if Koch's theory is well-founded—though it seems to correspond very little to the experience of the epidemic here!—then there is no guarantee that we members of other social classes will not be struck down by the disease as well …

Almost a month later, on 20 September, the Burgomaster was still unconvinced. Writing to his son, he reported:

Recently I have had long and interesting sessions with Professor Koch, who expounded his theory in a very clear and ingenious manner. It is logically unassailable, if one grants the premises. But that is where the big question comes: is the comma bacillus the sole cause of the sickness, and is it only transmitted in a specific way? Koch says 'yes!'—and then everything else follows of itself …[3]

Mönckeberg's further remarks on the subject did little to indicate that he had been won over to Koch's point of view. Similarly, on 8 September Senator Gustav Hertz also attacked 'the ridiculous exaggerations about our water.'[4]

Local hostility to Koch's contagionism found support among medical opinion too. Professor Ferdinand Hueppe, of Prague, who had been in Hamburg during the epidemic, was soon in print with a series of articles criticizing Koch's views. His decisive conclusion: the 1892 epidemic proved

[1] StA Hbg, FA Versmann F4, 1893 entry.
[2] StA Hbg, Senat. Cl. VII, Lit. Ta, Pars 2, Vol. 11, Fasc. 16, Inv. 27: *Hamburger Fremdenblatt*, 16 Jan. 1893.
[3] Mönckeberg, *Bürgermeister Mönckeberg*, pp. 20, 22.
[4] StA Hbg, FA Gustav Hertz B17: Gustav to Else Hertz, 8 Sept. 1892

that 'Asiatic cholera is an essentially miasmatic disease.'[5] Another writer, Dr W. Krebs, backed this up with 'ground-water observations in the lower Elbe region', published in December 1892 in support of Pettenkofer's views.[6] Pettenkofer was also defended by Professor Jäger in an article complaining bitterly of the 'modern surfeit of bacteriology.'[7] Another supporter of Pettenkofer, Dr Gläser, produced a whole series of articles attacking Koch as a 'fanatic'. 'Robert Koch's comma bacillus', he declared, 'is not the cause of cholera', and he railed against 'the presumption of Herr Koch and the failure of his measures against cholera.'[8] Cholera, argued *Sanitätsrat* Dr Lachmann from Krotoschin, was carried through the air.[9] This view was repeated in a long series of letters sent to the Hamburg authorities by a senior military physician in Hanover, *Oberstabsarzt* Dr August Dyers.[10] Koch was also attacked by the homeopaths, who argued that the 1892 epidemic was 'generated' in Hamburg itself. The local cuisine was too fatty, and the inhabitants of the city drank too much.[11] Another writer, who described himself as a Social Democrat, attacked the practice of disinfection as a product of the machinations of the chemicals industry. The best remedy, he declared, in terms reminiscent of Pettenkofer at his most enthusiastic, was exposure to air, sunshine, and fresh water, and he concluded by urging people to sleep with the bedroom windows open.[12] He was followed by another author, H. Fischer, in a pamphlet published in Dresden in 1893 and entitled 'Saprophytes, our natural, up to now unrecognized allies against cholera'. Fischer's view was that the 'relative humidity of the air' was the 'cardinal point of the whole cholera question.'[13] Another writer claimed in the *Kölnische Zeitung* on 28 August that the epidemic was caused not only by 'the notorious Hamburg Elbe-mains-water' but also by 'roadworks, which were carried out on a massive scale this summer, exposing gas pipes which have been causing bad

[5] See F. Hueppe's articles in *Berliner Klinische Wochenschrift*, 30, 4, 5, 6, and 7 (23 and 30 Jan. and 6 and 13 Feb. 1893).

[6] W. Krebs, *Grundwasser-Beobachtungen im unterelbischen Gebiete*, reviewed in *Hamburgischer Correspondent*, 31 Dec. 1892 in StA Hbg, PP S3490 Bd. 1.

[7] *Prof. Dr. G. Jägers Monatsblatt. Zeitschrift für Gesundheitspflege und Lebenslehre*, 12, 3 (March 1893), p.45. See also ibid., 12, 1 (Jan. 1893); and the contribution by Prof. Rosenbach in *Aerztliche Rundschau*, 29 Oct. 1892, along the same lines.

[8] J. A. Gläser, 'Kritische Bemerkungen zu Herrn Robert Kochs Aufsatz: Die Cholera in Deutschland während des Winters 1892–93', *Zeitschrift für Hygiene*, 15 (reprint, Hamburg, 1893); 'Gemeinverständliche Anticontagionistische Betrachtungen bei Gelegenheit der letzten Cholera-Epidemie in Hamburg 1892' (reprint, Hamburg, 1893); 'Robert Kochs Komma-Bacillus ist nicht Ursache der Cholera' (reprint, Hamburg, 1894), 'Die Ueberhebung des Herrn Robert Koch und due Erfolglosigkeit seiner Massregeln gegen Cholera' (reprint, Hamburg, 1894).

[9] StA Hbg, Mk III A 16, Bd. 1, Bl. 281.

[10] Ibid., Bl. 199 (27 Sept. 1892), *et seq.*

[11] *Pionier. Zeitschrift für volkswirtschaftlichen und sittlichen Fortschritt, für Schulwesen, Hygiene und Medizin*, 8, 17 (7 Sept. 1892), p. 134 (copy in StA Hbg, MK III A 16, Bd. 1).

[12] *Die Cholera, unser Bürgertum und die Sozialdemokratie* (Leipzig, 1892), pp. 5, 9, 17, 29.

[13] H. Fischer, *Die Saprophyten, unsere natürlichen, bisher noch nicht gewürdigten Helfer gegen die Cholera* (Dresden, 1893), p. 11.

air under the earth for decades' and the 'hundreds of courtyards, alley-ways and "terraces" which give out noxious vapours year in, year out.'[14]

Above all, Koch's theories met with widespread scepticism among medical men in the city where their practical consequences were most keenly felt—Hamburg. At least one local doctor disregarded Koch's advice altogether and carried on eating raw fruit, while on 9 September 1892, for example, the *Hamburgischer Correspondent*, generally regarded as reflecting the views of the Senate, carried a strong attack by Dr Erman, of the Eppendorf General Hospital, on Koch's view that the disease was carried by the public water-supply.[15] An account of the epidemic in Wilhelmsburg, just outside Hamburg, by the local doctor, Hans Wolff, was also written from an explicitly miasmatist standpoint, while another local doctor, Dr Doering, on the Veddel island in the Hamburg harbour area, criticized the 'assiduous hunt for the comma bacillus' and urged that more attention should be paid to 'the warnings of Pettenkofer, our tried hygienic veteran', because contagionism led to a 'mad fear of cholera' which caused 'enormous damage' to Hamburg's 'trade and industry.'[16] Dr Otto Paulsen, in a more general survey of the Hamburg epidemic, published in 1892, was of the opinion that cholera could only be found in still or stagnant pools, and that it could not possibly be present in the city's water-mains.[17] Miasmatists were quick to claim that the trickle of fresh cases reported in November and December proved the correctness of their theory, for they could only be explained by the fact that parts of the miasma were still lingering on after the main epidemic was over.[18] Particularly striking was the fact that the most substantial report on the epidemic to be published, by a number of Hamburg doctors and statisticians, was thoroughly miasmatist in spirit, with thirty pages devoted to an elaborate discussion of the water-table and the weather, and many more to trying to disprove the views of Robert Koch.[19]

Chief among Koch's medical critics in 1892–3 was, predictably enough, Max von Pettenkofer. As late as 1884 the Bavarian social hygiene expert had still exercised a powerful influence on the Imperial Health Office's instructions to local medical officers on cholera, directing them to pay particular attention to climatic conditions and the state of the ground-water in affected areas.

[14] StA Hbg, Senat, Cl. VII, Lit. Ta, Pars 2, Vol. 11, Fasc. 17, Inv. 4: *Kölnische Zeitung*, 30 Aug. 1892.

[15] StA Hbg, FA Lippmann A4 Vol. 2, p. 32, citing Dr Türkheim, who regarded official ordinances as 'superfluous'; StA Hbg, Senat, Cl. VII, Lit. Ta, Pars 2, Vol. 11, Fasc. 16, Inv. 9, *Hamburgischer Correspondent*, 9 Sept. 1892.

[16] Hans Wolff, 'Die Cholera-Epidemie 1892 in Wilhelmsburg' *Berliner Klinische Wochenschrift*, 17 Oct. 1892, p. 1061; StA Hbg, MK I K 6 Bd. 3, Bl. 188–93.

[17] O. Paulsen, *Ueber die Ursachen der diesjährigen Cholera-Epidemie in Hamburg* (Hamburg, 1892).

[18] StA Hbg, PP, S3490 Bd. 2: *Hamburger Fremdenblatt*, 16 Dec. 1892.

[19] Von Halle *et al.*, *Die Cholera*; Wolter subsequently wrote another attack on Koch in his *Die Entstehungsursachen der Gelsenkirchener Typhusepidemie von 1901* (Munich, 1903) and collaborated with Pettenkofer's pupil Emmerich.

Now, a mere eight years later, all this was changed. The entire management of the fight against the epidemic lay in the hands of Koch, the measures taken—quarantine, isolation, disinfection, the boiling of drinking-water—were precisely those which Pettenkofer had been condemning as utterly useless for the previous three decades.[20] As if to rub home this triumph, Koch also set in motion a plan which the Imperial Health Office had been considering for years, but had hitherto lacked the opportunity to put into effect: the introduction of a national Epidemics Law (*Reichsseuchengesetz*)[21] which would make the policies consequent upon his contagionist theories mandatory in all the federated states by law. An Expert Commission was hurriedly called together, consisting of medical specialists from various departments and institutions. One of their number was Max von Pettenkofer, who now travelled up from Munich for his last great confrontation with his old rival. The Commission sat for six days, from 26 September to 1 October 1892, and went through all the clauses of the proposed law, drafted in the Imperial Health Office, one by one.[22]

Already on the second day of deliberations Pettenkofer began to voice his objections. All the proposed quarantine measures, he said, were 'only sedatives for the populace. They have never been able to prevent the disease coming in, because it is impossible to control human traffic so tightly that even microbes cannot get through.' But he was speaking from the experience of a past age. 'Koch', continued the minutes of the meeting, 'believed that it would indeed be possible to control traffic as tightly as this, if the measures were strictly and appropriately applied.' With all the resources of the modern state at his disposal, he was probably right. The meeting, assured by the chairman that the measures were necessary, voted along the lines proposed by Koch.[23] Pettenkofer returned to the attack on the next point, which dealt with the isolation of epidemic victims in hospital. The minutes continued:

Pettenkofer sees no advantage to be gained in favour of preventing the spread of the disease by hospitalizing a victim of cholera, because all such compulsory measures are superfluous. In 1836 a cholera epidemic in Munich took a particularly mild form even though the authorities declared that the disease was not infectious and explicitly forbade all special measures of prevention. Indeed a market was held in Munich at that time and attended by 40,000 people without cholera being spread further by it. In Hamburg by contrast cholera is spreading further and further although the most energetic measures have been taken to prevent this.

[20] See Chapter 3c, above.

[21] The full title was the *Reichsgesetz zur Bekämpfung der gemeingefährlichen Krankheiten* (Law concerning the combating of diseases which constitute a common danger), a fact which (possibly coincidentally) allowed papers on it to be filed next to those on the *Reichsgesetz zur Bekämpfung der gemeingefährlichen Bestrebungen der Sozialdemokratie*, the Anti-Socialist Law of 1878–90.

[22] BA Koblenz R86/975 Bd. 1, for the minutes of the Commission's deliberations.

[23] Ibid., Bd., 2. Verhandlungstag, pp. 9–10. Even the Spanish government was able to impose an effective cordon sanitaire by 1894 (M. V. Ortiz, *Epidemias de Cólera en Vizcaya en el Siglo XIX* (Bilbao, 1978)).

Koch, however, stepped in immediately to rebut this last point. He denied 'that the measures taken in Hamburg up to now have been energetic.' The measures taken in no way satisfied 'the demands which,' he said, implying sarcastically that Pettenkofer was behind the times, 'must be made from the scientific standpoint of today.'[24]

This exchange continued the next day, as Pettenkofer continued to pour scorn on the idea of quarantine and isolation. He launched into a long and detailed argument, giving various examples of cases where the absence of isolation had not led to an epidemic outbreak, and urging that in any case 'the restriction of traffic should not be taken too far.' Again Koch rebutted him sharply, asserting that the cases described by Pettenkofer were probably not cholera anyway; and again Pettenkofer was voted down. Matters on the Commission were now clearly coming to a head.[25] As Koch moved on to demand that far-reaching measures to close down infected water-supplies and arrange for deliveries of pure drinking-water be included in the law, Pettenkofer, ever anxious to restrict the legislation's scope, asked 'would it not be appropriate merely to close down those water-supplies in which cholera bacilli have been found?' Koch, clearly enraged at these constant objections to his views, replied bitingly that 'that is not practicable, since, as everyone who deals with tracing cholera bacilli in water knows, this process is uncommonly difficult and time-consuming.'[26]

He went on to argue in favour of a very sharply formulated clause, clearly directed against Hamburg, which demanded what he called a 'central institution' for sanitary reform:

Sanitary conditions (water-supply, refuse disposal, cleanliness) must not only be kept under observation during epidemics, but rather all the time. They must be constantly improved, and for this purpose local health boards must be created, to supervise and improve the circumstances of their locality, and the medical officers of the state government or possibly even of the Reich must be entrusted with the carrying out of general sanitary reforms.

This was a very far-reaching proposal which would have given wide-ranging powers to the Reich to interfere in the internal affairs of the federated states. Pettenkofer immediately introduced a counter-proposal, whereby 'in all places where poor sanitary conditions have been confirmed in connection with epidemics, measures are to be taken to remove local nuisances after the end of the epidemic.' Thus were encapsulated the centralist and localist essences of Koch's and Pettenkofer's theories. No wonder Koch felt it necessary to step in to rescue the original proposal. 'Pettenkofer's proposal,' he said, 'seeks to shut the stable door after the horse has bolted. He could only accept it as a

[24] BA Koblenz R86/975 Bd. 1, p. 14.
[25] Ibid., 3. Verhandlungstag, p. 3.
[26] Ibid., p. 25.

payment on account, in the eventuality that nothing more could be achieved at the moment.' The Commission was unable, or unwilling, to continue with this clearly quite fundamental difference of opinion, and referred the clause to a four-man subcommittee, to which Pettenkofer and Koch were both appointed; but there is no evidence that it ever met, and the dispute on the point continued, though in a more muted way, the following day.[27]

By now, however, the heat was clearly beginning to go out of the confrontation. Probably Koch and his supporters had met behind the scenes and agreed to deal with Pettenkofer simply by ignoring him. On 30 September, the fifth day of the meeting, Koch once more dominated the discussion, which revolved around the question of who should be isolated during a typhoid epidemic, and how. Pettenkofer, clearly irritated by the general assumption on the Commission that isolation was effective, was moved to deliver yet another tirade against the practice ('on the whole no great success can be expected from it'); but the Commission simply went straight on to vote for isolation without even bothering to reply to the points he made. Next, the members voted through a whole list of detailed provisions on disinfection, isolation, and all the measures on which Pettenkofer had lavished such contempt and ridicule in his voluminous writings on epidemic disease.[28] Pettenkofer must clearly have felt that it was not worth trying to resist any further, for he only opened his mouth once more, on the final day, and that was on a minor procedural point, on which Koch actually supported him, perhaps in an attempt to mollify his feelings. But the whole meeting was a humiliating experience for Pettenkofer. First made the butt of Koch's sarcasm, then simply ignored by a Commission consisting mostly of his juniors, he was forced to sit idly by and watch the drafting of a law the provisions of which amounted to the institutionalized destruction of his whole life's work in the field in which he had made his reputation.

Back in Munich shortly after the beginning of October, Pettenkofer turned over in his mind how he could strike back at Koch. Perhaps, indeed, he had already decided in the train on the way down; or even before he left Berlin. He remained as convinced as ever that the 'X' factor (the cholera bacillus) would remain without influence if it was simply ingested through the mouth; on the contrary, he continued to believe that it operated exclusively by infecting the ground-water, under locally specific hygienic and climatic conditions, which he called the 'Y' factor, in such a way as to produce a specifically *miasmatic* infection (the 'Z' factor). It still seemed irrefutable to him that cholera had broken out in Hamburg in 1892 but not elsewhere because only in Hamburg had the climatic conditions and the hygienic circumstances combined to produce an infection of the ground-water. But how could he prove his point? Driven to desperation by his humiliation at

[27] Ibid., pp. 23–4, 27.
[28] Ibid., 5. Verhandlungstag, pp. 4–5.

the meeting of 26 September–1 October, Pettenkofer now resolved on a last, startling gamble to try and rescue the situation.

II

Early in October, Koch's colleague Georg Gaffky, who had stayed on in Hamburg as director of a newly founded epidemiological institute, was alarmed to receive in his morning mail a letter from Max von Pettenkofer in Munich requesting a sample of the bacillus culture for purposes of scientific experimentation. As a responsible but still relatively junior medical scientist, Gaffky was in no position to refuse such a request, coming as it did from one of the doyens of the profession. So he sent it. No sooner had Pettenkofer received the sample than he opened it and swallowed it. He was careful to do so on an empty stomach and with a quantity of alkaline solution which he added in order to neutralize the stomach acids which Koch asserted were particularly hostile to the bacillus. The drink, he reported, tasted 'like the purest water.' His students, aware of his intention, had offered to perform the experiment for him, but he had refused, remarking

I have the right to regard myself as a 'vile body'. I am 74 years old, ... I have not a single tooth left and use my false teeth only when I have to speak distinctly and at length, not while I am eating; and I also feel the other burdens of old age. Even if I were deceiving myself and the experiment put my life at risk, I would look death calmly in the eye, for it would be no irresponsible or cowardly suicide that I underwent, I would be dying in the service of science, like a soldier on the field of honour.

Two days after taking the bacillus, on 9 October, Pettenkofer began to have diarrhoea. On 10 October he was obliged to go to the lavatory at 1 a.m., 1.35 a.m., and 4 a.m. By this time his evacuations, as he reported, had the colour and consistency of pale red wine. Pettenkofer felt all the time a strong 'squeaking in the intestine' and a 'squeaking and rumbling in the abdomen.' Most of his account consisted of a detailed description, which we can safely pass over, of his bowel movements over the next few days. The evacuations, which he immediately subjected to microscopic examination, contained masses of bacilli up to 14 October. On 15 October, his bowel movements returned to normal and by the 16th his stool showed a complete absence of the cholera germ. Pettenkofer's experiment, which was conducted in private, was then, in a graphic demonstration of the power of the German professor over his assistants, repeated by his disciple Emmerich on 17 October before a hundred witnesses. Emmerich's symptoms were more severe than Pettenkofer's—indeed, they were said to be more severe than those of the patient from whom the sample had been taken—but he too managed to survive. These experiments, declared Pettenkofer triumphantly, showed that though the 'X' factor (the bacillus) was present, the absence of a 'Y' factor (the infected ground-water) in Munich meant that there was no onset of the disease (the 'Z' factor in Pettenkofer's terminology).[29]

Many commentators have devoted a great deal of ingenuity to explaining the genesis and result of this most celebrated of medical auto-experiments. One writer, for example, claimed to have been told on unimpeachable authority that Pettenkofer had previously suffered a serious attack of cholera, and so probably possessed some residual immunity.[30] But there is no corroborative evidence to support this claim. Another writer has speculated that the tension and excitement which Pettenkofer undoubtedly experienced during the experiment may have stimulated the activity of his stomach acids and so reduced the effectiveness of the bacillus.[31] In fact, Georg Gaffky, who supplied the sample, later told Pettenkofer's biographer that he and his colleagues had had a shrewd idea of what Pettenkofer intended to do with it when the old man's request came in, so they had sent him a diluted culture in the hope that it would have a mild effect. The story was confirmed by the military physician who had taken the sample down to Munich and handed it over.[32] Subsequent experiments have established that quite a powerful dose of the bacillus is usually required to produce the classic symptoms.[33] So it seems probable that Pettenkofer escaped because Koch's assistant took pity on him. Nevertheless, as Carl Fraenkel pointed out, the symptoms exhibited by Pettenkofer and Emmerich indicated that they had indeed suffered a mild attack of the disease.[34]

Moreover, Pettenkofer's auto-experiment was undertaken, as it later emerged, for reasons considerably more complex than scientific dedication or personal pride. Already in his description of the event, Pettenkofer, as we saw, made clear his distaste for the physical infirmities of old age. This distaste grew with the years. By the turn of the century, his friends and disciples were becoming seriously alarmed by the old man's state of mind, which had become obsessed with the symptoms of bodily decay. They were right to be worried when he purchased a revolver with ammunition and started talking of killing himself. On 10 January 1901, evading the attentions of those close to him, Max von Pettenkofer put the gun to his head and blew out his brains.[35]

[29] M. von Pettenkofer, 'Ueber die Cholera von 1892 in Hamburg und über Schutzmassregeln,' *Archiv für Hygiene*, 18 (1893), 94–132; and the same author's article 'Ueber Cholera mit Berücksichtigung der jüngsten Choleraepidemie in Hamburg', *Münchener Medizinische Wochenschrift*, 46 (1892). For other examples of the power of German professors and the submissiveness of their assistants, see M. P. Kater, 'Professionalization and Socialization of Physicians in Wilhelmine and Weimar Germany,' *Journal of Contemporary History*, 20 (1985), 671–701, esp. pp. 680–1.

[30] A. S. Evans, 'Pettenkofer Revisited,' *Yale Journal of Biology and Medicine*, 46 (1973), 171.

[31] N. Longmate, *King Cholera* (London, 1965), pp. 28–30.

[32] K. Kisskalt, *Max von Pettenkofer* (Stuttgart, 1948), p. 118.

[33] R. G. Feachem, 'Environmental Aspects of Cholera Epidemiology, III: Transmission and Control', *Tropical Diseases Bulletin*, 99 (1982), 25.

[34] StA Hbg, PP S3490 Bd. 1: *General-Anzeiger* (Hamburg), 6 Dec. 1892.

[35] Longmate, *King Cholera*, pp. 228–30; Kisskalt, *Max von Pettenkofer*.

In retrospect, therefore, the daring auto-experiment which he undertook in 1892 can be seen as an early manifestation of the death-wish that was ultimately to consume him.

In the meantime, however, his survival of the cholera bacillus gave Pettenkofer added zest in the fight against contagionism. From his base in Munich he now began to mobilize support against the proposed Epidemics Bill. His influence was sufficient to ensure, as the *Berliner Tageblatt* noted, 'that government circles in Munich essentially if not unconditionally take their cue from the theories of Pettenkofer.'[36] The Munich Medical Board criticized the Bill as impossible to carry out and its provisions for disinfection and isolation as 'excessive' and 'exaggerated many times over.'[37] And Bavaria's representatives on the Federal Council proposed that the Bill should be limited to cholera and the isolation and disinfection clauses emasculated or deleted altogether.[38] This official resistance was buttressed by a substantial campaign in the Bavarian press. 'What use is it anyway,' asked the *Augsburger Abendzeitung* rhetorically, 'if the authorities block off access to drinking-water and the typhoid is situated in the ground, or vice versa?' Koch's theory of contagion, the paper complained, 'has given rise in the whole country to a fear and dread such as have not been seen in earlier epidemics.'[39] But these views had little influence over the governments of the other federated states. On 23 March 1893 Pettenkofer announced that he still believed 'the burdensome provisions of the Bill, namely isolation, disinfection, sealing of the borders and quarantines, to be completely wrong, and confirms that Bavaria opposed the Bill in the Federal Council but was voted down.'[40]

Apart from the Bavarians, whose stance was partly particularist, partly a reflection of the entrenched institutional supremacy of Pettenkofer and his school in the South German Kingdom,[41] the critics of the Bill were a more than usually motley example of the *ad hoc* coalitions of interests that provided the driving-force of legislative and electoral politics in Wilhelmine Germany. The Catholic Centre Party objected to the proposals not only, it was reported, for particularist reasons,[42] but also because, as one of its deputies said to the applause of his colleagues in the Reichstag debate on 21 April, referring to the powers of forcible hospitalization by the Bill, 'the most holy right of the family, to care for one of its own members who has fallen ill within its bosom,

---

[36] BA Koblenz R86/946 Bd. 2: *Berliner Tageblatt* 4 Feb. 1893.

[37] Ibid.: *Berliner Lokal-Anzeiger*, 1 Mar. 1892.

[38] Ibid.: Anträge Bayerns zu dem Gesetzentwurf ..., 4 Mar. 1893.

[39] Ibid.: *Augsburger Abendzeitung*, 26 Feb. 1893.

[40] Ibid.: *Münchener Neueste Nachrichten*, 23 Mar. 1893. See also M. von Pettenkofer, 'Ueber die Cholera von 1892 in Hamburg und über Schutzmassregeln,' *Archiv für Hygiene*, 18 (1893) pp. 94–132. For Pettenkofer's more pessimistic views on the fate of his theory, see H. Breyer, *Max von Pettenkofer* (Leipzig, 1980), pp. 208–9.

[41] BA Koblenz R86/946 Bd. 2: *Augsburger Abendzeitung*, 8 Feb. 1893, for the particularist argument.

[42] Ibid.: *Berliner Lokal-Anzeiger*, 12 Apr. 1893; R86/946 Bd. 5: *National-Zeitung*, 1 June 1900.

will be undermined by this measure in a manner that I for myself cannot approve of, a manner which goes against my own feelings.'[43] The Conservative Party was also unhappy about the Bill because it meant East-Elbian Junker landowners would have to surrender some of their police powers to medical officials.[44] Further out towards the fringes of politics, there were strong objections from a *Mittelstand* organization known as the *Mittelpartei* or the *Volkswirtschaftlicher Verband*, which claimed the Bill contained 'unbelievable attacks on personal freedom, on trade, and on economic life in general,' and also subsequently from the Anti-Semites, who attempted to use the debate as a vehicle for populist attacks on 'dubious scientific experiments on the part of doctors,' as one of their leaders, Otto Böckel, put it on a later occasion. The Anti-Semites had long been favourably inclined towards fringe medicine, and Böckel also took the opportunity to attack compulsory vaccination for smallpox and the scientific use of vivisection.[45]

Most extreme were the views expressed in *Professor Dr G. Jägers Monatsblatt*, a 'natural healing' magazine whose editor described himself as 'Prof. Dr. Gustav Jäger, the man of the wool regime'. It argued that nothing should be done at all: cholera and other epidemics were a 'natural phenomenon' that performed a useful natural selection function, as had, it claimed, been demonstrated by the Hamburg epidemic, which removed 'cowards, weaklings, or libertines' from the 'better classes' and in the rest of the population killed only 'people who already had death sitting at their shoulder, or who faced unavoidable, incurable, lingering poverty and sickness, and among whom many must certainly have regarded death as a release from evil.'[46] These views were naturally anathema to the medical profession, whatever stand its individual members might take on the aetiology of cholera. But even the doctors were not happy with the Bill. They objected to the fact that it did not restrict the duty of reporting cases of infectious diseases to the medical profession but made it mandatory for anyone who was aware of their existence. This indeed was the main burden of Rudolf Virchow's contribution to the debate, indicating the central importance he attached to the interests of the medical profession by this time. The Federation of German Doctors' Clubs (*Deutscher Aerztevereinsbund*), regretting that it had not been formally consulted during the preparation of the Bill, declared that the freedom to report cases would only serve to legitimize 'quackery.'[47] The Doctors' Congress

[43] RT 21 Apr. 1893, col. 1960: speech of deputy Fritzen (Düsseldorf); cf. also Centre Party reactions to the similar speech of the Polish deputy Dr Rzepnikowski (col. 1964).

[44] BA Koblenz R86/946 Bd. 5: *National-Zeitung*, 1 June 1900.

[45] Ibid., Bd. 2: *Hamburger Freie Presse*, Extra-Abdruck: 'Die Mittelpartei und das Seuchengesetz'; RT 12 June 1900, cols. 6010 ff.

[46] BA Koblenz R86/946, Bd. 3: *Prof. Dr. G. Jägers Monatsblatt* (May 1893), pp. 81, 86, 90.

[47] Ibid. Bd. 2: *Tägliche Rundschau*, 8 Mar. 1893.

on 27 June 1893 went further and demanded that reports of cases be submitted to the medical boards and not the police.[48]

But it was not this strange coalition of interests that stopped the Bill from becoming law, so much as the declining urgency of the issue as the memory of the 1892 epidemic receded. The dissolution of the Reichstag and the elections of June 1893 meant that the Bill was lost for the time being and had to be reintroduced into the newly elected legislature in November.[49] But the press of urgent business relegated it to a low priority and it failed to reach the floor of the house during the legislative period of 1893–8. Just when it looked as if the Epidemics Bill, like the Revolution Bill, the Prison Bill, and the Lex Heinze, was to become one of the numerous legislative casualties that littered the parliamentary history of the 1890s, a new scare arose that was sufficiently urgent to reactivate it: in 1899 bubonic plague threatened Europe from the Middle East, and the medical theory that it was carried by rats gave the government the scientific legitimation to reintroduce the Epidemics Bill.[50] When it came to the Reichstag, there was little mention of cholera. The fronts lined up much as before. The Centre Party was appeased by a clause allowing relatives to visit patients on isolation wards. The doctors continued to demand the exclusive right to report cases to the authorities, with as little success as before. The Social Democrats used the occasion to launch renewed attacks on housing and living conditions among the working classes, and also to criticize the state of Germany's hospitals. But most of them supported the Bill on a free vote. And so it finally passed onto the statute book, coming into effect on 30 June 1900.[51]

Thus, ironically, a centralized law to deal with epidemics came into force just at the time when epidemics had ceased to be a real threat any more. Cholera, typhoid, and smallpox had dropped to negligible proportions by the turn of the century, and typhus, bubonic plague, and yellow fever were not remotely likely to occur on a major scale in Germany at this time. No wonder the *National-Zeitung* was moved to complain in 1900 that the law was directed only against 'exotic plagues' and went on to demand preventive measures against 'the indigenous plagues which are a general danger to all and cost us hundreds of millions of marks year in, year out.'[52] Initially brought before the Reichstag as an instant reaction to the cholera epidemic of 1892, the Bill disappeared as soon as the danger of a renewed cholera epidemic was past,

[48] Ibid. Bd. 4: *Verhandlungen des XXI. Deutschen Aerztetages am 27. Juni 1893 in Breslau*, p. 27.
[49] RT, 1893 Session, Drucksache 104.
[50] BA Koblenz R86/946 Bd. 4 contains the relevant documents tracing the legislative history of the Bill between 1893 and 1898. The new draft was printed in RT, 10. Leg. Per., 1. Sess. (1898–1900), Drucksache 690.
[51] RT, 10. Leg. Per., 179. Sitzung (24 Apr. 1900) col. 5060–75; 180. Sitzung (25 Apr. 1900), col. 5989–6003; 208. Sitzung (11 June 1900), col. 5989–6003; 209. Sitzung (12 June 1900), col. 6010–77; *Reichsgesetzblatt*, 1900, p. 306.
[52] BA Koblenz R86/946 Bd. 5: *National-Zeitung*, 5 May 1900.

and it was only reactivated in 1900 as a by-product of Wilhelmine *Weltpolitik*, in which increased involvement with Middle Eastern and overseas territories was thought to bring with it an increased danger of infection with the exotic diseases prevalent in these areas. As originally conceived, the Bill had provided the Imperial Chancellor with powers to order the federated states to implement the measures decided upon in Berlin. The role of Robert Koch in Hamburg in 1892 showed that these powers already had a *de facto* existence; and the experience was in practice unlikely to be repeated. What the states could expect instead was a steady increase in the daily interference of the Imperial Health Office in their affairs.[53] But this was happening anyway. The history of the Epidemics Bill was thus another demonstration of the limited and temporary impact of the cholera epidemic on medical and sanitary reform.

III

One of the most significant aspects of the debate over the reactivated Epidemics Bill in 1899–1900 was the absence of any serious objections from Munich. Pettenkofer's advanced age and declining powers robbed anticontagionism of its most doughty champion; and even the Bavarian government seems to have paid increasing heed to the contagionist point of view in the intervening period. Yet Pettenkofer's miasmatism did not die with its author. The unfortunate Rudolf Emmerich, who had repeated Pettenkofer's auto-experiment before a lecture class, maintained his faith in his teacher's ground-water theory to the end of his life. Well after the turn of the century, Emmerich and his colleagues published a massive six-volume survey of epidemic diseases in which they poured scorn on Koch's views and asserted once more that local soil conditions were the decisive factor. Typhoid, dysentery, and cholera were all ascribed principally to this cause. In volume three, which ran to 750 pages, Emmerich and five colleagues concluded that 'drinking-water plays no part in the causation of cholera epidemics ... the propagation of cholera depends chiefly on the properties of the soil.'[54] In 1904, indeed, Emmerich and Koch presented their rival theories in a court of law, in a celebrated case in which the directors, the engineer, and the chief mechanic of the waterworks in the Ruhr town of Gelsenkirchen were prosecuted for having allegedly let polluted river-water into the supply in 1901, resulting in a typhoid epidemic in which some 240 people had died. Called as a witness for the defence, Emmerich disputed the connection drawn by Koch between the pollution and the typhoid, with the result that the most serious of the charges against the four men were dropped.[55] Even as late as 1912 Georg Sticker, in a 600-page

[53] Ibid. Bd. 2: *National-Zeitung*, 8 Feb. 1893.

[54] C. E. A. Winslow, *The Conquest of Epidemic Disease. A Chapter in the History of Ideas* (Princeton, 1944), pp. 331–4.

[55] N. Howard-Jones, 'Gelsenkirchen Typhoid Epidemic of 1901, Robert Koch and the Dead Hand of Max von Pettenkofer,' *British Medical Journal* (1973), 103–5.

work on cholera, reported that Emmerich and his colleague F. Wolter 'have finally liquidated the drinking-water hypothesis.'[56]

In the longer run, miasmatism may have been transformed into a general concern with the environment, above all with air pollution, which, as we saw in Chapter 2, aroused widespread anxiety from the 1890s. But as early as 1893 Pettenkofer and Emmerich were described as 'completely isolated' in the medical profession.[57] Laymen who disliked the practical consequences of Koch's theories, most notably the merchant oligarchs of Hamburg, could continue to grumble about them. Yet even in 1892, as we have seen, they were unable to mount any effective resistance. The nationwide, indeed world-wide outcry against the Hamburg authorities in 1892 ensured that they could not afford to translate their opposition to quarantine, isolation, disinfection, or bacteriological diagnosis into public policy any more. After the resignation of Johann Caspar Kraus, they were faced with the fact that their own leading medical officials, Reincke and Rumpf at their head, no longer opposed Koch's views either, whatever more junior medical men might continue to think. Koch, together with Pasteur, had succeeded, one might argue, in establishing a *paradigm*, to use the concept developed by Thomas Kuhn: a general theory which could serve as the organizing principle for research, directing scientists where to look and telling them what problems were to be solved. Like all scientific paradigms, the bacteriological model of infectious disease was not immediately or universally accepted. But by the turn of the century those who ignored or opposed it can fairly be described as professionally margi-nalized. From the general historian's point of view, however, while Kuhn's own paradigm of the history of science is more fruitful than a simple linear model of cumulative discovery, it still has one major drawback: that is, it views scientific paradigms in isolation. Kuhn describes the process of paradigm formation, crisis, and scientific revolution strictly within the confines of scientific thought; indeed, different sciences—optics, electrical research, astronomy, and so on—are treated by Kuhn largely in isolation from each other, as well as in isolation from the broader historical context of the society within which they operate. Scientific theory in a field such as physics or pure mathematics may well develop entirely according to its own inner, paradigmatic logic; and scientific revolutions in these fields may well be entirely unrelated to social, economic, or political factors operating in the

---

[56] G. Sticker, *Abhandlungen aus der Seuchengeschichte und Seuchenlehre, ii. Die Cholera* (Giessen, 1912), quoted in Howard-Jones, 'Gelsenkirchen Typhoid Epidemic.' See also the positive account of Pettenkofer's theory in F. Weiling, 'J. G. Mendel sowie die von M. Pettenkofer angeregten Untersuchungen des Zusammenhanges von Cholera- und Typhus-Massenerkrankungen mit dem Grundwasserstand', *Südhoffs Archiv* 59 (1975), 1–19. On the struggles between the pupils of Pettenkofer and those of Koch, see W. Artelt *et al.* (eds.), *Städte-, Wohnungs- und Kleiderhygiene des 19. Jahrhunderts in Deutschland* (Stuttgart, 1969), pp. 17 ff.

[57] BA Koblenz R86/946 Bd. 2: *Berliner Tageblatt*, 14 Feb. 1893 (letter from an anonymous German bacteriologist).

world at large. But the same cannot be maintained of the social sciences, which is one reason why the application of Kuhn's approach to them is so problematical.[58]

Whether medicine should be placed within the 'pure' or the social sciences, and consequently whether medical theory develops according to its own inner logic or whether it develops in response to a broader social and political determination, is ultimately perhaps the fundamental theoretical question at issue in the debate on nineteenth-century theories of cholera. Neither contagionism nor miasmatism had any real effect on the efficacy of treatment of the disease, which remained minimal or negative throughout the nineteenth century. But while miasmatists had no hope of offering a breakthrough in this area, at least the bacteriological model offered the ultimate—though as it turned out in the short and medium term illusory—prospect of developing an antidote once the causative organism was identified. Similarly, while miasmatists remained openly sceptical about the possibility of effective prevention, contagionists were able to demonstrate on the Russian border throughout the 1890s that quarantine could stop the spread of the disease.[59] Ironically, railways and steamboats, which so speeded up the transmission of cholera, also enabled the authorities to control traffic more easily, at fewer points, and with greater rapidity. Water-filtration and hygienic precautions were enough to do the rest. Bacteriology triumphed, therefore, not least because, in reality and in potential, it was clearly seen to be more effective than the miasmatic approach.

Yet this very effectiveness was itself a result, as much as a cause, of the general acceptance of Koch's views. Indeed, the measures that confirmed the persuasiveness of the bacteriological model would have been unthinkable—as they were in the era of Pettenkofer's dominance two decades before—without such a general acceptance. So while Koch's account of cholera might well have been discredited had it not been confirmed in this way, its initial acceptance was a result of other factors. These included of course the general helplessness of miasmatism in the face of cholera, but there were also other influences too. Koch's bacteriological approach was ideally suited to an age of discovery; his achievement in isolating the bacillus was hailed as a national triumph; the quarantine and disinfection measures his theory demanded were in tune with the protectionist, centralizing temper of the German government of the time. In this case at least, therefore, medical science was clearly strongly influenced by social, economic, and political factors, and the Kuhnian concept of the paradigm is of limited use in explaining its development.[60]

Like the Epidemics Law to which it gave birth, bacteriological theory also seemed in many ways to be mainly useful in dealing with diseases which had

[58] For a more positive view, see B. Barnes, *T. S. Kuhn and Social Science* (London, 1982).

[59] See Map 25, above.

[60] For a fuller development of the argument recapitulated here, see Chapter 3d, above.

ceased to be a real threat by 1900. Subsequent experience, above all during the First World War, when typhus, dysentery, typhoid, and cholera were effectively contained by epidemiological strategies devised in the late nineteenth century, clearly vindicated Koch's approach. But the era of *Weltpolitik* that began at the very end of the 1890s took medical attention away from epidemics and refocused it on the problem of the German birth-rate, which was just entering its steep, long-term decline at this time. Reforming officials in Berlin were increasingly concerned to counteract this tendency both by educating the public in their 'national duty' to have children and by taking steps to lower the country's high rate of infant mortality. They sponsored the rapid spread of public health dispensaries to deal with specific afflictions such as tuberculosis, for which the first dispensary opened in 1899, with no fewer than 320 having been established by 1910; or more general problems such as the improvement of infant care, for which the first dispensary began work in 1905 and was followed by 1,000 more in the next decade. This new strategy of scientific hygiene was aimed partly at creating a numerous people fit for war, and partly at moralizing the working population, above all in the countryside, who were required to provide the loyal Imperial armies of the future.[61]

At the same time the medical profession became rapidly converted to more thoroughly collectivist and state interventionist strategies of health care than it had previously countenanced (for example in the era when Pettenkofer's voluntaristic conception of social hygiene was dominant). A vast range of medical or paramedical pressure groups emerged, from the Society for Public Hygiene (1900) to the Society Against Infant Mortality (1907). They co-operated with the state in extending the network of institutions designed to improve public health and hygiene, nutrition, and morality. Schools were increasingly used as centres for health investigation and improvement from the turn of the century on. All these voluntary associations were, as Paul Weindling has suggested, a medical equivalent of the burgeoning nationalist associations founded at the same time, such as the Navy League (*Flottenverein*) or the Society for the Eastern Marches (*Ostmarkenverein*). And like these officially backed nationalist movements, they had to face not only opposition from other parts of the Imperial bureaucracy but also an increasingly vociferous challenge from even more radical groups beyond them, in this case the eugenicists and Social Darwinists who urged a more comprehensive state policy of racial hygiene and selection.[62]

[61] F. Prinzing, *Epidemics Resulting from Wars* (Oxford, 1916); W. His, *Die Front der Ärzte* (Bielefeld and Leipzig, 1931). See also P. Weindling's important paper on 'The Medical Profession, Social Hygiene and the Birth Rate in Germany 1914–1918' (Cambridge Conference on the European Family and the Great War, 1983). The dates are misleading; much of the paper deals with the period before 1914.

[62] Ibid.; cf. also G. Eley, *Reshaping the German Right: Radical Nationalism and Political Change After Bismarck* (New Haven, 1980) and Adelheid Gräfin zu Castell-Rüdenhausen, 'Die Überwindung der Armenschule. Schülerhygiene an den Hamburger öffentlichen Volksschulen im Zweiten Kaiserreich,' *Archiv für Sozialgeschichte*, 22 (1982), 201–26.

These new movements emerged among other reasons because the Social Democrats at this time were mounting an increasingly explicit challenge to the existing structure of health care. Early socialist approaches to disease argued that its ultimate causes lay in the social inequalities of the capitalist mode of production. Correspondingly, in the 1870s Social Democrats tended to stress the need for state action to improve the sanitary infrastructure. Water-supplies, sewage disposal, street cleaning, food adulteration, housing conditions, and the hours, conditions, and pay of wage labour—all were the subject of the Social Democrats' attention at this time. The state take-over and reform of water-supplies and waste disposal remained constant demands of the party up to the turn of the century and beyond. By the 1890s, however, the Social Democrats were also demanding the creation of a National Health Service with free treatment and hospital care, the nationalization of apothecaries, and the conversion of doctors from private entrepreneurs into state functionaries. They devoted much attention—for instance, in the final debates on the Epidemics Bill—to criticizing the state of German hospitals. They were well aware of social inequalities in the face of death and disease and argued that a universally healthy society would only be possible after a socialist revolution ('socialism is the best doctor,' as a popular slogan put it).[63] And although some of these demands were eventually realized, it remained unlikely that most of them would be fulfilled under the existing capitalist order.

As the Social Democrats became increasingly involved in the affairs of municipalities where the local electoral system was sufficiently democratic to allow their election to the town council, so they began to develop an increasingly detailed set of further demands that could not immediately be dismissed as revolutionary nonsense. By the turn of the century Social Democratic town councillors in many parts of Germany were demanding measures to lower infant mortality, fight tuberculosis, and protect pregnant mothers. More than this, they wanted special local health offices set up with wide-ranging powers to reform the 'unnatural, unhealthy conditions of life' which they believed were the cause of all disease. They demanded an elaborate network of controls to improve food hygiene and nutrition. They urged the free distribution of disinfectants. And they pressed for the construction of sanatoria, baths, infant care dispensaries, and a whole range of other public health institutions at state expense.[64] These demands in many ways took up and amplified the social theory of disease advanced by democratic-liberal doctors such as Rudolf Virchow in 1848. They constituted a serious challenge to the existing status

[63] A. Labisch, 'Die gesundheitspolitischen Vorstellungen der deutschen Sozialdemokratie von ihrer Gründung bis zur Parteispaltung (1863–1917),' *Archiv für Sozialgeschichte*, 16 (1976), 325–70; and the same author's 'Das Krankenhaus in der Gesundheitspolitik der deutschen Sozialdemokratie vor dem Ersten Weltkrieg,' *Medizinsoziologisches Jahrbuch* (1981), pp. 126–51.

[64] Labisch, 'Die gesundheitspolitischen Vorstellungen.'

of the medical profession and would have required a substantial shift of resources to be implemented to their full extent.

Yet in some ways they were not the ideal mixture of reformist and revolutionary demands that they seemed at first sight to be. It was easy enough to distinguish them from the racist and eugenicist proposals of social hygiene propagandists such as Alfred Grotjahn, although subsequent historians have sometimes unfortunately failed to do so.[65] And although German doctors often gained a good deal of their income from state employment as local or district medical officers, the Social Democratic proposals would have removed their private fees which were often an even more important source of income for them.[66] The militarist thrust behind the state interventionist policies pushed by reforming bureaucrats after the turn of the century was also quite alien to the egalitarian impulses behind the Social Democratic programme. Nor did the Social Democrats ever share either Pettenkofer's pessimism about the possibilities of preventing epidemics, or—despite their immediate acceptance of his theories—Koch's exclusive emphasis on bacteriological causation.

In a practical sense, seen from the point of view of those at whom these policies were directed, the results of many of these divergent theories might be very similar in the end. For in broad political terms, it was in a way not so much Koch's view that triumphed in 1892 as Virchow's. Medical scientists continued to argue about cholera, albeit with diminishing passion as the years went by; the promise of an Epidemics Law, contagionist in spirit and practice, was not realized until the turn of the century, and then for reasons that had little to do with cholera; and the vigilance enjoined by Koch in the face of threatened epidemics was sacrificed in the autumn of 1893 to the interests of overseas trade and the stock exchange. While the consequences of the great cholera epidemic for medical science and medical practice were thus less dramatic than might at first sight have been supposed, there was on the other hand no doubting the importance of its consequences for social policy. Virtually everyone agreed in 1892 that social inequality, poverty, poor housing, inadequate nutrition, and lack of public and private hygiene were major causes of the disaster. The will to do something about these problems in Hamburg as the epidemic receded was virtually unanimous. We turn now to see how quickly, and in what ways, it was turned into practice.

---

[65] K. H. Roth, 'Schein-Alternativen im Gesundheitswesen: Alfred Grotjahn (1869–1931)— Integrationsfigur etablierter Sozialmedizin und nationalsozialistischer "Rassenhygiene"', in K. H. Roth (ed.), *Erfassung zur Vernichtung. Von der Sozialhygiene zum "Gesetz über Sterbehilfe"* (Berlin, 1984), pp. 31–56.

[66] For the background to this, see C. Huerkamp and R. Spree, 'Arbeitsmarktstrategien der deutschen Ärzteschaft im späten 19. und frühen 20. Jahrhundert. Zur Entwicklung des Marktes für professionelle ärztliche Dienstleistungen,' in T. Pierenkemper and R. Tilly (eds.), *Historische Arbeitsmarktforschung* (Göttingen, 1982), pp. 77–116.

c. *Poverty and the State*

I

The task of sanitary reform in the wake of the 1892 epidemic was initially taken up by a Joint Commission of the Senate and Citizens' Assembly for the Examination of Health Problems in Hamburg. It met on 15 September with the President of the Imperial Health Office and Robert Koch in attendance as representatives of Imperial Chancellor Caprivi. The meeting proved to be another occasion for the exercise of Koch's power over the city. He criticized the disinfection arrangements in Hamburg and secured immediate agreement to acquire proper disinfection machines. He told Chief Engineer Meyer how to maintain the sand filtration of the central water-supply. He persuaded the Joint Commission to organize a campaign to disinfect, relocate, or remove all the tanks (*Wasserkasten*) in which many of the city's inhabitants stored their drinking-water (they were, he said, 'breeding-places for bacilli, places where they could also easily last through the winter'). He urged another, even more comprehensive programme of general housing inspection and disinfection. All this was put into practice. Koch's disciple Georg Gaffky was appointed as hygienic adviser to the city at a substantial salary, and Gaffky acted on Koch's behalf at subsequent meetings of the Commission. By 28 October the Commission's deliberations had begun to take on a wide-ranging character. It decided that a major effort would have to be made to improve the sanitary condition of the housing stock, not only by tightening up planning regulations and establishing a housing inspectorate but also by initiating a slum clearance programme.[1] These proposals soon resolved themselves into a major public debate on the problem of the Alley Quarters.

Already in the early days of the 1892 epidemic, Koch's description of the 'Asiatic' conditions he perceived in the Alley Quarters of Hamburg's inner city, added to the popular memory of earlier epidemics in these areas, their visibility to bourgeois observers, and the undoubtedly high incidence of cholera in some blocks and streets within them, combined to focus general attention on the danger they represented. Vivid descriptions of the Alley Quarters soon filled the local, national, and international press. The *Hamburger Freie Presse* railed against the 'plague-spots of the inner city'; the *National-Zeitung* complained about 'everything that lies behind the façades, with old, crooked, dingy, airless houses, the abodes of the poor, crammed with people, and full of dirt and miasmas';[2] and the roving correspondent of

[1] StA Hbg, MK III A 12, §§ 1–58, 70.
[2] StA Hbg, PP S3496 Bd. I: *Hamburger Freie Presse*, 20 Nov. 1892; StA Hbg, Senat, Cl. VII, Lit. Ta, Pars 2, Vol. 11, Fasc. 17, Inv. 4: *National-Zeitung*, 28 Aug. 1892.

the London *Times* called Hamburg 'the dirtiest town I had ever seen on this side of the Mediterranean', criticized the 'tall houses excluding light and air from the narrow roadways' and found the 'walls and pavements greasy, dingy, and forbidding. And then', he added, 'those dreadful canals. You could almost fancy the cholera rising in visible shape from the foul and stagnant water bordered by black slime'.[3] Among medical men, contagionists saw the dampness, overcrowding, and lack of proper hygiene and sanitation in the Alley Quarters as major sources of infection, while anticontagionists saw their low elevation, proximity to the fleets and the river, and lack of light and air as ideal conditions for the creation of deadly miasmas.[4]

The pressure on the Senate to take radical steps to deal with the threat posed by the Alley Quarters was thus immense. Already in November 1892, the *Hamburger Freie Presse* was demanding 'the pulling down of the Alley Quarters and the construction of broad streets'.[5] The Social Democrats concurred in demanding the improvement of these areas and the construction of cheap and healthy accommodation for the working class. A general sense of shocked discovery was evident in wide circles of the Hamburg bourgeoisie. Jakob Loewenberg's comment must stand as representative for countless similar statements made in published and private writings by Hamburg's citizens in the autumn of 1892: 'Never', he wrote, 'had I ... realized what poverty concealed itself behind the proud and resplendent buildings of the great city, how dreadful was the chasm that separated the frontage and the houses behind. Those were not even people of the same era, the same land, the same race.'[6] In the Reichstag, Senator Burchard, faced with the threat of an Imperial Housing Law, was forced to promise radical reforms to improve living conditions in the inner city.[7] In Hamburg, the Senate and Citizens' Assembly quickly agreed to the establishment of a joint 'Slum Clearance Commission' (*Sanierungskommission*) to undertake the improvement of the Alley Quarters. Legislative powers already existed in the shape of the expropriation laws used as the basis for the construction of the new harbour in the 1880s. Further precedents lay in the construction of the Wexstrasse, breaking through part of the Alley Quarters in the Neustadt, in 1865–6, and the Kaiser Wilhelm Strasse built to join it in the summer of 1892.[8] The Slum Clearance Commission soon began to organize the pulling down of some of the houses worst affected by cholera in 1892.[9] The radical reforms promised by Burchard thus seemed to be getting under way.

[3] Ibid.: *The Times*, 27 Sept. 1892.
[4] For further comments, see above, Chapter 5b.
[5] StA Hbg, PP S3496 Bd. I: *Hamburger Freie Presse*, 26 Nov. 1892.
[6] Loewenberg, *Aus zwei Quellen*, p. 283.
[7] Cf. Chapter 4d, above.
[8] H. Speckter, 'Die grossen Sanierungsmassnahmen Hamburgs seit der zweiten Hälfte des 19. Jahrhunderts', *Raumforschung und Raumordnung*, 6 (1967) 257–68.
[39] Wischermann, *Wohnen in Hamburg*, pp. 94–5.

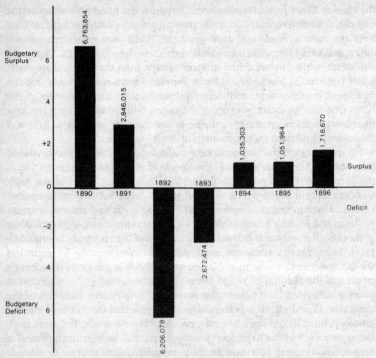

Source: Statistisches Handbuch für den Hamburgischen Staat, 1920 (Hamburg, 1921)

FIG. 29. Hamburg state budget: surplus and deficit 1890–6 (in Marks)

But as the immediate impact of the epidemic began to fade, so too did the reforming zeal of the Joint Commission. 'At the moment', wrote Burgomaster Johann Georg Mönckeberg in October 1892, 'everything is sailing under the flag of hygiene: but there will soon be a reaction once more when people have forgotten their fear and the colossal expenditure which is naturally bound up with the projects at present under consideration comes to the foreground.' As Figure 29 indicates, the cost to the Senate of fighting the epidemic brought a serious budgetary deficit in 1892 and prevented the state finances from recovering for another year after that. In order to improve its financial situation, indeed, the Senate was forced to propose a major increase in direct taxation, which came into effect in 1895 and almost doubled the level of tax in the higher income brackets, while at the same time raising the lowest tax threshhold from 600 Marks to 900. In these circumstances the Senate soon thought twice before undertaking costly projects that might necessitate a further rise in taxation. Moreover, the property-owners in the Citizens' Assembly quickly ranged themselves against proposals which, they thought, showed 'what ruinous progress socialist notions have already made in the wake of the most recent German social policy'.[10] So nothing of significance was done for over four years. Then, suddenly, the Senate and Citizens' Assembly leapt into activity again. In December 1896 the Assembly voted for far-reaching proposals for slum clearance in the inner city, to be financed by the state. Early in 1897 a new 'Commission for the Improvement of Housing Conditions' (*Kommission für die Verbesserung der Wohnverhältnisse*) was set up. Within two years it had produced a comprehensive plan to tear down the three main Alley Quarters in the Altstadt and Neustadt, and to replace them with model 'healthy dwellings' for the inhabitants.

The reason for this dramatic turn-about lay in the reaction of the dominant classes to the massive port strike of 1896-7. Beginning on 20 November 1896, the strike soon involved over 16,000 harbour workers and seamen, and lasted until 6 February, when the strikers finally admitted defeat. These events aroused nation-wide, indeed world-wide attention: the long and bitter struggle became the most celebrated in the history of labour conflict in nineteenth-century Germany after the miners' strike of 1889. It administered a shock to the dominant classes in Hamburg even more severe than that of the cholera epidemic four years previously.[11] The strike was not led by the regular trade unions or the Social Democrats: as a contemporary police report noted: 'throughout the whole strike movement not a single factor could be found to indicate the direct responsibility of the Social Democratic party'.[12] On the contrary, it was mainly pushed forward and sustained by the mass of unorganized casual port labourers, whose chances of finding employment during the winter months were not very good in any case. But while the Social Democrats and the trade unions attempted throughout to bring the strike to an end, even in the absence of concessions from the employers, the tough stance taken by the employers' association aroused widespread sympathy for the strikers not only in the Social Democratic Party itself—in the rest of Germany as much as in Hamburg—but also in a minority of the bourgeoisie. Feminists such as Lida Gustava Heymann organized free meals for the wives and children of the strikers, and large sections of the petty

[10] Mönckeberg, *Bürgermeister Mönckeberg*, p. 24; StA Hbg, Senat, Cl. VII, Lit. Ta, Pars 2, Vol. 11, Fasc. 16, Inv. 22: *Hamburger Echo*, 2 Nov. 1892 (reporting a meeting of the Hohenfelde Citizens' Club). For the tax reform, see StA Hbg, PP S3496 Bd. 2, 'Einkommenssteuer 1893–1918', *passim*.

[11] Among numerous accounts of this famous strike, the most recent and informative are M. Grüttner, 'Mobilität und Konfliktverhalten. Der Hamburger Hafenarbeiterstreik 1896/97', in K. Tenfelde and H. Volkmann (eds.), *Streik* (Munich, 1984), pp. 143–61; the same author's *Arbeitswelt an der Wasserkante: Sozialgeschichte der Hamburger Hafenarbeiter 1886–1914* (Göttingen, 1984), pp. 165–75; and H.-J. Bieber, 'Der Hamburger Hafenarbeiterstreik 1896/97', in A. Herzig, D. Langewiesche, and A. Sywottek (eds.), *Arbeiter in Hamburg: Unterschichten, Arbeiter und Arbeiterbewegung seit dem ausgehenden 18. Jahrhundert* (Hamburg, 1983), pp. 229–45.

[12] Grüttner, *Arbeitswelt*, p. 293 n. 134, citing Gustav Roscher.

bourgeoisie, especially innkeepers, brewers, artisans, and small shopkeepers dependent on the working class for custom, ranged themselves behind the strikers, while substantial parts of the merchant community and indeed even the Senate initially attempted to mediate. As the strike grew more bitter, however, the authorities took increasingly harsh measures to try and suppress it. Conflict reached a height immediately after the strike was ended, when the frustrated strikers attacked strike-breakers in the harbour area and the Neustadt Süd. A riot erupted, and as the police moved in, striking out in all directions with their sabres in their now customary style of military confrontation, their progress was met with a hail of stones, bottles, rubbish, and other objects from the houses of the Alley Quarter in which they found themselves. Several thousand people, including not only the strikers but also their womenfolk, engaged with the massed forces of the Hamburg police in two days of bitter fighting which shocked not only the bourgeois public but also the trade union leadership.[13]

These events led to a renewed concentration of public attention on the Alley Quarters as centres of moral contagion and social disorder. As the *Hamburgischer Correspondent* declared on 3 April 1897, the 'brutal outrages of so-called "young rowdies" in the last strike' were carried out by 'coarse youths, such as only the air-, light-, and loveless Alley Quarters of a great city can breed'. The petty criminals and disorderly elements who lived in the Alley Quarters were commonly described as a 'light-shy rabble' (*lichtscheues Gesindel*); and just as this phrase was clearly metaphorical, so too the demand for 'more air! more light!' to be brought into these areas also carried a heavy burden of symbolic meaning.[14] More explicitly than ever before, the health hazard allegedly posed by these quarters now moved into the centre of discussion as a symbolic expression of the socio-political threat revealed in the strike of 1896–7. Soon the employers' association was urging the bodily removal of the 'dangerous classes' from the inner city to the outer suburbs and the construction of a suburban railway to provide them with cheap and rapid transport to their workplace in the harbour. It wanted the Senate to undertake a thorough slum clearance programme and to improve the street paving so that workers living outside the city could bicycle to work instead of having to walk for over an hour, through which 'a great part of their capacity for work is lost'.[15] The Chamber of Commerce, for its part, informed the Senate in February 1897 that it was important after the strike

[13] Ibid., pp. 169–75.
[14] StA Hbg, MK II G 4, Bd. 1, 116: *Hamburgischer Correspondent*, 3 Apr. 1897; ibid., Bl. 113: *General-Anzeiger*, 13 Mar. 1897. For similar motives among housing reformers in 1850, see Wischermann, *Wohnen in Hamburg*, p. 48.
[15] 'Eingabe des Arbeitgeberverbandes', 3 Mar. 1897, in StA Hbg, Kommission für die Verbesserung der Wohnverhältnisse 24. See also the direct links with the 'excesses of young vandals (*Halbstarken*)' drawn in 'Bedeutung der Wohnungsfrage für die Verbilligung der Arbeitskräfte' in

that the workers are removed from the influences that lead to their embitterment against the employers and that contentment is encouraged among them. The most effective means to this end seems to be the provision of cheap and good-quality dwellings, especially of dwellings in the open, beyond the stifling confines of the streets and the bustle of the big city. Modern economic development brings with it the concentration of ever-larger masses of people in centres of communication. This has deleterious effects on health and morality, on the spirit and on the soul. These can only be compensated for by a decentralization of living-places which enables workers to create for themselves friendly homes in an open environment.[16]

In the public debate that ensued, it was the sanitary evils of the Alley Quarters, expressed above all through their role as the 'plague spots' (*Seuchenherde*) of the cholera epidemic of 1892, that held the stage: but behind this discourse, the hidden agenda of the removal of these quarters as centres of social and political discontent was clearly understood. It was not by accident, indeed, that parallels were now drawn with the great clearance schemes of Haussmann in Paris under Napoleon III, for these too had been guided by political as much as sanitary and other motives.[17]

As the slum clearance plan got under way, it quickly became—like every other major act of urban renewal in nineteenth-century Hamburg—the focus of a sharp conflict of interest between different fractions of capital within the city. While the merchants and employers, backed by the Senate, wanted social peace through the provision of cheap and healthy dwellings, both in the city centre and the suburbs, the property-owners were naturally interested in getting the best terms for compulsory purchase and the most profitable form of housing in the subsequent reconstruction. The property-owners' representation in the Citizens' Assembly made it certain that the Senate would not be able to realize its plans without substantial concessions, since the purchase price had to be approved by both the sovereign organs of the Hamburg state. The price was set so high that the Senate had to abandon its plan of imposing a legal maximum rent in the clearance areas because this would have lowered the price of resales after reconstruction so much that the state would have emerged from the deal with substantial losses. So it was decided instead to reserve 1,700 out of the 3,700 dwellings in the first clearance area, in the Neustadt, for small dwellings. However, when they were eventually constructed, their rents were double those of the old slums, and so the former inhabitants were unable to move back in. Thus the clearance of the Alley Quarters in the Neustadt, which took place between 1900 and 1908, certainly improved housing conditions there—not least

Hamburgischer Correspondent, 3–4 Apr. 1897 (copies ibid., 20). For an earlier version of these arguments, see J. H. Heidmann, *Hamburgs Verkehrsmittel und Wohnungsverhältnisse* (Hamburg, 1891).

[16] StA Hbg, Kommission für die Verbesserung der Wohnverhältnisse, 20: Eingabe des Handelskammers, 20 Feb. 1897. See also Plate 33.

[17] See the discussion of these points in Wischermann, *Wohnen in Hamburg*, pp. 94–5.

through raising ground levels to prevent a recurrence of the flooding that had been such a plague in the 1890s. But it was achieved at the cost of driving over 20,000 people from their homes without any practical steps being taken to find them alternative accommodation. A sustained boom in the construction of small dwellings which began from the turn of the century was concentrated in the outer suburbs and failed to fill the gap left by the clearance schemes.[18]

The sharp rise in rents in the improved areas had consequences delineated with considerable honesty by an official report in 1911:

The Neustadt Süd gives an example of the success with which the erection of small dwellings in the inner city has met. Not a single one of the families who used to inhabit the area has returned to live there, because the rents for small dwellings are too high despite the low price of the land. In order to be able to pay the rent, even the better-situated worker has to sublet to unmarried lodgers and thus reduce the living space of his own family in a manner that is quite alarming. The problem of lodgers, with all its moral repulsiveness, has arisen once more in the Neustadt to an unforeseen extent, and it is bound to reach the same extent in the slum-clearance area of the Altstadt if small dwellings are erected there as well.[19]

Whereas the proportion of households with lodgers was 28% in the Neustadt Süd in 1890, by 1910 it had climbed to 32%, and a similar growth was observable in the other Alley Quarter districts, reaching 37% in the Neustadt Nord and 34% in the Altstadt Nord by the latter date.[20] Moreover Hamburg retained the highest proportion of cellar dwellings of any town in Germany. 42,000 people lived in cellars in Hamburg as late as 1910. Ironically, therefore, a clearance scheme which had among its principal objects the reduction of overcrowding, the elimination of lodgers, and the creation of a contented working class based on the small family apartment, in the end did little to achieve any of these aims.[21]

The Senate realized that it would not be possible on financial grounds alone to continue with the ambition of settling displaced slum-dwellers in the reconstructed inner city. The next area marked for clearance was situated in the Altstadt, near to the city's main public buildings and so ideally placed for the construction of office-blocks. These would have the added advantage of providing the state with a better return on its investment in clearance than the creation of healthy labourers' dwellings could do. And indeed while the

[18] Ibid., pp. 111–13, 117–27; and M. Grüttner, 'Soziale Hygiene und Soziale Kontrolle: Die Sanierung der Hamburger Gängeviertel 1892–1936', in Herzig *et al.*, *Arbeiter in Hamburg*, pp. 359–71.

[19] StA Hbg, Kommission für die Verbesserung der Wohnverhältnisse, 51: Baudeputation I. Sektion, Zentralbureau des Ingenieurwesens Hamburg, 21 April 1911, Bericht betr. Sanierung der Altstadt südlich der Steinstrasse.

[20] Grüttner, 'Soziale Hygiene', p. 360.

[21] StA Hbg, PP S3496 Bd. I: *Hamburger Nachrichten*, 7 Mar. 1897. For cellar dwellings, see Wischermann, *Wohnen in Hamburg*, p. 145.

first phase of the clearance, in the Neustadt Süd, brought the state a net loss of some 20 million Marks, the second phase, involving the beginnings of a clearance of the Alley Quarters of the Altstadt, had cost a mere 2.75 million in all by the outbreak of the First World War. It was at this stage, from 1908 to 1911, that the long-awaited suburban railway was constructed to bring workers from the suburbs into the harbour, although a petition for the quick construction of such a railway had already gathered 11,000 signatories in November 1892. In the Altstadt too, thousands more people were forced to leave their homes and find their own accommodation elsewhere. If rents were cheaper in the outlying districts, the cost and inconvenience of commuting to work easily counterbalanced the improvement the move brought about— as the authorities themselves readily admitted (though only in private). Moreover, the widespread 'passive resistance' of the inhabitants of the Alley Quarters to forcible resettlement confirmed that for many, as an official employed on the scheme remarked, 'their home has become dear to them despite the lack of sunlight and the dilapidation of the houses, and they leave it with a heavy heart for the loveless, jerry-built multi-storey tenement blocks in the suburbs. Some of them had to be forcibly evicted by the bailiffs or the police.'[22]

II

While the physical removal of the 'dangerous classes' from the city centre marked the clear culmination of the fear of social contagion which had built up in the dominant classes since the 1860s, it was not the only strategy adopted at the end of the century to sanitize the living quarters of the proletariat. The dilapidated state of many of the buildings whose inhabitants had suffered most from cholera brought widespread calls for the tightening up of the planning regulations (*Baupolizeigesetze*). These were well known to be inadequate, since the property-owners had been able to frustrate all attempts to introduce strict planning regulations through their representation in the Citizens' Assembly. Fire precautions had naturally been tightened up after 1842, but twenty years later the addition of sanitary and health requirements advocated by the Doctors' Club was rejected by the Assembly 'in particular in order not to restrict the use of valuable building land too much, and in order not to encroach upon the freedom of the individual more

---

[22] Grüttner, 'Soziale Hygiene', pp. 364–6. The clearance of the Altstadt Alley Quarter was also in part a response to serious rioting there in 1906. See R. J. Evans, ' "Red Wednesday" in Hamburg: Social Democrats, Police and Lumpenproletariat in the Suffrage Disturbances of 17 January 1906', *Social History*, 4 (1979), 1–31. Heidmann, *Hamburgs Verkehrsmittel*, provides an interesting prediction of these developments. See StA Hbg. PP S3490 Bd. I: *General-Anzeiger*, 11 Nov. 1892 for the railway question.

than is necessary'.[23] The regulations introduced in 1865 did little more than
fix minimum norms for the size of passageways, courtyards, and building
storeys, and for the level of cellar floors. They were characterized as 'very
mild in comparison with similar laws in other large cities', and they were not
even extended to the outer suburbs until 1872.[24] In 1882 the regulations
were tightened up, and a requirement for all rooms to have windows opening
on to the outside world was introduced. The 1882 regulations laid down
quite detailed requirements for the provision of light and ventilation, and
were a good deal tougher than those of 1865. But they applied only to new
buildings, and so many exceptions were made that complaints were soon
heard that 'the fact that the existing laws are full of loopholes' was being
exploited 'in an almost unbelievable manner'.[25] The Senate moved quickly
after the cholera epidemic of 1892 to remedy this situation. The exceptions
were reduced, and new sanitary requirements added. The new regulations
were still not very effective, however, and the property-owners saw to it that
the 1882 regulations (as amended in 1893) remained in force until after the
First World War. Moreover, in 1902 a new law was passed, this time with
the full support of the Senate, which sought to encourage the construction
of small dwellings by relaxing planning regulations even further. Thus things
had changed very little in all.[26]

Planning regulations were by contrast immediately tightened up in the
'villa quarters', which were kept rigidly clear of factories and other buildings
which might disturb the peace which the grand bourgeoisie hoped to achieve
by living there.[27] For by the 1890s even the 'villa quarters' around the Alster
were being invaded by the working class. An attempt was made in a special
law of 20 December 1892 to plan the growth of the suburbs north of the Elbe
in an orderly way, and in 1896 a new general plan attempted not only to
lay down street lines to ensure the orderly distribution of traffic but also to
protect the 'villa quarters' from the contagious invasion of tenement blocks.
But these measures, mainly because of lax definitions, did little to counteract
the northward expansion of cheap housing. With the decline in the availability of housing in the city centre came a tendency for building speculators
to buy up plots in the sparsely populated areas immediately to the north,
where the better-off lived in large, detached villas surrounded by plenty of
empty ground. This development was gradually changing the character of
these areas, in a way which their original inhabitants did not like. The Health

---

[23] Bericht des von der Bürgerschaft am 20. Juni 1862 niedergesetzten Ausschusses zur Prüfung
des Antrages des Senats (1862, Nr. 54) betreffend das Baugesetz, Aug. 1863, p. 3 (copy in StA
Hbg, MK II G 3 Bd. 1).

[24] Wischermann, *Wohnen in Hamburg*, p. 71 (citing a contemporary source).

[25] StA Hbg, MK II G 3 Bd. 1: *Hamburgischer Correspondent*, 13 Sept. 1894.

[26] Wischermann, *Wohnen in Hamburg*, pp. 83, 117–27.

[27] See pp. 53–6 above.

Commission for Harvestehude, for example, complained in its second report on the epidemic:

Harvestehude is regrettably to a large extent no longer what it was in 1870. Since then a gradual transformation has taken place in Harvestehude. This process seems likely to destroy the district's good sanitary reputation. Slowly to begin with, then as time has passed by, more and more rapidly, colossi of stone have reared up between the villas, housing blocks with 4, 5, or 6 storeys, courtyards, passages, rear houses, and terraces.

Correspondingly, the grand bourgeoisie was on the move again, and this time it made sure that its peace could not be disturbed by such an unwelcome invasion of socially dubious elements by going to live in remoter suburbs further down the Elbe.[28]

It was not enough, however, to try and improve the housing stock by tightening up the planning laws. Already in October 1892 one commentator declared: 'experience shows that new, bright, and airy dwellings are often so neglected by their inhabitants that within a short space of time it is no longer healthy to live in them'. He therefore urged financial penalties for tenants who failed to keep their houses in order.[29] The first steps were taken during the epidemic itself, as the Citizens' Clubs set up local Health Commissions to organize disinfection and dispense advice on prevention. They operated in tandem with the Emergency Committees, but tended in the nature of things to be more dominated by the medical profession. On 20 September the Senate's Cholera Commission instructed them to carry out a comprehensive inspection of all the infected houses in their respective districts, and to check that they had been thoroughly disinfected. They were also required to notify the police of general living conditions in these houses. The police provided them with legitimation cards, and if they were refused entry they were advised to obtain police support. The status of the Commissions was thus made official. One report, for the Neustadt Nord, noted that while they usually got a friendly reception from tenants in the houses they visited, landlords were generally hostile, correctly reckoning that the disinfection procedure would cost them a good deal of money. In the whole area of the Altstadt Nord the Health Commission managed to deal with 100 households itself, but had to call the police in to deal with a further 66. In the Niedernstrasse, an Alley Quarter street notorious as a centre of prostitution and petty crime, the Health Commission was only able to disinfect 5 households without assistance from the police, who carried out the task in no fewer than 17 cases. This hostility was characteristic of the way the inhabitants of the Alley Quarters dealt with

[28] StA Hbg, MK III A 13, XI: Gesundheitskommission Harvestehude, pp. 7–8; Wischermann, *Wohnen in Hamburg*, pp. 284–5.
[29] StA Hbg, Senat, Cl. VII, Lit. Ta, Pars 2, Vol. 11, Fasc. 17, Inv. 1a: *Hamburger Tageblatt*, 21 Oct. 1892.

outsiders. But it also seems to have reflected an accurate perception of the Health Commssions' function of control.[30]

After the epidemic the Health Commissions became more or less dormant again, although in formal terms they continued in existence until the end of the century at least. But the Senate sought to institute a permanent, rigorous state control of health and sanitation by proposing a Housing Inspection Law (*Gesetz betreffend die Wohungspflege*) on 12 May 1893. This ran into immediate opposition from the property owners, who shunted it into a committee of the Citizens' Assembly, which rejected it altogether in June 1894 on the grounds that it proposed an unacceptable degree of interference in landlords' rights. Certainly the Law's stipulations about the permissible size and maintenance standards of dwellings would have committed the landlords to considerable expenditure, particularly since, in one of its most controversial points, it proposed to apply the new regulations to existing buildings as well as new ones. Like so many of the reforms set in motion in the aftermath of the epidemic, it ground to a halt within a very short space of time. Only after the harbour strike of 1896 were the proposals revived. This time even more comprehensive measures of inspection and control were envisaged.[31] Chief Medical Officer Johann Julius Reincke noted, in commenting on the slum clearance plans then under discussion, 'that a high mortality rate in unfavourable living conditions is not brought about by the dwelling alone but is also conditioned by the inhabitants' mode of life, nutritional standards, income, trade, and size of family'.[32] Measures would therefore have to be taken to improve these features of working-class life. As the Medical Board put it,

In poor and unhealthy dwellings people lapse into ill humour and listlessness, they lose their joy in their home and become alienated from it. Yet a home of one's own provides for adults what the parents' house provides for children, namely a centre of calm in the restlessness of life, a centre from which they can increasingly draw fresh strength for the struggles and burdens of the day. Contentment with one's home, love of one's own home, and pride in one's own home are the starting-points for all the civic virtues. Blessed is the city, therefore, which succeeds in providing healthy dwellings for its inhabitants.[33]

It proposed therefore to fix verifiable minimum hygienic standards for dwellings and to enforce them through a body of paid officials, the housing inspectors (*Wohnungspfleger*).

The Medical Board envisaged wide-ranging powers for the housing inspectors. They amounted to a *carte blanche* to reorganize the entire life-style of the working class. The inspectors were empowered to enter dwellings at will, and

---

[30] See the relevant reports in StA Hbg, MK III A13.

[31] Wischermann, *Wohnen in Hamburg*, pp. 85–93.

[32] StA Hbg, Kommission für die Verbesserung der Wohnverhältnisse, 25: Reincke to Hachmann, 13 July 1897.

[33] StA Hbg, MK II G 13, p. 8.

had instructions to inspect them for light and ventilation, the size and height of the rooms, the existence of steep or dark stairways that would be difficult to clean, the sanitary condition of the bathroom and toilet, damp, fungal infestations, and—in significant juxtaposition—the presence of animals, vermin, and lodgers. Working-class funeral rites were assailed in the belief that 'corpses which remain in the dwelling after the day of death pollute the air'. Even the few decorations with which working-class families could attempt to improve the drabness of their surroundings were not to be allowed. 'The cultivation of flowers', declared the instructions severely, 'can cause damp in dwellings and create foul air in them. Strong-smelling flowers in living-rooms cause headaches and other ailments.'[34] But the proposals also involved a far-reaching assault on the position of the landlords. Reincke and the Medical Board wanted to subject all dwellings in the city to medical inspection by paid state officials, they wanted the right to declare dwellings unfit for habitation, and above all they wanted to set minimum legal standards for healthy dwellings.[35] Those landlords whose properties did not conform to the exact and measurable requirements of the law in respect of lighting, windows, ventilation, sanitation, and the minimum space per inhabitant would have to pay for the necessary improvements. Not surprisingly, the landlords were plunged into 'panic-stricken terror' by these proposals.[36]

The Property-Owners' Association mobilized its forces in the Citizens' Assembly to frustrate the aims of the reformers. During the Bill's passage through the Assembly, all the quantitative stipulations were removed, leaving only vague and unenforceable general exhortations to provide a 'sufficient' number of toilets, light and ventilation 'in an adequate manner', and so on. The requirements for minimum space were reduced and restricted to subtenants, lodgers, and servants. The proposed paid housing inspectors were replaced by honorary inspectors on the lines of the Poor Law overseers. These, as we have seen, were drawn from the same middle-class and petty-bourgeois circles that provided the bulk of the membership of the Citizens' Clubs and indeed the Property-Owners' Association itself. In fact, when the law finally came into effect, there were widespread complaints 'that very many landlords are being called to the office of housing inspector'.[37] Just in case anyone apart from the landlords should manage to get himself appointed, the inspectors' powers of entry were confined to the daytime (9 a.m. to 8 p.m.), when most lodgers would be out of the house. The resulting law, which came into effect on 15 April 1899, was 'hopelessly mutilated', according to the semi-official *Hamburgischer Correspondent*.[38] 'The mountain has heaved', commented

[34] Ibid., pp. 13, 16, 55, 57.
[35] Wischermann, *Wohnen in Hamburg*, pp. 85–6.
[36] StA Hbg, PP S3496 Bd. I: *Neue Hamburger Zeitung*, 5 May 1898.
[37] Wischermann, *Wohnen in Hamburg*, pp. 87–93; StA Hbg, PP V273 Bd. 2: *Hamburger Nachrichten*, 14 June 1902.
[38] Ibid.: *Hamburgischer Correspondent*, 27 May 1898.

another newspaper, 'and brough forth a mouse.'[39] Revisions subsequently made in 1907 brought in more precise requirements, which were acceptable not least because the slum clearance programme was decisively altering the housing stock in the inner city anyway. But this made no difference to the ineffectiveness of the law, as the subsequent reports of the housing inspection authority made clear. Relatively few dwellings were inspected; the number of successful prosecutions only exceeded a hundred in two years before the First World War; and not surprisingly, these prosecutions were mainly connected with rent disputes.[40]

The policy of control was also frustrated, as Clemens Wischermann has pointed out, by the shortage and expense of small dwellings at this period, which forced tenants to sublet and take in lodgers, and provided landlords with irresistible grounds for allowing overcrowding so as to maximize their profits.[41] A possible alternative lay in the creation of building societies or co-operatives, which some saw as an important instrument for achieving social peace. As the *Hamburger Nachrichten* put it in March 1897,

The existence of an unbridgeable gulf between the educated and propertied on the one hand, and the propertyless on the other, is the cancerous growth of our modern social order. The well-off are totally separated from the propertyless nowadays, so that it almost seems as if the two classes are standing in opposite, enemy camps. This hostile relationship must vanish, and the very best opportunity for opening the way to friendly relations between all humanity is offered by Buildings and Savings Societies.[42]

But the Property-Owners' Association objected to building societies because their intention of constructing cheap workers' dwellings would lower housing values. In a meeting of the Association held on 11 May 1897, one of its leading members accordingly 'declared that he would seek in the Citizens' Assembly to ensure that no support would be given to Building Societies'.[43] Housing co-operatives provided little more than 3% of new dwellings in Hamburg from 1895 to 1913; the dwellings they provided were far from cheap in general, and the threatened intrusion of the Social Democrats into their affairs led one co-operative to convert itself into a limited company with shares at 1,000 Marks each in 1903. The concern of the property-owners with housing values also showed that the Property-Owners' Association was no longer quite the petty-bourgeois institution it had been in former days. Already in 1885 it had begun to arrange excursions for its members to nearby resorts, and by the turn of the century they were going on organized trips, lasting up to a fortnight, to London, Paris, Norway, and the casino at Monte

[39] Ibid.: *Hamburger Neueste Nachrichten*, 25 May 1898.
[40] Wischermann, *Wohnen in Hamburg*, pp. 90–3.
[41] Ibid.
[42] StA Hbg, PP S3490 Bd. I: *Hamburger Nachrichten*, 7 Mar. 1897.
[43] Ibid.: *Hamburgischer Correspondent*, 13 May 1897.

Carlo. These excursions cost each member who went on one as much as the entire annual rent of a three-room apartment in a building co-operative. As the Association's official *Festschrift* declares, 'these trips certainly did not provide very convincing support for claims about the "destitution of the property-owners"'. The parties, balls, and masquerades held by the Association had by this time attained a similar level of conspicuous consumption, with up to a thousand members attending on each occasion. The continued rapid growth of working-class tenements built and rented on a large scale in the outer suburbs had brought an equally rapid growth in landlord income. More and more better-off landlords joined the Association because of the increased threat of restrictive legislation after 1892. Rents became a primary rather than a secondary income for many of the members, and landlordism became professionalized.[44]

The attitude of the Social Democrats to these disputes was ambivalent. They accepted the general belief that the Alley Quarters were unhealthy and needed clearing. But they demanded that the task be carried out by the state and that the state should provide dwellings in the inner city to resettle those who had to be evicted. They were well aware of the social and psychological problems caused by the destruction of the old way of life in the Alley Quarters and publicized the consequences of eviction for these people in the *Hamburger Echo*. The Hamburg Social Democrats were inclined, therefore, to support the Senate's plans and to accept the medical justification for them, but wanted to carry them further and to provide state housing for the working population. Their hostility was directed above all at the Property-Owners' Association, which they regarded as the main obstacle to reform. Significantly, they differed on the question of building regulations from the views of their party comrades in Berlin. The draft Housing Inspection Law was sharply criticized as the 'grossest humbug' by the Berlin Social Democrats' *Vorwärts*. 'Anything as vacuous and miserable in respect of housing control', declared the paper, could scarcely be imagined. But the Hamburg police noted that 'the article went against the view taken by the members of the Social Democratic Party here'. In fact the *Hamburger Echo* considered the proposals a 'healthy step forward'[45] which had once more been frustrated by the property-owners in the Citizens' Assembly. The party in general wanted tough measures to protect tenants' rights and ensure the provision of decent accommodation. Ordinary party members in Hamburg were highly critical of the building inspectors: 'What do we have a Buildings Police for in any case?' asked one: 'they ought to make sure that such unhealthy conditions aren't present in

---

[44] R. Hauschild-Thiessen, *150 Jahre Grundeigentümer-Verein in Hamburg von 1832 e. V. Ein Beitrag zur Geschichte der Freien und Hansestadt Hamburg* (Hamburg, 1982), p. 214; Wischermann, *Wohnen in Hamburg*, pp. 136–7, 171–81, 220.

[45] StA Hbg, PP S 3490 Bd. I: *Vorwärts*, 2 May 1893 (with marginal note); *Hamburger Echo*, 16 June 1894.

new buildings, but the gentlemen don't worry themselves about that, they just spend the whole day sauntering around and if possible getting drunk with the owners.'[46] State control and supervision was thus seen as the key to housing improvement. Indeed Social Democratic doctors such as Ignaz Zadek demanded the establishment of a network of hygienic supervision of working-class families, especially women, that was little short of totalitarian. But the demand for public housing schemes which the Social Democrats advanced went far beyond anything that bourgeois opinion, even in the Hamburg Senate, was prepared to accept.[47]

Cholera thus provided an initial if short-lived impulse in favour of housing reforms. Even more important, it delivered a metaphorical justification for the reforms proposed after the further, decisive stimulus of the harbour strike. But the idea that the epidemic provided the motor of social reform in the 1890s is untenable. The reforms of 1892–3 were begun in order to defend Hamburg's autonomy and prevent a Reich take-over of part or even all of its powers of self-government. As the danger of Reich intervention receded, the will to reform receded as well. One local newspaper commented sadly in 1898

that the zeal with which the performance of these great tasks was begun is dying down more and more the further we get from the year of the disaster in 1892. As the immediate impressions [of the epidemic] fade, so the gaze which was fastened on the common good is being dimmed to a noticeable degree; special interests are coming to the fore, and out of the original idea, that the interests of individuals must stand back in favour of the common good, the principle has now become fixed in the minds of many members of the Citizens' Assembly that the common interest has to take account of the interests of individuals.[48]

Moreover, even the reforms that were eventually produced reflected a characteristic compromise between the fractions of capital in Hamburg achieved at the cost of the working class. Senior officials in the Finance Deputation, indeed, thought little of any of these schemes. Its Secretary, Leo Lippmann, subsequently argued that Hamburg's major housing requirement before 1914 was not the provision of healthy, cheap dwellings for the working class, but the 'creation of new building plots for villas for the better-off sections of the population', because there was no more space left in the city, and the wealthy were beginning to build their houses on Prussian territory, outside Hamburg's boundaries, thus depriving the city of valuable income by becoming Prussian tax-payers.[49] Given such attitudes, it is therefore hardly surprising that little was done to improve the housing of the working class.

[46] Ibid.: Wirtschaftsvigilanzbericht 30 Dec. 1893.

[47] Ibid.: Versammlungsbericht 5 Nov. 1892. Zadek's demands are quoted in F. Tennstedt, *Vom Proleten zum Industriearbeiter* (Cologne, 1983), pp. 485–6.

[48] StA Hbg, PP S3490 Bd. I: *Hamburger Neueste Nachrichten*, 21 Dec. 1897; *Hamburger Neueste Nachrichten*, 25 May 1898.

[49] StA Hbg, FA Lippmann A4 Bd. 1, p. 254.

III

Many of the reforms initiated in the wake of the cholera epidemic of 1892 were intended to demonstrate Hamburg's willingness to undertake long-term preventive measures to stop a similar outbreak happening again. But the city faced serious short-term problems as well. Most pressing among these was the mass unemployment caused by the quarantines. These were already having an effect by the end of August and continued to depress trade well into the New Year. On 12 September it was reported that 'labour conditions in the harbour have been really miserable since the outbreak of cholera. The number of unemployed is growing from day to day.' Workers were reported to be waiting for work on the quayside in groups of several hundred each at various places. The collapse in trade quickly brought on a crisis in processing industries. Over a thousand tobacco workers were laid off in September.[50] Already by the end of August it was reported that 2,000 tailors were without work because 'under the present circumstances, customers have gone out of town, and those who were already out of town have not come back'.[51] Barbers were reported to be without custom,[52] and there were numerous dismissals among house-painters, carpenters, and other artisan trades.[53] The Hamburg–America Line cut wages in December in the wake of the collapse in shipping.[54] By January 1893 the shipbuilders Blohm and Voss had reduced their work-force from 3,000 before the epidemic to 700,[55] and the cold winter brought building and engineering work to a virtual standstill through January. 'Innumerable unemployed' were to be seen waiting for work on the quaysides.[56] 70 workers occupied the City Engineer's Department in December demanding employment,[57] and on 18 January a crowd which had gathered outside a labour exchange shouted 'We want work!' in a 'riotous manner' so that mounted police were sent in to maintain order.[58] In January nearly 18,000 men were recorded seeking work on the quays; fewer than 5,000 of them found jobs. From 3 to 5 January a thousand people were counted outside the street-cleaning depot, where they were looking for work; only 260 jobs were available.[59] It was reported that street begging, thefts from bakeries, and other symptoms of poverty were reaching unprecedented

[50] StA Hbg, PP, S3420 Bd. 3: *Hamburger Nachrichten*, 12 Sept. 1892; ibid.: *Hamburger Fremdenblatt*, 'Freundschafts-Club der Cigarren Sortirer' (n.d.).

[51] Ibid.: Vigilanzberichte über die hiesige Arbeitslosigkeit 7274/5/92.

[52] Ibid.: 7967/5/92, 20 Sept.

[53] StA Hbg, Senat. Cl. XI, Gen. No. 2, Vol. 61. Fasc. 7: Senatskommission zur Prüfung der gegenwärtigen Arbeitslage, 1. Sitzung (3 Nov. 1892), § 3.

[54] StA Hbg, PP S3420 Bd. I: *Hamburger Echo*, 18 Dec. 1892.

[55] Ibid.: *General-Anzeiger*, 20 Jan. 1893.

[56] Ibid.: *Hamburger Tageblatt*, 29 Jan. 1893.

[57] Ibid.: *Hamburgischer Correspondent*, 18 Dec. 1892.

[58] Ibid.: *Hamburger Nachrichten*, 18 Jan. 1893.

[59] Ibid., Bd. 2: 'Berichte und Notizen', 17 Dec. 1892, 2–5 Jan. 1893.

dimensions.[60] Here was another aspect of the socially uneven impact of the epidemic.

Privately, leading Senators and city officials noted that the crisis had led to a dramatic increase in unemployment; and in its campaign to secure the removal of quarantine regulations the Chamber of Commerce made great play with the argument that 'the curtailment of manufacturing activity and the reduced movement of goods has affected very many groups in the population through redundancies and dismissals'.[61] However, this argument was given quite a different twist by the Social Democrats and trade unions, who pinned the blame for throwing thousands out of work on the Senate because of its responsibility for the epidemic. The unions tried to gather statistics to back up their contention, but less than 10% of the 172,000 questionnaires were filled in and the whole enterprise was rightly regarded by the authorities as something of a fiasco.[62] None the less, the Social Democrats and their trade union allies continued to press for state labour schemes to provide the unemployed with jobs. The police argued in November 1892 that the labour market was returning to normal and there was no need for special schemes of this sort. They even claimed that the Social Democrats were importing people into Hamburg just in order to make the situation look worse.[63]

Others took an even harder line. In November 1892, in a formal submission to the Senate, a prominent middle-class voluntary association, the Society against Begging (*Verein gegen Bettelei*) drew a sharp distinction between the 'industrious, i.e. the workers with regular employment, and the casual labourers'. The former, including building workers, who saved in the summer months enough to see them through the winter, formed the 'healthy stock of the labouring people'. 'When one enters the homes of such people, it is always a pleasure to see a well-ordered, attractive household; there is always a so-called "parlour", which is tastefully furnished in accordance with the household's circumstances.' These workers, especially building workers, formed 'the basic stock of the Social Democratic Party', while the party's 'voting fodder' consisted in large measure of casual workers. These were characterized by the Society as men who worked for a few days then spent the rest of their time drinking. 'A regular way of life', it declared, 'goes with regular work.' So it was not surprising that their homes were disorderly, with

[60] Ibid.: *Hamburger Fremdenblatt*, 6 Jan. 1895, *General-Anzeiger*, 20 Jan. 1893.

[61] Mönckeberg, *Bürgermeister Mönckeberg*, p. 23; F. Koch (ed.), 'Die Tagebuchaufzeichnungen Georg Kochs über die Hamburger Cholera-Epidemie des Jahres 1892', *Die Heimat. Monatsschrift zur Pflege der Natur- und Landeskunde in Schleswig-Holstein und Hamburg*, 79 (1972), 353–4, 30 (1973), 23–4, entry for 2 Sept; StA Hbg. Senat, Cl. VII, Lit. Ta, Pars 2, Vol. 11, Fasc. 16, Inv. 25: Präses der Deputation für Handel und Schiffahrt, Eingabe, 19 Dec. 1892.

[62] Cf. the account in J. Flemming, 'Wege zum "sozialen Frieden"? Anfänge staatlicher Arbeitsmarktpolitik in Hamburg', in Herzig *et al.*, *Arbeiter in Hamburg*, pp. 283–98.

[63] StA Hbg, Senat, Cl. XI, Gen. No. 2, Vol. 61, Fasc. 1: Denkschrift 4 Nov. 1892, pp. 8–9; ibid., Fasc. 7: Senatskommission zur Prüfung der gegenwärtigen Arbeitslage, § 4.

'ragged, starving children, miserable furniture, the beds consist of rather ambiguous coverlets, little or no rent is paid and so one eviction comes after another'. The cause of their permanent misery lay not in epidemics or economic depressions, but in the life-style they led. They carried the 'bacillus of dissatisfaction' into the solid working class and repeatedly provoked organized Social Democrats into adopting radical policies in order to retain their votes. Their 'demands' were 'endless and insatiable'. In this view, unemployment was caused by idleness and led to political radicalism. The unemployed therefore should only be helped by the Poor Law; since this robbed them of the right to vote, they would thereby be 'rendered politically harmless'.[64]

Given the high cost and administrative difficulty of implementing this policy at a time when the Elberfeld system was only just coming into operation in Hamburg, it was unlikely to meet with much approval in the Senate. Nor did Senators accept the police contention that unemployment was a Social Democratic fiction. As Senator Johannes Versmann wrote on 20 December,

The constantly recurring mass attempts to obtain employment in clearing snow and ice, the notorious quiescence of the building trade, the unquestioned weakening of the economic strength of the labouring classes by the epidemic—the need to take measures to deal with the temporary freezing up of the harbour in the cold spell that is probably on its way—all these are factors which make it inappropriate to regard complaints about the present and even more the coming mass unemployment as mere Social Democratic bluster.

Versmann therefore urged a serious effort to provide the Hamburg workers with more opportunities for employment. He argued that a project to remove earthworks on the line of the old city walls should go ahead, combined with a 'planned assignment of work to those in search of jobs'. Native workers should be given preference over foreign (i.e. non-Hamburg) ones; married men should be given preference over unmarried. Older men should not be turned away. Versmann saw long-term advantages in this, since it could only be achieved if the state construction authority, the City Engineer's Department (*Bau-Deputation*), set up an employment exchange for this purpose, in conjunction with the Emergency Committee, which had offered to bear the costs of establishing the exchange. This offer should not be refused. 'Such a labour exchange will probably develop into a permanent institution.'[65]

However, it was soon pointed out that Hamburg workers were disinclined to take up the offer of employment as labourers in the new construction schemes, including the speeded-up completion of the filter-beds. Police Commissioner Rosalowsky complained

[64] Ibid., Fasc. 2c: 'Der Arbeiterstand Hamburgs, socialpolitische und socialwirthschaftliche Bemerkungen in Bezug auf den Nothstand', 10 Nov. 1892.

[65] Ibid., p. 3.

that money could certainly be earned on the earthworks but Hamburg's workers do not want to be employed in earthworks at all. The labour is too heavy, and the wages too low. 'What is the Emergency Committee there for anyway?' Hamburg's workers have expressed their disinclination for earthworks in repeated meetings, and if Hamburg workers have reported for employment on the filter-beds, it has mostly been masons who have done so in their capacity as such.[66]

The problem of finding jobs for them remained. So Versmann's proposal was acted on and the Emergency Committee set up a labour exchange along the lines he suggested. It was subsequently taken over by a prominent voluntary association, the Patriotic Society. The aim was to further the cause of social peace by providing a service acceptable to workers and employers alike. This was all the more necessary because of the widespread unrest that had occurred at the beginning of 1892, as syndicalists in Berlin and elsewhere attempted to mobilize the already numerous unemployed in a political movement to the left of the Social Democrats. These activities had culminated in the famous riots of February 1892, immortalized by Heinrich Mann in his novel *Der Untertan*. Similarly a small group of syndicalists and anarchists in Hamburg attempted to turn the debate on the cholera epidemic into a mass mobilization of the unemployed. As the police were quick to note,

The Social Democrats here, or at least their leaders ... resisted ... the summoning of meetings of the unemployed, and as these led in many places to demonstrations and even disturbances of the peace, they fought against the calling of such meetings with all the influence at their command. Reichstag deputy Frohme, who is domiciled in this city, even thought it appropriate to warn the police about one demonstration that he feared would be mounted by the unemployed, and to tell them that if it should none the less take place, they could be sure that the demonstrators were not members of the Social Democratic organization.

The police were naturally not displeased with such actions, which made it easier for them in their aim to 'work towards ensuring that the party remains in the hands of moderate elements'. Nevertheless, the winter months of 1892–3 did see a number of mass meetings and small demonstrations by the unemployed in Hamburg, which made the questions of solving the problem all the more urgent.[67]

The strategy of defusing the unemployment issue through the provision of a state-sponsored labour exchange was wrecked by the hostile attitude of the employers. Because they refused to use it, the labour exchange was restricted

[66] Ibid., Fasc. 1: Denkschrift 4 Nov. 1892, pp. 7–8. For further comments of this issue, see the minutes cited in n. 64 above (e.g. pp. 10, 16, 17, etc.).

[67] StA Hbg, Senat, Cl. XI, Gen. No. 2, Vol. 61, Fasc. 1: Denkschrift 8 Dec. 1893, pp. 5, 9; StA Hbg, PP S3420 Bd. I: *Hamburgischer Correspondent*, 18 Dec. 1892, *Hamburger Nachrichten*, 18 Jan. 1893, and ibid. Bd. 2, *passim*. Frohme was the Social Democratic deputy for the neighbouring Altona constituency and an influential joint editor of the *Hamburger Echo*.

mainly to the state quay, and even here there were complaints from the director that

the labour exchange does not check those who are looking for jobs to see if they are suitable for work on the quays, whether they have previously come into conflict with the law on account of crimes against property, or whether they have perhaps been previously dismissed from a job on the quay for drunkenness or other offences.

But the Senate stuck to its policy of neutrality because it hoped thereby 'to be able to exercise an influence on the opposing positions of employers and workers in favour of compromise'. The state clearly separated itself from the employers here in the interests of reducing labour conflict and so keeping trade and business on an even keel. But its refusal to conform to the wishes of the employers did not mean the abandonment of every intention of social discipline: on the contrary the authorities used the labour exchange as a means of removing the 'work-shy' from the system of poor-relief, for those who applied for relief were now directed to the labour exchange, and if they failed to seek a job there, they were refused benefits on the grounds that they were not willing to work.[68]

The efforts of the Senate to increase the popularity of the labour exchange seemed by 1895 to be meeting with some success. Some of the employers were beginning to see the advantages of the scheme, and the leadership of the harbour workers' union and the local Social Democrats also favoured recognizing it. But the ordinary workers and union members were unhappy about several aspects of the exchange; and in any case the great harbour strike of 1896–7 quickly put paid to any further thoughts of social peace. After the strike was over, the employers set up their own labour exchange and used it to weed out undisciplined or radical workers. The Senate abandoned its former policy of neutrality in the wake of the strike and supported the new labour exchange. Meanwhile the employers moved to establish a core of carefully controlled permanent workers and reduce their previous dependence on unreliable casual labour. Initially this succeeded, but as time went on, the middlemen who did the actual hiring of port labour were forced by the passive resistance of the workers to revert to the old forms of *ad hoc* hiring, and by 1905, as Michael Grüttner has shown, the new labour exchange had lost most of its capacity to discipline the workforce. Ultimately, this was from the perspective of the 1890s yet another example of the failure of reforms originating in the cholera epidemic. The initial attempt of the state to mediate between workers and employers proved to be short-lived. By the turn of the century, under the impact of the harbour strike, the state had abandoned even the pretence of neutrality.[69]

[68] Grüttner, *Arbeitswelt*, pp. 157–8.
[69] Ibid.

IV

In following the chequered history of these various projects of reform from their origins in the cholera epidemic of 1892 to the turn of the century and beyond, it has become clear that none of them got very far before the port strike of 1896, nor did any of them ultimately achieve the goals envisaged when they were first proposed. To be understood in their true significance, they have to be seen not as consequences of the cholera epidemic, but as part of a broader and longer-term process going back to the middle of the 1880s. As we saw in Chapter 1, the growing social antagonisms and political conflicts of this period led to the rapid deployment of new strategies of control by the state, ranging from the increasingly elaborate representation of state authority to the militarization of the police force. By the 1890s the political police in Hamburg commanded a comprehensive network of agents and informers whose knowledge of political opinion in the German working class was unrivalled, even in Berlin. Parallel to this extension of the formal agencies of state authority was the emergence of formal or voluntary agencies of social control among the dominant classes, from the Elberfeld system of poor-relief to the creation of a powerful and united organization of the major employers in the city to combat labour unrest.

This last development—the foundation of the employers' association—was made possible largely by the increasing concentration of capital in the industrial and trading boom that followed Hamburg's entry into the Customs Union. The power of mercantile, banking, and industrial interests in the city continued to be very extensive. Mediated through the Senate and expressed in the hegemonic ideology of the primacy of trade, it ensured that the state would continue to regard the protection of business as its first priority, as indeed the tactics of Senator Hachmann and his colleagues in the first phase of the cholera epidemic so graphically demonstrated. When the state attempted to act independently in the interests of social peace, as in the port strike of 1896, it was unable to win over the employers to its side and eventually fell in with their wishes. On the other hand, when it proposed a reform of the building regulations, the creation of a housing inspection service, and the clearance of the Alley Quarters, in an attempt to counter the threat of social disorder and labour unrest, the backing of the mercantile and employers' interest was unable to secure success unless—as in the clearance of the Altstadt and its conversion to a business quarter—the interests of the property-owners were served as well.

The fate of the legislation introduced in the wake of the cholera epidemic shows that even the strong pressure exerted from Berlin was sometimes unable to escape being weakened, diverted, or dissipated altogether as it was filtered through the organs of Hamburg's self-governing constitution. Nevertheless, the epidemic did force a retreat in some of the remaining areas of *laissez-faire* ideology within the city. This was inevitably true in the field of public health, where the impact of world opinion and criticism from Berlin was most direct. A Hygienic Institute was immediately established, fully equipped for bacteriological investigation, backed by new laws against adulteration and supported by a proper system of enforcement. By 1906 it employed 20 chemists with 10 assistants and 5 clerks, working closely with the police.[70] Its systematic investigations of food and drink samples and the resulting publicity and prosecutions did a good deal to reduce adulteration and improve hygiene, so that nutritional standards began to experience an improvement that was already evident by the turn of the century. By the 1920s, for example, less than 3% of the milk samples tested were found to be adulterated, while cooling and refrigeration were having a major impact on the condition of all perishable foodstuffs. The Senate also introduced a Bill to vote funds for the construction of a rubbish incineration plant; a previous Bill along these lines had been rejected in 1889. It aroused furious opposition, based on the argument that rubbish should be sold to farmers for profit. Chief Engineer Meyer, typically, called these ideas 'childish and immature'. In 1896 he eventually secured a narrow vote in favour; the plant came into operation in 1898.[71]

After the epidemic, steps were also taken to improve the sewage system. But it was only under the impact of a renewed epidemic threat in 1899 that regulations were introduced requiring the hospitals to disinfect their wastes before they joined the main sewer. At the same time, the city made a serious attempt to ensure quicker and better mixing of the untreated sewage with the river at the outlet on the border with Altona: 'A device was installed in front of the outflow point of the main Hamburg sewers, to catch floating debris and larger submerged items, and the outflow itself was channelled into several different pipes, of which one discharged into the river near the north bank, one near the south, and one in the middle.'[72] In 1895 work began on an experimental treatment plant near the island of Finkenwerder. Not for many years, however, was a full treatment process actually introduced. Meanwhile further measures were also instituted to improve the quality of drinking-water. By 1900, notices had been placed all along the waterfront warning people against drinking the river-water, and 150 taps connected to the central, sand-filtered water-supply had been set up along the quaysides.[73]

The 1892 epidemic also called forth a serious attempt by the Senate to establish a new set of medical regulations to replace the existing ones in force since 1818. The new regulations did not come into effect until 1900. They

[70] StA Hbg, MK II A 1 Bd. 1, Bl. 87: *Hamburger Fremdenblatt*, 13 Oct. 1906.
[71] *Bürgerschaft*, 5 June and 12 June 1893; *Hygiene und Soziale Hygiene in Hamburg* (Hamburg, 1928), pp. 538–47.
[72] *Die Gesundheitsverhältnisse Hamburgs im 19. Jahrhundert* (Hamburg, 1901), pp. 44–5.
[73] Ibid.

finally increased the medical profession's numerical superiority on the Medical Board, with ten physicians as against seven lay members and one apothecary. The Chief Medical Officer's function remained an advisory one, but in practice the Medical Board and its medical officials had a good deal of independence in the control they exercised over the various subordinate medical authorities, from the new Hygienic Institute to the Harbour Medical Officer (*Hafenarzt*), also established in 1893 (against the wishes of the Finance Deputation, which thought that health checks in the harbour would damage shipping interests). In 1897, moreover, two City Medical Officers (*Stadtärzte*) were appointed to oversee public health in Hamburg itself. In these respects at least, therefore, the epidemic contributed to some gains in influence and status for the local medical profession.[74]

At the same time, the doctors were fighting less welcome developments on another front. The epidemic revealed the inadequacy of the Doctors' Club as a professional organization and led to the foundation of local Doctors' Associations, which eventually came together to form a Chamber of Doctors (*Ärztekammer*). This body then became responsible for professional matters while the Doctors' Club became exclusively a society for scientific lectures and demonstrations. However, the real reason for the formation of the Chamber was to organize the medical profession in Hamburg as elsewhere in defence of its rights against the growing power of the sickness insurance funds.[75] Up to the 1880s, sickness insurance had depended largely on a myriad of small funds whose membership covered a maximum of 5% of the German population in 1880 and whose resources were too meagre to deal with major disasters. These continued to exist to the end of the century and beyond, but their limitations were clearly revealed by the fact that a number of them in Hamburg were unable to meet the demands made on them in the epidemic of 1892.[76] Sickness benefits were thus mostly paid by poor-relief agencies, with all the civil disabilities this implied for claimants. The absence of a separate health insurance scheme was one reason for increasing expenditure on poor relief in many cities in the third quarter of the nineteenth century. In the 1880s, Bismarck introduced a series of social insurance schemes, above all for accidents at work, illness, and old-age pensions. These provided graded benefits in return for graded contributions, and so bypassed the poor relief system with all its unpopular implications for civil rights and social reputation. The law ensured that the sickness insurance scheme rapidly

[74] H. Rodegra, *Das Gesundheitswesen der Stadt Hamburg im 19. Jahrhundert. Unter Berücksichtigung der Medizinalgesetzgebung (1586–1818–1900)* (Wiesbaden, 1979), pp. 152–72.

[75] J. Michael, *Geschichte des ärztlichen Vereins und seiner Mitglieder* (Hamburg, 1896), pp. 207–8.

[76] G. A. Ritter, *Sozialversicherung in Deutschland und England. Entstehung und Struktur im Vergleich* (Munich, 1983), p. 31; StA Hbg, Versicherungsbehörde 1 Bd. 23, Bl. 377–9, and Sterbekasse 293 for examples of failures during the 1892 epidemic.

gained significant dimensions. By 1890, it covered over 6.5 million Germans.[77]

It is impossible to say exactly how many of the cholera victims in the epidemic of 1892 were paid for by sickness insurance, but over the year as a whole, about half of all hospital patients in Hamburg were supported by sickness funds (either public or voluntary); the great majority of the rest were paid for by the Poor Law authorities or the police.[78] In practice this latter category probably accounted for a majority of cholera patients. 1892 was still relatively early in the history of sickness insurance; by 1900 it covered over 9.5 million people, by 1914, over 15.5 million, or almost a quarter of the entire German population, including virtually the whole of the wage-labour force. This rapid growth of compulsory sickness insurance provided the basis for an increasing medicalization of the German population. As Gerhard A. Ritter has remarked, it was largely responsible for the increase in medical provision from 35 doctors per 100,000 inhabitants in 1885 to 51 by 1913, helped more than double the availability of hospital beds per head of population, and was the essential factor underlying the growth of the dispensary movement and the fight against infant mortality and tuberculosis mentioned earlier. By bringing the medical profession—though not without protest—into the orbit of a state insurance system, and by emphasizing preventive measures (to save expenditure) as well as therapeutic ones, the scheme perhaps encouraged those working-class people who entered it to adopt a less fatalistic attitude towards illness and disease, by giving them an incentive to obtain a return on their compulsory contributions if they fell ill.[79]

This growing medicalization of the working class[80] took place at a time when the environment was continuing to deteriorate. Broadly speaking, what had happened by the end of the nineteenth century was that the state had been obliged to control the traditional types of pollution which had been made worse by rapid urban growth, that is to say the disposal of organic waste produced by individual humans and animals. This had been achieved largely by abandoning established recycling procedures, which had by now become uneconomic, and by substituting incineration or purification under state management for private disposal by individuals or entrepreneurs. Significant steps had also been taken towards protecting food and water-supplies from the influence of this kind of pollution. But just as these problems were being brought under control, new ones were arising. From the 1890s at the latest, new forms of chemical pollution were replacing sewage and organic

[77] Ritter, *Sozialversicherung*, p. 32.

[78] *Jahrbuch der Hamburgischen Staatskrankenanstalten* (1892–3), p. xxiv.

[79] Ritter, *Sozialversicherung*, p. 54, Table 1: pp. 64–5.

[80] U. Frevert, 'Professional Medicine and the Working Classes in Imperial Germany', *Journal of Contemporary History*, 20 (1985), 637–58.

waste as the major threats to the purity of the rivers.[81] Above all, the rapid growth of the potash industry raised the saline content of the Elbe by its by-products, and municipal water-supplies, fishing interests, breweries, paper-makers, and other interests dependent on pure water-supplies were seriously threatened well before the outbreak of the First World War. The state of water pollution can be illustrated by the example of the river Bille. Already polluted by untreated sewage, it was made even more unbearable in the early 1900s by Sthamer's chemical factory, which poured large quantities of arsenic and sulphuric acid into it. When the river overflowed its banks and flooded the adjoining fields in 1906, the grass turned black.[82] By this stage the river was 'permanently full of slimy, decomposing, and stinking water'.[83] Below the chemical factories it was deep blue and covered in oil. By 1922 the Bille was colouring the Doveelbe blue as well. A report issued in that year referred starkly to 'the scarcely surpassable pollution of the lower Bille'.[84]

Atmospheric pollution also reached unprecedented heights after the turn of the century through the growth of chemical and other industries. In 1909 Ernst Müller issued a series of complaints about the situation in the Billwärder Ausschlag, which are worth quoting at some length:

In the heart of the district is the former Walkhoff fish factory ... which very often pollutes the environs with a stink of rotten fish ... Among the local chemical plants the one in the Markmannstrasse emits sulphuric acid fumes, so that windows are turned blue and people's lungs are damaged. Right next to this heavily built-up part of town there is now situated the great goods and railway shunting yard, whose locomotives send clouds of smoke into the air, stinging the lungs and olfactory organs and shrouding whole streets in smoke. At the far end lies the city gasworks, which ... emit strong fumes ... The refuse incineration plant on the Billerdeich creates a great deal of dust and sends strong, kilometre-long clouds of smoke streaming over the nearby parts of town ...

Other factories, he said, sent 'bright blue vapour clouds across the Bille valley', or gave off smells so powerful that the inhabitants had to close their windows. 'Is then a factory-owner worth more than many thousands of the city's population?' he asked. The answer he received, predictably, was that if he did not like the district he should not live in it. In any case, added the medical authorities, the vapours of which he complained did not pose any real health hazard.[85] This was unlikely. Müller's evidence showed once again how new sources of pollution were emerging just as the old ones seemed to be coming under control.

[81] Cf. Chapter 2 above.
[82] StA Hbg, MK II O 2 Bd. 2, Bl. 98–9.
[83] Ibid., Bl. 69.
[84] Ibid., Bd. 3, Bl. 181.
[85] StA Hbg, MK II H 10, Bl. 88 (Müller to Medizinalkollegium, 18 Sept. 1909, and reply 16 Dec. 1909).

Nevertheless, sanitary reform in this period did have some impact. Most dramatic of all were the improvements in public health brought about by the filtration of the water-supply in the spring of 1893. Not only was there no subsequent visitation of cholera in Hamburg, but the incidence of typhoid, previously the highest in Germany, immediately dropped to negligible proportions, as Figure 4 showed. Infant mortality, which had increased since the early part of the century to a point in the 1880s and early 1890s where nearly one in three children died before reaching the age of one, now fell to a lower rate than at any time since the 1820s, and from the turn of the century it began a steady decline that has continued with only one interruption, in the years immediately following the end of the Second World War, until our own day. Significantly, deaths from 'vomiting and diarrhoea', which had increased since the late 1850s, fell after the filtration of the water-supply to a lower level than any experienced since the 1860s.[86]

This improvement of health standards reflected not only the introduction of filtrated water in 1893 but also improvements in nutrition, encouraged by the campaign against adulteration launched by the new Hygienic Institute, and, from the turn of the century, the growth of the dispensary movement, which sought, often for nationalistic reasons, to improve the survival rate of infants and the health of mothers now that Germany's birth rate was beginning to decline. The influence of environmental improvement and medical intervention on lowering morbidity and mortality rates also has to be seen in the broader context of improving living standards. From 1870 to 1890 the proportion of taxpayers earning between 900 and 1,800 Marks a year remained static at 74–75%, but from 1890 to 1900 it declined to 69%, while the proportion of taxpayers earning from 1,800 to 6,000 Marks rose from 18 to 24%. This trend continued up to the First World War.[87] These gains were not evenly distributed, of course; for example, real wages for most port workers stagnated from 1895 until 1913; but as Michael Grüttner has pointed out, within the group the growing number of regularly employed workers was able to improve its income by working for an increasing number of days in the week, leaving a steadily impoverished and marginalized casual labour force to take the brunt of the impact of increased living costs. Improved real wages and living standards were also concentrated in sectors such as the building trades, which formed the active core of the Social Democratic movement.[88]

Many social indicators showed a significant upturn from the end of the nineteenth century to the First World War, from average density of occupation, which fell from a peak of 4.8 persons per dwelling in 1889 to 4.5 in the late 1890s and 4.1 and below by 1910, to average per capita

[86] See Figure 5, p. 198 above.
[87] *SHS* 22 (1904), 30.
[88] Grüttner, *Arbeitswelt*, pp. 54–5.

income, which rose from 533 Marks in 1885 to 875 by 1910.[89] These improvements were accompanied by a sharp fall in the birth rate. Births per 1,000 inhabitants in Hamburg had stayed at a level between 37 and 40 for most of the 1870s and 1880s, but beginning in 1894 the figure began to fall sharply, to 30 in 1900 and 22 by 1913.[90] In little over 15 years, the birth rate was well on the way to being halved. This affected overall statistics based on per capita reckoning, including density of occupation and average income. Mortality per 1,000 inhabitants, which stood at 25 to 30 for most of the second half of the nineteenth century, was already beginning to fall perceptibly just before the epidemic of 1892; in 1893 it was down to 20, by 1906 to 15, and by 1913 it had dropped below 13. As we have seen, some of these changes reflected improved sanitation. The decline in density of occupation and the rise in per capita income were accompanied by a steady improvement in nutritional standards. Rising incomes, better nutrition, and improved living conditions helped tuberculosis mortality, static for most of the 1870s and 1880s, to fall quite rapidly, just as they contributed to the simultaneous fall in infant deaths.[91]

Nevertheless, the general improvement in standards of living and health that was noticeable in the city from just before the turn of the century up to the First World War did not lead to any significant lessening of social inequality. On the face of it one might suppose, perhaps, that the gap between rich and poor grew less in this period. But this was not so. In terms of income per head of population, for example, the gulf between the better-off districts and the worse-off districts of Hamburg narrowed only slightly. The average per capita income of the poorest district was 8.9% of that of the richest district in 1889; by 1910 it was still only 10.4%, which represented a narrowing of the income gap of only 0.5% in a quarter of a century. The best measure of the general diversity of income between the districts—the so-called coefficient of variation—actually grew slightly over the period, from 83.3 to 84.7. The rich were getting richer just as quickly as the poor were beginning to attain a modest degree of economic security. Residential segregation was as marked as ever on the eve of the First World War. Indeed, the Alley Quarters still relatively unaffected by slum clearance—the Altstadt Nord and Neustadt Nord—experienced a very low rate of income growth in this period, as Map 36 shows, while average income in the better-off districts round the Alster was increasing by leaps and bounds.[92]

General mortality rates, as Map 37 indicates, actually increased by 17% between 1890 and 1910 in the Altstadt Nord; they declined by only 5% in the Neustadt Nord, and by 21% in the Neustadt Süd. In the newer working-

[89] Wischermann, *Wohnen in Hamburg*, p. 186.
[90] Ibid., p. 439.
[91] Ibid., p. 439; see also Figures 2 and 3 above.
[92] For a fuller discussion of the figures, see Part VIII of the Statistical Appendix.

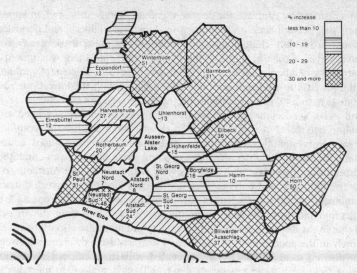

Sources: calculated from *SHS 18* (1895), 8 and *MS 1912*, Plate 1

MAP 36. Average increase in per capita income, by district, Hamburg 1889–1910

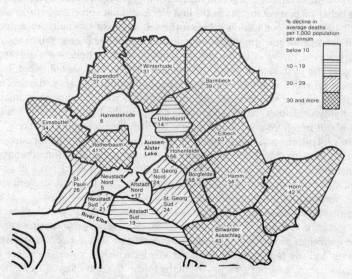

Sources: calculated from *MS 1890*, Table 13a, and *MS 1910*, 83

MAP 37. Mortality decline, by district, Hamburg 1890–1910

class districts, by contrast, the decline was more significant—37% in Eppendorf, 39% in Barmbeck, and over 50% in Hohenfelde, Eilbeck, and Borgfelde, though a possibly changing social composition of these districts may also have played a role. In terms of the overall death rate there was indeed a narrowing of differentials between the districts, as the coefficient of variation fell from 24.5 to 17.9 and mortality in the district with the lowest rate rose from 31% to 45% of that of the district with the highest rate between 1890 and 1910. Yet declining mortality rates were not significantly correlated with falling birth rates or rising income. Map 38 indicates that while the wealthiest areas—Harvestehude, Rotherbaum, and Hohenfelde—experienced a dramatic decline in the birth rate from 1890 to 1910, of 49%, 42%, and 48% respectively, the poorer areas did less well, with 36% for the Altstadt, 40% for the Neustadt, and only 30% for Barmbeck. Differences between districts remained, with the coefficient of variation increasing slightly from 24.1 to 28.4 and natality in the district with the lowest rate falling from 36% to 35% of that in the district with the highest rate. Infant mortality also fell relatively slowly in the poorest districts, as Map 39 suggests. Here differences between the districts seem actually to have increased, with the coefficient of variation rising from 22.7 to 27.1 between 1894 and 1910, and infant mortality in the district with the lowest rate falling from 45% to 19% of the figure for the district with the highest rate. The improvements in infant health care which were so important in this period thus seem to have been to the advantage of the better-off parts of the city in the first place, and not surprisingly there was little observable connection between the fall in infant mortality by district and average income growth in each district. By far the biggest fall in infant mortality—63%—was in the richest district—Harvestehude—while a 37% drop in the birth rate in one of the poorest districts, the Altstadt Nord, had almost no effect on infant mortality. Indeed, generally speaking, the decline in the birth rate was not significantly correlated with the decline in infant mortality by district, which casts some doubt on the hypothesis that health standards improved principally because families were becoming smaller.

In general, the persistent poverty of the older city districts was very apparent. As Map 40 shows, the richest areas—Harvestehude and Rotherbaum—experienced a decline in tuberculosis mortality from 1894 to 1910 of 61% and 53% respectively, while in the old parts of the city, the Altstadt Nord and the Neustadt Süd, the decline was only 30% and 45% respectively, and in the newer working-class suburbs it was not much better (46% in Barmbeck, for instance, and 39% in Uhlenhorst). Social inequalities grew here too, with the coefficient of variation increasing from 21.9 to 32.4 between 1894 and 1910, and the tuberculosis rate in the district with the lowest incidence of the disease falling from 43% to 29% of the rate in the district with the highest incidence. There was a mild negative correlation, indeed, between income growth and tuberculosis mortality decline by district (-0.52). The general

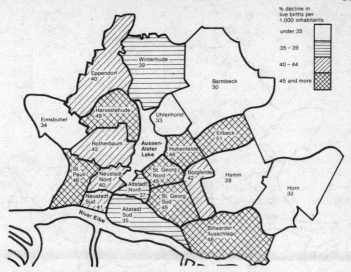

Sources: calculated from *MS 1890*, Table 13g, and *MS 1910*, 10

MAP 38. Decline in birth rate, by district, Hamburg 1890–1910

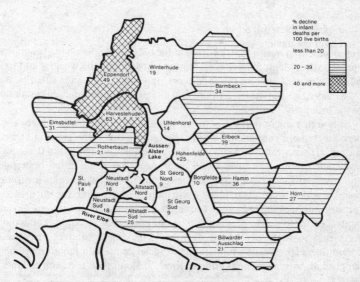

Sources: calculated from *SHS 20* (1902), 26–7; *SHS 27* (1918), 79; and *MS 1894*, 44

MAP 39. Decline in infant mortality, by district, Hamburg 1894–1910

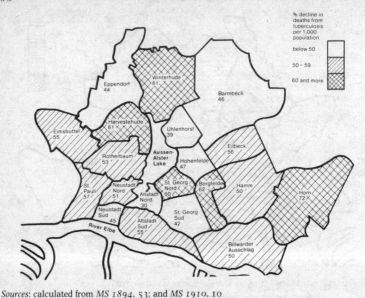

% decline in
deaths from
tuberculosis
per 1,000
population

below 50

50 - 59

60 and more

Eppendorf
44

Winterhude
61

Barmbeck
46

Harvestehude
61

Uhlenhorst
39

Eimsbuttel
55

Rotherbaum
53

Aussen-
Alster
Lake

Hohenfelde
47

Eilbeck
56

St.
Pauli
57

Neustadt
Nord
51

St. Georg
Nord
60

Borgfelde
62

Hamm
50

Horn
72

Neustadt
Sud
45

Altstadt
Nord
30

Altstadt
Sud
55

St. Georg
Sud
42

Billwarder
Ausschlag
50

River Elbe

Sources: calculated from *MS 1894*, 53; and *MS 1910*, 10

MAP 40. Decline in tuberculosis mortality, by district, Hamburg 1894–1910

improvement in health that occurred in the two decades following the cholera epidemic thus seems to have been most marked among the wealthy and well-off, less dramatic among the solid working class in the outer suburbs, and least evident in the poverty-stricken and increasingly marginalized population of the inner city.[93]

Although a major purpose of the health and other insurance schemes had been to create a contented working class and weaken the political basis of the Social Democrats, the result was rather the opposite. The Social Democrats and trade unions welcomed social insurance, after some initial hesitation, and involved themselves actively in elections to the local health insurance boards, which were open to all contributors. Soon after the turn of the century, the sociologist Florian Tennstedt has estimated, the unions already controlled up to 6,000 posts in the health insurance funds; by 1902 there were said to be nearly half a million elected representatives on various committees of the sickness funds, and the Social Democratic labour movement supplied an increasing proportion of them.[94] Along with the slum clearance

[93] For source references see Maps 36–40.
[94] Ritter, *Sozialversicherung*, p. 51.

schemes, which brought a sizeable reduction in the presence of the 'dangerous classes' of the Alley Quarters, and the proportional decline of casual labour with the growth of a more differentiated industrial structure and the emergence of a core of permanently employed workers in the docks, this brought about in Hamburg a shift in the structure of the working class in favour of the better-paid, more respectable sectors, who tended to be concentrated in outer suburbs such as Barmbeck, and who provided the backbone of the active cadres of the Social Democratic labour movement and its organizations. Yet this did not bring about any lessening of social and political conflict. On the contrary, as employers were increasingly inclined to complain, schemes such as the sickness funds only made the workers demand even more.[95] As we shall now see, this applied in Hamburg in a wider sense as well.

d. *Hamburg, Germany, and the World*

I

The most serious of the many pressures exerted on Hamburg in the wake of the cholera epidemic of 1892 was the pressure to reform its suffrage laws. It was widely agreed that a major cause of the disaster was the dominance of the Senate and Citizens' Assembly by the mercantile interest, which had thus been able to effect the fatal delay in bringing the existence of the epidemic to public notice in order as far as possible to prevent the imposition of quarantine. Not only was there strong comment in the Reichstag and the national press in this direction, there was also widespread debate in Hamburg itself, as discontented groups sought to use the epidemic to mobilize opinion in favour of desired political reforms. Already in the immediate aftermath of the epidemic, the Social Democrats, normally concerned with national issues, turned their attention to the Hamburg constitution, arguing 'that if we had been represented in the Hamburg Citizens' Assembly there would have been no need to have carried 10,000 people to the cemetery'.[1] At several mass meetings held immediately after the epidemic, the party demanded universal suffrage for the Citizens' Assembly, and the abolition of the compulsory 30-Mark fee and five years' residence qualification for citizens.[2] It argued that these reforms would not only counteract the influence of the patricians but

[95] Ibid., pp. 53, 71–2.

[1] StA Hbg, PP S3625 Bd. 3: Versammlungsbericht 1 June 1895 (meeting of 27 May). For the lack of interest of the Social Democrats in municipal problems before the 1890s, see D. Rebentisch, 'Die deutsche Sozialdemokratie und die kommunale Selbtverwaltung. Ein Überblick über Programmdiskussion und Organisationsproblematik 1890–1975', *Archiv für Sozialgeschichte*, 25 (1985) 1–78.

[2] StA Hbg, PP S3496: *Hamburger Echo*, 22 Apr. 1893 (speech by Otto Stolten) for a reiteration of these demands.

also do away with 'the most shameful exploitation of all the tenants' by the property-owners.[3] It was 'scandalous' that there was not a single Social Democrat in the Citizens' Assembly at a time when Social Democratic deputies sat for all three Hamburg Reichstag constituencies.[4] 'The decisive storming of this regime has begun', announced the *Hamburger Echo* on 21 September 1892: 'it is taking place under the banner of the Social Democratic movement, which has now been followed by a crushing majority of the population for years.'[5]

The demand for constitutional reform did not stop with the Social Democrats. The Caucus of Leftists, closely tied to the Property-Owners' Association, also argued that a change in the constitution was required, and managed to secure widespread support for its views among the local Citizens' Clubs. The ideas put forward ranged from the direct election of the Senate by the Assembly and the removal of the 30-Mark citizenship fee to the abolition of the notables' elections and the inclusion of a minimum number of representatives of 'other trades and professions' in the Senate besides merchants and lawyers.[6] Differences of opinion soon emerged within the Caucus of Leftists over how far the reform should go. Some wanted to stop short of throwing open the suffrage to men who had been resident in the city for less than five years; others pointed out that abolishing the notables' elections would leave the property-owners' elections open to attack; still others urged explicitly that the citizenship fee should at all costs be retained.[7] It was not surprising that observers were soon complaining 'that this caucus does not know what it wants'. As a letter to the semi-official *Hamburgischer Correspondent* pointed out early in the new year, the demand that the Senate should be directly appointed by an Assembly elected by a general vote alone would mean that the next three Senators would be called 'Bebel, Dietz, and Metzger'. The far-reaching proposals put forward by 'democrats' such as Heinrich Gieschen were not widely supported even in the Caucus of Leftists. The key point, concluded the writer, was that 'the forthcoming revision of Hamburg's constitution must not lead to the Senate and the Citizens' Assembly being composed of Social Democrats'.[8]

The Caucus of Leftists and the Citizens' Clubs were caught between fear of letting the Social Democrats in and fear of 'discontent among the labouring population'.[9] An unmistakably serious petty-bourgeois assault on the constitutional position of the grand bourgeoisie and the middle class was in

[3] Ibid.: *Hamburger Echo*, 18 Sept. 1892.

[4] Ibid.: *Hamburger Echo*, 22 Apr. 1893 (Stolton).

[5] Ibid.: *Hamburger Echo*, 21 Sept. 1892.

[6] Ibid.: *Hamburger Tageblatt*, 12 Nov. 1892, *Hamburgischer Correspondent*, 20 Dec. 1892, *Hamburger Fremdenblatt*, 16 Jan. 1893, and further reports.

[7] Ibid.: *Hamburger Tageblatt*, 16 Dec. 1892, *Hamburgischer Correspondent*, 14 Jan. 1893.

[8] Ibid.: *Hamburgischer Correspondent*, 22 Jan. 1893.

[9] Ibid.: *Hamburger Freie Presse*, 24 Apr. 1894.

progress, and throughout the winter and spring of 1892–3 the Citizens' Clubs repeatedly argued about the precise form the assault should take. Soon the division of opinion was formalized in the creation of an Association for Constitutional Reform (*Verein für Verfassungsreform*) led by seven of the more radical Citizens' Clubs.[10] The debate was interrupted by the Reichstag elections of 1893, when the dominant classes closed ranks against the Social Democrats, but it refused to die down; in October the Social Democrats held another series of mass public meetings on the subject. By the spring of 1894 the reformers had got so far as to persuade the Central Committee of Citizens' Clubs to back their plans, including the abolition of the citizenship fee and the introduction of 'other trades and professions' into a Senate elected by the Citizens' Assembly alone.[11]

The revival of the debate in April 1894 resulted from the appearance of a report on constitutional reform prepared by a Joint Commission of the Senate and the Citizens' Assembly. The Commission had met 29 times since its establishment on 30 January 1893. The five Senatorial representatives, Versmann, Mönckeberg, O'Swald, Lehmann, and Burchard, and their supporters among the delegates of the Citizens' Assembly, including Arthur Lutteroth and Albert Wolffson, were by no means disinclined to countenance constitutional changes.[12] Already in November 1892 the *Börsen-Halle*, the newspaper of the Chamber of Commerce, produced jointly with the semi-official *Hamburgischer Correspondent*, had conceded the need for constitutional reforms, through which 'necessary measures can be put into effect more expeditiously than hitherto'. It continued:

In addition these changes will arouse and maintain an active participation in the affairs of the state among many groups in the population ... [for] the lower classes have not committed even the tiniest excess, but have recognized and supported the activities of the authorities; while the better-placed classes have done everything to alleviate distress, organize assistance and do whatever is appropriate to end the emergency.

So the sense of community which it believed had been demonstrated in the epidemic could be used as a basis for the extension of citizenship further down the social scale.[13] The strategy behind this was clearly directed at reducing the power of the property-owners in favour of an extension of the general vote.

Thus while the property-owners used the opportunity to demand the reduction of the 'notables' in the Assembly,[14] the Senate used it to assail the

[10] Ibid.: *General-Anzeiger*, 7 Mar. 1893, *Hamburger Echo*, 2 Apr. 1893.

[11] Ibid.: *Hamburger Echo*, 8 Oct. 1893, *Hamburger Freie Presse*, 24 Apr. 1894, *Hamburger Nachrichten*, 7 May 1895.

[12] Ibid.: *Neue Hamburger Zeitung*, 14 Jan. 1897.

[13] StA Hbg, PP S3490 Bd. I: *Börsen-Halle*, 17 Oct. 1892.

[14] StA Hbg, Senat, Cl. VII, Lit. Ta, Pars 2, Vol. 11, Fasc. 17, Inv. 1a: *Hamburger Fremdenblatt*, 29 Oct. 1892.

position of the property-owners. For, as the *Hamburgischer Correspondent* declared, the blame for the epidemic should be ascribed

not to the Senate, not to the administration; here there was no doubt about the real facts, no, those to blame were the gentlemen who currently believe themselves more than anyone else entitled to perorate about the mismanagement of the city. Those who were in leading positions were clear about the damage being inflicted, but they knew just as well that the introduction of an effective planning and housing law into the Citizens' Assembly was a futile undertaking. It was the property-owning interest dominant there, and not the notables, that had already placed the most serious obstacles in the way of the planning bill of 1878. At that time it proved impossible to push through a whole number of very important sanitary reforms, because the property-owners thought that these would all too severely restrict their opportunities to exploit housing sites and building plots. The chances of getting such a bill through have not changed in the meantime, and plans which take insufficient account of the wishes of the house-owners could not reckon on a very friendly reception. 'The suggestions are very good, but they stand no chance of success', was a sentiment often heard; if the property-owners do not stand to make any money out of a proposal, it will not get through the Citizens' Assembly![15]

Once more, a major reform proposed in the wake of the epidemic became the object of a struggle between the different fractions of the bourgeoisie in the city.[16]

The result, as usual, was a compromise. The Joint Commission conceded the abolition of the citizenship fee, but proposed instead to set a minimum average annual income of 1,500 Marks a year sustained over five years' residence in Hamburg as the basic condition of citizenship. The rest of the Citizens' Clubs' demands, not surprisingly, were rejected; and subsequent attempts during the debate on the proposals to get the notables' seats abolished were roundly defeated. However, the Assembly did approve the lowering of the income requirement to 1,200 Marks. The Senate was able in the end to persuade the Assembly that in these circumstances the abolition of either the notables' or the property-owners' elections—above all the abolition of both—would throw the Assembly's doors wide open to the Social Democrats. The reduction of the minimum qualifying income to 1,200 Marks would inevitably bring in not only the whole of the petty bourgeoisie but also a substantial section of the working class as well.[17]

But the majority of the poor, transient, and the casual workers would still be excluded, and the five-year residential and average income requirement would mean that only the solid, middle-aged family man would get the vote. As the *Hamburger Fremdenblatt* commented,

[15] Ibid., Fasc. 16, Inv. 22: quoted in *Hamburger Echo*, 2 Nov. 1892.

[16] *Bürgerschaft*, 16 Nov. 1892.

[17] StA Hbg, PP S3496 Bd. 3: *Hamburgischer Correspondent*, 29 Mar. 1893. Cf. ibid.: *Hamburger Nachrichten*, 10 Dec. 1892 for a description of the petty-bourgeois interests behind these proposals.

There is no need to be afraid of these well-behaved, settled workers who have paid their taxes for at least five years and done their duty to family and state. If they really do vote some of their own numbers into the Citizens' Assembly, what of it? The local distribution of the constituencies will prevent Social Democratic elements from securing a majority.[18]

Here residential segregation was evidently seen as contributing to political stability. Another newspaper commented that the extension of the suffrage could be used by the Senatorial party to bring enough Social Democrats into the Assembly to force the Caucus of Leftists round to its line: 'the Leftists are to be brought to heel through terror of the Social Democrats'.[19] And to underline this point, some members of the Caucus of Rightists, including its leader Dr Albert Wolffson, went even further and demanded the extension of the suffrage to all male taxpayers irrespective of income.[20] This proposal alarmed the Caucus of Leftists not least because, as the *Hamburger Echo* reported, 'the Leftists believe that if the franchise to the Citizens' Assembly is extended as far as Dr Wolffson's motion aims to extend it, they will be squeezed to death between the notables on their right and the Social Democrats on their left'.[21]

Speculation and anxieties of this kind dominated the thinking of all parties to the discussion. Long and convoluted debates on the issue went on through 1894 and 1895 and well into 1896.[22] The final outcome could not be seen as the result of any subtle or devious calculation. All agreed that the highly restrictive franchise had to be extended; all were anxious that it should not be extended beyond the solid ranks of the respectable working class and the petty bourgeoisie; all were determined for one reason or another that it should not give too much leeway to the Social Democrats. By 1896 it was clear that the only generally acceptable compromise was the abolition of the citizenship fee and the introduction of the five-year minimum income requirement of 1,200 Marks, with a stipulation that anyone earning over 2,000 Marks a year for three years in a row should be obliged to take up citizenship added on to ensure that the maximum possible weight was given to the middling and upper income groups. This was necessary because under the previous rules many had not troubled to obtain citizenship, since they wanted to avoid being co-opted into time-consuming honorary administrative work in the Deputations. The new proposal was duly voted through by an overwhelming majority and came into effect on 2 November 1896. Its acceptance was unaffected by the harbour strike, which only broke out towards the end of November. It has a claim, therefore, to be regarded as one of the few genuine

18 Ibid., *Hamburger Fremdenblatt*, 19 May 1894.
19 Ibid.: *Hamburger Freie Presse*, 15 May 1894.
20 Ibid.: *Hamburger Echo*, 7 Dec. 1894.
21 Ibid.: *Hamburger Echo*, 7 Dec. 1894.
22 Ibid.: *Hamburger Nachrichten*, 14 Nov. 1895.

reforms that owed their existence above all to the cholera epidemic of 1892. It involved no serious expenditure of extra money, and it seemed to make no potential difference to the balance of forces in the state once it had been decided to keep intact the distribution of seats between the notables, the property-owners, and the deputies elected in the general vote. Its primary purpose was thus to increase the legitimacy of the existing political system by anchoring it more firmly in popular consent among the respectable classes. As Burgomaster Johannes Versmann noted in his diary when the reform was finally passed in 1896, 'if the action which was set off by the cholera epidemic and has now continued for 3 years had finally run into the sands, it would have been regarded by the whole world both within Hamburg and without as proof of political impotence, and rightly so'.[23]

This amendment of the citizenship requirement was accompanied by a wide-ranging reform of the administrative system, and indeed the fact that both were parts of the same legislative package was a major reason for the four-year delay in pushing them though. The epidemic had brought widespread criticism of Hamburg's amateur system of government, and those Senators, such as Johannes Versmann, who had long sought in vain to introduce a paid professional higher civil service into the city administration, now seized the opportunity to do so. The Joint Commission which reported on constitutional change in April 1894 also put forward far-reaching proposals for administrative reform. In some quarters this was regarded as a way of diverting public attention from the rejection of all the more radical proposals made in respect of the reform of the Senate and the Citizens' Assembly.[24] The idea of a professional higher civil service met with considerable opposition in the Assembly. There were fears that it would mean the introduction of a Prussian-style bureaucracy able to act independently from the legislature and the Deputations. The *Hamburgischer Correspondent* was forced to defend the proposals by claiming that 'we certainly want to have nothing to do with any bureaucratic style or impudent bureaucratic arrogance'.[25] The officials were needed to remove the burden of 'unpleasant, low-level, and mechanical business' from the Senate.[26] Others, however, saw in them something much more sinister: 'the building up of the administration in a bureaucratic sense, the extension of the powers of the Senate, the regulation of the careers of senior civil servants along Prussian lines—these are the characteristic features of this reform'.[27] After repeatedly rejecting these measures, the Citizens' Assembly was finally persuaded in 1896 to accept the package with some

[23] H. W. Eckardt, *Privilegien und Parlament. Die Auseinandersetzungen um das allgemeine und gleiche Wahlrecht in Hamburg* (Hamburg, 1980), pp. 35–6; StA Hbg, FA Versmann VI A 6: entry for 13. Oct. 1896.

[24] StA Hbg, PP S3496 Bd. 4: *Hamburger Fremdenblatt*, 17 July 1913.

[25] Ibid.: *Hamburgischer Correspondent*, 21 Oct. 1894.

[26] Ibid.: *Hamburgischer Correspondent*, 16 May 1894.

[27] Ibid.: *Hamburger Nachrichten*, 13 Nov. 1895.

minor concessions from the Senate on issues such as elections to the Depu-tations.[28] Once again, by tacking issues together—this time the citizenship fee and the adminstrative reform—the Senate had got its way, although at the cost of several years' delay.

The reform of 1896 established for the first time in Hamburg a higher civil service with a career structure modelled on Prussian lines. In 1898, indeed, officials with a legal degree were given the right to take decisions on their own without having to consult the Senate on every matter that came up. In 1912, finally, Prussian titles were introduced for the Hamburg bureaucracy.[29] This meant a further decline in the importance of the merchant Senators. Senator Mönckeberg remarked in 1902 that 'above all they find it difficult to work with legally or technically trained senior civil servants. The gentlemen either believe and follow the civil servants unconditionally or they develop an independence that overrides all the forms of orderly administration.'[30] Nevertheless, the Senate now took on something of the character of a ministry. The reform set up departments within the Senate which had the right to take legally binding decisions on minor matters without referring them to a full meeting of the Senate, as had been customary before.[31] Departments of external affairs, trade, shipping, and customs (I), building, education, and justice (II), and finance, police, and internal affairs (III) were charged with preparing detailed drafts of bills to lay before the Senate as well as dealing with day-to-day administration. Each consisted of at least five Senators, two Syndics or Secretaries, and one higher civil servant. The full session could thus concentrate on important matters of general policy, the discussion of final drafts of laws, announcements and communications to the Citizens' Assembly, and so on. The Senators still had to preside over a total of nearly a hundred different Deputations, committees, and commissions, however, many of which would have been chaired by civil servants in Prussia. Some remnants of the old patriarchal image remained. Senators, for example, were still carrying out civil marriages after the turn of the century, for a fee of 50 Marks a time. The reform was also by no means smoothly implemented. Senators took a long time to accustom themselves to senior civil servants, and these were also 'all too often the "scapegoats"' of the Citizens' Assembly. Nevertheless, there was no doubting the significance of the change.[32] It was a decisive abandonment of the old system of self-government by the citizenry. It did indeed mark a real increase in the power of the Senate, and this was further buttressed by the inclusion of significant new powers for the police to 'protect persons and property against emergencies and dangers' which one

[28] Ibid.: *Hamburger Echo*, 30 Nov. 1896, *Hamburger Fremdenblatt*, 12 Nov. 1896.
[29] StA Hbg, FA Lippmann A4 Bd. 1, p. 3. See also Plate 34.
[30] Ibid., FA Mönckeberg 21a, p. 276.
[31] Ibid., FA Buehl 2c, pp. 31–2.
[32] Ibid., pp. 34–7.

critic regarded as creating 'a police regime ... that is able ruthlessly to interfere in the citizens' private life'.[33] These innovations seemed to provide ample
security against any further growth in the political importance of the Social
Democrats which the reform of the citizenship law might be thought to imply.

II

Reporting on the constitutional reform of 1896, the liberal *Berliner Tageblatt*
predicted the following spring that the next elections to the Citizens' Assembly
would bring at least half a dozen Social Democrats into the chamber. 'The
debates', it warned, 'will, however, take on a different tone' from the existing,
mostly polite discussion of differences within the bourgeois-liberal camp.[34] In
fact, the 1898 elections did not bring any Social Democrats into the Citizens'
Assembly. But the lowering of the citizenship fee led to an immediate increase
in the registration of citizens, and soon 700 or 800 were being sworn in
every week. In 1893–4 there were only 23,000 citizens; by 1902–4 the
number had grown to 44,000, making up 23% of the Reichstag electors in
the city as against a mere 14% ten years before.[35] Moreover, it soon became
apparent that substantial numbers of workers were declaring a taxable
income in excess of their real income, solely in order to acquire the vote.[36]
Given the five-year qualification required for the citizenship, these workers
could expect to participate if not in the 1898 elections, then certainly in those
of 1901. Far from being weaned away from the Social Democrats by their
newly acquired privilege, they used it to elect the party's first deputy in 1901
and 12 more in 1905, when the Social Democrats gained no less than 38%
of the vote in the general elections to the Citizens' Assembly.[37]

Just as the *Berliner Tageblatt* had predicted, the new deputies brought about
a radical change in the Assembly's tone of debate. Where sharp words and
serious criticisms of the state had previously been heard only on the rarest
of occasions, they now became the norm as far as the Social Democratic
group of deputies was concerned. Unlike the old Caucuses, the Social Democratic deputies were part of an organized national political party with all the
trappings including a party programme and party discipline. The leisurely
achievement of compromises between the different fractions of capital which
had been the main feature of legislative business in the past was now disputed
at every stage in the name of the neglected majority. The Senate and the
Caucuses faced the alarming prospect of having to co-opt Social Democrats
on to commissions and Deputations, where they would be able to interfere in

---

[33] StA Hbg, PP S3496 Bd. 3: *Hamburger Fremdenblatt*, 17 Oct. 1894.

[34] Ibid.: *Berliner Tageblatt*, 21 Mar. 1897.

[35] Eckardt, *Privilegien und Parlament*, p. 37.

[36] E. Lüth and H.-D. Loose, *Bürgermeister Carl Petersen* (Hamburg, 1971), pp. 5–6.

[37] Eckardt, *Privilegien und Parlament*, p. 38.

administrative as well as legislative processes. Already in 1904, therefore, the Senate and Citizens' Assembly rushed through a measure widely discussed in the mid-1890s but not so far implemented: the requirement that to be elected for an individual constituency in the general elections a candidate had to obtain an absolute instead of (as previously) only a relative majority. This would allow the Caucuses to bury their differences in a second-round run-off and defeat the Social Democratic candidate should this be necessary. It incidentally offered the same possibility with regard to the Anti-Semites, who had also benefited from the reform of 1896 and had three deputies in the Assembly by 1901.[38]

This measure did not go far enough in the eyes of most of the bourgeois groups. For the elections of 1904 had only, of course, covered half the constituencies, and the elections for the other half, due to be held in 1907, would certainly double the number of Social Democratic deputies in the Assembly, if not more than double it. Ultimately it was not likely that all 80 generally elected seats would be filled by the Social Democrats, giving them a blocking power over legislative and especially constitutional change. This created a real panic in the old Caucuses. A representative of the Caucus of Rightists feared that the 'classes ... upon whose entrepreneurship, industriousness, and efficiency the prosperity of our city ... has been built, the merchants, industrialists, etc. ... will hardly be represented any more, or indeed not at all'. The workers, another writer argued, should 'be represented, but they must not take power here'. A flood of newspaper and magazine articles in the bourgeois press enlarged upon these arguments. A Social Democratic majority in the Assembly, it was alleged, would 'bring our whole state machine to a stop'. The Assembly thereupon—in language that was already highly expressive of their anxieties—formally requested the Senate to establish a commission to investigate 'how and possibly by what means an excessive intrusion of Social Democratic elements into the Citizens' Assembly can be prevented'.[39]

In 1905 therefore, the Senate proposed a division of the general electorate in the city into three classes of voter according to income, so that 24 deputies would be elected by those earning over 6,000 Marks taxable income a year on a three-year average, 24 by those earning 3,000 to 6,000 and 24 by all the other male taxpayers. The Social Democrats would—it was believed—be unable to obtain more than a handful of votes from the top two classes and so they would never get more than 24 or 30 seats at the most. Interestingly, as Hans Wilhelm Eckardt has pointed out, the old regulations were to continue to apply to the eight constituencies in the rural areas belonging to Hamburg,

[38] Ibid., pp. 37–8.
[39] Quoted in ibid., pp. 39–40. See also U. Seemann, 'Die Kämpfe der Hamburger Arbeiter gegen die Verschlechterung ihres Wahlrechts in den Jahren 1905/06'. *Wissenschaftliche Zeitschrift der Universität Rostock, gesellschafts-und sprachwissenschaftliche Reihe*, 10 (1961).

where it was thought that the electorate would continue to remain immune to the socialist appeal. Even these proposals did not go far enough for the Citizens' Assembly, which amended them so that there were only two classes in the general elections, with a minimum annual income of 2,500 Marks for the first and 1,200 for the second. Thus the vote continued to be reserved for the more solid upper levels of the working class, and even they were only to elect 24 deputies, while those earning over 2,500 Marks elected 48. Eight seats were reserved for the rural territories on the old basis, and the notables and property-owners continued to have 40 seats each as before. Moreover, by introducing proportional representation for the general elections, the Assembly proposed to ensure that a minority of seats in the second class would continue to be held by the bourgeois Caucuses. The notables continued to have three votes and the property-owners two, but their position was strengthened because their vote in the general elections now fell into the first class. Thus it has been calculated that under the new system a property-owning notable's electoral power was 59 times more effective than that of a citizen in the second class, and an ordinary property-owner's 17 times more effective.[40]

These proposals opened up unprecented political divisions in the dominant classes. In the Senate, the ability of the merchants to bring the lawyers to heel in an emergency was once more graphically demonstrated. Six of the legal Senators, led by the two Burgomasters Johann Georg Mönckeberg and Johann Heinrich Burchard, opposed the reform, while the merchant Senators, and a minority of the lawyers, led by Senator Predöhl, supported it. Burchard and Mönckeberg considered that it would only create more bitterness and extremism in the working class. When the Senate eventually rejected their pleas and decided to go ahead with the plan, Mönckeberg lost his temper— it was said to be the only occasion on which this ever happened at a Senate meeting—and declared that he was not going to 'prostitute' himself by defending it in the Assembly. Burchard, by constrast, remained calm, but he too flatly refused to defend the reform in public.[41] While 120 Assembly deputies from all the Caucuses eventually voted for the change, 35 voted against, and the non-Social Democratic members of the minority, who came from all three of the old Caucuses, now broke away to found a new-style political party of their own, the United Liberals (*Vereinigte Liberalen*). The new group set up a permanent organization and put forward a full political programme.[42]

Significantly, they were led by Carl Petersen, a younger member of one of

[40] Eckardt, *Privilegien und Parlament*, pp. 40–9.

[41] StA Hbg, FA Buehl 2c, p. 75; StA Hbg, Senat, Cl. VII, Lit. Bd., No. 45, Vol. 12b, reports of 11 May 1904, 23 Jan. 1905, 24 Mar. 1905. The death of Hachmann in 1904 seriously weakened the opponents of the move. Among the merchant Senators, O'Swald, who opposed the reform in 1904, had come round to support it a year later.

[42] Eckardt, *Privilegien und Parlament*, pp. 42–4.

Hamburg's great Senatorial families, and formerly an important figure in the Caucus of Rightists, who pointed out that the Social Democrats had generally 'voted with the Rightists or even, as with the recent Housing Inspection Law, stuck through thick and thin with the Senate', and that it was the property-owners who stood to gain most from the change.[43] The United Liberals were no friends of the Social Democrats either. Influenced by the left-liberal revival being led in Germany by Friedrich Naumann, they declared:

We are fundamentally of the opinion ... that the fight against the Social Democrats cannot be won by following the recipes of Prussian-conservative statesmanship, by exceptional ordinances, injustice, and narrow-mindedness. On the contrary, these will only increase the numbers of their hangers-on. Only a just, liberal policy towards the workers on the part of the state, which also co-opts this stratum of the population and its party-political representatives into collaboration within the state, is capable of overcoming the Social Democrats' radicalism.[44]

By choosing to link themselves to a national political movement with this object in mind, the United Liberals contributed to a further politicization of the Citizens' Assembly.

By 1913, 30 deputies belonged to this party, and 20 to the Social Democrats, while the strength of the Caucuses who relied heavily on the general elections (Left and Left-Centre) had declined to 68 seats (from 115 in 1895) and the Caucus of Rightists had become entirely dependent on the notables' elections. These changes also represented the end of the old mercantile domination of the Assembly; by 1913 the proportion of independent merchants in the Assembly—an absolute majority throughout the nineteenth century—had sunk to less than a third. The middle-class professional element declined from 18% in 1896 to 14% in 1913, and the old petty bourgeoisie lost heavily, with artisans and small tradesmen sitting in the Assembly declining from 17% to 10% in the same period. Those who gained were the new white-collar groups, civil servants, schoolteachers, clerks, and officials working for businesses, voluntary associations, or trade unions: their proportion among the deputies rose from 6% in 1896 to no less than 32% by the eve of the First World War. Although they were distributed across the three Caucuses and two parties represented in the Assembly, their presence contributed to a further decline in the old 'unpolitical politics' based on the balancing of interests between 'fixed and mobile capital' in the city.[45]

Thus the improvement of working-class living standards in the late 1890s

[43] Quoted in ibid.

[44] U. Büttner, 'Vereinigte Liberale und Deutsche Demokraten in Hamburg 1900–1930', *ZHG* 63 (1977), 1–34, quoted pp. 7–8.

[45] A. Cord, 'Die soziale Schichtung der Hamburger Bürgerschaft von 1859 bis zum Jahre 1921. Ein Beitrag zur parlamentarischen Geschichte des Kaiserreichs' (StA Hbg, Handschriftensammlung 1023, Wiss. Prüfung für das Lehramt an Gymnasien, Hamburg, 1961), pp. 66–7.

and 1900s did not lead to greater stability in the Hamburg political scene: it merely provided the basis for the election of Social Democrats to the Assembly as more and more workers managed to rise into the income tax brackets where they could register as citizens. The 'suffrage robbery' of 1906 caused deep embitterment in the Hamburg working class. The Social Democrats called a political general strike—the first ever in Germany—to protest against the decision; it was followed by massive demonstrations outside the Town Hall, where the aggressive tactics of the now thoroughly militarized police force led to violent clashes with the crowd. While Social Democratic stewards tried in vain to restore order, the casual port labourers and other inhabitants of the Alley Quarters in the Altstadt set up barricades, stoned the police, and looted a number of jewellers' shops. These events called forth a sharp response from the police, who instituted a brief reign of terror in the city centre, sabring down virtually anyone they came across, killing two people and wounding many others in the process. The rioting was portrayed by the police as a dress rehearsal for the revolution, deliberately staged by the Social Democrats; it was used by the bourgeois press as a heaven-sent opportunity to justify the disfranchisement of the social class held responsible, namely the proletariat.[46]

The truth was more complex. The Social Democratic party organization demonstrated its continued moderation by appealing for calm and condemning the rioters as lumpenproletarian elements who had nothing to do with the organized labour movement.[47] The consistent, undeviating reformism of the Social Democratic party organization in Hamburg—so automatically accepted that it was hardly the subject of internal party debate—remained unaffected by the disfranchisement of 1906. It would be tempting to ascribe it to the English-style liberalism of the Hamburg polity, in contrast to the authoritarian state structures that dominated the Prussian towns, such as Düsseldorf, where the local Social Democratic Party was far more radical in outlook. In some respects, indeed, things were easier in Hamburg: the authorities did nothing to stop the party's May Day celebrations, for example, as they did elsewhere, regarding them as a harmless way for the labour movement to let off steam once a year. But as the 'suffrage robbery' and the militarization of the police force showed, the face turned towards the Social Democrats by the dominant classes in Hamburg could be no less authoritarian than that which is alleged to have been so important in producing a radical Social Democratic Party elsewhere. Moreover, Hamburg's sister Hanseatic city of Bremen had one of the most radical branches of the Social Democratic party anywhere in the Empire by 1914.[48] The intransigence of an authoritarian state and an aggressive and highly organized group of industrial employers which Molly Nolan has argued in her study of the labour movement

---

[46] See Evans, ' "Red Wednesday" in Hamburg' (n. 22, p. 515 above).

[47] Ibid., pp. 14–15, 26–7.

[48] K.-E. Moring, *Die Sozialdemokratische Partei in Bremen 1890–1914* (Hanover, 1968).

in Düsseldorf did so much to fuel the radicalism of the local party seems to have produced nothing but reformism in Hamburg.[49]

Nor were the social bases of the party very different in the two cities, for in Düsseldorf as well as Hamburg the party rested essentially on the active support of the permanent labour force of skilled workers in the construction and other industries, with the mass of the unskilled, the casual, and the transient largely absent from the party's ranks.[50] Nolan seems at various points in her book to suggest that the Düsseldorf Social Democrats were able to bridge the gap between the skilled and unskilled, and achieve an identification of interests in which they actively 'made' the local working class. Yet there are theoretical difficulties involved in arguing that class is principally constituted by politics, and other factors—such as the experience of exploitation and inequality—are merely secondary. This leads, as Geoff Eley has pointed out, to an identification of the party militants with ordinary workers, which begs the question of their failure to win more than 50% of the vote in a town such as Düsseldorf where the overwhelming majority of adult males were manual labourers. And it ignores the question of whether the local party dismissed the casual, transient, and unskilled as 'lumpenproletarian' to the extent that the Hamburg Social Democrats did.[51] The presence of a serious competitor for working-class allegiance in Düsseldorf in the form of the Catholic Centre Party and its social organizations certainly provided a contrast with the solidly Protestant background of the working class in Hamburg, but as Friedhelm Boll has shown, the labour movement in a Protestant town such as Brunswick was every bit as militant as it was in a 70% Catholic town like Düsseldorf.[52]

Tentatively, perhaps, one might suggest four basic reasons for the persistent reformism of the Hamburg Social Democrats.[53] The first was the sharply defined residential segregation between the steady, 'respectable' elements of the labour force in the outer suburbs and the 'rough', casual, unskilled elements in the Alley Quarters near the harbour. Ultimately, indeed, this gulf found its expression in the Weimar Republic through the abandonment of the Social Democratic Party by more than two-thirds of the voters in the last

---

[49] M. Nolan, *Social Democracy and Society. Working-class Radicalism in Düsseldorf, 1890–1920* (Cambridge, 1981).

[50] D. Fricke, *Die deutsche Arbeiterbewegung 1869 bis 1914. Ein Handbuch über ihre Organisation und Tätigkeit im Klassenkampf* (Berlin, 1976), pp. 256–61.

[51] G. Eley, 'Combining Two Histories: The SPD and the German Working Class before 1914', *Radical History Review*, 28–30 (1984), 13–44, here esp. p. 28.

[52] F. Boll, *Massenbewegungen in Niedersachsen 1906–1920* (Bonn–Bad Godesberg, 1981).

[53] There has so far been no systematic archival research on the Social Democratic Party in Hamburg except for the periods of the First World War and the end of the Weimar Republic. Attempts to write one have been defeated by the overwhelming mass of primary source material available. Laufenberg's classic *Geschichte der Arbeiterbewegung in Hamburg-Altona und Umgegend* (2 vols.; Hamburg, 1911–31) stops at the end of the 1880s. (See the remarks on this point by Dieter Langewiesche in Herzig *et. al.*, *Arbeiter in Hamburg*, p. 17.) The following theses should therefore be seen as speculative and provisional in character.

remaining Alley Quarter, the Neustadt Nord, in favour of the Communists.[54] In the 1890s, significantly, by far the strongest district in the Hamburg party was Barmbeck-Uhlenhorst, with 2,300 members. The Social Democrats showed by supporting the clearance of the Alley Quarters that they shared the general aversion to the disorderly and unruly nature of their inhabitants; indeed, trade union functionaries were sometimes reluctant to enter the Alley Quarters to collect their dues because, dressed in their Sunday best, they were taken by the locals to be police agents in disguise and subjected to a corresponding degree of threat and abuse.[55] The theft, prostitution, illegitimacy, drunkenness, unemployment, casual violence, and occasional mass insurrections to which these quarters were prone, became the negative standards against which the active Social Democrats of Barmbeck or Winterhude measured their self-perception of social and political seriousness and responsibility. Residential segregation within the working class owed a lot to the peculiarities of the labour market in a major seaport, and was probably present to the same degree in few other German cities.[56]

Secondly, Hamburg's labour movement could look back on a history that was virtually unique in its length and continuity. Labour organizations and socialist political societies had emerged as early as the 1840s, and institutions such as the Educational Association for Workers had carried on this tradition to link up with the Lassalleans in the 1860s and the Social Democrats a decade later. Hamburg's status as a great city, second only to Berlin, at a time when most towns in the Ruhr were still mere villages, made it inevitable that it should become a centre of the labour movement very early on.[57] This continuity ensured an unusually powerful transmission of artisan traditions and values into the local Social Democratic Party later in the century, helped by the fact that the guilds were not abolished in Hamburg until 1865, in contrast to Prussia, where they declined much earlier. In a town such as Remscheid, the 'Sheffield of Germany', where similar traditions of highly skilled manual work and craft consciousness also existed, the labour movement was more radical, but it was not confronted, as it was in Hamburg, by a substantial number of unskilled and casual labourers whose values were in numerous respects not only different from those which dominated skilled consciousness but also seriously threatened to undermine them. Moreover, in Hamburg the tradition of the labour movement as transmitted through

---

[54] Grüttner, 'Soziale Hygiene und Soziale Kontrolle', in Herzig *et al.*, *Arbeiter in Hamburg*, pp. 359–72, here p. 367.

[55] Ibid., p. 361; for the Barmbeck branch, see StA Hbg, PP V334a Bd. 31: Zusammenfassung der Mitgliedschaft ... January 1892.

[56] Cf. J. Reulecke, *Geschichte der Urbanisierung in Deutschland* (Frankfurt, 1985), p. 95, on the normal heterogeneity of inner-city areas, and the class solidarity of industrial suburbs as a basis for the labour movement.

[57] See the contributions by T. Offermann and J. Breuilly in Herzig *et al.*, *Arbeiter in Hamburg*, pp. 121–52.

the 1850s and 1860s was specifically reformist and moderate in character; this indeed was the condition upon which its survival in these years was predicated.[58]

Thirdly, it would be wrong to ignore the influence of ideological factors on the reformism of the Hamburg Social Democrats: ideological not in the sense of their theoretical stance or their formal aims and goals and understanding of the capitalist world, which was entirely conventional in Social Democratic terms, but rather in the sense of their everyday assumptions about the role they had to play in the political life of the city they lived in. As a Hanseatic town with a tradition of independence in the past and a claim to autonomy in the present, Hamburg offered its inhabitants far more to identify with than a Prussian municipality such as Remscheid or Düsseldorf. Its status as Germany's major port allowed it to continue a particularist resistance to integration in the German Empire far longer than smaller, comparable towns like Bremen and Lübeck, and even as the reality of autonomy became more frayed, the growing elaboration of the state's representation of its own authority, which had no parallel in either of the other two Hanseatic cities, placed ever-greater stress on Hamburg's identity as an individual community.[59] The powerful hegemonic ideology developed and propagated at every opportunity by the Senate and the mercantile grand bourgeoisie was not wholly without influence on the labour movement.

The stress of this ideology on the primacy of trade was far from totally accepted by the Social Democrats, and its emphasis on the community of interests of all classes in the city was recognized for the deception it was.[60] On the other hand, the city's identification with free trade offered a very real material basis with which the party could identify, and the Social Democrats were consistently and openly hostile to protectionist policies which pushed up the cost of living. Local patriotism does seem to have been stronger in the Social Democratic party organization in Hamburg than in other German cities. The political significance of this could be double-edged, as in the party's oft-repeated claim to have stood by the city in its hour of need in 1892 while the bourgeoisie either fled or assailed the Senate with hysterical accusations. But in the long run such local patriotism bred an identification with the city and its traditions, and proved to be an important influence in favour of reformism. In 1918, when the revolution broke out in Hamburg and brought a democratic constitution to the city, the Social Democrats were elected with an absolute majority and found themselves in a position to constitute the Senate, now an ordinary party government responsible to the electorate,

---

[58] E. Lucas, *Arbeiterradikalismus. Zwei Formen von Radikalismus in der deutschen Arbeiterbewegung* (Frankfurt, 1976), and J. Breuilly and W. Sachse, *Joachim Friedrich Martens (1806–1877) und die deutsche Arbeiterbewegung* (Göttingen, 1984), esp. chs. 7–9.

[59] See Chapters 1a and 1d, above.

[60] See Chapter 1b, above, for a discussion of this ideology.

entirely from their own ranks. Instead of this, however, they considered it appropriate spontaneously to invite a member of one of the old Senatorial families, the liberal Werner von Melle, to become First Burgomaster and thus effective head of government, and to give the chair of the Finance Deputation to a prominent merchant on the grounds that it was in the city's best interests for its financial affairs to be controlled by those responsible for its commerce and trade. In addition, the representatives of the United Liberals were also co-opted into the Senate by the Social Democrats so that each party had nine Senators; the First Burgomaster retained the casting vote. It is impossible not to see in this policy, which soon lost the party many thousands of votes as large sectors of a disillusioned working class turned to the Communists instead, the influence of the hegemonic ideology of the balancing of interests and the primacy of trade that went far back beyond the First World War and may well have helped incline the party to reformism before the turn of the century.[61]

Finally, Hamburg's Social Democrats, above all when they came to contest the elections to the Citizens' Assembly, were confronted with the need to extend their appeal at least to the lower sections of the petty bourgeoisie if they were to maximize their support. Otto Stolten argued, for instance, 'that the party needs small businessmen ... only the reactionary element in small business is a hinderance for our movement'; thus he was critical of the Hamburg co-operatives, which the petty bourgeoisie disliked, and in general indeed the party distanced itself from the co-operative movement (which had 70,000 members in Hamburg by 1914) for this very reason.[62] There are indications, indeed, that this consideration even played a role in Reichstag elections, at least while the party's hold over the three Hamburg constituencies was still relatively insecure. For most of the 1890s the Social Democrats had to compete for petty-bourgeois voters with the Anti-Semites, who won substantial support in districts where the social composition was very mixed; and it was widely believed in the city administration that the Social Democrats' campaign to extend the local franchise was in large part aimed at potential petty-bourgeois supporters. In solidly working-class areas there was good reason for small shopkeepers, artisans and handymen, inn-keepers, and others whose livelihood depended on working-class customers, to nail their colours to the Social Democrats' mast. A local history of the Billwärder Ausschlag, the poorest district in the city, referred significantly in 1902 to the 'number of Social Democrats among the workers and Anti-Semites among the civil servants, and the following of business men and

[61] U. Büttner, *Hamburg in der Staats- und Wirtschaftskrise 1928–31* (Hamburg, 1982), pp. 24–82.

[62] W. Ahrens, 'Das sozialistische Genossenschaftswesen in Hamburg 1890–1914. Ein Beitrag zur Sozialgeschichte der Arbeiterbewegung', Ph.D. thesis (Hamburg, 1970), p. 182.

shopkeepers in both camps'.[63] But given the large and rapidly growing number of white-collar workers in the city, it was, not surprisingly, this group to which the Social Democrats devoted most attention.

In the Reichstag election of 1893, for example, the party held special meetings for white-collar workers on themes such as 'which candidate must white-collar workers give their vote to in the forthcoming Reichstag election?' Much of the propaganda in these meetings was devoted to attacking the Anti-Semites, but Social Democratic speakers also tried to persuade the audience that it was only their party that had done anything to legislate in the Reichstag for improvements in the position of white-collar workers, not least because liberals of all shades were too closely identified with the employers. The growing importance of this group in Hamburg—indicated for example in the rapidly increasing number of white-collar deputies in the Citizens' Assembly—not only encouraged the Social Democrats to appeal to their interests and attempt to provide them with trade union and other organizational outlets for their aspirations; it also strengthened the tendency in the party to dissociate itself from the 'rougher' side of working-class life and project an image of stolid and sensible reformism. The rise of the United Liberals indicated a continuing need to win the allegiance of this group, above all after the reform of the suffrage limited the effectiveness of the working-class vote in city elections after 1906.[64]

Unlike the Social Democratic Party in some parts of Germany, therefore, it is difficult to see in the Hamburg case any gradual development towards a reformist position which might require explanation by reference to phenomena such as the bureaucratization of the party apparatus, the growth of a labour aristocracy, or the integration of the party into the state. The Hamburg Social Democrats were reformist from the very beginning. When the opportunity arose to demonstrate their moderation, as in the cholera epidemic of 1892, they took it up with almost indecent alacrity. The overwhelming majority of the working class continued to follow them at the polls while there was no viable alternative. But on repeated occasions, from the harbour strike of 1896–7 through the suffrage demonstrations of 1906 to the shipyard strikes of 1911–12, large sectors of it ignored the attempts of Social Democrats and trade unionists to restrain them and demonstrated a radicalism that went far beyond anything the formal organizations of the labour movement were prepared to initiate. This pattern found its most dramatic expression of all in

---

[63] E. Müller, *Kleine Beiträge zur Geschichte des Billwärder Ausschlags* (Hamburg, 1902), p. 29.

[64] StA Hbg, PP S3625, Bd. 3: *Hamburger Echo*, 16 June 1893. More generally on relations between the Social Democrats and the petty bourgeoisie, see D. Blackbourn, 'The *Mittelstand* in German Society and Politics 1871–1914', *Social History*, 2 (1977), 409–33, and H.-G. Haupt, *Die radikale Mitte. Lebensweise und Politik von Handwerkern und Kleinhändlern in Deutschland seit 1848* (Munich, 1985), pp. 7–31, 188–234.

the Revolution of 1918.[65] Social Democratic ideology of course played a role in all this, as it was transmitted in the ceaseless round of public meetings, newspaper articles, discussions at work, and conversations in the pub. Even on the unorganized it was bound to have some effect in raising expectations and structuring a view of the capitalist world. But the motor of working-class aspirations was provided by the daily experience of injustice, inequality, and exploitation. In the end, this proved more powerful than the loyalty which the party had so carefully fostered over the years. The compromises which the party made in the Weimar Republic lost it so much working-class support not least because they snatched away at the last minute the victory for which the bulk of the working class had waited for so long, and which the party itself had encouraged workers to expect. The legacy of these compromises was not only a deep division within the labour movement that fatally weakened any policy of concerted action against the Nazis, but also a political blindness that culminated in the attempt by a substantial part of the trade union movement to join the Nazis early in 1933. Small wonder, therefore, that the Social Democrats' role in opposing the Third Reich after its foundation was in some respects eclipsed by that of the Communists.[66]

III

If Hamburg's bourgeois-liberal traditions did not allow it to escape the challenge thrown down to every major German province and municipality by the rise of Social Democracy, still less did they enable the city to escape the troubles that assailed the fragile democratic order of the Weimar Republic. Despite Hamburg's constitutionalist history and long-established liberal ideology, and despite the willing participation of the Social Democrats in all the elected Senates of the period, Hamburg succumbed in the end with no more resistance than anywhere else in the Reich. Thousands flocked to the Nazi camp even though Hitler's promise to bring about Germany's self-sufficiency in an 'autarkic' economic order threatened the very basis of Hamburg's existence as an international trading centre.[67] The Nazi voters included not only the disaffected petty bourgeoisie but also a significant proportion of the middle class and the grand bourgeoisie as well. Among the electoral strongholds of Nazism in the city before 1933 were, significantly, the substantial middle-class districts of Rotherbaum and Harvestehude.[68] Although

[65] V. Ullrich, *Die Hamburger Arbeiterbewegung vom Vorabend des Ersten Weltkrieges bis zur Revolution 1918–19* (2 vols., Hamburg, 1976); and the same author's *Kriegsalltag. Hamburg im Ersten Weltkrieg* (Cologne, 1982), esp. pp. 51–62, 68–72.

[66] K. Ditt, *Sozialdemokraten im Widerstand: Hamburg in der Anfangsphase des Dritten Reiches* (Hamburg, 1984).

[67] Büttner, *Hamburg*, pp. 501–4.

[68] R. F. Hamilton, *Who Voted for Hitler?* (Princeton, 1982), with a detailed analysis of the Nazi vote in the various districts of Hamburg.

many of the grand bourgeoisie had by now gone to live downriver, there was no doubting the fact that Hitler enjoyed substantial support in the city's former ruling families. Continuity was secured by the presence of yet another member of an old Senatorial family in the Burgomaster's seat. Following Werner von Melle (1919–24) and Carl Petersen (1924–30, 1931–3), the post of Burgomaster now went, in the Third Reich, to Wilhelm Amsinck Burchard-Motz (1933–45).[69]

By this time, however, such continuities had become little more than symbolic. While von Melle and Petersen still had real power thanks to their position as First Burgomaster, Burchard-Motz fulfilled a mainly ceremonial and ornamental role, as Second Burgomaster. The city was in any case dominated not by the First Burgomaster, the Nazi Carl Krogmann, but by the local party leader, Gauleiter Karl Kaufmann, who acted as Reich Commissioner, carrying out orders sent from Berlin, while the last remaining vestiges of Hamburg's autonomy were quickly being stamped out.[70] Yet so powerful was the symbolic resonance of the old Senatorial families that the British had no hesitation in installing another of their members, the previously unpolitical businessman Rudolf Petersen, brother of Carl, as First Burgomaster in the provisional government of 1945–6. Continuity was further represented in the holding of the same office in 1953–7 by Kurt Sieveking at the head of a centre-right coalition dominated by the conservative Christian Democrats. All this helped the creation of a long-standing myth, in which it was alleged that Hamburg had managed to hold itself aloof from the worst excesses of Hitler's 'Third Reich'.[71]

The truth was very different. Not only did Hitler visit Hamburg thirty-one times during the 'Third Reich', but in more than one respect the city proved to be a model example of a local cog in the Nazi machine. By 1933, for example, not least at the prompting of the Social Democrats, it had extended its network of social services and built up its files on 'anti-social' elements to such a pitch of elaboration that it proved easier to implement the discrimination, sterilization, and extermination policies of the Third Reich in Hamburg than almost any other part of Germany. This was the logical if by no means predestined conclusion of the eugenic ideas and policies developed after the turn of the century. It also represented the culmination of the fear and contempt with which the state, the bourgeoisie, and increasingly the apparatus of the Social Democratic Party had come to regard people such as the denizens of the Alley Quarters—the last parts of which were pulled down in

[69] M. Bruhns et al., '*Hier war doch alles nicht so schlimm*'. *Wie die Nazis in Hamburg den Alltag eroberten* (Hamburg, 1984).

[70] U. Büttner, and W. Jochmann, *Hamburg auf dem Weg ins Dritte Reich* (Hamburg, 1983); H. Timpke (ed.), *Dokumente zur Gleichschaltung des Landes Hamburg 1933* (Hamburg, 1964).

[71] GAL-Fraktion in der Hamburger Bürgerschaft (ed.), '*Es ist Zeit für die ganze Wahrheit*' (K. v. Dohnanyi). *Aufarbeitung der NS-Zeit in Hamburg: Die nichtveröffentlichte Senatsbroschüre* (Hamburg, 1985).

the Third Reich—until they were ultimately disqualified as human beings altogether.[72]

Middle-class merchants, business men, and civil servants in Hamburg co-operated willingly in all these policies up to and including the extermination of the Jews.[73] It is tempting, therefore, to place Hamburg squarely in the context of recent interpretations which regard the collapse of the Weimar Republic and the coming of the Third Reich as above all the work of the old, anti-democratic élites.[74] Yet the grand bourgeoisie of Hamburg was by no means traditionally hostile to parliamentarism—quite the opposite, in fact, as we have seen. Even less was it burdened by a legacy of past hostility to free-market capitalism, industrial society, or bourgeois-liberal values, such as the Junkers are commonly supposed to have suffered under. Nor was it itching to put into effect any long-held dreams of military conquest, any deep-rooted anti-Semitic prejudices, or any heartfelt need to revive a society dominated by feudal notions of honour and nobility. As always, it was sober calculation that moved the Hamburg bourgeoisie to action: fear of the Communist Party, which had grown so large in the city during the Depression; disbelief in the ability of the Weimar Republic to solve the business crisis of 1929–33; desperation with the untenable situation of the city's finances, stretched beyond their limits by the task of supporting Hamburg's 130,000 unemployed.[75] Much as the myth of 'Hamburg's Heyday' before 1914, propagated by men such as Carl August Schröder in his best-selling book of the same title, published in 1921, may have done to discredit the Weimar Republic in the city,[76] few can have imagined that the old system would be restored, and it was for negative rather than positive reasons that so many of the city's grand bourgeoisie welcomed the coming of the Third Reich in 1933.

How can we categorize the grand bourgeoisie of the wealthy Senatorial and mercantile families in Hamburg in the nineteenth century? Was it, as one contemporary wrote in the middle of the nineteenth century, a 'Hamburg Junkerdom, partly belonging to the mercantile, partly to the legal profession', which had 'every characteristic and manifestation of life of the former German Junkerdom', being 'insolent', 'blown-up', and suffering from 'squander-mania'?[77] Or was it a quintessential bourgeoisie, the incorporation of every bourgeois virtue and value? Was it an urban equivalent of the feudal element

---

[72] A. Ebbinghaus, H. Kaupen-Haag, and K. H. Roth, *Heilen und Vernichten im Mustergau Hamburg. Bevölkerungs- und Gesundheitspolitik im Dritten Reich* (Hamburg, 1984).

[73] Ibid.

[74] See G. Eley, *From Unification to Nazism: Reinterpreting the German Past* (London, 1986), pp. 254–82.

[75] Büttner, *Hamburg*, and more generally the same author's *Politische Gerechtigkeit und sozialer Geist. Hamburg zur Zeit der Weimarer Republik* (Hamburg, 1985).

[76] Schröder, *Blütezeit*.

[77] J. W. Christern, cited in W. Schmidt, *Hamburger in der Revolution von 1848/49* (Ergebnisse, Vol. 22, Hamburg, 1983), p. 15.

in German politics?[78] Or was it an alien, 'English' obtrusion into German public life? Questions such as these are difficult to answer not least because of the slippery, protean character of the categories at issue. But however we define 'feudal' it hardly seems reasonable to apply it to a group of people whose economic basis was capitalist to the very core. Even if we make a distinction, as it seems permissible to do in the 1840s and before, between merchant capital and industrial capital, and concede that the mercantile interest was distinctly hostile to the development of industry in some respects, still, capital was capital, and neither the economic activity nor the social world nor finally the political beliefs and actions of the Hamburg merchants corresponded to anything that has ever been defined, however remotely, as 'feudal'.

Were the Hamburg merchants then simply an untypical subgroup within the German bourgeoisie? Much of the work that has been done on the history of the middle classes in Germany would certainly seem to support this view.[79] The characteristic bourgeois in nineteenth-century Germany is often assumed to have been a professional—ideally, a teacher, a university professor, a doctor, a lawyer, or a civil servant. Later, the centre of historical attention shifts to the industrialists, who are then depicted, in certain sectors such as coal and iron and steel, as a class as 'feudalized' in its way as the university professors whose one social ambition was to become an officer in the army reserve.[80] If merchants, bankers, and the like ever get a mention in this context, then it is usually as outsiders, like Ballin or Bleichröder.[81] We have seen throughout this book, however, that there were close economic, social, and family ties between the legal profession and the mercantile interest in nineteenth-century Hamburg; merchants and merchant bankers were often virtually indistinguishable; and in the second half of the century there was a further merging of interests between merchants, bankers, shipowners, and industrialists. It is in reality a skewed vision that sees the bourgeois only in terms of the factory-owner or the professional.

The centrality of merchants to the nineteenth-century bourgeoisie become much more obvious when we look at the English experience. For as W. D. Rubinstein has shown, the very rich in Victorian England were not factory-owners but merchants and financiers.[82] Fortunes were made, not by northern

---

[78] Cf. the remarks by Otto Stolten, comparing the patricians with the Junkers, in StA Hbg, PP S3625 Bd. 3: *Hamburger Echo*, 6 June 1893.

[79] For a recent survey, see U. Frevert and J. Kocka, 'La borghesia tedesca nel XIX secolo. Lo stato della ricerca', *Quaderni storici*, 56 (1984), 549–72.

[80] For one example among many, cf. M. Kitchen, *The Political Economy of Germany 1815–1914* (London, 1978), pp. 75–8, 126–9 (note the absence of 'merchants' from the index).

[81] L. Cecil, *Albert Ballin. Business and Politics in Imperial Germany, 1888–1918* (Princeton, 1967), and F. Stern, *Gold and Iron. Bismarck, Bleichröder and the Building of the German Empire* (London, 1977).

[82] W. D. Rubinstein, *Men of Property: The Very Wealthy in Britain since the Industrial Revolution* (London, 1981).

manufacturers but, as Gareth Stedman Jones has observed, 'by merchants, bankers and stock and insurance brokers mainly in the home counties'.[83] While the English rich adopted a basically aristocratic life-style, following the ideal of the 'gentleman', spending their money on conspicuous consumption, purchasing landed property, deferring to the titled aristocracy, and if possible joining them,[84] the wealthy of nineteenth-century Hamburg were for the most part stern republicans, abhorring titles, refusing to accord any deference to the Prussian nobility, and determinedly loyal to their urban background and mercantile heritage. Aristocratic values dominated in nineteenth-century England not least because of the growth of the Empire, which quickly bred ideas of superiority; but Hamburg's close involvement in the imperialism of free trade and, from the 1880s, the building of the German overseas empire, provided no plausible substitute because it involved no commitment to colonial administration.

The patrician families which dominated Hamburg's politics for generation after generation were essentially creations of the nineteenth century. They were the equivalents of the '200 families ' of the *grandes dynasties bourgeoises* who have been made responsible for so much that happened in France in that era.[85] The hereditary principle was never alien to the bourgeois world; but it had to be confirmed in every generation by renewed evidence of hard work, responsible behaviour, and moral self-discipline. Such was the power of the socializing process through which the Hamburg merchants put their offspring that this was usually the case in the nineteenth century. As Percy Ernst Schramm, born into the centre of one of the Senatorial kinship networks in Hamburg in the 1890s, remarked of Thomas Mann's great novel *Buddenbrooks*,

When I was still at High School I got to know Thomas Mann's *Buddenbrooks*. The context within which his characters were portrayed was very familiar to me, and comparisons between them and my own relatives virtually forced themselves upon me. Below the surface there was no correspondence: while among the 'Buddenbrooks' one after the other fails in life or gives up the struggle, my relations stood up to it and even enjoyed it: 'decadence' was a foreign word to them, and for those who failed in life they had nothing but contempt, or at most pity.[86]

After the turn of the century there were signs that the republican independence of the grand bourgeoisie in Hamburg, perhaps the most un-English of all its social characteristics, was beginning to crumble. Men who had already gained titles and orders began to take up residence in Hamburg and to join the city's ruling circles. Even members of old Hamburg families began

---

[83] G. S. Jones, 'Poor Laws and Market Forces', *New Statesman*, 27 May 1983, p. xiii.
[84] R. Samuel, 'Soft Focus Nostalgia', ibid., p. iii, and for the following.
[85] T. Zeldin, *France 1848–1945*, i: *Ambition, Love and Politics* (Oxford, 1973), pp. 12–13.
[86] P. E. Schramm, *Neun Generationen. Dreihundert Jahre deutscher 'Kulturgeschichte' im Lichte der Schicksale einer Hamburger Familie* (1648–1948) (Göttingen, 1964), ii. 408.

to accept distinctions from the Emperor. Most prominent among them were Karl Freiherr von Merck, Rudolph Freiherr von Schröder and Freiherr John von Berenberg-Gossler (who actually became a Senator). Titles remained concentrated among the very richest; yet of the twenty men in Hamburg in 1912 with an annual income of more than a million Marks, only six had titles (including two *Kommerzienräte*).[87] And John von Berenberg-Gossler's sister, Susanne Amsinck, is said to have exclaimed on being told of his ennoblement, 'But John, our good name!'[88]

Limited though it was, this assimilation of the republican grand bourgeoisie of Hamburg to the German middle class was largely a function of Hamburg's increasing integration into the Empire, as the city's merchants, industrialists, and financiers acquired increasing interests in the rest of Germany, as more wealthy outsiders came to take up residence in the city, as the rapidly thickening communications network overcame local isolationism, and above all as national politics, with the arrival of the Social Democrats and the United Liberals, began to penetrate more permanently into the local scene. A characteristic individual example of these new tendencies is provided by the man who was, alongside Johann Georg Mönckeberg, the leading member of the Senate from the turn of the century, Johann Heinrich Burchard. While the Old Hamburg Particularists were railing against the Prussians in 1870-1, Burchard was fighting on the front lines in France. His principal aim as Hamburg's representative on the Federal Council (*Bundesrat*) was not to defend Hamburg's particular interests, but on the contrary 'to give to the Reich on Hamburg's part what was due to it, and above all in questions of internal policy not to interfere too much with the Reich Chancellor and the leading federal state'.[89] Although he was said to have been critical of Wilhelm II's impulsiveness and lack of any sense of political proportion, he was also, like Versmann before him, personally acquainted with the monarch, and once wrote: 'The Kaiser is an important factor in my life. My life would be poorer if this relationship did not exist. When I have not seen the Kaiser for a long time, I long for an early meeting. Like so many others, I am under the spell of his personality.'[90] Burchard was probably no more frequently in Berlin than had been Versmann and Kirchenpauer, but Berlin after the turn of the century was the grandiose capital of a major world power, far removed from the relative modesty of a few decades before, and Burchard was accordingly far easier to impress.

None of this amounted to anything like a 're-feudalization' of the Hamburg bourgeoisie, even if such a thing had been possible for a class that had never

[87] R. Martin, *Jahrbuch des Vermögens und Einkommens der Millionäre in den drei Hansestädten* (Berlin, 1912).

[88] R. Hauschild-Thiessen, *Bürgerstolz und Kaisertreue. Hamburg und das Deutsche Reich von 1871* (Hamburg, 1979), p. 97.

[89] H. Merck, *Begegnungen und Begebnisse* (Hamburg, 1958), pp. 17–18.

[90] Ibid., p. 20.

been feudal in the first place except in the relationship between the Senate and its rural possessions. The process of assimilation to the world of court ceremony, titles, honours, and military precedence centred in Berlin never went very far. Under the circumstances, indeed, the extent to which the Hamburg grand bourgeoisie succeeded in remaining aloof from the pomp and circumstance of the Reich was very impressive. It said a good deal for its self-confidence, even more perhaps for the social and moral power of the ideals of conduct it had made its own. In these respects, however, Hamburg's bourgeoisie was not untypical of the entrepreneurial upper-middle class in Germany as a whole. On average relatively few merchants, financiers, and industrialists in Imperial Germany were ennobled, or married into the nobility, or indulged in an aristocratic life-style, in contrast to their counterparts in Victorian England. The middle and upper-middle classes in Hamburg—and Germany in general—were far less affected by aristocratic sentiments than their counterparts in nineteenth-century England. The English cult of manly chivalry that created heroes of the stamp of Gordon of Khartoum or Scott of the Antarctic was quite alien to the calculating mercantile rationality of the Hamburg merchants. German nationalism, and especially the colonial and naval ideal, came in Hamburg to have a power and fascination of its own, above all from the end of the 1890s. But the appeal it exerted was specifically bourgeois. It was based not only on a concomitance with Hamburg's maritime traditions and an undeniable attraction in terms of the economic benefits which it offered, but also on a moral claim to a civilizing world mission that sought to replace England's colonial hegemony with something ultimately not so very dissimilar to it in character and intent.[91]

Hamburg thus represented a remarkably undiluted form of the bourgeois state. It remained for a long time relatively free from feudal or aristocratic influence, far more than England did. As in England, bourgeois hegemony rested on the exclusion of the working class from political participation through the restriction of voting rights. As in England, there was a strong belief in the market as a system of distributive justice, where hard work would be rewarded and idleness would meet its just deserts. Sound finance, a low rate of income tax, and a commitment to the policy of free trade all testified to the power of Gladstonian fiscal ambitions on the banks of the Elbe. The liberal-conservative policies of Victorian England in its heyday were intended not so much to foster industrial growth as to prevent it from causing social

---

[91] For the relative absence of 'feudal' propensities among the rich in Germany, see H. Kaelble, 'Wie feudal waren die deutschen Unternehmer im Kaiserreich? Ein Zwischenbericht', in R. Tilly (ed.), *Beiträge zur quantitativen vergleichenden Unternehmensgeschichte* (Stuttgart, 1985), pp. 148–71. More generally, see D. Blackbourn, 'The Discreet Charm of the Bourgeoisie: Reappraising German History in the Nineteenth Century', in D. Blackbourn and G. Eley, *The Peculiarities of German History: Bourgeois Society and Politics in Nineteenth-century Germany* (Oxford, 1984), pp. 159–292.

and political disruption; and so too were they in Hamburg.[92] English too, in a very literal sense, was the attitude of the Hamburg authorities to sanitary reform. The innovations of the 1840s——the consequence not of a systematic plan, but of a chance disaster——made Hamburg a pioneer on the Continent in this field. As we have seen, they included the construction of a centralized water-supply, sewage system, public bathhouses, and much more. They were introduced not by a German but by an Englishman, William Lindley. When his successor, Franz Andreas Meyer, wanted to improve the water-supply, it was to England that he turned for his example. The far-reaching proposals for a housing inspection service that Chief Medical Officer Johann Julius Reincke and his associates put forward in the 1890s were a direct imitation of measures Reincke had observed on an official tour of housing authorities across the North Sea.

These parallels serve as a reminder that it is too simple to regard state intervention in society as 'Prussian' and *laissez-faire* policies as 'English'. The ideal of the night-watchman state rested on a strong element of moral discipline to make sure the night-watchman was not disturbed too much. The system of poor-relief introduced in England in the 1830s imposed harsh penalties on those thought to be idle or undeserving; it was buttressed by the transformation of the ideal of imprisonment from a form of punishment into an instrument of moral education; and it emerged alongside the creation of a uniformed police force, above all in London, that was subject to government rather than community control. Sanitary reform provided a further weapon in this disciplinary arsenal, as well as ministering to growing fears of moral and social contagion among a bourgeoisie confronted with a rapidly growing urban proletariat. All these measures demanded a considerable degree of state intervention in society; but it was a form of intervention directed against the lower orders, leaving the propertied classes as free as possible to continue their pursuit of profits and dividends undisturbed. The combination of the free-market economy, the moral disciplining of the poor, and the construction of powerful and intrusive instruments of state coercion in the face of the threat from below was a characteristic of the liberal capitalist social order in England as it was in Hamburg: it has returned in Britain in the 1980s, indeed, in the policies of the Thatcher government.

No system of rule is ever free from contradictions; nor has any capitalist society, not even that of Victorian England, ever existed in isolation from the forces of the world economy and the international diplomacy of the states surrounding it. Grand-bourgeois and middle-class rule in Hamburg was only able to survive the mid-century crisis by co-opting a substantial sector of the petty bourgeoisie. From 1860 onwards this group, represented above all in the Property-Owners' Association, was able to frustrate many of the reforms

[92] Jones, 'Poor Laws and Market Forces', p. xi.

which the merchant-dominated Senate tried to introduce at its expense. The liberal-conservative ideal of state–society relations pursued by the grand bourgeoisie was never translated into practice in more than a fragmented, imperfect way. Much the same could be said about its implementation in England, where, as Gareth Stedman Jones has observed, 'the attainment of a self-regulating mechanism which by its own momentum would inculcate "Victorian values" always remained tantalisingly just over the horizon'.[93] In Hamburg it was frustrated above all by internal contradictions among the dominant classes. The city also had to contend with repeated and, from 1866 onwards, increasingly sustained intervention from without. Its incorporation into the North German Confederation and then the German Empire removed many of its peculiarities and assimilated it gradually to the Prussian model. Up to the late 1880s, Hamburg managed to preserve most of the formal and even more the informal institutions of its system of class domination intact. Even the ending of the free trade era was achieved by a compromise that paid due respect to the economic liabilities that would have resulted from a complete absorption of the city into the Customs Union. The rapid deepening of social conflict in the city in the second half of the 1880s brought on a crisis to which the dominant classes responded by massively increasing the coercive and disciplining power of state, and by moving as quickly as possible to organize business defence against labour unrest. This transformation of the state involved a further assimilation to Prussian forms, but the purposes it served, as indicated by its timing, were very much local ones. And it still left wide areas of social life untouched, above all where state intervention was thought to be potentially damaging to the interests of trade.

One such area was, crucially as it turned out, the organization of medical ideology and administrative practice in the face of epidemic threats. The resulting cholera epidemic of 1892 exposed the city to the condemnation of world opinion. Like all epidemics, it was not an autonomous, chance occurrence beyond the reach of human power: cholera, more than most diseases, indeed, was the product of human agency, of social inequality and political unrest, of industry and empire. It came at a time when economic and social inequalities in the city had reached unprecedented dimensions. Among a substantial part of the working class, probably the majority, living standards and conditions had been worsening for years, and were probably little better than half a century before. Social conflict and political unrest had increased sharply since the middle of the 1880s. Analysis of the cholera victims reveals patterns of inequality that were probably more marked than at any time since the late 1840s. Those who suffered most, significantly, were those who were least likely to be politically organized: the old and the very young, casual dock labourers, domestic servants, women (compared to normal times), and

[93] Ibid., p. xiii.

in general the very poor, the inhabitants of the Alley Quarters near the harbour and of the poorly built tenement blocks in the working-class suburbs.

The epidemic entered local mythology as a turning-point in the city's history. 'The cholera epidemic', as the doctor Max Nonne wrote, 'meant the caesura, the great divide, between the old Hamburg and the new.'[94] 'For a long time afterwards', as another observer remembered, 'the time of the cholera served as a way of dividing the past ("before" or "after the time of the cholera"), until it was replaced by the Great War.'[95] But just as were its causes, so too were its effects mediated through the social, political, and indeed intellectual context in which it occurred. Only in the matter of constitutional and administrative reform did it provide a decisive impulse for change; other developments which it began, from slum clearance to labour market control, had to wait for the port strike of 1896 before being brought to fruition, while the inadequacies of sanitary reform which had done so much to bring the epidemic about were for the most part already on the way to being made good by the time the disaster happened. Much of the same points hold good on the national level. The major legislative consequence of the disaster, the Epidemics Bill, was soon buried, to be disinterred nearly a decade later for quite different reasons. The intellectual and political supremacy of the contagionist and bacteriological approach had already effectively been achieved almost everywhere except in Hamburg and Munich before the disaster occurred. However tempting it may be, therefore, to regard disasters such as the Great Fire of 1842 and the cholera epidemic half a century later as engines of social and sanitary reform, the reality, as so often, was a good deal more complex.

The significance of the 1892 epidemic lay elsewhere, in the realm of politics. It demonstrated, with a graphic and shocking immediacy, the inadequacy of classical liberal political and administrative practice in the face of urban growth and social change. Hamburg's system of government was tried at the bar of local, national, and even international public opinion in 1892, and found wanting. It was not the *laissez-faire* state that was ultimately convicted, but the domination of the executive, legislature, and administration by local notables: and correspondingly the major consequences of the epidemic lay less in any increase in state intervention in society in the name of sanitary reform than in the undermining of the old system of *Honoratiorenpolitik*. Within four years, reforms were introduced which spelled the end of the old amateur administration and 'unpolitical politics' which had run the city for so long. Within a decade and a half the local political scene had become unrecognizable.

These processes were not unique to Hamburg. All over Germany the 1890s

[94] M. Nonne, *Anfang und Ziel meines Lebens* (Hamburg, 1972), p. 96.
[95] StA Hbg, FA Buehl 2c, pp. 38–9. See also Plate 35.

saw a profound transformation of the structure of politics, as the newly mobilized masses made their influence felt. A *laissez-faire* attitude to problems of urban growth was not unique to Hamburg either, and here too it was the 1890s that saw its legitimacy beginning to be seriously undermined. Municipal administration took on a more professional character in many German towns, as the sense of local community among the citizenry, which had given towns their identity, began to be replaced by a national class consciousness which reflected not least a growing fear of the proletariat.[96] But in few other cities did this process take place so dramatically as in Hamburg. The cholera epidemic of 1892 highlighted—and symbolized—the helplessness of the politics of notables in the face of the challenge posed by the social and environmental consequences of rapid industrial and urban growth. Administrative professionalism on the Prussian model offered itself as a solution not only because pressures were already being exerted in its favour before 1892, not just because it was the only real political alternative, but also because it worked. But by itself it was not enough. In the crucible of cholera, the fusion of class interests held together since the 1860s by the liberal ideology of free trade, the primacy of merchant enterprise, and the reconciliation of divergent interests by qualified parliamentary government, came unstuck.

The attempt to reforge it in the constitutional changes of 1896 lasted little more than a decade. When the dust cleared, after the 'suffrage robbery' of 1906, the character of liberalism had itself undergone a change. The running was increasingly made by the new United Liberals. Unlike the old Caucuses they had a programme of their own and took a far more interventionist line in using the state as an instrument for dealing with the consequences of economic growth and social change. The peculiarities of old-style liberalism in Hamburg, even more different from liberalisms in other parts of Germany that they were from each other, began to fade. The new liberalism of the younger Carl Petersen was not so very different from that of Friedrich Naumann. Liberals in Hamburg became more like liberals elsewhere. Yet this change was only partially realized. The old Senatorial party remained in power. It was not until the Weimar Republic that the warring factions of bourgeois liberal politics in Hamburg finally buried their differences in the

---

[96] Although Hamburg did not fall into the category of a 'home town' as described by Mack Walker in his account of small-town society in the 19th century, some parallels can nonetheless be discerned (M. Walker, *German Home Towns. Community, State and General Estate* (London, 1971), pp. 79, 405–31). For further considerations on the role of 'unpolitical politics' and the associational life of the urban middle class in this period, see R. Koshar, *Social Life, Local Politics, and Nazism: Bourgeois Marburg, 1880 to 1935* (Chapel Hill, 1986). For changes in municipal politics and society at this time, see in particular W. Hofmann, *Die Bielefelder Stadtverordneten. Ein Beitrag zu bürgerlicher Selbstverwaltung und sozialem Wandel 1850 bis 1914* (Lübeck and Hamburg, 1964), and more generally, Reulecke, *Urbanisierung*, pp. 131–9, on the general crisis of the rule of notables in the cities.

face of a Social Democratic majority brought to power by the coming of universal suffrage.[97]

In this process of political realignment and transformation, the cholera epidemic of 1892 did indeed form a decisive turning-point: the event which released the forces of political change to work through a series of consequences which few foresaw at the time. By concentrating into a few weeks a sequence of environmental, social, and political events which might under other circumstances, in other places and doubtless in other ways have taken years to work through, the disaster of the epidemic magnified them and made them easier to anatomize. It was one of those events that, as Lenin once put it, may perhaps be ultimately insignificant in themselves, but nevertheless, as in a flash of lightning, illuminate a whole historical landscape, throwing even the obscurest features into sharp and dramatic relief. The immense amount of written source material, both public and private, generated by the catastrophe, enables us to examine in detail the life of a great European city at the height of of the industrial age. The structures of social inequality, the operations of political power, the attitudes and habits of mind of different classes and groups in the population, come to light with a clarity of profile unimaginable in more normal times. By enabling us to see day by day, sometimes hour by hour, how people behaved under the stress of a terrible and unexpected disaster, the sources that have come down to us from the epidemic of 1892 also bring into our vision the nature of the everyday lives out of which people were torn in the crisis: more important still, they dispel the historical obscurity that in other circumstances so often shrouds the ways in which those lives were structured.

As we contemplate the intricate and sometimes disturbing patterns thus revealed, we can ponder too the lessons they provide for our own times. The great cities of the industrial age are so advanced in the complexity and fragility of their existence that even relatively small-scale disasters can plunge them into a state of chaos and helplessness. For in the end, the outbreak of cholera which so devastated Hamburg in the autumn of 1892, grave though its consequences were for those it affected, only killed a small proportion of the population. How much more helpless, then, would be an urban society in the face of a really serious disaster, such as a major earthquake or a nuclear

---

[97] For the general context of German liberalism in the late 19th and early 20th century, see J. J. Sheehan, *German Liberalism in the Nineteenth Century* (Chicago, 1978); G. Eley, 'James Sheehan and the German Liberals: A Critical Appreciation', *Central European History*, 14 (1981), 273–88; W. J. Mommsen, 'Der deutsche Liberalismus zwischen "Klassenloser Bürgergesellschaft" und "Organisiertem Kapitalismus". Zu einigen neueren Liberalismusinterpretationen', *Geschichte und Gesellschaft*, 4 (1978), 77–90; and J. C. Hunt, 'The Bourgeois Middle in German Politics, 1871–1933. Recent Literature', *Central European History*, 11 (1978) 83–106. There is a detailed local study of a very different region from Hamburg in G. Zang (ed.), *Provinzialisierung einer Region. Zur Entstehung der bürgerlichen Gesellschaft in der Provinz* (Frankfurt, 1978), dealing with Konstanz in the 19th century.

attack. If there was some justification in the claim of Hamburg's defenders in 1892 that no city anywhere would have been capable of coping smoothly with such a catastrophe, then how much more justification there must be in the scepticism with which the civil defence preparations which municipal authorities in our own time are being asked to undertake are commonly regarded. More immediately, the study of popular and official reactions to cholera in the nineteenth century reveals many similarities to public attitudes towards AIDS, the epidemic that is threatening society in the last part of the twentieth century. In both cases, socially stigmatised groups have been blamed, fear of contagion has produced panic reactions, and official responses have varied from the coercive to the indifferent. Medical opinion has been divided, and prevention has been more widely discussed than cure. The limits of public education have been clearly revealed when medical advice has clashed with deep-rooted lifestyles. Both cholera and AIDS contain in their history grim warnings for those who would assume that medicine's powers are unlimited, or that medical science operates in a socially neutral context.

The epidemic of 1892 has lessons of a less dramatic kind, too. Cholera both revealed and reflected patterns of inequality that had a longer-term impact in terms of health and sickness, life and death. If we are to confront these problems with any hope of reducing their power and removing their causes, then a willingness to involve the state in the shaping of society, essential though it is, is not enough. That involvement must also be based on a recognition that the fundamental issue to be tackled is social inequality, not wealth creation or moral improvement. Above all, state intervention must be subject to democratic control. Otherwise it can all too easily become an authoritarian, disciplining force which pays scant regard to the needs of the community as a whole, and ends by assaulting people's bodies and minds instead of healing them.

STATISTICAL APPENDIX

I

BEHIND the solid-looking maps, tables, graphs, and diagrams presented in the text lie many uncertainties. It would take up far too much space to discuss them all: the reader who is interested in pursuing them further is invited to consult the original publications of the *Medizinische Statistik für den Hamburgischen Staat*, the *Statistik des Hamburgischen Staates*, and the other series from which the figures are drawn. The main purpose of the present Appendix is to assess the reliability of the statistics, particularly those relating to cholera and presented in Chapter 5, and to explain as far as possible how they have been arrived at.

For most of the nineteenth century, it is not possible to work out reliable, detailed statistical measures for the impact of cholera in Hamburg. There are no easily available figures for the composition of Hamburg's population by age or sex against which the cholera statistics could be measured, except for the epidemic of 1873. Even in 1892, statisticians made no attempt to calculate occupation-specific morbidity and mortality rates, and for earlier epidemics the task proved altogether impossible. Occupational data for cholera victims in 1832 and 1848 are available in profusion, but attempts to match them with the contemporary estimate of the occupational structure of the city in F. H. Neddermeyer's *Zur Statistik und Topographie der Freien und Hansestadt Hamburg und deren Gebietes* (Hamburg, 1847) proved fruitless. Neddermeyer's figures also have their own problems (see Antje Kraus, *Die Unterschichten Hamburgs in der ersten Hälfte des 19. Jahrhunderts. Entstehung, Struktur und Lebensverhältnisse* (Stuttgart, 1965)). The categories he used differed substantially from those employed in the occupational breakdown of cholera victims in 1832 and 1848 (available in J. C. Rothenburg *Die Cholera-Epidemie des Jahres 1832 in Hamburg* (Hamburg, 1836), and in a manuscript list in StA Hbg, MK III A 2 Bd. 1, Bl. 84). Moreover, although the authorities in 1848 went to some trouble to note the occupation of each of the victims, they failed to do so in over 1,000 of the 3,687 cases that occurred. In 1873, the occupational breakdown of the victims was very crude and in no way matched the complexity of the categories used in the occupational census of 1871 (see SHS 7 (1873)). The numbers of victims in 1873 were very low in comparison to the population of the city as a whole, so that the margin of error in the comparison is too great for any resulting figures to claim even a small degree of plausibility.

A second obstacle to the compilation of statistically reliable estimates of morbidity and mortality rates in earlier epidemics at any level below that of the city as a whole lies in the varying categories into which the lists of victims were divided. The districts used for the epidemic of 1892 are too large to be of any use in analysing earlier epidemics, when the population was much smaller and confined almost exclusively to the Altstadt, Neustadt, St Pauli, and St Georg. Within this area statistics were compiled sometimes by taxation district (available for the epidemics of 1848, 1859, and 1866) and sometimes by recruitment district, of which there were fewer, with different boundaries (available for 1848). Street-by-street figures of cases and deaths are available for the three mid-century epidemics, but at present the composition of the population of each street by age, sex and occupation is not known, although the sources for calculating it are available in manuscript, and a computer-assisted analysis of them is being undertaken at the University of Manchester.

Fourthly, there is a general problem of reliability. Given the uncertainties of diagnosis in earlier epidemics, it would be unwise to place too much reliance on a detailed statistical analysis of the figures below the city level. This is an important point because of the likelihood that infant cholera deaths were to a large extent diagnosed as caused by something else. For example, scarlet fever, which was accompanied in infants and young children by vomiting, increased from 4 cases in October 1830 to 54 in October 1831, while infant deaths from 'difficult teething' increased from 1 to 7 between the same two months, 'convulsions' from 27 to 31, 'apoplexy' from 31 to 42, diarrhoea from 2 to 4, 'hardening of the stomach' from 2 to 5, 'gastric fever' from 3 to 5, 'nervous fever' from 10 to 14, and scrofula from 23 to 33. October 1831 was a cholera month, unlike October 1830, and many of these cases may have been misdiagnosed. (K. G. Zimmermann, *Die Cholera-Epidemie in Hamburg während des Herbstes 1831. Historisch nach ihrer Entwickelung und Verbreitung so wie in ihrem pathologischen und therapeutischen Verhalten dargestellt* (Hamburg, 1831), pp. 110–14.) The problems of diagnosis can be gauged by the fact that only 363 of the 640 cholera cases reported to the Doctors' Club between 12 September and 9 November 1832 were eventually diagnosed as 'real cholera'. In other words, 43% of the cases which ordinary people considered to be displaying the symptoms of cholera, which were well enough known by this time, were adjudged by the medical profession to be something else altogether (StA Hbg, MK III A 2 Bd. 1, Bl. 93). Debates in the Doctors' Club in 1831 were inconclusive. Not only were the members unable to decide how cholera was transmitted, 'there was just as little unanimity in respect of the differential diagnosis of *Cholera asiatica* and *Cholera nostras*' (J. Michael, *Geschichte des ärztlichen Vereins und seiner Mitglieder* (Hamburg, 1896), p. 124). It was widely supposed in the 1830s and 1840s that cholera was preceded by 'premonitory diarrhoea' and followed in many cases by typhoid, all in the same individual (ibid., pp. 146–7). The idea that cholera was an extreme form of other diseases was also common in 1831. Zimmermann reported that he had treated a woman for three days with scarlet fever, when she suddenly developed severe cramps, vomiting and diarrhoea, which led to death within three hours (op. cit., pp. 40–1). In these circumstances it does not seem exaggerated to claim that cholera statistics in 1831–2 were very unreliable.

Finally, there is the problem of reconciling the different figures provided by different writers on the earlier epidemics. This was compounded by the fact that from 1832 onwards the Senate washed its hands of cholera and left everything to the Doctors' Club, including the compilation of the statistics. Rather than comparing all the available figures, I have simply taken those which seemed to me to be the fullest (usually, those compiled at or after the end of the relevant epidemic). The best figures for 1831 give 613 male cases with 328 deaths and 311 female cases with 170 deaths. The best figures for 1832 give a total of 1,626 male cases with 877 deaths and 1,443 female cases with 732 deaths (though the number in Figure 7 is slightly higher).

The best-documented earlier epidemic is that of 1873, during which the names of victims were carefully recorded on individual cards, giving age, sex, address, and dates of the first appearance of symptoms and (where it occurred) death. The compilation of these cards was relatively unproblematical because the epidemic proceeded quite gradually. Only on three days were more than 50 new cases reported, and there was no 'explosive' outbreak as there was in 1859 or 1892. The cards were used to compile quite full statistics on the victims, who numbered 1,729 in all (1,005 of them died). These were presented and discussed in volume vii of the official *Statistik des Hamburgischen Staates*, 1875, in an article written by J.C.F. Nessmann. In keeping with the prevalent theories of a miasmatic causation of cholera, the report paid considerable attention to meteorological phenomena. But Nessmann also compiled age- and sex-specific morbidity and mortality rates, and attempted a social geography of the disease. As a basis for the total population figures by age, sex, district, and street he used the census material of 1871, adding 5% to all the 1871 figures on the grounds that the population was increasing by an average of 3% a year. This obviously introduced some error, since all age-groups were not increasing in number at the same rate. Moreover, many of the same points made below in relation to the 1892 figures probably also apply to 1873, although Nessmann did not provide the same detail as his successors did on how the figures were compiled. Nessmann also provided occupational details for the male victims of the 1873 epidemic. Unfortunately the occupational categories he used for cases did not correspond to those used for deaths, so that a true comparison could not be attempted. Again, Fig. 7 gives a slightly higher number of deaths.

II

The 1892 Hamburg figures are by far the best for any epidemic of the nineteenth century. They too present considerable problems, but none of them is insurmountable, and there is plenty of information on how the figures were compiled. Of the many problems which confront the historian in attempting to assess the incidence of cholera in 1892, the most serious is undoubtedly that of diagnosis. I have already pointed out the difficulties which contemporaries had in reaching a firm diagnosis of cholera earlier in the century. Even in 1892, these difficulties affected not only the announcement of the arrival of the disease in the city but the eventual calculation of the numbers of those affected. After the outbreak of the epidemic it quickly became impossible to institute a bacteriological investigation of any but a tiny fraction of cases. At the height of the epidemic, diagnosis was often hasty, involving on-the-spot decisions without recourse to serious investigations. In effect, diagnosis was often according to the symptoms.

Diagnosis in such circumstances would be based not least on expectations. Physicians would tend to use their previous experience in coming to a conclusion. As Figure 12 indicates, normal, non-cholera mortality was highest among infants and small children, and among the major causes was 'vomiting and diarrhoea' (sometimes known as 'summer diarrhoea'). There were 2,793 deaths from this cause recorded in 1892, all for children below the age of 5: 2,298 of these deaths were among infants aged 0–1. The great majority of these—1,830—occurred in August and September. In fact, 20% of all deaths in August and 16% in September were attributed to vomiting and diarrhoea among children (*MS 1892*, Table 15h/n). These were of course the months of the great cholera epidemic; but they were also the months when normal deaths from 'vomiting and diarrhoea' could be expected to be high in number, especially if the weather was hot, as it was in 1892. It is possible to get a rough idea of how many cholera deaths among infants were wrongly diagnosed as deaths from 'vomiting and diarrhoea' by comparing the death rate from the latter cause in 1892 with average annual deaths from the same cause in 1882–91. Deaths among infants and children aged 0–5 from all major causes were higher in 1892 than on average in 1882–91, but deaths from 'vomiting and diarrhoea' were much higher as Table 10 indicates. In general, a comparison between infant mortality in 1892 and the average for the previous ten years suggests that a great many fatal cases of cholera were diagnosed as 'vomiting and diarrhoea' or other 'illnesses' in 1892, as Figure 6 further indicates.

Table 10. Excess mortality in Hamburg, 1892, from selected causes, among children aged 0–5

Cause	Deaths per 1,000 inhabitants of all ages, 1892	Average annual deaths per 1,000 inhabitants of all ages, 1882–91	Excess mortality in 1892 (1882–91 = 100)
Weakness of the newborn	1.65	1.56	106
Infant convulsions	1.41	1.35	104
Wasting	2.62	2.08	126
Vomiting and diarrhoea	4.35	2.53	172

Source: SHS 20 (1902), Uebersicht IF, p. 14.

Deaths from 'old age and gangrene' were in fact lower in 1892 than on average in 1882–91. The rate per 1,000 inhabitants of all ages was 0.96 in 1892 as against an annual average of 1.07 for the ten previous years, a fall of 11%. But deaths from this cause had a marked seasonal pattern, rising sharply in the winter months and falling to a low point in the summer and early autumn. Since deaths among the old, as among infants, were common, expectation may have led

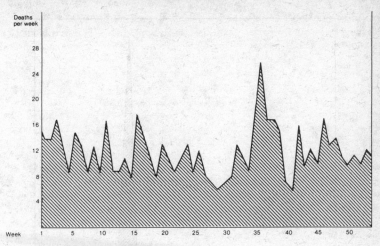

Week

Source: *MS 1892*, Table 19

FIG. 30. Weekly deaths from old age, Hamburg 1892

physicians to diagnose cholera cases as something else. The unseasonal rise in deaths from old age in August and September 1892 suggests that between 20 and 30 of these were in fact the result of cholera, as Figure 30 shows. There are no other causes of death involving significant numbers of people where misdiagnosis of cholera cases is evident. Given the expectation of physicians of a low death rate among the adolescent and the middle-aged, it is probable that few fatal cases of cholera in these age-groups would have been diagnosed as something else.

With non-fatal cases, matters were different. There was some likelihood that physicians would register almost any disease among the adolescent and middle-aged as cholera, providing it included vomiting and diarrhoea. But we have already seen that this was not the case for infants and young children; in fact expectations of fatality could just as easily lead physicians to diagnose mild cases of cholera as 'cholerine' or *cholera nostras*, as Figure 31 indicates. Indeed the medical statistics for 1892 recognized this by including in the statistics of deaths from cholera all fatal cases of 'cholerine', amounting to 149, and all cases of infant mortality from 'vomiting and diarrhoea', amounting to 400, in families where cholera cases were diagnosed among other members at the same time. This procedure was incorporated into the official statistics, where only 19 fatal cases of 'cholerine' appear for 1892. But, as we have seen, it still leaves many cases of infant mortality and deaths from old age unaccounted for. Indeed, if infant and child deaths from 'vomiting and diarrhoea' in 1892 had been the same as usual for the previous decade, there would (as Table 10 suggests) have

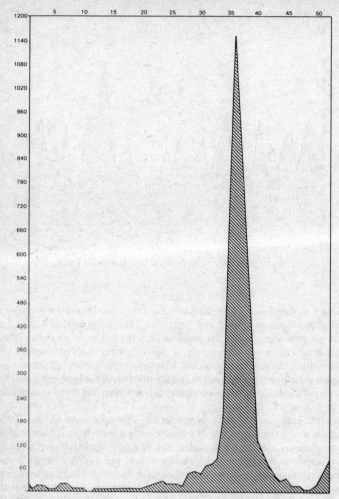

Source: MS 1892, Table 29a

FIG. 31. Cases of *cholera nostras* in Hamburg, 1892, by week

been only 1,623, so that as many as 1,170 deaths may have been wrongly diagnosed and may in fact have been due to cholera. These would of course have been in families where there were no other cholera cases, so not all of them are likely to have been cholera. The exceptionally hot weather of August and early

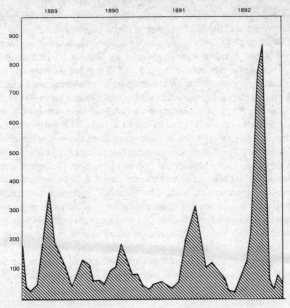

Source: MS 1892, Table 20a

FIG. 32. Deaths from diarrhoea and 'summer cholera' of infants under one year of age, by month, Hamburg 1889–92

September 1892 may well have increased the 'normal' death rate among the very young from digestive orders, since food contamination of the sort discussed in Chapter 2d, above, was likely to have been more widespread than usual. Infant mortality from digestive orders was already increasing sharply in July 1892, well before the outbreak of the cholera epidemic, as Figure 32 suggests. But even if we take a very cautious and conservative estimate, and accept that only a half of these deaths were due to cholera, we still come up with 585 'hidden' cholera deaths. With the addition of the cholera deaths ascribed to 'old age', this makes a round 600. The official death toll was 8,616. So we can say with confidence that there were at least 9,000 deaths and we can suggest that the final death toll may even have been as high as 9,800.

Contemporaries were aware of such problems. In Uhlenhorst, while the official statistics gave 581 cases and 277 deaths, the local Health Commission found 719 cases and 343 deaths, and remarked that there were another 206 cases and 21 deaths which may well have been cholera attacks. In other words, it considered morbidity to have been underestimated by 24% and possibly as much as 31% (*Bericht des Gesundheitskomites für den Bezirk Uhlenhorst über ihre Tätigkeit während der Cholera-Epidemie 1892*, Hamburg, 1892). If the figures for Hamburg as a whole had been underestimated by as much as 24%, the final death toll would have been 10,684 and the final number of cases 21,368.

After 1 October 1892, only cases where bacteriological investigations resulted in cultures of the bacillus were registered as cholera (cf Reincke's account, *Deutsche Medizinische Wochenschrift*, 314 (1893), p. 12). Given the difficulties which contemporary medical men experienced in producing such cultures, it is thus likely that the figures of morbidity and mortality for October–December 1892 were too low. Moreover, false diagnosis was probably less common in fatal cases among adolescents and adults than in milder attacks where the symptoms were less extreme and so more difficult to distinguish from those of other diseases. For instance, cases of typhoid showed little variation, as Figure 33 indicates. Similarly, it seems likely that many of the mild non-fatal cases of 'cholerine' were in fact cholera; modern medical science rejects any sharp distinction between the two, for the bacillus is present in both. The Health Commission for Harvestehude argued that 'one should not distinguish between cholera cases and cases where there is merely a suspicion of cholera, but one must include all cases relating to the epidemic'. On this basis, the Committee added to the official figure of 81 cases another 89 cases of 'cholerine', 14 of 'vomiting with diarrhoea', 52 cases of 'diarrhoea', and 3 of 'stomach catarrh', none of any of these being fatal. This made 239 in all and of course drastically reduced the case-specific mortality rate for the area (StA Hbg, MK III A 13, XI: Harvestehude, p. 10). This was certainly going too far, and such practices were not adopted by the official statistics. It is not really necessary, however, to go through such elaborate procedures to arrive at an estimate. (inevitably rough in any case) of cholera morbidity in 1892. All we have to do is take the estimated figure of deaths from cholera and double it. Taking the four figures we have suggested, this would yield an estimate of 16,944 (official figures), or 18,000, or 19,600, or 21,368, depending on which figure we adopt. In conclusion, therefore, we can say that the official figures considerably underestimated the actual number of cholera deaths and cholera cases, perhaps by as much as a quarter.

This immediately raises the problem of whether the calculations of mortality and morbidity rates should be revised. There are several reasons, however, why such a procedure would be inadvisable. In the first place there is no knowing whether or not the underestimate is consistent across all age-groups and classes, and by sex. Given the evidence I have reviewed so far, it would seem that the underestimate was concentrated among infants. This means that rates for all other age groups are unlikely to be seriously affected by any upward revision on this basis. There is a further point to note, and that is that the global population figures that formed the basis for the calculation of morbidity and mortality rates were derived from censuses taken in the month of December. Because of seasonal migration, the population, especially in the working class, was lower in December that it was in August and September. This meant that morbidity and mortality rates would be artificially inflated because the cases and deaths which occurred in August and September were not expressed as a proportion of the population actually present in August and September, but as a proportion of the rather

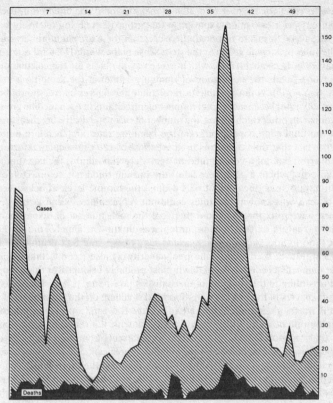

Source: MS 1892, Table 30

FIG. 33. Typhoid in Hamburg 1892: cases and deaths per week

smaller population estimated to have been present in December. This factor goes some way to counterbalancing the underestimate in morbidity and mortality rates caused by misdiagnosis. It provides another reason for using the official statistics as a basis for calculation, since there is no way of correcting for the seasonal factor which I have mentioned.

III

In Figure 18, wives and children who fell victim to cholera are counted in the income group of the husband. This means that the rates given are high, because they give in effect the number of deaths of men, women, and children in each income group per 1,000 male taxpayers in that group (there being relatively few female taxpayers). It has to be noted, therefore, that these are *not* morbidity and mortality rates by income group in the strict sense of the word. The total number of taxpayers in December 1891, which is used as the basis for the calculation, was 147,604, while the population of Hamburg (state) at the same time was roughly 600,000. It is not possible to recalculate the figures as true morbidity and mortality rates because the total number of inhabitants in each income group is not known. In other calculations, the number of cases and deaths are measured against the total state population, and the resulting rates are therefore much lower. The fact that the tax returns used are those of 1891 introduces a further source of error, but not a very significant one. More important is the fact that in 3,168 cases (of whom 1,226 were fatal) the income could not be ascertained, while in 3,347 cases (including 1,648 deaths) the income level, at below 600 Marks a year, was known, but rates could not be calculated because they fell below the lowest tax threshold and therefore the total number of taxpayers or potential taxpayers in that income group was unknown. Finally, the lowest bracket (600 to 800 Marks a year) yielded 1,575 cases and 873 deaths, but is too inaccurate to be used because the great majority of those 3,168 victims whose income, name, or abode were unknown most probably belonged to this group, at least according to the compiler of the statistics (*MS 1892*, p. 38). There were 47,447 taxpayers in the bracket 600–800 Marks; adding on the 'unknowns', for what it is worth, gives a morbidity rate of exactly 100 per 1,000 taxpayers and a mortality rate of 44.2, which roughly accords with the rates for the income groups up to 2,000 Marks a year. As one would expect from tax returns, then, the very poor are not included and meaningful figures can only be compiled for those acutally earning a decent living for themselves and their families.

With this limitation, however, the figures none the less present a striking trend towards lower morbidity and mortality with higher income, even though the trend may have been rather less marked in reality than the figures suggest. The fact that infant mortality was higher in the lower income groups, as was general mortality, would tend to even out family size by reducing the number of dependants. The better-off had fewer children, but a much higher proportion of them survived infancy. The birth rate of the richest districts may have been about half that of the poorest, but cholera rates were only a third or even a quarter as great (see Maps 22, 32, and 33). Thus the difference in the incidence of cholera between income groups was more than a mere statistical illusion.

IV

The intitial basis for Figure 19 is provided by the list of occupations of cholera victims, given in the medical statistics for 1892. Here they are divided according to the conventional classification used in the German occupational census, except that the paper and leather industries are taken together and trade and insurance are also placed in the same category. The victims assigned to the various occupational categories included dependants, but not the domestic servants of people engaged in the various categories. In all, 8,047 people who caught cholera were dependants not actually engaged in the occupations listed but assigned to them on the basis of the occupation of the head of household. 4,497 of these dependent victims died, a case-specific mortality rate of 53.49%. It is not possible to separate these people out of the statistics, since the original material has been destroyed. This means, of course, that the value of the occupational classification of victims is greatly reduced. It can be assumed, however, that a good many victims caught the disease at work and then infected their families, so that the classification is not entirely without value. An added complication lies in the fact that dependants were unevely distributed across occupations, partly because some occupations (e.g. the free professions) had lower birth rates than others, partly because occupations varied in age structure, as can be seen most clearly in the case of domestic servants, who were predominantly young and unmarried. Here again, it is not really possible to recalculate the figures in any convincing or reliable way. We may reasonably suppose, however, that the distortions introduced here only had a relatively minor effect on the overall occupational distribution of cases.

A further problem lies in the fact that the personal details of the victim were obviously taken very hastily and superficially at the height of the epidemic. Thus a great many victims were simply classified as 'workers', no further details being available at the time. Altogether there were 4,056 victims in this category, of whom 2,056 died. In the official occupational census taken in 1895, however, the city's inhabitants were required to be very careful and precise in describing their occupation. Thus the 'workers' became a residual category, containing only a very small number of people, 438 in Hamburg all told, for whom it was absolutely impossible to discover an occupation, but who were obviously in some sense or other manual labourers. A rough estimate of occupation-specific morbidity and mortality can be arrived at by comparing the number of victims by occupation with the number of people (including dependants but not including 'servants for domestic services') in each occupational group in 1895. Such an estimate is not possible for 'workers'. The category 'workers' of the 1892 figures, containing roughly 25% of all victims, was in effect redistributed across all the other categories in the census of 1895.

A similar problem is encountered in the occupational groups 'no trade' and 'no trade given'. Those without a trade suffered 419 cases (296 fatal) in 1892. No trade was given in 2,547 cases (997 fatal). The 1895 occupational census lumped these two groups together and arrived at a total of 46,161 occupied persons and dependants. The cholera morbidity rate for these groups, combined, works out at an implausibly high 64.3 per 1,000. Clearly in many cases the authorities simply lacked the time to establish the victim's trade. The mortality rate, at 28.0 per 1,000, is more plausible because the bureaucratic procedures set in motion by a death were more successful in identifying the occupation of these people and so in lowering the number of deceased individuals in the 'no trade' and 'no trade given' categories. It seems likely that a majority of the 2,547 cases

Statistical Appendix

where no trade was given were manual labourers or their dependants. The people who fell under this heading in the 1895 census numbered a mere 1,275 and represented the sum total of the census-takers' failure to identify people's occupation. Those with 'no trade' in the 1895 figures were mainly widows living off properties, inheritance, or pensions. University students, paupers, and lunatics also fell into this category. So the figures in the cholera statistics especially for those with no trade given bore no relation to the kinds of people included in this category in the 1895 census.

In these circumstances it seemed advisable to attempt a redistribution of all these unidentified individuals into the other occupational categories. In all, this involved 6,603 cases and 3,053 deaths from the categories 'no trade given' and 'workers'. I assumed that all these people fell into the category described in the 1895 occupational census as manual workers (*sonstige Gehulfen, Lehrlinge, Fabrik-, Lohn- und Tagearbeiter*). That is, I assumed they did *not* include white-collar and supervisory personnel (*Beamte, Handwerksmeister, Directoren, Eigentümer, Geschäftsleiter, überhaupt das wissenschaftlich, technisch und kaufmännisch gebildete Verwaltungs- und Aufsichtspersonal*). These manual workers are listed in the census as 'c' category workers (except in occupations IX–XXIII, where there are more subdivisions, and the manual labourers all fall into category c3). I calculated the number of 'c' or 'c3' workers and dependants (not including domestic servants) in each occupational group, then calculated what percentage of the total number of these people fell into each occupational group. Then I divided the extra 6,603 cholera cases and 3,053 deaths into the various occupational groups, excluding the *Fabrikanten* (or unidentified labourers) but including the 'no trade' and 'no trade given' groups, according to these percentages. These were added to the cases and deaths which had already been identified in the medical statistics, divided by the number of employed people and dependants (excluding domestic servants), in each category as listed in the 1895 occupational census, and multiplied by 1,000 to arrive at occupation-specific morbidity and mortality rates. Thus—to take an example at random—the medical statistics listed 1,006 cases and 567 deaths in the clothes manufacture and cleaning trade. The 1895 census lists 22,350 'c' category workers in this trade, which is 6.5% of the total number of such workers in Hamburg in 1895 (with dependants but excluding domestic servants). 6.5% of 6,603 cases is 429, of 3,053 deaths is 198, which when added to the original figures in the medical statistics gives a total of 1,435 cases and 765 deaths in this occupational group. The sum total of all occupied people (*Erwerbstätige*) is this category (who included many with their own businesses)—plus dependants but minus servants—was 55,132 in 1895. When this sum is divided into the estimated number of cases and deaths in this group and multiplied by 1,000 the result is a morbidity rate of 26‰ and a mortality rate of 13.9‰

There is no denying that this procedure has a number of disadvantages. The number of people in most groups increased between 1892 and 1895, but

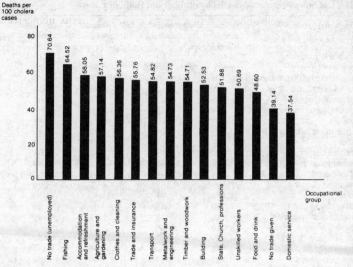

Deaths per
100 cholera
cases

Value	Occupational group
70.64	No trade (unemployed)
64.52	Fishing
58.05	Accommodation and refreshment
57.14	Agriculture and gardening
56.36	Clothes and cleaning
55.76	Trade and insurance
54.82	Transport
54.73	Metalwork and engineering
54.71	Timber and woodwork
52.53	Building
51.88	State, Church, professions
50.69	Unskilled workers
48.60	Food and drink
39.14	No trade given
37.54	Domestic service

Source: MS 1892, p. 32.

FIG. 34. Case-specific cholera mortality in selected occupational groups, Hamburg 1892.

unevenly. It is not possible to calculate back figures for 1892 because the previous occupational census had been held as far back as 1882, and in any case the occupational structure was also affected temporarily by the economic downturn of the early 1890s. This is not a very serious problem, however, and will have affected the eventual figures only by making the estimated occupation-specific morbidity and mortality rates marginally on the low side. A more serious source of error lies in the levelling effect of the procedure used to estimate these rates. The extra 6,603 cases and 3,053 cholera deaths have been redistributed among the occupational groups as if all occupations were equally affected, or rather, as if the 'c' and 'c3' workers in all occupational groups were equally affected. It is very unlikely that this was the case. Still, there is no knowing what factors determined the failure of the medical authorities to identify cases and deaths by occupation, or how these factors varied by occupational group, so it seemed safest to distribute the extra cases and deaths simply according to the proportion of 'c' and 'c3' workers in each group. At least the figures thus arrived at are less implausible than the ones that would be worked out solely on the basis of the cases and deaths identified in the medical statistics.

There are so many figures and statistics relating to the occupational distribution of cholera in 1892 that it seemed unwise to burden the text with them, and instead they are presented here in the form of a table. Table 11 contains a full list of the sources used in calculating occupation-specific morbidity and mortality

Table 11. Cholera cases and deaths by occupation, Hamburg 1892

Occupational group	Officially listed cases	Officially listed deaths	Estimated cases	Estimated deaths
Agriculture, gardening	105	60	296	149
Fishing and forestry	31	20	38	23
Mining, iron smelting, saltworks	0	0	13	6
Stone and earth industries	15	7	68	32
Metal processing	549	293	912	461
Machines, tools, instruments	255	147	506	263
Chemicals	20	10	119	56
Lighting materials, fats, oils	16	9	102	46
Textiles	25	12	71	33
Paper and leather	171	85	342	164
Woodworking	669	366	1,052	543
Food and drink	393	191	763	362
Clothes and cleaning	1,006	567	1,435	766
Building	1,114	601	2,019	1,019
Printing	90	45	196	94
Painting and sculpture	44	23	57	29
Workers (no more details)	4,056	2,056	†	†
Trade and insurance	1,537	857	2,468	1,287
Transport	1,824	1,000	2,498	1,311
Hotels, refreshments	441	256	500	284
Domestic service	855	321	1,271	513
State and Church, free professions	744	386	896	456
No trade	419	296	1,704	705
No trade given	2,547	997	†	†
TOTAL	16,926	8,605	16,926	8,605

† = redistributed among the other groups

Sources: calculated from *MS 1892*, p. 32, from *SHS* 18 (1898), I, pp. 102–18; *SHS* 21 (1903), pp. 114–16.

rates. Comparing Figure 34 and Table 11 (both official figures) with my own calculations (Figure 19), it will be noted that the redistribution of the extra cases and deaths alters the rank-order of the occupational groups in some respects, moving 'hotels, refreshments' down the scale, for example, and 'food and drink' up. But the general features remain constant, and it seems reasonable to conclude that they are broadly correct: that is, high morbidity rates for domestic service, transport, woodworking, and metal processing, low morbidity rates for agriculture, gardening, trade and insurance, state, church, and free professions, tools and instruments, with the rest somewhere in between. The mean morbidity rate by occupation according to these calculations works out at 27.3 per 1,000, or 26.9 not including the last category ('no trade given'), which fits in quite well with the mean morbidity rate by age group (28.6).

V

Figures 22 and 25, indicating respectively sex-specific cholera mortality by age-group, Hamburg, 1892, and sex-specific excess mortality in Hamburg, 1892, by age-group (1882–91 = 100), are both calculated from *SHS* 20 (1902), Uebersicht IE (pp. 12–13). The basic problem of calculating rates such as these is that a full census was only taken every five years, on 1 December 1885, 1890, 1895, and so on, so figures for the age and sex distribution of population are not available for the intervening years. The official statistics provide absolute numbers by deaths, by age and sex, and according to cause of death, for 1892, and construct death rates by assuming a steady increase in population between 1890 and 1895 and calculating the population for 1892 on this basis, according to age-group. I have selected out the absolute numbers of deaths by sex and age-groups from Uebersicht IE and expressed them as a rate (deaths per 1,000 of the respective population). Unfortunately there are no estimates available for the absolute numbers of males and females in each age-group in 1892, so I have calculated back the original absolute figures from the global death rates provided. Thus for example Uebersicht IE provides a death rate of 343.7 per 1,000 males aged 0–1 for 1892, which gives an estimated male population of 11,470 in that age-group (1,000 − 343.7 × 4,035). There are slight differences between the numbers in Figure 22, which derive from the official statistics published in 1902, and those in Figure 20, which derive from the medical statistics published in 1893. The discrepancies arise mainly from the different basis of calculation for the total population in each age-group. The figures from the medical statistics are based on taking the global population count for December 1891 and dividing it among the different age-groups in the same proportion as it was divided in the census of 1890. The global population figure used was thus generally lower than that used in the official statistics published in 1902. So the morbidity and mortality rates are generally higher.

It will be noted that the difference declines with each higher age-group (6.9% for 0–1, 3% for 1–2, 0.6% for 2–5, and so on down to 0.09% for 80 and over). The difference between the two sets of figures is not significant for any age-group except infants aged 0–1, where it is 6.9%. This can be partly explained by fluctuations in the birth rate, as shown in Table 12. The rise in the birth rate between 1890 and 1891 meant that the medical statistics slightly underestimated the number of infants present in 1892 and so gave morbidity and mortality rates that were slightly too high. The marked decrease in the birth rate by 1895 meant that the official statistics noticeably overestimated the number of infants present in 1892 and so gave morbidity and mortality rates that were clearly too low.

The official statistics are also used as a basis for calculating sex-specific excess

Table 12. Live births per 1,000 population, Hamburg 1890–95

Year	1890	1891	1892	1893	1894	1895
Births	37.11	37.44	37.05	37.27	36.42	35.13

Source: SHS 20 (1902), p. 1.

mortality, in Figure 25, showing deaths per 1,000 population by age and sex in 1892 as a percentage of the equivalent death rates for an average year in the previous decade. Since the death rate was declining, albeit slowly, during this period, the excess mortality for 1892 is likely to be slightly underestimated; or, to put it another way, the estimate for what mortality rates for 1892 would have been had the cholera epidemic not taken place, is probably a little too high. In comparing these figures with those in the original tables, it should also be noted that some of the original figures have been corrected or rounded up. How much of the excess mortality was the result of cholera cannot be calculated with absolute certainty. Some other diseases were certainly recorded as killing more people in 1892 than in an average year, but this may simply be a result of wrong diagnosis. It is highly probable that by far the greatest cause of excess mortality in 1892 was cholera.

The age distribution of cholera was connected with other aspects of the social distribution of the disease in a number of ways. In the first place, the wealthier classes had fewer children than their poorer counterparts. The birth rate was negatively correlated with the proportion of economically independent occupied persons (-0.69) and positively with the population of manual labourers (0.67) in each district. The birth rate in a bourgeois district such as Rotherbaum or Harvestehude as we saw in Map 22, was much lower than in a poorer district such as the Altstadt Nord or the Billwärder Ausschlag. Consequently the number of infants was also smaller. Map 41 shows the number of infants per 1,000 inhabitants by district in Hamburg, using statistics from the 1890 census. Since infants were by far the most susceptible sector of the population to cholera, it would seem reasonable to suppose that the higher proportion of infants in the population of a district, the higher the proportion of cholera cases, and even more, of cholera deaths, in that population was likely to be. In fact, the relationship between these two factors was not a very strong one. The correlation between infants per 1,000 inhabitants and the cholera morbidity rate, by district, works out at only 0.25, which is weak. Given the high proportion of infants who died of the disease, once they caught it, it is not surprising that the same test, when applied to the cholera mortality rate and the number of infants per 1,000 population, by district, comes out a little higher, at 0.44, but this is still not very impressive. The correlation between children aged 0–5 per 1,000 population by district, and cholera morbidity is 0.13, for cholera mortality 0.33, which is again very weak. The correlations between the birth rate and cholera morbidity (0.21) and mortality (0.39) are similarly low.

If we look more closely at Map 41, it becomes clear that the districts fall rather neatly into two groups. First, there is a group of inner-city districts and inner suburbs with a relatively low proportion of infants, including not only the well-off areas of Harvestehude, Rotherbaum, and Hohenfelde but also the much less prosperous areas such as the Altstadt and the Neustadt, St Pauli, and St Georg. Then, in a band stretching round the outskirts of the city from Eimsbüttel and Eppendorf in the north-west through Winterhude, Barmbeck, and Uhlenhorst in the north down through all the eastern suburbs to the Billwärder Ausschlag,

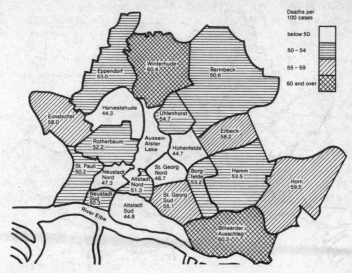

Deaths per
100 cases

below 50

50 – 54

55 – 59

60 and over

Source: MS 1892, 40

MAP 41. Infants per thousand inhabitants, by district, Hamburg 1890

there is a second group of districts with a higher proportion of infants. This reflects the fact that these newly built-up districts were experiencing rapid population growth during this period, as young married couples were moving out of the overcrowded inner city to more spacious accommodation where it was easier to house and bring up children. The high case-specific mortality among infants thus provides a good explanation for the pattern of case-specific mortality by district revealed in Map 42, where once again the outlying districts show the highest figures. And in fact the correlation between case-specific mortality and the proportion of infants by district works out at 0.58, which is a more convincing level than the correlations cited in the last paragraph.

Correlations, of course, do not by themselves say anything about causation, but it would seem reasonable to suppose that infants and small children constituted to some extent an independent source of infection, so it is likely that infant deaths contributed disproportionately to the mortality rate in all districts. On the other hand, given the greater supervision and better hygiene of bourgeois infant care, we would expect infant morbidity rates to be somewhat lower in the better-off districts, and the same may have applied, though probably to a lesser degree, to infant case-specific mortality rates as well. When these considerations are taken together with the weak correlations between infants per 1,000 population and cholera morbidity and mortality rates, we can conclude that the distribution of

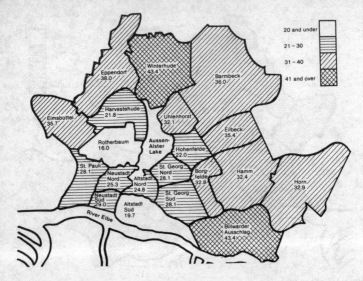

Source: calculated from *MS 1892*, Tables 33g, 33c.

MAP 42. Case-specific cholera mortality rate, by district, Hamburg 1892

cholera by district in Hamburg in 1892 cannot be explained, except to a very small extent, by the proportion of infants by district.

A further set of problems relates to the sex-specific typhoid morbidity and mortality rates among adults by district, Hamburg 1885–8 (given in Table 2). These were calculated on the basis of the absolute numbers of cases by sex in J. J. Reincke, *Der Typhus in Hamburg. Mit besonderer Berücksichtigung der Epidemieen von 1885 bis 1889* (Hamburg, 1890), p. 19, and *SHS* 16 (1894), pp. 24–5. The figures for the adult population (age 15 and over) were arrived at by working out the percentage of each district aged under 15 in 1890 and subtracting this percentage from the 1886 population figures supplied by Reincke, an approximate procedure made necessary by the fact that a detailed census was taken only every five years. The average annual number of adult cases by district was then divided into the estimated adult population by district, omitting the districts south of the river for reasons discussed in Section VI of this Appendix, and multiplied by 1,000 to arrive at the morbidity rate. These calculations were necessary because the number of children varied substantially by district, following the variations in the birth rate. Once children under 15 are included, the picture takes on a rather clearer outline. Case-specific mortality was higher in the inner city (8.4%) and inner suburbs (7.7%) than in outlying districts such as Harvestehude (6.0%), and

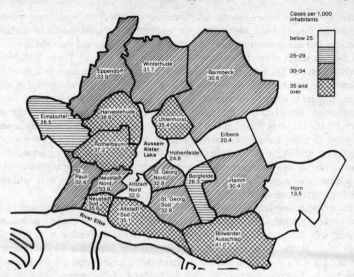

Cases per 1,000
inhabitants

below 25

25–29

30–34

35 and
over

Source: MS 1892, Table 31

MAP 43. Typhoid morbidity rate, by district, Hamburg 1892

Uhlenhorst (4.5%). Unfortunately the very small number of deaths in some districts (only an average of 3 a year in Winterhude, 4 a year in Eppendorf, and 8 a year in the Billwärder Ausschlag in this period, for example) brings the figures for many if not most districts well within the margin of error.

Map 43 raises the further possibility that middle-class cholera victims in 1892 classified their disease, with the connivance of their doctors, as typhoid, which was more socially acceptable. The wealthiest districts, round the Alster, clearly had the highest rates. Such a procedure would not have been so easy in fatal cases.

VI

Maps 32 and 33, showing cholera morbidity and mortality by district in 1892, are constructed from the medical statistics for 1892, and so of course follow the general principles of those statistics as explained earlier in this Appendix. It should be noted that cases and deaths in hospitals and institutions were registered by the permanent address of the victim. Some minor adjustments have been made to achieve consistency between the different sets of figures: in particular, I have averaged out the figures for St Pauli Nord and Süd, where these are available, to provide a figure for the whole of St Pauli; I have split St Georg into two parts, with the same figure for each in the few cases where only a global figure is given; and I have ironed out the differences between 'Marsch' and 'Geest' where individual figures have been given for each of these subdivisions of certain districts. But the most drastic step I have taken is the removal from the maps of all districts south of the Elbe. There were in fact five of these: Peute, Kaltehofe, Veddel, Steinwärder, and Kleiner Grasbrook. Some of these areas only appear in a few of the statistics and not in the rest, so that they had to be eliminated in any case, in order to achieve consistency between the different sets of statistics. All of these areas, however, by 1892, were effectively occupied by the new harbour built for the Customs Union in the 1880s. There were thus too few people living in most of them for cholera statistics to be at all significant. An even more important reason for eliminating these areas from the maps and correlations is their character as workplaces rather than living quarters. This affects the statistics in a number of ways that would render them more or less useless even without the further problems mentioned above.

For example, we know that morbidity and mortality rates were arrived at in the medical statistics by comparing the absolute number of cholera cases and deaths, which occurred overwhelmingly in August and September, with the total population figures derived from the census taken in December 1891. Seasonal population shifts were very marked in these areas, however; many workers still engaged in harbour construction left at the end of the season, so that the population figure for Veddel in particular was much too low, and yielded implausibly high morbidity and mortality rates. At 119 per 1,000 indeed, the official morbidity rate for Veddel was three times as high as that of the worst-affected area north of the river, the Billwärder Ausschlag. The same goes for Peute and Kaltehofe, where the morbidity rate was officially calculated at the utterly implausible level of 140 per 1,000. At the other extreme were Kleiner Grasbrook and Steinwärder. According to the factory inspectorate, there were 120 deaths from cholera recorded among the 7,676 male factory workers employed in the two areas. These 120 deaths, however, were registered in other parts of the city, where the victims lived. Thus Kleiner Grasbrook appeared in the official statistics with the lowest morbidity rate of any district, at 6.9, and with no fatalities at all, while Steinwärder also recorded a mortality rate of 5.9, the next lowest after Harvestehude if one disregards the Kleiner Grasbrook. It might be possible to correct these figures, but not with any degree of accuracy or completeness.

VII

Figure 14 tried to give an impression of the number of people who fled the 1892 cholera epidemic by looking at the issue of railway tickets in Hamburg during the early days of the epidemic. Of course, some of the very rich may have left in their own private carriages; whilst the very poor may simply have walked out of the city. Small traders and country people staying in Hamburg at the time may have travelled in wagons or carts. But by and large the railway was at this period the most common means of long-distance transport. Without exception, all the people who mentioned in their letters, diaries, or memoirs travelling either to or from Hamburg in August and September 1892 gave the railway as their mode of transportation. Moreover, there was no local suburban railway in Hamburg at this time. Some people may have travelled towards the city boundaries by tram. But they could only get further if they were met by cart or carriage or proceeded from the end of the tramline on foot. Such means of escape were cumbersome and slow. The trams were still horse-drawn in 1892.

Figure 14(a) shows the total number of railway tickets bought in Hamburg and Altona on 20, 21, and 22 August, the three days immediately preceding the official announcement of the epidemic. The figures for the last three days combined are shown for each of the four years 1889, 1890, 1891, and 1892. The average annual increase in 1889–91 was 10.5%, so the number of railway tickets we would expect to have been issued on these three days in 1892 would be 34,390. In fact no fewer than 56,554 tickets were issued on 20–2 August 1892, or some 22,164 more than we would have expected. Traffic dropped off sharply in the period 23 August to 3 September (Fig. 14(b)). We would have expected a total of 208,340 tickets to have been purchased; but in the event, only 102,567 were, or 105,773 fewer than expected. To put this another way, in the three days immediately before the official announcement of the epidemic there was a 64% increase in the number of tickets issued over the number we would have expected; while in the period immediately after the official announcement, from 23 August to 3 September inclusive, there was a 49% drop. Figure 14(c) shows that 16,275 more people travelled on 21 August 1892 than on the same day in 1891, though much of the increase must have been Sunday traffic rather than cholera refugees. On the other hand, 23 August was a Sunday in 1891, so the number of tickets issued was high, and the decrease in 1892 was a consequence of the fact that 23 August 1892 was a weekday. Obviously the 'Sunday factor' distorts the statistics and must be accounted for. 23 and 30 August were Sundays in 1891, while 24 and 31 August were Sundays in 1890 (21 and 28 August were Sundays in 1892). A further complication is introduced by the fact that there was a relatively small increase in traffic on the last Sunday of the month in both 1890 and 1891, probably because the harvest season, during which many migrant workers left the city every Sunday, was largely over by this time. Taking these factors into account we can estimate that the expected increase in tickets issued on Sunday 21 August 1892 was 16,003 and the expected increase on Sunday 28 August 1892 was 5,891; while the expected decrease on 23 August 1892 and 30 August 1892 as against the same dates the previous year (a Sunday) would be, respectively, the same. This leaves out of account of course the question of whether the difference was increasing or decreasing over time. Figures are only available for 1889–92; no trends of any kind are discernible over the period 1889–91. The statistics excluded tickets issued at the small Lübecker Bahnhof in 1889 and 1890.

There was normally a considerable increase in railway passenger traffic on Sundays, as people used their only day off work to visit friends and relatives, to spend a day in the country, or by the sea, or to buy farm produce, or to move to a new job (especially if they were migrant labourers). Thus we can say with a fair degree of certainty that few people fled the city on Saturday 20 August 1892. Though there was a considerable increase in railway traffic on 21 August, almost all of this was regular Sunday traffic. There was little or no evidence of a serious panic until Monday 22 August. On that day some 9,290 more railway tickets were purchased in Hamburg and Altona than on the same day (also a weekday) the previous year. As we have already seen, railway traffic in mid to late August was increasing at a rate of about 10.5% a year at this time, so we can say with some confidence that the great majority of these tickets, certainly 8,000 and perhaps as many as 9,000 were bought by people fleeing the city because of the epidemic. More speculatively, we can also suggest that perhaps 3,000 or 4,000 more people fled the city on 23 August to escape infection, because the decrease in the number of railway tickets issued on 23 August 1892 as compared with the number of tickets issued on 23 August 1891—a Sunday—was three or four thousand less than would normally be expected.

As Figure 14(c) indicates, some 4,968 fewer railway tickets were purchased in Hamburg on 24 August 1892 than on 24 August the previous year, and fewer tickets were also purchased on 25 and 26 August. On 27 August the figure for 1892 exceeded that for 1891 by a mere 98, which given the fact that railway passenger traffic was increasing by an annual average of 10.5% during these years, suggests a fairly significant drop (around 900, in fact). On Sunday 28 August perhaps 3,000 or 4,000 fewer tickets were purchased than one would have expected, since Sunday 30 August 1891 had seen 8,417 more tickets purchased than on the same date (a weekday) in 1890, and the excess was only 5,027 in 1892. Some of the papers talked of 'thousands' leaving the city on 25–8 August, but the statistics of tickets issued seem to indicate this was an exaggeration, even if—as was probably the case—many of those who left on these days did so to escape the cholera.

During this period is was still possible for people to leave the city if they wished. Neither the Hamburg Senate nor the Reich government announced any quarantine or disinfection measures for railway passengers other than those already in force since earlier in the summer, until 28 August. These did not come into effect until 29 August. Their announcement may have persuaded some people that this was their last chance to escape, while others may by now have come round to the view that the situation was in fact far more serious than they had imagined on the 24th. For whatever reason, railway traffic on Monday 29 August was about the level expected, that is to say, roughly 10% up on the same day the previous year, and some of those travelling may have been using this last opportunity to flee the epidemic, though it is impossible, of course, to say precisely how many.

VIII

In Chapter 5 some mention was made of correlations between cholera mortality and morbidity in 1892 and independent variables such as households with living-in servants, households with bathrooms and so on, across the 20 Hamburg districts. The usual procedure was used to obtain Pearson's product-moment coefficient of correlation for the variables. The rank-order of independent variables correlating with the cholera mobidity rate is given in Table 13; the procedure was repeated for 19 districts excluding Horn, which as a rural area was anomalous in most respects, as explained in Chapter 5b. The main difference made by the removal of Horn is to improve the correlations, particularly at the top end of the scale, but the rank order is not significantly affected, except in the case of population density, and rent levels, reflecting on the one hand the fact that many cases occurring in Horn were imported from the city and spread by overcrowding

Table 13. Rank-order of cholera morbidity correlations, Hamburg 1892

Rank-order for 20 districts		Rank-order for 19 districts (excluding Horn)	
1. Households with bathrooms	−0.66	Households with bathrooms	−0.80
2. Households with servants	−0.65	Households with servants	−0.80
3. % manual workers	0.62	% manual workers	0.77
4. Average per capita income	−0.57	% white-collar workers	−0.72
5. % white-collar workers	−0.56	Average per capita income	−0.71
6. Population density	0.54	% rents below 300 M	0.69
7. % economically independent	−0.53	% economically independent	−0.65
8. Households without heating	0.51	Households without heating	0.61
9. % rents below 300 M	0.42	Population density	0.49
10. Households with lodgers	0.42	Households with lodgers	0.38
11. Infants per 1,000 population	0.25	Infants per 1,000 population	0.31
12. Birth rate	0.21	Birth rate	0.26

Sources: as for Maps 3, 4, 5, 6, 7, 10, 11, 12, 17, 22, 32, 33, 42, and *SHS* 16 (1894), p. 57.

Table 14. Rank-order of cholera mortality correlations, Hamburg 1892

Rank-order for 20 districts		Rank-order for 19 districts (excluding Horn)	
1. Households with servants	−0.71	Households with servants	−0.84
2. % manual workers	0.70	% manual workers	0.83
3. Households with bathroom	−0.69	Households with bathroom	−0.80
4. % economically independent	−0.66	% economically independent	−0.76
5. Average per capita income	−0.61	% rents below 300 M	0.75
6. Population density	0.59	Average per capita income	−0.72
7. % white-collar workers	−0.56	% white-collar workers	−0.69
8. % rents below 300 M	0.51	Population density	0.56
9. Infants per 1,000 population	0.44	Infants per 1,000 population	0.50
10. Households without heating	0.37	Households without heating	0.44
11. Birth rate	0.39	Birth rate	0.44
12. Households with lodgers	0.31	Households with lodgers	0.28

Sources: as for Table 13.

rather than through the water-supply, and on the other the untypical nature of the housing stock in a rural area. The correlations between the same independent variables and the cholera mortality rate for the 20 Hamburg districts are generally higher, as shown in Table 14, reflecting perhaps the influences of variables such as bathrooms, servants, and especially the presence of infants on the case-specific mortality rate. Here too the procedure has been repeated for 19 districts excluding Horn. As far as mortality is concerned, excluding Horn has a similar effect on the position of rental levels and population density in the rank-order, but does not affect the place of white-collar workers and the economically independent.

Chapters 1 and 5 cited correlations between cholera rates and various socio-economic indicators across the Hamburg districts.

BIBLIOGRAPHY

I. MANUSCRIPT SOURCES

A. *Bundesarchiv Koblenz*

R86   *Reichsgesundheitsamt*

9 Bd. 1	Denkschrift über die Tätigkeit des Kaiserlichen Gesundheitsamtes 1877
864	Reichskommissar für die Gesundheitspflege im Stromgebiet der Elbe 1892–1904
946 Bd. 2	Reichs-Seuchengesetz 1893
Bd. 3	Reichs-Seuchengesetz 1893
Bd. 4	Reichs-Seuchengesetz 1894–1900
Bd. 5	Reichs-Seuchengesetz 1900–1923
954 Bd. 1	Ausführung des Reichsseuchengesetzes in Hamburg
975 Bd. 1, Bd. 2	Verhandlungen der Sachverständigen-Commission über ein Volksseuchen-Gesetz
1041 Bd. 1	Flecktyphus im Königreich Preussen
1048 Bd. 1	Flecktyphus in der Provinz Posen
1097 Bd. 1	Pocken im Deutschen Reiche
1215 Bd. 1	Impfgesetz im Deutschen Reiche
1337	Tierkrankheiten in Hamburg
2068 Bd. 1, Bd. 2	Lebensmittelfälschungen im allgemeinen
2104 Bd. 1–2	Die im Jahre 1879 im Deutschen Reiche vorhandenen Lebensmittel-Untersuchungs-Anstalten
2107 Bd. 3	Lebensmittel-Untersuchungs-Anstalten im Deutschen Reich
2114	Lebensmittel-Untersuchungsanstalt in Hamburg
2215 Bd. 1	Kindermilch
2271	Vergiftungen durch Fische
2273 Bd. 1	Vergiftungen durch Genussmittel
2657	Sitzungsberichte der Cholera-Commissionen (Generalia) 1892–1902

B. *Geheimes Staatsarchiv Berlin-Dahlem*

Rep. 84a   *Preussisches Justizministerium*

4178	Die Verordnung wegen der Quarantaine-Anstalten 1804–1831
4179	Die Verordnung wegen der Quarantain-Anstalten, intus: die gegen die Cholera morbus getroffenen Sicherheits-Maassregeln 1831

4180 Die Verordnung wegen der Quarantain-Anstalten

2182 Die gegen die Cholera morbus getroffenen Sicherheits-Maassregeln 1832–1835

C. *Staatsarchiv Bremen*

2-M. 6. 1. 4k. 7 Gelbfieber, Cholera, insb. Abwehrmassnahmen gegen die Einschleppung solcher im Ausland ausgebrochenen Krankheiten 1872–1888

3-M. 1. r. 18–1 Akte, betreffend den Ausbruch der Cholera in Russland, Hamburg etc. und Anordnungen zum Schutze gegen die Einschleppung derselben—Allgemeines. 1892–1895

        2 Akte, betreffend den Vertrag mit dem Zimmermeister Th. Jung über den Bau einer Cholerabaracke 1892

        4 Akte, betreffend den Ausfall des Freimarkts 1892 in Rücksicht auf die Choleragefahr

        5 Cholera 1892. Tägliche Bulletins und Zeitungsberichte

        8 Akte, betreffend Gesuche von Wirten, Kellnern und Musikern um Wiederaufhebung des wegen der Choleragefahr erlassenen Verbots von öffentlichen Tanzmusiken 1892

3-Q. 1. b. 1 Feststellung der Voranschläge für das Preussisch-Oldenburgisch-Bremische Quarantäneamt zu Bremerhaven, 1884

        3 Preussisch-Oldenburgisch-Bremisches Quarantäne-Amt zu Bremerhaven, 1883–1888

D. *Stadtarchiv Berlin* (*Hauptstadt der DDR*)

Rep. 01 GB Magistrat der Stadt Berlin: Generalbüro

       217 Massregeln gegen die Cholera 1830–1831

       218 Die Massregeln gegen die Cholera 1831–1834

       219 Die Massregeln gegen die Cholera 1851–1867

       220 Massregeln gegen die Cholera 1867—1883

       257 Massnahmen gegen die Cholera 1831–1838

       258 Cholera specialia: Massregeln und Massnahmen gegen das Auftreten der Cholera (1831) 1849–1883

E. *Kirchenarchiv Hamburg*

D166 Pastor Friedrich Werner, 'Erinnerungen aus meiner Amtstätigkeit in der Gemeinde Süd-Hamm' (MS 1937)

Kirchenrat B. X. d. 11   Ausserordentliche Gottesdienste in der Cholerazeit 1892

     B. X. d. 12   Dankfest anlässlich des Erlöschens der Cholera am Buss- und Bettage 1892

     B. XVI. a. 2   Bericht über die Arbeit der Kirche bei der Choleraepidemie 1892

F. *Staatsarchiv Hamburg*

Allgemeine Armenanstalt II

211 Massnahmen aus Anlass der Choleraepidemie von 1892

Auswanderungsamt

I	E	I	No. 2	Bd. 1–2	Cholera–Epidemie 1892
II	E	I	No. 1a2	Bd. 1	Grenzsperre
			No. 1a3		Grenzsperre
			No. 3	Bd. 10	Statistik 1892
		II	No. 4	Bd. 1	Unterbringung von Auswanderern in der Baracke am Amerikakai
		IV	No. 1	Bd. 1	Bekämpfung der Cholera in den Jahren 1886–1900
			No. 9	Bd. 1	Massnahmen gegen die Einschleppung epidemischer Krankheiten durch russische Auswanderer 1891–1921
		V	No. 1	Beiheft 2	Verzeichnisse, betr. die Revisionen der Auswanderer-Logierhäuser vom Jahre 1888
				Bd. 2	Beherbergung von Auswanderern in Logierhäusern

Baudeputation

B 513 Einrichtung und Betrieb von Bedürfnisanstalten auf öffentlichem Grund 1841–1920

1547 Entfernung von angehäuften Unrat in den Strassen 1821–60

1548 Verpachtung der Gassenreinigung in der Stadt 1824–62

1549 Verpachtung der Gassenreinigung in St Georg 1825–36

1550 Reinigung der Strassen von Eis und Schnee 1829–65, 1890

1553 Wassersprengungen in den Strassen

1745 Gutachten und Berichte über des Sielwesen

1748 Fäkalienverwertung 1869–96

1749 Untersuchung über die Bedeutung von Sielanlagen bei Epidemien 1870

Cholerakommission

1 Protokolle

6 Namentliche Liste der während der Cholera-Epidemie im Jahre 1892 in die öffentlichen Leichenhallen eingebrachten Choleraleichen

9 Statistische Erhebungen

11 Statistik der Choleraepidemien

13 Flüchtlinge aus Hamburg

27 Berichte der Polizeibehörde

Familienarchive

Beneke	M 2	Urkunde über Freiheit von Choleraverdacht
	94	Briefwechsel mit Familie Amsinck 1878–1948
Bertheau	E 4a IV	Briefe an Carl II Bertheau von Familienmitgliedern
Birt	6	Tagebuch von Friedrich Birt, 1807–91, Kaufmann, fortgesetzt von der Hand seiner Tochter Friederike 1891–6

Buehl	2c	Lebenserinnerungen des Stadtrats Dr. Adolf Buehl
Goverts	76 Bd. 17	Dr. Ernst Friedrich Goverts 1851–1932: Tagebuch 1892
Gustav Hertz	B17	Abschriften einer Auswahl des privaten Briefwechsels von Dr. Gustav Hertz 1842–1910
	D9 Bd. 2	Heinrich Rudolf Hertz: Versandte Briefe
Lippmann	A4 Bd. 1, Bd. 2	Leo Lippmann (Staatsrat, 1881–1943), 'Mein Leben und meine amtliche Tätigkeit, Erinnerungen und ein Beitrag zur Finanzgeschichte Hamburg' (Lebenserinneringen, bis 1928)
	A20	'Aus dem Leben eines Hamburger Kaufmanns', Tagebücher Hermann Robinow's, von Adele Jaffé, 1837–1920
Merck	II 9 Konv. 4a Heft II, Heft III	Erinnerungen und Aufzeichnungen von Heinrich Merck 1877–1958
Meyer	B6	Ehrungen (Franz Andreas Meyer, 1837–1901)
	7a	Absterben von Franz Andreas Meyer: Nachrufe
	7b	Absterben von Franz Andreas Meyer: Zeitungsausschnitte
	11	Stellungnahme zu dem Bericht von Dr. Gerson: In welcher Weise ist eine verbesserte Wasserversorgung Hamburgs herzustellen 1878
Mönckeberg	21a	Johann Georg Mönckeberg 1854–1908: Aufzeichungen und Reden
Neubauer	1	Ida Neubauer: Erinnerungen einer alten Hamburgerin (1938)
Petersen	D23	Carl Friedrich Petersen (1809–92), letzte Krankheit und Tod
	30 Bd. 2	Carl Friedrich Petersen (1809–92): Briefwechsel
	G5	Anna Marie Petersen: Briefe von dem Ehemann Gustav Petersen
Refardt	G1	Edith Refardt (1873–1900) Briefe
Ritter	D2	Aus dem Leben von Henny Ritter (1842–1911)
Roscher	Ia1	Lebenserinnerungen Heinrich Roschers bis 1914
Schramm	K10/1	Olga Schramm, geb. O'Swald (1869–1965): Autobiographische Aufzeichnungen (1946/47)
Versmann	F4	Aufzeichnungen betr. Massnahmen und Forderungen bei Verlust der Selbständigkeit Hamburgs 1870–93
	VI A6	Tagebuch Johannes G. A. Versmann (1820–99)
	XI 313	Arnold Versmann. Briefe von den Geschwistern 1872–98
Voigt	B68	Johann Friedrich Voigt (1833–1920): Manuskript über die Wohnungen hamburgischer Senatsmitglieder 1712–1911

Westenholz   B XV 2   Albert Westenholz (1879–1940): Memoiren

Hafenarzt

I 77   Cholera auf Schiffen während der Reise, mit Einzelfällen 1892–1939

Kommission für die Verbesserung der Wohnverhältnisse

20   Von der Kommission gesammelte Zeitungsausschnitte und Veröffentlichungen, mit vereinzelten Sitzungsberichten der Bürgerschaft und des Reichstags 1892–1904

24   Vorschläge des Arbeitgeberverbandes Hamburg-Altona und der Handelskammer zur Verbesserung von Wohnverhältnissen und Verkehrsverbindungen der Arbeiter 1897

25   Statistiken und Berichte über Bevölkerungs-, Wohn- und Gesundheitsverhältnisse in den zu sanierenden Gebieten

26   Statistiken und Berichte über Bevölkerungs-, Wohn- und Gesundheitsverhältnisse in den zu sanierenden Gebieten

51   Vierter Bericht: Sanierung der beiderseits der Steinstrasse liegenden Teile der Altstadt 1903–1915

Medizinalkollegium

I	K	6	Bd. 3	Jahresberichte der Districtärzte der Vororte, Ritzebüttel und Bergedorfs
II	A	1	Bd. 1	Verkehr mit Nahrungsmitteln, etc.
		2	Bd. 1	Controle der Nahrungs- und Genussmittel
		3a	Bd. 1	Milch: Allgemeines
		3g	Bd. 1	Milch-Gesetzgebung 1888–1903
		9a		Küchengewürze, Obst, Pilze u. dergl., Hülsenfrüchte, Marmelade
		13a	Bd. 1	Fleisch: Allgemeines
	C	2	Bd. 1	Kostkinderwesen
		3	Bd. 1	Öffentliche Gesundheitspflege in Bezug auf Kinder in den ersten Lebensjahren
	D	1	Bd. 1	Impfwesen: Allgemeines
		5	Bd. 1	Impfgegner
	E	6	Bd. 1	Rauchverhütung, gesundheitsschädliche Gase etc.
	F	5		Gesundheitliche Überwachung der Auswanderer anlässlich von Seuchen
	G	3	Bd. 1	Baupolizei-Gesetzgebung
		4	Bd. 1	Wohnungswesen-Allgemein
		6	Bd. 1	Stallungen in der Nähe von Wohnungen
		13		Leitfaden für Wohnungspfleger
		15	Bd. 1	Milben, Käfer u. dergl. in den Wohungen
	H	10		Sanitäre Angelegenheiten einzelner städtischer und der ländlichen Bezirke: Billwärder Ausschlag
		12		Schutz der Neustadt gegen Sturmfluthen

N	3	Bd. 1	Das Kranken-Transportwesen in Hamburg. Seine Entwicklung und Organisation, 1892
O	1	Bd. 1	Die Alster und deren Zuflüsse
		Bd. 2	Die Alster und deren Zuflüsse
		Bd. 4	Die Alster und deren Zuflüsse
		Bd. 5	Die Alster und deren Zuflüsse
	2	Bd. 1	Die Bille und deren Zuflüsse
		Bd. 2	Die Bille und deren Zuflüsse
		Bd. 3	Die Bille und deren Zuflüsse
	3	Bd. 4	Die Elbe
		Bd. 5	Die Elbe
III A	2	Bd. 1	Choleraepidemien 1832–55
		Bd. 2	Choleraepidemien 1859–86
	3	Bd. 1	Cholera-Materialien 1892–1913
	12		Cholera: Protokolle, Drucksachen und Berichte der Senats- und Bürgerschaftskommission für die Prüfung der Gesundheitsverhältnisse Hamburgs
	13		Cholera: Gesundheitskommissionen
	16	Bd. 1	Cholera Schutz- und Heilmittel
B	1	Bd. 1	Pocken: Allgemeines 1818–1901
C	2	Bd. 1	Pest: Massnahmen gegen Ratten pp.
G	1	Bd. 1	Tuberculose: Allgemeines
H	12	Bd. 1	Bekämpfung der Krätze- und Läuseplage
W	4		Cholera-Statistik

Meldewesen

B43 Generalakte betr. gerichtliche Erkenntnisse und besondere Entscheidungen in Gesindestreitsachen 1873–1918

Polizeibehörde I

44		Gassenreinigung und Abfuhr in der Stadt und der Vorstadt St. Pauli 1870–85
49	Bd. 1, Bd. 2	Cholera-Epidemien 1859 und 1866
60		Gassenreinigung u. Abfuhr in den Vororten Hamburgs, sowie auf dem kleinen Grasbrook u. Steinwerder
84		Vorsichtsmassregeln zur Verhütung ansteckender Krankheiten: Blattern-Epidemie u. Pocken 1871

Politische Polizei

S	576 I	Bd. 1	Zeitungsausschnitte: Antisemitische Angelegeneiten 1890–2
	1365	Bd. 1	Zeitung 'Hamburger Echo': Meineids-Prozesse 1889–1903
	2424	Bd. 1	Antisemitische und Christlich-soziale Vorträge in Hamburg
	3420	Bd. 1 Bd. 3	Arbeitslose von 1892/93: Zeitungsausschnitte

3469		Tätigkeit der Sozialdemokratie während der Cholera-Epidemie 1892
3490	Bd. 1	Cholera 1892/93: Zeitungsausschnitte
	Bd. 2	Cholera 1892/93: Zeitungsausschnitte
	Bd. 3	Cholera 1892/93: Zeitungsausschnitte
3496	Bd. 1	Wohnungswesen, Verbesserung der Wohnverhältnisse, Wohnungspflege, Wohnungsnot
	Bd. 2	Einkommensteuer 1893–1918
	Bd. 3	Reorganisation der Verwaltung und Verfassung: Stellungnahmen der Bürgervereine 1892–1896
	Bd. 4	Verfassung und Verwaltung in Hamburg—Allgemeines Verhältnis zwischen Senat und Bürgerschaft, Stellung der Verwaltungsbehörden, historische Abhandlungen 1891–1918
	Bd. 5	Sozialdemokratische Versammlungen am 4.11.1892
3625	Bd. 3	Reichstagswahl 1893: Versammlungen der Sozialdemokratie
	Bd. 4	Reichstagswahl 1893: Versammlungen der Ordnungsparteien
	Bd. 5	Reichstagswahl 1893: Berichte und Notizen für Hamburg
4296	Bd. 1	Antisemitischer Wahlverein von 1890, Deutsch-Soziale Reformpartei
V 164		Verein Hamburgischer Staatsangehöriger 1886–1891
273	Bd. 2	Miether-Verein zu Hamburg 1901–1918
327–30		Öffentliche Versammlungen der Desinfektions- und Kolonnenarbeiter 1892
		Öffentliche Versammlungen der Leichenträger 1892–93
334a	Bd. 31	Sozialdemokratischer Verein für den 3. Hbg. Wahlkreis–Stadtgebiet. Zusammenfassungen
494		Verein Sanitäts-Kolonne von 1892
495		Verein der Hilfskrankenwärter und Wärterinnen von 1892

Senat

Cl. VII, Lit. Bd, No. 45, Vol. 12b	Beratungen der Senatskommission zur Erwägung der Frage, ob und eventuell durch welche Mittel einem übermässigen Eindringen sozialdemokratischer Elemente in die Bürgerschaft vorgebeugt werden könne 1904/08
Lit. Cc, No. 3b, Vol. 32	Die Verhandlungen der Gassen-Reinigungs-Pacht

	48	Gassenreinigung
	54	Gassenreinigung
	56	Gassenreinigung
	58a, Fasc. 1	Gassenreinigung
	Fasc. 2	Gassenreinigung
	Fasc. 3	Gassenreinigung
	Fasc. 4	Gassenreinigung
	59	Gassenreinigungs-Ordnung
	61	Gassenreinigung
Lit. Lb, No. 23a,	Vol. 1	Einführung der Medicinal-Ordnung von 1818
	Vol. 75, Fasc. 1a	Medicinalwesen: Protocolle der Commission zur Revision der Medicinalordnung von 1818
	Fasc. 3	Medicinalwesen: Acta, betr. die bei Reorganisation des Gesundheitsraths erfolgte Versetzung des Physicus Dr. Med. Heinrich Wilhelm Buek mit jährlich 3000f. in den Ruhestand (1871)
	Vol. 88, Fasc. 7	Medicinalwesen-Physicatswesen. Entlassung des Medicinalrathes Dr. Kraus
Lit. Mb, No. 1,	Vol. 1a2, Bd. 2	Acta, die auf Veranlassung des erledigten Physicats belebte gänzliche Revision der Medizinal–Policey betreffend 1796–1804
	Vol. 1a4	Papiere, die Revision der Medicinal-Ordnung, wie sie im Jahre 1797 proponiret worden, betreffend
	Vol. 1	Contagiones und Epidemien: Acta, betreffend das im Jahre 1848 stattgehabte epidemische Grassiren der s.g. asiatischen Cholera in Hamburg, gegen welche keine Absperrungsmittel, keine Hospitäler oder sonstige bedeutende Vorkehrungen und Massnahmen angewandt worden sind
Lit. Ta, Pars 2,	Vol. 6	Contagiones: Acta, betr. die Cholera-Epidemie im Jahre 1859 u. 1865
	Vol. 11, Fasc. 1b	Cholera-Epidemie 1892/93: Einzelne Aktenstücke, Drucksachen und Zeitungsausschnitte
	Fasc. 3a	Cholera-Epidemie im Jahre 1892/93
	Fasc. 14	Cholera. Acta des Herrn Syndicus Dr. Leo betr. die Cholera-Epidemie im Jahre 1892/93

Fasc. 16, Inv. 9 Cholera. Acta, betr. den Zeitpunkt des Auftretens der Cholera

Inv. 22 Cholera: Acta, betr. die Verwaltungsreform

Inv. 24 Cholera: Acta, betr. Verteidigung gegen die Angriffe auf Hamburg wegen angeblicher Verheimlichung der Cholera 1892

Inv. 25 Cholera: Acta, betr. die Schädigung Hamburgs durch die Choleraepidemie 1892

Inv. 26 Cholera: Acta, betr. die Wasserversorgung Hamburgs 1892–1894

Inv. 27 Cholera: Verschiedene Aktenstücke, betr. die Cholera, als Material für die Reichstagsverhandlungen 1892/93

Fasc. 17, Inv. 1a Cholera: Sammlung der Zeitungsartikel betr. die Cholera-Epidemie in Hamburg 1892

Inv. 2 Cholera: Sammlung der Zeitungsartikel, betr. die Cholera-Epidemie 1892 (Sprechsaal-Artikel)

Inv. 3 Sammlung der in Hamburg erlassenen amtlichen Bekanntmachungen betr. die Cholera

Inv. 4 Cholera: Sammlung der Zeitungsartikel, betr. die Cholera-Epidemie 1892 (auswärtige Presse)

Inv. 5 Cholera: Zeitungsartikel, betr. die Cholera. Allgemeines 1892/93

Inv. 6 Einsendung von Zeitungsartikel, welche Schmähungen gegen Hamburg enthalten

Inv. 7 Contagiones. Sechs Hefte Zeitungsartikel über die Cholera d. J. 1892

Fasc. 24 Contagiones. Zeitungsartikel, betr. die Aeusserungen des Abgeordneten Bebel im Reichstage über das Verhalten des Hamburger Bürgertums während des

Auftretens der Cholera im Jahre 1892

Cl. XI, Gen. No. 2   Vol. 61, Fasc. 1   Gewerbewesen: Prüfung der gegenwärtigen Arbeitslage

Fasc. 2c   Akte des Bürgermeisters Dr. Versmann als Vorsitzender der Senatskommission zur Prüfung der gegenwärtigen Arbeitslage und der etwa erforderlichen Abhilfemassregeln, Arbeitslage

Fasc. 7,   Inv. Ia Acta, betr. die Bewilligung von Staatlichen Beihülfen an den Arbeitsnachweis der Gelegenheitsarbeiter, später Arbeitsnachweis der Patriotischen Gesellschaft, 1892–1898

Versicherungsbehörde 1

Bd. 23   Sitzungsprotokolle der Totenladen-Deputationen

Zeitungsausschnitt-Sammlung

A760   Pastor Albrecht Krause

G. *Private Possession*

Tagebuch Elise Mönckeberg
Tagebuch Tilli Mönckeberg
(in possession of Mrs Ruth Evans, Oxford)

H. *Deutsches Volkslied-Archiv, Freiburg*

A 95/463   Aufzeichnungen der Mathilde Bünz, Oldenburg (Holstein), 1892

II. PRINTED SOURCES

Aerztliche Rundschau (1892–3)

Amtsblatt der Freien und Hansestadt Hamburg

Anweisung zur Erhaltung der Gesundheit und Verhütung der Ansteckung bei etwa eintretender Choleraepidemie. Von der Königl. Preussischen obersten Medicinal-Behörde in Berlin zum Druck befördert (Hamburg, 1831).

Behrmann, Christian Konrad Georg, *Erinnerungen* (Berlin, 1904).

Beiträge zur Statistik Hamburgs (Verein für hamburgische Statistik, Hamburg, 1854).

Bericht der Gesundheits-Commission für den Bezirk Uhlenhorst über ihre Tätigkeit während der Cholera-Epidemie 1892 (Hamburg, 1892).

Berichte des Medizinal-Inspectorats (Medizinalrathes) über die Medicinische Statistik des Hamburgischen Staates 1872–1914.

Bernhard, Johannes, *Ich bin der Herr, dein Arzt! Eine Zeitpredigt über das Evangelium des 14. Sonntages* (Lübeck, 1892).

Beruhigung für Jedermann und Ermahnung an Viele. Zur Verminderung der Furcht von der Cholera morbus, und Befestigung des Vertrauens auf die Güte Gottes, von einem mitfühlenden und zur Beruhigung Anderer gern beitragenden Mitbürger geschrieben (Hamburg, 1831).

von Brandenburg, F., *Der Sturz der Cholera morbus nebst den sie begleitenden Attributen des Irrthums und des Vorurtheils oder die gediegene Antwort auf die Frage: Woher entstand die Cholera?—Was war deren Character? (angesehen als Krankheitsstoff), und welches waren die eigentlichen Mittel zu deren Beseitigung? Alles aus grossen Natur-Ereignissen hergeleitet,—in dieser Schrift erklärt und zur bessern Verständlichkeit in Gesprächsform abgefasst* (Hamburg, 1832).

Buchheister, Dr. J. F., and C. Noodt Apotheke, *Erfahrungen über die Cholera Asiatica in Hamburg im Herbste 1831* (Hamburg, 1832).

Buek, Heinrich Wilhelm, *Die bisherige Verbreitung der jetzt besonders in Russland herrschenden Cholera. Erläutert durch eine Karte und eine dieselbe erklärende kurze Geschichte dieser Epidemie* (Hamburg, 1831).

Cohnstein, Wilhelm, *Trost- und Beruhigungsgründe für die durch das Herannahen der Cholera aufgeschreckten Gemüther, nebst Angabe aller gegen diese Krankheit bisher empfohlenen Schutzmittel* (Glogau and Lissa, 1831).

Conrad, J., *Beitrag zur Untersuchung des Einflusses von Lebenshaltung und Beruf auf die Mortalitätsverhältnisse, auf Grund des statistischen Materials zu Halle a. S. von 1855–74* (Jena, 1874).

Das Deutsche Reich in gesundheitlicher und demographischer Beziehung. Festschrift, den Teilnehmern am XIV. Internationalen Kongresse für Hygiene und Demographie Berlin 1907 gewidmet vom Kaiserlichem Gesundheitsamte und vom Kaiserlichen Statistischen Amte (Berlin, 1907).

Das öffentliche Armenwesen in Hamburg während der Jahre 1893–1903. Darstellung seiner Reorganisation und weiteren Entwickelung, herausgegeben vom Armenkollegium (Hamburg, 1903)

Degener, H. A. L. (ed.), *Wer Ist's?* (Berlin, 1909).

Deneke, Theodor, 'Nachträgliches zur Hamburger Cholera-Epidemie von 1892', *Münchener Medizinische Wochenschrift*, 41 (1895).

—— 'Die Hamburger Choleraepidemie 1892', *ZHG* 49 (1949), 124–58.

Der Hamburgische Beobachter (1831).

Der Herr, Dein Arzt, auch in der Cholerazeit, von H. G. Hamburg, 1892).

Die Cholera, unser Bürgertum und die Sozialdemokratie (Leipzig, 1892).

Die Gesundheitsverhältnisse Hamburgs im 19. Jahrhundert (Hamburg, 1901).

Die Misserfolge der Staatsmedicin und ihre Opfer in Hamburg (Hamburg, 1892).

Dunbar, J., 'Zum derzeitigen Stand der Wasserversorgungsverhältnisse im hamburgischen Staatsgebiet', *Vierteljahresschrift für öffentliche Gesundheitspflege*, 37 (1905), 537–80.

von Eckardt, Julius, *Lebenserinnerungen* (2 vols., Leipzig, 1910).

'Ein Blick in die Haushaltung einer Hamburger Arbeiterfamilie', *Mitteilungen aus der Arbeit der Hamburger Stadtmission*, 20 (1899), 77–85.

Ein Spaziergang durch Hamburgs City (Hamburg, 1897).

Entdeckung und Beleuchtung des bisher unbekannt gebliebenen Wesens und eigentlichen Sitzes der Cholera morbus nebst der Darstellung der Behandlungsart und der Schutzmittel gegen dieselbe für Gesunde. Für Jedermann fasslich dargestellt von einem erfahrnen praktischen Arzt nach den sehr ausführlichen und bestimmten Aussagen einer besonders hellsehenden Somnambule (Schlafwachenden) (Hamburg, 1831).

Entwurf zum Hamburgischen Staats-Budget für das Jahr 1892.

Export. Organ des Centralvereins für Handelsgeographie und Förderung deutscher Interessen im Auslande (Berlin, 1892).

Fiege, Hartwig, 'Aus dem Leben eines unteren Postbeamten vor dem Ersten Weltkrieg', *Hamburgische Geschichts- und Heimatblätter*, 10. 5 (1978), 119–32.

Fischer, H., *Die Saprophyten, unserer natürlichen, bisher noch nicht gewürdigten Helfer gegen die Cholera* (Dresden, 1893).

Frank, Johann Peter, *System einer vollständigen medicinischen Polizey* (6 vols.: Mannheim, 1779–88).

Fricke, J. C. G., *Geschichtliche Darstellung des Ausbruchs der asiatischen Cholera in Hamburg* (Hamburg, 1831).

Führer durch Hamburg zum III. Allg. Deutschen Journalisten- und Schriftstellertage 1894 Hamburg, 1894).

(Gaffky, Georg), *Amtliche Denkschrift über die Choleraepidemie 1892* (Kaiserliches Gesundheitsamt, Berlin, 1895).

Gernet, Hermann Gustav, *Auch ein Votum über die Medizinal-Reform* (Hamburg, 1863).
—— *Die öffentliche Gesundheitspflege in Hamburg* (Hamburg, 1870).

Gläser, J. A., 'Kritische Bemerkungen zu Herrn Robert Kochs Aufsatz: Die Cholera in Deutschland während des Winters 1892–93', *Zeitschrift für Hygiene*, 15 (reprint, Hamburg, 1893).
—— 'Gemeinverständliche Anticontagionistische Betrachtungen bei Gelegenheit der letzten Cholera-Epidemie in Hamburg 1892' (reprint, Hamburg, 1893).
—— 'Robert Kochs Komma-Bacillus ist nicht Ursache der Cholera' (reprint, Hamburg, 1894).
—— 'Die Ueberhebung des Herrn Robert Koch und die Erfolglosigkeit seiner Massregeln gegen Cholera' (reprint, Hamburg, 1894).

Glückliche Heilung der Cholera asiatica auf homöopatischem Wege, nach einem Schreiben des Dr. Schröter in Lemberg an die Versammlung homöopatischer Aerzte zu Naumburg (Leipzig, 1831).

Hahnemann, Samuel, *Sicherste Heilung und Ausrottung der asiatischen Cholera* (Leipzig, 1831).

von Halle, L., F. Wolter, and G. Koch, *Die Cholera in Hamburg in ihren Ursachen und Wirkungen. Eine ökonomisch-medicinische Untersuchung* (Hamburg, 1895).

Hamburger Cholera-Tropfen: Blüthen-Lese von Curiositäten aus ernster Zeit (Hamburg, 1892).

Hamburger Echo, Aug.–Sept. 1892.

Hamburger Fremdenblatt, Aug–Sept. 1892.

Hamburgischer Correspondent, Aug.–Sept. 1892.

Hamburg und seine Bauten (Architekten- und Ingenieur-Verein zu Hamburg, Hamburg, 1890 and 1913).

Heidmann, J. H., *Hamburg's Verkehrsmittel und Wohnungsverhältnisse* (Hamburg, 1891).

Hirsch, August, 'Die Cholera-Epidemie des Jahres 1866 in Berlin. Vom statistischen Standpunkte geschildert', *Berliner Stadt- und Gemeindekalender und Städtisches Jahrbuch*, 1 (1867), pp. 297–331.

Horn, E., and W. Wagner, *Wie hat man sich vor der Cholera zu schützen und was hat man bei ihrem Eintritt zu ihrer Heilung und zur Verhütung der weiteren Verbreitung zu thun? Zur Beruhigung des Publikums beantwortet vom dem Geheimen Medizinal-Rath und Professor Dr. Ernst Horn und dem Professor und Stadt-Physikus Dr. Wilhelm Wagner in Berlin* (Berlin, 1831).

Hueppe, Ferdinand, 'Die Cholera-Epidemie in Hamburg, 1892', *Berliner Klinische Wochenschrift*, 30 (1893), Nos. 4–7.

—— and Else Hueppe, *Die Cholera-Epidemie in Hamburg 1892. Beobachtungen und Versuche über Ursache, Bekämpfung und Behandlung der asiatischen Cholera* (Berlin, 1893).

Hygiene und soziale Hygiene in Hamburg (Hamburg, 1928).

Jahrbücher der Hamburgischen Staatskrankenanstalten (1892–3).

Jahresbericht des Armenpflegevereins zu Harvestehude für das Jahr 1897.

Jensen, Thomas H., *Belehrungen, Ermunterungen und Tröstungen für den Bürger und Landmann wegen der Cholera. Von einem Landprediger* (Altona, 1831).

Joachim, Hermann, *Handbuch der Wohltätigkeit in Hamburg*, (2nd edn., Hamburg, 1909).

Jungclausen, J., *Acht Tage Cholerakrankenpflege* (Hamburg, 1892).

Kaisen, Wilhelm, *Meine Arbeit, mein Leben* (Munich, 1967).

Kaiser, C., *Zur Frage der Strassen-Reinigung* (Stuttgart, 1884).

Koch, Friederike, (ed.), 'Die Tagebuchaufzeichnungen Georg Kochs über die Hamburger Cholera-Epidemie des Jahres 1892', *Die Heimat. Monatsschrift zur Pflege der Natur- und Landeskunde in Schleswig-Holstein und Hamburg*, 79 (1972), 353–4; 80 (1973), 23–4.

Koch, Georg, *Beiträge zur Statistik der Löhne und Preise in Hamburg* (Hamburg, 1891).

Koch, Robert, 'Über den augenblicklichen Stand der Cholera-Diagnose', *Zeitschrift für Hygiene und Infektionskrankheiten*, 14 (1893), 319–23.

Kraeplin, Karl, *Die Fauna der Hamburger Wasserleitung* (Separatabdruck aus dem IX. Band der Abhandlungen des Naturwissenschaftlichen Vereins in Hamburg; Hamburg, 1885).

Kraus, Johann Caspar Theodor, *Die Cholera in Hamburg im Jahre 1873* (Hamburg, 1873).

Krause, Albrecht, *Hamburgs Anfechtung, Bewährung, Errettung: Predigt über Jacobus I. 12 aus der Zeit des Kampfes mit der Cholera am 2. Oktober 1892* (2nd edn., Hamburg, 1892).

Lindley, William, *Bericht über die Anlage eines neuen Siel-Systems zur Entwässerung der Stadt Hamburg* (Hamburg, 1843).

—— *Erläuterungen zu seinem Berichte über die Anlage eines neuen Sielsystems zur Entwässerung der Stadt Hamburg*, (Hamburg, 1843).

—— *Oeffentliche Wasch- und Bade-Häuser* (Hamburg, 1851).

Loewenberg, Jakob, *Aus Zwei Quellen* (Berlin, 1914).

Manchot, Carl, *Wie wir in unserer Noth nach Gottes Willen leiden* (Hamburg, 1892).

Martin, Rudolf, *Jahrbuch des Vermögens und Einkommens der Millionäre in den drei Hansestädten* (Berlin, 1912).

Merck, Heinrich, *Begegnungen und Begebnisse* (Hamburg, 1958).

Mitglieder der Bürgerschaft (typescript biographical files in StA Hbg).

Mönckeberg, Carl (ed.), *Bürgermeister Mönckeberg. Eine Auswahl seiner Briefe und Aufzeichnungen* (Stuttgart and Berlin, 1918).

Müller, Ernst, *Kleine Beiträge zur Geschichte des Billwärder Ausschlags* (Hamburg, 1902).

Müller, J. A. P., *Verhaltungsregeln gegen Cholera morbus* (Hamburg, 1831).

Münchmeyer, C., *Kurzgefasste Rathschläge für Familienväter zu Vorbereitungsmassregeln und die diätische und ärztliche Behandlung von Cholera-Kranken in Privathäusern zu erleichtern und zu beschleunigen* (Lüneburg, 1831).

Nagel, C. F., *Nachricht an das Publikum über die zweckmässigsten Verhaltungsmaassregeln bei einer etwaigen Erscheinung der morgenländischen Brechruhr (Cholera morbus). Auf Befehl sr. Exzellenz des Herrn Geheim-Conferenzraths Grafen von Blücher, Altona, entworfen von Dr. C. F. Nagel* (Altona, 1831).

Neddermeyer, F. H., *Zur Statistik und Topographie der Freien und Hansestadt Hamburg und deren Gebietes* (Hamburg, 1847).

Neddermeyer, Robert, *Es begann in Hamburg ... Ein deutscher Kommunist erzählt aus seinem Leben* (East Berlin, 1980).

Nessmann, Johann, C. F., *Ein Beitrag zur Statistik der Löhne und Preise* (Hamburg, 1876).

Nonne, Max, *Anfang und Ziel meines Lebens* (Hamburg, 1972).

Noth- und Hülfsbüchlein bey der Cholera-Epidemie für den Landmann und für diejenigen, denen nicht gleich ärztliche Hülfe zu Gebote steht (Hamburg, Gesundheits-Rath, Hamburg, August 1831).

Paulsen, Otto, *Ueber die Ursachen der diesjährigen Cholera-Epidemie in Hamburg* (Hamburg, 1892).

Pettenkofer, Max von, *Untersuchung und Beobachtung über Verbreitung der Cholera, nebst Betrachtungen über Massregeln derselben Einhalt zu thun* (Munich, 1855).

—— 'Causes of Cholera', *Medical Press* (London, 1869), p. 405.

—— 'Rudolf Virchow's Choleratheorie', *Berliner Klinische Wochenschrift*, 21 (1884), 485–91.

—— 'Cholera', *The Lancet*, 2 (1884), 769–71, 861–5, 904–5, 992–4, 1042–3, 1086–8.

—— 'Zum gegenwärtigen Stand der Cholera-Frage', *Archiv für Hygiene*, 4 (1886), 249–354, 397–545; 5 (1886), 353–445; 6 (1887), 1–84, 129–233, 303–58, 373–441; 7 (1887), 1–81.

—— 'Ueber Cholera mit Berücksichtigung der jüngsten Choleraepidemie in Hamburg'. *Münchener Medizinische Wochenschrift*, 46 (1892).

—— 'Ueber die Cholera von 1892 in Hamburg und über Schutzmassregeln', *Archiv für Hygiene*, 18 (1893), 94–132.

Pieper, P., *Kirchliche Statistik Deutschlands* (Freiburg, 1899).

Preu, Karl, *Was haben wir won der Cholera morbus zu fürchten? Ein Versuch, die aufgeschreckten Völker zu beruhigen* (Nuremberg, 1831).

Prof. Dr. G. Jägers Monatsblatt. Zeitschrift für Gesundheitspflege und Lebenslehre (1892–3).

Protocoll-Extracte der ersten bis sechsten Sitzung sämmtlicher Aerzte Riga's in Betreff der daselbst herrschenden Cholera-Epidemie vom 30. May bis 4. July 1831.

Rambach, Johann J., *Versuch einer physisch-medizinischen Beschreibung von Hamburg* (Hamburg, 1801).

Dr Reck, *Die Gesundheitsverhältnisse der Stadt Braunschweig in den Jahren 1864–1873 und die Verbreitung der Cholera daselbst in den Jahren 1850 und 1855*. Brunswick, 1874).

Reichsgesetzblatt

Reincke, J. J., *Der Typhus in Hamburg, mit besonderer Berücksichtigung der Epidemieen von 1885 bis 1888* Hamburg, 1890).

—— 'Die Cholera in Hamburg', *Deutsche Medizinische Wochenschrift*, 34 (1893).

Report on Labour and Social Conditions in Germany: Working Men's Tours III, 3 (1910–11).

Reuss-Löwenstein, Harry, *Kreuzfahrt meines Lebens. Erinnerungen* (Hamburg, 1962).

Rothenburg, J. N. C., *Die Cholera-Epidemie des Jahres 1832 in Hamburg* (Hamburg, 1836).

Rumpf, Theodor, 'Die Cholera in den Hamburgischen Krankenanstalten', *Jahrbuch der Hamburgischen Krankenanstalten*, 3 (1891–2), 34–8.

—— *Lebenserinnerungen* (Gotha, 1925).

Runge, F. F., *Vom Chlor, seinem Nutzen, seiner Anwendung und ausserordentlichen Wirksamkeit zum Reinigen der Luft und zur Abhaltung ansteckender Stoffe; besonders auch in Bezug auf die uns bedrohende Cholera. Nach den 'Grundlehren der Chemie für Jedermann' des Herrn Professor F. F. Runge in Breslau* (Hamburg, 1831).

Scheffler, Karl, *Der junge Tobias. Eine Jugend und ihre Umwelt* (Hamburg and Munich, 1962).

von Schinkel, Max, *Lebenserinnerungen* (Hamburg, 1929).

Scholz, J. H., *Freimüthige und bescheidene Rügen einer hamburgischen Polizei-Mängel nebst unmassgeblichen Vorschlägen zu ihrer Abstellung. Eine patriotische Schrift zur Beherzigung für Gesetz-Geber und Gesetz-Pflichtige* (Hamburg, 1810).

Schröder, Carl August, *Aus Hamburgs Blütezeit* (Hamburg, 1921).

Schurek, Paul, *Das Leben geht weiter* (Stuttgart, 1940).

Schüssler, Hugo, *Ein praktisches Mittel zur Verhütung der Cholera-Epidemie* (Köpenick, 1894).

Schütz, A., 'Über den Einfluss der Cholera auf Menstruation, Schwangerschaft, Geburt und Wochenbett', *Jahrbuch der Hamburgischen Staatskrankenanstalten*, 3 (1891–2), 63–95.

Siedenburg, A. B., *Dr. A. B. Siedenburg's Heilverfahren bei der Cholera morbus nebst krankengeschichtlichen Belegen* (Hamburg, 1831).

Siemerling, F., *Entschleierung der Cholera nebst dem sprechendsten Beweise ihrer Nicht-Contagiosität, und Angabe der Heilmittel, sowie des einzig und allein auf Vernunft basirten Vorbeugungsverfahrens gegen das Einathmen der Malaria animata (belebten Sumpfluft). Auf den Altar der Menschheit niedergelegt von Dr. Fr. Siemerling zu Stralsund* (Hamburg, 1831).

Sigerist, Henry (ed. and trans.), 'The Value of Health to a City. Two Lectures. Delivered in 1873, by Max von Pettenkofer', *Bulletin of the History of Medicine*, 10 (1941), 473–503, 593–613.

Simon, Friedrich, *Abfertigung und Warnung vor einem gewissen Krüger-Hansen und seinem, im Hamburger Correspondenten vom 7. September d. J. empfohlenen Mittel gegen die Cholera, von Scheue-Niemand* (Hamburg, 1831).

—— *Schutzmassregeln gegen die asiatische Cholera* (Hamburg, 1848).

Sitzungen der Hamburger Bürgerschaft (*Hamburger Nachrichten*, bound copies in StA Hbg).

'Stammbaum der Familie Reincke, zusammengestellt für den Familientag am 29. xii. 1899.

Statistisches Handbuch für den Hamburgischen Staat, 1885, 1891.

Statistik des Hamburgischen Staates.

Steinheim, S. L. *Bau- und Bruchstücke einer künftigen Lehre von den Epidemieen und ihrer Verbreitung, mit besonderer Rücksicht auf die asiatische Brechruhr* (Altona, 1831).

Stenographische Berichte über die Verhandlungen des deutschen Reichstags.

Stimme aus Danzig die Cholera. Zur Beruhigung Aller, die sie fürchten (Danzig, 1831).

Stubbe, Christian, *Hamburg und der Branntwein. Die ältere Mässigkeits- und Enthalts- amkeitsbewegung in Hamburg* (Berlin, 1911).

'Ueber die Tuberkulose in Hamburg und ihre Bekämpfung', *Sonder-Abdruck aus dem Hamburgischen Correspondent* (Hamburg, 1896).

Unfehlbares Mittel gegen die Cholera (Hamburg, 1831).

Untersuchungsplan zur Erforschung der Ursachen der Cholera und deren Verhütung. Denk- schrift verfasst im Auftrage des Reichskanzler-Amts von der Cholera-Kommission für das Deutsche Reich (Bundesrath 1873, Drucksache 151).

Verhandlungen des ärztlichen Vereins zu Hamburg 1881–1890 (Hamburg, 1890).

Verordnung, betreffend die Organisation des Gesundheits-Polizeywesens für die Freie und Hanse-Stadt Hamburg, deren Vorstädte und Gebiet, für den Fall des Ausbruches der Asiatischen Cholera (Hamburg, 1831).

Verständlichste und bewährteste Belehrungen über die mit Gefahr bedrohende pestartige Krankheit Cholera morbus. Mit einem Recepte versehen, welches das sicherste Schutz- mittel wider die Cholera lehrt, und alle hierüber schon erschienene und vielleicht noch erscheinende Büchlein übertrifft und überflüssig macht. Nach den Hauptresultaten ärzt- licher, in Indien, Persien, Russland und Polen gemachten Erfahrungen sorgfältig zus- ammengestellt. Nur nicht ängstlich! (Hamburg, 1831).

Viersbeck, Doris, *Erlebnisse eines Hamburger Dienstmädchens* (Munich, 1907).

Wachendorf, Helmut, 'Im Gängeviertel stand meines Vaters Wiege' (typescript, StA Hbg).

Wie ist das Erkranken bei der herrschenden Cholera-Epidemie zu vermeiden, wie erkennt man die Krankheit, und was ist bei derselben bis zur Ankunft eines Arztes zu thun? Zur Beruhigung und Belehrung des Publicums hg. von dem Hamburgischen Gesundheits-Rath September 1848 (Hamburg, 1848).

Wolff, Hans, 'Die Cholera-Epidemie 1892 in Wilhelmsburg', *Berliner Klinische Woch- enschrift*, 29 (1892).

Wolter, Friedrich, 'Die Cholera in Hamburg', *Berliner Klinische Wochenschrift*, 29 (1892), 1062–3.

——*Die Entstehungsursachen der Gelsenkirchener Typhusepidemie von 1901* (Munich, 1903).

Zimmerman, K. G., *Die Cholera-Epidemie in Hamburg, während des Herbstes 1831. Historisch nach ihrer Entwicklung und Verbreitung sowie in ihrem pathologischen und therapeutischen Verhalten dergestellt von K. G. Zimmermann, Dr. med. et chir.* (Hamburg, 1831).

——*Nachtrag zu der geschichtlich-medicinischen Darstellung der Cholera-Epidemie in Hamburg im Herbste und Winter 1831–1832* (Hamburg, 1832).

Zubereitung auf die Cholera (Bergedorf, 1831).

Zur Beruhigung für Jedermann bei Annäherung der Cholera. Schreiben eines Familienvaters in St. Petersburg an seinen Freund in Deutschland (Hamburg, 1831).

III. SECONDARY WORKS

A. *Hamburg*

Ahrens, Werner, 'Das sozialistische Genossenschaftswesen in Hamburg 1890–1914. Ein Beitrag zur Sozialgeschichte der Arbeiterbewegung', Ph.D. thesis (Hamburg, 1970).

Aust, Alfred, 'Vor 80 Jahren: Die Cholera in Hamburg. Soziale und hygienische Missstände und ihre Folgen', *Die Heimat. Monatsschrift des Vereins zur Pflege der Natur- und Landeskunde in Schleswig-Holstein und Hamburg*, 79 (1972), 302–11.

Baasch, Ernst, *Geschichte Hamburgs 1814–1918* (2 vols.; Gotha and Stuttgart, 1925).

Bavendamm, Dirk, '"Keine Freiheit ohne Mass". Hamburg in der Revolution von 1848/9', in Berlin, *Das andere Hamburg* (q.v.), pp. 69–92.

Bergemann, Hans Georg, *Staat und Kirche in Hamburg während des 19. Jahrhunderts* (Hamburg, 1985).

Berlin, Jörg, *Das andere Hamburg, Freiheitliche und demokratische Bestrebungen in der Hansestadt seit dem Spätmittelalter* (Hamburg, 1981).

Beselin, Oskar, *Franz Andreas Meyer* (Hamburg, 1974).

Bieber, Hans-Joachim, 'Der Hamburger Hafenarbeiterstreik 1896/97', in Herzig *et al.*, *Arbeiter in Hamburg* (q.v.), pp. 229–45.

Böhm, Ekkehard, *Überseehandel und Flottenbau. Hanseatische Kaufmannschaft und deutsche Seerüstung 1879–1902* (Düsseldorf, 1972).

—— 'Wirtschaft und Politik in Hamburg zur Zeit der Reichsgründung', *ZHG* 64 (1978), 52–73.

Böhme, Helmut, *Frankfurt und Hamburg. Des Deutschen Reiches Silber- und Goldloch und die allerenglischste Stadt des Kontinents* (Frankfurt, 1968).

Breuilly, John, 'Kontinuität in der Hamburger Arbeiterbewegung 1848–1860', in Herzig *et al.*, *Arbeiter in Hamburg* (q.v.), pp. 139–52.

—— and Wieland Sachse, *Joachim Friedrich Martens (1806–1871) und die deutsche Arbeiterbewegung* (Göttingen, 1984).

Bruhns, Maike, *et al.*, '*Hier war doch alles nicht so schlimm'. Wie die Nazis in Hamburg den Alltag eroberten* (Hamburg, 1984).

Büttner, Ursula, 'Vereinigte Liberale und Deutsche Demokraten in Hamburg 1900–1930', *ZHG* 63 (1977), 1–34.

—— *Hamburg in der Staats- and Wirtschaftskrise 1928–31* Hamburg, 1982).

—— *Politischer Gerechtigkeit und sozialer Geist. Hamburg zur Zeit der Weimarer Republik* (Hamburg, 1985).

—— and Werner Jochmann, *Hamburg auf dem Weg ins Dritte Reich* (Hamburg, 1983).

Cattaruzza, Marina, 'Das "Hamburgische Modell" der Beziehung zwischen Arbeit und Kapital. Organisationsprozesse und Konfliktverhalten auf den Werften 1890–1914', in Herzig *et al.*, *Arbeiter in Hamburg* (q.v.), pp. 247–60.

Castell-Rüdenhausen, Adelheid Gräfin zu, 'Die Überwindung der Armenschule. Schülerhygiene an den Hamburger öffentlichen Volksschulen im Zweiten Kaiserreich', *Archiv für Sozialgeschichte*, 22 (1982), 201–26.

Cecil, Lamar, *Albert Ballin. Business and Politics in Imperial Germany 1888–1918* (Princeton, 1971).

Cord, Alix, 'Die soziale Schichtung der Hamburger Bürgerschaft von 1859 bis zum Jahre 1921. Ein Beitrag zur parlamentarischen Geschichte des Kaiserreichs' (Wiss.

Prüfung für das Lehramt an Gymnasien, Hamburg, 1961; StA Hbg, Hand-schriftensammlung 1023).

Dasey, Robyn, 'Women's Work and the Family: Women Garment Workers in Berlin and Hamburg before the First World War', in Evans and Lee (eds.), *The German Family* (q.v.), 221–56.

—— 'Women Workers. Their Employment and Participation in the Labour Movement. Hamburg 1880–1914', Ph.D. thesis (Institute of Slavonic and East European Studies, University of London, 1985).

Ditt, Karl, *Sozialdemokraten im Widerstand. Hamburg in der Anfangsphase des Dritten Reiches* (Hamburg, 1984).

Dworak, Sabine, *Die Entwicklung des Impfwesens der Stadt Hamburg. Die Entwicklung der Pockenschutzimpfung von 1800 bis 1940*, M.D. thesis (Hamburg, 1984).

Ebbinghaus, Angelika, Heidrun Kaupen-Haag and Karl-Heinz Roth, *Heilen und Ver-nichten im Mustergau Hamburg. Bevölkerungs- und Gesundheitspolitik im Dritten Reich* (Hamburg, 1984).

Eckardt, Hans Wilhelm, *Privilegien und Parlament. Die Auseinandersetzungen um das allgemeine und gleiche Wahlrecht in Hamburg* (Hamburg, 1980).

Engels, Hans-Werner, '"Wo ein St Paulianer hinhaut, wächst so leicht kein Gras wieder". St Pauli und die Revolution von 1848/9', in Berlin, *Das andere Hamburg* (q.v.), pp. 93–115.

Evans, Richard J., '"Red Wednesday" in Hamburg: Social Democrats, Police and Lumpenproletariat in the Suffrage Disturbances of 17 January 1906', *Social History*, 4 (1979), 1–31.

—— 'Die Cholera und die Sozialdemokratie: Arbeiterbewegung, Bürgertum und Staat in Hamburg während der Krise von 1892', in Herzig *et al.*, *Arbeiter in Hamburg* (q.v.), pp. 203–14.

Flemming, Jens, 'Wege zum "sozialen Frieden"? Anfänge staatlicher Arbeits-marktpolitik in Hamburg', in Herzig *et al.*, *Arbeiter in Hamburg* (q.v.), pp. 283–98.

Freitag, Hans-Günther, *Von Mönckeberg bis Hagenbeck. Ein Wegweiser zu denkwürdigen Grabstätten auf dem Ohlsdorfer Friedhof* (Hamburg, 1973).

Frevert, Ute, [review of Heinrich Rodegra, *Das Gesundheitswesen* (q.v.), in] *Archiv für Sozialgeschichte*, 23 (1983), 772–4.

GAL-Fraktion in der Hamburger Bürgerschaft (ed.), *'Es ist Zeit für die ganze Wahrheit'* (*K. v. Dohnanyi*). *Aufarbeitung der NS-Zeit im Hamburg: Die nichtveröffentlichte Sen-atsbroschüre* (Hamburg, 1985).

Gelberg, Birgit, *Auswanderung nach Übersee. Soziale Probleme der Auswan-dererbeförderung in Hamburg und Bremen von der Mitte des 19. Jahrhunderts bis zum Ersten Weltkrieg* (Hamburg, 1973).

Grüttner, Michael, 'Soziale Hygiene und Soziale Kontrolle. Die Sanierung der Ham-burger Gängeviertel 1892–1930', in Herzig *et al.*, *Arbeiter in Hamburg* (q.v.), pp. 359–71.

—— *Arbeitswelt an der Wasserkante. Sozialgeschichte der Hamburger Hafenarbeiter 1886–1914* (Göttingen, 1984).

—— 'Mobilität und Konfliktverhalten. Der Hamburger Hafenarbeiterstreik 1896/97', in Klaus Tenfelde and Heinrich Volkmann (eds.), *Streik* (Munich, 1984), pp. 143–61.

Hauschild-Thiessen, Renate, 'Der Freiherr von Homayer und die Hamburger', *ZHG* 63 (1967), 55–6.

—— *Bürgerstolz und Kaisertreue. Hamburg und das Deutsche Reich von 1871* (Hamburg, 1979).

—— *150 Jahre Grundeigentümer-Verein in Hamburg von 1832 e. V. Ein Beitrag zur Geschichte der Freien und Hansestadt Hamburg* (Hamburg, 1982).

Henze, Willi, ' "Dem Nachtwächter wird hiemit anbefohlen ...": aus "Reglements", "Instructionen", alten Dienstvorschriften und über Organisationsformen der Hamburger Polizei', in *Hundertfünfzig Jahre Hamburger Polizei (1814–1964)* (Hamburg, 1964).

Herzig, Arno, 'Organisationsformen und Bewusstseinsprozesse. Hamburger Handwerker und Arbeiter in der Zeit 1790–1848', in Herzig *et al.*, *Arbeiter in Hamburg* (q.v.), pp. 95–108.

—— Dieter Langewiesche, and Arnold Sywottek (eds.), *Arbeiter in Hamburg. Unterschichten, Arbeiter und Arbeiterbewegung seit dem ausgehenden 18. Jahrhundert* (Hamburg, 1983).

Hintze, Otto, *Die Niederländische und Hamburgische Familie Amsinck*, iii (Hamburg, 1932).

150 Jahre Hamburger Polizei (Hamburg, 1964)

Hundertfünfzig Jahre Hamburger Polizei (1814–1964) (Hamburg, 1964).

Husung, Hans-Gerhard, 'Volksprotest in Hamburg zwischen Restauration und Revolution 1848', in Herzig *et al.*, (eds.), *Arbeiter in Hamburg* (q.v.), pp. 79–88.

Jensen, Jürgen, *Presse und politische Polizei. Hamburgs Zeitungen unter dem Sozialistengesetz 1878–1890* (Hanover, 1966).

Jochmann, Werner, and Hans-Dieter Loose (eds.), *Hamburg. Geschichte der Stadt Hamburg und ihrer Bewohner*, i, ed. Hans-Dieter Loose (Hamburg, 1982).

Just, Michael, 'Hamburg als Transithafen für osteuropäische Auswanderer', in *'Nach Amerika!': Auswanderung in der Vereinigten Staaten* (Museum für Hamburgische Geschichte, Schausammlungen Heft 5; Hamburg, 1976).

Kellenbenz, H. W., 'Die Hansestädte', in G. W. Sante (ed.), *Geschichte der deutschen Länder*, ii (Würzburg, 1971).

Klessmann, Eckart, *Geschichte der Stadt Hamburg* (Hamburg, 1981).

Kopitzsch, Franklin, *Grundzüge einer Geschichte der Aufklärung in Norddeutschland* (Hamburg, 1984).

Kraus, Antje, *Die Unterschichten Hamburgs in der ersten Hälfte des 19. Jahrhunderts. Entstehung, Struktur, Lebensverhältnisse. Eine historisch-statistische Untersuchung* (Sozialwissenschaftliche Studien, 9; Stuttgart, 1965).

—— 'Unterschichten und Sozialpolitik in Hamburg, 1815–1848', in Herzig *et al.*, *Arbeiter in Hamburg* (q.v.), pp. 71–7.

Krohn, Helga, *Die Juden in Hamburg 1800–1850* (Frankfurt, 1967).

—— *Die Juden in Hamburg 1850–1914* (Hamburg, 1974).

Kutz-Bauer, Helga, 'Arbeiterschaft und Sozialdemokratie in Hamburg vom Gründerkrach bis zum Ende des Sozialistengesetzes', in Herzig *et al.*, *Arbeiter in Hamburg* (q.v.), pp. 179–92.

Laufenberg, Heinrich, *Geschichte der Arbeiterbewegung in Hamburg-Altona und Umgegend* (2 vols.; Hamburg, 1911–31).

Leo, Gustav, *William Lindley: Ein Pionier der Technischen Hygiene* (Hamburg, 1969).

Lessat, Afred, 'Vom "Corps der Nachtwache" zur modernen Schutzpolizei. Aus der 150 jährigen Geschichte der Polizeibehörde Hamburg', in *Hundertfünfzig Jahre Hamburger Polizei (1814–1964)* (Hamburg, 1964).

Lessat, Alfred, 'Alte Kameraden ... Aus der Geschichte Hamburger Polizeiuniformen', in *Hundertfünfzig Jahre Hamburger Polizei (1814–1964)* (Hamburg, 1964).

Lindemann, Mary, 'Love for Hire: The Regulation of the Wet-nursing Business in 18th-century Hamburg', *Journal of Family History* 6 (1981), 379–92.

——'Producing Policed Man: Poor Relief, Population Policies and Medical Care in Hamburg, 1750–1806', Ph.D. thesis (Cincinnati, 1980).

Lüth, Erich, and Hans-Dieter Loose, *Bürgermeister Carl Petersen* (Hamburg, 1971).

von Marchtaler, Hildegard, *Aus Alt-Hamburger Senatorenhäusern. Familienschicksale im 18, und 19. Jahrhundert* (Hamburg, 1958).

Matti, Werner, 'Bevölkerungsvorgänge in den Hansestädten Hamburg und Bremen vom Anfang des 19. Jahrhunderts bis zum Ersten Welthrieg', *ZHG* 69 (1983), 103–56.

Mehnke, Bernhard, *Armut und Elend in Hamburg. Eine Untersuchung über das Öffentliche Armenwesen in der ersten Hälfte des 19. Jahrhunderts* (Ergebnisse, Heft 17; Hamburg, 1982).

Melhop, Wilhelm, *Alt-Hamburgisches Dasein* (Hamburg, 1899).

Meyer-Delius, Hugo, 'Die Säuglingssterblichkeit in Hamburg seit dem Jahre 1820', *Hamburger Ärzteblatt*, 19 (1965).

Michael, J., *Geschichte des ärztlichen Vereins und seiner Mitglieder* (Hamburg, 1896).

Naumann, Horst, *Wilhelm Koenen* (Halle, 1973).

Obst, Arthur, *Geschichte der Hamburger Bürgervereine* (Hamburg, 1911).

Offermann, Toni, 'Arbeiterbewegung, Bürgertum und Staat in Hamburg 1850–1862/63', in Herzig *et al.*, *Arbeiter in Hamburg* (q.v.), pp. 121–37.

Pelc, Ortwin, '"... Geräuschloses Pflaster wäre wünschenswert". Die Bemühungen einer Hamburger Schule um Lärmschutz zu Beginn dieses Jahrhunderts', *Hamburgische Geschichts- und Heimatblätter*, 11 (1982), 13–24.

Plagemann, Volker, (ed.), *Industriekultur in Hamburg. Des Deutschen Reiches Tor zur Welt* (Munich, 1984).

Riquarts, Knut-Gerhard, 'Der Antisemitismus als politische Partei in Schleswig-Holstein und Hamburg, 1871–1914', Ph.D. thesis (Kiel, 1975).

Rodegra, Heinrich, *Das Gesundheitswesen der Stadt Hamburg im 19. Jahrhundert unter Berücksichtigung der Medizinalgesetzgebung (1586–1818–1900)* (Sudhoffs Archiv, Supplement 21, Wiesbaden, 1979).

Schlegel, Katharina, 'Mistress and Servant in Nineteenth-Century Hamburg: Employer/Employee Relationships in Domestic Service 1880–1914', *History Workshop Journal*, 15 (1983), 60–77.

Schmidt, Wolfgang, *Die Revolution von 1848/49 in Hamburg* (Ergebnisse, Vol. 22, Hamburg, 1983).

Schönhoff, Hans-Georg, *Hamburg im Bundesrat. Die Mitwirkung Hamburgs an der Bildung des Reichswillens 1867–1890* (Hamburg, 1967).

Schramm, Percy Ernst *Hamburg, Deutschland und die Welt. Leistung und Grenzen hanseatischen Bürgertums in der Zeit zwischen Napoleon I, und Bismarck. Ein Kapitel deutscher Geschichte* (Munich, 1943).

——*Neun Generationen. Dreihundert Jahre deutscher 'Kulturgeschichte' im Lichte der Schicksale einer Hamburger Familie (1648–1948)*, ii (Göttingen, 1964).

——*Hamburg. Ein Sonderfall in der Geschichte Deutschlands* (Hamburg, 1964).

Schult, Johannes, *Geschichte der Hamburger Arbeiter 1890–1919* (Hamburg, 1968).

Seemann, Ulrich, 'Die Kämpfe der Hamburger Arbeiter gegen die Verschlechterung ihres Wahlrechts in den Jahren 1905/06', *Wissenschaftliche Zeitschrift der Universität, Rostock, gesellschafts- und sprachwissenschaftliche Reihe*, 10 (1961).

Sieveking, G. Hermann, 'Nachklänge aus der Cholerazeit 1892', *Deutsche Medizinische Wochenschrift*, 51 (1899), 1–5.

von Simson, John, *Kanalisation und Städtehygiene im 19. Jahrhundert* (Düsseldorf, 1983).

Speckter, Hans, 'Die grossen Sanierungsmassnahmen Hamburgs seit der zweiten Hälfte des 19. Jahrhunderts', *Raumforschung und Raumordnung*, 6 (1967), 257–68.

Stein, Hans-Konrad, 'Interessenkonflikte zwischen Grosskaufleuten, Handelskammer und Senat in der Frange des Zollanschlusses an das Reich 1866–1881', *ZHG* 64 (1978), 55–89.

Stühmke, Hans-Georg, ' "Wo nix ist, hett de Kaiser sien Recht verlor'n" oder "Der Stein auf dem Sofa der Frau Senatorin". Die Hamburger Unruhen vom 31. August bis 5. September 1830', in Berlin, *Das andere Hamburg* (q.v.), pp. 48–68.

Teuteberg, Hans-Jürgen, 'Die Entstehung des modernen Hamburger Hafens (1866–1896)', *Tradition*, 17 (1976), 257–91.

Timpke, Henning (ed.), *Dokumente zur Gleichschaltung des Landes Hamburg 1933* (Hamburg, 1964).

Trautmann, Günter, 'Das Scheitern liberaler Vereinspolitik und die Entstehung der sozialistischen Arbeiterbewegung in Hamburg zwischen 1862 und 1871', in Herzig *et al.*, *Arbeiter in Hamburg* (q.v.), pp. 163–76.

Treue, Wilhelm, 'Zur Geschichte einer Hamburgischen Anwaltssocietät 1812–1972', *Tradition*, 2 (1972), 48-83.

Ullrich, Volker, *Die Hamburger Arbeiterbewegung vom Vorabend des Ersten Weltkrieges bis zur Revolution 1918–19* (2 vols; Hamburg, 1978).

——*Kriegsalltag. Hamburg im Ersten Weltkrieg* (Cologne, 1982).

——'Massenbewegungen in der Hamburger Arbeiterschaft im Ersten Weltkrieg', in Herzig *et al.*, *Arbeiter in Hamburg* (q.v.).

Washausen, H., *Hamburg und die Kolonialpolitik des Deutschen Reiches 1880–1890* (Hamburg, 1968).

Whaley, Joachim, *Religious Toleration and Social Change in Hamburg 1529–1819* (Cambridge, 1985).

Winkle, S., 'Chronologie und Konsequenzen der Hamburger Choleraepidemie von 1892', *Hamburger Ärzteblatt*, 12 (1983), 421–30; 1 (1984), 16–23.

Wischermann, Clemens, *Wohnen in Hamburg vor dem Erstem Weltkrieg* (Münster, 1983).

Wiskemann, Erwin, *Hamburg und die Welthandelspolitik* (Hamburg, 1929).

Wohlwill, Adolf, *Hamburg während der Pestjahre 1712–14* (Hamburg, 1893).

——*Die Hamburgischen Bürgermeister Kirchenpauer, Petersen, Versmann* (Hamburg, 1903).

——'Johannes Versmann. Zur Geschichte seiner Jugendjahre und seiner späteren Wirksamkeit', *ZHG* 15 (1910), 166–252.

Zimmermann, Mosche, 'Antijüdischer Sozialprotest? Proteste von Unter- und Mittelschichten 1819–1835', in Herzig *et al.*, *Arbeiter in Hamburg* (q.v.), pp. 89–94.

B. General

Ackerknecht, Erwin H., 'Anticontagionism between 1821 and 1867', *Bulletin of the History of Medicine*, 22 (1948), 562–93.

—— *Rudolf Virchow. Doctor, Statesman, Anthropologist* (Madison, Wisconsin, 1953).

Albrecht, Günter, 'Das Bremer Haus. Ein Sonderfall in der deutschen Baugeschichte um 1900', in Lutz Niethammer (ed.), *Wohnen im Wandel* (Wuppertal, 1979).

Alvarez, A., *The Savage God: A Study of Suicide* (Harmondsworth, 1981).

Anderson, Michael, *Approaches to the History of the Western Family, 1500–1914* (London, 1980).

Ariès, Philippe, *Centuries of Childhood* (London, 1975).

—— *The Hour of our Death* (Harmondsworth, 1981).

Artelt, Walter, *et al.* (eds.), *Städte-, Wohnungs- und Kleiderhygiene des 19. Jahrhunderts in Deutschland* (Stuttgart, 1969).

Baehrel, René, 'Épidémie et terreur. Histoire et sociologie', *Archives Historiques de la Revolution Française*, 23 (1951), 113–46.

Barker, T. C. and H. Drake (eds.), *Population and Society in Britain 1850–1980* (London, 1982).

Barnes, Barry, *T. S. Kuhn and Social Science* (London, 1982).

Beaver, M. W., 'Population, Infant Mortality and Milk', *Population Studies*, 27 (1973), pp. 243–54.

Berghahn, Volker R., *Germany and the Approach of War in 1914* (London, 1973).

Bilson, Geoffrey, *A Darkened House: Cholera in Nineteenth-century Canada* (Social History of Canada, 31; Toronto, 1980).

Biraben, Jean-Noël, *Les hommes et la peste en France et dans les pays européens et méditerranéens* (Paris, 2 vols., 1975–6).

Blackbourn, David, 'The *Mittelstand* in German Society and Politics 1871–1914', *Social History*, 2 (1977), 409–33.

—— and Geoff Eley, *The Peculiarities of German History: Bourgeois Society and Politics in Nineteenth-century Germany* (Oxford, 1984).

Blasius, Dirk, ' "Volksseuchen": Zur historischen Dimension von Berufskrankheiten', *Sozialwissenschaftliche Informationen für Unterricht und Studium*, 6 (1977), 55–60.

Boccaccio, Giovanni, *The Decameron* (London, n.d.).

Boll, Friedhelm, *Massenbewegungen in Niedersachsen 1906–1920* (Bonn and Bad Godesberg, 1981).

Bourdelais, Patrick, and J. Y. Raulot, 'Sur le rôle des contacts interhumains dans la transmission du choléra, épidémies de 1832 et 1854', *Bulletin de la Société de Pathologie Exotique*, 71 (1978), 119–30.

Braudel, Fernand, *The Mediterranean and the Mediterranean World in the Age of Philip II* (2 vols.; London, 1972).

Breyer, Harald, *Max von Pettenkofer* (Leipzig, 1980).

Briggs, Asa, 'Cholera and Society in the 19th Century', *Past and Present*, 19 (1961), pp. 76–96.

Brink, André, *The Wall of the Plague* (London, 1984).

Burnett, John, *Plenty and Want. A Social History of Diet in England from 1815 to the Present Day* (Harmondsworth, 1968).

Camus, A., *La Peste* (Paris, 1947).

Cannadine, David, 'The Context, Performance and Meaning of Ritual: The British Monarchy and the "Invention of Tradition", *c.* 1820–1977', in Hobsbawm and Ranger (eds.), *The Invention of Tradition* (q.v.), pp. 101–64.

Cartwright, F. F., *A Social History of Medicine* (London, 1977).

Charbonneau, Hubert, and André Larose (eds.), *The Great Mortalities: Methodological Studies of Demographic Crises in the Past* (Liège, 1979).

Checkland, Olive, and Margaret Lamb (eds.), *Health Care as Social History: The Glasgow Case* (Aberdeen, 1982).

Chevalier, Louis (ed.), *Le choléra. La première épidémie du XIXe siècle* (Paris, 1958).

Childs, C., 'Obituary: Geheimrath Max von Pettenkofer, of Munich', *Transactions of the Epidemiological Society*, NS 20 (1901), 118–25.

Conrad, Christoph, 'Sterblichkeit im Alter, 1715–1975—am Beispiel Berlin: Quantifizierung und Wandel medizinischer Konzepte', in Konrad (ed.), *Der alte Mensch in der Geschichte* (q.v.).

Conze, Werner, and Ulrich Engelhardt (eds.), *Arbeiterexistenz im 19. Jahrhundert* (Suttgart, 1981).

——— and Jürgen Kocka (eds.), *Bildungsbürgertum im 19, Jahrhundert*, i (Stuttgart, 1985).

Cooter, Roger, 'Anticontagionism and History's Medical Record', in Treacher and Wright (eds.), *The Problem of Medical Knowledge* (q.v.), pp. 87–108.

Corbin, Alain, *Pesthauch und Blütenduft. Eine Geschichte des Geruchs* (Berlin, 1984).

Crew, David F., *Town in the Ruhr. A Social History of Bochum 1860–1914* (New York, 1979).

Cronjé, Gillian, 'Tuberculosis and mortality decline in England and Wales, 1851–1910', in Woods and Woodward, *Urban Disease and Mortality* (q.v.).

Crosby, A., *Epidemic and Peace 1918* (Westpoint, Conn., 1976).

Dechêne, Louis, and Jean-Claude Robert, 'Le choléra de 1832 dans le Bas-Canada: Mesure des Inegalités devant la mort', in Charbonneau and Larose (eds.), *The Great Mortality* (q.v.), pp. 229–56.

Defoe, Daniel, *A Journal of the Plague Year* (London, 1722, repr. 1966).

Delaporte, François, *Disease and Civilization: The Cholera in France, 1832* (London, 1986).

Delumeau, Jean, *Angst im Abendland. Die Geschichte kollektiver Ängste im Europa des 14. bis 18. Jahrhunderts* (2 vols; Reinbek bei Hamburg, 1985).

Dickler, Robert A., 'Labor Market Pressure—Aspects of Agricultural Growth in the Eastern Region of Prussia, 1840–1914. A Case Study of Economic-Demographic Transition', Ph.D. thesis (University of Pennsylvania, 1975).

Dineur, M., and C. Engrand, 'Épidémie et pauperisme: le choléra à Lille en 1832', in Gillet (ed.), *l'Homme, la vie et la mort* (q.v.), pp. 41–78.

Douglas, Mary, *Purity and Danger* (London, 1975).

Dubois, R., *The White Plague. A History of Tuberculosis* (London, 1961).

Durey, Michael, *The Return of the Plague. British Society and the Cholera 1831–32* (Dublin, 1979).

Dyos, H. J., and M. Wolff (eds.), *The Victorian City: Images and Realities* (London, 1973).

Eley, Geoff, *Reshaping the German Right: Radical Nationalism and Political Change After Bismarck* (New Haven, 1980).

Eley, Geoff, 'James Sheehan and the German Liberals: A Critical Appreciation', *Central European History*, 14 (1981), 273–88.

—— 'Combining Two Histories: The SPD and the German Working Class before 1914', *Radical History Review*, 28–30 (1984), 13–44.

—— *From Unification to Nazism: Reinterpreting the German Past* (London, 1986).

Elias, Norbert, *Über den Prozess der Zivilisation* (2 vols.; Frankfurt, 1969).

Eulner, H.-H., 'Hygiene als akademisches Fach', in W. Artelt *et al.* (eds.), *Städte-, Wohnungs-und Kleidungshygiene* (q.v.), pp. 17–33.

Evans, Alfred S., 'Pettenkofer Revisited', *Yale Journal of Biology and Medicine*, 46 (1973), 161–76.

Evans, Richard J., *Sozialdemokratie und Frauenemanzipation im deutschen Kaiserreich* (Bonn and Berlin, 1979).

—— (ed.), *The German Working Class 1888–1933: The Politics of Everyday Life* (London, 1982).

—— and W. R. Lee (eds.), *The German Family: Essays on the Social History of the Family in Nineteenth and Twentieth Century Germany* (London, 1981).

—— —— (eds.), *The German Peasantry. Conflict and Community in Rural Society from the Eighteenth to the Twentieth Centuries* (London, 1986).

Falliner, H., 'Zur historischen Entwicklung des Bremischen Quarantänedienstes', *Bremer Ärzteblatt*, 9 (1978), 36–52.

Feachem, Richard G., 'Environmental Aspects of Cholera Epidemiology, III: Transmission and Control', *Tropical Diseases Bulletin*, 99 (1982), pp. 1–30.

Ferenczi, Imre, (ed.), *International Migrations*, i (New York, 1929).

Fischer, Alfons, *Geschichte des deutschen Gesundheitswesens*, ii (Berlin, 1933).

Fischer, Ilse, *Industrialisierung, sozialer Konflikt und politische Willensbildung in der Stadtgemeinde. Ein Beitrag zur Sozialgeschichte Augsburgs 1840–1914* (Augsburg, 1977).

Fleischer, Georg, *Die Choleraepidemien in Düsseldorf* (Düsseldorf, 1977).

Frieden, Nancy M., 'The Russian Cholera Epidemic, 1892–93, and Medical Professionalisation', *Journal of Social History*, 10 (1977), 538–59.

Frevert, Ute,' "Fürsorgliche Belagerung": Hygienebewegung und Arbeiterfrauen im 19. und 20. Jahrhundert', *Geschichte und Gesellschaft*, 11 (1980), 420–46.

—— *Krankheit als politisches Problem 1770–1880. Soziale Unterschichten in Preussen zwischen medizinischer Polizei und staatlicher Sozialversicherung* (Kritische Studien zur Geschichtswissenschaft, 62; Göttingen, 1984).

—— 'Professional Medicine and the Working Classes in Imperial Germany', *Journal of Contemporary History*, 20 (1985), 637–58.

—— and Jürgen Kocka, 'La borghesia tedesca nel XIX secolo. Lo stato della ricerca', *Quaderni storici* 56 (1984), 549–72.

Fricke, Dieter, *Die deutsche Arbeiterbewegung 1869 bis 1914. Ein Handbuch über ihre Organisation und Tätigkeit im Klassenkampf* (Berlin, 1976).

Fritzsche, Bruno, 'Der Quartier als Lebensraum', in Conze and Engelhardt (eds.), *Arbeiterexistenz im 19. Jahrhundert* (q.v.), pp. 92–113.

Gellately, Robert, *The Politics of Economic Despair: Shopkeepers and German Politics 1890–1914* (London, 1974).

Gillet, M. (ed.), *L'Homme, la vie et la mort dans le nord au XIXe siècle* (Lille, 1972).

Gins, Heinrich A., *Krankheit wider den Tod. Schicksal der Pockenschutzimpfung* (Stuttgart, 1983).

Gleichmann, Peter, 'Die Verhäuslichung körperlicher Verrichtungen', in Peter Gleichmann, Johan Goudsblom, and Hermann Korte (eds.), *Materialien zu Norbert Elias' Zivilisationstheorie* (Frankfurt-on-Main, 1977).

Göckenjan, Gerd, *Kurieren und Staat machen. Gesundheit und Medizin in der Bürgerlichen Welt* (Frankfurt, 1985).

Grote, Heiner, *Sozialdemokratie und Religion. Eine Dokumentation für die Jahre 1860 bis 1875* (Tübingen, 1968).

Hall, Alex, *Scandal, Sensation and Social Democracy. The SPD Press and Wilhelmine Germany* (Cambridge, 1977).

Hamilton, Richard F., *Who Voted for Hitler?* (Princeton, 1982).

Haupt, Heinz-Gerhard, *Die radikale Mitte. Lebensweise und Politik von Handwerkern und Kleinhändlern in Deutschland seit 1848* (Munich, 1985).

Heischkel-Artelt, Edith, (ed.), *Ernährung und Ernährungslehre im 19. Jahrhundert* (Göttingen, 1976).

Helm, Dietrich, *Die Cholera in Lübeck. Epidemieprophylaxe und -bekämpfung im 19. Jahrhundert* (Kieler Beiträge zur Geschichte der Medizin und Pharmazie, 16; Neumünster, 1979).

Hemmings, John, *The Conquest of the Incas* (London, 1970).

van Heyningen, W. E., and John R. Seal, *Cholera. The American Scientific Experience 1947–1980* (Boulder, 1985).

His, W., *Die Front der Ärzte* (Bielefeld and Leipzig, 1931).

Hobsbawm, Eric, and Terence Ranger (eds.), *The Invention of Tradition* (Cambridge, 1983).

Hofmann, Wolfgang, *Die Bielefelder Stadtverordneten. Ein Beitrag zu bürgerlicher Selbstverwaltung und sozialem Wandel 1850 bis 1914* (Lübeck and Hamburg, 1964).

Hoffmann, Walther G., *Das Wachstum der deutschen Wirtschaft seit der Mitte des 19. Jahrhunderts* (Berlin, Heidelberg and New York, 1965).

Hohorst, Gerd, Jügen Kocka, and Gerhard A. Ritter, *Sozialgeschichtliches Arbeitsbuch II* (Munich, 1975).

Howard-Jones, Norman, 'Cholera Therapy in the Nineteenth Century', *Journal of the History of Medicine*, 27 (1972), 373–95.

—— 'Gelsenkirchen Typhoid Epidemic of 1901, Robert Koch and the Dead Hand of Max von Pettenkofer', *British Medical Journal* (1973), 103–5.

—— 'Choleranomalies', *Perspectives in Biology and Medicine*, 15 (1975), 422–33.

Huber, Ernst Rudolf, *Deutsche Verfassungsgeschichte seit 1789*: i. *Reform und Restauration 1789–1830* (2nd edn., Stuttgart, 1975); ii. *Der Kampf um Einheit und Freiheit 1830–1850* (2nd edn., Stuttgart, 1978); iv. *Struktur und Krisen des Kaiserreichs* (Stuttgart, 1969).

Huerkamp, Claudia, 'Ärzte und Professionalisierung in Deutschland. Überlegungen zum Wandel des Arztberufs im 19. Jahrhundert', *Geschichte und Gesellschaft*, 6 (1980), 349–82.

—— 'Die preussisch-deutsche Ärzteschaft als Teil das Bildungsbürgertums: Wandel in Lage und Selbstverständnis vom ausgehenden 18. Jahrhundert bis zum Kaiserreich', in Conze and Kocka (eds.), *Bildungsbürgertum im 19. Jahrhundert*, i (q.v.), pp. 358–88.

Huerkamp, Claudia, 'The History of Smallpox Vaccination in Germany: A First Step in the Medicalization of the General Public', *Journal of Contemporary History*, 20 (1985), 617–35.

——and Reinhard Spree, 'Arbeitsmarktstrategien der deutschen Ärzteschaft im späten 19. und frühen 20. Jahrhundert. Zur Entwicklung des Marktes für professionelle ärztliche Dienstleistungen', in Pierenkemper and Tilly (eds.), *Historische Arbeitsmarktforschung* (q.v.), pp. 77–116.

Hume, Edgar E., 'Max von Pettenkofer's Theory of the Etiology of Cholera, Typhoid Fever and Intestinal Diseases: A Review of his Arguments and Evidence', *Annals of Medical History*, 7 (1925), 319–53.

Hunt, James C., 'The Bourgeois Middle in German Politics, 1871–1933. Recent Literature'. *Central European History*, 11 (1978), 83–106.

Imhof, Arthur E., 'Mortalität in Berlin vom 18. bis 20. Jahrhundert', *Berliner Statistik*, 31 (1971), 138–45.

——(ed.), *Mensch und Gesundheit in der Geschichte* (Husum, 1980).

——*Die gewonnenen Jahre. Von der Zunahme unserer Lebensspanne seit dreihundert Jahren, oder, von der Notwendigkeit einer neuen Einstellung zu Leben und Sterben. Ein historischer Essay* (Munich, 1981).

——'Unterschiedliche Säuglingssterblichkeit in Deutschland, 18, bis 20. Jahrhundert—Warum?', *Zeitschrift für Bevölkerungswissenschaft*, 7 (1981), 343–82.

——'Mensch und Körper in der Geschichte der Neuzeit: Reflexionen über eine internationale Tagung in Berlin vom 1.–3. Dezember 1981', *Beiträge zur Wissenschaftsgeschichte*, 5 (1982), 195–207.

Jasper, Karlbernhard, *Der Urbanisierungsprozess dargestellt am Beispiel der Stadt Köln* (Cologne, 1977).

Jones, Gareth Stedman, *Outcast London. A Study in the Relations between Classes in Victorian England* (Oxford, 1975).

——'Poor Laws and Market Forces', *New Statesman*, 27 May 1983.

Kaelble, Hartmut, *Industrialisierung und soziale Ungleichheit. Europa im 19. Jahrhundert. Eine Bilanz* (Göttingen, 1983).

——'Wie feudal waren die deutschen Unternehmer im Kaiserreich? Ein Zwischenbericht', in Tilly (ed.), *Beiträge* (q.v.), pp. 148–71.

Kater, Michael H., 'Professionalization and Socialization of Physicians in Wilhelmine and Weimar Germany', *Journal of Contemporary History*, 20 (1985), 677–701.

Karl Kisskalt, *Max von Pettenkofer* (Stuttgart, 1948).

Kitchen, Martin, *The Political Economy of Germany 1815–1914* (London, 1978).

Koch, Rainer, *Grundlagen bürgerlicher Herrschaft. Verfassungs- und sozialgeschichtliche Studien zur bürgerlichen Gesellschaft in Frankfurt am Main (1612–1866)* (Wiesbaden, 1983).

Konrad, Helmut (ed.), *Der alte Mensch in der Geschichte* (Vienna, 1982).

Koshar, Rudy, *Social Life, Local Politics, and Nazism: Bourgeois Marburg, 1880 to 1935* (Chapel Hill, 1986).

Krabbe, Wolfgang, *Gesellschaftsveränderung durch Lebensreform* (Göttingen, 1974).

Kropf, Rudolf, and Horst Rauter, 'Erklärungsansätze zum Einfluss der Ernährung auf die Gesundheit und Lebenserwartung der Menschen im 19. Jahrhundert', in Konrad (ed.), *Der alte Mensch in der Geschichte* (q.v.), pp. 185–204.

Labisch, Alfons, 'Die gesundheitspolitischen Vorstellungen der deutschen Sozialdemokratie von ihrer Gründung bis zur Parteispaltung (1863–1917)', *Archiv für Sozialgeschichte*, 16 (1976), 325–70.

—— 'Das Krankenhaus in der Gesundheitspolitik der deutschen Sozialdemokratie vor dem Ersten Weltkrieg', *Medizinsoziologisches Jahrbuch* (1918), pp. 126–51.

—— 'Selbsthilfe zwischen Auflehnung und Anpassung: Arbeiter-Sanitätskommission und Arbeiter-Samariterbund', in *Alternative Medizin* (Argument-Sonderband, 77; Berlin, 1983), pp. 11–26.

—— ' "Hygiene ist Moral—Moral ist Hygiene". Soziale Disziplinierung durch Ärzte und Medizin', in Sachsse and Tennstedt, *Soziale Sicherheit und soziale Disziplinierung* (q.v.), pp 265–85.

Leca, Ange-Pierre, *Et le choléra s'abattit sur Paris 1832* (Paris, 1982).

Lee, W. R., 'Primary Sector Output and Mortality Changes in Early XIXth Century Bavaria', *Journal of European Economic History*, 6 (1977), pp. 130–62.

—— 'Bastardy and the Socioeconomic Structure of South Germany', *Journal of Interdisciplinary History*, 7 (1977), 403–25.

—— 'A Commentary on Reinhard Spree: Determinanten des Sterblichkeitsrückgangs in Deutschland seit der Mitte des 19. Jahrhunderts' (typescript; contribution to conference, 'Neuere Ergebnisse und Entwicklung einer Sozialgeschichte der Medizin und des Gesundheitswesens', Bielefeld, 1982).

Leuschen-Seppel, Rosemarie, *Sozialdemokratie und Antisemitismus im Kaiserreich* (Bonn, 1978).

Longmate, Norman, *King Cholera* (London, 1965).

Loschky, D. J., 'Urbanisation and England's Eighteenth-century Crude Birth and Death Rates', *Journal of European Economic History*, 1 (1972), 697–712.

Lucas, Erhard, *Arbeiterradikalismus. Zwei Formen von Radikalismus in der deutschen Arbeiterbewegung* (Frankfurt, 1976).

Luckin, Bill, 'Death and Survival in the City: Approaches to the History of Disease', *Urban History Yearbook* (1980), pp. 53–62.

—— 'Evaluating the Sanitary Revolution: Typhus and Typhoid in London, 1851–1900', in Woods and Woodward, *Urban Disease and Mortality* (q.v.).

—— 'States and Epidemic Threats', *Bulletin of the Society for the Social History of Medicine*, 34 (June, 1984), 25–7.

Lüdtke, Alf, 'Hunger, Essens-"Genuss" und Politik bei Fabrikarbeitern und Arbeiterfrauen. Beispiele aus dem rheinisch-westfälischen Industriegebiet 1910–1940', *Sozialwissenschaftliche Informationen* 14 (1985), 118–26.

McGrew, Roderick, *Russia and the Cholera 1823–32* (Wisconsin, 1965).

McKeown, Thomas, *The Modern Rise of Population* (London, 1976).

McLeod, 'Protestantism and the Working Class in Imperial Germany', *European Studies Review*, 12 (1982), 323–44.

McManners, John, *Death and the Enlightenment: Changing Attitudes to Death among Christians and Unbelievers in 18th-century France* (Oxford, 1981).

McNeill, William H., *Plagues and Peoples* (Oxford, 1977).

Madai, Lajos, 'Les crises de mortalité en Europe dans la deuxieme moitié du XIXe siècle', in Charbonneau and Larose, *The Great Mortalities* (q.v.), 157–70.

Mann, Thomas, *Buddenbrooks* (Penguin edn.; Harmondsworth, 1968).

Mann, Thomas, *Death in Venice* (Penguin edn.; Harmondsworth, 1955).

Marschalck, Peter, *Deutsche Überseeauswanderung im 19. Jahrhundert* (Stuttgart, 1973).

Matessian, Mary K., 'Death in London, 1750–1909', *Journal of Interdisciplinary History* (1985), 183–98.

May, Jacques M., *The Ecology of Human Disease* (New York, 1958).

Möller, Bernhard, *Robert Koch. Persönlichkeit und Lebenswerk 1843–1910* (Hanover, 1950).

Moltmann, Günter (ed.), *Deutsche Amerikaauswanderung im 19. Jahrhundert* (Stuttgart, 1976).

Mommsen, Hans, and Winfried Schulze (eds.), *Vom Elend der Handarbeit. Probleme historischer Unterschichtenforschung* (Stuttgart, 1981).

Mommsen, Wolfgang J., 'Der deutsche Liberalismus zwischen "Klassenloser Bürgergesellschaft" und "Organisiertem Kapitalismus". Zu einigen neueren Liberalismusinterpretationen', *Geschichte und Gesellschaft*, 4 (1978), 77–90.

Moring, Karl-Ernst, *Die Sozialdemokratische Partei in Bremen 1890–1914* (Hanover, 1968).

Morris, R. J., *Cholera 1832: The Social Response to an Epidemic* (London, 1976).

Niethammer, Lutz (ed.), *Wohnen im Wandel* (Wuppertal, 1979).

Nipperdey, Thomas, *Deutsche Geschichte 1800–1866* (Munich, 1983).

Nohl, Johannes, *The Black Death: A Chronicle of the Plague. Compiled from Contemporary Sources* (London, 1961).

Nolan, Molly, *Social Democracy and Society. Working-class Radicalism in Düsseldorf, 1890–1920* (Cambridge, 1981).

Ocaña, Esteban Rodriguez, 'La dependencia social de un comportamiento cientifico: Los medicos españoles y el cólera de 1833–35', *Dynamis*, 1 (1981), 101-30.

—— 'Hygiene y terapeutica anticóléricas en la primera epidemia de cólera en España 1833–1835', *Asclepio*, 24 (1982), 71–100.

—— *El cólera de 1834 en Granada. Enfermedad catastrófica y crisis social* (Granada, 1983).

Oddy, D. J., 'The Health of the People', in Barker and Drake, *Population and Society* (q.v.).

Ortiz, M. V., *Epidemias de Cólera en Vizcaya en el Siglo XIX* (Bilbao, 1978).

Panzac, Daniel, 'Aix-en-Provence et le choléra en 1835', *Annales du Midi*, 86 (1975), 419–44.

Pelling, Margaret, *Cholera, Fever and English Medicine 1825–1865* (Oxford, 1978).

Pennington, Carolyn, 'Tuberculosis', in Checkland and Lamb, *Health Care as Social History* (q.v.).

Perrenoud, Alfred, 'Contribution à l'histoire cyclique des maladies. Deux siècles de variole à Genève (1580–1810)', in Imhof, *Mensch und Gesundheit* (q.v.), pp. 175–98.

Pierenkemper, Toni, and Richard Tilly (eds.), *Historische Arbeitsmarktforschung* (Göttingen, 1982).

Prinzing, F., *Epidemics Resulting from Wars* (Oxford, 1916).

Rebentisch, Dieter, 'Die deutsche Sozialdemokratie und die kommunale Selbstverwaltung. Ein Überblick über Programmdiskussion und Organisationsproblematik 1890–1975', *Archiv Für Sozialgeschichte*, 25 (1985), 1–78.

Reulecke, Jürgen, *Geschichte der Urbanisierung in Deutschland* (Frankfurt, 1985).

—— and Wolfhard Weber (eds.), *Fabrik, Familie, Feierabend. Beiträge zur Sozialgeschichte des Alltags im Industriezeitalter* (Wuppertal, 1978).

Ritter, Gerhard A., *Sozialversicherung in Deutschland und England. Entstehung und Struktur im Vergleich* (Munich, 1983).

Robbins, Richard G. *Famine in Russia 1891–1892* (New York, 1975).

Robert, Jean-Claude, 'Le Choléra de 1832 dans le Bas-Canada: mesures des Inégalités devant la mort', in Charbonneau and Larose, *The Great Mortalities* (q.v.).

Roberts, James S., *Drink, Temperance and the Working Class in 19th-century Germany* (London, 1984).

Röhl, John C.G., 'Kaiser Wilhelm II., Grossherzog Friedrich I. und der "Königs-mechanismus" im Kaiserreich. Unzeitgemässe Betrachtungen zu einer badischen Geschichtsquelle', *Historische Zeitschrift*, 236 (1983), 539–77.

Rollet, C., and A. Souriac, 'Le choléra de 1832 en Seine-et-Oise', *Annales ESC* 29 (1974), 935–65.

Rosen, George, 'Disease, Debility and Death', in Dyos and Wolff, *The Victorian City* (q.v.).

——— *From Medical Police to Social Medicine. Essays on the History of Health Care* (New York, 1974).

Rosenberg, Charles, *The Cholera Years. The United States in 1832, 1879 and 1866* (Chicago, 1962).

Roth, Karl Heinz (ed.), *Erfassung zur Vernichtung. Von der Sozialhygiene zum "Gesetz über Sterbehilfe"* (Berlin, 1984).

——— 'Schein-Alternativen im Gesundheitswesen: Alfred Grotjahn (1869–1931)— Integrationsfigur etablierter Sozialmedizin und nationalsozialistischer "Rassenhygiene" ', in id., *Erfassung zur Vernichtung* (q.v.), pp. 31–56.

Rubinstein, W.D., *Men of Property. The Very Wealthy in Britain since the Industrial Revolution* (London, 1981).

Sachsse, Christoph, and Florian Tennstedt (eds.), *Soziale Sicherheit und soziale Disziplinierung. Beiträge zu einer historischen Theorie der Sozialpolitik* (Frankfurt-on-Main, 1986).

von Saldern, Adelheid, *Vom Einwohner zum Bürger. Zur Emanzipation der Städtischen Unterschicht– Göttingens 1890–1920. Eine sozial- und kommunalhistorische Untersuchung* (Berlin, 1973).

Samuel, Raphael, 'Soft Focus Nostalgia', *New Statesman*, 27 May, 1983.

Schipperges, Heinrich, 'Zur "Wirtschaftslehre von der Gesundheit" bei Max von Pettenkofer', *Die Heilkunst*, 89 (1976), 321–3.

Schmauderer, E., 'Die Beziehungen zwischen Lebensmittelwissenschaft, Lebensmittelrecht und Lebensmittelversorgung im 19. Jahrhundert, problemgeschichtlich betrachtet', in Heischkel-Artelt (ed.), *Ernährung* (q.v.), pp. 131–97.

Schramm, Engelbert, *Ökologie-Lesebuch. Ausgewählte Text zur Entwicklung Ökologischen Denkens* (Frankfurt, 1984).

Schwarzwälder, Herbert, *Geschichte der Freien Hansestadt Bremen*, ii (Bremen, 1976).

Sheehan, James J., 'Liberalism and the city in 19th-century Germany', *Past and Present*, 51 (1971), 116–37.

——— *German Liberalism in the Nineteenth Century* (Chicago, 1978).

Shorter, Edward, *The Making of the Modern Family* (London, 1976).

——— *A History of Women's Bodies* (London, 1983).

Sieferle, Rolf-Dieter, *Der unterirdische Wald. Energiekrise und industrielle Revolution* (Munich, 1982).

von Simson, John, 'Die Flussverunreinigungsfrage im 19. Jahrhundert', *Vierteljahr-schrift für Sozial- und Wirtschaftsgeschichte*, 65 (1978), pp. 370–90.

——*Kanalisation und Städtehygiene im 19. Jahrhundert* (Düsseldorf, 1983).

Slack, Paul, *The Impact of Plague in Tudor and Stuart England* (London, 1985).

Smith, F. B., *The People's Health 1830–1910* (London, 1979).

Sontag, Susan, *Illness as Metaphor* (Harmondsworth, 1983).

Spelsberg, Gerd, *Rauchplage: Hundert Jahre Saurer Regen* (Aachen, 1984).

Spree, Reinhard, *Soziale Ungleichheit vor Krankheit und Tod: Zur Sozialgeschichte des Gesundheitsbereichs im Deutschen Kaiserreich* (Göttingen, 1981).

——'Erwiderung zum Comment von Robert W. Lee' ('A Commentary on Reinhard Spree', q.v.) (typescript, contribution to conference, 'Neuere Ergebnisse und Entwicklung einer Sozialgeschichte der Medizin und des Gesundheitswesens', Biele-feld, 1982).

Steel, David, 'Plague Writing. From Boccaccio to Camus', *Journal of European Studies*, 11 (1981), 85–110.

Stenz, Wilfried, *et al.*, 'Zu den Beziehungen zwischen Gesellschaft und Umwelt von der Industriellen Revolution bis zum Übergang zum Imperialismus', *Jahrbuch für Wirtschaftsgeschichte* (1984) pp. 81–132.

Stern, Fritz, *The Politics of Cultural Despair* (New York, 1966).

——*Gold and Iron. Bismarck, Bleichröder and the Building of the German Empire* (London, 1977).

Stollenwerk, A., 'Die Cholera im Regierungsbezirk Koblenz (1832)', *Jahrbuch für westdeutsche Landesgeschichte*, 5 (1979), pp. 241–72.

Stone, Lawrence, *The Family, Sex and Marriage in England, 1500–1800* (London, 1975).

Struve, Walter, *Elites Against Democracy* (Princeton, 1973).

Tenfelde, K. and Heinrich Volkmann (eds.), *Streik* (Munich, 1984).

Tennstedt, Florian, *Sozialgeschichte der Sozialpolitik in Deutschland. Vom 18. Jahrhundert bis zum Ersten Weltkrieg* (Göttingen, 1982).

——*Vom Proleten zum Industriearbeiter* (Cologne, 1983).

Teuteberg, Hans-Jürgen, 'Die Nahrung der sozialen Unterschichten im späten 19. Jahrhundert', in Heischkel-Artelt, *Ernährung und Ernährungslehre* (q.v.), pp. 205–87.

——'Der Verzehr von Nahrungsmitteln in Deutschland pro Kopf und Jahr seit Beginn der Industrialisierung (1850–1975). Versuch einer quantitativen Langzeitanalyse', *Archiv für Sozialgeschichte*, 19 (1979), 331–88.

——'Wie ernährten sich Arbeiter im Kaiserreich?', in Conze, *Arbeiterexistenz im 19. Jahrhundert* (q.v.), pp. 57–73.

——and Günter Wiegelmann, *Der Wandel der Nahrungsgewohnheiten unter dem Einfluss der Industrialisierung* (Göttingen, 1972).

——and A. Bernhard, 'Wandel der Kindernahrung in der Zeit der Industrialisierung', in Reulecke and Weber, *Fabrik, Familie, Feierabend* (q.v.), pp. 183–97.

Thompson, Barbara, 'Infant Mortality in Nineteenth-century Bradford', in Woods and Woodward (q.v.), pp. 120–47.

Thompson, F. M. L., *Victorian England: The Horse-drawn Society* (London, 1970).

Tilly, Richard (ed.), *Beiträge zur quantitativen vergleichenden Unternehmensgeschichte* (Stuttgard, 1983).

Tjaden H. (ed.), *Bremen in hygienischer Beziehung* (Bremen, 1907).

—— *Bremen und die Bremische Ärzteschaft seit dem Beginne des 19. Jahrhunderts* (Bremen, 1932).

Treacher, A., and P. Wright (eds.), *The Problem of Medical Knowledge* (Edinburgh, 1982).

Walker, Mack, *German Home Towns. Community, State and General Estate* (London, 1971).

Wehler, Hans-Ulrich, *The German Empire 1871–1918* (Leamington Spa, 1985).

Weiling, Franz, 'J. G. Mendel sowie die von M. Pettenkofer angeregten Untersuchungen des Zusammenhanges von Cholera- und Typhus-Massenerkrankungen mit dem Grundwasserstand', *Sudhoffs Archiv*, 59 (1975), 1–19.

Weindling, Paul, 'The Medical Profession, Social Hygiene and the Birth Rate in Germany 1914–1918' (unpub. paper, Cambridge Conference on the European Family and the Great War, 1983).

—— 'Was Social Medicine Revolutionary? Rudolf Virchow and the Revolutions of 1848', *Bulletin of the Society for the Social History of Medicine*, 34 (1984), 13–18.

Weisbrod, Bernd, 'Wohltätigkeit und symbolische Gewalt in der Frühindustrialisierung. Städtische Armut und Armenpolitik im Wuppertal', in Mommsen and Schulze (eds.), *Vom Elend der Handarbeit* (q.v.).

Westwood, J. N., *A History of Russian Railways* (London, 1964).

Klaus-Georg Wey, *Umweltpolitik in Deutschland. Kurze Geschichte des Umweltschutzes in Deutschland seit 1900* (Opladen, 1982).

Wilson, Adrian, 'The Infancy of the History of Childhood: An Appraisal of Philippe Ariès', *History and Theory*, 19 (1980), 132–53.

Wilson, Stephen, 'The Myth of Motherwood a Myth: The Historical View of European Child-rearing', *Social History*, 9 (1984), 181–98.

Winslow, Charles Edward Amory, *The Conquest of Epidemic Disease. A Chapter in the History of Ideas* (Princeton, 1944).

Wohl, Anthony S., *Endangered Lives. Public Health in Victorian Britain* (London, 1983).

Woods, Robert, and John Woodward (eds.), *Urban Disease and Mortality in Nineteenth-century England* (London, 1984).

Woodward, John, *To Do the Sick No Harm: A Study of the British Voluntary Hospital System to 1875* (London, 1974).

Zacke, Brita, *Koleraepidemien i Stockholm 1834. En Socialhistorisk Studie* (Monografien utgivne av Stockholms Kommunalforvaltning, 32, Stockholm, 1971).

Zang, Gert (ed.), *Provinzialisierung einer Region. Zur Entstehung der bürgerlichen Gesellschaft in der Provinz* (Frankfurt, 1978).

Zeldin, Theodore, *France 1848–1945, i. Ambition, Love and Politics* (Oxford, 1973).

Index

Index

FOR THE BEST IN PAPERBACKS, LOOK FOR THE 🐧

In every corner of the world, on every subject under the sun, Penguin represents quality and variety – the very best in publishing today.

For complete information about books available from Penguin – including Puffins, Penguin Classics and Arkana – and how to order them, write to us at the appropriate address below. Please note that for copyright reasons the selection of books varies from country to country.

In the United Kingdom: Please write to *Dept E.P., Penguin Books Ltd, Harmondsworth, Middlesex, UB7 0DA.*

If you have any difficulty in obtaining a title, please send your order with the correct money, plus ten per cent for postage and packaging, to *PO Box No 11, West Drayton, Middlesex*

In the United States: Please write to *Dept BA, Penguin, 299 Murray Hill Parkway, East Rutherford, New Jersey 07073*

In Canada: Please write to *Penguin Books Canada Ltd, 2801 John Street, Markham, Ontario L3R 1B4*

In Australia: Please write to the *Marketing Department, Penguin Books Australia Ltd, P.O. Box 257, Ringwood, Victoria 3134*

In New Zealand: Please write to the *Marketing Department, Penguin Books (NZ) Ltd, Private Bag, Takapuna, Auckland 9*

In India: Please write to *Penguin Overseas Ltd, 706 Eros Apartments, 56 Nehru Place, New Delhi, 110019*

In the Netherlands: Please write to *Penguin Books Netherlands B.V., Postbus 195, NL–1380AD Weesp*

In West Germany: Please write to *Penguin Books Ltd, Friedrichstrasse 10–12, D–6000 Frankfurt/Main 1*

In Spain: Please write to *Longman Penguin España, Calle San Nicolas 15, E–28013 Madrid*

In Italy: Please write to *Penguin Italia s.r.l., Via Como 4, I-20096 Pioltello (Milano)*

In France: Please write to *Penguin Books Ltd, 39 Rue de Montmorency, F-75003 Paris*

In Japan: Please write to *Longman Penguin Japan Co Ltd, Yamaguchi Building, 2–12–9 Kanda Jimbocho, Chiyoda-Ku, Tokyo 101*